# Strategic Knowledge Management in Multinational Organizations

Kevin O'Sullivan
*New York Institute of Technology, USA*

**INFORMATION SCIENCE REFERENCE**

Hershey · New York

| | |
|---|---|
| Acquisitions Editor: | Kristin Klinger |
| Development Editor: | Kristin Roth |
| Senior Managing Editor: | Jennifer Neidig |
| Managing Editor: | Sara Reed |
| Copy Editor: | Maria Boyer |
| Typesetter: | Michael Brehm |
| Cover Design: | Lisa Tosheff |
| Printed at: | Yurchak Printing Inc. |

Published in the United States of America by
Information Science Reference (an imprint of IGI Global)
701 E. Chocolate Avenue, Suite 200
Hershey PA 17033
Tel: 717-533-8845
Fax: 717-533-8661
E-mail: cust@igi-pub.com
Web site: http://www.igi-pub.com/reference

and in the United Kingdom by
Information Science Reference (an imprint of IGI Global)
3 Henrietta Street
Covent Garden
London WC2E 8LU
Tel: 44 20 7240 0856
Fax: 44 20 7379 0609
Web site: http://www.eurospanonline.com

Library of Congress Cataloging-in-Publication Data

Strategic knowledge management in multinational organizations / Kevin O'Sullivan, editor.
   p. cm.
 Summary: "This book presents a comprehensive set of investigations of a wide range of environmental factors, both internal and external, that contribute to the key challenge of complexity in KM. These factors include culture, technology, communications, infrastructure, and learning and leadership structures"--Provided by publisher.
 Includes bibliographical references and index.
 ISBN-13: 978-1-59904-630-3 (hardcover)
 ISBN-13: 978-1-59904-632-7 (ebook)
 1. Knowledge management. 2. International business enterprises. 3. Intercultural communication. 4. Corporate culture. I. O'Sullivan, Kevin, 1967-
 HD30.2.S7885 2007
 658.4'012--dc22
                 2007016963

British Cataloguing in Publication Data
A Cataloguing in Publication record for this book is available from the British Library.

All work contributed to this book set is new, previously-unpublished material. The views expressed in this book are those of the authors, but not necessarily of the publisher.

# Table of Contents

**Detailed Table of Contents** ................................................................................................ vi

**Preface** ........................................................................................................... xv

### Section I
### Organization

**Chapter I**
HRM Practices and Knowledge Transfer in Multinational Companies / *Dana B. Minbaeva* ............... 1

**Chapter II**
Knowledge Creation in Commitment-Based Value Networks in Multinational Organizations /
*Leslie Gadman* .......................................................................................................... 28

**Chapter III**
The Impact of Group Relationships on Knowledge Sharing: A Cross-Cultural Study /
*Qiping Zhang, Vincent M. Ribiere, and Thippaya Chintakovid* ............................................... 40

**Chapter IV**
Why First-Level Call Center Technicians Need Knowledge Management Tools / *Joe Downing* ........ 53

**Chapter V**
KAFRA: A Context-Aware Framework of Knowledge Management in Global Diversity /
*A. Okunoye and N. Bertaux* .......................................................................................... 63

**Chapter VI**
The Role of Culture in Knowledge Management: A Case Study of Two Global Firms /
*D. Leidner, M. Alavi, and T. Kayworth* ............................................................................ 83

# Section II
## Technology

**Chapter VII**
KM Technologies and the Organizational LOE: The Unintended Consequence of Constant
Organizational Change / *Victoria M. Grady and James D. Grady III*................................................. 104

**Chapter VIII**
Architecting Knowledge Management Systems / *Shankar Kambhampaty*........................................ 119

**Chapter IX**
Global Knowledge Management Technology Strategies and Competitive Functionality /
*William Schulte and Kevin J. O'Sullivan*........................................................................................ 126

**Chapter X**
Comparing Cultural and Political Perspectives of Data, Information, and Knowledge Sharing
in Organisations / *D. Hart and L. Warne* ...................................................................................... 137

**Chapter XI**
Technology Trends in Knowledge Management Tools / *G. Balmisse, D. Meingan, and
K. Passerini*.................................................................................................................................... 152

# Section III
## Learning

**Chapter XII**
Improving Global Knowledge Management Through Inclusion of Host Country Workforce Input /
*Yongsun Paik, Charles M. Vance, Jeffrey Gale, and Cathleen A. McGrath* ........................................ 167

**Chapter XIII**
Developing a Standardization Best Practice by Cooperation Between Multinationals /
*Henk J. de Vries* ................................................................................................................................ 183

**Chapter XIV**
The Building of the Intellectual Capital Statements in Multinationals: Challenges for the Future /
*Miltiadis D. Lytras and Patricia Ordóñez de Pablos* .......................................................................... 195

**Chapter XV**
Knowledge Management in Research Joint Ventures / *Elena Revilla*............................................... 207

**Chapter XVI**
CRM Practices and Resources for the Development of Customer-Focused
Multinational Organizations / *Luciano C. Batista* ............................................................................ 227

**Chapter XVII**

Organizational Learning Process: Its Antecedents and Consequences in Enterprise System

Implementation / *W. Ke and K. Kee Wei* .......................................................................... 256


**Section IV**
**Leadership**


**Chapter XVIII**

Managing Knowledge Diversity in Distributed Organizational Structures /

*Claude Paraponaris* .......................................................................................................... 275


**Chapter IXX**

Knowledge Management Success: Roles of Management and Leadership /

*Vittal S. Anantatmula* ....................................................................................................... 299


**Chapter XX**

Strategic Knowledge Management in Matrix Multinational Organizations /

*Alan M. Thompson* ............................................................................................................ 311


**Chapter XXI**

A Cross-National Comparision of Knowledge Management Practices in Israel,

Singapore, the Netherlands, and the United States / *Ronald D. Camp II, Leo-Paul Dana,*

*Len Korot, and George Tovstiga* ...................................................................................... 323


**Chapter XXII**

Developing a Global CRM Srategy / *M. Shumanov and M. Ewing* .................................. 342


**Compilation of References** ........................................................................................... 356


**About the Contributors** ............................................................................................... 397


**Index** ............................................................................................................................. 403

# Detailed Table of Contents

**Preface** ................................................................................................................................... XV

## Section I
## Organization

**Chapter I**
HRM Practices and Knowledge Transfer in Multinational Companies / *Dana B. Minbaeva* ................ 1

*This chapter introduces human resource management (HRM) practices that help multinational companies (MNCs) overcome knowledge transfer barriers (knowledge-driven HRM practices). It argues that MNCs can institute various HRM practices that impact knowledge transfer barriers associated with behavior of knowledge senders and receivers. HRM practices relevant for absorptive capacity of subsidiary employees form two groups—cognitive (job analysis, recruitment, selection, international rotation, career management, training, and performance appraisal) and stimulative (promotion, performance-based compensation, internal transfer, orientation programs, job design, and flexible working practices). The application of cognitive HRM practices enhances the ability of knowledge receivers to absorb transferred knowledge, while the use of stimulative HRM practices increases their motivation. Temporary and permanent types of international assignments respectively influence the ability and motivation of expatriate managers to share their knowledge.*

**Chapter II**
Knowledge Creation in Commitment-Based Value Networks in Multinational Organizations /
*Leslie Gadman* ................................................................................................................................ 28

*The digital networked economy has gone global and is reshaping traditional business models. "Free" and "open source" software (Raymond, 1999), along with more recent successes in the private, public, and social sectors, offer a vision of a radically new globally networked economy. This economy is characterized by new sources of value creation and competition, as barriers to entry are lowered and substitution made easier. It also requires a more stratified, localized approach to the marketplace (Hart & Milstein, 2003) to meet more specialized demands from customers and the societies and environments within which they live. These challenges have implications for almost every aspect of a firm's strategy and business model, especially its ability to leverage these networks to create value through innovation. Yet, most multinational firms are ill-equipped to take advantage of the knowledge creation derived from high-value relationships with suppliers, complementors, and customers. This chapter shows the importance of developing a corporate strategy which takes into account ways in which an innovation focus must integrate with installed business processes. The chapter considers the challenges associated with knowledge disclosure, diffusion, and utilization (Snowdon, 2002; Spinosa, Flores, & Dreyfus, 2001) across value networks and concludes that while successful examples exist in "free" and "open source" software projects (Raymond, 1999), commercialization of innovation becomes more challenging when increasing levels of personal and financial commitment are required (Mauer, Rai, & Sali, 2004). Choosing the most appropriate value networking strategy can have serious implications for success. This chapter adds to studies on knowledge creation and knowledge transfer in multinational corporations by proposing a conceptual model of commitment-based value networking strategy. It is hoped this will contribute to future research by offering a theoretical foundation upon which this research may be based, and explains why and under what conditions people in commitment-based value networks share knowledge.*

**Chapter III**

The Impact of Group Relationships on Knowledge Sharing: A Cross-Cultural Study /
*Qiping Zhang, Vincent M. Ribiere, and Thippaya Chintakovid*............................................................ 40

*Organizations nowadays typically have several locations geographically dispersed around the world. Organizations distribute their resources around the world to reduce cost and remain competitive. As a consequence, globally distributed working teams are common, thereby rendering a need for knowledge sharing cross-culturally. This chapter presents a series of studies investigating the impact of cultures on how people handle knowledge management issues. It shows how in-group/out-group relationships determine people's attitudes towards knowledge sharing in a global working environment. Findings of this project would help organizations' executives understand better how to encourage their members to reap benefits from using the knowledge management systems.*

**Chapter IV**

Why First-Level Call Center Technicians Need Knowledge Management Tools / *Joe Downing*........ 53

*This chapter argues that first-level call center technicians are the new knowledge worker of the 21st century. As such, these technicians are ideal candidates for knowledge management tools. The objective of the chapter is to introduce these technicians to the IT community and, by way of a case study, show how decision-tree-type help tools can increase technicians' productivity. The chapter ends with recommendations for IT practitioners who are interesting in implementing these tools in their call centers.*

**Chapter V**

KAFRA: A Context-Aware Framework of Knowledge Management in Global Diversity /
*A. Okunoye and N. Bertaux*................................................................................................................ 63

*Multiple case studies in India, The Gambia, and Nigeria are the background for an empirically grounded framework of knowledge management (KM). Cultural diversity and gaps in the provision of infrastructure make managing knowledge challenging but necessary in developing countries. These cultural and infrastructural issues are also related to governmental, educational, political, social, and economic factors. These environmental factors interact with organizational variables and information technology to enable or constrain knowledge management processes in the creation and protection of knowledge resources. The framework can help organizations to prepare their KM projects, to reveal problems during the project, and to assess its outcomes.*

**Chapter VI**

The Role of Culture in Knowledge Management: A Case Study of Two Global Firms / *D. Leidner, M. Alavi, and T. Kayworth* ................................................................................................ 83

*Knowledge management (KM) approaches have been broadly considered to entail either a focus on organizing communities or a focus on the process of knowledge creation, sharing, and distribution. While these two approaches are not mutually exclusive and organizations may adopt aspects of both, the two approaches entail different challenges. Some organizational cultures might be more receptive to the community approach, whereas others may be more receptive to the process approach. Although culture has been cited widely as a challenge in knowledge management initiatives, and although many studies have considered the implications of organizational culture on knowledge sharing, few empirical studies address the influence of culture on the approach taken to knowledge management. Using a case study approach to compare and contrast the cultures and knowledge management approaches of two organizations, the study suggests ways in which organizational culture influences knowledge management initiatives as well as the evolution of knowledge management in organizations. Whereas in one organization, the KM effort became little more than an information repository, in the second organization, the KM effort evolved into a highly collaborative system fostering the formation of electronic communities.*

**Section II**
**Technology**

**Chapter VII**

KM Technologies and the Organizational LOE: The Unintended Consequence of Constant Organizational Change / *Victoria M. Grady and James D. Grady III* ................................................ 104

*The potential benefits of utilizing knowledge management (KM) technologies in multinational and global organizations are of particular significance due to the inherent geographic distance and diversity of such organizations. Unfortunately, the process of constantly changing technology can be extremely disruptive at both the individual and organizational level. This chapter explores the relationship between KM technology change within the organization and the Theory of Organizational Loss of Effectiveness (LOE). "The general Theory of Organizational Loss of Effectiveness is predicated upon organizational behavior resulting from a loss of stability, e.g. technology change, within an organization." (Grady, 2005) The loss of stability, in the context of this theory, occurs when a defined set of symptoms develop in individuals and groups undergoing a change in technology. The assertion is that the development of these symptoms is predictable, and when viewed collectively, results in an organizational loss of effectiveness.*

**Chapter VIII**

Architecting Knowledge Management Systems / *Shankar Kambhampaty* ......................................... 119

*Organizations need well-architected systems for knowledge management (KM). This chapter begins with a review of approaches adopted by organizations for developing KM solutions. It defines a set of components that can form the building blocks for developing a knowledge management system. The relevance of the principles of Service-Oriented Architecture (SOA) to KM solutions is explained. It presents the architecture of a generic knowledge management system based on the components defined and the principles of SOA. It then discusses the patterns for implementing the architecture, followed by maturity levels of knowledge management systems.*

**Chapter IX**

Global Knowledge Management Technology Strategies and Competitive Functionality /
*William Schulte and Kevin J. O'Sullivan* ......................................................................................... 126

*Information and knowledge management technologies and globalization have changed how firms in service industries formulate, implement, and sustain competitive advantage. This research project contributes to our understanding of the relationships between global knowledge management technology strategies and competitive functionality from global IT. Based on field research, this study found that global knowledge management technology strategies have a positive impact on competitive advantage from information technology applications functionality from global IT. This study provides recommendations to international engineering, procurement, and construction industry executives regarding the impact of knowledge management strategies and global information technology on competitive advantage of firms in their industry.*

**Chapter X**

Comparing Cultural and Political Perspectives of Data, Information, and Knowledge Sharing
in Organisations / *D. Hart and L. Warne* ....................................................................................... 137

*This chapter raises issues concerning data, information, and knowledge sharing in organisations and, in particular, compares an organisational cultural analysis of why such sharing is often difficult to achieve with an organisational political one. The issues raised are often insufficiently attended to by practitioners who are attempting to build technological information and knowledge management systems. The driver for the chapter is that despite impressive advances in technology and its now almost ubiquitous presence in organisations, as well as academic study over several decades, many of the benefits originally expected concerning improved data, information, and knowledge sharing have not materialised as expected. Basic reasons for this lie in the lack of attention to the cultural foundations of organisations and because matters relating to organisational power and political matters are often misunderstood, overlooked, or ignored. These different perspectives are discussed and contrasted in order to tease out the important differences between them and assess the prospects for a synthesis. It is concluded that while there are important commonalities between the two perspectives there are also fundamental differences, notably regarding what are causes and what are effects and, therefore, how to go about effecting change regarding data, information, and knowledge sharing.*

**Chapter XI**

Technology Trends in Knowledge Management Tools / *G. Balmisse, D. Meingan, and
K. Passerini*.................................................................................................................................. 152

*A large number of tools are available in the software industry to support different aspects of knowledge
management (KM). Some comprehensive applications and vendors try to offer global solutions to KM
needs; other tools are highly specialized. In this chapter, state-of-the-art KM tools grouped by specific
classification areas and functionalities are described. Trends and integration efforts are detailed with
a focus on identifying current and future software and market evolution.*

**Section III
Learning**

**Chapter XII**

Improving Global Knowledge Management Through Inclusion of Host Country Workforce Input /
*Yongsun Paik, Charles M. Vance, Jeffrey Gale, and Cathleen A. McGrath* ...................................... 167

*Within a framework of international strategy for multinational corporations, this chapter examines the
important opportunities afforded by taking a more inclusive approach to the foreign subsidiary host
country workforce (HCW). It argues that past international management writing and practice, with its
expatriate bias, has neglected consideration of this important resource. Not only can the HCW help
expatriate managers be more successful and have a better experience in the host country, but it can
contribute to and benefit from the corporate knowledge base, leading to more effective global knowledge
management. The authors discuss means by which a multinational corporation can effectively include
the HCW in its knowledge management activities.*

**Chapter XIII**

Developing a Standardization Best Practice by Cooperation Between Multinationals /
*Henk J. de Vries* ............................................................................................................................. 183

*This chapter presents a case of knowledge sharing between multinational companies. The companies
cooperated to develop a common best practice for the development of company standards through sharing
their practices. The chapter describes how this best practice was developed and tested. Experiences in
this successful project may help other multinationals also profit from knowledge sharing. Critical success
factors are the willingness to be open, the culture of cooperation, and the involvement of academia.*

**Chapter XIV**

The Building of the Intellectual Capital Statements in Multinationals: Challenges for the Future /
*Miltiadis D. Lytras and Patricia Ordóñez de Pablos* ........................................................................ 195

*Multinational companies (MNCs) are facing important challenges within the current economic context.
Rapid technological changes, the globalization of the economy, the existence of increasingly demanding
consumers are, among other factors, the origin of the difficulties involved in achieving and sustaining a*

*competitive advantage in the long term. One of the keys for overcoming these difficulties is to manage knowledge-based resources appropriately. However, in order to be able to manage these resources, the multinationals need to know, with complete transparency, just what these resources are, and this is achieved by quantifying them. The quantification of knowledge-based resources and the preparation of intellectual capital statements represent two strategic challenges for the MNCs.*

**Chapter XV**
Knowledge Management in Research Joint Ventures / *Elena Revilla*................................................ 207

*As innovation and technology management grow in complexity, the need for interorganizational cooperation increases. Part of this cooperation requires the understanding of how knowledge management and learning processes may function to support a successful research and development collaboration in multinational enterprises. To further this understanding we introduce a typology to help categorize various collaborative efforts within a research joint venture environment. The typology is based on two dimensions: the locus of the research joint venture knowledge and the knowledge management approach. This matrix leads us to deduce that different research joint venture (RJV) strategies can emerge as a result of these two dimensions. Finally, an evaluation of this relationship is completed using information and practices from data acquired from a broad-based study of European-based RJVs. Implications for research and management of these types of projects are also introduced throughout the chapter.*

**Chapter XVI**
CRM Practices and Resources for the Development of Customer-Focused
Multinational Organizations / *Luciano C. Batista*............................................................................ 227

*This chapter aims to provide a complete characterization of the different perspectives of customer relationship management (CRM) and its potentialities to support knowledge management practices in a multinational context. It describes the strategic and technological dimensions of CRM and how its adoption supports the development of a learning and customer-focused organization, with special emphasis on multinational corporations. CRM strategic approach entails the adoption of customer-focused initiatives and the development of learning relationships with customers. On the other hand, its technological dimension integrates a variety of different information and communication technologies, which makes a powerful system for improving the process of knowledge acquisition. This way, different subsidiaries of a multinational corporation can develop their learning capability so that they can better identify local market demands. As a result, the corporation is able to more accurately create a global knowledge stock about its different markets in different regions of the world.*

**Chapter XVII**
Organizational Learning Process: Its Antecedents and Consequences in Enterprise System
Implementation / *W. Ke and K. Kee Wei*........................................................................................ 256

*This chapter uses organizational learning as a lens to study how firms implement enterprise system. The core research questions are: what are the critical organizational factors affecting organizational learning in ES implementation? How do these elements shape the learning process and thereby influence ES implementation outcomes? To address these questions, we conducted comparative case study with two organizations that have recently adopted ES and achieved significantly different results. Based on the empirical findings, we propose a framework that describes how organizational factors affect the four constructs of organizational learning in ES implementation context—knowledge acquisition, information distribution, information interpretation and organizational memory.*

## Section IV
## Leadership

### Chapter XVIII
Managing Knowledge Diversity in Distributed Organizational Structures /
*Claude Paraponaris*.................................................................................................................275

*Knowledge in organizations can be compared with human memory. There is no unique place for creating and conserving knowledge. Knowledge in multinationals realizes its potential with various tools of management. The diversity of tools leads to the issue of coordinating levels of management. How can one manage different tools of KM without disrupting the knowledge creating process? To address this issue we analyze several knowledge management strategies of high-technology industries (computer, telecommunications, and pharmacy). In these cases diversity encourages implementation of knowledge management tools. The precision of these tools indicates the firm's competence in managing and diffusing knowledge. An important conclusion that can be drawn is that several factors (redundancy, diversity, discussion, and duration) can reinforce these competences and, in fact, network mechanisms in organizations.*

### Chapter IXX
Knowledge Management Success: Roles of Management and Leadership /
*Vittal S. Anantatmula* ............................................................................................................299

*Globalization and free market philosophy characterize the current economic environment of increased competition, and it has posed far greater challenges than ever for organizations to meet customer needs and demands. The global competition is compelling organizations to develop products and services faster, cheaper, and better in order to sustain competitive advantage in the marketplace.*
*Twenty-first century economy is setting new trends and unique styles of business operations because of continuous advancement of information technology and communication technologies. These technologies have offered more avenues to conduct business effectively and efficiently. Many organizations participating in the global economy have two distinct features associated with their operations, outsourcing and virtual teams, which have become feasible because of these technological advances. These two features have an impact on how organizations manage knowledge, and they deserve further discussion.*

**Chapter XX**

Strategic Knowledge Management in Matrix Multinational Organizations /

*Alan M. Thompson* ................................................................................................................. 311

*This chapter looks at managing knowledge workers within the business environment of a matrix-organized multinational organization, using oil and gas contractor Production Services Network for illustration. It looks at the influence of business needs, and human and organizational culture and strategic factors on KM; the importance of communicating business drivers; and adverse demographics; it also outlines some future trends that managers and KM staff in multinational matrix organizations should be preparing for. It is hoped that discussing examples of KM in practice, within the context of globalization, demographic changes, and rapid developments in technology, markets, and business relationships, will ground some familiar theory in some new and evolving territory, providing interest to both academics and practitioners.*

**Chapter XXI**

A Cross-National Comparision of Knowledge Management Practices in Israel,
Singapore, the Netherlands, and the United States / *Ronald D. Camp II, Leo-Paul Dana,
Len Korot, and George Tovstiga* ................................................................................................ 323

*The purpose of this chapter is to explore organizational knowledge-based practices. A distinguishing feature of the successful post-Network Age enterprise is its intrinsic entrepreneurial character that manifests itself in key organizational knowledge practices relating to organizational culture, processes, content, and infrastructure. The chapter reports on the outcome of field research in which entrepreneurial firms in four geographic regions were analyzed with the help of a diagnostic research tool specifically developed for profiling organizational knowledge-based practices. The diagnostic tool was applied in firms located in the U.S.'s Silicon Valley, Singapore, The Netherlands, and Israel. Key practices that were found to be common to leading-edge firms in all regions included: a propensity for experimentation, collective knowledge sharing, and collective decision making. The chapter describes the research in terms of a cross-cultural comparison of the four regions, derives key determinants of competitiveness, and profiles regional characteristics that enhance innovation and entrepreneurship.*

**Chapter XXII**

Developing a Global CRM Srategy / *M. Shumanov and M. Ewing* ...................................... 342

*While the managerial rationale for adopting customer relationship management (CRM) has been fairly well articulated in the literature, research on strategy development is scant. Moreover, reports of "CRM failures" in the popular business press have done little to inspire confidence. To date, what little research has been conducted in the area of CRM strategy development has been confined to a single country (often the U.S.). Global CRM strategy development issues have yet to be specifically addressed, particularly which elements of CRM strategy should be centralised/decentralised. The present study examines the complexities of global CRM strategy using the case of a leading financial services company. Interviews are conducted in 20 countries. Global Head Office and external IT consultant perspectives are also considered. Our findings confirm that a hybrid approach has wide practical appeal and that subsidiary orientation towards centralisation/decentralisation is moderated by firm/market size and sophistication.*

**Compilation of References** ................................................................................................. 1

**About the Contributors** ..................................................................................................... 1

**Index** ..................................................................................................................................... 1

# Preface

At the beginning of the 21$^{st}$ century, we enter into a new era of both globalization and the use of knowledge management (KM) in achieving strategic objectives. This book is designed to bring the theory, research, and thought leaders together in establishing both the salient capabilities of KM in multinational organizations as well as the approaches that may be employed in attaining those objectives.

In approaching the topic of multinational knowledge management, it was apparent from the beginning that the book needed to be based on the experience and knowledge of practitioners and researchers from wide and diverse backgrounds and from different parts of the globe. To this end we have brought together leaders from Australia, Canada, Denmark, France, Hong Kong, India, New Zealand, Scotland, Spain, Switzerland, the United Kingdom, The Netherlands, and the United States to share their knowledge and research on the topic of strategic knowledge management in the multinational organization.

Targeted at KM practitioners, researchers, and students of knowledge management, the text is divided into four general sections:

- Organization
- Technology
- Organizational Learning
- Leadership

The approach is consistent with the Four Pillars of Knowledge Management, first postulated by Baldanza and Stankosky in 1999. The approach to describing knowledge management has sustained the test of time and has been the basis of numerous papers, research projects, and books, and ultimately is highly suited to examining knowledge management in this setting.

## ORGANIZATION

The first section deals with organizational consideration in utilizing knowledge management in a multinational setting. Obviously, the level of complexity associated with the multinational are much increased over that of an organization operating in a single market.

In Chapter I we start by examining the human aspect of KM and in particular the human resource management (HRM) component in facilitating knowledge transfer. HRM practices relevant for absorptive capacity of subsidiary employees form two groups—cognitive (job analysis, recruitment, selection, international rotation, career management, training, and performance appraisal) and stimulative (promotion, performance-based compensation, internal transfer, orientation programs, job design, and flexible working practices). The application of cognitive HRM practices enhances the ability of knowledge receivers to absorb transferred knowledge, while the use of stimulative HRM practices increases their motivation. Temporary and permanent types of international assignments respectively influence the ability and motivation of expatriate managers to share their knowledge.

In Chapter II we examine knowledge creation techniques facilitated by commitment-based value systems within the multinational organization, and in particular the implications for almost every aspect of a firm's strategy and business model, especially its ability to leverage these networks to create value through innovation. Most multinational firms are ill-equipped to take advantage of the knowledge creation derived from high-value relationships with suppliers and customers. This chapter shows the importance of developing a corporate strategy which takes into account ways in which an innovation focus must integrate with installed business processes. Choosing the most appropriate value networking strategy can have serious implications for success. In this chapter we add to studies on knowledge creation and knowledge transfer in multinational corporations by proposing a conceptual model of commitment-based value networking strategy.

The objective of Chapter III is to assist executives in understanding how to encourage their members to reap benefits from using the knowledge management systems within the multinational setting by examining the cultural aspects of knowledge sharing. Organizations distribute their resources around the world to reduce cost and remain competitive. As a consequence, globally distributed working teams are common, thereby rendering a need for knowledge sharing cross-culturally. The chapter presents a series of studies investigating the impact of cultures on how people handle knowledge management issues. It shows how in-group/out-group relationships determine people's attitudes towards knowledge sharing in a global working environment.

In Chapter IV we examine the organization from the knowledge worker perspective: using the case study approach, we examine the case of the first-level call center technician. Such technicians are ideal candidates for knowledge management tools. The chapter ends with recommendations for IT practitioners who are interesting in implementing these tools in their call centers.

The move to the multinational setting for most organizations comes through the establishment of both an international customer base and through the use of outsourcing. Chapter V continues the case study approach examining cases in India, The Gambia, and Nigeria as a background for an empirically grounded framework of KM. Cultural diversity and gaps in the provision of infrastructure make managing knowledge challenging but necessary in developing countries. These cultural and infrastructural issues are also related to governmental, educational, political, social, and economic factors. These environmental factors interact with organizational variables and information technology to enable or constrain knowledge management processes in the creation and protection of knowledge resources. The framework is designed to assist organizations to prepare their KM projects, to reveal problems during the project, and to assess its outcomes.

In the final part of our section on Organization, Chapter VI continues the examination of culture in the multinational organization. We examine the factors contributing to process-based approaches and community-based approaches. Although culture has been cited widely as a challenge in knowledge management initiatives, and although many studies have considered the implications of organizational culture on knowledge sharing, few empirical studies address the influence of culture on the approach taken to knowledge management. Using a case study approach to compare and contrast the cultures and knowledge management approaches of two organizations, we postulate different ways in which organizational culture influences knowledge management initiatives as well as the evolution of knowledge management in organizations.

## TECHNOLOGY

In Section II we examine the technological aspects of KM in the multinational setting. The potential benefits of utilizing KM technologies in multinational and global organizations are of particular significance due to the inherent geographic distance and diversity of such organizations. Unfortunately, the process of constantly changing technology can be extremely disruptive at both the individual and organizational level. In Chapter VII, we explore the relationship between KM technology change within the organization and the Theory of Organizational Loss of Effectiveness (LOE). The Theory of Organizational Loss of Effectiveness is predicated upon organizational behavior resulting from a loss of stability (e.g., technology change) within an organization.. The loss of stability, in the context of this theory, occurs when a defined set of symptoms develop in individuals and groups undergoing a change in technology. The assertion is that the development of these symptoms is predictable, and when viewed collectively, results in an organizational loss of effectiveness.

Organizations need well-architected systems for effective KM. Chapter VIII begins with a review of approaches adopted by organizations for developing KM solutions. It defines a set of components that can form the building blocks for developing such systems. The relevance of the principles of service-oriented architecture (SOA) to KM solutions is demonstrated. The author presents the architecture of a generic knowledge management system based on the components defined and the principles of SOA, and then discusses the patterns for implementing the architecture followed by maturity levels of knowledge management systems.

Having established in Chapter IX the need for well-formed and sustainable architectures for knowledge management systems within the multinational setting, Chapter IX now examines the use of such technologies from an industry perspective: how information and knowledge management technologies and globalization have changed how firms in service industries formulate, implement, and sustain competitive advantage. The authors underline this with results from a research project that contributes to our understanding of the relationships between global knowledge management technology strategies and competitive functionality from global IT. Based on field research this study found that global knowledge management technology strategies have a positive impact on competitive advantage from information technology applications functionality from global IT. This study provides recommendations to international engineering, procurement, and construction industry executives regarding the impact of knowledge management strategies and global information technology on competitive advantage of firms in their industry.

In Chapter X raises issues concerning data, information, and knowledge sharing in organizations, and in particular compares an organizational cultural analysis of why such sharing is often difficult to achieve with an organizational political one. The issues raised are often insufficiently attended to by practitioners who are attempting to build technological information and knowledge management systems. The driver for the chapter is that despite impressive advances in technology, and technology's now almost ubiquitous presence in organizations, as well as academic study over several decades, many of the benefits originally expected concerning improved data, information, and knowledge sharing have not materialized as expected. Basic reasons for this lie in the lack of attention to the cultural foundations of organizations, and because matters relating to organizational power and political matters are often misunderstood, overlooked, or ignored. These different perspectives are discussed and contrasted in order to tease out the important differences between them and assess the prospects for a synthesis. It is concluded that while there are important commonalities between the two perspectives, there are also fundamental differences, notably regarding what are causes and what are effects and, therefore, how to go about effecting change regarding data, information, and knowledge sharing.

Finally for this section, we examine the trends that are evolving in terms of technologies that can be used to enable knowledge management in multinational organizations. In Chapter XI we examine the large number of tools available in the software industry to support different aspects of knowledge management. Some comprehensive applications and vendors try to offer global solutions to KM needs; other tools are highly specialized. In this chapter, state-of-the-art KM tools grouped by specific classification areas and functionalities are described. Trends and integration efforts are detailed with a focus on identifying current and future software and market evolution.

## LEARNING

In Section III we examine the concept of organizational learning in the multinational setting. Chapter XII examines the important opportunities afforded by taking a more inclusive approach to the foreign subsidiary host country workforce (HCW). The authors argue that past international management writing and practice, with its expatriate bias, has neglected consideration of this important resource. Not only can the HCW help expatriate managers be more successful and have a better experience in the host country, but it can contribute to and benefit from the corporate knowledge base, leading to more effective global knowledge management. The authors discuss means by which a multinational corporation can effectively include the HCW in its knowledge management activities.

Chapter XIII deals with the concepts of standardization in the multinational setting. The chapter presents a case of knowledge sharing between multinational companies. The companies cooperated to develop a common best practice for the development of company standards through sharing their practices. The chapter describes how this best practice was developed and tested, and experiences in this successful project may help other multinationals also profit from knowledge sharing.

One of the keys for overcoming these difficulties is to manage knowledge-based resources appropriately. However, in order to be able to manage these resources, the multinationals need to know, with complete transparency, just what these resources are, and this is achieved by quantifying them. The quantification of knowledge-based resources and the preparation of intellectual capital statements represent two strategic challenges for the multinational organization. In Chapter XIV we discuss the approaches to quantify such knowledge, given the complexity of the multinational setting and then the presentation of quantified knowledge through the use of intellectual capital statements. This chapter has two basic aims. First, it analyzes the complex dynamics of knowledge flow transfers in multinational firms. Second it addresses the measuring and reporting of knowledge-based resources in multinational organizations.

As innovation and technology management grow in complexity, the need for inter-organizational cooperation increases. Part of this cooperation requires the understanding of how knowledge management and learning processes may function to support a successful research and development collaboration in multinational organizations. To further this understanding, Chapter XV introduces a typology to help categorize various collaborative efforts within a research joint venture environment. The typology is based on two dimensions—the locus of the research joint venture knowledge and the knowledge management approach. This matrix leads us to deduce that different research joint venture (RJV) strategies can emerge as a result of these two dimensions. Finally, an evaluation of this relationship is completed using information and practices from data acquired from a broad-based study of European-based RJVs.

Chapter XVI aims to provide a complete characterization of the different perspectives of customer relationship management (CRM) and its potentialities to support knowledge management practices in a multinational context. It describes the strategic and technological dimensions of CRM and how its adoption supports the development of a learning and customer-focused organization, with special emphasis on multinational corporations. CRM strategic approach entails the adoption of customer-focused initiatives and the development of learning relationships with customers. On the other hand, its technological dimension integrates a variety of different information and communication technologies, which makes a powerful system for improving the process of knowledge acquisition. This way, different subsidiaries of a multinational corporation can develop their learning capability so that they can better identify local market demands. As a result, the corporation is able to more accurately create a global knowledge stock about its different markets in different regions of the world.

In Chapter XVII we use organizational learning as a lens to study how firms implement the enterprise system (ES). In approaching this topic the authors discuss the critical organizational factors affecting organizational learning in ES implementation, and how these elements shape the learning process and thereby influence ES implementation outcomes. In approaching this, the authors conducted a comparative case study with two organizations that recently adopted ES and achieved significantly different results. Based on the empirical findings, we propose a framework that describes how organizational factors affect the four constructs of organizational learning in ES implementation context—knowledge acquisition, information distribution, information interpretation, and organizational memory.

## LEADERSHIP

In the final section of the book, we examine the role of leadership in the development, utilization, and management of knowledge in the multinational setting. Central to this aspect is the understanding that without appropriate leadership knowledge, management initiatives are destined to fail to meet expectations. Given the complexities of the multinational setting, the need for strong leadership is even more essential than in the context of a single market system.

The discussion in Chapter XVIII begins with an analysis of several knowledge management strategies in high-technology industries (computer, telecommunications, and pharmacy). In these cases diversity encourages implementation of knowledge management tools. The precision of these tools indicates the firm's competence in managing and diffusing knowledge. An important conclusion that can be drawn is that several factors (redundancy, diversity, discussion, and duration) can reinforce these competences and, in fact, network mechanisms in organization.

Chapter IXX focuses on two distinct challenges for leaders in the multinational organization: outsourcing and virtual teams. Both of these have become feasible because of technological advances and have features that have an impact on how organizations manage knowledge and consequently have strategic significance. In addressing these two challenges, we examine how they impact the way organizations run their business operations and how they impact the leader's role. Both these distinct features—outsourcing and virtual teams—have one thing in common: the explicit and tacit knowledge of the organization is no longer confined within the organization.

In the 21st century, the move towards customer-oriented, team-based organizational structures is becoming more pronounced in the marketplace. Chapter XX examines the practice of managing knowledge workers within the business environment of a matrix-organized multinational organization, using oil and gas contractor Production Services Network (PSN) for illustration. We look at the influence of business needs and human, organizational culture and strategic factors on KM; the importance of communicating business drivers; adverse demographics; and outline some future trends that managers and KM staff in multinational matrix organizations should be preparing for. It is hoped that discussing examples of KM in practice, within the context of globalization, demographic changes, and rapid developments in technology, markets, and business relationships, will ground some familiar theory in some new and evolving territory, providing interest to both academics and practitioners.

In ChapterXXI we look at knowledge management practices in the context of the international setting. In particular we examine knowledge management practices in Israel, Singapore, The Netherlands, and the United States. A distinguishing feature of the successful post-Network Age enterprise is its intrinsic entrepreneurial character that manifests itself in key organizational knowledge practices relating to organizational culture, processes, content, and infrastructure. This chapter reports on the outcome of field research in which entrepreneurial firms in four geographic regions were analyzed with the help of a diagnostic research tool specifically developed for profiling organizational knowledge-based practices. The diagnostic tool was applied in firms located in the United States, Singapore, The Netherlands, and Israel. Key practices that were found to be common to leading-edge firms in all regions included: a propensity for experimentation, collective knowledge sharing, and collective decision making. The chapter describes the research in terms of a cross-cultural comparison of the four regions, derives key determinants of competitiveness, and profiles regional characteristics that enhance innovation and entrepreneurship.

Finally in Chapter XXII we look at establishing a global customer relationship management strategy. To date, what little research has been conducted in the area of CRM strategy development has been confined to a single country (the United States). Global CRM strategy development issues have yet to be specifically addressed, particularly which elements of CRM strategy should be centralized/decentralized. This study examines the complexities of global CRM strategy using the case of a leading financial services company. Interviews were conducted in 20 countries. Global head office and external IT consultant perspectives are also considered. Our findings confirm that a hybrid approach has wide practical appeal and that subsidiary orientation towards centralization/decentralization is moderated by firm/market size and sophistication.

## CONCLUSION

In conclusion, it must be said that many books and articles could and will be written on the four major elements of knowledge management outlined in this book. Knowledge management is, for many organizations, still in the process of development; and the true capabilities of KM, especially in the context of multinationals and in the global economy, may be a source of great competitive advantage. As such this book is designed to enlighten the reader to these capabilities and demonstrate that not only is KM desirable in the multinational setting, it is all but required.

## REFERENCE

Baldanza, C., & Stankosky, M. (1999). Knowledge management: An evolutionary architecture toward enterprise engineering. *Proceedings of the Mid-Atlantic Regional Conference of the International Council on System Engineering (INCOSE).*

# Section I
# Organization

# Chapter I
# HRM Practices and Knowledge Transfer in Multinational Companies

**Dana B. Minbaeva**
*Copenhagen Business School, Denmark*

## ABSTRACT

*This chapter introduces human resource management (HRM) practices that help multinational companies (MNCs) overcome knowledge transfer barriers (knowledge-driven HRM practices). It argues that MNCs can institute various HRM practices that impact knowledge transfer barriers associated with behavior of knowledge senders and receivers. HRM practices relevant for absorptive capacity of subsidiary employees form two groups—cognitive (job analysis, recruitment, selection, international rotation, career management, training, and performance appraisal) and stimulative (promotion, performance-based compensation, internal transfer, orientation programs, job design, and flexible working practices). The application of cognitive HRM practices enhances the ability of knowledge receivers to absorb transferred knowledge, while the use of stimulative HRM practices increases their motivation. Temporary and permanent types of international assignments respectively influence the ability and motivation of expatriate managers to share their knowledge.*

## INTRODUCTION

Previous research has found that the competitive advantage that multinational corporations (MNCs) enjoy over national firms is contingent upon the MNCs' ability to exploit knowledge internally across organizational units. A common theme in this line of research is that MNCs can develop knowledge in one location and then exploit it in other locations, requiring an internal transfer of knowledge. It should not be assumed that internal knowledge transfer is ever unproblematic. The transfer impediments that have attracted researchers' attention to date are: the characteristics of the transferred knowledge (Zander & Kogut, 1995; Szulanski, 1996; Simonin, 1999a, 1999b), knowledge sources (Foss & Pedersen, 2002), absorptive capacity (Szulanski, 1996; Lyles & Salk, 1996; Lane & Lubatkin, 1998; Gupta & Govindarajan, 2000; Lane, Salk, & Lyles, 2001; Minbaeva, Pedersen, Bjorkman, Fey, & Park, 2003), and the organizational context in which the transfer takes place (Szulanski, 1996; Simonin, 1999a, 1999b; Bresman, Birkinshaw, & Nobel, 1999; Gupta & Govindarajan, 2000). Taken together, the findings suggest several generalizations about what is known regarding the process of knowledge transfer and its determinants. However, there are several areas that have been bypassed which therefore create shortcomings in our understanding of the knowledge transfer process. For example, until recently, transfer of knowledge has been rarely taken to be endogenous to organizational processes and arrangements (Foss & Pedersen, 2002). Despite an increasing interest in the subject, it is surprising how little empirical research has actually been conducted on the topic. In the conclusions of the few studies that included organizational practices (e.g., Lane & Lubatkin, 1998; Gupta & Govindarajan, 2000), we often find calls for further research on "the learning capacities of organizational units," "more explicit description of the motivation and cooperative choices of the organizational individuals," "organizational mechanisms to facilitate knowledge acquisition," and so forth. This study has undertaken the task of addressing these calls by considering the following question: *What human resource management (HRM) practices could MNCs employ to enhance knowledge transfer from the headquarters to the overseas subsidiaries and in which combination?* In particular, the chapter suggests that MNCs can institute various organizational policies and practices to overcome transfer barriers associated with knowledge transfer determinants, thereby facilitating internal knowledge transfer. It differs from the existing limited work on HRM and knowledge transfer by introducing a wider range

of HRM practices and considering them as a set of interrelated activities.

To clearly present the assumed relationships between HRM practices and knowledge transfer, I start by reviewing the findings of HRM-performance research to identify HRM practices that help organizations overcome knowledge transfer barriers. Once the question of *what* HRM practices are important is addressed, the next step is to determine *in which combination* HRM practices matter to knowledge transfer. Rather than using statistical techniques to group HRM practices such as factor and cluster analysis, it was recommended to try to *theoretically* identify groups of HRM practices (Guest, 1997; Delery, 1998). In this regard, literature points to the possibility of expanding the framework linking HRM practices and organizational outcomes by introducing mediating variables—that is, determinants of knowledge transfer (Minbaeva, 2007). Two determinants related to the behavior of individuals were identified in the MNC knowledge transfer literature—absorptive capacity of knowledge receivers (ability and motivation to absorb knowledge) and disseminative capacity of knowledge senders (ability and motivation to disseminate knowledge). These are considered as mediating variables in the relation between HRM practices and knowledge transfer, both of which in turn enhance the degree of knowledge transfer to the focal subsidiary.

The first set of hypotheses on the link between HRM practices and knowledge transfer examines the relationships between HRM practices and absorptive capacity of knowledge receivers (subsidiary employees). The use of *cognitive HRM practices* (job analysis, recruitment, selection, international rotation, career management, training, and performance appraisal) is expected to be positively related to the receivers' ability to absorb knowledge, while the employment of *stimulative HRM practices* (promotion, performance-based compensation, internal transfer, orientation programs, job design, and flexible working practices) is expected to enhance the receivers' motivation to absorb knowledge.

The study further investigates how four types of expatriate assignments influence the knowledge-sharing behavior of expatriates in terms of their ability and motivation. It was expected that *long-term assignments* affect an expatriate's motivation. On the other hand, *temporary assignments* (short-term assignments, international commuters, and frequent flyers) positively influence the expatriate's ability to transfer knowledge across the MNC.

The hypotheses were tested using a data set of 92 subsidiaries of Danish MNCs located in 11 countries.

## BACKGROUND

HRM is a highly diverse and often controversial field. In this study, HRM is defined as a process of "developing, applying and evaluating policies, procedures, methods and programs relating to the individual in the organization" (Miner & Crane, 1995, p. 5). HRM is a highly dynamic process where environmental forces continually impinge on all policies, procedures, methods, and programs, thereby forcing HRM to adapt. HRM practices can vary across organizations (e.g., Pfeffer & Cohen, 1984) and countries (e.g., Brewster, 1993).

Researchers working in the field of HRM called for the transformation of the HRM system more than a decade ago, at which time they identified support to the process of organizational learning as the key strategic task facing the HRM function in many MNCs today (Pucik, 1988). Lado and Wilson (1994) suggested that HRM practices "can contribute to sustained competitive advantage through facilitating the development of competencies that are firm specific, produce complex social relationships...and generate organizational knowledge" (Lado & Wilson, 1994, p. 699). However, few studies have recognized that

the traditional prescriptions of high-performance HRM practices[1] do not fit the emerging knowledge-related goals of organizations. For example, Keegan and Turner (2002) argued that formal planning and job analysis procedures were not used by knowledge-intensive firms since they were engaged in uncertain, ambiguous tasks and dealt with highly turbulent and expertise-demanding environments. They, together with later researchers, argued for a new HRM task—to be centered around the process of learning and enhance the capacity of organizational members to contribute to knowledge-related organizational goals.

To identify which HRM practices could be employed to help organizations to achieve knowledge-related outcomes, a brief review of representative case-based and existing empirical studies undertaken by scholars from different research fields (international HRM, innovation, strategy, international business, etc.) on the link between HRM practices and various knowledge-related outcomes is necessary. My purpose is to determine what HRM practices organizations could employ to enhance knowledge-related outcomes, otherwise referred to as knowledge-driven HRM practices.

Using an illustrative case study, Gupta and Singhal (1993, pp. 41-42) investigated how companies manage human resources to foster innovation and creativity. They conceptualized HRM practices along four dimensions:

- **Human resource planning**, which includes creating venture teams with a balanced skill-mix, recruiting the right people, and voluntary team assignment. This strategy analyzes and determines personnel needs in order to create effective innovation teams.
- **Performance appraisal**, which includes encouraging risk taking, demanding innovation, generating or adopting new tasks, peer evaluation, frequent evaluations, and auditing innovation processes. This strategy appraises individual and team performance

so that there is a link between individual innovativeness and company profitability. Which tasks should be appraised and who should assess employees' performance are also taken into account.

- **Reward systems**, which includes freedom to do research, freedom to fail, freedom to form teams, freedom to run businesses, balancing pay and pride, noticeable pay raises, dual career tracks, promoting from within, recognition rewards, and balancing team and individual rewards. This strategy uses rewards to motivate personnel to achieve an organization's goals of productivity, innovation, and profitability.
- **Career management**, which includes empowering people, leading by example, and continued education. This strategy matches employees' long-term career goals with organizational goals through continuing education and training.

Recently, international business researchers have identified the role of HRM practices in the organizational learning as one subject of inquiry. For instance, Lane and Lubatkin (1998) looked at the similarities and differences between the student and teacher firms in their study on relative absorptive capacity and interorganizational learning. Among other factors, researchers considered *compensation practices* and found that a firm's ability to learn from another firm depends on the relative similarities of compensation policies in the student and teacher firms. Lyles and Salk (1996) and Lane et al. (2001) reported *training programs* to be an important knowledge acquisition mechanism. They claimed that when properly organized, the training programs are also important vehicles for establishing contacts between local and parent companies' employees, and thus promote collaboration and knowledge exchange. In Minbaeva et al. (2003) an effort was made to diverge from the previous work on knowledge transfer within MNCs by integrating

this stream more closely with the HRM-performance literature. The results of the study indicated that investments in the development of absorptive capacity of knowledge receivers through the extensive use of *training, performance appraisal, performance-based compensation,* and *internal communication* contribute to MNCs' knowledge transfer.

Similar discussions have been undertaken in the innovation literature. Laursen and Foss (2003) investigated the link between HRM practices and innovation performance, and argued that HRM practices are "most conducive to innovation performance when adopted, not in isolation, but as a system of mutually reinforcing practices" (p. 249). Researchers tested the hypotheses on a large dataset of 1,900 privately owned Danish firms in both manufacturing and non-manufacturing industries. Applying principal component analysis, they identified two HRM systems that influence innovation performance. The first one consists of HRM practices, which matter for the ability to innovate. They are interdisciplinary workgroups, quality circles, systems for collection of employees' proposals, planned job rotation, delegation of responsibility, integration of functions, and performance-related pay. The second system is dominated by firm-internal and firm-external training. The overall conclusion is that "while the adoption of individual HRM practices may be expected to influence innovation performance positively, the adoption of a package of complementary HRM practices could be expected to affect innovation performance much more strongly" (Laursen & Foss, 2003, p. 257).

In international HRM studies, it was found that the employment of formal HRM practices hinders flexibility, while employment of new HRM practices aimed at promoting flexibility facilitate organizational learning and innovation (Brewster et al., 2001). The use of a full range of *flexible working arrangements* may lead to the better innovation performance in organizations since:

- Flexible employees are more adaptive to new or unfamiliar experiences.
- Flexibility, with its emphasis on the efficient deployment of labor, increases multi-skills and cross-functional knowledge of employees, granting individuals the freedom to innovate.
- Flexibility can be seen as a way of gaining the commitment of the workforce.
- Flexible organizations are more successful in building a supportive learning environment, which helps to create continuous learning opportunities.

Tsang (1999) evaluated the HRM practices adopted by 12 Singapore MNCs operating in China, taking the view of the knowledge-based and learning perspectives. He focused on the *role of expatriates* in replicating organizational routines in a foreign subsidiary, and concluded that effective expatriation (including selection of expatriates, pre-assignment training, rotation, and their learning experience) in combination with inter-operation communication and training help in achieving knowledge diffusion within MNCs. This conclusion was later supported and further developed by other researchers focusing on expatriation, including Downes and Thomas (2000) and Bonache and Brewster (2001).

Downes and Thomas (2000) studied expatriation in the different stages of MNCs' international experience. It was found that "in the early stages of the subsidiary establishment, the expatriate acts as a vehicle for facilitating the transfer of SOP (standard operating procedures), technical and managerial expertise, corporate philosophy, and overall 'best practices'" (p. 137). As systems and practices of HQ are imparted, the role of expatriates may temporarily be diminished. Later, the expatriation practice picks up again as subsidiaries' ages increase. "It is likely that a renewed practice of expatriation is either the result of technological advancements and/or product and service innovations, which may

render previous knowledge obsolete and perhaps dictate updates in subsidiary learning" (Downes & Thomas, 2000, p. 146).

Bonache and Brewster (2001) put forward propositions regarding the significant impact of knowledge characteristics on expatriation policies. They proposed that if knowledge has a tacit nature, the organization must assign expatriate employees to the foreign operation; if knowledge to be transferred among MNC units is specific, the recruitment source of expatriates will be the organization itself; if knowledge to be transferred among MNC units is complex, the duration of the assignment will be longer.

In summary, the literature indicates that there are certain knowledge-driven HRM practices, the extensive use of which enhances knowledge-related outcomes. They are *job analysis, job design, recruitment, selection, career management, promotion from within, expatriation, international rotation, training, orientation programs, lateral transfer, performance appraisal, performance-based compensation, and flexible working practices.*

The interest of the knowledge management and organizational learning researchers in these HRM practices is extremely divergent. Not all practices receive equal attention. To illustrate this point, a review of articles with empirical evidence published in management and personnel-related journals was carried out on the ABI/Inform database. The search was conducted comparing the defined HRM practices and cross-searching with subjects "knowledge," "learning organizations," and "knowledge management." The results are presented in Figure 1, showing that training, expatriation, and selection are the three HRM practices that attracted the most attention in terms of their impact on knowledge-related outcomes. However, there are a number of other HRM practices that an MNC could employ to enhance knowledge-related outcomes. Therefore, more empirical investigations are needed to address other knowledge-driven HRM practices identified in the theoretical literature.

*Figure 1. HRM practices in studies on knowledge, innovation, and learning*

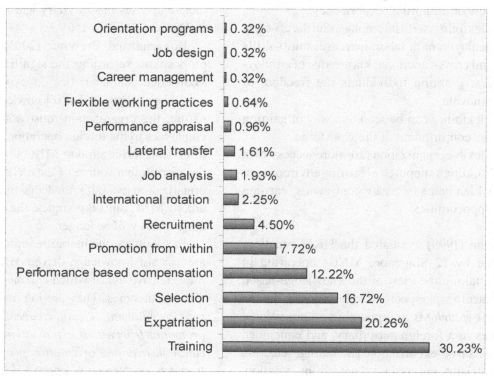

The next step is to determine *in which combination* HRM practices matter to knowledge transfer. As mentioned earlier, the literature recommends theoretically identifying groups of HRM practices by looking at mediating variables. In this study two behavioral determinants of knowledge transfer are chosen as mediating variables in the relation between HRM practices and knowledge transfer. These are absorptive capacity of knowledge receivers (ability and motivation to absorb knowledge) and disseminative capacity of knowledge senders (ability and motivation to transfer knowledge) (see Textbox 1). The next section investigates how HRM practices influence the behavior of knowledge receivers which in turn enhances the degree of knowledge transfer to the focal subsidiary.

## HRM PRACTICES AND KNOWLEDGE RECEIVERS' ABILITY AND MOTIVATION TO ABSORB KNOWLEDGE

Taking the above recommendation into consideration, the following sections argue *theoretically* for the choice of HRM practices affecting absorptive capacity of knowledge receivers. As indicated in Textbox 1, absorptive capacity has two elements: prior knowledge and intensity of effort (Cohen & Levinthal, 1990; Kim, 2001). "Prior knowledge base refers to existing individual units of knowledge available within the organization" (Kim, 2001, p. 271). Thus, the employees' ability, their educational backgrounds, and their job-related skills might represent the

*Textbox 1. Behavioral determinants of knowledge transfer*

Szulanski (1996, 2000, 2003) defines knowledge transfer as a process of dyadic exchanges of knowledge between the sender and the receiver, where the effectiveness of transfer depends to some extent on the disposition and ability of the source and recipient, on the strength of the tie between them, and on the characteristics of the object that is being created (Szulanski, 2003). Given the definition, Szulanski suggests the *signaling metaphor* as an approach of how to classify the determinants of knowledge transfer. "This metaphor specifies the basic elements of a transfer: source, channel, message, recipient and context" (Szulanski, 2000, p. 11). There are barriers associated with the each of the named elements. They are the characteristics of knowledge, characteristics of knowledge receivers, characteristics of knowledge senders, and characteristics of the relationships between the senders and receivers (Minbaeva, 2007). Two of the named variables are behavioral. They are:

1.  **Characteristics of Knowledge Receivers:** An implicit consensus exists about the importance of knowledge receiver behavior with respect to the absorption of transferred knowledge exists. The inability of knowledge receivers to absorb new knowledge (low absorptive capacity) is one of the most often cited impediments to internal knowledge transfer (e.g., Cohen & Levinthal, 1990; Lyles & Salk, 1996; Szulanski, 1996; Lane & Lubatkin, 1998; Gupta & Govindarajan, 2000; Lane et al., 2001). Following Cohen and Levinthal (1990) and Kim (2001), this study defines absorptive capacity as having two elements: prior knowledge and intensity of effort. Prior knowledge includes basic skills, a shared language, relevant prior experience, and up-to-date information on knowledge domains (Cohen & Levinthal, 1990; Szulanski, 1996, 2003). The term refers to the existing individual units of knowledge available within the organization (Kim, 2001). Employees need to have combinations of skills that enable them to find, acquire, manage, share, and apply knowledge that the organization needs.
    The second element of absorptive capacity, as proposed by Kim (2001), is the intensity of effort. Employees' intensity of effort is well researched in cognitive process theories, such as the expectancy theory of work motivation (Vroom, 1964). Overall, motivated employees want to contribute to organizational performance. Even though the organization may consist of individuals with significant abilities to learn, the organization's ability to utilize the absorbed knowledge will be low if employee motivation is low or absent (Baldwin, Magjuka, Loher, 1991).
2.  **Characteristics of Knowledge Senders:** Minbaeva and Michailova (2004) term the behavior of knowledge senders as "disseminative capacity." They argue that ability and willingness of organizational actors to share their knowledge are crucial to the success of knowledge transfer. Valuable knowledge is often tacit in nature. Transferring tacit knowledge requires teaching (Winter, 1987). Moreover, knowledge sharing is marked by different interpretations of the same idea, false starts, and disruptions (Zellmer-Bruhn, 2003). Therefore, knowledge senders should have well-developed abilities to articulate and communicate knowledge. These abilities could be acquired through education, training, observation, and involvement. On the other hand, knowledge senders may be capable but unwilling to share knowledge for the reasons outlined by Husted and Michailova (2002). The greater an individual's influence on the work carried out—how it is done and by whom—the greater the sense of responsibility the individual tends to feel for these decisions and the greater commitment knowledge senders exhibit.

"prior related knowledge" that the organization needs to assimilate and use (Cohen & Levinthal, 1990). The subsidiary employees' ability to absorb knowledge is related to such factors as prior achievement, initial skills level, and aptitudes. HRM practices that influence employees' ability have been a focus of research on high-performance HRM practices for some time. The overall conclusion of those studies is much the same: HRM practices "enhance employees' knowledge, skills, and abilities and thereafter provide a mechanism through which employees can use those attributes in performing their role" (Huselid, 1995, p. 645). Thus, organizations interested in achieving better individual ability should employ those HRM practices that aim at acquiring, developing, and

retaining human capital, hereafter referred as *cognitive* HRM practices.

Even highly skilled employees will not perform effectively if they are not motivated to do so (Huselid, 1995). Indeed, few would question that "if individuals possess the prerequisite ability to learn…performance will likely be poor if motivation is low or absent" (Baldwin et al., 1991, p. 52). In this context, there are HRM practices that recognize and reinforce employee behavior by providing incentives that elicit the appropriate behavior. Hereafter, these practices are referred to as *stimulative*[2] HRM practice.

The hypotheses on the effect of cognitive and stimulative HRM practices are developed below (Hypotheses 1 and 2 respectively).

## Cognitive HRM Practices

The findings of studies on the impact of cognitive HRM practices on ability are not consistent. Moreover, the majority of the studies did not examine relationships between cognitive HRM practices and employee ability. Instead, they used employee ability as a criterion for collapsing practices in a composite index. Table 1 presents the findings of high-performance HRM practice research on the cognitive HRM practices. The review is supplemented by findings from recent studies on HRM and knowledge-related outcomes.

Seven out of 14 knowledge-driven HRM practices were often identified as being related to employee ability. These are: *job analysis, recruitment, selection, international rotation, career management, training,* and *performance appraisal.* Specifically, an analysis of the competencies needed for different positions, together with an analysis of the firm's current pool of employee competencies, helps the organization specify the

*Table 1. Cognitive HRM practices*

| Author(s) | HRM Practices | Findings (influence on ability) |
|---|---|---|
| MacDuffie (1995) | Work teams. Problem-solving groups. Employee suggestion made and implemented. Job rotation. Decentralization of quality-related tasks. Recruitment and hiring. Training of new employees. Training of experienced employees. | The direct impact of HRM practices on employees' ability was not tested. Some of the HRM practices related to skills/knowledge were linked as well to motivation/commitment: work teams, problem-solving groups, employee suggestion made and implemented, recruitment and hiring, training of new employees, and training of experienced employees. |
| Huselid (1995) | A formal job analysis. A formal information-sharing program. Recruitment from within. Attitude survey. Quality of work life program, quality circles, and labor-management teams. Incentive plans, profit-sharing plans, and gain-sharing plans. Training. A formal grievance procedure and complaint resolution system. Enhanced selectivity. | The list of HRM practices emerged from the factor analysis of 13 items from the domain of High Performance Work Practices identified by the U.S. Department of Labor. The direct impact of HRM practices on employees' ability was not tested. Instead, the HRM practices were collapsed to get a composite index for an "employee skills and organizational structures" variable (Cronbach's alpha 0.67). The variable was later used to define its impact on organizational performance (turnover, productivity, and corporate financial performance). |
| Youndt et al. (1996) | Selective staffing. Selection for technical and problem-solving skills. Developmental and behavior-based performance appraisal. External equity. Group incentives. Skill-based pay. Salaried compensation. | The direct impact of HRM practices on employees' ability was not tested. The practices were collapsed into the index for the human-capital-enhancing HR system with a Cronbach's alpha of 0.68. |
| Delaney and Huselid (1996) | Staffing selectivity: number of applications for CORE, GSS, and managerial openings (Cronbach's alpha 0.66). Training effectiveness: formal job training, number of employees participating in training, training effectiveness (Cronbach's alpha 0.88). | The direct impact of HRM practices on employees' ability was not tested. There was suggestive evidence for complementarity between training effectives and staffing selectivity. |
| Guest, 1997 | Selection. Socialization. Training and development. Quality improvement programs. | The practices are conceptually defined. Instead of using the term "performance," it is more sensible to use the word "outcomes." HRM practices should be designed to lead to HRM outcomes of high-performance employee commitment, high-quality staff, and highly flexible staff. |
| Minbaeva et al. (2003) | Training: the number of days of formal training managerial and non-managerial employees (Cronbach's alpha 0.83). Competence/performance appraisal: the proportion of the workforce that regularly receives a formal evaluation of their performance, the proportion of jobs where a formal job analysis has been conducted, the proportion of new jobs for which a formal analysis of the desired personal skills/competencies/characteristics is carried out prior to making a selection decision (Cronbach's alpha 0.66). | Training has a significant relationship with employees' ability ($p<0.01$). The effect of performance appraisal on employees' ability is marginally significant ($p<0.10$). |

desired skills and knowledge. Recruitment and selection procedures aim to bring people with the previously identified skills and knowledge into vacant positions. Training, when organized as a systematic process, helps organizational individuals master their skills and influences their development. There is extensive evidence that investment in employee training enhances the human capital of the organization, which later results in a positive relationship between employee training and organizational performance (see also Delaney & Huselid, 1996). In MNCs, international rotation helps to best allocate the individual employee's need for growth and development. Performance appraisal (or performance management) systems provide employees with feedback on their performance and competencies, and give directions for enhancing their competencies to meet the needs of the organization. An integrated part of most performance appraisal systems is the establishment of objectives and targets for career management, self-development, and training of employees. Thus:

*Hypothesis 1. The more the subsidiary employs cognitive HRM practices, the higher the subsidiary employees' ability to absorb knowledge.*

## Stimulative HRM Practices

In the research on high-performance HRM practices, close attention was paid to HRM practices influencing employee behavior (see Table 2). For example, Huselid (1995) defined stimulative HRM practices as those that "affect employee motivation by encouraging them to work both harder and smarter" (p. 637). Among these stimulative practices are formal performance appraisal, performance-based criteria for compensation, internal promotion systems based on merit, and

the average number of qualified applicants per position. Organizational practices influencing employees' motivation to share knowledge have also been analyzed in some studies on HRM and knowledge. For example, Hislop (2002) suggested that HRM practices could be used to shape the willingness of employees to share their knowledge through their impact on organizational commitment. Among the HRM practices that make such an impact, Hislop (2002) named job design, performance appraisal, reward system, job security and career opportunity, among others. Minbaeva et al. (2003) suggested that HRM practices such as merit-based promotion and performance-based compensation may influence the motivation of knowledge receivers by providing incentives that elicit appropriate behaviors.

The reviewed studies are more or less in agreement regarding which HRM practices influence employees' willingness to perform (see Table 2). Among these are *performance-based compensation* and the use of *internal promotion* systems that focus on employee merit and help employees to overcome invisible barriers to their career growth (Arthur, 1994; Huselid, 1995; MacDuffie, 1995; Delery & Doty, 1996). *Internal transfer,* aiming at allocating and retaining the best people with their knowledge and skills, allows an organization to sustain and accumulate its human capital pool. *Orientation programs* are designed to help new people adjust quicker to the new environment and become a part of the "big picture." *Flexible working practices* and *job design* can be beneficial for such employees, allowing them to balance their work and other aspects of their lives. Thus:

*Hypothesis 2. The more the subsidiary employs stimulative HRM practices, the higher the subsidiary employees' motivation to absorb knowledge.*

*Table 2. Stimulative HRM practices*

| Author(s) | HRM Practices | Findings (influence on motivation) |
|---|---|---|
| Arthur (1992) | Broadly defined jobs. Employee participation. Formal dispute resolution. Information sharing. Highly skilled workers. Self-managed teams. Extensive skills training. Extensive benefits. High wages. Salaried workers. Stock ownership. | Commitment HRM practices were characterized by higher levels of employee involvement in managerial decisions, formal participation programs, training in group problem solving, socializing activities, and by a higher percentage of maintenance, or skilled, employees and average wage rates. |
| MacDuffie (1995) | Work teams. Problem-solving groups. Employee suggestion made and implemented. Recruitment and hiring. Contingent compensation. Status differentiation. Training of new employees. Training of experienced employees. | The direct impact of HRM practices on employees' motivation was not tested. Some HRM practices related to skills/knowledge were linked as well to motivation/commitment: work teams, problem-solving groups, employee suggestion made and implemented, recruitment and hiring, training of new employees, training of experienced employees. |
| Huselid (1995) | Performance-based compensation. Formal performance appraisal. Merit-based promotion, seniority-based promotion (reverse coded). Number of qualified applicants per position. | The list of HRM practices emerged from the factor analysis of 13 items from the domain of High Performance Work Practices identified by the U.S. Department of Labor. The direct impact of HRM practices on employees' motivation was not tested. Instead, the HRM practices were collapsed to get a composite index for an "employee motivation" variable (Cronbach's alpha 0.66). The variable was later used to define its impact on organizational performance (turnover, productivity, and financial performance). |
| Delaney and Huselid (1996) | Incentive compensation: performance-related earnings of managers and administrators, COREs, and GSS (Cronbach's alpha 0.83). Grievance procedure: formal procedures for resolving disputes. | The direct impact of HRM practices on employees' motivation was not tested. Complementarity among HRM practices influencing employees' motivation was not observed. |
| Guest, 1997 | Single status. Job security. Internal promotion. Individualized reward systems. | The practices are conceptually defined. Instead of using the term "performance," it is more sensible to use the word "outcomes." HRM practices should be designed to lead to HRM outcomes of high-performance employee commitment, high-quality staff, and highly flexible staff. |
| Hislop (2002) | Fair decision making. Appraisal and reward system. Job design. Type of organizational culture. Job security. Internal promotion and career opportunities. | The motivation of employees to share their knowledge may be shaped by their level of organizational commitment. The list of HRM practices influencing commitment is conceptually defined. |
| Minbaeva et al. (2003) | Merit-based promotion: the opportunity to be promoted to positions of greater pay and/or responsibility within the subsidiary, the importance on merit for promotion decisions, the extent to which upper-level vacancies are filled from within (Cronbach's alpha 0.63). Performance-based compensation: the proportion of employees who have the opportunity to earn individual, group, or company-wide bonuses, whether the company uses performance-based compensation and whether the compensation systems are closely connected to the financial results of the subsidiary (Cronbach's alpha 0.61). | Performance-based compensation is a highly significant (p<0.001) determinant of employee motivation. |

## HRM PRACTICES AND KNOWLEDGE SENDERS' ABILITY AND MOTIVATION TO TRANSFER KNOWLEDGE

In Textbox 1, the ability and motivation of knowledge senders to transfer knowledge were identified as important determinants of MNC knowledge transfer. In addition to job-related competencies, knowledge senders should have the ability to articulate and communicate knowledge, stimulate the learning environment, and motivate receivers to assimilate and utilize knowledge. At the same time, the senders' willingness to share knowledge is associated with commitment and involvement in the day-to-day life of the organizational unit.

One of the knowledge-driven HRM practices identified earlier and related to the behavior of knowledge senders was expatriation. In this section, therefore, hypotheses on how different types of expatriation assignment relate to expatriates' knowledge-sharing behavior in terms of their ability and willingness to share knowledge are presented and tested.

### Expatriates as Vehicles for Knowledge Dissemination

Traditionally, expatriation has been associated with the ethnocentric approach and indicated the practice of using parent-country nationals for staffing key positions in overseas subsidiaries. The primary goal of expatriation has been control and coordination: by reallocating expatriates, parent organizations have been able to exert control and achieve global integration across subsidiaries (Edstrom & Galbraith, 1977).

The goals of expatriate assignment have been changing gradually (Evans, Pucik, & Barsoux, 2002). Nowadays, the old motto of expatriation—"just get the job done"—is no longer relevant. The role of expatriates as vehicles for disseminating knowledge across MNCs' units has become a new area of inquiry for international HRM literature (Tsang, 1999; Downes & Thomas, 2000; Delios & Bjorkman, 2000; Bonache & Brewster, 2001). Expatriates are expected to be engaged in local staff development and support skills transfer from HQ. Some researchers argued that the knowledge-related function of expatriates is complementary to the traditional function of coordination and control. For example, Delios and Bjorkman (2000) noted that under the control and coordination function, "the expatriate works to align the operations of the unit with that of the parent organization" (p. 279), while the complementary knowledge function requires the expatriate to transfer the parent company's knowledge to the foreign subsidiary under conditions "in which the parent has greater proprietary knowledge" (p. 281). Research revealed a list of possible strategic targets for expatriates in the area of knowledge transfer: to develop top talent and future leaders of the company; to improve the trust/commitment of the subsidiary; to train host-national employees in order to improve individual skills; to improve team skills; to implement knowledge practices; to develop, share, and transfer best practices; and to develop an international leadership (Bonache & Fernandez, 1999; Harris, Brewster, & Sparrow, 2003).

Changes in the expatriate profile and increasing awareness of relocation challenges for international managers and their families led organizations to experiment with alternative forms of expatriate assignments (Harris, 2002). The *traditional (long-term) expatriate assignment* is usually defined as an assignment where the international manager and his or her family move to the host country for over one year (in the majority of cases, for approximately three years). Alternative forms to the traditional assignment include (Harris, 2002; Harris et al., 2003):

- **Short-Term Assignment:** An assignment with a specified duration, usually less than one year. Family may accompany the employee.
- **International Commuter:** An employee who commutes from the home country to a place of work in another country, usually on a weekly or bi-weekly basis, while the family remains at home.
- **Frequent Flyer:** An employee who undertakes frequent international business trips but does not relocate.

The New Forms of International Working survey was carried out by the Center for Research into Management of Expatriation (Cranfield School of Management, UK) with the purpose to increase understanding of the management issues surroundings alternative forms of international working. Key findings from the survey were that all types of international assignment, including the alternative forms of international assignment, are increasing in number, but the reasons for using each type of assignment vary (see Table 3).

*Table 3. New forms of international working: Survey findings*

| Type of Assignment | Number of Employees | Changing Patterns and Trends in the Number of Employees | | Reasons for Use (top 3) | Usual Length of Assignment (majority) | Main Problems Encountered |
|---|---|---|---|---|---|---|
| | | In the last 2 years | For the next 5 years | | | |
| Long-Term Assignment | 53% of respondents have more than 50 employees on this type of assignment | 62% of respondents reported an increase | 48% of respondents reported an increase | Skills transfer (74%), managerial control (62%), and management development (60%) | 3 years (57%) | Mobility barriers/ unwillingness to go to unattractive locations. Dual career/family issues. Repatriation/career issues. Cost assignment/administration. Compensation package/terms and conditions |
| Short-Term Assignment | 18% of respondents have more than 50 employees on this type of assignment | 67% of respondents reported an increase | 66% of respondents reported an increase | Skills transfer (69%), management development (39%), and managerial control (12%) | Up to 1 year (55%) | Work/life balance. Difficult to establish policy and practice. Tax management issues and compensation terms and conditions. |
| International Commuter | 6% of respondents have more than 50 employees on this type of assignment | 52% of respondents reported an increase | 50% of respondents reported an increase | Skills transfer (32%), family reasons (32%), and managerial control (25%) | Up to three months (15%) | High costs. Work/life balance. Defining policy terms. Tax management. Cultural differences. |
| Frequent Flyer | 26% of respondents have more than 50 employees on this type of assignment | 52% of respondents reported an increase | 50% of respondents reported an increase | Managerial control (40%), skills transfer (26%), and developing an international cadre (20%) | Up to one week (31%) | Cost management. Burnout. No established policies. |

What remains largely unknown is whether different types of expatriation assignments influence knowledge transfer. As indicated, the traditional form of expatriate assignment is changing due to cost and family constraints. In addition to the traditional long-term assignment, expatriates are sent abroad on more temporary assignments. However, the literature is silent on whether the new forms of international working influence knowledge transfer. This study addresses this gap by looking at why and how four types of expatriation assignments influence the knowledge-sharing behavior of expatriates and thereby enhance the degree of knowledge transfer to overseas subsidiaries.

In particular, an assignment that required the relocation of the manager and his or her family for a specified period was assumed to affect expatriates' motivation. Temporary assignments (short-term assignment, international commuters, and frequent flyers) would increase expatriates' ability to transfer knowledge across the MNCs. More detailed discussion of these relationships is presented in the next section.

## Permanent and Temporary Expatriate Assignments

Harris (2002) defined a long-term expatriate assignment as an assignment where the employee and his or her family move to the host country for a specified period of time, usually more than one year. Expatriates employed on long-term assignments are permanently stationed at the overseas subsidiary. They experience high-task autonomy, greater responsibilities, and other factors, which in the behavioral literature are known as role discretion (Stewart, 1982). The greater an individuals' discretion as to "what work gets done, how it gets done and by whom," the greater the sense of responsibility the individual will feel for these decisions and the greater commitment an expatriate will exhibit (Gregersen & Black, 1992). "It seems logical that task autonomy,

which is similar to role discretion, should lead to greater satisfaction, since the expatriate manager has the freedom to modify the role to fit his/her abilities" (Downes, Thomas, & McLarney, 2000, p. 124). Organizational commitment originally focused on an individual's emotional attachment to an organization (Mowday & McDade, 1979). If someone has high levels of affect toward their job or organization, it could be expected that they would be motivated to perform better. Therefore, permanently placed expatriates, who are abroad for a specified duration, may show higher willingness to contribute to the organizational goals. Thus:

*Hypothesis 3. The more the MNC uses permanent expatriate assignments, the higher the expatriates' motivation to transfer knowledge.*

Expatriates on temporary assignments (short-term assignments, international commuters, and frequent flyers) are the tools by which MNCs obtain and maintain their global knowledge to a great extent. These expatriates have a greater opportunity to learn from their experience of managing the subsidiaries. "People moving around the company's operations worldwide are expected to learn from each other, acquire globally applicable skills, deepen expertise and expand their networks" (Center for Research into Management of Expatriation, 2002, p. 7). For example, highly mobile teams of experts—troubleshooters—are often seen on short-term assignments (Center for Research into Management of Expatriation, 2002). They are sent on a temporary basis to different locations to work together with local employees and help them solve a particular operational problem. They also enhance their competencies by extracting the best solutions from different locations, they increase their individual understanding and vision of international operations, they continuously increase their skills and develop competencies, they improve their language

*Figure 2. Conceptual model*

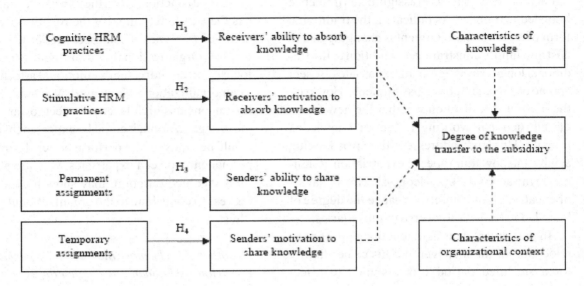

abilities, and they learn how to communicate in different cultures. Thus:

*Hypothesis 4. The more the MNC uses temporary expatriate assignments, the higher the expatriates' ability to transfer knowledge.*

The hypotheses are summarized in the conceptual model presented in Figure 2.

## MEASURES

Measures for high-performance HRM practices were developed and very well described in Huselid (1995), Huselid, Jackson, and Schuler (1995), and Delaney and Huselid (1996). These studies served as the main source of inspiration. In addition, scales were adopted from the Cranet survey on International Human Resource Management (car-

ried out in 1991, 1995, and 1999). The measures for the four types of expatriate assignments were adopted from the previously mentioned survey on the New Forms of International Working which was carried out in 2000. Measures were then crosschecked with the conclusions of theoretical papers, findings from the case studies, and limited empirical work on the link between HRM and knowledge-related outcomes. This resulted in the list of HRM practices presented in Table 4. The same table contains measures for mediating variables. For all variables, the understanding of the operationalization was checked during the piloting of the questionnaire.

The hypotheses are tested on the data set of 92 subsidiaries of Danish MNCs. For the description of the survey instrument development, research strategy, data collection, and sample, see Textbox 2. SPSS statistical analysis software was used for the analyses. Descriptive statistics for variables are presented in Table 5.

*Table 4. Measures*

| Variables | Label | Description |
|---|---|---|
| Job Analysis | Analysis | Please mark the number that best indicates the degree to which each statement describes the HRM practices employed within your subsidiary (Likert-type scale ranging from 1–never to 5–always):<br>- Job analysis identifies the required educational background, previous experience, the general competency information, etc. |
| Job Design | Design | - We use different approaches to job design such as job enlargement, job rotation, and team-based job design. |
| Flexible Practices | Flexible | - We use flexible working arrangements—such as flextime, job sharing, and part-time work—to accommodate best the individual working arrangement preferences. |
| Recruitment | Recruitment | - The purpose of our recruitment procedures is to generate a pool of qualified external candidates for a particular job. |
| Promotion | Promotion | - When a vacancy occurs, we carry out a search within the company before turning to the various outside sources. |
| Selection | Selection | - We use various selection procedures to determine the characteristics required for effective job performance. |
| Orientation Programs | Orientation | - All new employees will be oriented in the philosophy, ethics, values, and business priorities of the company. |
| Lateral Transfer | Transfer | - Employee lateral transfer is considered a development activity and one of the best ways to retain talented people. |
| International Rotation | Rotation | - Local nationals are often transferred to headquarters or other international operations. |
| Career Management | Career | - Career development in our company represents an ongoing and formalized effort of corporate management. |
| Training | Training | - Our training programs aim to provide employees with specific skills and help them correct deficiencies in their performance. |
| Performance-Based Compensation | Compensation | - Employees are generally rewarded on the basis of the value of the job and their personal contribution to organizational performance. |
| Performance Appraisal | Appraisal | - The performance management system in our company has a developmental purpose of providing information and direction to individuals. |
| Receivers' Ability to Absorb Knowledge | ReAb | Compared to your industry competitors, how do you rate your subsidiary's employees on the following dimensions (Likert-type scale ranging from 1–very low to 5–outstanding):<br>- Job-related abilities<br>- Overall competence<br>Please evaluate the ability of the knowledge receivers (your subsidiary's employees) to absorb new knowledge (Likert-type scale ranging from 1–very low to 5–outstanding). |
| Receivers' Motivation to Absorb Knowledge | ReMot | Compared to your industry competitors, how do you rate your subsidiary's employees on the following dimensions (Likert-type scale ranging from 1–very low to 5–outstanding):<br>- Motivation<br>- Involvement<br>- Job satisfaction<br>Please evaluate motivation of the knowledge receivers (your subsidiary's employees) to absorb new knowledge (Likert-type scale ranging from 1–very low to 5–outstanding). |

*Table 4. Continued*

| | | Please mark the number that best indicates the degree to which each statement describes HRM practices employed across all subsidiaries within the MNC (Likert-type scale ranging from 1–no or very little extent to 5–very great extent): |
|---|---|---|
| Long-Term Expatriation | LTexpat | - Presence of expatriates on long-term assignments (usually over one year). |
| Short-Term Expatriation | STexpat | - Presence of expatriates on short-term assignments (usually less than one year). |
| International Commuters | ICexpat | - Presence of international commuters (expatriates who commute from country to country usually on a weekly basis). |
| Frequent Flyers | FFexpat | - Presence of frequent flyers (expatriates who undertake frequent international business trips but do not relocate). |
| Senders' Ability to Transfer Knowledge | SeAb | Please evaluate the ability of the knowledge senders to transfer new knowledge (Likert-type scale ranging from 1–very low to 5–outstanding). |
| Senders' Motivation to Transfer Knowledge | SeMot | Please evaluate motivation of the knowledge senders to transfer new knowledge to the rest of the corporation (Likert-type scale ranging from 1–very low to 5–outstanding). |

*Table 5. Descriptive statistics*

| Variables | Min. | Max. | Means | St. Dev. |
|---|---|---|---|---|
| Analysis | 1.00 | 5.00 | 3.30 | 1.12 |
| Design | 1.00 | 5.00 | 2.57 | 1.10 |
| Flexible | 1.00 | 5.00 | 2.66 | 1.23 |
| Recruitment | 1.00 | 5.00 | 3.32 | 1.17 |
| Promotion | 1.00 | 5.00 | 3.41 | 1.15 |
| Selection | 1.00 | 5.00 | 3.20 | 1.08 |
| Orientation | 1.00 | 5.00 | 3.60 | 1.20 |
| Transfer | 1.00 | 5.00 | 3.37 | 1.20 |
| Rotation | 1.00 | 5.00 | 2.01 | 1.10 |
| Career | 1.00 | 5.00 | 2.52 | 1.24 |
| Training | 1.00 | 5.00 | 3.42 | 1.03 |
| Compensation | 1.00 | 5.00 | 3.49 | 1.18 |
| Appraisal | 1.00 | 5.00 | 3.18 | 1.14 |
| ReAb | 2.00 | 5.00 | 3.6848 | 0.52149 |
| ReMot | 2.00 | 5.00 | 3.6277 | 0.62379 |
| LTexpat | 1.00 | 5.00 | 2.9778 | 1.25401 |
| STexpat | 1.00 | 5.00 | 2.1957 | 1.07150 |
| ICexpat | 1.00 | 4.00 | 2.0769 | 1.12774 |
| FFexpat | 1.00 | 5.00 | 2.4565 | 1.16178 |
| SeAb | 1.00 | 5.00 | 3.2857 | 0.80672 |
| SeMot | 1.00 | 5.00 | 3.1196 | 0.93577 |

*Textbox 2. Data collection*

The Hermes CD Direct from KOB (Kobmandstandes Oplysnings Bureau) was used to construct the data set.[3] The database query was initiated by selecting those firms that were headquartered in Denmark, and then the sample was reduced to those that had two or more subsidiaries abroad. The procedure resulted in a list that was crosschecked with the Børsen 500[4] to ensure that the population was as complete and relevant as possible. The MNCs included in the sample were further limited to those whose subsidiaries employ more than 30 employees as small-scale companies in general, and small subsidiaries in particular, and which do not utilize a wide range of formal HRM practices (Miner & Crane, 1995).

The final data set consisted of 305 Danish subsidiaries. Questionnaires were addressed to the HRM manager/general manager of the focal subsidiary. If the approached manager was unable to complete the survey, he or she could forward the questionnaire to a senior or middle manager with sufficient knowledge regarding the themes of this study.

A Web-based survey was chosen for data collection due to the time and cost considerations. The respondents were approached by a cover letter sent via e-mail, which explained the purpose of the survey, detailed the research process and analysis procedures, offered follow-up reports and related working papers, and provided straightforward directions completing the questionnaire. In addition, a Web site was established to back up the survey. Respondents were invited to visit the Web site and read more on the survey subjects and related themes. A link to the questionnaire was provided within the text of the cover letter, and the survey was only available through that link, which decreased the risk of potential error.

The above strategy resulted in achieving a response rate of 30% (92 out of 305 subsidiaries). Twenty responding subsidiaries were located in Germany, 17 in the United States, 15 in Russia, 14 in China, 10 in Sweden, 6 in the UK, 6 in France, and 1 each in Sri Lanka, the Philippines, Spain, and Portugal. The response rates in various countries reflect the general geographical distribution of Danish subsidiaries abroad.

## RESULTS

### Results for Cognitive and Stimulative HRM Practices

The correlation matrix is presented in Table 6. There were a high number of associations among HRM practices, as was expected—58 significant correlations of different degree out of 78 possible. Factor analysis creates a set of factors to be treated as uncorrelated variables in one approach to handling multicollinearity in regression. Following Huselid (1995), I factor-analyzed HRM practices using the principal component analysis with varimax rotation. Factor loadings for each factor are reported in Table 7.

Three factors with eigenvalues more than 1 emerged from the analysis.[5] As expected, Factor 1 included a range of cognitive HRM practices employed to improve the ability of knowledge receivers. The factor included job analysis, recruitment, selection, international rotation, career management, and training and performance appraisal. Factor 2 contained stimulative HRM practices aiming at enhancing motivation of knowledge receivers. The factor was composed of promotion, orientation programs, lateral transfers, and

compensation. Factor 3 also contained stimulative HRM practices, namely flexible working practices and job design.

Table 8 provides examination of the relationship between the HRM practices and the ability and motivation of knowledge receivers to absorb knowledge (absorptive capacity). Unstandardized coefficients were reported. Model 1 presents the results of the regression analysis of the impact of HRM practices on the ability of knowledge receivers. The model is statistically significant with an R-square of 0.111. As predicted, Factor 1 (the group of cognitive HRM practices) showed a positive, significant effect on the dependent variable ($p<0.05$). Hypothesis 1 is confirmed. Model 2 tested the effect of HRM practices on the motivation of knowledge receivers to absorb knowledge. The model is significant with $p<0.001$ and the R-square of 0.23. Factor 2—promotion, orientation, transfer, and compensation—showed positive effect with strong significance ($p<0.001$). In Model 2, Factor 1 also showed a positive effect, but with the smaller significance than in Model 1. The hypothesized effect of flexible working practices and job design (Factor 3) on the dependent variable was in the expected direction but insignificant. Hypothesis 2 is partially confirmed.

*Table 6. Correlation matrix (1)*

| | 1 | 2 | 3 | 4 | 5 | 6 | 7 | 8 | 9 | 10 | 11 | 12 | 13 | 14 | 15 |
|---|---|---|---|---|---|---|---|---|---|---|---|---|---|---|---|
| 1. Analysis | 1.000 | | | | | | | | | | | | | | |
| 2. Design | 0.379*** | 1.000 | | | | | | | | | | | | | |
| 3. Flexible | -0.071 | 0.265* | 1.000 | | | | | | | | | | | | |
| 4. Recruitment | 0.300** | 0.261* | 0.108 | 1.000 | | | | | | | | | | | |
| 5. Promotion | 0.272* | 0.083 | 0.171 | 0.282* | 1.000 | | | | | | | | | | |
| 6. Selection | 0.410*** | 0.262* | 0.117 | 0.411*** | | 1.000 | | | | | | | | | |
| 7. Orientation | 0.296* | -0.007 | 0.123 | 0.134 | 0.316** | 0.343** | 1.000 | | | | | | | | |
| 8. Transfer | 0.292* | 0.264* | 0.158 | 0.258* | 0.483*** | 0.425*** | 0.124 | 1.000 | | | | | | | |
| 9. Rotation | 0.178† | 0.358*** | 0.219† | 0.179 | 0.149 | 0.176*** | 0.094 | 0.114 | 1.000 | | | | | | |
| 10. Career | 0.378*** | 0.273* | 0.227† | 0.427*** | 0.375*** | 0.608*** | 0.264* | 0.578*** | 0.433*** | 1.000 | | | | | |
| 11. Training | 0.393*** | 0.411*** | 0.003 | 0.362*** | 0.293** | 0.422*** | 0.181 | 0.418*** | 0.306** | 0.390*** | 1.000 | | | | |
| 12. Compensation | 0.337** | 0.349*** | 0.089 | 0.261* | 0.335** | 0.396*** | 0.304** | 0.477*** | 0.123 | 0.385*** | 0.544*** | 1.000 | | | |
| 13. Appraisal | 0.252* | 0.310** | 0.043 | 0.293* | 0.294* | 0.661 | 0.194† | 0.531*** | 0.292* | 0.560*** | 0.476*** | 0.440*** | 1.000 | | |
| 14. ReAb | 0.259* | 0.148 | -0.020 | 0.124 | 0.075 | 0.166 | 0.053 | 0.007 | -0.008 | 0.082 | 0.134 | 0.214* | 0.111 | 1.000 | |
| 15. ReMot | 0.190† | 0.004 | 0.052 | -0.079 | 0.162 | 0.162 | 0.183 | 0.384*** | 0.007 | 0.232* | 0.223* | 0.320** | 0.193 | 0.535*** | 1.000 |

*\*\*\* - p<0.001, \*\*- p<0.01, \* - p<0.05, † - p<0.1*

*Table 7. Factor loading for cognitive and stimulative HRM practices (extraction method: principal component analysis. varimax rotation)*

| Variables | HRM1 | HRM2 | HRM3 |
|---|---|---|---|
| Analysis | 0.588 | 0.234 | -0.261 |
| Design | 0.524 | 0.099 | 0.527 |
| Flexible | -0.097 | 0.189 | 0.897 |
| Recruitment | 0.584 | 0.158 | 0.029 |
| Promotion | 0.246 | 0.758 | 0.073 |
| Selection | 0.606 | 0.482 | 0.038 |
| Orientation | 0.038 | 0.668 | -0.136 |
| Transfer | 0.447 | 0.602 | 0.206 |
| Rotation | 0.528 | -0.184 | 0.375 |
| Career | 0.710 | 0.366 | 0.173 |
| Training | 0.665 | 0.304 | 0.015 |
| Compensation | 0.448 | 0.574 | 0.204 |
| Appraisal | 0.699 | 0.298 | 0.086 |
| Initial eigenvalues | 4.960 | 1.371 | 1.043 |
| % of variance | 38.15 | 10.54 | 8.024 |

*Table 8. Regression analyses for ability and motivation of knowledge receivers to absorb knowledge*

| Variables | Model 1 (ReAb) | | Model 2 (ReMot) | |
|---|---|---|---|---|
| | β | s.e. | β | s.e. |
| Constant | 3.682*** | 0.060 | 3.693*** | 0.064 |
| Factor 1 | 0.155* | 0.060 | 0.134* | 0.065 |
| Factor 2 | 0.054 | 0.060 | 0.244*** | 0.065 |
| Factor 3 | -0.035 | 0.060 | 0.014 | 0.065 |
| R-square | 0.111 | | 0.230 | |
| F | 2.587† | | 6.178*** | |

*\*\*\* - p<0.001, \*\* - p<0.01, \* - p<0.05, † - p<0.1*

## Results for Types of Expatriate Assignments

The correlation matrix for all variables used in this section is presented in Table 9. In the correlation matrix, four types of expatriate assignments showed a high degree of association. Some of the correlation coefficients indicated the possibility of multicollinearity (i.e., r>0.5). To uncover the underlying factor structure associated with four independent variables, they were factor-analyzed using the principal component analysis as an extraction method (following Huselid, 1995). The previous choice of factor analytic solution is proven to be useful since it provided a possibility to decrease the number of independent variables and reduced problems associated with multicollinearity. Moreover, similar to the factor analytic solution used in the previous section, this factor analysis had a confirmative rather than an explorative nature. It was expected that four types of expatriate assignments would form two groups:

*Table 9. Correlation matrix (2)*

| | | 1 | 2 | 3 | 4 | 5 | 6 |
|---|---|---|---|---|---|---|---|
| 1. | LTexpat | 1.000 | | | | | |
| 2. | STexpat | 0.367*** | 1.000 | | | | |
| 3. | ICexpat | 0.098 | 0.483*** | 1.000 | | | |
| 4. | FFexpat | -0.071 | 0.219* | 0.590*** | 1.000 | | |
| 5. | SeAb | -0.008 | 0.049 | 0.183† | 0.201† | 1.000 | |
| 6. | SeMot | 0.278** | 0.261* | 0.034 | 0.091 | 0.495*** | 1.000 |

*** - p<0.001, **- p<0.01, * - p<0.05, † - p<0.1

*Table 10. Factor loading for four types of international assignments (extraction method: principal component analysis)*

| Variables | Factor 1 | Factor 2 |
|---|---|---|
| LTexpat | 0.332 | 0.821 |
| STexpat | 0.740 | 0.418 |
| ICexpat | 0.880 | -0.222 |
| FFexpat | 0.692 | -0.558 |
| Initial eigenvalues | 1.912 | 1.209 |
| % of variance | 47.79 | 30.23 |

*Table 11. Regression analyses for knowledge senders' ability and motivation to transfer knowledge*

| Variables | Model 1 (SeAb) | | Model 2 (SeMot) | |
|---|---|---|---|---|
| | β | s.e. | β | s.e. |
| Constant | 3.284*** | 0.086 | 3.101*** | 0.096 |
| Factor 1 | 0.161† | 0.086 | 0.200* | 0.097 |
| Factor 2 | -0.096 | 0.086 | 0.211* | 0.097 |
| R-square | 0.053 | | 0.095 | |
| F | 2.387† | | 4.538* | |

*** - p<0.001, * - p<0.05, † - p<0.1

permanent and temporary assignments. Indeed, two factors with eigenvalues >1 were determined from the factor analysis. Factor 1 included temporary expatriate assignments employed to improve ability of knowledge receivers. Among these were short-term expatriates, international commuters, and frequent flyers. Factor 2 was represented by one type of assignment—long-term expatriation. This type of assignment was expected to influence the willingness of knowledge senders to transfer knowledge. Factor loadings for each factor, eigenvalues, and percentages of variance explained by each factor are reported in Table 10.

To test the hypotheses, regression analyses were run with permanent and temporary assignments (factor-analyzed) as independent variables. The results are presented in Table 11. Model 1 showed some statistical significance with p<0.10 and the R-square 0.053. The model provided support for Hypothesis 4: the employment of expatriates on the short-term basis, use of international

commuters, and frequent flyers positively influence the ability of knowledge senders to transfer knowledge (p<0.10). Model 2 tested the effect of permanent expatriate assignments (Factor 2) on the motivation of knowledge senders while controlling for Factor 1. The model showed higher significance with the R-square of about 10%. The influence of Factor 2 (long-term assignments) was positive and significant (p<0.05). Hypothesis 3 was confirmed.

## DISCUSSION

HRM practices and knowledge transfer are associated, but some important aspects of this interpretation and empirical support for the link are missing. This chapter aimed to take steps towards understanding why this association exists and how various HRM practices influence knowledge transfer.

In particular, it was hypothesized that the use of cognitive HRM practices is positively related to the receivers' ability to absorb incoming knowledge, while stimulative HRM practices develop knowledge receivers' motivation. The group of cognitive HRM practices includes job analysis, recruitment, selection, international rotation, career management, training, and performance appraisal, while stimulative HRM practices contain promotion, performance-based compensation, internal transfer, orientation programs, job design, and flexible working practices.

Before testing the hypothesis, HRM practices were classified into the factors theoretically. The specific factor structure was then confirmed through the factor analysis. Factor analysis was not used as an exploratory technique, but rather as a method of comparing the classification initially suggested by non-statistical arguments or evidence. It was also needed to reduce a number of independent variables and to handle the multicollinearity problem. Moreover, the hypotheses were developed in such a way that they assumed the simultaneous effect of HRM practices on the dependent variable and not the effect of individual practices. Such an assumption was recommended in the literature since HRM practices applied in combination were found to have a greater effect on organizational outcomes than the sum of the individual effects from each practice alone (Ichniowski, Shaw, & Prennushi, 1997). Results of the factor analysis indicated the existence of three groups of HRM practices conducive to the behavior of knowledge receivers—the first factor was marked by higher loadings on the cognitive HRM practices (Factor 1), the second and third factors were marked by high loadings on the stimulative factors (Factor 2 and Factor 3).

To test the hypothesis, following Huselid (1995), factors were entered as independent variables into the regressions on the dependent variable. The simultaneous effect of job analysis, recruitment, selection, international rotation, career management, training, and performance appraisal (Factor 1) on the receivers' ability was positive and significant ($p<0.05$). Job analysis investigates the competencies needed for different positions, based on how the needed competencies are acquired through recruitment and selection procedures. Those organizations that carry out the formal job analysis, and employ extensive recruitment and selection procedures are able to generate a pool of skilled external candidates with the desired level of knowledge and skills. Members of this pool then show the higher ability to absorb knowledge. Career management and international rotation best allocate the individual employee's need for growth and development. Performance appraisal provides employees with feedback on their performance and competencies, and offers direction for enhancing their competencies to meet the changing needs of the firm. An integrated part of most performance appraisal systems is the establishment of objectives and targets for the self-development and training of employees. When organized as a systematic process, training helps to eliminate skill deficiencies identified through performance appraisals.

The simultaneous effect of only some stimulative HRM practices at improving the receivers' motivation to absorb knowledge was positive and significant ($p<0.001$). Those organizations that send new employees through extensive orientation programs, in which they receive realistic information about the job and the organization, should expect a higher level of employee motivation to absorb knowledge. Orientation programs aim to provide general support and reassurance for the new employees, help them to cope with inevitable stresses of transition, and help them adjust quickly in the new organizational environment. Promoting employees from within the firm is likely to provide a strong motivation for employees. Internal transfers aim to better allocate individual needs for growth and development. In addition to the learning experience, employees achieve higher commitment and involvement. There is a clear linkage between individual effort and reward.

Formation of performance-based compensation systems that reward employees for the value of their job and their personal contribution to organizational performance is a strong incentive. The effect of job design and flexible working practices (Factor 3) was in the expected direction, but insignificant.

This chapter also considered how different types of expatriate assignments may contribute to the expatriates' ability and motivation to share knowledge. The four types of assignments are defined as long-term expatriate assignment, short-term expatriate assignment, international commuters, and frequent flyers. According to the Center for Research into Management of Expatriation on the New Forms of International Working (2002), organizations appear to be making increasing use of all four types of expatriate assignments. Moreover, skills/knowledge transfer is among the main reasons for using each type of assignment. The needs for knowledge transfer were highest for long-term assignments and the lowest for frequent flyers. This chapter proceeded further, suggesting that although all four types are connected to knowledge transfer, there are different types of assignments that increase expatriates' ability and motivation to transfer knowledge to the subsidiaries. It was suggested that expatriates' willingness to transfer knowledge can be enhanced through the employment of long-term expatriation practices, while expatriates' ability to transfer knowledge may be increased through their involvement in temporary assignments, such as short-term assignments, frequent flyers arrangements, and international commuters practices. The classification of the types of expatriate assignments was verified through factor analysis.

The results of hypotheses testing indicated that by moving among several countries, expatriates deepen their knowledge, acquire globally applicable skills, become better teachers, and so forth. Moreover, expatriates are often expected to have both the skills to quickly and continuously transfer knowledge and be highly motivated to do so. In other words, by sending expatriates on various types of international assignments, MNCs could develop the expatriates' disseminative capacity. The analysis provided support for Hypothesis 4, namely that opting for long-term assignments influences positively expatriates' willingness to transfer knowledge across MNCs' subsidiaries. When permanently stationed at an overseas subsidiary, expatriates experience greater autonomy and responsibility for their employees' performance, and they exhibit greater commitment and willingness to perform better. The data analysis also confirmed Hypothesis 3, that the expatriates' ability to transfer knowledge is positively associated with the employment of practices such as short-term expatriation, international commuters, and frequent flyers.

## CONCLUSION

The goal of knowledge transfer is that the receiving unit accumulates and utilizes new knowledge, a goal that is a major managerial challenge. MNCs could employ formal organizational mechanisms—HRM practices—to enhance knowledge transfer. However, HRM practices do not influence knowledge transfer directly, but rather through their impact on the behavior of process participants: knowledge senders and receivers. Those subsidiaries interested in enhancing the ability and motivation of their employees to absorb transferred knowledge should employ cognitive and stimulative HRM practices. The employment of cognitive HRM practices—namely job analysis, recruitment, selection, international rotation, career management, training, and performance appraisal—positively influences the receivers' ability to absorb knowledge. Some stimulative HRM practices were identified as being positively related to the motivation of knowledge receivers—promotion, orientation programs, transfer, and compensation.

Managing the transfer process becomes more complicated when the problems associated with knowledge transfer are considered from the international dimension. MNCs rely heavily on expatriation practices when dealing with coordination and control, breaking down the barriers between the parent company and subsidiaries, fostering the parent corporate culture, solving technical problems, and developing local talents. In addition to the traditional long-term expatriate assignments, companies engage actively in temporary international assignments such as short-term assignments, international commuters, and frequent flyers. It was also found that MNCs are "unsure whether alternative forms of international assignments are helping or hindering them in meeting their global strategic objectives" (Center for Research into Management of Expatriation on the New Forms of International Working, 2002, p. 1). The results of this study argue that MNCs may consider applying different expatriation practices depending on whether the aim is to increase expatriates' willingness or ability to transfer knowledge to the subsidiaries. Expatriates' willingness to transfer their knowledge can be enhanced through the employment of long-term expatriation practices, while their ability to transfer knowledge may be increased through involvement in short-term assignments, frequent flyers arrangements, and international commuters practices.

This study has certain limitations and shortcomings. The recent literature also recommends examination of the complementarity/system effect, resulting from a combination of several groups of HRM practices. In this study, the potential for complementarity was indicated by the presence of pairwise correlations among individual HRM practices. As expected, the correlations were generally positive and substantial. One should further investigate whether HRM practices when applied as an integrated system are mutually reinforcing and hence more effective for knowledge transfer than isolated individual practices. One possible

response could be a test of a full set of interaction terms among all HRM practices while controlling for the individual practices. That solution would require a larger sample and sufficient number of degrees of freedom.

Further, in the framework offered by Szulanski (1996, 2000, 2003) and used here, there are four determinants of knowledge transfer (see Textbox 1). Only two of those—related to the behavior of knowledge senders and knowledge receivers—were used in this study as mediating variables. Can HRM practices influence the characteristics of knowledge? There is some evidence that MNCs employ various organizational mechanisms given the characteristics of knowledge. For example, Brewster and Bonache (2001) addressed the question of whether knowledge characteristics explain expatriation policies. Among other things, they suggested that "if the knowledge to be transferred among units of an MNC is tacit collective knowledge, then that transfer will involve the team" and " if the knowledge to be transferred among units of the MNC is specific, the recruitment source of expatriates will be the company itself" (Bonache & Brewster, 2001, pp. 160-161). However, "the possibility of a reverse causality, in which organizational arrangements are chosen so that they influence the relevant characteristics, has not previously been investigated" (Foss & Pedersen, 2003, p. 13). In this study, there were significant associations between knowledge characteristics and HRM practices. Obviously, the correlation only indicates that the two variables co-vary, but never assumes that a change in one variable causes a change in another. More research is needed to understand the direction of causality of the relationships.

Another determinant of knowledge transfer— characteristics of organizational context—could also be considered as being influenced by HRM practices. Rigid organizational boundaries impose high barriers, which impede knowledge flows at all levels of the MNC. By employing HRM practices that remove traditional boundaries, melt the bureaucratic structures, and support learning, organizations may establish the environment that promotes knowledge transfer. Indeed, Hansen (1999) concludes that the lack of direct relations between people from different departments within the organization inhibits knowledge transfer. Crossing traditional organizational boundaries is important for effective use of obtained knowledge through common projects, decentralized and autonomous groups, flexible working arrangement, and so forth. In the empirical studies, flexibility was found to be associated with learning opportunities, an organizational climate for innovation and development, higher capacities to absorb knowledge, and so forth. Lyles and Salk (1996) postulate that flexibility promotes the knowledge transfer process "by encouraging greater receptivity of organizational members to new stimuli from the outside, by promoting collaboration and exchanges of information within the organization and by granting members greater latitude in altering activity patterns and ways of doing things to adopt to perceived changing needs an conditions" (pp. 881-882).

Finally, there is no reason to assume that the results obtained in this study are generalizable to other countries, other functional areas, and so forth. The model developed here does represent a reasonable starting point. But it was tested on a rather small data set of Danish subsidiaries. That definitely has some implications for the generalizability of the findings. For instance, a small sample did not offer a desirable number of degrees of freedom, which was necessary to fully explore the possible impact of control variables, such as subsidiary size (Lyles & Salk, 1996; Bresman et al., 1999; Lane et al., 2001; Foss & Pedersen, 2002; Minbaeva et al., 2003), industry characteristics (Lane & Lubatkin, 1998; Gupta & Govindarajan, 2000; Lane et al., 2001; Subramaniam & Venkatraman, 2001; Minbaeva et al., 2003), mode of entry (Foss & Pedersen, 2002; Martin & Salomon, 2003), ownership (Lyles & Salk, 1996; Mowery, Oxley, & Silverman, 1996;

Lane et al., 2001), subsidiary age (Lyles & Salk, 1996; Bresman et al., 1999; Simonin, 1999a, 1999b; Minbaeva et al., 2003), and previous experience (Simonin, 1999a, 1999b). Clearly, there is a need for a similar study with a much larger sample and country representation, in the hope that some of the overlooked relations will be possible to consider. If that is possible, the above mentioned limitations become opportunities to be explored.

# REFERENCES

Arthur, J. (1994). Effects of human resource systems on manufacturing performance and turnover. *Academy of Management Journal, 37,* 670-687.

Baldwin, T., Magjuka, R., & Loher, B. (1991). The perils of participation: Effects of choice of training on trainee motivation and learning. *Personnel Psychology, 44,* 51-65.

Bonache, J., & Fernandez, Z. (1997). Expatriate compensation and its link to the subsidiary strategic role: A theoretical analysis. *International Journal of Human Resource Management, 8*(4), 457-475

Bonache, J., & Brewster, C. (2001). Knowledge transfer and the management of expatriation. *Thunderbird International Business Review, 43*(1), 145-168.

Bresman, H., Birkinshaw, J., & Nobel, R. (1999). Knowledge transfer in international acquisitions. *Journal of International Business Studies, 30*(3), 439-462.

Brewster, C. (1993). Developing a "European" model of human resource management. *International Journal of Human Resource Management, 4*(4), 765-785.

Brewster, C., Communal, C., Farndale, E., Hegewisch, A., Johnson, G., & van Ommeren, J. (2001). *The HR healthcheck. Benchmarking HRM practices across the UK and Europe* (report published by Cranfield University School of Management and Financial Times). Englewood Cliffs, NJ: Prentice Hall.

Center for Research into Management of Expatriation on the New Forms of International Working. (2002). *Executive report*. Cranfield, UK: Cranfield School of Management.

Cohen, W., & Levinthal, D. (1990). Absorptive capacity: A new perspective on learning and innovation. *Administrative Science Quarterly, 35*, 128-152.

Delaney, J., & Huselid, M. (1996). The impact of human resource management practices on perceptions of organizational performance. *Academy of Management Journal, 39*(4), 949-969.

Delery, J. (1998). Issues of fit in strategic human resource management: Implications for research. *Human Resource Management Review, 8*, 289-309.

Delery, J., & Doty, H. (1996). Modes of theorizing in strategic human resource management: Tests of universalistic, contingency, and configurational performance predictions. *Academy of Management Journal, 39*(4), 802-835.

Delios, A., & Bjorkman, I. (2000). Expatriate staffing in foreign subsidiaries of Japanese multinational corporations in the PRC and the United States. *International Journal of Human Resource Management, 11*(2), 278-293.

Downes, M., & Thomas, A. (2000). Knowledge transfer through expatriation: The U-curve approach to overseas staffing. *Journal of Management Issues, 12*(2), 131-149.

Downes, M., Thomas, A., & McLarney, C. (2000). The cyclical effect of expatriation satisfaction on organizational performance: the role of firm international orientation. *The Learning Organization, 7*(3), 122-134.

Edstrom, A., & Galbraith, J. (1977). Transfer of managers as a coordination and control strategy in multinational organizations. *Administrative Science Quarterly, 22,* 248-263.

Evans, P., Pucik, V., & Barsoux, J. (2002). *The global challenge*. New York: McGraw-Hill Irwin.

Foss, N., & Pedersen, T. (2002). Transferring knowledge in MNCs: The role of sources of subsidiary knowledge and organizational context. *Journal of International Management, 8,* 49-67.

Gregersen, H., & Black, J. (1992). Antecedents to commitment to a parent company and a foreign operation. *Academy of Management Journal, 35*(1), 65-90.

Guest, D. (1997). Human resource management and performance: A review and research agenda. *International Journal of Human Resource Management, 8*(3), 263-276.

Gupta, A., & Govindarajan, V. (2000). Knowledge flows within MNCs. *Strategic Management Journal, 21,* 473-496.

Gupta, A., & Singhal, A. (1993). Managing human resources for innovation and creativity. *Research Technology Management, 36*(3), 41-48.

Hansen, M. (1999). The search-transfer problem: The role of weak ties in sharing knowledge across organization subunits. *Administrative Science Quarterly, 44,* 82-111.

Harris, H. (2002). Strategic management of international workers. *Innovations in International HR, 28*(1), 1-5.

Harris, H., Brewster, C., & Sparrow, P. (2003). *International human resource management*. London: CIPD

Hislop, D. (2002). Linking human resource management and knowledge management via commitment: A review and research agenda. *Employee Relations, 25*(2), 182-202.

Huselid, M. (1995). The impact of human resource management practices on turnover, productivity, and corporate financial performance. *Academy of Management Journal, 38*(3), 635-672.

Huselid, M., Jackson, S., & Schuler, R. (1997). Technical and strategic human resource management effectiveness as determinants of firm performance. *Academy of Management Journal, 40*(1), 171-188.

Husted, K., & Michailova, S. (2002). Diagnosing and fighting knowledge sharing hostility. *Organizational Dynamics, 31*(1), 60-73.

Ichniowski, C., Shaw, K., & Prennushi, G. (1997). The effects of human resource management practices on productivity: A study of steel finishing lines. *The American Economic Review,* (June), 291-313.

Keegan, A., & Turner, J. (2002). The management of innovation in project-based firms. *Long Range Planning, 35,* 367-388.

Kim, L. (2001). Absorptive capacity, co-operation, and knowledge creation: Samsung's leapfrogging in semiconductors. In I. Nonaka & T. Nishiguchi (Eds.), *Knowledge emergence—social, technical, and evolutionary dimensions of knowledge creation* (pp. 270-286). Oxford: Oxford University Press.

Lado, A., & Wilson, M. (1994). Human resource systems and sustained competitive advantage: A competency-based perspective. *Academy of Management Review, 19,* 699-727.

Lane, P., & Lubatkin, M. (1998). Relative absorptive capacity and interorganizational learning. *Strategic Management Journal, 19,* 461-477.

Lane, P., Salk, J., & Lyles, M. (2001). Absorptive capacity, learning, and performance in inter-national joint ventures. *Strategic Management Journal, 22*(12), 1139-1161.

Laursen, K., & Foss, N. (2003). New HRM practices, complementarities, and the impact on innovation performance. *Cambridge Journal of Economics, 27,* 243-263.

Lyles, M., & Salk, J. (1996). Knowledge acquisition from foreign parents in international joint ventures: An empirical examination in the Hungarian context. *Journal of International Business Studies,* (Special Issue), 877-903.

MacDuffie, J. (1995). Human resource bundles and manufacturing performance: Flexible production systems in the world auto industry. *Industrial & Labor Relations Review, 48*(2), 197-221.

Martin, X., & Salomon, R. (2003). Knowledge transfer capacity and its implications for the theory of the multinational corporation. *Journal of International Business Studies, 34*(4), 345-356.

Minbaeva, D. (2007). Knowledge transfer in MNCs. *Management International Review,* (forthcoming).

Minbaeva, D., Pedersen, T., Bjorkman, I., Fey, C., & Park, H. (2003). MNC knowledge transfer, subsidiary absorptive capacity and knowledge transfer. *Journal of International Business Studies, 34*(6), 586-599.

Minbaeva, D., & Michailova, S. (2004). Knowledge transfer and expatriation practices in MNCs: The role of disseminative capacity. *Employee Relations, 26*(6), 663-679.

Miner, J., & Crane, D. (1995). *Human resource management: The strategic perspective.* HarperCollins College.

Mowday, R., & McDade, T. (1979). Linking behavioral and attitudinal commitment: A longitudinal analysis of job choice and job attitude. *Academy of Management Proceedings.* Atlanta: AOM.

Mowery, D., Oxley, J., & Silverman, B. (1996). Strategic alliances and interfirm knowledge transfer. *Strategic Management Journal, 17,* 77-91.

Pfeffer, J., & Cohen, Y. (1984). Determinants of internal labor markets in organizations. *Administrative Science Quarterly, 29*(4), 550-573.

Pucik, V. (1988). Strategic alliances, organizational learning, and competitive advantage: The HRM agenda. *Human Resource Management, 27*(1), 77-93.

Simonin, B. (1999a). Transfer of marketing know-how in international strategic alliances: An empirical investigation of the role and antecedents of knowledge ambiguity. *Journal of International Business Studies, 30*(3), 463-490.

Simonin, B. (1999b). Ambiguity and the process of knowledge transfer in strategic alliances. *Strategic Management Journal, 20*(7), 595-623.

Stewart, R. (1982). A model for understanding managerial jobs and behavior. *Academy of Management Review, 7*(1), 7-14.

Subramaniam, M., & Venkatraman, N. (2001). Determinants of transnational new product development capability: Testing the influence of transferring and deploying tacit overseas knowledge. *Strategic Management Journal, 22,* 359-378.

Szulanski, G. (1996). Exploring internal stickiness: Impediments to the transfer of best practice within the firm. *Strategic Management Journal, 17*(Winter Special Issue), 27-43.

Szulanski, G. (2000). Appropriability and the challenge of scope: Banc One routinizes replication. In G. Dosi, R. Nelson, & S. Winter (Eds.), *The nature and dynamics of organizational capabilities.* New York: Oxford University Press

Szulanski, G. (2003). *Sticky knowledge: Barriers to knowing in the firm.* Thousand Oaks, CA: Sage.

Tsang, E. (1999). The knowledge transfer and learning aspects of international HRM: An empirical study of Singapore MNCs. *International Business Review, 8,* 591-609.

Vroom, V. (1964). *Work and motivation.* New York/London/Sydney: John Wiley & Sons.

Winter, S. (1987). Knowledge and competence as strategic assets. In D. Teece (Ed.), *The competitive challenge.* Ballinger.

Zander, U., & Kogut, B. (1995). Knowledge and the speed of the transfer and imitation of organizational capabilities, *Organization Science, 6*(1), 76-92.

Zellmer-Bruhn, M. (2003). Interruptive events and team knowledge acquisition. *Management Science, 49,* 514-528.

## ENDNOTES

[1] The high-performance/"best practices" approach aims at determining HRM practices "whose adoption generally leads to valued firm-level outcomes" (Huselid, 1995, p. 643). The findings of empirical studies on this subject are similar: either across industries or within a specific sector, the more high-performance HRM practices used, the better the various performance measures, such as productivity, labor turnover, and financial indicators (e.g., Huselid, 1995; Huselid et al., 1997; Delaney & Huselid, 1996; Arthur, 1994, Ichniowski et al., 1997, MacDuffie, 1995).

[2] In some studies, this type of HRM practice is referred to as "behavioral." In this study, the word "stimulative" is used instead to emphasize that the HRM practices in question aim to develop the motivational part of individual behavior.

[3] The KOB dataset is a comprehensive, continuously updated data set of domestic and international Danish firms (*www.kob.dk*).

[4] *Børsen* is the Danish business sector's global, national, and regional newspaper. Every year the newspaper publishes an annual status report on Danish businesses (*www.borsen.dk*).

[5] A common rule for dropping the least important factors from the analysis is the Kaiser criterion, by which all components with eigenvalues under 1.0 are dropped.

# Chapter II
# Knowledge Creation in Commitment–Based Value Networks in Multinational Organizations

**Leslie Gadman**
*London South Bank University, UK*

## ABSTRACT

*The digital networked economy has gone global and is reshaping traditional business models. "Free" and "open source" software (Raymond, 1999), along with more recent successes in the private, public, and social sectors, offer a vision of a radically new globally networked economy. This economy is characterized by new sources of value creation and competition, as barriers to entry are lowered and substitution made easier. It also requires a more stratified, localized approach to the marketplace (Hart & Milstein, 2003) to meet more specialized demands from customers and the societies and environments within which they live. These challenges have implications for almost every aspect of a firm's strategy and business model, especially its ability to leverage these networks to create value through innovation. Yet, most multinational firms are ill-equipped to take advantage of the knowledge creation derived from high-value relationships with suppliers, complementors, and customers. This chapter shows the importance of developing a corporate strategy which takes into account ways in which an innovation focus must integrate with installed business processes. The chapter considers the challenges associated with knowledge disclosure, diffusion, and utilization (Snowdon, 2002; Spinosa, Flores, & Dreyfus, 2001) across value networks and concludes that while successful examples exist in "free" and "open source" software projects (Raymond, 1999), commercialization of innovation becomes more challenging when increasing levels of personal and financial commitment are required (Mauer, Rai, & Sali, 2004). Choosing the most appropriate value networking strategy can have serious implications for success. This chapter adds to studies on knowledge creation and knowledge transfer in multinational corporations by proposing a conceptual model of commitment-based value networking strategy. It is hoped this will contribute to future research by offering a theoretical foundation upon which this research may be based, and explains why and under what conditions people in commitment-based value networks share knowledge.*

## BACKGROUND

Information and communications technology (ICT) is enabling new organizational models based on value networking (Ridderstrale & Nordstrom, 2004; Flores, 1998). Business drivers include increased speed to market, access to world-class technology, focus on core competence and total cost savings, and balance sheet improvement (Sveiby & Roland, 2002; Savage, 1996; Gadman, 1996). Allee (2004) describes value networks as webs of relationships that generate material or social value through complex dynamic exchanges of both tangible and intangible goods, services, and benefits. Examples include James Maxxmin's business strategy, fashioned on a single logistics platform enabling functioning with zero-working capital while making huge profits. When the inspiration dies, they disappear as suddenly as they arise (Loveman & Anthony, 1996; Turkle, 1995). Other examples include user innovation networks like Zero Attribution, Linux, and Apache, which design and build products for their own use—and also freely reveal their designs to others (Harhoff, Henkel, & von Hippel, 2002).

Value networks challenge existing theories of transaction cost economics, which regard organizations as efficient contractual instruments (Coase, 1937; Williamson, 1985) by demonstrating that efficient contracting depends upon effective cooperation, coordination, and collaboration, without which successful competition would be impossible. Indeed, existing concepts of competition as survival of the fittest are being replaced by new models of collaboration and co-opetition which are characterized by an openness and transparency that allows ideas, data, services, products, and markets to flow more seamlessly across an ever-widening and inclusive landscape of participants. The purposes and principles behind value networking are more consistent with theories of organization as effective appliers of valuable knowledge to business activity (Kogut & Zander, 1992; Conner & Prahalad, 1996; Grant 1996). In

that, they comprise individuals capable of self-organizing to a point where there is no breakdown in the cost and quality of the contract. They do this through orchestrating the "speech acts" (Austin, 1962; Searle, 1975) that make up a network of commitments (Winograd & Flores, 1987) which drive and coordinate action among the members of that network. These examples suggest a more synergistic relationship between a transaction cost (Coase, 1937) reason to organize and one that is more commitment and knowledge based (Conner & Prahalad, 1996) in that they both offer some economic advantage to members. Conner and Prahalad (1996, p. 478) go so far as to say that the primary contribution of the knowledge-based view is to round out transaction cost theory by recognizing "knowledge-based transaction costs." Unfortunately, because the organizational models supporting this approach tend to be highly nuanced and pluralistic (Hock, 1999; von Hippel, 2002), many firms—fearing loss of control and leakage of intellectual property—tend to ignore them and consequently fail to leverage the potential existing in well-coordinated and committed networks of people. This chapter takes a deeper look into this potential by considering the relationship between market instability and the demand for knowledge disclosure, diffusion, and utilization (Snowdon, 2002; Spinosa et al., 2001). It concludes that while successful examples exist in "free" and "open source" software projects (Raymond, 1999), commercialization of innovative ideas becomes more challenging when increasing levels of personal and financial commitment are required (Mauer, Rai, & Sali, 2004). Choosing the most appropriate value networking strategy based on these factors can have serious implications for success.

Based on a review of empirical studies into commitment-based value networking, this chapter explores the notion of shared culture and commitment to a common purpose in value networks and proposes a model of business strategy based on the synergistic interactions between requirements for knowledge innovation, extent of environmental disruption, and quality of commitments among network participants. One view is that such interaction happens because network participants identify with one another (Kogut & Zander, 1996) through the shared values, beliefs, and assumptions that define their cultural identity (Schein, 1992; Laine-Sveiby, 1991). This disclosive space (Spinosa et al., 2001) is made up of shared coding schemes (Hansen, Nohria, & Tierney, 1999), and language and cognitive schema (Winograd & Flores, 1997), which make up the background against which coordinated actions take place (McKinney & Gerloff, 2004), (Flores, 1993). In other words it reflects committed participation in a shared cultural identity (Weeks & Galunic, 2003).

A core assumption underpinning value networks is that participants and stakeholders participate by converting what they know, both individually and collectively, into tangible and intangible value that they contribute to the network. Participants accrue value from their participation by converting value inputs into positive increases of their tangible and intangible assets, in ways that allow them to continue producing value outputs in the future. In a successful value network, every participant contributes and receives value in ways that address their concerns and the concerns of network participants as a whole, and in so doing an identity or selfhood is realized by those individuals and the enterprise as a whole. Successful value networking requires trusting relationships and a high level of integrity and transparency on the part of all participants. This is evidenced in companies like Southwest Airlines, Dell, IKEA, Lastminute.com, and Google, which are defined by strong brand identity, talented and authentic leadership and followership, and elegant and agile organizational designs supported by a global network of trusted and trusting partners and suppliers. Advancing this idea further, Weeks and Galunic (2003) propose a theory which takes the notion of business as a knowledge-bearing entity to that of a culture-bearing entity, wherein

the concept of culture includes not just shared knowledge, but also the ability of its members to achieve selfhood or personal authenticity by committing themselves to the network in ways that position them in the culture as people who make a difference because they can be "counted on." They do this by conforming to norms of shared beliefs, meanings, values, behaviors, language, and symbols of the culture, while experiencing a greater sense of selfhood (Heidegger, 1962). The core commitment structures and identities of value networks (Flores, 1998) dedicated to innovation development like the Tropical Disease Initiative (TDI) and the Human Genome Project (HGP) have not been well established, let alone compared to those dedicated to production, distribution, and consumption like IKEA, Lastminute, and Amazon. As a preliminary step toward that project, this chapter attempts to explain how each is different and why knowing the difference is essential to corporate strategy. The main challenge of both approaches to transaction cost and knowledge-based theories of the firm is the taken-for-granted view that they are a single unified entity rather than a network of commitment-based identity-forming relationships. Consequently, theories of value networking need to take seriously the idea that they are more than just knowledge-creating and knowledge-sharing entities. They are fundamentally cultural in nature, and it is the degree to which this culture, with its beliefs, meanings, values, behaviors, language, and symbols, supports the selfhood and identity needs of its members (Heidegger, 1962 [1937], pp. 352-358; 434-444) that determines the success of its mission.

## DETERMINANTS OF VALUE NETWORKING STRATEGY

Drawing on the works of Heidegger (1962 (1937)), Kierkegaard (1985), and Hegel (1979), Flores and Spinosa (1998) offer an account of personal and corporate identity that shows how identities that matter lead us to open a new shared world in which the concerns of our identity can matter to others. They believe that identities are maintained by carrying out two interrelated activities: interpreting which actions are appropriate given our intense concerns, and positioning our actions so that we are interpreted in ways that attract favorable attention. This perspective helps explain why managers choose value networking strategies based on a more or less open or more or less closed position to the outside world. Gadman (2003) proposes two positioning strategies, each with its own unique style of knowledge sharing modes of thinking, externalization (Nonaka & Takeuchi, 1995), and networking. These are *closed source adaptation* and *open source innovation*.

## Closed Source Adaptation

Companies adopting this approach are challenged to continuously improve existing products and services through strategies that lead to increased knowledge creation and dissemination. This allows them to deepen penetration of existing and new markets with the same products/services. Organizational models built on a closed source adaptation strategy create their identities through a strong brand image and then orchestrate and front networks of outsourced suppliers, partners, and distributors. Intellectual assets are considered vital since competitive advantage is gained through intellectual property protection, lean and elegant business processes, and outstanding responsiveness to customer needs. For example, Dell holds the record for numbers of patents pending on its manufacturing processes, and Boeing intentionally built the 777 to be "service ready" from day one.

## Open Source Innovation

Companies taking this approach attempt discontinuity by producing products and services that are "history making" (Spinosa et al., 2001), in that they create a need where none previously existed.

Like Caxton's printing press or Omidyar's eBay, competitive advantage is gained through a highly responsive "build it and they will come" very early adoption approach. Led by a very special kind of entrepreneur (Spinosa et al., 2001), these businesses are highly competent at introducing new products/services into existing and new markets. Innovation at high velocity is possible because the people who make up these organizations identify with the values and mission of the founder/s and are themselves authentic identity seekers who thrive in natural and spontaneous experimentation. "Free" and open source (F/OSS) software development communities are a prime example where products are created by a globally networked volunteer community of independent software users and developers (Lee & Cole, 2003), but they are not exclusive to software development and can be found elsewhere in enterprises like Project ALS and Southwest Airlines (Gittell, 2003).

Both examples illustrate that while the two positioning strategies of open source innovation and closed source adaptation might not be mutually exclusive, one takes precedence and receives support from the other. For example, in Open Source and Free Software communities like GNU and Linux, an open source innovation strategy is primary with closed source adaptation ensuring commercialization of the source code. As one programmer put it, "Linux started with Linus (Torvalds). He released an operating system for us to play with. You need someone great in the field to release something for everyone else to play with." From a commitment-based perspective, this image of "greatness" can be understood as Torvalds being authentic, talented, and a critical factor in attracting like-minded people and ensuring a symmetry, synchrony, and syntopy (Richardson, 2004) of idea generation among multiple perspectives. Similarly, in Freenet, a project aimed at developing a decentralized and anonymous peer-to-peer electronic file sharing network, closed source adaptation tools like CVS (Concurrent Versioning System) synchronize work and keep track of changes in the source code performed by developers working on the same set of files. A further closed source adaptation is seen in the way final decisions to commercialize are restricted to the project founder and some early developers (von Krogh, Spaeth, & Lakhani, 2003). Microsoft's "shared source" strategy is another example of closed source adaptation where the company allows selected governments and technology businesses, known as MVPs or most valued professionals, to gain access to some of its proprietary source code. In return the MVPs supply Microsoft with the outputs from their product development. In this way, Microsoft expands its range of programs, while continuing to place limitations on where and with whom it shares its intellectual property.

## TOWARDS A MODEL OF VALUE NETWORKING

By combining a closed source adaptation strategy with an open source innovation strategy, companies leverage the creativity that comes from opening up to multiple sources of new ideas while imposing a form of natural selection to nurture those ideas that best fit its strategic mission, core competence, and needs for identity creation (Grove, 1996). Remarkable companies like Boeing, P&G, 3M, Intel, Oracle, and IKEA routinely set up innovation networks for a wide variety of purposes, and through this unique blend of committed coordination create unique competitive advantage. They integrate the authenticity-seeking nature of their people with sufficient control to maintain their uniqueness and direction, while maintaining sufficient flexibility for creative improvisation. This is illustrated in Figure 1, describing four types of value networking strategy from *simple adaptive* to *complex integrative*. Each is based on complex interaction between the pace of environmental change, innovation demand, and adaptation/innovation culture.

*Figure 1. Value networking strategies*

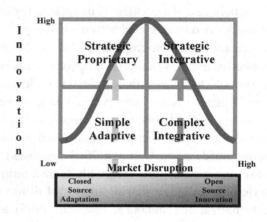

The four strategic choices are *simple adaptive, strategic proprietary, strategic integrative,* and *complex integrative.*

### Simple Adaptive

Strategies are appropriate in situations where there is little requirement for innovation, and the business environment is relatively stable and predictable. On the other hand, strategic integrative strategies, like those adopted by user innovation networks, must manage multiple connections of the highest quality in highly dynamic environments. As the velocity of change increases, so too must the scope of the value networks across and between organizations. This is especially so in the case of strategic integrative and complex integrative strategies where success depends heavily on the quality of commitment among participants. Such quality is determined by the nature of relationships making up the commitment nets and the level of trust shared among participants. Without a shared belief in the sincerity, competence, and reliability of network members to act upon and resolve individual concerns and the overarching concerns of the network, there can be no value network. It is this essential quality of trusting commitment which defines authenticity from both a selfhood and 'otherhood' perspective (Raymond, 1999). When combined with enabling capacities such as resource and time allocation, inspirational space, and supporting informatics (Palmer, 2004), organizational performance can be outstanding.

## Simple Adaptive

In slow-changing environments where innovation is not considered mission critical, networking is not a priority. The objectives of strategic management in these situations is to maintain tight control by managing the input–output relationship between the company and its environment through ensuring clear product–market positioning, resource allocation, planning, organizing, performance management, and control. Management practices and organizational design principles favor task specialization and individual rather than collaborative endeavors. Consequently, self-organization among workers, if considered at all, is discouraged. Detailed plans rather than guidelines tend to be the norm. Knowledge connectivity is low. Relationships tend to be based on power, control, and hierarchy. Interaction essential to the generation of new knowledge and problem solving are captured, categorized, and stored for retrieval. Knowledge networking is neither valued nor encouraged. Banking, insurance, utilities, transportation, telecommunications, and retail sectors have, at various times in their lives, manifested this kind of behavior. Some still do, especially those with a history of monopoly protection or favorable trading arrangements. One significant downside to this approach is its lack of responsiveness to shifts in environmental change velocity. Retail banking is one example of a sector that has struggled to respond to the challenges presented by the entry of Tesco in the United Kingdom and Wal-Mart in the United States into their markets. These retail giants were able to steal market share by providing choice, convenience, lower costs, and better service. Simple adaptive

strategies pose real dangers if they ignore pricing and partnering strategies, product ranges, infrastructure, and customer needs.

## Strategic Proprietary

In situations where there is a relatively stable environment yet a high need for innovation, for example healthcare and computer product manufacturing, value networking strategies do exist, but demands for high skill levels and fears for intellectual property leakage keep them firmly within the four walls of the business. Communication and information technology, combined with innovative leadership and elegant business processes, increase the capacity for creative interaction and a culture which maintains high-quality interactions and authentic behavior. Networks provide strategic and operational benefits by enabling members to collaborate effectively inside the business. While boundaries are to some extent permeable, the number and quality of connections is limited to those which speed information flow and adaptation. Inside the business information is transparent and diversity of opinions, and experience to speed innovation is promoted. An excellent example of such an organization is the stroke unit of St Luke's Hospital in Kansas City, Missouri (Palmer, 2004), where a focus on value networking has resulted in world-class performance. According to Medicare, stroke patients at Saint Luke's Hospital have a severity-of-illness index of 252, indicating that St. Luke stroke patients are two-and-a-half times as complicated as the average stroke patient. Medicare assigns an index number of 100 for average mortality rates. St. Luke's mortality rate for stroke was 85, indicating St. Luke patients are more likely to survive their stroke and that the health system has 15% fewer deaths from stroke than expected. Forty-seven percent of St. Luke's stroke victims return to their homes at discharge. This is twice the national average. If a stroke victim reaches St. Luke's in time, he or she is 10 times more likely to get stroke reversal treatment than the national average. In computer products manufacturing, similar leadership skills are practiced in the Dell Corporation, where Michael Dell established an authentic and strategic proprietary culture. Dell's preference for working alone is evident in its desire to eliminate middle people in almost every area of its operation. A retail foray a decade ago confirmed this view, and recent partnership break-ups show. Also, operating in the highly commoditized personal computer market, Dell's strategy was not to innovate or spend on research and development, but to apply existing knowledge to build on the ideas of competitors and then enter the market later with cheaper prices enabled by an extremely efficient in-house manufacturing process.

## Strategic Integrative

In environments of high change velocity requiring maximum levels of innovation, strategic integrative strategies combine inter- and intra-organizational networking intended to enable self-organization to recombine and to reinvent. People are encouraged to borrow and share ideas and practices liberally, making every product or service upgradeable, breeding ideas and processes early and often, and viewing interchangeable modules for people and products essential for mass customization. Strategic identity is based on continuously upgraded performance of services and products, understanding the requirements of customers, knowing where to target products, how to market and sell products, and developing new channels to market. Strategic management's role is to integrate control with experimentation. Consequently, guidelines rather than detailed plans tend to be articulated. Knowledge connectivity is an essential aspect of relationship building because it enables interaction essential to the generation of new knowledge and problem solving. In such a culture, group memory is the holy grail of knowledge management efforts. However, the effort to capture and categorize is often more

hassle than people are willing to put up with. If the organization or team culture is suitable to a conversational working style, the best IT solutions offer a combination of synchronous collaboration tools, such as videoconferencing, instant messaging, and screen sharing, with asynchronous environments that allow teams to work across geographic and chronological boundaries. In this way, they can quickly produce both a highly effective online workspace and an instant archive that becomes searchable group memory.

New team members can easily get up to speed and ask questions that have not already been answered. Managers can tune in and get a solid pulse on the state of the project. Customers can be an integral part of the project team, viewing the process and giving feedback along the way. Trusting and stronger working relationships are established for future contracts. And everything is embedded in a clear context (the flow of the conversation), which makes for better, more integrated work and learning. For example, following the inaugural flight of the Boeing 777, United Airlines declared it as its best ever, first flight experience with a new plane. The 777 had been delivered "service ready" on day one. This unique collaboration was identified by a core commitment to "work together to design, produce, and introduce an airplane that exceeds the expectations of flight crews, cabin crews, and maintenance and support teams and ultimately our passengers and shippers" (Palmer, 2004). The effective and efficient cultivation, and superior application, of its value networks enabled Boeing, its customers, suppliers, and consumers to fulfill that declaration and create the 777. Boeing effectively shortened by six months the process of designing and introducing into service, a sophisticated, $150 million price tag plane. This brought forward significant future cash flows amounting to several billion dollars. Millions of dollars of re-work costs were avoided by the online understanding and anticipation of possible design incompatibilities, and service and maintenance issues that might occur in actual use. Unfortunately, many of the lessons learned at Boeing were not picked up during the construction of the Airbus A380 with its highly publicized cost overruns and time delays.

## Complex Integrative

In situations where the pace of environmental change is high, but there is a relatively low requirement for innovation, complex integrative enterprises invent new worlds alongside existing ones and ultimately bring about lasting change. For example, the iPod has replaced the tape recorder, and the USB has replaced the floppy disk. The transistor replaced the valve and calculating machine. Ultimately, the products replaced will be wiped from our memory. Complex integrative cultures thrive on "Internet time" and redefine how individuals, businesses, and technologists view the Internet. They exceed customer demands for better, faster, cheaper products and services. They attract and retain highly committed identity seekers who are not only skilled in their roles, but knowledge driven in that they are willing and able to embed individual-based knowledge and make it accessible and useful to the entire organization. This focus on internal knowledge creation through commitment networking means that formal reporting structures and detailed work processes have a diminished role in the way important work is accomplished.

Informal networks are at the forefront, and the general health and "connectivity" of these groups has a significant impact on strategy execution and organizational effectiveness. Google's declaration to "never settle for the best" reflects this approach, and though acknowledged as the world's leading search technology company, Google's goal is to provide a much higher level of service to all those who seek information, wherever they are. They persistently pursue innovation and push the limits of existing technology to provide a fast, accurate, and easy-to-use search service that can be accessed from anywhere. Similarly, 3M's culture

has fostered creativity and given employees the freedom to take risks and try new ideas. This culture has led to a steady stream of products. With no boundaries to imagination and no barriers to cooperation, one good idea swiftly leads to another. So far there have been more than 50,000 innovative products brought to market.

Value networks built on a culture of trust and committed coordinated action improve knowledge sharing, innovation, and organizational effectiveness. Several authors link trust, collaboration, and knowledge sharing: Urch-Druskat and Wolff (2001) argue that trust, identity, and efficacy are the core elements for collaboration, and Huener, von Krogh, and Roos (1998) regard the level of trust as the most important factor affecting the willingness to share knowledge. It is a critical role of strategic management to understand and value these qualities and capacities, and to align financial and intellectual resources accordingly. In so doing, decisions regarding variations on closed source adaptation and open source innovation may be discussed and agreed. Emphasizing the wrong strategy can have a profound impact on the successful outcomes of a knowledge creating collaboration and hence, business results (von Krogh & Roos, 1996).

## FUTURE TRENDS

The Internet is revolutionary because its two-way communications technology allows large numbers of people to interact with each other. While some interactions might be considered casual, many more are purposefully designed to satisfy concerns. The quality of these interactions can be measured by the strength of commitments generated as one person or group promises to deliver results to address the concerns of another person or group in such a way that they are looked upon as authentic people both by the society within which they operate and their own self-assessment (Winograd & Flores, 1987; Flores & Spinosa,

1998). Commitment-based value networks deliver value because they are bound by the strength of the collective words of their members and identity built on the extent to which a person's word can be "counted upon." For example, FedEx and Amazon.com use the Internet to establish an identity through conversation-based interactions where they commit to be reliable. They do this by positioning strategies such as letting customers know what is going on—alerting customers if problems occur and offering counter-proposals designed to resolve the problem to a customer's satisfaction. Using customer and inventory databases and well-integrated financial and logistical systems, they use the Internet to build identity through core commitment structures based on trust (Winograd & Flores, 1987). This rich network of commitments delivers value by addressing the deep concerns of those involved and ultimately those who receive the benefits of their work.

The essential purpose of value networks is the achievement of synergistic interactions among participants which produce results greater than the sum of the individual parts (Richardson, 2004). Value networks rely on that most unique of human qualities, which is the ability to give their word, and for those willing and able to keep their word, to gain a unique identity as authentic people. This is reflected in a recent speech by Apple's Steve Jobs who said:

"The only way to be truly satisfied is to do what you believe is great work, and the only way to do great work is to love what you do. If you haven't found it yet, keep looking, and don't settle. As with all matters of the heart, you'll know when you find it, and like any great relationship it just gets better and better as the years roll on. So keep looking. Don't settle."

Richly synergistic communities are made up of like-minded people who seek authenticity (Heidegger, 1977) by giving freely of themselves into a culture that values their offer and thrives on the resulting products. Whether it is a discovery to unblock drains or to cure ALS, these people position themselves in such a way that they "show up to the world" by the quality of their committed speaking and action, and as a consequence, become identified "by the world" as people who make a difference. The difference they make changes history because the world they inhabit is not the same as a result of their "authentic being in the world" (Heidegger, 1962). The benefits of participation are capability development as potential meets opportunity and ultimately identity creation by association with a history-making event (Richardson, 2004; Olson, 1965). According to von Hippel and von Krogh (2003), newcomers to such communities share with existing developers and derive greater benefits of revealing their innovations than those outside the community (Callhoun, 1986; Taylor & Singleton, 1993). This is possible because their ideas can be reviewed and commented upon by other developers and users, and in terms of learning benefits, the group's feedback can be direct and specific to the newcomer. Such architectures of participation (Raymond, 1999) include low barriers to entry by newcomers and some mechanism for balancing the need for control with the need for improvisational innovation. This architecture of participation allows for a free market of ideas in which anyone can put forward proposed solutions to problems; it becomes adopted, if at all, by the organic spread of its usefulness. Ultimately, the reward for such rich networking is the ability to progress toward levels of knowledge and discovery beyond those achieved by conventional means, especially awareness of one's own identity through core commitment revelation. By better understanding the *closed adaptation* and *open innovation* options and their relative merits, business leaders who are attempting to make history with innovative products and services may be better informed about the best way to invest their time and money.

## CONCLUSION

The conceptual model proposed presents a theoretical foundation upon which a future research agenda can be based. One area that has high potential for exploration is the question of how and under what circumstances firms manage the qualities and capacities of interaction that maintain commitment-based value networks. Also, how much a part does information and communications technology play in the success of these networks and is there a point at which networks naturally break down without its support? Is there a limit to the numbers of connections that can be made within a network and what qualities are required to reach that limit? Finally, what contribution is required from managers to build and maintain these networks in the face of increasing pace of change when the natural reaction is to "over control" and consequently restrict the flow of innovation? Researching these questions will require a methodology that takes into consideration the problems associated with uncertainty (Chakravarthy & Doz, 1992; Lorange et al., 1993). As von Krogh, Roos, and Slocum (1996) point out, this is in accordance with the principle of indeterminism discovered by Werner Heisenberg in the mid-1920s. As a result, any approach to inquiry must acknowledge that observation influences what is seen and vice versa, and the problematic and recursive nature of organizational research will require a more qualitative grounded approach to develop analytical categories and propositions (Glaser & Strauss, 1967; Meyers, 1997; Strauss & Corbin, 1990). One approach might be to synthesize applied practice and empirical research based on a single case in order to increase the depth of the analysis, and acquire and report experience with the gathering of new and unfamiliar data (Numagami, 1998). It will also avoid the trap of generalizing the findings to other subjects and encourage readers to see for themselves how the results apply to themselves as in an action research approach. Whatever the method adopted, there can be no doubt that this field of inquiry will change our view of the world and emphasize the importance of identity and authenticity in achieving high performance. From this new understanding, possibilities for action will emerge that increase dialogue in situations of conflict, and improve skills to bring unlike-minds into meaningful work and experience together, and encourage and nurture increased collaborations among competing organizations doing the same. Who knows what new worlds will develop alongside the old and what new actions will become possible?

## REFERENCES

Allee, V. (2004). 360-degree transparency and the sustainable economy. *World Business Academy, 18*(2).

Austin, J.L. (1962). *How to do things with words.* Cambridge, MA; Harvard University Press.

Coase, R.H. (1937). The nature of the firm. *Economica, 4*(16), 386-405.

Conner, K.R., & Prahalad, C.K. (1996). A resource based theory of the firm: Knowledge versus opportunism. *Organization Science, 7*(5), 477-501.

Flores, F., & Spinosa, C. (1998) *Information technology & people* (vol. 11, no. 4, pp. 351-372). MCB University Press (0959-3845 Reflections).

Gadman, S. (2003) Adaptive innovation: Interdependent approaches to knowledge creation and organisational transformation. *Journal of Management Systems.*

Gittell, J. (2003). *The Southwest Airlines way.* New York: McGraw Hill.

Grant, R.M. (1996). Toward a knowledge based theory of the firm. *Strategic Management Journal, 17,* 109-122.

Grove, A. (1996). *Only the paranoid survive—how to exploit the crisis points that challenge every company and career.* New York: Doubleday.

Hansen, M., Nohria, N., & Tierney, T. (1999). *What's your strategy for managing knowledge?* HBR.

Harhoff, D., Henkel, J., & von Hippel, E. (2002, May). *Profiting from voluntary information spillovers: How users benefit by freely revealing their innovations.* Working Paper, MIT Sloan School of Management, USA.

Hart, S.L., & Milstein, M.B. (2003). Creating sustainable value. *Academy of Management Executive, 17*(2).

Hegel, G.W.F. (1979). *The phenomenology of spirit* (A.V. Miller, trans.). Oxford: Oxford University Press.

Heidegger, M. (1962 [1937]). *Being and time* (J. Macquarrie & E. Robinson, trans.). Oxford: Basil Blackwell.

Heidegger, M. (1977). The question concerning technology. In *The question concerning technology and other essays.* New York: Harper and Rowe.

Huener, L., von Krogh, G., & Roos, J. (1998). Knowledge and the concept of trust. In von Krogh, Rood, & Klein (Eds.), *Knowing in firms, understanding, managing and measuring knowledge.* London: Sage.

Kierkegaard, S. (1985). *Fear and trembling* (A. Hannay, trans.). London: Penguin.

Kogut, B., & Zander, U. (1992). Knowledge of the firm, combinative capabilities and the replication of technology. *Organization Science, 3*(3), 383-397.

Kogut, B., & Zander, U. (1996). What firms do. Coordination, identity and learning. *Organization Science, 7*(5), 502-518.

Laine-Sveiby, K. (1991). *Foretagil kulturmoten. tre finlandska foretag och ders svenska dotterbolag.* En Etnologisk Studie (diss) Akedemitryck Edsbruk.

Lee, R., & Cole, R. (2003). The Linux model of software quality development and improvement." In International Association of Quality (Ed.), *Quality in the 21st century: Perspectives on quality and competitiveness sustained performance.* ASQ Press.

McKinney, V., & Gerloff, E. (2004). *Interorganizational systems partnership effectiveness.* Retrieved from *http://hbs.baylor.edu*

Nonaka, H., & Takeuchi, I. (1995). *The knowledge creating company.* Oxford: Oxford University Press.

Palmer, J. (2004). Qualities and capacities of interaction. *Proceedings of the Mindful Leadership Program,* Isle of Man, UK.

Raymond, E.S. (1999). *The cathedral and the bazaar: Musings on Linux and open source by an accidental revolutionary.* Cambridge, MA: O'Reilly.

Richardson, R. (2004). *The whole and its parts.* Retrieved from *www.Dr.Rob.info*

Ridderstrale, J., & Nordstrom, K. (2004). *The Karaoke capitalism: Management for mankind.* Financial Times.

Schein, E. (1992). *Organizational culture and leadership.* San Francisco: Jossey-Bass.

Schein, E. (2003). *DEC is dead, long live DEC: Lessons on innovation, technology and the business gene.* San Francisco: Berrett-Koehler.

Searle, J.R. (1975). *Speech acts.* Cambridge: Cambridge University Press.

Spinosa, C., Flores, F., & Dreyfus, H.L. (2001). *Disclosing new worlds—entrepreneurship, democratic action and the cultivation of solidarity.* Cambridge, MA: MIT Press.

Turkle, S. (1995). *Life on the screen: Identity in the age of the Internet.* New York: Simon and Schuster.

Urch-Druskat, V., & Wolff, B.S. (2001). *Building the emotional intelligence of groups.* HBR.

Von Hippel, E. (2002). Innovation by user communities: Learning from open source software. *Sloan Management Review, 42*(4), 82-86.

Von Hipple, E., & Von Krogh, G. (2003). Exploring the open source software phenomenon: Issues for organization science. *Organization Science.*

Von Krogh, G. (2002). The communal resource and information system. *Journal of Information Systems, 11*(2).

Von Krogh, G., & Roos, J. (Eds.). (1996). *Managing knowledge: Perspectives on cooperation and competition.* London: Sage.

Von Krogh, G., Roos, J., & Slocum, K. (1996). In G. Von Krogh & J. Roos (Eds.), *Managing knowledge: Perspectives and cooperation and competition.* London: Sage.

Von Krogh, G., Spaeth, S., & Lakhani, K.R. (2003). Community joining and specialization in open source software innovation: A case study. *Research Policy, 32,* 1217-1241.

Weeks, J., & Galunic, C.A. (2003). *Theory of the cultural evolution of the firm: The interorganizational ecology of memes.* INSEAD.

Williamson, O.E. (1985). *The economic institutions of capitalism.* New York: The Free Press.

Winograd, T., & Flores, F. (1987). *Understanding computers and cognition.* Norwood, NJ: Ablex.

# Chapter III
# The Impact of Group Relationships on Knowledge Sharing:
## A Cross–Cultural Study

**Qiping Zhang**
*Long Island University, USA*

**Vincent M. Ribiere**
*New York Institute of Technology, USA*

**Thippaya Chintakovid**
*Drexel University, USA*

## ABSTRACT

*Organizations nowadays typically have several locations geographically dispersed around the world. Organizations distribute their resources around the world to reduce cost and remain competitive. As a consequence, globally distributed working teams are common, thereby rendering a need for knowledge sharing cross-culturally. This chapter presents a series of studies investigating the impact of cultures on how people handle knowledge management issues. It shows how in-group/out-group relationships determine people's attitudes towards knowledge sharing in a global working environment. Findings of this project would help organizations' executives understand better how to encourage their members to reap benefits from using the knowledge management systems.*

## INTRODUCTION

Previous research exhibits that a knowledge management system solely is not the answer for successful knowledge management in an organization (Damodaran & Olphert, 2000; Thomas, Kellogg, & Erickson, 2001). Rather, social factors are an essential part in influencing how the knowledge management system would be utilized (Damodaran & Olphert, 2000). Specifically, social factors influence knowledge management practices, among which knowledge sharing plays an important role.

Many factors influence people's attitudes towards knowledge sharing. First, organizational culture, particularly the reward policy, is an obvious factor. If the group outcome is encouraged, the knowledge sharing within the group will be encouraged as well. Certainly, people will not share their unique knowledge with everyone in the organization. Studies show that people tend to share their knowledge only with their in-group members (Chow, Deng, & Ho, 2000). However, it is not clear what factors determine the boundary of in-group/out-group relationships in an organization. Second, at the individual level, personal values like altruism, power, and risk tolerance also play an important role in knowledge sharing. Individuals' value systems are deeply rooted in their national cultures. People, in general, would be aware of their cultural values, which are different from others, when they encounter a different culture.

In the rest of the chapter, we will first review the literature on influences of culture and in-group/out-group relationships on knowledge sharing. Then we will report two cross-cultural studies on knowledge sharing. We will conclude the chapter with a discussion on future directions in knowledge sharing in a global virtual environment.

## Influences of Cultures on Knowledge Sharing

Culture, a set of values governing the way people think and behave, is one of the significant social factors influencing people's attitudes towards knowledge sharing.

Figure 1 shows the influences of cultures in a global corporate. For each global corporate, the influences of cultures come from multiple layers: national culture, corporate culture, and corporate sub-cultures. Cultures can be categorized as weak or strong (Deal & Kennedy, 1982). A strong culture will highly influence its sub-cultures (making them almost uniform), whereas a weak culture will have a low impact on its sub-cultures and disparities will appear in terms of behaviors and values between various groups in the organization. In this project, we focus on the outer layer—national culture. We

*Figure 1. Influences of cultures on knowledge sharing in a global corporate*

previously conducted research on the role of trust at the corporate culture level (Ribiere, 2005), and in the future we would continue our studies on the other layers and their interactions.

The most influential work on national cultural dimensions is by Hofstede (1980, 2001), who conducted a work value survey in a large multinational business organization (IBM) in 72 countries. Based on the data from IBM surveys and other subsequent IBM-unrelated value surveys, five cultural dimensions were identified: power distance (PDI), individualism/collectivism (IND), masculinity/femininity(MAS), uncertainty avoidance(UAI), and long-term orientation (LTO). These cultural dimensions have become an established framework for later cross-cultural research.

Figure 2 shows the cultural value indexes of the United States, Bahrain, and China based on the data we collected in this project. The United States and China differ dramatically on power distance and individualism/collectivism, and have been frequently used as a representative of western culture and eastern culture in cross-cultural studies. A strategic position between the East and the West makes the Kingdom of Bahrain a good candidate for a mixed culture of western and eastern cultures. As shown in Figure 2, Bahrain shows similarities with both the U.S. and China.

- **PDI:** Power distance is defined as the extent to which the less powerful members of institutions and organizations within a society expect and accept that power is distributed unequally.
- **IDV:** Individualism is the opposite of collectivism. Individualism stands for a society in which the ties between individuals are loose: a person is expected to look after himself or herself and his or her immediate family only. Collectivism stands for a society in which people from birth onwards are integrated into strong, cohesive in-groups, which continue to protect them throughout their lifetime in exchange for unquestioning loyalty.
- **MAS:** Masculinity is the opposite of femininity. Masculinity stands for a society in which emotional gender roles are clearly distinct: men are supposed to be assertive, tough, and focus on material success; women are supposed to be more modest, tender, and concerned with the quality of life. Femininity stands for a society in which emotional gender roles overlap: both men and women are supposed to be modest, tender, and concerned with the quality of life.
- **UAI:** Uncertainty avoidance is defined as the extent to which the members of institutions and organizations within a society feel threatened by uncertain, unknown, ambiguous, or unstructured situations.
- **LTO:** Long-term orientation is the opposite of short-term orientation. Long-term orientation stands for a society that fosters virtues oriented towards future rewards, in particular perseverance and thrift. Short-term orientation stands for a society that fosters virtues related to the past and present, in particular respect for tradition, preservation of "face," and fulfilling social obligations.

*Figure 2. Hofstede's cultural value indexes of the United States, China, and Bahrain*

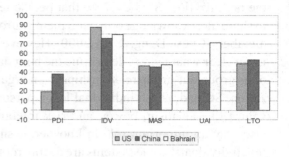

## Influences of In-Group/Out-Group Relationships on Knowledge Sharing

Group members' relationship (in-group vs. out-group) is another social factor shown to impact different behavior patterns in different cultures. Earley (1993) studied the impact of group members' relationships on individual performance of individualists and collectivists in a group setting. This study found that individualists working alone performed better than those working in an in-group or out-group context, while collectivists working in an in-group context performed better than those working alone or in an out-group context. In addition, Chow et al. (2000) found that Chinese compared to Americans were less willing to share knowledge with a co-worker who was considered an out-group member. These results suggest that people from collectivism cultures such as Chinese and Middle Eastern cultures, emphasizing harmony relationships and putting group interests before individual interests, are more willing to share knowledge with in-group members than out-group members, while people from individualism cultures such as American culture, emphasizing individual achievements, will not treat in-group or out-group members differently. They just focus on accomplishing their work no matter whether they need to share knowledge with in-group members or out-group members.

While several factors such as family, hometown, shared school or company affiliation, and national culture define the boundaries of an in-group member (Triandis, 1989), there are no consistent definitions of in-group/out-group relationships. In Earley's study (1993), an in-group was defined as "an aggregate of people sharing similar trait and background characteristics" (p. 321). It further stated that "this definition does not require that in-group members have direct contact with one another while working or that they work interdependently" (p. 321). In Chow et al.'s study (2000), however, in-group/out-group relationships were defined based on whether members successfully worked together. In other words, an in-group relationship was defined as people having successfully worked together on some tasks, whereas an out-group relationship was defined as people having met just once or twice at meetings. One objective of our study is to identify which factor defining in-group/out-group relationships will more significantly influence people's attitudes towards knowledge sharing: shared working experience or shared cultural background. To examine this question, four in-group/out-group conditions were included: out-group condition (neither shared working experience nor shared cultural background), in-group culture condition (shared cultural background, but no shared working experience), in-group work condition (shared working experiences, but different cultural background), and in-group condition (shared both working experiences and cultural background).

## Research Hypotheses

Given the above literature review, our hypotheses are as follows:

- *Hypothesis A: Chinese will be more willing to share knowledge with in-group members than out-group members.*

- *Hypothesis B: American will be equally willing to share knowledge with both in-group and out-group members.*
- *Hypothesis C: Bahraini will be more willing to share knowledge with in-group members than out-group members.*

## STUDIES

## Study 1: Comparison of the Americans and Chinese on the Effect of In-Group/Out-Group Relationships on Knowledge Sharing

## Method

This study is a 2 x 4 mixed experimental design: one between-subject factor *national culture* with two levels, American vs. Chinese, and one within-subject factor *the group members' relationships* with four levels (combining two values of whether sharing the same culture or not and whether sharing previous work experience or not): out-group, in-group (culture), in-group (work), and in-group, as shown in Figure 3.

*Figure 3. Experiment design of the factor: group members' relationships*

**Previous work experience**

|  | | Yes | No |
|---|---|---|---|
| **Same culture** | Yes | In-group | In-group culture |
| | No | In-group work | Out-group |

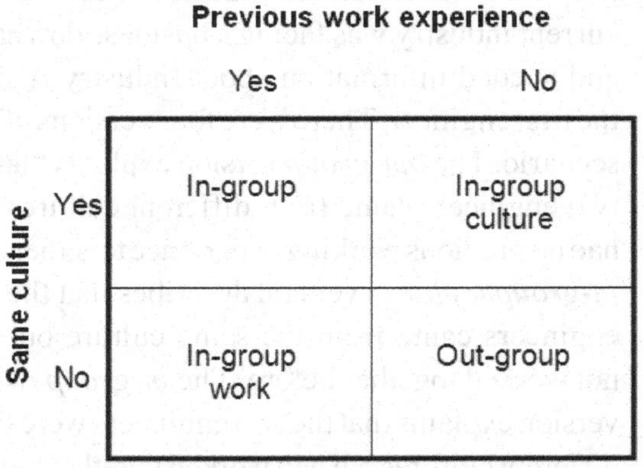

## Materials

A set of questionnaires and scenarios were used in this study. The questionnaires included Hofstede's Values Survey Module (Hofstede, 2001, pp. 494-497) and the Personal Values Questionnaire (Hay Acquisition Company I, 1993). These questionnaires were intended to investigate cultural differences on personal values in general instead of the attitudes towards knowledge sharing.

Two scenarios, similar to the ones in Chow et al. (2000), were used in the study. The first scenario examines attitudes towards sharing knowledge of mistakes either made by themselves or by others. It depicts a situation in a company where a newly promoted department manager underestimated the cost of a new technology and introduced it to the department upon his becoming a manager. In one version of the scenario, the mistake was made by the new manager himself/herself, whereas in the other version of the scenario, the mistake was made by a friend of the new manager who co-workers in the company did not know. The second scenario measures people's attitudes towards knowledge sharing with in-group and out-group members. In our study, versions of the second scenario were modified to include both culture and working experience as factors determining an in-group relationship. The second scenario describes two engineers: one who previously dealt business with Industry A and now shifted to Industry B, and the other who was interested in dealing business with Industry A because his current industry was facing a business downturn and needed information about Industry A from the first engineer. There were four versions of this scenario. The *out-group* version explains that the two engineers came from different cultures and had no previous working experience together. The *in-group (culture)* version describes that the two engineers came from the same culture but had not worked together before. The *in-group (work)* version explains that the two engineers were from different cultures but had worked together before.

Finally, the *in-group* version describes that the two engineers were from the same culture and had worked together before. Participants were asked to evaluate to what degree they are willing to share the knowledge with group members for each version of the scenario. Participants were asked to give their opinion not only on sharing work-related knowledge or professional knowledge, but also on sharing personal information (e.g., educational background, family information, hobbies, etc.) to co-workers in order to facilitate the work.

## Procedure

The study was a one-time session and conducted in a lab setting. Participants came to the specified room to complete the set of questionnaires and two scenarios. During each session, each participant read and signed a consent form, gave responses to the cultural values questionnaires, read and completed questions of the two scenarios, and received a stipend at the end of the study.

## Participants

A total of 111 American undergraduate students and 197 Chinese undergraduate students were recruited, through class announcements and campus flyers, from prestigious universities in the United States and China. Both American and Chinese undergraduate students were recruited from four majors: Engineering, Business, Information Technology, and Arts and Sciences. The number of participants for each major and gender was balanced across two cultural groups.

## Results

In this chapter, we only report the data from the second scenario focusing on the impact of in-group/out-group relationships on attitudes towards sharing professional knowledge and personal information.

**Professional knowledge**

Figure 4 shows the means of attitudes towards sharing professional knowledge among four in-group/out-group relationships for Americans and Chinese. The MANOVA analysis with repeated measures revealed both two main effects and an interaction effect (F (3, 304) = 3.73, $p$ < .05).

The analysis reveals significant main effects of culture: F(1, 306) = 4.52, $p$ < .05. American participants were more willing to share professional knowledge than Chinese ones (refer to Table 1 for means and standard deviations).

The analysis also shows significant main effects of in-group/out-group relationships: F(3, 304) = 35.71, $p$ < .05. Both American and Chinese participants were more willing to share professional knowledge with in-group members than out-group members. The results of further paired t-tests among four in-group/out-group conditions are reported in Table 2. There are no differences between in-group (culture) and out-group condition, suggesting that participants treat members with shared cultures in the same way as out-group members. Similarly, there are no differences between in-group (work) and in-group condition, suggesting that participants treat members with shared working experiences in the same way as in-group members.

*Figure 4. Means of attitudes towards sharing professional knowledge among group members' relationships*

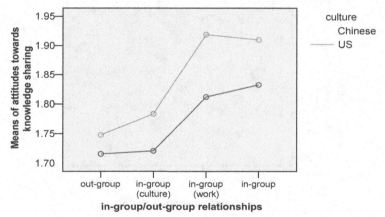

*Table 1. Means (standard deviations) of attitudes towards sharing professional knowledge in Study 1*

|  | Out-Group | In-Group (Culture) | In-Group (Work) | In-Group |
|---|---|---|---|---|
| Chinese | 1.72 (0.45) | 1.72 (0.45) | 1.81 (0.39) | 1.83 (0.37) |
| American | 1.75 (0.44) | 1.78 (0.41) | 1.92 (0.27) | 1.91 (0.29) |

*Table 2. Paired samples t-tests among four group members' relationships in Study 1 (professional knowledge)*

|  | Chinese | | American | |
|---|---|---|---|---|
| Pairs | t | Sig. (2-tailed) | t | Sig. (2-tailed) |
| In-Group (Culture) vs. Out-Group | 0.31 | 0.76 | 1.65 | 0.10 |
| In-Group (Culture) vs. In-Group | **-3.45** | **0.00** | **-3.46** | **0.00** |
| In-Group (Culture) vs. In-Group (Work) | **-2.39** | **0.02** | **-3.62** | **0.00** |
| Out-Group vs. In-Group | **-3.34** | **0.00** | **-4.34** | **0.00** |
| Out-Group vs. In-Group (Work) | **-3.01** | **0.00** | **-4.49** | **0.00** |
| In-Group vs. In-Group (Work) | 0.93 | 0.35 | -1.00 | 0.32 |

**Personal information**

Figure 5 shows the means of attitudes towards sharing personal information among four in-group/out-group relationships for both Americans and Chinese.

The MANOVA analysis with repeated measures revealed a significant main effect of in-group/out-group relationships: $F(3, 304) = 44.10$, $p < .05$ and a significant interaction effect (culture and group members' relationships): $F(3, 304) = 6.36$, $p < .05$. However, the main effect of culture is not statistically significant: $F(1, 306) = 2.23$, $p > .05$.

Table 3 shows means (standard deviations) of attitudes towards sharing personal information for both Americans and Chinese.

Both American and Chinese participants were more willing to share personal information with in-group members than out-group members. The results of further paired t-tests among four in-group/out-group conditions are reported in Table 4. With $p < .05$ for both Chinese and Americans, there are no differences between in-group (work) and in-group condition, suggesting that participants treat members with the same working experiences in the same way as in-group members. Moreover, for Americans only, there is no difference between

*Figure 5. Means of attitudes towards sharing personal information among group members' relationships*

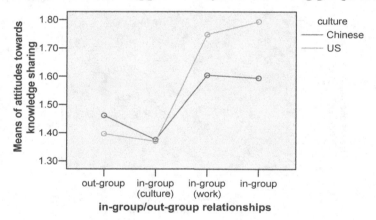

*Table 3. Means (standard deviations) of attitudes towards sharing personal information in Study 1*

| | Out-Group | In-Group (Culture) | In-Group (Work) | In-Group |
|---|---|---|---|---|
| Chinese | 1.46 (0.50) | 1.38 (0.49) | 1.60 (0.49) | 1.59 (0.49) |
| American | 1.40 (0.49) | 1.37 (0.48) | 1.75 (0.44) | 1.79 (0.41) |

*Table 4. Paired samples t-tests among four group members' relationships in Study 1 (personal information)*

| | Chinese | | American | |
|---|---|---|---|---|
| Pairs | t | Sig. (2-tailed) | t | Sig. (2-tailed) |
| In-Group (Culture) vs. Out-Group | -2.41 | 0.02 | -1.35 | 0.18 |
| In-Group (Culture) vs. In-Group | **-6.08** | **0.00** | **-8.81** | **0.00** |
| In-Group (Culture) vs. In-Group (Work) | **-5.96** | **0.00** | **-8.02** | **0.00** |
| Out-Group vs. In-Group | **-3.33** | **0.00** | **-8.50** | **0.00** |
| Out-Group vs. In-Group (Work) | **-4.31** | **0.00** | **-7.72** | **0.00** |
| In-Group vs. In-Group (Work) | -0.17 | 0.87 | 1.68 | 0.10 |

in-group (culture) and out-group condition, suggesting that American participants treat members who only share the same culture in the same way as out-group members. However, the Chinese were more willing to share their personal information with an American stranger (out-group) than a Chinese stranger (in-group (culture)) ($p < .05$).

## Discussion

Based on the results, Hypothesis A was supported. Chinese were more willing to share both professional knowledge and personal information with in-group members than out-group members. However, Hypothesis B was not confirmed. Americans were also more willing to share both professional knowledge and personal information with in-group members than out-group members. Our explanation is that even though individual achievement is emphasized in American culture, people tend to build higher levels of trust with those whom they have worked with than those whom they have not worked with before. As a result, they are more willing to share their knowledge with people having shared working experience (in-group) than those without such common grounds (out-group). Further, they limit sharing personal information with the safest and strongest social ties.

Nevertheless, when dealing with sharing personal information with an out-group member, Chinese and American participants showed significantly different attitudes. Chinese participants were more willing to share personal information with an American stranger (out-group) than a Chinese stranger (in-group (culture)), while Americans showed no such difference. In other words, the weakest social tie varies for Chinese participants and American participants. Possible explanations behind this result are as follows.

When Chinese share personal information with a Chinese stranger, there is a great chance of losing face because they are from the same culture and aware that the same cultural framework is applied.

On the contrary, an out-group member applying a different cultural framework has different views of acceptable behaviors. Therefore, Chinese would feel that there is less chance of losing face when sharing personal information, especially face-sensitive information, with an out-group member than with an in-group (culture) member.

In addition, Chinese more concern about face-saving than Americans (Hu, 1944; Bond, 1996). Psychologically, people tend to share personal information in order to release inner stress and anxiety. They usually choose to share such information via either the most trusted channel like the strongest social ties or the channel with the least chance to leak such information like the weakest social ties. Compared to an American stranger, a Chinese may more easily find a relationship with a Chinese stranger through several connections in his or her social network. Therefore, his or her personal information will have a better chance to be leaked through a Chinese stranger than through an American stranger. This might lead Chinese participants to be more reluctant to share personal information with an in-group (culture) member than an out-group member. For American participants, however, they do not care about face-saving as much as Chinese. Our results further suggest that American participants treat an American stranger and a Chinese stranger equally as the least leaking channel to share personal information.

Interestingly, the results exhibit that shared working experience was a more important factor than shared cultural background in determining an in-group relationship for a knowledge sharing attitude. Both Americans and Chinese tend to perceive people with whom they have worked as in-group members, whereas they tend to perceive people who only share the same culture as out-group members. Initially, the result seems rather surprising. It is widely known that people from the same culture share common characteristics and beliefs. With this shared background, people should be more comfortable and willing to share knowledge with each other than with those from different cultures. However, this belief was not supported by the results found in this study. People seem to be more comfortable and willing to share knowledge with those they have shared working experiences with rather than shared cultural background. Is this because our scenario is in a business environment where working experience is more relevant to the task? Further study with a task emphasizing more cultural experiences will be able to answer this question.

## Study 2: The Effect of In-Group/ Out-Group Relationships on Knowledge Sharing in Bahrain

The United States and China represent typical western and eastern cultures. However, many other cultures are not typical of western or eastern cultures. Therefore, we ran the study two with the Kingdom of Bahrain, which is physically located in the Middle East but culturally influenced by both eastern and western cultures. Following are some facts about the Kingdom of Bahrain:

*In a region currently experiencing an oil boom of unprecedented proportions, the United Nations Economic found in January 2006 that Bahrain is the fastest growing economy in the Arab world, the United Nations Economic and Social Commission for Western Asia found in January 2006. Bahrain also has the freest economy in the Middle East according to the 2006 Index of Economic Freedom published by the Heritage Foundation/Wall Street Journal, and is twenty-fifth freest overall in the world. Bahrain is sometimes described as the 'Middle East lite': a country that mixes thoroughly modern infrastructure with a definite Persian Gulf identity, but unlike other countries in the region its prosperity is not solely a reflection of the size of its oil wealth, but also related to the creation of an indigenous middle class. This unique socio-economic development in the Persian Gulf has meant that Bahrain is generally*

*more liberal than its neighbours. While Islam is the main religion, Bahrainis have been known for their tolerance, and alongside mosques can be found churches, a Hindu temple, a Sikh Gurud-wara and a Jewish synagogue. Bahrain was the first place on the Arabian side of the Gulf where oil was discovered. It couldn't have come at a better time for Bahrain as it roughly coincided with the collapse of the world pearl market. Unfortunately, it was also the first country in the area where oil ran out. The British withdrew from Bahrain on August 15, 1971, making Bahrain an independent emirate. In 2004, Bahrain signed the U.S.-Bahrain Free Trade Agreement, which will reduce certain barriers to trade between the two nations. (Wikipedia, 2006)*

## Method

We used the same materials and procedure as those in Study 1.

## Participants

A total of 108 Bahraini graduate students enrolled in an MBA program in an American university located in the Kingdom of Bahrain volunteered to participate in the study, but only 70 participants completed all questions in the questionnaires.

## Results

Table 5 and Figure 6 show the result of Study 2 with participants from Bahrain.

The ANOVA analysis with repeated measures shows the significant main effect of in-group/out-group relationships on attitudes towards sharing personal information: ($F(3, 198) = 4.48, p < .01$). However, there is no significant main effect of in-group/out-group relationships on attitudes towards sharing professional knowledge: ($F(3, 204) = .93, p > .05$).

The results of further pairwise comparisons among four in-group/out-group conditions are reported in Table 6. For personal information, there is a significant difference between in-group and out-group condition ($p < .01$), and in-group (work) and out-group condition ($p < .03$), but for professional knowledge, there are no differences between any of the combinations of in-group/out-group relationships.

## Discussion

Hypothesis C was partially confirmed. Bahrainis were more willing to share personal information with in-group members than with out-group members, but they did not show such difference for sharing professional knowledge.

*Figure 6. Means of attitudes towards knowledge sharing in Study 2*

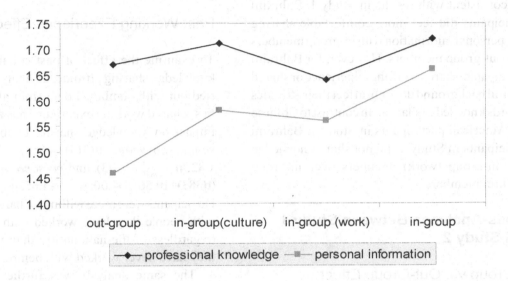

*Table 5. Means (standard deviations) of attitudes towards knowledge sharing in Study 2*

| | Out-Group | In-Group (Culture) | In-Group (Work) | In-Group |
|---|---|---|---|---|
| Professional Knowledge | 1.67 (.45) | 1.71 (.46) | 1.64 (.46) | 1.72 (.45) |
| Personal Information | 1.46 (.47) | 1.58 (.50) | 1.56 (.47) | 1.66 (.48) |

*Table 6. Pairwise comparisons among four group members' relationships in Study 2 (p value)*

| | Bahraini (Middle East) | |
|---|---|---|
| Pairs | Professional Knowledge | Personal Information |
| In-Group (Culture) vs. Out-Group | 0.44 | **0.04** |
| In-Group (Culture) vs. In-Group | 0.81 | 0.20 |
| In-Group (Culture) vs. In-Group (Work) | 0.30 | 0.64 |
| Out-Group vs. In-Group | 0.33 | **0.00** |
| Out-Group vs. In-Group (Work) | 0.63 | **0.03** |
| In-Group vs. In-Group (Work) | 0.06 | 0.08 |

The finding on professional knowledge in Study 2 can be explained by the fact that Bahrainis do not see out-group members (foreigners) as a threat/competitor for their job because they know that it will take them a long time to adjust and to understand the subtleties of their culture and to become as essential as they are. Therefore, level of vulnerability is low even though level of trust is low.

The finding on personal information in Study 2 is consistent with results in Study 1. Bahraini participants did feel more comfortable sharing their personal information with in-group members than out-group members. However, for Bahraini participants, shared working experience or shared cultural background does not affect their attitudes towards knowledge sharing. In contrast to Chinese and American participants in Study 1, Bahraini participants in Study 2 did not share knowledge with in-group (work) members over in-group (culture) members.

## Cross-Analyses Between Study 1 and Study 2

### In-Group vs. Out-Group Effect

To measure the effect of in-group/out-group relationships, an analysis was conducted to compare data from the combined three types of in-group conditions with the out-group condition. The analysis, all nationalities combined, shows a significant difference between the in-group and out-group relationships on both professional knowledge sharing: $(t(381)= 4.25, p < .00)$, and personal information sharing: $(t(377)=6.32, p < .00)$. Participants were more willing to share with in-group members than out-group members: *professional knowledge:* $(\mu_{in} = 1.79, \mu_{out} = 1.71)$ and *personal information:* $(\mu_{in} =1.59, \mu_{out} =1.44)$.

The same analysis was also conducted at each nationality level. The analysis reveals that this difference remains significant for the Chinese: *professional knowledge:* $(t(199) = 2.73, p < .01,$

$\mu_{in} = 1.78, \mu_{out} = 1.71)$, and *personal information:* $(t(196) = 2.06, p < .04, \mu_{in} = 1.53, \mu_{out} = 1.46)$, as well as for the American: *professional knowledge:* $(t(110)=4.35, p < .00, \mu_{in} = 1.87, \mu_{out} = 1.75)$, and *personal information:* $(t(110)=7.80, p < .00, \mu_{in} = 1.64, \mu_{out} = 1.40)$. The effect is mixed for the Bahraini: not significant for *professional knowledge:* $(t(70)=.47, p > .05, \mu_{in} = 1.69, \mu_{out} = 1.67)$, but significant for *personal information:* $(t(69)=3.10, p < .00, \mu_{in} = 1.60 \mu_{out} = 1.47)$.

### Past Working Experience Effect

To examine the effect of past collaboration on knowledge sharing attitude, an analysis was carried out with combined data from all nationalities. Shared working experience has a significant impact on knowledge sharing for both *professional knowledge:* $(t(315)=4.85, p < .00, \mu_{work} = 1.82, \mu_{non-work} = 1.73)$, and *personal information:* $(t(383)=10.56, p < .00, \mu_{work} = 1.65, \mu_{not-work} = 1.43)$. Participants were more willing to share knowledge with people they have worked with in the past (regardless of the nationality) than with people they have never worked with before.

The same analysis was further conducted at each nationality level. The analysis reveals that this difference remains significant for the Chinese participants: *professional knowledge:* $(t(199)=3.77, p < .00, \mu_{work} = 1.82, \mu_{non-work} = 1.71)$, and *personal information:* $(t(198)=6.29, p < .00, \mu_{work} = 1.60, \mu_{not-work} = 1.42)$, as well as for the American participants: *professional knowledge:* $(t(111)=4.20, p < .00, \mu_{work} = 1.92, \mu_{non-work} = 1.77)$, and *personal information:* $(t(111)=8.90, p < .00, \mu_{work} = 1.77, \mu_{not-work} = 1.38)$. The analysis shows a mixed effect of shared working experience on knowledge sharing for Bahraini participants: not significant for *professional knowledge:* $(t(73)=.21, p > .05, \mu_{work} = 1.70, \mu_{not-work} = 1.71)$, but significant for *personal information:* $(t(72)=2.80, p < .01, \mu_{work} = 1.63, \mu_{not-work} = 1.52)$.

## CONCLUSION

Results of a comparative study on people's attitudes towards knowledge sharing between Chinese, Americans, and Bahrainis are reported in this chapter. Various factors can define group members' relationships (Triandis, 1989). It is significant to know which factor is a strong determinant of group members' relationships so that organizational knowledge management could concentrate more on that factor in order to encourage knowledge sharing in the organization. A scenario investigating the impact of in-group/out-group relationships on people's attitudes towards knowledge sharing was given to Chinese, American, and Bahraini participants. The results show that shared working experience is a stronger determinant of an in-group relationship than shared cultural background for both Chinese and Americans. For Bahrainis, shared working experience and shared cultural background are both strong determinants of an in-group relationship.

In summary, our study implies that global organizations should focus on building community of practice rather than a localization approach, in which the cultural uniqueness is emphasized in designing knowledge management systems and practices. Encouraging people to interact with each other will not only help promote knowledge sharing culture, but also form *knowledge ecologies* (Brown, Denning, Groh, & Prusak, 2005, pp. 83-85), where people from different disciplines work together by interacting and exchanging their knowledge. Such knowledge ecologies help facilitate cross-fertilization of ideas, and enable innovation beyond a fixed and rigid knowledge management system.

## REFERENCES

Bond, M.H. (Ed.). (1996). *The handbook of Chinese psychology.* New York: Oxford University Press.

Brown, J.S., Denning, S., Groh, K., & Prusak, L. (2005). *Storytelling in organizations: Why storytelling is transforming 21$^{st}$ century organizations and management.* Burlington, MA: Elsevier Butterworth-Heinemann.

Chow, C.W., Deng, F.J., & Ho, J.L. (2000). The openness of knowledge sharing within organizations: A comparative study in the United States and the People's Republic of China. *Journal of Management Accounting Research, 12,* 65-95.

Damodaran, L., & Olphert, W. (2000). Barriers and facilitators to the use of knowledge management systems. *Behaviour & Information Technology, 19*(6), 405-413.

Deal, T.E., & Kennedy, A.A. (1982). *Corporate cultures: The rites and rituals of corporate life.* Boston: Addison-Wesley.

Earley, P.C. (1993). East meets west meets mideast: Further explorations of collectivistic and individualistic work groups. *Academy of Management Journal, 36*(2), 319-348.

Hay Acquisition Company I. (1993). *Personal values questionnaire.*

Hofstede, G. (1980). *Culture's consequences: International differences in work-related values.* Beverly Hills, CA: Sage.

Hofstede, G. (2001). *Culture's consequences: Comparing values, behaviors, institutions, and organizations across nations.* Thousand Oaks, CA: Sage.

Hu, H.C. (1944). The Chinese concept of "face." *American Anthropologist, 46*(1), 45-64.

Ribiere, V. (2005). Building a knowledge-centered culture: A matter of trust. In M.A. Stankosky (Ed.), *Creating the discipline of knowledge management.* Elsevier/Butterworth-Heinemann.

Thomas, J.C., Kellogg, W.A., & Erickson, T. (2001). The knowledge management puzzle: Human and social factors in knowledge management. *IBM Systems Journal, 40*(4), 863-884.

Triandis, H.C. (1989). The self and social behavior in differing cultural contexts. *Psychological Review, 96,* 506-520.

Wikipedia. (2006). *Bahrain.* Retrieved November 16, 2006, from *http://en.wikipedia.org/wiki/Bahrain*

# Chapter IV
# Why First–Level Call Center Technicians Need Knowledge Management Tools

**Joe Downing**
*Southern Methodist University, USA*

## ABSTRACT

*This chapter argues that first-level call center technicians are the new knowledge workers of the 21ˢᵗ century. As such, these technicians are ideal candidates for knowledge management tools. The objective of the chapter is to introduce these technicians to the IT community and, by way of a case study, show how decision-tree-type help tools can increase technicians' productivity. The chapter ends with recommendations for IT practitioners who are interesting in implementing these tools in their call centers.*

## INTRODUCTION

The goal of this chapter is to introduce readers to first-level call center technicians who staff the phones for countless banks, financial institutions, credit card companies, and help desks around the world (Datamonitor, 2003). The intense knowledge demands required of first-level technicians make them ideal candidates for *knowledge management tools.* Knowledge management tools refer to communication technologies that index and structure an organization's "corporate memory" (Walsh & Ungson, 1991; Yates & Orlikowsky, 2002).

This chapter is structured as follows. First, I provide a brief historical overview of the call center industry, including the outsourcing trend that began in the late 1990s. Next, I describe why first-level technicians must have knowledge tools to perform their jobs effectively. Then, I discuss two popular types of help interfaces that are used in call center environments. I conclude the chapter with my recommendations and by noting future trends that I see will affect the industry.

## BACKGROUND

Until the late 1980s, most organizations handled their customer service and technical support functions in-house. First-level call center technicians who staffed the phones were often full-time employees who handled only a single product or service (Bagnara & Marti, 2001). However, organizations soon realized it was cheaper, and often more effective, to outsource these support functions to third-party call center providers. The global call center industry was born.

## Call Centers: From the Help Desk to the Sales Center

Until recently, call center providers had distinct goals for their inbound and outbound operations. Inbound operations focused mainly on resolving customers' product or service issues. Conversely, organizations used their outbound (telemarketing) operations to attract new customers.

In the last five years, though, consumer hostility towards telemarketing practices has increased. According to a study commissioned by the American Teleservices Association (2002), about 40% of U.S. consumers subscribe to a caller ID service. Between 2003-2004, U.S. consumers also registered more than 64 million telephone numbers with the Federal Trade Commission's National Do Not Call Registry.

The negative public sentiment against telemarketers has led some providers to move away from their outbound call center operations. Instead, these organizations use their call centers to generate revenue from existing customers (Lieber, 2002; McDaniel, 2006). Turek (2002) reported that in certain financial sectors, approximately 70% of all upselling and reselling transactions in the United States now take place through one of these centers.

## Reducing Labor Costs

Over the past 20 years, U.S.-based call center providers have struggled to reduce their growing labor costs and to curb the high employee turnover that plagues their industry. According to a study conducted by researchers from Purdue University's Center for Customer-Driven Quality, annual turnover in U.S. centers averages 26% for full-time technicians. Further, call centers incur one year's salary to replace each technician who leaves the company (Hillmer, Hillmer, & McRoberts, 2004).

## OUTSOURCING CALL CENTER TECHNICIAN POSITIONS TO INDIA

In the late 1990s, call center providers addressed these rising labor costs by outsourcing part or all of their operations to India (McDaniel, 2006). India was a popular destination because of the country's highly educated workforce (Fairell, Kaka, & Stürze, 2005). Also, nearly three million English-speaking college students graduate from India's universities every year (Ebsco, 2005a).

Initially, organizations found that relocating their call center operations to India reduced their operating costs. However, these same multinational companies soon experienced problems attracting and retaining qualified technicians. Across India's call centers, employee turnover now approaches 50% a year (Clarke, 2006).

Privacy laws in India are less strict than in the United States (Ebsco, 2005a). This has resulted in a series of widely publicized public relations snafus involving India's outsourcing community. For instance, in March 2004, Capital One canceled its telemarketing contact with Wipro, one of India's largest call center providers, when an internal investigation found technicians had misled U.S. consumers by providing them unauthorized promotions to sign up for credit cards (Krebsbach, 2004).

Most troubling to U.S. companies, though, has been the rising number of customer service complaints directed at overseas technicians. In 2004, *Call Center Magazine,* a key industry trade publication, surveyed call center providers from countries that included both India and the Philippines (Dawson, 2004). Managers in these centers reported that achieving "higher customer satisfaction" was the single most important metric (75%) they used to gauge success in their business (p. 18). Further, the outsource providers estimated that 65% of their customers went away "highly satisfied." Consumers, however, reported they were "highly satisfied" only 22% of the time (p. 16). Chief among their complaints: technicians who were poorly trained and unable to resolve their problem (Dawson, 2004, p. 18). Customers have also reported issues understanding technicians. These communication barriers are most problematic in certain regions of India where English-speaking technicians have thick accents (Fairell et al., 2005).

## From Outsourcing to Nearsourcing

Some multinational corporations responded to customers' complaints by moving their technical support operations out of India. In the most publicized case, Dell Inc. pulled two of its business product lines out of a Bangalore, India, call center and relocated the operation back to the United States (Chittum, 2004; Edwards, 2004; Heller, 2004). Other companies have moved their centers from India to the Philippines because English-speaking Filipino technicians have accents closer to individuals who live in the United States (Fairell et al., 2005).

The current trend is for multinational corporations to adopt a *nearsourcing* strategy where they open centers in Canada, Mexico, and Latin America (Beasty, 2005). Datamonitor, a leading industry research firm, reported that three Latin American countries—Argentina, Brazil, and Chile—offer call center providers the most

qualified applicant pool at the lowest possible wage (Ebsco, 2005b). Whether this nearsourcing strategy will be effective remains to be seen.

## CALL CENTER TECHNICIANS AS THE 21ST KNOWLEDGE WORKER

As I have argued, the knowledge demands of call center work are intense. Technicians who once provided support for a single product line increasingly field calls for multiple clients. As product development cycles shrink, there is also increased complexity *within* the products or services first-level technicians' support. The challenge facing call center management is how to keep these low-paid, rather unskilled first-level technicians up to date on the rapidly changing technologies they support.

A related problem is that individuals who apply for these first-level technician positions often lack the necessary computer skills and requisite product or service knowledge to address customers' issues effectively. In response, call center providers spend millions of dollars each year to train these new first-level technicians (Downing, 2004). However, even the best designed training curriculum rarely provides incoming first-level technicians with the details they will need to correctly diagnose, and then answer, their customers' questions. Consequently, technicians, like any knowledge worker, use various strategies to search for the information they need to perform their jobs effectively. In most centers, management has developed formal knowledge tools, also called *online help systems,* for this purpose (Das, 2003).

The quality of these knowledge management tools varies widely across the industry. This helps explain the surprising results from a recent study conducted at *Consumer Reports'* National Research Center. In that study, researchers found that only 55% of consumers who contacted their computer manufacturer for technical support had their problem resolved (Consumer Reports, 2006).

There are several possible reasons why this could happen; however, I will address two of the most likely scenarios. First, it is possible technicians failed to use the knowledge tools management had made available to them. Instead, they relied on more interactive search strategies such as face-to-face communication with colleagues or participating in chat room sessions. Second, even if call center management mandates the use of such tools, the tools simply may have been too difficult for first-level technicians to use.

## The Problems Associated with Technicians Asking Colleagues for the Answer

When customers call with questions first-level technicians cannot immediately answer, technicians' natural tendency is to ask their colleagues who sit nearby if they know the answer (Downing, 2004). It is usually easier for employees to ask someone they know and trust a question rather than rely on printed manuals or to call someone outside their immediate communication network (Holman, Epitropaki, & Fernie, 2001).

In a call center environment, customer satisfaction depends, in large part, on how quickly technicians can solve customers' problems. The first problem with technicians' asking their colleagues for answers is it requires first-level technicians to place their customers on hold. This, in turn, increases talk time on the call. Low talk time is important since customers placed on hold are up to 25% less likely to repurchase a product or service from the company (Clegg, 2004).

The call center management also evaluates its first-level technicians on whether they can successfully answer customers' questions on the first call (high first-call resolution rate). First-call resolution, along with talk time, are both positively related to increased customer satisfaction on an account (Feinberg, Kim, Hokama, de Ruyter, &

Keen, 2000). Yet another issue associated with asking colleagues for help is that there is no guarantee they will provide a correct solution to the customer's problem. If this proves to be the case, the customer will have to contact the center again to resolve the issue. This, in turn, negatively affects first call resolution scores.

## Alternative Strategies First-Level Technicians Use to Find Solutions

Sometimes call center management will develop interactive channels that allow technicians to share knowledge. For example, in a synchronous chat room environment, first-level technicians can request help from their more experienced colleagues who are second-level technicians. Using Microsoft Chat or a similar technology, technicians can either talk to the entire community of technicians that are logged on to the system or they can *whisper* to individual users. Second-level technicians also can monitor first-level technicians' talk times. If a first-level technician's talk time reaches a critical threshold, experienced second-level technicians can jump in to ask if the technician needs help with the call.

## KNOWLEDGE MANAGEMENT TOOLS IN CALL CENTERS

Instead of having first-level technicians' ask their colleagues for answers or developing "informal" knowledge tools like chat rooms, call center providers are better off developing formal knowledge tools that their first-level technicians will voluntarily adopt. A formal knowledge management tool is viable in a call center environment since roughly 80% of the support calls first-level technicians field have already been answered by another technician on the account (Hollman, 2002).

As I argued in the previous section, if these tools are already in place but technicians have chosen not to use them, one likely culprit is that the tools are too difficult to use. Indeed, researchers (Davis, 1989; Rogers, 1995) have long argued that for a new technology to be successfully adopted in the workplace, the technology must not only be easy to use (*perceived ease of use*), but employees also must see how using it will help them perform their jobs more efficiently (*perceived usefulness*). Thus, a new knowledge tool must help first-level technicians meet their performance metrics, which include achieving high first-call resolution scores and low talk and average handle times. (*Average handle time* is the average amount of talk time a technician spends with his or her customer, including any time customers' spend on hold.) The problem, as we shall soon see, is that traditional (Web-based) knowledge tools in use at many call centers fail to meet this criterion.

## Two Types of Formal Knowledge Tools

### Online Help Tool with a Search Box Query

Most knowledge tools use a Web-based interface that requires users to enter a keyword query directly into the tool's search box. The tool then searches for documents housed in its help database that match these keywords. Microsoft's Online Help (*support.microsoft.com*) provides an example of this type of knowledge tool.

A knowledge tool's effectiveness is related to the accuracy and comprehensiveness of the documents that software engineers have selected to populate the tool. Typically, product engineers, technical writers, and learning design specialists create this technical documentation.

Interestingly, first-level technicians often use the same help tool the client makes available for free to its consumer end user. Both first-level technicians and consumers share a common trait: both are novice users. Tsoukas and Vladimirou (2001) argued that novice users have difficulty using this type of help interface because they lack

the requisite technical knowledge and cognitive complexity to enter "correct" keywords into the search box. To illustrate, Juniper Research, a market research firm, surveyed more than 2,700 consumers and found that among the 80% of respondents who had used this type of knowledge tool, fully 46% had difficulty constructing their search queries (Daniels, 2003).

After the tool searches the database, it returns the title and often a brief abstract of technical documents that match the keywords. Users can then click on the hyperlink to receive the full text of the document. A second and related problem with this type of interface is it returns too many documents to be helpful to the user (Daniels, 2003).

### Decision-Tree-Type Help Interfaces

Software designers also can develop an alternative knowledge tool for call center technicians that use a decision-tree-type help interface. As with the other tool, first-level technicians ask their customers to describe the symptom(s) of the problem they are experiencing with the product or service. Technicians then type the symptom into the tool. After technicians hit *Enter,* the software application that drives the tool directs technicians to ask their customers a series of questions, one symptom-related issue at a time. This serves to narrow down the likely cause of the problem. Initially, the scope of these questions is broad. However, the tool uses case-based logic—also called a *decision tree*—to narrow down possible solutions to the customer's problem. At the end of this deductive process, the tool interprets the probability level of its proposed solutions.

In his recent study, Downing (in press) reported how ClientLogic, a global call center provider based in the United States, worked with one of its clients to develop a knowledge tool that incorporated a decision-tree-type help interface. The new tool replaced an existing search box interface ClientLogic technicians already used on the account.

Approximately 600 first-level ClientLogic technicians used the new knowledge tool for four months. ClientLogic officials then applied internal performance metrics (average handle time and first-call resolution) to compare the decision-tree-type interface with the more traditional search box tool. At the end of four months, average handle time on the account decreased by 2%. Further, over the course of the study, issue resolution rates increased by an average of 1% a week. Downing concluded that a decision-tree-type interface holds special promise in call center environments because of the limited knowledge required of first-level technicians to use this type of tool properly.

## Keeping Knowledge Tools Up to Date

Regardless of what type of knowledge tool first-level technicians' use, they will still field non-routine calls from their customers. Since the answer to a customer's problem is not yet included in the tool, first-level technicians will have to escalate the call to second-level technicians who support the account. The second-level technician, in turn, may have to conduct outside research to find a solution to the customer's problem.

Call center management must have a process in place where second-level technicians take this (often tactic) knowledge and make this knowledge explicit. Only then can this knowledge later be added to the tool. Further, management also must gather information from chat room transcripts, e-mails, and other material collected through informal search procedures, catalog it, and then index the information so it can later be incorporated into the system.

## The Importance of Securing Buy-In from Second-Level Technicians

An important success criterion is for second-level technicians to participate in the decision-making process to adopt any new knowledge tool that is brought into the center. In many call center environments, second-level technicians earn the esteem of their first-level colleagues because of the specialized knowledge they have learned on the job. A formal knowledge tool tries to codify this specialized knowledge and include its contents in the tool. Once first-level technicians discover that the tool contains this knowledge, second-level technicians' informational power can dissipate quickly.

Second-level technicians, then, often have the most to lose if a knowledge tool is implemented in their center. This creates a paradox for center management. Second-level technicians' technical savvy and expertise position them as excellent candidates to be early adopters of new technologies in the center. At the same time, how these opinion-leaders frame the new tools to their first-level technician colleagues will go a long way to determining if the knowledge tools will reach a critical mass of users within the center.

## Incentives for First-Level Technicians to Use the Tools

For call center management to implement a tool that will achieve this critical mass, management needs to understand the incentives that drive employee behavior. Unfortunately, little is known about first-level technicians' subjective experience with knowledge management tools. However, IT scholars have published many empirical studies that investigate why employees choose to adopt different technologies in the workplace. Earlier, I argued that perceived usefulness and perceived ease of use of a new innovation (Yi, Fiedler, & Park, 2006) are perhaps the two most critical factors in this adoption decision. In a call center, a knowledge tool that takes too long to answer a customer's question, and worse, does not include relevant knowledge for this purpose, is unlikely to be used by technicians (Downing, 2004).

Moore and Benbasat (1991) have claimed that to be successfully adopted in an organization, employees' use of the new innovation must be visible to others in the company. Thus, the adoption will be successful to the extent it strengthens employees' social status in their work group (Venkatesh & Davis, 2000). Another interesting line of research seeks to understand why employees voluntarily adopt a new technology. For instance, the *perceived enjoyment* employees' gain from using the innovation, Chin and Gopal (1995) argued, helps explain why a particular technology succeeds or fails in the workplace.

A related research area that holds much promise is studying how the structure of a particular job task—in this case, the use of a knowledge tool—invites employees to become immersed in the task. Csikszentmihalyi (1997) calls this state of total attention to the task at hand *flow*. To achieve flow, employees must undertake job tasks that include clear and achievable goals. Further, employees must receive immediate and relevant feedback about how they have achieved these goals. Employees' individual skill levels must also meet the cognitive demands of the task. Tasks must be demanding enough to challenge the employee, but not so demanding that completing the job task leads to increased employee stress.

A productive line of future study for call center researchers will be to study how the structure of a particular knowledge tool—that is, using an online help tool with search box vs. a decision-tree-type help interface—affects first-level technicians' feelings of personal accomplishment to solve their customer's problems. Further, researchers must continue to study how differences across cultures (Heijden, 2003; Igbaria, Livari, & Maragahh, 1995) affect first-level technicians' decisions to adopt and continue to use online knowledge tools in call centers.

## RECOMMENDATIONS

For multinational organizations to attract and retain their call center operations, companies must develop knowledge tools technicians can quickly and accurately use to answer their customers' issues. Call center research is in its infancy; as a result, few empirical research studies have investigated this phenomenon. Indeed, most call center research consists of individual case studies. Clearly, more longitudinal research is needed on this topic. Nevertheless, the following three recommendations can help ensure this process flows as smoothly as possible:

1.  Ask key opinion-leaders to participate in the decision to adopt the knowledge tool. Second-level technicians who participate in the process are also more likely to later contribute knowledge into the tool (Klein & Ralls, 1995).

2.  Develop a tool that is easy for technicians to use and that provides technicians with a quick solution to their customer's problem. Management also should consider using a decision-tree-type help interface, not a traditional search box tool, if first-level technicians on the account lack the technical knowledge needed to enter the "correct" keywords into the tool. If the tool takes too long for first-level technicians to use, they may regress to the more informal search process, where customers are placed on hold and technicians ask colleagues who sit nearby if they know the answer to the customer's problem.

3. Design a formal reward and recognition system that acknowledges those technicians, especially second-level technicians, who often contribute new information into the tool. If users are allowed to "sign" their contributions to the knowledge tool, they may be more motivated to share their information.

## FUTURE TRENDS AND CONCLUSION

The U.S. Department of Labor, Bureau of Labor Statistics (2005) expects customer service positions, which include call center technicians, to grow by 18-26% by 2014. To decrease costs, call center providers are investigating online support channels like e-mail and chat—both of which are less expensive than having a technician speak with a customer on the phone (Hollman, 2002). Regardless of what form the communication takes, first-level technicians will still have to use some type of formal knowledge tool to answer their customers' questions.

In many ways, the key to building a successful knowledge tool is tied to innovations in *natural language search protocols* (Daniels, 2003). Natural language search will allow technicians to construct a search query using their own vocabulary and will not require technicians to learn the complex technical lexicon that is needed to use most of the knowledge tools in use today.

In this chapter I have argued how formal knowledge tools can help first-level call center technicians perform their job more effectively. Technicians who work in these centers offer researchers a different type of "knowledge worker" relative to the engineers, consultants, and other types of "professional" knowledge workers that most researchers study. As such, call center environments hold promise for researchers interested in how knowledge workers use help tools to perform their jobs more efficiently.

## REFERENCES

American Teleservices Association. (2002). *Consumer study.* Retrieved February 17, 2006, from *http://www.ataconnect.org/IndustryResearch/ ConsumerStudy2002.html*

Bagnara, S., & Marti, P. (2001). Human work in call centers: A challenge for cognitive ergonomics. *Theoretical Issues in Ergonomic Science, 2*(3), 223-237.

Beasty, C. (2005). Outsourcing south of the border. *Customer Relationship Marketing,* (April), 13.

Chin, W., & Gopal, A. (1995). Adoption intention in GSS relative importance of beliefs. *Data Base, 26*(2/3), 42-63.

Chittum, R. (2004). Call centers phone home. *Wall Street Journal,* (June 9), B1.

Clarke, T. (2006). Why Indian summer is drawing to a close. *PrecisionMarketing,* (May 12), 14-15.

Clegg, C.H. (2004). *Best practices in telephone customer service.* Portland, OR: Portland Research Group.

Consumer Reports. (2006). Computer technical support survey. *Consumer Reports,* (June), 21.

Csikszentmihalyi, M. (1997). *Finding flow: The psychology of engagement with everyday life.* New York: Basic Books.

Daniels, D. (2003). Self-service: Creating value with natural language search. *Call Center Magazine, 16,* 8-9.

Das, A. (2003). Knowledge and productivity in technical support work. *Management Science, 49*(4), 416-431.

Datamonitor. (2003). *Call centers in the United States. Industry profile.* New York: Author (reference code: 00720758).

Davis, F.D. (1989). Perceived usefulness, perceived ease of use, and user acceptance of information technology. *MIS Quarterly, 13,* 319-340.

Dawson, K. (2004). Customers: Not as happy as you think. *Call Center Magazine, 17,* 16-22.

Downing, J. (in press). Using customer contact center technicians to measure the effectiveness of online help systems. *Technical Communication.*

Downing, J. (2004). 'It's easier to ask someone I know:' Call center technicians' adoption of knowledge management tools. *Journal of Business Communication, 41*(2), 166-192.

Ebsco. (2005a). Busy signals. *Economist,* (September 9), 60. Retrieved March 3, 2005, from *http://www.ebsco.com*

Ebsco. (2005b). Offshore contact centers. *MarketWatch: Global Round-Up, 4*(October), 229-230. Retrieved February 15, 2006, from *http://www.ebsco.com*

Edwards, L. (2004). Overseas call centers can cost firms goodwill. *Marketing News,* (April 15), 21.

Fairell, D., Kaka, N., & Stürze, S. (2005). Ensuring India's offshoring future. *McKinsey Quarterly,* 74-83.

Feinberg, R.A., Kim, I., Hokama, L., de Ruyter, K., & Keen, C. (2000). Operational determinants of caller satisfaction in the call center. *International Journal of Service Industry Management, 11,* 131-141.

Heijden, H. (2003). Factors influencing the usage of Web sites: The case of a generic portal in The Netherlands. *Information & Management, 40,* 541-549.

Heller, M. (2004). Outsourcing. *Workforce Management, 83,* 95-97. Retrieved May 17, 2006, from *http://www.ebsco.com*

Hillmer, S., Hillmer, B., & McRoberts, G. (2004). The real costs of turnover: Lessons from a call center. *Human Resource Planning, 27*(3), 34-41. Retrieved February 17, 2006, from *http://www.ebsco.com*

Hollman, L. (2002). The power of knowledge management software. *Call Center Magazine, 15*(1), 30-38.

Holman, D., Epitropaki, O., & Fernie, S. (2001). Understanding learning strategies in the workplace: A factor analytic investigation. *Journal of Occupational and Organizational Psychology, 74,* 675-681.

Igbaria, M., Livari, J., & Maragahh, H. (1995). Why do individuals use computer technology? A Finnish case study. *Information & Management, 29*(5), 227-238.

Klein, K.J., & Ralls, R.S. (1995). The organizational dynamics of computerized technology implementation: A review of the literature. In M.W. Lawless & L.R. Gomez-Media (Eds.), *Advances in global high-technology management* (pp. 31-79). New York: JAI Press.

Krebsbach, K. (2004). Lessons from the dark side: Avoiding mistakes in overseas outsourcing. *Bank Technology News,* (May), 31, 54.

Lieber, R. (2002). 'Operator, I demand an automated Menu.' *Wall Street Journal,* (July 30), D1.

McDaniel, C. (2006). *2006 call center employment outlook.* Available from M.E.R. Inc., 866-991-3555.

Moore, G., & Benbasat, I. (1991). Development of an instrument to measure the perceptions of adopting an information technology innovation. *Information Systems Research, 2*(3), 192-222.

Rogers, E.M. (1995). *Diffusion of innovations* (4th ed.). New York: The Free Press.

Tsoukas, H., & Vladimirou, E. (2001). What is organizational knowledge? *Journal of Management Studies, 38,* 973-993.

Turek, N. (2002). Call centers: Here, there, and everywhere. *InformationWeek,* (October 23), 168-174.

U.S. Department of Labor, Bureau of Labor Statistics (2005). *Customer service representatives.* Retrieved February 17, 2006, from *http://www. bls.gov/oco/ocos280.htm*

Venkatesh, V., & Davis, F.D. (2000). A theoretical extension of the Technology Acceptance Model: Four longitudinal field studies. *Management Science, 46*(2), 186-204.

Walsh, J.P., & Ungson, G.R. (1991). Organizational memory. *Academy of Management Review, 16,* 57-91.

Yates, J., & Orlikowski, W. (2002). Genre systems: Structuring interaction through communicative norms. *Journal of Business Communication, 39,* 13-35.

Yi, M.Y., Fiedler, K.D., & Park, J.S. (2006). Understanding the role of individual innovativeness in the acceptance of IT-based innovations: Comparative analyses of models and measures. *Decision Sciences, 37*(3), 393-426.

# Chapter V
# KAFRA:
## A Context–Aware Framework of Knowledge Management in Global Diversity

**A. Okunoye**
*Xavier University, USA*

**N. Bertaux**
*Xavier University, USA*

## ABSTRACT

*Multiple case studies in India, The Gambia, and Nigeria are the background for an empirically grounded framework of knowledge management (KM). Cultural diversity and gaps in the provision of infrastructure make managing knowledge challenging but necessary in developing countries. These cultural and infrastructural issues are also related to governmental, educational, political, social, and economic factors. These environmental factors interact with organizational variables and information technology to enable or constrain knowledge management processes in the creation and protection of knowledge resources. The framework can help organizations to prepare their KM projects, to reveal problems during the project, and to assess its outcomes.*

## INTRODUCTION

KM frameworks assist us in establishing a focus for KM efforts (Earl, 2001). These frameworks can also help organizations to approach KM methodically and consciously. They can help to identify a specific approach to KM, to define goals and strategies, to understand the various knowledge management initiatives, and then to choose the best ones for the particular circumstances (Earl, 2001; Maier & Remus, 2001). There have been several proposed frameworks to guide KM efforts in organizations. However, these frameworks do not address KM across the full spectrum of organizational needs (Calaberese, 2000) but instead address certain KM elements. There is, therefore, a need for a comprehensive KM framework that considers the full range of organizational dimensions.

Three reviews (Holsapple & Joshi, 1999; Lai & Chu, 2000; Rubestein-Montano, Liebowitz, Buchwalter, McCaw, Newman, & Rebeck, 2001) have discussed the components and assumptions of the frameworks proposed to date. There appears to be a consensus on the need for a more generalized framework, and, consequently, these authors also outline recommendations regarding such a framework. All agree that the basic components should be knowledge resources, KM processes, and influences. Even though the existing and the suggested frameworks recognize varying organizational contexts, they have not considered differences in the operating environmental contexts. This is similar to the information systems (IS) literature, where very few studies address global diversity (Avgerou, 2002; Walsham, 2001).

The importance of the local operating environmental context has already received some attention in e-commerce (Simon, 2001), ERP (Wassenar, Gregor, & Swagerman, 2002), and IS development methodology research (INDE-HELA Project, 1999). Also, King, Gurbaxani, Kraemer, McFarlan, Raman, and Yap (1994) comprehensively discuss institutional factors in information technology innovation. In knowledge management, however, there is a basic need for consideration of the diverse environmental context and how it could influence other issues involved. The framework described here is designed to address that need, by focusing on the local cultural and infrastructural factors that could interact with organizational factors and information technology and the resultant effect on knowledge processes and resources.

## GLOBAL DIVERSITY AND SIGNIFICANCE OF A NEW FRAMEWORK

Our view on global diversity recognizes the existence of different organizational contexts and that assumptions cannot be simply made about the pattern of organizational performance and innovations (Avgerou, 2002). For example, the wide gap in the availability and use of ICT across the world, and the influences ICT exerts on globalization, raise questions about the feasibility and desirability of efforts to implement the development of ICT through the transfer of best practices from Western industrialized countries to developing countries, and whether organizations can utilize such ICT in accordance with the socio-cultural requirements of the contexts (Avgerou, 1998; Morales-Gomez & Melesse, 1998; Walsham, 2001). Previous research (Avgerou, 2002; Bada, 2000; Walsham, 2001) concludes that diversity and local context does matter, and that the global techniques employed in western industrialized countries should not be implemented mechanically in developing countries without consideration for the local context (Bada, 2000).

The concept of description proposed by Akrich (2000) also expresses our understanding of global diversity and the significance of a context-aware framework. Akrich argues that when technologists define the characteristics of their object, they necessarily make hypotheses about the entities that make up the world into which the object is to be inserted. They also assume that the designers define actors with specific tastes, competences, motives, aspirations, political prejudices, and the rest. They assume that morality, technology, society, and the economy will evolve in particular ways. In a nutshell, they inscribe their vision, or prediction about the world, into the technical content of the new object. Karsten (2000, p. 21) also suggests that "the functions of these (technical) systems[1] are not predetermined, but only evolve within specific, socio-political contexts." Focusing on specific contexts will help to move away from unfruitful general claims and all-encompassing pictures, enabling us to see a technical change as embedded in a larger system of activity, having consequences that depend on peoples' actual behavior, and taking place in a social world in which the history of related changes may influence the new change.

We are aware of the force of globalization and its assumed homogeneity. However, globalization does not mean imposing homogenous solutions in a pluralistic world. It means giving a global vision and strategy, but it also means cultivating roots and individual identities. It means nourishing local insights, but it also means re-employing communicable ideas in new geographies around the world (Das, 1993). The adoption and usage of such a technology framework will vary according both to local socio-cultural and organizational contexts, and to the national context, including government, economic, and political systems, educational systems, and history, culture, and infrastructure (Schneider & Barsoux, 1997).

A KM framework can be seen as an IS innovation (Avgerou, 2001), a technology (Walsham, 2001), or a technical object (Akrich, 2000). Considering the context in which they are designed and their designers, it can be argued that some basic assumptions (to be discussed later) about the KM processes and influences have been inscribed into these frameworks. An attempt to describe and apply the framework in another context might be problematic. Hence, a context-aware framework, with specific consideration for the operating environmental factors and for the organizational factors that are closely related to the environment, could help to move us toward a more universally applicable KM framework, as well as increasing our sensitivity to the importance of global diversity.

## TOWARD A CONTEXT-AWARE FRAMEWORK

### Theoretical Background

In this paper, we synthesize some of the insights from our studies to build a context-aware framework, including an explanation of its components. The framework is called KAFRA (an abbreviation of Kontext Aware FRAmework). In building KAFRA, we relied on some well-known concepts and theories in organization studies in order to

support our arguments. Leavitt (1965) calls for interdependence of organizational variables for effective organizational change, and Scott (1998) asserts that environment and organization are inseparable. The institutionalist perspective of Powell and DiMaggio (1991) also supports the argument on the need to consider the operating environment in a KM framework. Following Pettigrew's contextualist approach (1987), for a study on change to contribute toward a robust theory or framework that can guide practice, it must examine change as a process and in a historical and contextual manner (Bada, 2000). Hofstede's (1997) cultural model and Galbraith's (1977) concept of organization design are also brought in to strengthen the arguments for the KAFRA framework. Initially, the design of the study, data collection and analysis and subsequent theorizing and building of the framework was influenced by socio-technical systems (STS) theory. Thus, we next present a brief overview of the STS theory and knowledge management.

### Socio-Technical Systems Theory and Knowledge Management

A socio-technical system is defined as a combination of a social and a technical subsystem (Trist, 1981). Rather than insisting that individual and social units must conform to technical requirements, the socio-technical systems theory emphasizes the needs of both (Scott, 1998). One of the guiding premises of this approach is that work involves a combination of social and technical requisites and that the object of design is to jointly optimize both components without sacrificing one to others. This approach provides a broad conceptual foundation as well as insights into the nature of routine and non-routine work design. STS has been applied both in systems development practice and in the analysis of ICT functionality and organizational changes (Avgerou, 2002; Lyytinen Mathiassen, & Ropponen, 1998; Mumford & Weir, 1979). There has also been application of socio-technical systems theory in KM (Coakes Willis, & Clarke, 2002; Pan & Scarbrough, 1998; Sena & Shani, 1999).

In a similar manner, Leavitt (1965) recognized the complexity and diversity of organizations by identifying four socio-technical variables (structure, task, technology, and people) that need to interact together in a balanced way to bring about organizational change. Scott (1998) added environment as another element, suggesting that organizations and environments are interdependent in terms of information systems and cognitive processes and in terms of environmental effects on organizational outcomes. They are also interdependent in more direct ways, since organizations attempt to directly influence environments and vice versa.

## Leavitt's Diamond Organization Model

The Leavitt Diamond (Figure 1) gives a balanced view of the complexities that affect KM framework by positioning technology in strong relationships to the tasks carried out, the people participating in these, and to the organization of the tasks and the people, for example, the structure. It has been widely adopted and cited (e.g., El Sawy, 2001; Mumford, 1993; Schäfer, Hirschheim, Harper, Hansjee, Domke, & Bjorn-Andersen, 1988; Wiggins, 2000) as a basis for understanding organizational changes.

*Figure 1. Leavitt's diamond organization model (Leavitt, 1965)*

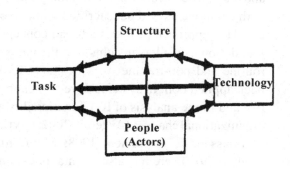

Leavitt's Diamond shows four sets of organizational variables: task, people (actors), technology, and structure. According to Leavitt (1965), these four groups of variables are highly interdependent, as indicated by the arrowheads, so that change in any one usually results in compensatory or retaliatory change in others. Technologies are considered tools that help organizations to get work done and mechanisms for transforming inputs to outputs.

This view corresponds to ours: knowledge management is not only about managing knowledge-work processes or the people that carry out these processes, since technology and organizational structure are also affected. A position explored in the framework is that by studying the balance of all these variables, it is possible to bring out the value of the knowledge management efforts in an organization. Therefore, rather than trivializing any one of the variables or neglecting one set (such as technology), the framework considers all equally and gives priority to all the variables so that knowledge management efforts can achieve maximal success.

## Summary

The work of knowledge-based organizations is usually non-routine and needs to be supported by balancing all the variables mentioned earlier. Thus KM from the socio-technical perspective will require all activities that support the *social subsystems* (the nature of human capital, i.e., the people with knowledge, competencies, skills, experience, and attitudes), a *technical subsystem* (the production function, i.e., the inputs and the technology that convert inputs into outputs), and an *environmental subsystem* (including customers, competitors, and a host of other outside forces) (Sena & Shani, 1999). Any framework to support KM should integrate these main variables and put proper emphasis and consideration to diversity in various environments, since all organizations exist in a specific geographical, cultural, technological, and social environment to which they must adapt.

To these general theoretical perspectives on the influence of local diversity in an organization's environment, we add our own insights concerning cultural and infrastructure diversity and their influences on KM based on findings from the multiple case study. The diversity in our study organizations—which include national and international organizations in different research fields—formed the basis for the evidence on contextual issues in organizational variables and information technology. We next present the methodology and approaches to data collection.

## The Study

Most of the studies that form the basis of the existing frameworks have been carried out in organizations in Western industrialized countries where there can be similar assumptions about the components of the framework. To add a new perspective, we conducted our study in developing countries. These countries afford us an opportunity to see the differences in culture (Hofstede, 1997) and infrastructure provision (The World Bank Group, 2004) at the local level. An empirical study was conducted on KM in six research organizations in Nigeria and The Gambia and two research organizations in India. Nigeria is representative of countries in sub-Saharan Africa due to its large population and huge natural resources. Oil exploration has particularly attracted many multinational companies that are characterized by Western management styles. The Gambia presents a contrast to Nigeria as one of the smallest countries in sub-Saharan Africa but with a reliable infrastructure. India is representative of countries in South Asia, by population, culture, and business environment. India is a major site for offshore software production (Lateef, 1997), and it was anticipated this would be evident in both the environmental context and the organizational variables. The

advances of India in software business and the commitment of government in knowledge-based activities make it a strategic place to study KM. However, these industries are in the minority and could not be viewed completely as indigenous. The methodology used was a multiple case study (Yin, 1994) with data analysis carried out on the organizational level (Korpela, Mursu, & Soriyan, 2001). Both quantitative and qualitative data was collected using questionnaires, interviews, non-participant observation, and reviews of historical documents.

The discussion in this paper summarizes relevant aspects of these studies. The results show differences in assumptions on the influence of KM, especially when the local operating environment context is considered. Our study shows how the availability and use of information and communication technologies could support KM processes and how the Internet especially appears to provide a gateway to the international research community. This would suggest raising IT to be a major component in a comprehensive KM model. These findings also indicated some issues about leadership, structure, and culture that are contextual to each organization and the environment in which they operate. A conclusion of our study is that a KM framework needs to have contextual relevance for organizations in diverse social-cultural environments. It should align information technology, people, structure, knowledge processes, and socio-cultural and organizational influences to make knowledge management sustainable.

## Research Methods

The contextual issues in a KM framework were studied through a multiple-case study and analysis of eight different research organizations. Yin (1994) observed that the triangulation of multiple sources of evidence permits convergence and corroboration of findings and building a stronger, more convincing basis for conclusions. While the conduct of a multiple-case study can require extensive resources and time, the evidence is often considered more compelling than from a single case, and the study can be regarded as more robust. We carried out our study in two countries in sub-Saharan Africa, in Nigeria and The Gambia, and in two organizations in India. These countries have different levels of infrastructure and cultural differences. For example, in telecommunications, The Gambia has a significantly higher penetration (The World Bank Group, 2004). We assumed there would also be differences in organizational infrastructures across countries.

## The Case Organizations

Of the six organizations in Nigeria, three are international: International Institute of Tropical Agriculture (IITA), Medical Research Council Laboratories (MRC), and International Trypanotolerance Center (ITC). Three are national: National Agricultural Research Institute (NARI), Nigeria Institute of Social Economic Research (NISER) and Nigerian Institute of Medical Research (NIMR). The national organizations are mainly dependent on the national government for their basic funding. Usually the international organizations have a substantial number of expatriates working in them for the duration of their project. Three of the organizations are large, with more than 500 staff members. The smaller three have 100-200 staff members. All of the organizations carry out their research within several sites. Also, all of them have in-country and international collaboration with other institutions. Thus, they all work in a wide network of sponsors, customers, and cooperating institutions. India's two organizations are International Crop Research Institute for the Semi Arid Tropics (ICRISAT), an international organization with a staff of more than 500, and National Institute of Mental Health and Neuroscience (NIMHANS), a national organization also with a staff of more than 500.

The study used several methods of data gathering. The two main questionnaires were the KM diagnostic and the information technology infrastructure (ITI) services assessment instrument (see Okunoye & Karsten, 2001 for more details). These were complemented by semi-structured interviews and short-time on-site observations of knowledge management enablers.

Organizational documents and presentations by senior management about their KM-related initiatives were collected and analyzed. A similar approach in data gathering has been applied in a study on the relationship between IT infrastructure and business process re-engineering (Broadbent, Weill, & St. Clair, 1999). Between January and March 2001, we visited all six organizations in Nigeria and during the summer of 2002, we visited the two organizations in India. The visits lasted for about two weeks each. Some of the research sites of each organization were visited and as many as possible of the relevant people were interviewed, especially the heads of sections, the IT managers, and the librarians, to fill out the questionnaires and to provide the documents. Individual researchers provided valuable insight into the actual work processes. In the Nigeria study, a total of 48 people participated in the research: 29 were interviewed and did the questionnaire, eight did the questionnaire only, and 11 were interviewed only. However, only 31 out of the 37 questionnaires were included in the final analysis, because six of them had to be eliminated due to low responses to the questions. In India, 26 people participated: 16 people were interviewed and completed the questionnaire, six did the questionnaire only, and four were interviewed only; 19 out of 22 questionnaires were included in the final analysis and three had to be eliminated due to low responses to the questions. The interviews were recorded on audiotape and in a field diary and later transcribed. As the visits were brief and as all instruments had to be filled out with the researcher present, the time was only sufficient for observation of some KM practices (see Okunoye & Karsten, 2002a, 2002b, 2003; Okunoye, Innola, & Karsten, 2002 for detailed results).

## COMPONENTS OF KAFRA FRAMEWORK

### Environmental Factors

Environmental factors include those factors outside the organization that directly influence its activities. Holsapple and Joshi (2000) include governmental, economic, political, social, and educational factors (GEPSE) here. There are also indirect factors such as *culture* and *national infrastructure*. The operating environment varies from organization to organization, between countries, and also from one site to another within a country. Yet many frameworks that guide organizational strategies and development simply assume a homogeneous environment and thus exclude it from their design. A common assumption is that organizations will consider the GEPSE factors that have a direct economic impact on their operation but that indirect factors such as the culture and the infrastructure are irrelevant[2]. However, our empirical studies tell us that these indirect factors also significantly influence organizational variables. This is consistent with a growing literature in the U.S. that documents the importance of managing cultural diversity factors to improve organizational systems (Cox, 2001; Thomas, Roosevelt, Thomas, Ely, & Meyerson, 2002).

### Infrastructural Issues

The national infrastructure can be said to include education, banking, cooperatives, transportation, and communication systems. Scholars have pointed out the influence that these systems have on the organizational IT infrastructure (Weill & Vitale, 2002). The infrastructural issues are derivatives of several other environmental factors, and this discussion thus cuts across many other issues. The infrastructural capability of a country is likely to influence the kind of technology the organization can deploy. It could also determine the extent of the application and sustainability of this technology. The extent to which countries provide infrastructure at the national level clearly affects the infrastructure of organizations in these countries. Most of the technological problems associated with environmental factors are beyond the control of single organizations. There are considerable differences in the IT infrastructures globally between countries, that is, between Western and developing countries (The World Bank Group, 2004). The differences within developing countries are also wide, as illustrated in Table 1. Specifically, in our study and as evidenced in the literature (Barata, Kutzner, & Wamukoya, 2001; Darley, 2001; Odedra, Lawrie, Bennett,

*Table 1. Infrastructural differences between Nigeria, The Gambia, India, and the USA (The World Bank Group, 2004)*

| ICT infrastructure, computers, and the Internet | Nigeria | The Gambia | India | USA |
|---|---|---|---|---|
| Telephone mainlines/1000 people | 4 | 26 | 32 | 700 |
| Mobile phones/1000 people | 0 | 4 | 4 | 398 |
| Personal computers/1000 people | 6.6 | 11.5 | 4.5 | 585.2 |
| Internet users ('000) | 200 | 4 | 5,000 | 95,354 |
| Internet speed and access[3] | 2.5/7 | | 3.6/7 | 6.6/7 |
| Internet effect on business[1] | 3.3/7 | | 3.2/7 | 5.0/7 |

& Goodman, 1993) and available statistics (The World Bank Group 2004), the problem with the IT infrastructure is more pronounced in sub-Saharan Africa (SSA) than in India, where the government has invested heavily in it. Most of the problems in SSA can be attributed to the government's lack of preparedness to commit sufficient resources to develop the national infrastructure, which could as a consequence improve the infrastructures available to organizations. The low availability and utilization of IT infrastructure in sub-Saharan Africa and the lack of expertise to support the physical infrastructure has been widely discussed (e.g., Moyo, 1996; Odedra et al., 1993). According to our study, while the availability of IT infrastructure has the expected significant effect on the knowledge management efforts, its under-utilization and the lack of technical expertise to support its proper application to the knowledge management processes becomes an even bigger problem.

For example, in Nigeria, individuals were expected to bear the cost associated with Internet use in the national research organizations we studied:

*...if you understand, it [Internet] is not widely available for some reasons, cost, which implies that cost of access is high, even though you have opened it up to everybody, the cost is scaring them off and they are not using it. That is why I was a bit eh eh, but there is access. You have to pay N200 (about $2) for 15 minutes of browsing, some of them use it when it is very important and critical...* (Mr. B, NISER)

This was not the case in India and The Gambia. Also, the Indian government's long-term investment in educational and social infrastructures has provided a large pool of qualified IT practitioners (Lateef, 1997; Tessler & Barr, 1997). This has a high impact on the kinds of technology they are able to use in their organizations. They have been able to design the required KM applications

and to provide adequate support, sometimes at a cheaper cost when compared to Nigeria and The Gambia. This was not the case in SSA, where getting qualified IT support and management personnel continue to be a major problem (Odedra et al., 1993).

These examples show the kind of influence the provision of infrastructure in a particular environmental context can exert on the information technology that can be deployed within an organization. It also shows the effect on usage; where individuals are responsible for the cost of using technology, it is likely to discourage the use of this technology. Thus, a framework that could be applicable in this context should provide for the assessment of infrastructural provision in the environment where the organization operates.

## Cultural Issues

Several authors have demonstrated how national culture influences management practices. For example, Schneider and Barsoux (1997) relate culture to each of the organizational variables that have been identified as having a great influence on KM (American Productivity and Quality Center, 1996). Weisinger and Trauth (2002) have argued that cultural understanding is locally situated and negotiated by actors within a specific context. In information systems research, national culture has been noted to influence, among others, IT utilization (Deans et al., 1991), IT diffusion (Straub, 1994), and technology acceptance (Anandarajan, Igbaria, & Anakwe, 2000; Straub, Keil, & Brenner, 1997). As noted, earlier KM frameworks (Holsapple & Joshi, 1999; Lai & Chu, 2000; Rubenstein-Montano et al., 2001) recognize different organizational cultures, but they are generally silent on the effect of different national cultures.

The best-known and most widely used cultural model was developed by Hofstede based on a study conducted among IBM employees working in different countries in the late 1960s

(Hofstede, 1997). Hofstede included four dimensions of national culture: power distance, uncertainty avoidance, individualism-collectivism, and masculinity-femininity. He later added a fifth dimension, long- versus short-term orientation, based on a study carried out in Asian countries. The model helps bring out issues related to cultural differences, and it provides some universal measures with which to analyze them. According to Walsham (2001), however, such measures are too general and cannot be used to explain some cultural differences.

According to Hofstede, countries in West Africa differ culturally from the USA, especially in the power distance and individualism-collectivism dimensions. This study and our earlier experiences, however, report some differences within and between the countries in West Africa. In western Nigeria, where three of the study organizations are located, every village has a well-defined hierarchy and family structure. It is a societal norm to treat senior members with absolute respect and obedience. Their views and opinions are often accepted and their judgments are not to be publicly questioned.

*...To certain extent, given that for any particular area, the programme leader is the expert in that area, It is a requirement for whoever is heading a particular programme to try during the course of his tenure as the programme leader and get the team under him involve in the day to day activities...the people under you [the leaders] are really undergoing apprenticeship so to say...and they need to show respect.* (Dr. SBO, NARI)

There is thus a substantial gap between the leaders and their subordinates. Contrary behavior (even when not necessarily wrong) by any member of the community can be interpreted as disloyalty and attract punishment. In the Nigerian national research organizations located in western Nigeria, it was very easy to recognize the leaders and people in positions of power. Without careful

attention to this, implementing a framework that assumes that everyone has freedom of expression and equal rights could yield undesirable outcomes in these settings. Our argument here is that each organization should be studied in its own cultural context, and thorough knowledge of this should influence the application of the KM framework.

## Organizational Variables

The organizational variables as a necessary concern are recognized in our study as well as several other studies and frameworks (Holsapple and Joshi, 2000; APQC 1996). To succinctly describe all organization issues that could influence KM, the conceptual framework (Figure 2) developed by Galbraith (1977) is adopted and modified by adding organizational culture, which is another important component in organizational design (Schein, 1985). Task, culture, structure, information and decision processes, reward systems, and people are the commonly included organizational variables. These need to be aligned for optimal results (Galbraith, 1977; Leavitt, 1965).

Organizational structure is the distribution of power and the shape of the organizational form. People have competence, nature, and attitudes. Information and decision processes include especially the availability and accessibility of information. Reward systems tell how the organization compensates its members for effective performance (Nathanson, Kazanjian, & Galbraith, 1982). The task is the link between choices of strategy and organization structure; decision processes and individual personality vary systematically with the uncertainty of that task (Galbraith, 1977). The organizational culture includes the shared values, beliefs, norms, expectations, and assumptions that bind people and systems. The organizational culture is particularly important in KM because it gives people a basis for stability, control, and direction and helps them to adapt and integrate other variables and technology with the operating environmental factors. This

*Figure 2. Organizational variables (Adapted from concept of organization design, Galbraith, 1977)*

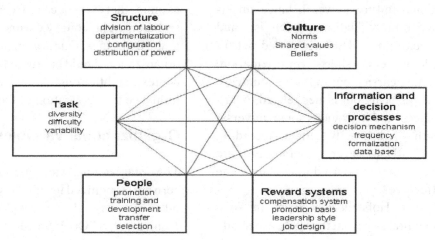

framework enables a complete representation of all the identified organizational enablers of knowledge management. Organizational changes could depend on how well the interrelationship of these variables can support an organization's core activities, considering the available information technology (Markus & Robey, 1988) and the influence of environmental factors.

Organizational variables and knowledge management processes are mutually dependent. For the success of a KM project, Davenport and Prusak (1998) include many of the organizational variables as important factors. We cannot be talking about KM even with all the processes without the organizational variables to support them (APQC, 1996). Due to several factors, such as strategic alliance, internationalization of firms and services, technology transfer, globalization, and recent advances in ICT, Western management styles and forms of organization have a great influence across the world. The success of multinational corporations and consulting firms add to the assumptions about the universality of management strategies, including KM. Nevertheless, significant differences due to cultural diversity exist, as illustrated in subsequent paragraphs.

The *people* dimension of KM enablers can be problematic in several respects; for example, in our case, the international, expatriate staff members tended to come and go and take their knowledge with them. This had resulted in discontinuity: knowledge could not be assessed, sustained, or divested in any systematic way, as illustrated by the quotes that follow:

*...When I came there was a tremendous knowledge gap... because there was no documentation at all...there was no written information, there was no information on the computer, the people who were there, were only able to provide a little bit of information, but there was an awful knowledge gap.* (Dr. SDL, MRC)

*...That's true, that sort of information rests with the individual involved. To handle this problem, we want people to be appointed before the previous person has already left to avoid creation of gap. It is a problem. You are right, most of that information is with people that left...Yes that is very true. I think you are right but the knowledge and the expertise is linked to some people. That is certainly true. Not only for us but also for other similar research institutions and local organizations. Institutional knowledge seems to be very fragile. I think that is right. But we have the*

*infrastructure that is required to make sure that knowledge is stored and accessible without really depending on people...* (Dr. SA, MRC)

The local staff members were often discouraged from ambitious projects as they were not considered able to perform beyond a certain level. They also often lacked the personal funds that the expatriates might have for supplementing the possibly meager resources at the institutes.

*...Surely there is a lot of obvious difference. For instance, the national research institutes and the universities, which we called NARS, we put them under NARS. They are handicapped by funding. Their budgets are in Naira which keeps depreciating every time. And for them to procure materials and whatever, they have to purchase from abroad in dollar which is not available to them, they have to convert, and buy at very high rates and which may not be available. Apart from the facts that they are under-funded, the little they have, they can't convert it to dollars, secondly, most of them do not have the expertise we have, thirdly they lack IT systems ...Even they don't have up-to-date books. Because they don't have enough funds to buy them, if you go to their library, they have outdated materials. So, that is why if you go to our library, you find many of them coming to use the library here. Many of their scientists and the lecturer of university come to use the library here...* (Mr. YA, IITA)

The people working in an organization are directly influenced by their own identity (Walsham, 2001), which could be influenced by societal norms and values and controlled by social, economic, and educational factors. For example, while training and learning without any formal certification could be acceptable for employees in Western industrialized countries, we found that employees in sub-Saharan Africa would normally like to have a certificate for their training. The reason is the importance attached

to a certificate as evidence of knowledge and the prospect of getting a well-paid job, based on the extent of certified training.

*...I think the financial incentive has mainly attracted people initially to do the on-the-job training (OJT) and it is also slightly more popular. But some of the main problems of OJT are still there. In the culture here, and I think in Africa in general, people don't see the same value in training unless there is a certificate or qualification attached to it. So that's one big part. Having a qualification attached to OJT is a big issue in giving OJT the credibility that it needs.* (Dr. SA, MRC)

Similarly, knowledge as a source of power has a different meaning to Western employees and their developing countries counterparts. In many developing countries, due to high unemployment rates, lack of social security and benefits, and the scarcity of well-paid jobs, employees may wish to protect their source of competitiveness and thus view sharing knowledge as giving away their power.

*...they should be jealous of their means of livelihood [their knowledge]...* (Professor HOTA, NIMR)

The basic concept of knowledge varies from one culture to another. This could impact the effectiveness of organizational KM initiatives. In each of the countries in our study, there is a long tradition of recognizing some people as a repository of knowledge; for example, the griot in The Gambia, the babalawo in Yorubaland, and the guru in India. Although it may not be formally recognized in research organizations, since it is basically overridden by the professional culture, attention needs to be paid to differences in people's notions of knowledge and the effect of this on organizations.

*...The Gurus are those with true knowledge and gives only to his beloved student, only one student. So since you ask about the knowledge and the India traditional culture, let us talk about "AMRITA" [Nectar of life], which if you drink you never die. The people who know the AMRITA never tell anybody. It automatically dies with them. Likewise the gurus committed, unknowingly, they committed...I cannot say sin, they just did not see the importance of their knowledge and never share it widely. They never share their full knowledge, if they did, we would have the entire traditional medicinal things we had in the past...* (Mr. Raju, ICRISAT)

One scientist in a national organization explained how ascription is being used to rate people's contributions instead of achievement; that is, people are judged by who they are and not necessarily by what they do.

*...There are some people who should be regarded as a source [of knowledge] and not a threat [to the leaders], but when you turn source to a threat, people become discouraged ...People are not always evaluated and promoted by what they know but by who they know.* (Professor HOTA, NIMR)

As research organizations, our case organizations shared many similar cultural features, and the scientists also shared a similar professional culture. Yet there are notable differences in the organizational culture of national versus international organizations. While international organizations exhibit combinations of cultures (Weisinger & Trauth, 2002), which include corporate culture, industrial culture, professional culture, and some national culture of the local environment, the national organizations are greatly influenced by the regional culture (e.g., western vs. northern Nigeria). Also, the diversity in workforce of international organizations reduces the effect of the interaction of national or societal culture with organizational culture when compared to national organizations.

*...The people here are highly educated. The illiterate thinks the moment they share the information, the value is lost. But ours is a different organization. Ours is a multicultural organization and this culture is influenced by western culture and there is free flow of information...* (Mr. V, ICRISAT)

The *task and structure* dimensions had to do with management, which was in some institutes better than in others, and with ability to carry out the tasks planned. Here the external circumstances had their strongest impact: If there is no electricity, no working phone, and very slow mail, work in general is slowed down. Communication between people not working at the same site is greatly hampered. Visiting and sending messengers are the only possibilities, and they take time.

*...Of course, when we have electricity blackout and telecommunication breakdown, we can't reach anywhere and we can't physically travel, we just have to wait...* (Dr. GE, MRC)

The organizational structure is closely related to the societal structure, and the style of leadership could be influenced by the orientation of the people (Korpela, 1996). In the leadership pattern in western Nigeria, we also observe that superiors are often inaccessible and the power holders are entitled to privileges in the organization. The hierarchies in the community are also reflected in the organization. This is in contrast to organizations in The Gambia. This has implications for KM, as the organizational structure could affect knowledge sharing and communication (Davenport & Prusak, 1998).

Taken together, each of these has implications for KM efforts in organizations. In KM research and practice, it has typically been suggested that particular attention be paid to organizational variables (often called enablers or influences), without which the success of KM cannot be guaranteed. With evidence that the assumptions about these variables are contextual, we contend here that any framework to support KM needs to consider each variable in the context of each organization, with due consideration also for the interaction with the operating environment.

## Information Technology

Information technology can support the processes for knowledge creation, sharing, application, and storage (Alavi & Leidner, 2001). It can also enhance the interaction of individual, group, organizational, and inter-organizational knowledge (Hedlund, 1994; Nonaka & Takeuchi, 1995). Information technology availability and use varies between countries, but also within countries and between organizations. When there is little funding for an organization, there are fewer computers and software applications for use, with less access time to the Internet and other IT services.

*...The researchers are willing to learn but in a situation where resources are not available, research cannot be carried out without money. It is a money gulping thing, it takes a lot of money and you don't expect immediate results, particularly medical research. It is not something like industrial research where you have a very big breakthrough and you publicize that you have been able to invent these things. I think medical research is not like that. I think the past government was not too keen on that. They didn't make money available for our researchers to work with. They keep on searching for funding, except some of them that are ready to spend their own money. Somebody was just telling me that she needed a reagent for her research work, she had to take a cooperative loan to get it, the loan is not meant for that kind of thing, but she had no alternative for her research work, so that is a kind of problem we have. Maybe with this present government, things may improve.* (Mr. A, NIMR)

In contemporary organizations, IT is not only considered to support other organizational processes but a source of competitive advantage and even organizational core capability. IT enables changes in the organizational structure and supports communication within and between organizations. IT can make the information and decision-making processes easier. There is hardly any aspect of organizations that IT has not affected, including the way people think and carry out their work processes (Lau, Wong, Chan, & Law; 2001).

According to Orlikowski and Barley (2001), the transformation in the nature of work and organizing cannot be understood without considering both the technological changes and the institutional (specifically environmental) context that are reshaping economic and organizational activities. They thus emphasize the interrelationship of the environment, organizational variable, and technology. They argue that collaboration between organizational issues and information technology could increase the understanding of changes taking place in the organization. In our study, we found that organizations with high information technology capability were generally able to support knowledge processes better. The application of technology also depends on skills and abilities of individuals and the support of management, which are also organizational issues.

Many technologies can support KM processes. However, these technologies require a basic IT infrastructure, such as local area networking and Internet connectivity, to function optimally. There is also a need for basic hardware and software. The provision of these IT infrastructures varies between organizations (Broadbent et al., 1999), and its use depends on the context of each organization. Apart from the statistic evidence, we also found in our study differences in level of IT capability between national and international organizations, which we attribute to differences in level of funding and other factors (discussed earlier):

*...An expatriate usually managed the IT units of the international organizations. The expatriate heads of the IT units were generally more experienced, and had knowledge of relevant modern technologies, due to their training in and access to the Western market. This usually had a positive influence on the performance of the IT unit and the adoption of technologies. The only international organization without a computer unit had an effective outsourcing strategy, which indirectly resulted in better services than national organizations with higher IT infrastructure services. The IT units of the international organizations were better staffed than the national organizations. Most of the staff had a university degree and had received some other special training. LAN and Intranet were only available in the international organizations...* (Okunoye & Karsten, 2003)

There were also differences in expertise to support these technologies. Although IT skill shortage is a global phenomenon, its extent varies between countries. Thus, it is important that a framework to support KM efforts in an organization recognizes these different levels of IT availability and use, and that it supports the organization in making the right decision of which technology is most appropriate in their circumstances.

## Knowledge Management Processes

Knowledge management processes are socially enacted activities that support individual and collective knowledge and interaction (Alavi & Leidner, 2001). These activities vary depending on which knowledge resources that the organization aims at improving. It is these activities that must be supported by the influences discussed earlier. Since each organization has a different focus, KM processes take place also in different contexts. These processes can be summarized as knowledge creation, knowledge storage/retrieval, knowledge transfer, and knowledge application. Thus the organization should consciously choose which of these activities they intend to support in order to choose appropriate organizational variables and technology to enable them.

For example, research organizations in SSA are particularly interested in knowledge creation and transfer, and they found the Internet to be an effective technology to support this process. One of our case organizations in India focuses on knowledge sharing among the scientists and the rural community, and they also are using a global intranet (ICRISAT, 2001).

## Knowledge Resources

The main targets of the knowledge management processes are the knowledge resources. Holsapple and Joshi (2001) present a comprehensive framework of organizational knowledge resources where they consider, including employee knowledge, knowledge embedded in physical systems (Leonard-Barton, 1995), human capital, organizational capital, customer capital (Petrash, 1998), external structures, internal structures, and employee competencies (Sveiby, 1996). Knowledge resources also include intellectual capital (Stewart, 1998). The main goal of knowledge management is the effective marshalling and use of these resources (Lai & Chu, 2000).

The benefit and strategic importance of KM is in the ability of an organization to correctly identify which knowledge resources it can improve to gain sustainable competitive advantage. This is a reason for the popularity of KM, as the process of identifying the resources and subsequent selection of processes are never the same. In addition, organizational variables and technology need to support these processes with varying complexity and with different levels of influence by the operating environment.

## CONTEXT-AWARE FRAMEWORK OF KM

In a context-aware KM framework, KM is seen as an effort to properly put all the organizational variables into best use, with the support of relevant information technology, in order to facilitate the knowledge processes. The main overall goals center on organizational productivity, responsiveness, innovation, and competency through the creation and protection of knowledge resources.

This framework (Figure 3) differs from those presented earlier in that it considers the relationships between and interdependency of all components with particular attention to the environmental context. This framework enables organizations to pay attention to the local context and how this affects the assumptions about each component. The method and research approach used to arrive at the assumption about the components also ensure that the projected users are the actual users and the gap between the world inscribed in it and the world that will be described by its displacement can be expected to be narrowed.

As explained earlier, all the organization-related influences that could enable or constrain KM can be put together as *organizational variables*. *IT* is a separate component due to its strategic importance in supporting *the knowledge processes* of knowledge creation, storage, sharing, and application. All these are directly affected by the *environmental factors* (e.g., culture and infrastructure in our discussion) where the organization operates. The organizational variables and information technology can influence each other, and they are both enablers of knowledge processes. On the other hand, the kind of knowledge to be created could determine which kind of information technology to be used and which variables in the organization need to be adjusted. Effective handling of knowledge processes yields the main aim of the KM, which is improving the *knowledge resources* in which the competitive advantage and all other benefits of KM lie. Also, knowledge resources could effectively affect knowledge processes. The double arrow that joins the organizational variables and the technology to the operating environment shows the interdependency between the organization

*Figure 3. KAFRA (Kontext Aware FRAmework), a context-based framework of knowledge management*

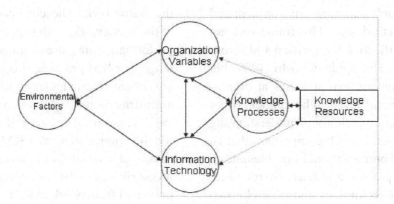

and the environment, ensuring that KM processes are consistent with the external environment in which the organization operates and that those activities meant to improve knowledge resources are undertaken in a coordinated manner. Each component is linked to the others in a cyclic manner, which indicates the continuous dependency and influence between them. There is also a possibility of direct interaction between knowledge resources and organizational variables and also with information technology.

## CONCLUSION

The KAFRA presented here represents a move toward a more universally applicable KM framework, one that increases our sensitivity to global diversity. The framework agrees with the recommendations of Leavitt (1965) that call for interdependence of the variables and with Scott (1998) in acknowledging that organizations and their environment affect each other. The consideration for environmental factors agrees with the institutionalist perspective of organizational challenges (Powell & DiMaggio, 1991). The emphasis on the importance of context within which the framework will be applied is informed by Pettigrew's contextualist approach (1987). Our framework recognizes the diversity in the organization's operating environment and utilizes it in its basic design. This framework not only achieves unification both within and across each component (Holsapple & Joshi, 1999) but also addresses the contextual issues at organizational and national levels. The application of this framework requires thorough understanding of the issues related to each component, that is, pre-knowledge of organizational variables and an ability to handle problematic areas are required. Knowledge of the technology and which knowl-edge processes it can support are also essential for the successful application of the framework. The organization also needs to identify the knowledge resources that are crucial to improving competitive advantage and which knowledge processes could best support this. The framework also requires cultural sensitivity, including cultural knowledge of the environment and a realistic assessment of the available infrastructure. The GEPSE factors are often assessed with easily obtained statistics, but such statistics do not reveal many important qualitative details. Thus, input from local sources and local people are essential.

The KAFRA framework could serve as a link between the organization and its environment, ensuring that KM is approached with consideration to the environment in which the organization operates. The framework also helps to ensure that the activities involved in KM are carried out in a well-guided manner. This framework shows the need for a multidisciplinary team when undertaking a KM project. In a multinational organization, a multicultural team is also required. As long as the world economy continues to tilt toward knowledge-based products and processes, developing countries will increasingly see the importance of KM. This framework could be a good starting point for them. The problems associated with inscription of the outsiders' beliefs, perception, and norms are addressed in the framework. The correct operationalization of the framework, with support from the in-built performance measures, represents a further challenge. For KM practice, this paper has sought to contribute to our understanding of the cultural and infrastructural interaction with organizational variables and technology. It also forms a basis for the composition of a KM team as well as a means of control and balance. For researchers, it contributes to the conceptualization of a more universal framework, which allows for localized specific assumptions.

## REFERENCES

Akrich, M. (2000). The description of technical objects. In W. Bijker & J. Law (Eds.), *Shaping technology/building society: Studies in socio-technical change* (pp. 205-224). Cambridge: The MIT Press.

Alavi, M., & Leidner, D. (2001). Knowledge management and knowledge management systems: Conceptual foundations and research issues. *MIS Quarterly, 25*(1), 107-136.

American Productivity and Quality Center (APQC). (1996). *Knowledge management: Consortium benchmarking study final report.* Retrieved on April 3, 2000, from http://www.store.apqc.org/reports/Summary/know-mng.pdf

Anandarajan, M., Igbaria, M., & Anakwe, U. (2000). Technology acceptance in the banking industry: A perspective from a less developed country. *Information Technology and People, 13*(4), 298-312.

Avgerou, C. (1998). How can IT enable economic growth in developing countries? *Information Technology for Development, 8*(1), 15-29.

Avgerou, C. (2001). The significance of context in information systems and organizational change. *Information Systems Journal, 11*(1), 43-63.

Avgerou, C. (2002). *Information systems and global diversity.* Oxford: Oxford University Press.

Bada, A. (2000). *Global practices and local interests: Implementing technology-based change in a developing country context.* Unpublished doctoral dissertation, London School of Economics and Political Science, London.

Barata, K., Kutzner, F., & Wamukoya, J. (2001). Records, computers, resources: A difficult equation for sub-saharan Africa. *Information Management Journal, 35*(1), 34-42.

Broadbent, M., Weill, P., & St. Clair, D. (1999). The implications of information technology infrastructure for business process redesign. *MIS Quarterly, 23*(2), 159-182.

Calaberese, F. (2000). *A suggested framework of key elements defining effective enterprise knowledge management programs.* Unpublished doctoral dissertation, George Washington University, Washington, DC.

Coakes, E., Willis, D., & Clarke, S. (Eds.). (2002). *Knowledge management in the sociotechnical world: The graffiti continues.* London: Springer-Verlag.

Cox, T. (2001). *Creating the multicultural organization: A strategy for capturing the power of diversity.* San Francisco, CA: Jossey-Bass.

Darley, W. (2001). The Internet and emerging e-commerce: Challenge and implications for management in sub-saharan Africa. *Journal of Global Information Technology Management, 4*(4), 4-18.

Das, G. (1993, March-April). Local memoir of a global manager. *Harvard Business Review,* 38-47.

Davenport, T., & Prusak, L. (1998). *Working knowledge: how organizations manage what they know.* Cambridge, MA: Harvard Business School Press.

Earl, M. (2001). Knowledge management strategies: Towards taxonomy. *Journal of Management Information Systems, 18*(1), 215-233.

El Sawy, O. (2001). *Redesigning enterprise processes for e-business.* Boston: Irwin/McGraw-Hill.

Galbraith, J. (1977). *Organizational design.* Reading, MA: Addison Wesley.

Hedlund, G. (1994). A model of knowledge management and the N-Form corporation. *Strategic Management Journal, 15*, 73-90.

Hofstede, G. (1997). *Cultures and organizations — Software of the mind*. New York: McGraw Hill.

Holsapple, C., & Joshi, K. (1999, January 3-6). Description and analysis of existing knowledge management frameworks. In *Proceedings of the Thirty-Second Hawaii International Conference on System Sciences*.

Holsapple, C., & Joshi, K. (2000). An investigation of factors that influence the management of knowledge in organizations. *Journal of Strategic Information System, 9*(2-3), 235-261.

Holsapple, C., & Joshi, K. (2001). Organizational knowledge resources. *Decision Support Systems, 31*(1), 39-54.

International Crops Research Institute for Semi-Arid Tropics (ICRISAT). (2001). *People first!* (Medium Term Plan 2002-2004). Patancheru AP, India.

INDEHELA-Methods project. (1999). Retrieved on March 2, 2003, from http://www.uku.fi/atkk/indehela/

Karsten H. (2000). *Weaving tapestry: Collaborative information technology and organizational change*. Doctoral dissertation, Jyvaskyla Studies in Computing, No 3.

King, J., Gurbaxani, V., Kraemer, K., McFarlan, F., Raman, K., & Yap, C. (1994). Institutional factors in information technology innovation. *Information Systems Research, 5*(2), 139-169.

Korpela, M. (1996). Traditional culture or political economy? On the root causes of organizational obstacles of IT in developing countries. *Information Technology for Development, 7*, 29-42.

Korpela, M., Mursu, A., & Soriyan, H. A. (2001). Two times four integrative levels of analysis: A framework. In N. Russo, B. Fitzgerald, & J. DeGross, (Eds.), *Realigning research and practice in information systems development. The social and organizational perspective* (pp. 367-377). Boston: Kluwer Academic Publishers.

Lai, H., & Chu, T. (2000, January 4-7). Knowledge management: A theoretical frameworks and industrial cases. In *Proceedings of the Thirty-Third Annual Hawaii International Conference on System Sciences* [CD/ROM].

Lateef, A. (1997). *A case study of Indian software industry*. International Institute for Labor Studies, New Industrial Organization Programme, DP/96/1997.

Lau, T., Wong, Y., Chan, K., & Law, M. (2001). Information technology and the work environment — Does IT change the way people interact at work? *Human Systems Management, 20*(3), 267-280.

Leavitt, H. J. (1965). Applied organizational change in industry: structural, technological, and humanistic approaches. In J. March (Ed.), *Handbook of organizations* (pp. 1144-1170), Chicago: Rand McNally & Co.

Leonard-Barton, D. (1995). *Wellsprings of knowledge: Building and sustaining the sources of innovation*. Cambridge, MA: Harvard Business School Press.

Lyytinen, K., Mathiassen, L., & Ropponen, J. (1998). Attention shaping and software risk — A categorical analysis of four classical risk management approaches. *Information Systems Research, 9*(3), 233-255.

Maier, R., & Remus, U. (2001, January 3-6). Toward a framework for knowledge management strategies: Process orientation as strategic starting point. In *Proceedings of the 34th Hawaii International Conference on Systems Sciences* [CD/ROM].

Markus, L., & Robey, D. (1998). Information technology and organizational change: Causal structure in theory and research. *Management Sciences, 34*(5), 583-598.

Morales-Gomez, D., & Melesse, M. (1998). Utilizing information and communication technologies for development: the social dimensions. *Information Technology for Development, 8*(1), 3-14.

Mumford, E. (1993). *Designing human systems for health care: The ETHICS method.* Chesire: Eight Associates.

Mumford, E., & Weir, M. (1979). *Computer systems in work design — The ETHICS method: Effective technical and human implementation of computer systems.* Exeter: A. Wheaton & Co.

Nathanson, D., Kazanjian, R., & Galbraith, J. (1982). Effective strategic planning and the role of organization design. In P. Lorange (Ed.), *Implementation of strategic planning* (pp. 91-113). Englewood Cliffs, NJ: Prentice Hall, Inc.

Nonaka, I., & Takeuchi, H. (1995). *The knowledge-creating company: How Japanese companies create the dynamics of innovation.* Oxford: Oxford University Press.

Odedra, M., Lawrie, M., Bennett, M., & Goodman, S. (1993). International perspectives: Sub-saharan Africa: A technological desert. *Communications of the ACM, 36*(2), 25-29.

Okunoye, A., Innola, E., & Karsten, H. (2002, September 24-25). Benchmarking knowledge management in developing countries: Case of research organizations in Nigeria, The Gambia, and India. In *Proceedings of the 3rd European Conference on Knowledge Management*, Dublin, Ireland.

Okunoye, A., & Karsten, H. (2001, June 10-12). Information technology infrastructure and knowledge management in sub-saharan Africa: Research in progress. In *Proceedings of the Second Annual Global Information Technology Management (GITM) World Conference*, Dallas, TX.

Okunoye, A., & Karsten, H. (2002a). Where the global needs the local: Variation in enablers in the knowledge management process. *Journal of Global Information Technology Management, 5*(3), 12-31.

Okunoye, A., & Karsten, H. (2002b, January 7-10). ITI as enabler of KM: Empirical perspectives from research organisations in sub-saharan Africa. In *Proceedings of the 35th Hawai'i International Conference on Systems Sciences*, Big Island, Hawaii.

Okunoye, A., & Karsten, H. (2003). Global access to knowledge in research: Findings from organizations in sub-saharan Africa. *Information Technology and People, 16*(3), 353-373.

Orlikowski, W., & Barley, S. (2001). Technology and institutions: What can research on information technology and research on organizations learn from each other. *MIS Quarterly, 25*(2), 145-165.

Pan, S., & Scarbrough, H. (1998). A socio-technical view of knowledge — Sharing at Buckman Laboratories. *Journal of Knowledge Management, 2*(1), 55-66.

Pettigrew, A. M. (1987). Context and action in the transformation of the firm. *Journal of Management Studies, 24*(6), 649-670.

Powell, W. W., & DiMaggio, P. J. (Eds.). (1991). *The new institutionalism in organizational analysis.* Chicago, University of Chicago Press.

Rubenstein-Montano, B., Liebowitz, J., Buchwalter, J., McCaw, D., Newman, B., Rebeck, K., & The Knowledge Management Methodology Team. (2001). A systems thinking framework for knowledge management. *Decision Support Systems, 31*(1), 5-16

Schäfer, G., Hirschheim, R., Harper, M., Hansjee, R., Domke, M., & Bjorn-Andersen, N. (1988). *Functional analysis of office requirements: A multiperspective approach.* Chichester: Wiley.

Schein, E. (1985). *Organizational culture and leadership.* San Francisco: Jossey-Bass.

Schneider, S. C., & Barsoux, J.-L. (1997). *Managing across cultures*. London: Prentice Hall.

Scott, W. (1998). *Organizations: Rational, natural and open systems*. Upper Saddle River, NJ: Prentice-Hall.

Sena, J., & Shani, A. (1999). Intellectual capital and knowledge creation: Towards an alternative framework. In J. Liebowitz, (Ed.), *Knowledge management handbook*. Boca Raton: CRC Press.

Simon, S. (2001). The impact of culture and gender on Web sites: An empirical study. *The DATA BASE for Advances in Information Systems, 32*(1), 18-37.

Stewart, T. (1997). *Intellectual capital: The new wealth of organization*. New York: Double Day.

Straub, D. (1994). The effect of culture on IT diffusion: Email and fax in Japan and the US. *Information Systems Research, 5*(1), 23-47.

Straub, D., Keil, M., & Brenner, W. (1997). Testing the technology acceptance model across cultures: A three country study. *Information & Management, 31*(1), 1-11.

Sveiby, K. (1996). *What is knowledge management?* Retrieved on March 4, 2000, from http://www.sveiby.com.au/KnowledgeManagement.html

Tessler, S., & Barr, A. (1997). *Software R&D strategies of developing countries* (Position Paper). Stanford Computer Industry Project.

The World Bank Group, Data and Map. (2004). Retrieved December 27, 2004, from http://www.worldbank.org/data/countrydata/ictglance.htm

Thomas, R., Roosevelt, R., Thomas, D., Ely, R., & Meyerson D. (2002). *Harvard Business Review on managing diversity*. Boston: Harvard Business Review Publishing.

Trist, E. (1981). The socio-technical perspective. The evolution of sociotechnical systems as conceptual framework and as an action research program. In A. Van de Ven, & W. Jotce (Eds.), *Perspectives on organization design and behavior* (pp. 49-75). New York: John Wiley & Sons.

Walsham, G. (2001). *Making a world of difference: IT in a global context*. New York: John Wiley and Sons.

Wassenar, A., Gregor, S., & Swagerman, D. (2002). ERP implementation management in different organizational and cultural settings. In *Proceedings of the European Accounting Information Systems Conference*, Copenhagen Business School, Copenhagen, Denmark.

Weill, P., & Vitale, M. (2002). What IT infrastructure capabilities are needed to implement e-business models? *MIS Quarterly Executive, 1*(1), 17-34.

Weisinger, J., & Trauth, E. (2002). Situating culture in the global information sector. *Information Technology and People, 15*(4), 306-320.

Wiggins, B. (2000). *Effective document management: Unlocking corporate knowledge*. Gower: Aldershot.

Yin, R. K. (1994). *Case study research: Design and methods* (2nd ed.). Newbury Park, CA: Sage Publications.

## ENDNOTES

[1] Framework in the context of this thesis.

[2] Multinational organizations now selectively consider some infrastructure when considering location of new subsidiaries; nevertheless, they often have the capability and resources to come with their own infrastructure. Thus, they pay more attention to other factors beyond their control.

[3] Ratings from 1 to 7; 7 is highest/best.

*This work was previously published in International Journal of Knowledge Management 2(2), edited by M. E. Jennex, pp. 26-45, copyright 2006 by IGI Publishing, formerly Idea Group Publishing (an imprint of IGI Global).*

# Chapter VI
# The Role of Culture in Knowledge Management:
## A Case Study of Two Global Firms

**D. Leidner**
*Baylor University, USA*

**M. Alavi**
*Emory University, USA*

**T. Kayworth**
*Baylor University, USA*

## ABSTRACT

*Knowledge management (KM) approaches have been broadly considered to entail either a focus on organizing communities or a focus on the process of knowledge creation, sharing, and distribution. While these two approaches are not mutually exclusive and organizations may adopt aspects of both, the two approaches entail different challenges. Some organizational cultures might be more receptive to the community approach, whereas others may be more receptive to the process approach. Although culture has been cited widely as a challenge in knowledge management initiatives, and although many studies have considered the implications of organizational culture on knowledge sharing, few empirical studies address the influence of culture on the approach taken to knowledge management. Using a case study approach to compare and contrast the cultures and knowledge management approaches of two organizations, the study suggests ways in which organizational culture influences knowledge management initiatives as well as the evolution of knowledge management in organizations. Whereas in one organization, the KM effort became little more than an information repository, in the second organization, the KM effort evolved into a highly collaborative system fostering the formation of electronic communities.*

## INTRODUCTION

Knowledge management (KM) efforts often are seen to encounter difficulties from corporate culture and, as a result, to have limited impact (DeLong & Fahey, 2000; O'Dell & Grayson, 1998). An Ernst and Young study identified culture as the biggest impediment to knowledge transfer, citing the inability to change people's behaviors as the biggest hindrance to managing knowledge (Watson, 1998). In another study of 453 firms, over half indicated that organizational culture was a major barrier to success in their knowledge management initiatives (Ruggles, 1998). The importance of culture is also evident from consulting firms such as KPMG who report that a major aspect of knowledge management initiatives involves working to shape organizational cultures that hinder their knowledge management programs (KPMG, 1998). These findings and others (Hasan & Gould, 2001; Schultze & Boland, 2000) help to demonstrate the profound impact that culture may have on knowledge management practice and of the crucial role of senior management in fostering cultures conducive to these practices (Brown & Duguid, 2000; Davenport, DeLong, & Beers, 1998; DeLong & Fahey, 2000; Gupta & Govindarajan, 2000; Hargadon, 1998; KPMG, 1998; von Krogh, 1998).

Studies on the role of culture in knowledge management have focused on such issues as the effect of organizational culture on knowledge sharing behaviors (DeLong & Fahey, 2000; Jarvenpaa & Staples, 2001) and the influence of culture on the capabilities provided by KM (Gold, Malhotra & Segars, 2001) as well as on the success of the KM initiative (Baltahazard & Cooke, 2003). More specifically, Baltahazard and Cooke (2003) ascertained that constructive cultures (emphasizing values related to encouragement, affiliation, achievement, and self-actualization) tended to achieve greater KM success. Similarly, Gold, et al. (2001) found that more supportive, encouraging organizational cultures positively influence

KM infrastructure capability and resulting KM practice. Finally, Jarvenpaa and Staples (2001) determined that organizational cultures rating high in solidarity (tendency to pursue shared objectives) will result in a perception of knowledge as being owned by the organization, which, in turn, leads to greater levels of knowledge sharing.

While studies have shown that culture influences knowledge management and, in particular, knowledge sharing, there is little research on the broader aspects of the nature and means through which organizational culture influences the overall approach taken to knowledge management in a firm. The purpose of this research is to examine how organizational culture influences knowledge management initiatives. We use a case study methodology to help ascertain the relationship of the organizational culture to the knowledge management approaches within two companies. The following section discusses knowledge management approaches and organizational culture. The third presents the methodology. The fourth section presents the two cases and the fifth, and discusses the case findings, implications, and conclusion.

## LITERATURE REVIEW: KNOWLEDGE MANAGEMENT APPROACHES AND ORGANIZATIONAL CULTURE

### Knowledge Management Approaches

Knowledge can be defined as a form of high value information (either explicit or tacit) combined with experience, context, interpretation, and reflection that is ready to apply to decisions and actions (Davenport et al., 1998). While all firms may have a given pool of knowledge resources distributed throughout their respective organization, they may be unaware of the existence of these resources as well as how to effectively leverage them for competitive advantage. Therefore, firms must engage in activities that seek to build, sustain, and leverage these intellectual resources. These types of activities, generally characterized as knowledge management, can be defined as the conscious practice or process of systematically identifying, capturing, and leveraging knowledge resources to help firms to compete more effectively (Hansen, Nohria, & Tierney, 1999; O'Dell & Grayson, 1998).

There are two fundamental approaches to knowledge management: the process approach and the practice approach. The process approach attempts to codify organizational knowledge through formalized controls, processes, and technologies (Hansen et al., 1999). Organizations adopting the process approach may implement explicit policies governing how knowledge is to be collected, stored, and disseminated throughout the organization. The process approach frequently involves the use of information technologies, such as intranets, data warehousing, knowledge repositories, decision support tools, and groupware (Ruggles, 1998), to enhance the quality and speed of knowledge creation and distribution in the organizations. The main criticisms of this process approach are that it fails to capture much of the tacit knowledge embedded in firms and that it forces individuals into fixed patterns of thinking (Brown & Duguid, 2000; DeLong & Fahey, 2000; Hargadon, 1998; von Grogh, 2000).

In contrast, the practice approach to knowledge management assumes that a great deal of organizational knowledge is tacit in nature and that formal controls, processes, and technologies are not suitable for transmitting this type of understanding. Rather than building formal systems to manage knowledge, the focus of this approach is to build social environments or communities of practice necessary to facilitate the sharing of tacit understanding (Brown & Duguid, 2000; DeLong & Fahey, 2000; Gupta & Govindarajan, 2000; Hansen et al., 1999; Wenger & Snyder, 2000).

These communities are informal social groups that meet regularly to share ideas, insights, and best practices.

Drawing from this discussion, some key questions emerge. First, how does culture affect organizations' approaches (e.g., process or practice) to knowledge management? Second, as organizations pursue these initiatives, how do cultural influences affect the KM activities of knowledge generation, codification, and transfer? To address these questions, it is necessary to explore the concept of organizational culture.

## Organizational Culture

Schein (1985) defines organizational culture as a set of implicit assumptions held by members of a group that determines how the group behaves and responds to its environment. At its deepest level, culture consists of core values and beliefs that are embedded tacit preferences about what the organization should strive to attain and how it should do it (DeLong & Fahey, 2000). These tacit values and beliefs determine the more observable organizational norms and practices that consist of rules, expectations, rituals and routines, stories and myths, symbols, power structures, organizational structures, and control systems (Bloor & Dawson, 1994; Johnson, 1992). In turn, these norms and practices drive subsequent behaviors by providing the social context through which people communicate and act (DeLong & Fahey, 2000). Putting this into the context of knowledge management, organizational culture determines the social context (consisting of norms and practices) that determines "who is expected to control what knowledge, as well as who must share it, and who can hoard it" (Delong & Fahey, 2000, p. 118). Figure 1 illustrates this conceptual linkage between culture and knowledge management behavior.

As Figure 1 depicts, the social context (consisting of norms and practices) is the medium for transmission of underlying values and beliefs into

*Table 1. The process vs. practice approaches to knowledge management*

|  | Process Approach | Practice Approach |
|---|---|---|
| **Type of Knowledge Supported** | Explicit knowledge — codified in rules, tools, and processes. | Mostly tacit knowledge — unarticulated knowledge not easily captured or codified. |
| **Means of Transmission** | Formal controls, procedures, and standard operating procedures with heavy emphasis on information technologies to support knowledge creation, codification, and transfer of knowledge. | Informal social groups that engage in storytelling and improvisation. |
| **Benefits** | Provides structure to harness generated ideas and knowledge.<br><br>Achieves scale in knowledge reuse. | Provides an environment to generate and transfer high value tacit knowledge.<br><br>Provides spark for fresh ideas and responsiveness to changing environment. |
| **Disadvantages** | Fails to tap into tacit knowledge. May limit innovation and forces participants into fixed patterns of thinking. | Can result in inefficiency. Abundance of ideas with no structure to implement them. |
| **Role of Information Technology** | Heavy investment in IT to connect people with reusable codified knowledge. | Moderate investment in IT to facilitate conversations and transfer of tacit knowledge. |

specific knowledge management behaviors. While Figure 1 is useful to explain the conceptual linkage between culture and knowledge management behavior, further explanation is needed to inform our understanding of the types of cultures that exist within organizations.

A number of theories have attempted to define culture at the organizational level. Wallach (1983) conceptualizes organizational culture as a composite of three distinctive cultural types: bureaucratic, innovative, and supportive. In bureaucratic cultures, there are clear lines of authority, and work is highly regulated and systematized. Innovative cultures are characterized as being creative, risk-taking environments where burnout, stress, and pressure are commonplace. In contrast, supportive cultures are those that provide a friendly, warm environment where workers tend to be fair, open,

and honest. From Wallach's (1983) standpoint, any given firm will have all three types of culture, each to varying levels of degree. Wallach's (1983) cultural dimensions were developed based upon a synthesis of other major organizational culture indices. Wallach's (1983) cultural dimensions were applied by Kanungo, Sadavarti, and Srinivas (2001) to study the relationship between IT strategy and organizational culture. Part of the attractiveness of Wallach's (1983) dimensions, in comparison with other commonly used cultural indices such as the Organizational Culture Profile scale (O'Reilly, Chatman, & Caldwell, 1991); the Competing Values Framework (Quinn & Rohrbaugh, 1983); and the Organizational Value Congruence Scale (Enz, 1986), is that it is highly intuitive. Managers readily can identify with the descriptions of the three general culture

*Figure 1. The impact of organizational culture on knowledge management behaviors*

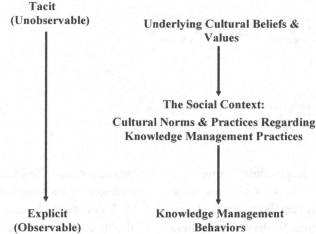

types. Consistent with Kanungo, et al. (2001), we will employ Wallach's (1983) approach to describe organizational cultures. Specifically, we are interested in the following question: How does organizational culture influence knowledge management initiatives?

## Methodology

A case study method involving multiple (two) cases was used. The approach of the study is depicted in Figure 2. The figure, based on the work of Yin (1994), displays the replication approach to multiple-case studies. As illustrated in Figure 2, the initial step in the study involved the development of a theoretical framework on the relationship between organizational culture and organizational knowledge management (KM) strategies. This step was then followed by the selection of the two specific cases (the data collection sites) and the design of the data collection protocol. Following the case selection and data collection steps, the individual case reports were developed. A cross-case analysis of the findings was then undertaken. This analysis provided the basis for the theoretical and normative discussions and implications presented in the final section of the article.

The two case studies involve two very large global corporations: Company A and Company B. Company A is a global consumer goods company with 369,000 employees worldwide. The company is headquartered in the U.S. and operates in four other regions: Europe, the Middle East and Africa, Central and South America, and Asia. Company revenues consistently exceed $20 billion. In Company A, large-scale knowledge management projects were initiated at the North American region in 1996. Company B is a high-tech global company with multiple product lines and services. Similar to Company A, Company B is headquartered in the U.S. and operates globally in other regions of the world. With approximately 316,000 employees, its revenues exceed $80 billion. Large-scale knowledge management projects were initiated in Company B in 1995.

These two companies were selected for the purpose of this study for the following reasons. First, significant opportunities and challenges are associated with knowledge management activities in large and geographically dispersed companies. Thus, identification of factors such as organizational culture that may influence KM outcomes in this type of organizations potentially can lead to high payoffs. Second, considering the high levels of organizational resources required

*Figure 2. Case study methodology (Adapted from Yin, 1994)*

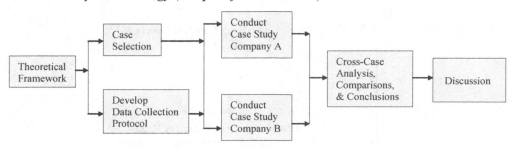

for implementation of large-scale knowledge management initiatives, these initiatives most likely are encountered in very large firms. Thus, the phenomenon of interest to these researchers could be best investigated in the context of very large firms with an established track record in KM projects. Finally, past contacts that one of the researchers had with these two firms facilitated their recruitment as case study sites.

## Data Collection

Data for this study were collected through semi-structured interviews with a small group of managers and professional employees at the two company locations in the U.S. Identical approaches to data collection were used at Company A and Company B1. Six individuals at each of the two companies were interviewed. In each of the two companies, three of the interviewees were the current or potential users of the KM systems. The remaining three interviewees in each company were the KMS sponsors or supporters. The interviews took between 45 and 85 minutes and were conducted between October 2001 and January 2002. All the interviews were tape recorded and then transcribed for data analysis. The interviews all followed the same protocol. The informants first were asked to characterize their organization's culture in their own words. The three cultures described by Wallach (1983) were then portrayed, and the informants were requested to identify which one best described their

organization. The interviewees next were asked to describe and characterize the KM practices in their company. A set of specific questions guided the discussions of these practices. For example, informants were asked to describe the specific KM activities that they engaged in and to discuss the effects of these activities on themselves and/or their peers. Informants were also asked to describe any resistance and impediments to KM that they might have noticed in the organization. The same interviewer, using identical data collection protocols, conducted all the interviews in Company A and Company B. The interviewer carefully read the transcripts to ensure accuracy.

## Data Analysis

An author not involved in the interviews and, hence, having no predisposed interpretation of the transcripts, conducted the data analysis. Based upon the transcribed interviews, 12 profiles were written, each one based upon the perspective of a single informant. These profiles described the informants' perspective of culture and their perspective of KM. The profiles of informants for Company A were compared and contrasted with each other, as were those of Company B. Cases for each company, reported in the next section, then were written, based upon the within-case analysis. The cases for each company then were interpreted from the perspective of how the culture appeared to be influencing the organizational KM initiative. This is also reported in the next section. After the two cases and their within-case analysis were complete, a cross-case comparison and contrast was undertaken, leading to the formulation of the discussion section.

## CASE DESCRIPTIONS AND ANALYSES

### Knowledge Management at Company

Knowledge management at Alpha began as a top-down idea, courted by senior management "as a way of helping the company become more leading edge" according to one informant. A small group of eight or nine individuals at headquarters was charged with driving knowledge management and facilitating knowledge sharing. As a result of larger issues surfacing, most notably the economic downturn that rocked U.S.-based businesses in early 2000, the top-level initiative fell into the background, and the small, dedicated group was disbanded. Thus, at the organizational level, KM was an idea that received neither funding nor action. However, at the business unit level, successful KM initiatives have been built around an intranet or around Lotus Notes team rooms.

### Intranet-Based KM Projects

One initiative in the marketing area of corporate headquarters is called MIC — marketing information center. MIC serves the global marketing community of several thousand individuals around the world. It is an intranet-based library containing links to agencies, compensations, human resource information, and contracts, among other things. MIC is opportunity-oriented rather than problem-oriented. The members do not use the community to post a problem inquiry and await responses but rather to look for ideas performed in other parts of the company and think about adopting the ideas to their local group.

*Table 2. Characteristics of culture, KM initiatives, and KM behaviors*

| Culture Characteristics | KM Characteristics | KM Behaviors |
|---|---|---|
| Dominant culture is bureaucratic | Intranet-based static repositories of information | Individuals access information on an as-needed basis |
| Emphasis on individual: *individuals are "risk averse" *individuals fear being criticized for ideas *individuals are uneasy and prefer to go unnoticed *individual relationships externally, particularly within the marketing unit, are perceived as critical to their success | Failed top-down effort Bottom-up initiatives largely targeted creation of repositories Some use of Lotus Notes to create team rooms Team rooms have high failure rate | Individuals reluctant to contribute information Individuals reluctant to own and maintain content Individuals uncomfortable using ideas from the systems, since they do not own the idea Individuals use repository when rules prohibit printing brochures Individuals reluctant to use tools that would result in a loss of touch points with customers |

MIC is intended to be a catalyst for collaboration and to propel a universal worldwide marketing community. Because the chief marketing officer no longer allows the budgeting of glossy manuals or brochures, MIC is widely accepted as the primary means of obtaining such static information. In fact, as attempts were made to include best practices in MIC, the initiative encountered resistance. Explains one informant, "We could never nudge the culture enough to have people understand and be motivated to enter their information." Another informant felt that there were challenges in overcoming "people's fear of being judged for their ideas and their indifference to yet another information site."

CM connection (CMC) is another KM initiative within the North American marketing unit. This is a Web-based marketing repository used to disseminate information so that wholesalers that are responsible for store-level execution can have access to the most recent information on how to merchandise the latest promotions. As with MIC, the major impact of CMC has been the reduction of the number of printed catalogs; in this case, by 80%. Among the challenges experienced with CM connection has been convincing content providers to own the information in the sense of both providing it and keeping it up-to-date. Another issue has been that CM connection is seen by some as distracting from their relationships with clients. Even while MCC may reduce the amount of time spent traveling, this is not necessarily welcome in "a sales and marketing oriented relationship company because you are taking away relationship points."

The Human Resources unit with the Corporate Functions unit also has an intranet-based KM, referred to as My Career. My Career is designed for managers and employees to help provide information about what tools, classes, and coaching are available for development. One of the goals of My Career has been to merge all of the training information into one place.

Many such intranet-based KM have been developed throughout Alpha, so many that the portal project was initiated to alleviate the problem of "too much information in too many places, different IDs and passwords for each database, having to remember what is in the database to even go to get the information." However, despite some initial receptiveness to the idea from the head of the New Business Ventures unit, IT budgets were frozen and the project never got underway.

The common thread running through the intranet-based KM projects at Alpha is that they all are geared to housing static information with the most major impacts being the reduction in printed catalogs. Among the greatest resistance, according to informants, is that these KM projects appear to try to standardize work practices in a company comprised of "creative assertive people who want to do it their way and make their own individual mark."

## Lotus Notes-Based KM

Lotus Notes forms the basis of other KM initiatives within Company A. What distinguishes the Lotus Notes-based KM projects from the intranet-based KM projects is the added focus on facilitating teamwork. The Lotus Notes-based initiatives developed independently from the intranet-based initiatives. The North-American marketing group developed a Lotus Notes-based community of interest. The system contains examples of briefs, shared research, shared examples of different sites, and information on internal research. This micro KM has 50 to 60 regular users. An important feature of the system is that whenever new information is added, community members receive an e-mail. In this way, members visit the community when new information that is relevant to them has been posted. This KM project has served as a means of sharing best practices. For example, a marketing manager from the UK posted information concerning a successful auction initiative, which was then emulated by five other countries. On an individual level, KM has helped to increase the frequency of communication among members of the community. Similarly, HR developed HR Source, a Lotus Notes-based general bulletin board, where meeting notes, follow-up action items, strategy documents, and work plans are placed. It is shared by the HR community on a global basis.

Lotus Notes is also the platform used to develop team rooms. The individual responsible for managing team rooms for North America has what he calls the six-month rule: if a team room is not getting regular utilization for more than six months, it is deleted so that they can save money on the server expense. He says that he deletes about 70 to 80% of team rooms. He thinks the lack of reward is the biggest barrier toward KM system usage: "People who don't have technology in their title don't take it upon themselves and are not generally rewarded for exploiting technology." Also, content management is a barrier: "This is the responsibility of the end user but it is perceived as the responsibility of the technology group." However, a marketing manager had another opinion, attributing lack of use of the team rooms to self-preservation: "Even if someone took the time to put something out there, even if I knew it was there, went and got it, had the time to review it, and understand it, I am going to create this other thing by myself. I might look at that as input, but then it is the new XYZ program and I created it."

## ANALYSIS OF ALPHA'S KNOWLEDGE MANAGEMENT: THE IMPACT OF CULTURE ON KM BEHAVIORS AND OUTCOMES

### The Perceptions of Culture

While each individual interviewed gave their own perception of the culture at Alpha, and while the perceptions naturally contain some variance, there is a marked theme running throughout the individuals' views. Informants describe Alpha as risk averse and bureaucratic. They speak of an environment where people don't want to be noticed, where direction is unclear, and where individual survival trumps teamwork. Moreover, informants state that people work in silos, feel isolated, and are afraid of being criticized for their ideas. The slow, bureaucratic, hierarchical culture at Alpha has resulted in silos of information. As a consequence, managers indicate that even though they have great consumer and customer information, they end up reinventing the wheel 1,000 times. However, our informants also maintained that although they characterize the culture as bureaucratic, they also sense that Alpha is striving to become more innovative and supportive.

### The Possible Impacts of Culture on KM

The statements and observations of our informants point to two largely shared perspectives: (1) the culture emphasizes the individual, and (2) the culture is in a state of transition. In understanding the impacts of KM, one can see the influence of the individuality within Company A. Table 2 lists the characteristics of culture, characteristics of the KM initiatives, and characteristics of KM behaviors as expressed by the informants.

At work within Alpha seems to be a tension between a culture that demands individuality and the communal aspects of KM. The informants talk about a culture that is one of "individual survival" where individuals "fear being judged for their ideas," where there is individual "isolation," and where individuals try to go unnoticed. The overall feeling is that of individuals trying to avoid being noticed. Such a culture does little to foster the sense of community that may be necessary to enable KM to move beyond static repositories of information into the kind of dynamic system envisioned by developers, where ideas flow freely and where KM provides a catalyst for collaborative engagement. Not only are individuals reluctant to share their information for fear of being criticized for their ideas, they also are reluctant to use information posted in a KM for lack of credit for the idea. Such behaviors can spring from a culture that emphasizes individual ideas and contribution.

The individual aspects of the culture go well beyond individuals behaving in a certain way because of a rewards system but reflects an underpinning notion that to succeed in a marketing-oriented organization, one must be creative and that creativity is perforce, of an individual nature, so that to survive as an individual, one must capture ideas and only share them if they are going to be favorably judged. One must not look to others for learning or for problem solving but might look to reuse creative ideas in some circumstances (like the auction site example from the UK) where one may tailor the idea to one's environment. It is telling that the informants speak of using outsiders (e.g., consultants) to assist with problem solving and learning instead of attempting to use any of the existing KM to post queries, and this in spite of the fact that it is recognized that the company reinvents the wheel 1,000 times.

Another tension within Alpha seems to stem from the expectations of what should occur in a bureaucratic culture and what was occurring. The top-down approach to KM, an approach that would be consistent with a bureaucratic organization, had failed at Alpha. Yet, despite the failure of the top-down approach to KM and the seeming success of several bottom-up approaches, such as MIC and the marketing team room for the community of 50, one informant still proffered the need for top management leadership to be the key to success with KM. He considered the bottom-up approaches as "band-aid-approaches." In his opinion, power within Alpha comes "from knowledge hoarding, not knowledge sharing." In order for KM to be assimilated in this environment, "behavior really has to come from the top. Leadership needs to walk the walk." In a bureaucratic culture, individuals become accustomed to clear guidance from senior management. The absence of clearly stated support from senior management may be sufficient to deter many from experimenting with the KM tools available to help them.

## Summary

Alpha has many KM initiatives that were developed largely as bottom-up initiatives. The KM tools seem well designed and housed with valuable information. The informants are able to use the tools to facilitate the retrieval of information that they need in the performance of their jobs. However, the tools have not progressed yet to the level of fostering collaboration. While there are some successful communities from the standpoint of providing a place to share meeting notes and plans, the majority of team rooms remain unused and, if used, become as much a library of information as a communication tool. In some ways, the culture of Alpha appears to foster the types of KM behaviors observed, in that the individual is seen as the primary source of innovation and ideas as opposed to the community being the ultimate source of success. Thus, individuals will use the systems as needed but are occupied mostly with their individual roles and work and do not attribute value to the collaborative features of technology.

## The Case of Beta

Beta is organized into seven major units. Our interviews were concentrated within the Innovations Services group of the consulting wing (referred to as Worldwide Services Group, or WSG) of Beta.

Knowledge management at Beta began in 1996 with the view that KM was about codifying and sharing information, leading to the creation of huge repositories of procedures and process approaches. It was assumed that people would go to a central site, called Intellectual Capital Management System (ICM), pull information down, and all would be more knowledgeable.

ICM is under the protection of the Beta Corporation. There is a process one must undertake to have information submitted and approved. The process is complicated by legalities and formalities. As a result, ICM is not used as widely as it could be. What was discovered from the initial foray into knowledge management was that the information was not being refreshed and that the approach was not complementing the way people really learned, which was through communities. Consequently, the KM initiative began to shift to providing tools to communities that would help foster collaboration both within teams and within locations and around the globe. Among the tools are team rooms and communities.

## Team Rooms

Lotus Notes-based team rooms are widely used at Beta to coordinate virtual teams and to share important documents. Access to team databases are limited to the members because of the confidential nature of a lot of the issues. The project manager or someone delegated by the project manager takes the responsibility of sanitizing the material and posting the most relevant parts to a community system such as OC-zone (to be discussed later) and/or to the ICM after the team's project has been completed.

The team rooms are valuable tools to help members keep track of occurrences as well as to help newly assigned members get quickly up to speed. Because of the itinerant nature of the Beta consultant's life, it is invaluable to have the documents they need stored in an easily accessible manner that does not require sending and receiving files over a network. Team room databases also are used for managing the consulting practices. It is important in helping new people with administrative tasks (e.g., how to order a piece of computer equipment, how to order business cards). The team rooms keep track of such metrics as utilization so that members of the team

know "who's on the bench and who's not." One informant gave the example of a recent project she was put on at the last minute that involved selling a project to a government department in another country. She was able to access all the documentation from the team room and become a productive member of a new team very quickly: "I can go in and start getting information about a particular topic and work with colleagues almost immediately. It allows me to work more easily with colleagues across disciplines."

Although team rooms are invaluable in organizing and coordinating project teams, there are also some potential drawbacks. Some view the team rooms as engendering "a false sense of intimacy and connectedness." This sense of intimacy can be productive for the team as long as things are going well. However, "if things go south," says an informant, "you don't have the history or skill set to really deal with difficult situations." As a result, instead of dealing with the conflict, the team is more likely to just take someone off the team and replace the person with another. In this sense, problems are not solved so much as they are avoided, and team members take on an expendable quality.

## Communities

Communities serve members based not upon project or organizational position but upon interest. By 2000, a group referred to as the organizational change (OC) group had established a successful community of 1,500 members cutting across all lines of business and was beginning to act as consultants to other groups trying to set up communities. The OC community has gone so far as to quantify the business return of such a community in terms of cycle time reductions and sophistication of responses to clients. The OC community is comprised of tools, events, and organization.

1. **Tools.** The technology tools at the disposal of the OC community are databases of information submitted by team rooms, including such things as white papers, projects, and deliverables, as well as client information. The databases also contain pictures of community members with personal information about the members.

2. **Events.** An important aspect of the OC community is the events that are organized for community members. These include monthly conference call meetings, which generally are attended by 40 to 90 members, and replay meetings, which draw another 40 to 70 members. In the past, the community has sponsored a face-to-face conference for members. Members often meet others for the first time, yet they already feel they know each other.

3. **Organization.** The organization of the community is managed by two community leaders. When people request information or have queries to post to members, they send their messages to one of the community leaders. The leader first tries to forward the message directly to a subject-matter expert (SME). If the leader does not know offhand of an appropriate SME, the leader will post the question to the entire group. In this event, the group members respond to the leader rather than to the community in order to avoid an inundation of messages. The leader normally receives responses within an hour. The leader then forwards the responses to the individual with the query. Later, the leader sends an e-mail to the person who made the inquiry, asking how the response was, how much time it saved, and so forth. The leader normally gets back as many as 28 responses to a particular inquiry. The leader has manually loaded a portion of what he or she has developed in the past seven months. There are 114 pieces of intellectual capital that the leader has loaded, and it is just a portion of what the leader has received.

The community has a structure that consists of a senior global board of 30 members representative of different parts of the business. There is a subject matter council that constantly scans the intellectual capital, as well as an expert council and the health check team.

The health check team examines such things as how well members communicate with each other. They conducted an organizational network analysis to help better understand the communication networks. The team has a series of questions to help assess how they are doing in terms of high performance teaming. They use a survey that measures perceptions from the community members about what they see is happening and do a gap analysis on what is actually happening. Finally, the team does a self-assessment of where it is compared to the community maturity model developed by the OC community leaders. There is a community mission, vision, and goals, and they are working on capturing data to support the metrics to demonstrate value to the company and community members.

The goal is to attain level-5 maturity, which is considered an "adaptive organization." There are 13 areas of focus at which the community leaders look in building a sustained community. While communities are felt to be organic, there is also a community developers kit with an assessment tool to determine at what level of maturity a community is and what steps need to be taken to move the community forward. One community leader says that the purpose of the development kit "is not to confine, but to provide a road map in which to navigate and build." For this leader, the essence of community is continuous learning. Of the initial KM efforts focused on information repositories, the leader says, "I could see the technology coming that was going to enslave people, like an intellectual sweat shop." By contrast, the primary tools for a community are "passion and environment."

## Impact of OC

Among the major impacts of the OC zone is that having a community helps people not feel isolated. "People feel they are affiliated, that they are part of the company." Thirty percent of Beta employees do not have offices and work from home or the client sites. Such a work environment easily can be associated with isolation. However, the community is claimed by some to provide clarity of purpose. "I see it as a conduit for both developing thought leadership and enabling thought leadership to get into the hearts and minds of the workers so that they all have a common vision, goals, and objectives."

Community members view the purpose of the community as a knowledge-sharing forum and as a means to create a sense of belonging. One member went so far as to suggest that she would "not be at Beta any longer if it wasn't for this community." The reason is that most of her connections at Beta have been made through the community. Also, being in the community helps her to get assigned to projects. For example, the leader of a new project will call someone in the community and say that they are looking for a person with a certain profile. She finds that she gets asked to work on projects this way.

Other members refer to the community as a supportive family and state that within the community is someone who has already encountered any issue they will encounter on a project, so the community keeps them from reinventing the wheel. The norms of operation exist to help the OC zone be as effective as possible. No one is under obligation to contribute, but individuals contribute in order to help other people. One member credits the success of the community to the two leaders, whom she feels "in their hearts, care about the members of the community." She feels that the community is more than a community of people who like the topic of organizational change, but it is a community of people who support one another.

The primary resistance to the OC community has been the practice managers. Most of the community members report to practice managers. The practice managers are used to thinking in terms of billable hours. Indeed, the performance evaluation system requires that an individual's goals support those of his or her boss, which support those of his or her boss, and so forth. The community leaders hope that one day, participating in a community will be included as a standard part of this evaluation system.

## ANALYSIS OF BETA KNOWLEDGE MANAGEMENT: THE IMPACT OF CULTURE ON KM BEHAVIORS AND OUTCOMES

### The Perceptions of Culture

All of the respondents from Beta work within the same business unit. The respondents describe the culture of Beta as a blend of hierarchical and innovative. The hierarchical aspects are evident in that little innovation is undertaken until senior management has officially supported the innovation, but once senior management does give the green light to an idea, "everybody jumps on it."

One aspect of culture that is highlighted by the informants is the importance of collaboration. Informants characterize the street values within Beta as win, team, and execute. Beta informants recognize a duality of culture that, on the one hand, gives individuals control over their work and, at the same time, is highly supportive of the individual. The culture is autonomous in the sense of not having someone looking over your shoulder and telling you what to do. While there is certainly competition (i.e., everyone has objectives that they are trying to meet), things "are always done in a collaborative helpful spirit."

The other dominant aspect of culture, as related by the informants, is hierarchy. The hierarchy is

*Table 3. Characteristics of Company B culture, KM initiatives, and KM behaviors*

| Culture Characteristics | KM Characteristics | KM Behaviors |
|---|---|---|
| Hierarchical, yet collaborative and innovative | Company-wide information repository consisting of hundreds of information databases | Team members actively coordinate via the team rooms |
| Individuals largely responsible for their own careers, yet competition is undertaken in a cooperative manner | Team rooms used by project teams | Community members obtain a sense of belonging to the community |
| The team is the unit of success, more so than the individual | Communities of practice emerging. These communities include tools, events, and structures | Community members post information from completed team projects to the community out of a sense of commitment, not coercion |
| Absence of extreme supervision of individuals' work — individuals have a sense of control | The OC community is used as an example of a successful community and as a consultant to other emerging communities | Community members are more loyal to the company (less likely to depart) because of their belonging to the community |
| | | Assignments to projects made through community references |

as much a hierarchy of experience as of structure. Community members, for example, proffered that becoming a subject matter expert is more about length of service to the company than to one's inherent knowledge. Another aspect of the bureaucratic culture is that "there is very much a correct way to do things."

Table 3 lists the characteristics of culture, KM initiatives, and KM behaviors expressed by the Beta informants.

Beta's emphasis on collaboration seems to have enabled the progression of KM from a static information repository system into active, vital communities of interest, wherein individuals feel a sense of belonging to the extent that they identify themselves first with the community and second, if at all, with their actual formal business units. One informant claimed to not identify herself at all with the Innovation Services unit. Of course, one could ponder whether such identity transfer from the business unit to the community serves the best interest of the unit.

At the same time, the bureaucratic and innovative aspects of the culture also have helped. Having senior management show interest in KM was a catalyst to individual groups undertaking KM initiatives with great enthusiasm. In addition, rather than ad hoc communities that are entirely organic, the community model emerging at Beta is a relatively structured one.

While one can make the argument that Beta's culture influences KM development and use, one also can argue that KM at Beta is influencing Beta's culture. OC members claim that without a sense of connection provided by the OC community, Beta would be nothing but a "big and scary" company in which individuals "get lost." The community, though, allows and enables a culture of connection. In effect, one informant believes that the OC community attempts to shift a very technical, phone-oriented, work-product-oriented way of communicating with each other into a more personal work-in-process movement toward what Beta refers to as "thought leadership." When asked why members take the time to participate in the community when there is no formal reward for doing so, one informant said simply, "It's just how we do business." Thus, the community has infused the culture of the members.

Yet, this does not suggest that an organizational utopia has been or will be achieved. While the culture is becoming more connected, there is another angle. One informant believes that when you have widespread access to knowledge management, you also can have a culture where people that know very little about something have access to enough information to be dangerous. People get too comfortable with having access to knowledge and then feel free to share it. This informant remained unconvinced that the knowledge one acquires through the network is as solid a foundation as the knowledge one has acquired through experience and traditional learning. Moreover, she feels that the notion of dialogue can get redefined in a way that you lose the quality of participation that one might be looking for.

## Summary

Beta has many KM databases, collectively referred to as Intellectual Capital Management. While these databases serve an important role of housing and organizing information in a huge organization, they do not go so far as to foster collaboration. Instead, team rooms and communities of interest, largely left to the discretion of team members and community members, have proven to be vital tools to achieving collaboration, community, and belonging. As the culture of Beta has been receptive to individual groups setting and pursuing their community agendas, the culture also is being subtly altered by the communities as members feel that they belong more to the community than to their business units.

## DISCUSSION

The two cases offer insights into the role that organizational culture plays in the inception and maturation of KM. This section summarizes the key findings that help us to answer the following question: How does organizational culture influence KM approaches? We suggest four responses to this question.

**1. Organizational culture influences KM through its influence on the values organizational members attribute to individual vs. cooperative behavior.** The two companies we examined share several similarities. Both huge multinational organizations are regarded widely by organizational members as being predominantly bureaucratic in culture. Both organizations had initial KM approaches that were strongly supported by senior management. And both had initial KM approaches focused on the creation of a large centralized repository of organizational knowledge to be shared throughout the organization. These two large bureaucratic organizations began their KM quests with the process approach. The most striking difference between the organizational cultures of these two companies was the emphasis at Alpha on the individual and the emphasis at Beta on collectivity — the team or community. This evinces itself even in the interpretation of innovation. While individuals at both companies spoke of the need for innovation in their organizations and of the striving of their organizations to develop an innovative culture, in the case of Alpha, innovation was perceived as an individual attribute, whereas at Beta, innovation was perceived as a team-level attribute.

The individualistic view of innovation at Alpha seemed to militate against the requisite sharing and cooperation that makes the evolution of KM from process approach to a community of practice approach possible. In both companies, micro-level experimentation of the various possibilities of KM was undertaken within teams or business units. The value placed on individualism vs. cooperativism seems to have played a significant role in the nature and form of the KM approach. The micro-level experimentations by teams or business units were carried out with their own assumptions about the usefulness of repositories of knowledge and the usefulness of communities or practice. We suggest that it is not organizational culture at the organizational level or even the subunit level that has the most significant influence on KM approach, but it is organizational culture as embodied in the individualistic vs. cooperative tendencies of organizational members. Thus, organizational culture influences KM approaches through its influence on individualism vs. cooperativism. From a theoretical view, it seems that Wallach's (1983) cultural dimensions and those of Earley (1994) were both valuable at explaining organizational level culture. However, Earley's (1994) cultural dimensions at the organizational level seem best able to explain why a KM approach tended to become more process or more practice-based.

**2. Organizational culture influences the evolution of KM initiatives.** Our findings suggest that firms do not decide in advance to adopt a process or practice approach to KM, but that it evolves. The most natural starting point is one of process, perhaps because the benefits seem more evident and because it can align more closely with the existing organizational structure. Moreover, the practice approach may not only fail to align with existing structure, but it may engender a virtual structure and identity. It is interesting that at Beta, a culture that is viewed dominantly as bureaucratic, once the initial organizational change community was established, the evolution of the community then became a highly structured process of maturation. The community leaders developed a toolkit to help other communities develop and developed a maturation model to help them to determine how mature a community was and to develop a plan to move the community forward. What some might see as an organic process (i.e., establishing and developing a community or practice) became a structured process in a bureaucratic organization. Even if the idea for the community emerged from inter-

ested potential members, the evolution took on a structured form with tools, kits, assessments, and plans. The cooperative aspect of culture at the individual level made the community possible; the bureaucratic elements of culture at the organizational level enabled the community to mature. Hence, the evolution of the community was highly dependent on the individual willingness of organizational members to sustain and nurture their community. This appeared tied to the importance they placed on cooperation with their community members, most of whom they had never met.

**3. Organizational culture influences the migration of knowledge.** In the case of Alpha, where the informants seemed to identify the individual as the ultimate unit of responsibility in the organization, the individuals also were viewed as the owners of knowledge and had the responsibility to share their knowledge. This, in fact, created a major challenge, since the individuals rejected this new responsibility. At Beta, where the team seemed to be the focus of responsibility, knowledge migrated from the team to the community to the organizational level system and back down to the team. The leader of the team would take responsibility for cleaning the team's data and submitting it to the community and to the central information repository. Thus, knowledge migrated upward from the team to the central repository. Interestingly, the most useful knowledge was claimed to be that at the team and community level. Once the knowledge had completed its migration to the central repository, it was seen primarily as an item of insurance for use in case of need. Knowledge sharing and transfer occurred primarily at the team and community level, whereas knowledge storage was the function of the central repository.

The migration of knowledge also is influenced by the structural processes put in place to ensure that knowledge finds its way to the appropriate persons. Of key importance seems to be the way

*Table 4. Summary of organizational culture's influence on KM*

| Cultural Perspective | Influence of Culture on Knowledge Management |
|---|---|
| Bureaucratic (Wallach, 1983) | Favors an initial process approach to KM<br><br>Creates expectation among members that senior management vision is essential to effective KM |
| Innovative (Wallach, 1983) | Enables subgroups in organizations to experiment with KM and develop KMs useful to their group |
| Individualistic (Earley, 1994) | Inhibits sharing, ownership, and reuse of knowledge |
| Cooperative (Earley, 1994) | Enables the evolution of process-oriented KM to practice-oriented KM<br><br>Enables the creation of virtual communities |

the queries are handled. The marketing group at Alpha adopted the approach of notifying individuals when new information had been added to the KMS. However, little interference was put in place to either guide people to the appropriate knowledge or to encourage people to contribute knowledge. Conversely, believing that the community should not become a bulletin board of problems and solutions, the leaders of the organizational change community at Beta worked arduously to learn the subject matter experts so that queries would be submitted to the community leader who would serve as an intermediary between the individual with the query and the expert.

It has been reported widely that the use of knowledge directories is a primary application of KM in organizations. Our study suggests that the facilitated access to experts rather than direct access via the location of an individual through a directory or via a problem posted to a forum may lead to a more favorable community atmosphere.

**4. Knowledge management can become embedded in the organizational culture.** Over time, as KM evolves and begins to reflect the values of the organization, the KM can become a part of the organizational culture. At Beta, individuals spoke of their community involvement and their team rooms as simply the "way we work." In fact, the communities became so much part of the culture that even though they were not part of the organizational structure, they were part of an individual's implicit structure. The sense of belonging that the individuals reported feeling toward their community suggests that the community had become an essential aspect of their value system and, hence, had become part of organizational culture. That the organizational change community members at Beta identified themselves first and foremost with their community, in spite of receiving neither reward nor recognition within their formal reporting unit for participating in the community, indicates the extent to which community participation had become a value and an aspect of the individual culture.

## Implications and Conclusion

The findings of our study suggest that a dominantly bureaucratic culture seems to tend toward an initial process-based KM approach. Furthermore, a bureaucratic culture seems to create the expectation among organizational members that senior management needs to provide a vision of purpose for KM before the organizational members should embark on KM activities. As well, the members view senior management support as validating any KM activities that they undertake. Innovative cultures, even if not the dominant culture at the organizational level, seem to enable subgroups to experiment with KM or create micro-KMs. In essence, in organizations having dominant bureaucratic cultures with traces of innovativeness, senior management support legitimizes KM, but the innovativeness of the culture enables it to expand far beyond an organization-wide repository. Specific KM behaviors such as ownership and maintenance of knowledge, knowledge sharing, and knowledge reuse seem to be influenced largely by the individualistic or cooperative nature of the culture. Individualistic cultures inhibit sharing, ownership, and reuse, while cooperative cultures enable the creation of virtual communities. Earley's (1994) work on organizational culture emphasized the individualistic and collectivistic aspects of culture. Organizations encouraging individuals to pursue and maximize individuals' goals and rewarding performance based on individual achievement would be considered to have an individualistic culture, whereas organizations placing priority on collective goals and joint contributions and rewards for organizational accomplishments would be considered collectivist (Chatman & Barsade, 1995; Earley, 1994). This dimension of organizational culture emerged as critical in our examination of the influence of culture on KM initiatives. These findings are summarized in Table 4.

This research set out to examine the influence of organizational culture on knowledge management approaches. Using a case study approach, we have gathered the perspectives of individuals in two firms that share some cultural similarities yet differ in other aspects. The findings suggest that organizational culture influences the KM approach initially chosen by an organization, the evolution of the KM approach, and the migration of knowledge. Moreover, the findings suggest that KM eventually can become an integral aspect of the organizational culture. Much remains to be discovered about how organizational cultures evolve and what role information technology takes in this evolution. This case study is an initial effort into a potentially vast array of research into the issue of the relationship of information technology and organizational culture.

## REFERENCES

Alavi, M., Kayworth, T., & Leidner, D. (2005). *Organizational and sub-unit values in the process of knowledge management* (Working Paper). Baylor University.

Baltahazard, P. A., & Cooke, R. A. (2003). *Organizational culture and knowledge management success: Assessing the behavior-performance continuum* (Working Paper). Arizona State University West.

Bloor, G., & Dawson, P. (1994). Understanding professional culture in organizational context. *Organization Studies, 15*(2), 275-295.

Brown, S. J., & Duguid, P. (2000). Balancing act: How to capture knowledge without killing it. *Harvard Business Review, 78*(3), 73-80.

Chatman, J. A., & Barsade, S. G. (1995). Personality, organizational culture, and cooperation: Evidence from a business simulation. *Administrative Science Quarterly, 40*(3), 423-443.

Davenport, T. H., De Long, D. W., & Beers, M. C. (1998). Successful knowledge management. *Sloan Management Review, 39*(2), 43-57.

DeLong, D. W., & Fahey, L. (2000). Diagnosing cultural barriers to knowledge management. *Academy of Management Executive, 14*(4), 113-127.

Earley. (1994). Self or group? Cultural effects of training on self-efficacy and performance. *Administrative Science Quarterly, 39*(1), 89-117.

Enz, C. (1986). *Power and shared values in the corporate culture.* Ann Arbor, MI: University of Michigan Press.

Gold, A. H., Malhotra, A., & Segars, A. H. (2001). Knowledge management: An organizational capabilities perspective. *Journal of Management Information Systems, 18*(1), 185-214.

Gupta, A. K., & Govindarajan, V. (2000). Knowledge management's social dimension: Lessons from Nucor Steel. *Sloan Management Review, 42*(1), 71-80.

Hansen, M. T., Nohria, N., & Tierney, T. (1999). What's your strategy for managing knowledge? *Harvard Business Review, 77*(2), 106-115.

Hargadon, A. B. (1998). Firms as knowledge brokers: Lessons in pursuing continuous innovation. *California Management Review, 40*(3), 209-227.

Hasan, H., & Gould, E. (2001). Support for the sense-making activity of managers. *Decision Support Systems, 31*(1), 71-86.

Jarvenpaa, S. L., & Staples, S. D. (2001). Exploring perceptions of organizational ownership of information and expertise. *Journal of Management Information Systems, 18*(1), 151-183.

Johnson, G. (1992) Managing strategic change — Strategy, culture and action. *Long Range Planning, 25*(1), 28-36.

Kanungo, S., Sadavarti, S., & Srinivas, Y. (2001). Relating IT strategy and organizational culture: An empirical study of public sector units in India. *Journal of Strategic Information Systems, 10*(1), 29-57.

KPMG Management Consulting. (1998). *Knowledge management: Research report.*

O'Dell, C., & Grayson, C. J. (1998). If only we know what we know: Identification and transfer of best practices. *California Management Review, 40*(3), 154-174.

O'Reilly, C. A., Chatman, J., & Caldwell, D. F. (1996). Culture as social control: Corporations, cults, and commitment. *Research in Organizational Behavior, 18*, 157-200.

Quinn, R. E., & Rohrbaugh, I. (1983). A spatial model of effectiveness criteria: Towards a competing values approach to organizational analysis. *Management Science, 29*(3), 363-377.

Ruggles, R. (1998). The state of the notion: Knowledge management in practice. *California Management Review, 40*(3), 80-89.

Schein, E. H. (1985). *Organizational culture and leadership.* San Francisco, CA: Jossey-Bass.

Schultze, U., & Boland, R. (2000). Knowledge management technology and the reproduction of knowledge work practices. *Journal of Strategic Information Systems, 9*(2-3), 193-213.

von Krogh, G. (1998). Care in knowledge creation. *California Management Review, 40*(3), 133-153.

Wallach, E. J. (1983, February). Individuals and organizations: The cultural match. *Training and Development Journal,* .

Watson, S. (1998). Getting to "aha!" companies use intranets to turn information and experience into knowledge — And gain a competitive edge. *Computer World, 32*(4), 1.

Wenger, E. C., & Snyder, W. M. (2000). Communities of practice: The organizational frontier. *Harvard Business Review, 78*(1), 139-145.

## ENDNOTE

[1] After this initial data collection, we returned to Company B a year later and conducted more widespread interviews across different business units. This data collection and analysis is discussed in Alavi, Kayworth, and Leidner (2005).

*This work was previously published in International Journal of e-Collaboration, 2(1), edited by N. Kock, pp. 17-40, copyright 2006 by IGI Publishing, formerly Idea Group Publishing (an imprint of IGI Global).*

# Section II
# Technology

# Chapter VII
# KM Technologies and the Organizational LOE:
## The Unintended Consequence of Constant Organizational Change

**Victoria M. Grady**
*George Washington University, USA*

**James D. Grady III**
*Oral and Maxillofacial Surgery of East Alabama, USA*

## ABSTRACT

*The potential benefits of utilizing knowledge management (KM) technologies in multinational and global organizations are of particular significance due to the inherent geographic distance and diversity of such organizations. Unfortunately, the process of constantly changing technology can be extremely disruptive at both the individual and organizational level. This chapter explores the relationship between KM technology change within the organization and the Theory of Organizational Loss of Effectiveness (LOE). "The general Theory of Organizational Loss of Effectiveness is predicated upon organizational behavior resulting from a loss of stability, e.g. technology change, within an organization." (Grady, 2005) The loss of stability, in the context of this theory, occurs when a defined set of symptoms develop in individuals and groups undergoing a change in technology. The assertion is that the development of these symptoms is predictable, and when viewed collectively, results in an organizational loss of effectiveness.*

## INTRODUCTION

*"Change is inevitable. Change is constant."*
-Benjamin Disraeli (1804-1881), Prime Minister, United Kingdom, 1874-1880

*Knowledge management (KM) is the name given to the set of systematic and disciplined actions that an organization can take to obtain the greatest value from the information available to it. 'Knowledge' in this context includes both experience and understanding of the people in the organization and the information artifacts, such as the documents and reports, available within the organization and in the world outside.* (Marwick, 2001)

Within organizations, KM and its associated technologies can be used to store and/or distribute types of information that may be useful to the organization in the present and the future. KM technologies, if properly implemented, change the fundamental principles by which organizational information is captured, stored, retrieved, organized, analyzed, and shared. These tools have the potential to improve the organization's effectiveness and can be used to enhance the long-term health of the organization.

However, implementation of new technologies and the changes faced by employees may also have an unintended and detrimental impact on the overall effectiveness of the organization. This chapter suggests reasons why a decision to implement new technologies should be accompanied by the anticipation that there may also be a significant negative impact on the employees affected by the change. This is because the implementation of a new technology can lead to the development of a specific set of symptoms in those employees affected by the change. This condition was first described in the Theory of Organizational Loss of Effectiveness (Grady, 2005), which states that when technology change results in the removal of systems that are familiar to the employee, and are replaced with new and unfamiliar technologies, these employees experience a loss of stability. This loss of stability is then manifested by the exhibition of symptoms which, if a sufficient number and intensity develop, will lead to an organizational loss of effectiveness (see Figure 1).

The Theory of Organizational Loss of Effectiveness in Grady (2005) as relates to the issues of KM technology change for multinational organizations can be restated as such:

*The change associated with adding a new KM technology within a multinational organization can be expected to cause a loss of stability among those employees affected by the change. This change results in the development of a predictable and measurable set of symptoms in this employee group. When a significant intensity and number of these symptoms are present simultaneously in employees of an organization, an organizational loss of effectiveness will occur.*

Now more than ever, organizational development is influenced by the rapidly changing technological environment and the impact these changes have on its workforce. This chapter will address the interface of KM and the organizational LOE, and will provide insights into a problem that can frustrate the efforts to enhance the competitive advantage of the multinational organization.

*Figure 1. Model of the Theory of Organizational LOE*

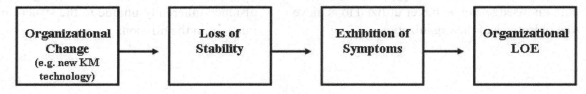

## Organizational Knowledge

Generally, discussions of organizational knowledge are classified knowledge into two categories, tacit or explicit. "Tacit knowledge, from the Latin, tacitare, refers to something that is very difficult to articulate, to put into words or images; typically highly internalized knowledge such as knowing how to do something or recognizing analogous situations" (Dalkir, 2005). Or, "Tacit knowledge refers to personal, context-specific knowledge that is difficult to formalize, record, or articulate; it is stored in the head of people. Tacit knowledge consists of various components, such as intuition, experience, ground truth, judgment, values, assumptions, beliefs, and intelligence" (Tiwana, 2002). The second classification of knowledge is referred to as explicit knowledge. "Explicit knowledge is that which has been rendered visible (usually through transcription into a document or an audio/visual recording); typically captured or codified knowledge" (Dalkir, 2005). Or, "Explicit knowledge is that component of knowledge that can be codified and transmitted in a systematic and formal language; documents, databases, webs, e-mails, charts, etc." (Tiwana, 2002).

"'Knowledge' in this context includes both the experience and understanding of the people in the organization and the information artifacts, such as documents and reports, available within the organization and in the world outside"(Marwick, 2001). "Knowledge management does not provide you with the answer to your problem rather it facilitates the learning of the answer" (Call, 2005).

The unique challenge facing multinational organizations is more effective capture of tacit knowledge and better organization of explicit knowledge. The intent of KM projects is to align this process so that technology, process, people, and knowledge can be better utilized to achieve the objectives of the organization.

## Purpose of KM Technologies

Knowledge management efforts gather, organize, share, and analyze information in terms of resources, documents, and people skills to harness organizational assets to overcome challenges and achieve goals. KM technologies facilitate the way in which organizational information is captured, stored, retrieved, organized, analyzed, and shared. "Examples of KM technologies that are common to multinational organizations include: decision support systems, document management systems, groupware, business modeling systems, messaging, search engines, workflow systems, Web-based training, information retrieval systems, electronic publishing, intelligent agents, knowledge-mapping tools, help-desk applications, database management technologies, enterprise information portals, data warehousing and data mining tools" (Park, Ribiere, & Schulte, 2004). When properly applied to match organizational resources to organizational needs, these tools have the potential to make the organization more effective by making information more readily available, and available information more accessible. In this way pertinent information can be rapidly retrieved and used to the benefit of the employees and the organization.

"Effective knowledge management typically requires an appropriate combination of organizational, social, and managerial initiatives along with deployment of the appropriate technology" (Marwick, 2001). It is significant that KM technologies, as discussed in the literature, are largely viewed as the catalyst to overcoming time and space barriers that otherwise limit effective knowledge utilization within the organization. Multinational organizations are particularly sensitive to this issue because of the geographic distance inherently unique to the structure and inherent in the mission.

# THEORY OF ORGANIZATIONAL LOSS OF EFFECTIVENESS

## Organizational Loss of Effectiveness

As organizations undertake KM projects, they should understand that substantial change of systems and processes used by its employees can cause symptoms which will have disruptive effects on the entire organization. The reduction in an organization's ability to function effectively was comprehensively studied in businesses that were undergoing changes in technology. The results of the study were presented in the Theory of Organizational Loss of Effectiveness by Grady (2005). The LOE theory states that organizational change creates a loss of stability when systems that are familiar to employees are removed and replaced with new and unfamiliar technologies or processes, as is often the case in KM projects. This study further demonstrated that loss of stability causes predictable and measurable symptoms in the affected employees and that those symptoms are related to those described in previous scientific studies on individual depression. The development of LOE as a theory for organization behavior more specifically evolves from scientific studies of anaclitic depression. The common link is that loss of a "leaned on" object leads to a loss of stability that in turn leads to the development of a predictable and measurable set of symptoms, either in the individual or in this case the employees of an organization. Because the Theory of an Organizational Loss of Effectiveness, and the anaclitic depression on which it is based, are critical to understanding obstacles to timely KM project implementation, the following sections are devoted to explaining the evolution and basis tenets of the theory.

## What is Anaclitic Depression?

The Theory of Organizational LOE is based on the research into anaclitic depression as identified by Rene Spitz and Katherine Wolf in 1945-1946. The term anaclitic originally comes from the Greek word *anaklitos,* which means 'to lean upon' (*www.m-w.com*) Anaclitic depression (AD) was initially identified in infants and young children in Romanian orphanages who experienced the loss of an object they had become accustomed to "leaning on." In this circumstance the object was the removal of their primary caregiver. The behavioral symptoms exhibited in these orphans include: frustration, apprehension, rejection of environment, withdrawal, refusal to participate, retardation of development, loss of appetite, and insomnia.

Aside from Spitz and Wolf, very little direct research has been conducted on anaclitic depression, per se (Grady, 2005). However, in 1969, John Bowlby published a related series highlighting the significance of "Attachment, Separation, and Loss" during childhood and its impact on the maturation process. Bowlby cited the studies conducted by Spitz and Wolf in addition to the work of several other researchers who had arrived at similar conclusions regarding the impact of attachment and the exhibition of predictable symptoms on the early childhood development process.

In his 1977 book, *The Medical Consequences of Loneliness,* James Lynch employs the work of Spitz and Bowlby to build on his hypothesis that significant loss does cross the previously defined age-specific boundaries to include adults who had suffered significant emotional or physical loss. In this work, Lynch outlines as the diagnostic criteria, a set of individual symptoms that are consistent with those described by Spitz and Bowlby.

## Connection from Individuals to Organizations

Historically, the primary focus of research on organizational change management was strictly linear in nature. Kurt Lewin (1951), often referred to as the "father" of change management, introduced the sequential concept of managing change by "freezing, mobilize, re-freeze." Lewin's model (1951) is often cited as the "gold standard" for change management initiatives. This school of thought is beginning to dissipate and is slowly being replaced with open acknowledgement of the complex nature of organizational change:

*Recent work suggests, ironically, that to understand organizational change, one must first understand organizational inertia, its content, its tenacity, and its interdependencies. Recent work also suggests that change is not an on-off phenomenon nor is its effectiveness contingent on the degree to which it is planned. Furthermore, the trajectory of change is more often spiral or open-ended than linear.* (Weick & Quinn, 1999)

Change management and other theories of organizational management have struggled to support continuous change in organizations for decades. The application of information that relates anaclitic depression to changes in organizational behavior is a relatively recent concept. In studies in the late 1990s, Dr. Jerry Harvey, professor emeritus at George Washington University, asserted that the concept of anaclitic depression not only applies to individuals, but also applies to the roles of those individuals as members of an organization. Dr. Harvey conducted extensive research that indicates that a form of depression is experienced "when individuals, organizations, or belief systems that we lean on or are dependent on for emotional support are withdrawn from us" (Harvey, 1999).

While Dr. Harvey's theory spanned many forms of organizational change (downsizing, departure of leaders, corporate reorganization, etc.), it is being applied in this chapter as it relates to employee response to KM technology change. Individuals in organizations who suffer the loss of a technology or process they have become accustomed to "leaning on" suffer a loss of stability and, as a result, symptoms that may combine to impact the organization as a whole. The Theory of Organizational LOE states that technology change within an organization has the potential to cause a loss of stability that may result in predictable and measurable symptoms, which can ultimately lead to an organizational loss of effectiveness (Grady, 2005).

## Mapping Individual Symptoms to Employee Behavior

An analysis of the previous studies of anaclitic depression reveals that each of the individual symptoms identified by Spitz and Wolf (1946) has an associated diagnostic category code as defined by the DSM IV (2000):

*Diagnostic criteria are essentially descriptions of symptoms that fall into one of four categories. In major depressive episodes for example,* **affective** *or mood symptoms include depressed mood and feelings of worthlessness or guilt.* **Behavioral** *symptoms include social withdrawal and agitation.* **Cognitive** *symptoms or problems in thinking include difficulty with concentration or making decisions. Finally,* **somatic** *or physical symptoms include insomnia (sleeping too little) or hypersomnia (sleeping too much) and eating disorders.*

For the application of anaclitic depression to organizational behavior and the Theory of Organizational Loss of Effectiveness, only six of the original eight symptoms have organizational equivalents. While still potentially affecting individuals within an organization, the somatic symptoms involving eating and sleeping disorders do not directly translate for the organization as a whole. The remaining symptoms associated with anaclitic depression include: frustration, apprehension, rejection of environment, withdrawal, refusal to participate, impeded development, loss of appetite, and insomnia.

*Table 1. Comparison of individual symptoms to organizational equivalent symptoms of a loss of effectiveness*

| Symptoms of Individual Anaclitic Depression for LOE Theory | Equivalent Symptoms in the Organizational Environment |
|---|---|
| Frustration | Loss of Productivity |
| Apprehension (Anxiety) | Morale |
| Rejection of the Environment | Conflict |
| Withdrawal | Turnover |
| Refusal to Participate | Absenteeism |
| Retardation of Development | Motivation |

In organizations, a change or changes that cause a loss of stability in employees can similarly lead to the development of a set of symptoms that include: decreased productivity, lower morale or motivation, increased conflict, absenteeism, and turnover. Further investigation has shown that symptoms in one group are analogous to the other group as shown in Table 1.

The connections are further explored and described in the paragraphs that follow. This discussion is based on the research of Grady (2005).

## Frustration: Loss of Productivity

The discussion of frustration, in terms of loss of productivity, begins with the dictionary definition of the root word *frustrate*. That is, to frustrate someone is to prevent them from doing or achieving something (*www.m-w.com*). This is the opposite of achieving something (i.e., being productive). Productive is defined as yielding results, benefits, or profits or devoted to the satisfaction of wants or the creation of utilities (*www.m-w.com*). To be productive an employee produces a product or an increase in quantity, quality, or value. Therefore, a loss of productivity corresponds to a decrease in quantity, quality, or value of a predefined metric such as a product, output, or activity.

Increased productivity is a key objective cited repeatedly in current literature as justification for implementation of KM programs and tech-nologies. The essence of KM is improvement of knowledge use through capture, organization, and dissemination.

*Modern organizations are investing heavily in information technology (IT) with the objective of increasing overall profitability and the productivity of their knowledge workers. Yet, it is often claimed that the actual benefits of IT are disappointing at best, and that IT spending has failed to yield significant productivity gains—hence the productivity paradox.* (Pinsonneault & Rivard, 1998)

The onset of the symptom *frustration* in the knowledge worker as a result of a change in KM technology can lead to a decrease in productivity and generate an outcome contrary to the original intent.

## Apprehension (Anxiety): Morale

*In and of itself, anxiety is neither functional nor dysfunctional. It is a keen state of readiness to do something that may or may not be appropriate in response to a threat that may or may not be perceived accurately.* (Miller, 2003, p. 11)

Organizational morale emerges as the reasonable equivalent to the AD symptom of apprehension/anxiety. Morale is defined as the mental and emotional condition (enthusiasm, confidence, or loyalty) of an individual or group with regard to the function/tasks at hand or as a sense of common purpose with respect to a group (*www.m-w.com*). "Morale can be considered an overall index of psychological strain" (Bliese & Britt, 2001, p. 430).

Stress is the body's reaction to the perception of a stressor. Psychologists have recognized the presence of both positive and negative stressors. Both positive and negative stressors result in increased levels of stress. However, positive stressors generally result in a lower absolute level of stress. In a 2001 research study of stress-strain relationships,

Bliese and Britt assessed the relationship between work stressors and morale. The research indicated a negative interaction between these two factors. A high level of work stressors or anxiety resulted in lower morale in the affected unit. While changes in KM technology could be perceived ultimately as positive stressors, this chapter focuses on the possible initial negative effects those technology changes have on an employees behavior.

The introduction of KM technology into the organizational environment can produce a negative work stressor. One example is, as the organizational unit struggles to learn and incorporate the new technology, it becomes a work stressor and contributes to a loss of stability. Another example is the introduction of a new KM technology that produces a perceived information overload. "Information overload is that state in which available and potentially useful information is a hindrance rather than a help" (Bawden, 2001). The loss of stability represents the perceived threat regardless of the perception's accuracy as stated by Miller (2003). Thus, it is the perception of a threat that results in a state of anxiety, and organizationally it is the existence of work stressors that results in lower morale.

## Rejection of Environment: Conflict

The organizational equivalent of the individual's symptom termed rejection of the environment closely parallels issues of conflict in the workplace. Conflict is commonly defined as the competitive or opposing action of incompatibles or the mental struggle resulting from incompatible or opposing needs, drives, wishes, or external or internal demands (*www.m-w.com*). Although conflict is usually thought of as "bad," it is a normal part of the functioning of an organization. Of concern with respect to this organizational symptom is when conflict does become negative, or destructive, and how it is handled. Destructive conflicts often have a detrimental effect and hinder organizational

development resulting in a loss of organizational control. (Virovere et al., 2002).

The literature highlights different root causes for workplace conflict. Examples include lack of communication, tenuous work relationships, questionable managerial authority, or unclear chain of command (Fortado, 2001), and bad information, lack of teamwork, or unclear work procedures/ rules (Virovere et al., 2002). With respect to the issue of conflict, the literature describes different methods individuals have of coping with conflict. These include avoidance, accommodation, competition, collaboration, and compromise. The symptom termed rejection of the environment closely correlates with the organizational behavior coping mechanism identified as avoidance in the conflict management literature.

Avoidance is the act of emptying, vacating, or clearing away. This action is consistent with the theoretical organizational reaction to the continuous adoption of KM technology that is perceived by the employees as unsolicited, inferior, or unnecessary. The result is organizational conflict driven by the attempt to avoid the proposed technological change.

## Withdrawal: Turnover

Employee withdrawal can be viewed as a "volitional response to perceived aversive conditions, designed to increase the physical and/or physiological distance between the employee and the organization" (Gupta & Jenkins, 1980). Gupta and Jenkins (1980) suggest that one of the most commonly studied organizational manifestations of withdrawal is turnover.

Turnover is defined as the continuous process of loss and replacement of a constituent of a living system or as the reorganization with a view to a shift in personnel (*www.m-w.com*). Traditional turnover theories identify job dissatisfaction and lack of organizational commitment as two central reasons for employee turnover (Mobley, 1977). However, Mobley emphasizes that job satisfaction measures alone are typically not sufficient enough to predict turnover. Instead, combining job satisfaction with other criteria such as job content or satisfaction with working conditions produces more predictable results. Additional research suggests that turnover predictors extend the generalized nature of traditional theories to include such demographic factors as education, marital status, gender, and tenure (Hom & Griffeth, 1995). The organizational extensions include compensation, leadership, co-worker cohesion, and stress (Hom & Griffeth, 1995). The more recent analysis of turnover predictors conducted by Hom et al. (2000) substantiated the earlier data and provided additional information about reducing turnover rates.

In an atmosphere of loss of stability created by a change in KM technology, there can be a resultant negative impact on employee job satisfaction and a weakening of the employees' commitment to the organization; these factors can therefore contribute to increased turnover.

## Refusal to Participate: Absenteeism

Turnover and absenteeism are frequently considered part of the same withdrawal process (Mobley, 1980). Gupta and Jenkins (1980) consider both turnover and absenteeism as manifestations of organizational withdrawal. One theory argues that withdrawal progresses from absenteeism to turnover. Another theory argues that they (turnover and absenteeism) are alternatives, and still another that absenteeism and turnover are unrelated (Gupta & Jenkins, 1980). For the purposes of this chapter, they are defined as separate symptoms with independent consequences that can occur within one organization to multiple individuals.

The root word of absenteeism is absence. Absence is defined as not present or attending or lost in thought and not attentive (*www.m-w.com*). The early literature highlights two basic themes for organizational absenteeism. The first is the rela-

tionship between absence and job satisfaction. The second is the link between personal characteristics and absence. Nicholson and Johns (1985) find both to be inadequate and instead focus their attention on the combination of individual characteristics of both the employee and the organization. This theory is based on the psychological contract and cultural absence salience. The comparison of these two characteristics yields two types of absenteeism that are relevant to the theory of organizational LOEs. The first is absence due to job satisfaction and the second is absence based on dysfunctional relations between the employee and employer.

As discussed in the analysis of turnover, multinational organizations functioning to maintain a competitive advantage in the 21st century are faced with perpetual KM technology change. The vulnerability of individual employees' response to those respective changes are factors impacting job satisfaction. If this response is negative and the level of job satisfaction is decreased, the probability of increased absenteeism as a response also increases. The relationship between individual employees and the employer is also a function of change resulting in a loss of stability. If the employee perceives the change as unjustly thrust upon them, the entitlement attitude emerges and absence results as rebellion. Increased absenteeism as well as the other symptoms presented above have a potential negative impact on effectiveness of the organization.

## Retardation of Development: Motivation

To motivate means to provide with a motive. A motive is a conscious or unconscious need or drive that produces an action or behavior—that is, causing or having the power to cause a motion (*www.m-w.com*). The expression *retardation of development* implies a lack of motion or impediment of development. If development is defined as growth, expansion, or progress (*www.m-w.com*), then retardation of development implies the opposite: decline, loss, or failure. Organizational growth, expansion, and progress would typically be supported by motivational factors that enable those results, that is, causes those things to happen.

The literature describing motivational theory is cumbersome and often difficult to apply in the absence of a stable environment. The nature of KM technology implementation in multinational organizations is somewhat volatile and requires theory that can accommodate flexibility. Self-determination theory as defined by Deci and Ryan (1985) is a plausible alternative.

*This theory discusses that all individuals have natural, innate, and constructive tendencies to develop an ever more elaborate and unified sense of self. It focuses on how individuals develop a coherent sense of self through regulation of their behavioral actions that may be self-determined, controlled, or motivated. Technologies of knowledge work require proactive engagement of users unlike the technologies of data processing and transaction processing.* (Malhotra, 2004)

Malhotra (2002) argued that tacit perspective of knowledge management should be managed and controlled mainly by self-control or intrinsic motivation as described in self-determination theory.

The basic tenets of self-determination theory focus on three "needs" that must be satisfied in order for the individual to remain sufficiently motivated to accomplish tasks. The needs are competence, relatedness, and autonomy. In the absence of any one of these needs, based on the theory, individual motivation will decline. Organizational change is a threat to all three of the defined needs. Reduction in any one of the needs is considered significant enough to warrant a temporary decline in motivation. "Human beings can be proactive and engaged or, alternatively, passive and alienated, largely as a function of the social conditions in which they develop and function"

(Deci & Ryan, 2000). If the symptoms leading to retardation of development exist, ultimately there would be an impediment to or reduction in motivation.

## Validation of LOE Symptoms

The theoretical basis by which we can relate a change in technology to symptoms which can lead to the organizational LOE is established in the preceding sections. The practical application evolves during analysis of the symptoms in the context of real data to determine the validity and relevance with respect to the proposed theory. The data for this research was initially collected by a project management consulting firm and was analyzed retrospectively. The mission of the consulting firm was to provide project management software and management consulting services that assist with the analysis and prediction of work. This consulting firm provides a comprehensive software package that provides statistical analysis by graphing progress on projects and tracking through to completion. The projects for this research were general new technology implementations, and the data collected was adapted for use in the initial phase of this research.

Data was analyzed from two independent databases. Each database contains multiple tables with detailed information about the projects, tasks (including estimated and actual task duration), risks, strategic objectives, priorities, personnel, and churn. The databases each contain several thousand records. The analysis was validated in interviews with the project manager of each database. The findings are briefly explained and summarized below.

Grady (2005) found that the data demonstrated strong correlations between evidence of symptoms of loss of stability and the introduction of the new software. The identification of the symptoms was based on the analysis of project churn. Churn is defined as slippage of milestones and deadlines relative to original schedules within the time-

*Figure 2. Date range of interest*

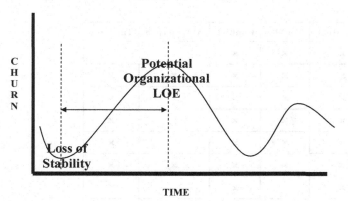

*Figure 3. Example database analysis*

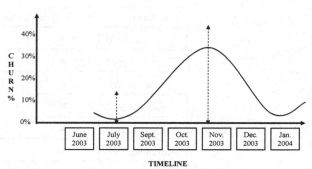

line for completion of a project. Each incidence of churn is assigned a "reason" code that was developed as an explanation of why the slippage occurred. Analysis of the reason codes revealed that many of the reason codes could be directly correlated to the symptoms that employees would be expected to develop as a result of the loss of stability.

The date range of interest (see Figure 2) is defined as the point at which a loss of stability occurs. The initial loss of stability generally coincides with the beginning of the new technology implementation phase; however, it was noted during the research analysis that loss of stability occasionally occurred prior to the implementation due to strong negative anticipation. The loss of stability is the point at which the symptoms begin to occur. During the date range of interest, the symptoms escalate in frequency and severity until reaching the associated maximum churn rate. Based on the project manager interviews, a maximum churn rate of greater than 30% constitutes a significant decline in the overall health of the organization. This is the point at which the potential is greatest for development of organizational LOE.

Further analysis of the reason codes for the churn was completed to determine whether or not a pattern of commonly occurring reason codes was present. The reason codes most commonly associated with slippage were related to the organizational LOE symptoms of productivity, morale, conflict, and motivation. A significant finding of

this study was that the churn occurrences included reason code designations that reflect the consistent exhibition of all six symptoms predicted in employees who were suffering from a loss of stability. The research demonstrated that with the implementation of new technology, the projects experienced a high rate of churn or slippage based on the original project completion timeline. The two databases represented in the study were equivalent. For illustration purposes, a graph of one of the databases is provided in Figure 3.

Table 2 represents the summary of the date range of interest and the association of the corresponding symptoms for the database. Interviews with principals of these two companies involved in this study revealed the organizations did in fact experience a decrease in profitability during the incidents of increased churn, as would be predicted by the Theory of Organizational LOE.

These results indicate an apparent correlation between the occurrence of negative and/or unanticipated project churn and the exhibition of the organizational behavior symptoms consistent with the Theory of Organizational LOE. The unique contribution of this research to the existing body of knowledge is specifically the relationship between the developments of "loss"-related symptoms in infants and adults and a similar set of symptoms in employees who are also experiencing a "loss." In this regard, the reported results of the analysis demonstrate the influence of the symptoms and the potentially negative impact on the organization.

*Table 2. Summary of date range of interest*

| Date Range | Productivity | Motivation | Morale | Conflict | Absenteeism | Turnover |
|---|---|---|---|---|---|---|
| June 2003 | ✗ | ✗ | ✗ | ✗ | | |
| July 2003 | ✗ | ✗ | ✗ | ✗ | ✗ | ✗ |
| August 2003 | ✗ | ✗ | ✗ | ✗ | ✗ | ✗ |
| September 2003 | ✗ | ✗ | ✗ | ✗ | ✗ | ✗ |
| October 2003 | ✗ | ✗ | ✗ | ✗ | ✗ | ✗ |
| November 2003 | ✗ | ✗ | ✗ | ✗ | ✗ | ✗ |
| December 2003 | ✗ | ✗ | | ✗ | | |
| January 2004 | ✗ | ✗ | | ✗ | | |

## BUILDING SUCCESSFUL KM PROJECTS

"According to the Standish Group, the implementation success rate for knowledge management systems runs at about 30%" (Schultze & Boland, 2000) The tendency to focus on the configuration of technology in KM projects often overshadows attempts to insure that the components of the effort are aligned with the goals of the organization and the needs of all impacted, including the workers, managers, customers, suppliers, and partners.

Multinational organizations are at a particularly high risk for problems with communication of information and management of expectations in KM technology projects. Because of the scope and importance of their KM efforts, and the need to gain a competitive advantage across geographic and cultural boundaries, this often means the core business processes of the organization must change. It is these processes that, when changed, have the potential to engender the greatest resistance from employees and may cause the greatest potential damage to the effectiveness of the multinational organization.

## The Heart of KM Is People, Not Technology

Today's advanced KM projects often incorporate a considerable amount of technology and innovation. It is often the technical focus of KM projects (the selection of software, hardware, systems integration, data translation, security architecture, deployment, maintenance, budget, etc.) that is treated as the most critical component of the project. Thus, knowledge management, on the surface, is often equated to a slightly more complicated function of information management. To the contrary, KM is much more than simply managing information. "It is important to note that knowledge management problems can typically not be solved by the deployment of a technology solution alone" (Ruggles, 1998) "Information technology, while critical for enabling the spread of information, cannot capture and store knowledge. Only people can do that" (Senge, Kleiner, Roberts, Ross, & Smith, 1999) The difficulty in implementing successful KM technology projects resides not only in the manner of documentation and archiving of information, but also in the ability of the organization to predict and manage the behavior of its employees during the process.

"The greatest difficulty in knowledge management…is changing people's behavior" (Ruggles, 1998). Thus, KM is much more than the management of knowledge; it is about a better understanding and an appropriate utilization all of its resources, including its people. It is in this respect that the Theory of Organizational LOE has the potential to make its greatest contribution. With this knowledge a critical component is identified that will ultimately lead to the ability of KM implementation projects to be more successful.

While in no way diminishing the intricacy of the technical issues of a major KM project, it has been demonstrated consistently that one of the most critical components to the success of KM technology projects is not found in the technology, but in the employees who will ultimately embrace or resist it. The focus of this chapter has been to show why troublesome changes in employee behavior can be expected to occur as a result of new KM technology projects, and the effects those resulting behaviors could have on the organization.

## Issues for Managers of KM Projects

Looming in the background of this discussion are secondary connections which may ultimately have a significant impact on other issues elsewhere in this book. Consider the employee perception of "personal" ownership of the organizational tacit knowledge they possess. The attempt to document tacit knowledge from experienced employees may be seen as an invasion of personal space or a threat to individual usefulness within the organization. The potential for this scenario is further validated in the research of Harvey (1988, 1999) and Noer (1993), who state that the employee perception of being insignificant, irrelevant, or ignored during change may have severe implications on the employee's performance. The perceived threat to

the employee surrendering tacit knowledge may be comparable in severity to the feelings of loss experienced when surrendering a "leaned on" technology. The potential for an organizational LOE is considerably increased in KM technology projects that expect employees not only to relinquish tacit knowledge, but simultaneously adopt new technologies.

This chapter has focused on the identification of the problem. We have shown that in the process of change, the removal of familiar technology can cause the development of symptoms related to a loss of stability in those employees impacted by that change. Unfortunately, at this point in the evolution of the Theory of Organizational LOE, it is still unclear what can prevent the symptoms from developing and how to lessen the organizational impact on proposed KM technology implementations. However, this research does validate with reasonable certainty that the symptoms will develop and why they are developing. Research that documents possible solutions to this problem has not yet occurred.

In the absence of specific recommendations to avoid these problems, it is still necessary to bring this perspective of change into management's awareness. The informed manager can move forward with more realistic expectations in planning an implementation process that is appropriate to the organization's culture. This can include various levels of employee involvement on one end of the scale and plans that adjust for possible delays in the implementation process on the other. The manager's awareness makes him or her a potential partner in observing and documenting the change process, and the identification of possible factors that will lead, ultimately, to solutions. Management acknowledgment of the link between employee psychology and new technology project success may improve the employee's perception of the KM project and enhance his or her ability to deal with the perceived loss, and thereby reduce the potential of an organizational LOE.

## Issues for the Future Study of KM

This chapter has called attention to specific dilemmas that may be encountered in the process of changing to new technologies, and research continues to further define the intricate relationship between technology change and behavioral psychology. Ongoing research into the issues discussed above and how to effectively deal with these scenarios may soon yield some preliminary answers to help improve the overall success rate of KM technology projects.

The LOE theory, borrowing from the advances in medical science and psychology, adds rigor and structure to the study of organizational behavior and its emerging science. The basic principles of change, psychology, and organizational management are there, but are potentially not aligned or optimized to effectively address the issues. Unfortunately, at this point in the evolution of the practice of management, we still struggle with the concept of establishing a universal foundation on which to build answers. The only certainty is that we have an obligation to take human nature into consideration at all levels of the organization. Knowledge management, and especially the endeavor to capture tacit knowledge, stands to benefit greatly from the continued research into change management and employee psychology related to KM technology projects.

## CONCLUSION

The organizational development aspects of the successful organization are no longer a function of acquiring skilled employees and assigning those employees in such a way that organizational objectives are met. Now more than ever, organizational development is challenged by a rapidly changing technological environment. These challenges will continue to escalate as more and more companies are forced to become multinational in order to compete. In order to sustain growth, in addition to new issues involving global marketing, production, distribution, and so forth, organizations must develop an inventory of knowledge assets and act to preserve and/or disseminate them in such a manner that they will be accessible everywhere in the organization.

At least one area needing attention is the development, in all levels of our organizations, of a continuous learning process that is intuitive and predictable in dealing with issues of employee acceptance of new technologies. In the absence of this integrative practice, the organization will be vulnerable to a loss of stability, which manifests itself in the form of symptoms that lead to the eventual decline into an organizational LOE.

To maximize success, organizations must expand their focus during the implementation of new KM projects to align their information technology and human capital for organizational benefit. This paradigm shift applies to the KM project scope, requirements development, technology solution selection, and project implementation. From a long-term perspective, organizations must also change their human resource and human capital programs to identify, acquire, foster, and develop traits in our employees that will allow them to be more open to continual change in the work environment.

The continued evolution of the research on the organizational LOE theory and similar others seeks to provide a scientific structure on which to influence the science of management and enhance the integration of successful KM technology projects. Questions such as those discussed in this chapter highlight the evolutionary nature of the study of management and emphasize the struggle to establish a true science. It is through the monitoring of these new discoveries in this emerging science, just as they monitor the health of the KM technology projects and the health of the overall organization, that managers can hope to achieve the competitive advantage of a well-engineered KM initiative and avoid the potential impacts of an organizational LOE.

# REFERENCES

Bawden, D. (2001). Information overload. *Library and Information Briefings,* 92.

Benbya, H., & Belbaly, N.A. (2005). Mechanisms for knowledge management system effectiveness: An exploratory analysis. *Knowledge and Process Management Journal, 12*(3), 203-216.

Bennett, J.L. (2001). Change happens. *HR Magazine,* 149-156.

Bowlby, J. (1969). *Attachment and loss* (vol. I). New York: Basic Books.

Burnes, B., & James, H. (1995). Culture, cognitive dissonance and the management of change. *International Journal of Operations and Production Management, 15*(8), 14-22.

Call, D. (2005). Knowledge management—not rocket science. *Journal of Knowledge Management, 9*(2), 19-31.

Dalkir, K. (2005). *Knowledge management in theory and practice.* Oxford: Elsevier Butterworth-Heinemann.

Deci, E., & Ryan R. (1985). *Intrinsic motivation and self-determination in human behavior.* New York : Plenum Press.

Delisi, P. (1990). Lessons from the steel axe: Culture, technology, and organizational change. *Sloan Management Review,* 83-93.

Goldschmidt, W.R. (1960). *Exploring the Ways of Mankind.* New York: Holt, Rinehart, and Winston.

Grady, V. (2005). *Studying the effect of loss of stability on organizational behavior: A perspective on technological change.* Unpublished Doctoral Dissertation, George Washington University, USA.

Grady (Goetz), V., & Hamner, M. (2004, October). The deterioration from an organizational loss of stability into an organizational LOE. *Proceedings of the 2004 American Society Engineering Management National Conference,* Alexandria, VA.

Grady (Goetz), V., & Hamner, M. (2004). The effect of technological change on organizational effectiveness. *American Society of Engineering Managers Practice Periodical, 1*(2).

Grady-Goetz, V., & Hamner, M. (2003, October). Identifying behavioral symptoms in the workplace that can evolve into an organizational loss of effectiveness. *Proceedings of the 2003 American Society Engineering Management National Conference,* St. Louis, MO.

Harvey, J.B. (1988). *The Abilene Paradox: And other meditations on management.* New York: John Wiley & Sons.

Harvey, J.B. (1999). *How come every time I get stabbed in the back my fingerprints are on the knife? And other meditations on management.* San Francisco: Jossey-Bass.

Hwang, Y. (2005). Investigating enterprise systems adoption: Uncertainty avoidance, intrinsic motivation, and the Technology Acceptance Model. *European Journal of Information Systems, 14,* 150-161.

Lewin, K. (1951). *Field theory in social science.* New York: Harper and Row.

Lynch, J.J. (1977). *The broken heart: The medical consequences of loneliness.* New York: Basic Books.

Malhotra, Y. (2004). Desperately seeking self-determination: Key to the new enterprise logic of customer relationships. *Proceedings of the Americas Conference on Information Systems,* New York.

Malhotra, Y. (2002). Is knowledge management really an oxymoron? Unraveling the role of organizational controls in knowledge management. In D. White (Ed.), *Knowledge mapping and management* (pp. 1-13). Hershey, PA: Idea Group.

Marwick, A.D. (2001). Knowledge management technology. *IBM Systems Journal, 40*(4), 814-830.

Noer, D.M. (1993). *Healing the wounds: Overcoming the trauma of layoffs and revitalizing downsized organizations.* San Francisco: Jossey-Bass.

O'Sullivan, K.J., & Stankosky, M. (2004). The impact of KM technology on intellectual capital. *Journal of Information and KM, 3*(4), 331-346.

Park, H., Ribiere, V., & Schulte, W.D. (2004). Critical attributes of organizational culture that promote KM technology implementation success. *Journal of KM, 8*(3), 106-116.

Pinsonneault, A., & Rivard, S. (1998). Information technology and the nature of managerial work: From the productivity paradox. *MIS Quarterly, 22,* 3.

Ribiere, V., & Sitar, A.S. (2003). Critical role of leadership in nurturing a knowledge-supporting culture. *KM Research and Practice,* 39-48.

Ruggles, R. (1998). The state of the notion: Knowledge management in practice. *California Management Review, 40*(9), 80-90.

Rybczynski, W. (1983). *Taming the tiger: The struggle to control technology.* New York: Viking Press.

Schultze, U., & Boland, R.J. Jr. (2000). Knowledge management and reproduction of knowledge work practices. *Journal of Strategic Information Systems, 9,* 193-212.

Senge, P., Kleiner, A., Roberts, C., Ross, R.G., & Smith, B. (1999). *The dance of change: The challenges to sustaining momentum in learning organizations* (1st ed.). New York: Doubleday.

Spitz, R.A. (1983). *Rene A. Spitz: Dialogues from infancy* (R.N. Emde, ed.). New York: International Universities Press.

Spitz, R.A., & Wolf, K. (1946). Anaclitic depression: An inquiry into the genesis of psychiatric conditions in early childhood, II. *The Psychoanalytic Study of the Child, 2,* 313-342.

Tiwana, A. (2002). *The knowledge management toolkit.* Englewood Cliffs, NJ: Prentice Hall.

Washington, M., & Hacker, M. (2005). Why change fails: Knowledge counts. *Leadership & Organization Development Journal, 26*(5/6).

Weick, K.E., & Quinn, R.E. (1999). Organizational change and development. *Annual Psychology Review, 50,* 361-386.

# Chapter VIII
# Architecting Knowledge Management Systems

**Shankar Kambhampaty**
*Satyam Computer Services Ltd., India*

## ABSTRACT

*Organizations need well-architected systems for knowledge management (KM). This chapter begins with a review of approaches adopted by organizations for developing KM solutions. It defines a set of components that can form the building blocks for developing a knowledge management system. The relevance of the principles of Service-Oriented Architecture (SOA) to KM solutions is explained. It presents the architecture of a generic knowledge management system based on the components defined and the principles of SOA. It then discusses the patterns for implementing the architecture, followed by maturity levels of knowledge management systems.*

## INTRODUCTION

Knowledge management (KM) is a practice for managing the intellectual assets of an organization. A successful knowledge management program increases employee productivity by providing systems that not only allow for information access and sharing of explicit knowledge, but also enable expression of tacit knowledge in the minds of the people through collaboration. Organizations that successfully implement knowledge management programs have well-architected systems supported by good training and cultural change management practices to ensure that the systems are leveraged fully for improved productivity and competitive edge (Calwell, 2004).

## KNOWLEDGE MANAGEMENT SOLUTIONS

Most organizations keen on implementing effective knowledge management solutions begin with a systematic process of defining KM requirements. A knowledge management team is formed with clearly defined objectives. The different approaches adopted by organizations in architecting and implementing KM solutions are as follows.

### Evolutionary Approach

Many organizations architect solutions in an evolutionary manner. A KM initiative is launched as part of an existing enterprise portal, and other systems in the enterprise are extended to meet KM goals.

### Product-Based Approach

The key aspect of this approach is to base the solution on products available from vendors or from open source. The different products that are needed to meet the KM objectives are identified, and the solution is architected based on customization of products.

### Hybrid Approach

In this approach, while existing systems are extended wherever appropriate, suitable products are also identified and customized to meet the KM objectives of the organization.

## COMPONENTS OF KNOWLEDGE MANAGEMENT SYSTEMS

While the knowledge management solutions discussed above address certain requirements, they provide very few insights into components that

could form the basis of a KM system independent of technology.

As knowledge management is a practice and not a technology concept (Rasmus, 2003), it becomes necessary to consider architectures for KM systems that are independent of technologies and are based on generic components that can be implemented using a variety of technologies and products.

A detailed study of requirements identified by practitioners and researchers, and a review of KM systems implemented in organizations revealed that generic components could be identified that could form the basis of the architecture of a KM system. The generic components identified are as follows:

- Aggregator
- Segregator
- Publisher
- Explorer
- Collaborator
- orchesTrator
- Storage & network

These components will be collectively referred to as ASPECTS of KM systems.

Figure 1 shows the components of the KM system. Each of the components shown in the figure has been defined to meet a specific requirement of the system.

The aggregator component accesses data in a number of sources of the organization and creates index information in the storage & network component.

The segregator component maintains taxonomy of knowledge topics and classifies the indexed information created by the aggregator component based on the categories defined for the enterprise.

The publisher component exposes the explicit knowledge created by the aggregator and segregator components through different mechanisms such as enterprise portals, newsletters, and train-

*Figure 1. Components of the KM system*

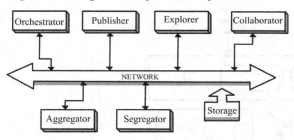

ing updates. This component is meant to update and generate interest in users who may not be looking for specific information or data.

The explorer component is the mechanism for the users in the enterprise who may be interested in information related to specific topics. It allows for search and retrieval of ranked lists of results for the search criteria indicated by the users.

While all of the above components address the needs of managing explicit knowledge, the collaboration component is specifically meant to facilitate communication, and sharing and transfer of tacit knowledge.

One of the challenges in KM is to have the systems continuously refreshed with new knowledge to maintain a high degree of richness that would make users repeatedly use and contribute to the KM system. The orchestrator component brings the dynamism to the KM system and ensures that all the other components perform continuously their respective functions in order to provide a live knowledge environment.

## ARCHITECTURE OF THE GENERIC KM SYSTEM

Using the ASPECTS defined in the earlier section, several architectures can be developed for KM systems based on different architectural styles that incorporate some or all of the components mentioned to address the requirements of an organization.

One of the architectural trends, Service-Oriented Architecture (SOA), is relevant to KM. Industry analysts such as Gartner (Abrams & Smith, 2003) predict that over 80% of the business applications sold between 2005 and 2008 will be based on the principles of (SOA).

Several key drivers are common to both SOA and KM:

a.   There is increasing demand on organizations for agility in their business processes in order to stay competitive in changing market situations. SOA is considered as a right fit for such requirements, as the services model allows for restructuring of business processes. Likewise, organizations that wish to leverage their intellectual assets for competitive advantage need also to bring together the relevant explicit and tacit knowledge in a form and shape that can be applied to gain the required advantage.

b.   Both SOA and KM aim at reuse of intellectual assets.

c.   When fully implemented, both SOA and KM, target the enterprise.

d.   While the focus of KM is on knowledge and that of SOA is on information, both SOA and KM need information integration (Frank, 2001). This is the driving convergence of KM and information management (IM) initiatives (Harris, 2004).

The following sub-sections discuss some of the key concepts of SOA and the architecture of KM system based on SOA.

### Service-Oriented Architecture

Service-Oriented Architecture is an architecture style that involves exposing reusable functionality of an application as services that can be consumed by other applications.

*Figure 2. Enterprise Strawman for SOA*

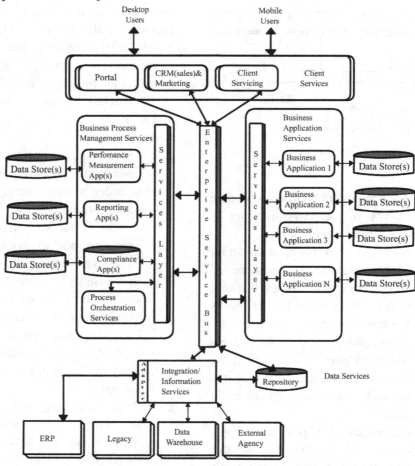

The following are some of the key aspects of SOA:

1.  Service provider applications expose services as per the published "contract" without knowledge of who the consumer is. Likewise, service consumer applications consume services as per the published "contract" without knowledge of who is providing the service. This brings about loose coupling between service provider and consumer.

2.  The four tenets of service orientation are (Evdemon, 2005):

    a.  Boundaries are explicit.
    b.  Services are autonomous.
    c.  Services share schema and contract.

    d.  Service compatibility is based on policy.

3.  Content routing, transformation, and delivery between service provider and consumer can be handled by a mediator pattern called the Enterprise Service Bus (ESB). The ESB, therefore, serves the purpose of connection and integration.

4.  The services in an organization can be grouped under four types of services (Kambhampaty & Chandra, 2006):

    a.  **Client Services:** Enable and deliver content to users.

    b.  **Business Process Management Services:** Handle orchestration of business processes implemented in business applications.

c. **Business Application Services:** Encapsulate access to the functionality of the business processes.
d. **Data Services:** Encapsulate access to data in various sources.

ESB integrates the service providers and consumers. The Enterprise Strawman for SOA based on the above classification is shown in Figure 2.

## Architecture of KM System Based on SOA

The components of KM, namely the ASPECTS, can be incorporated into the SOA architecture shown in Figure 2 resulting in an SOA-based architecture for KM. There are two advantages with such an approach:

1. The architecture would support and provide all the benefits of SOA.
2. The investments made by the organization in implementing SOA or KM can be leveraged by both.

Figure 3 shows the architecture of the KM system based on SOA.

Each of the ASPECTS is implemented as one or more services as per the services model of SOA. Aggregator services are part of the data services. On being invoked by the orchestrator services or as per a pre-defined schedule, the aggregator services access information and data in enterprise systems and typically create index information in storage. Segregator services are invoked by the orchestrator services or by editorial staff in the enterprise for classifying the information as per the taxonomy defined. This would involve creating metadata in storage that the publisher services can use as input. Publisher services (on being invoked by the orchestrator component or enterprise portal staff) use the content in storage to upload updated information for access by users.

Publisher services are client services and often invoke the explorer services when users wish to search for specific information. Publisher services also invoke collaboration services such as chat, instant messaging, and Web meetings, and the tacit knowledge brought out in such efforts can once again be acted upon by the aggregator services.

## PATTERNS FOR ASPECTS

Each of the ASPECTS of KM shown in Figures 1 and 3 can be implemented based on *design patterns*. This section discusses the applicable patterns that provide solutions to address the requirements of ASPECTS.

A design pattern is a solution to a recurring problem in specific design situations (Buschmann, Meunier, Rohnert, Sommerlad, & Stal, 1996). Identifying the design patterns applicable to each of the ASPECTS of KM would enable the solution related to each of the components to be applied repeatedly regardless of the technology used for implementation.

### Aggregator

The patterns applicable for the aggregator component are: composite pattern (Gamma, Helm, Johnson, & Vlissides 1994), cascade pattern (Foster & Zhao, 1999), whole-part pattern (Buschmann et al., 1996), and application patterns for information aggregation (IBM, 2004).

The aggregator would also need to index information aggregated. A full-text indexing and retrieval algorithm and implementation is discussed in Chellappa and Kambhampaty (1994).

### Segregator

*Topic map design patterns* for information architecture (Techquila, n.d.) address the requirements of a segregator effectively. Hierarchical classification pattern, hierarchical naming pattern, topic-per term thesaurus pattern, and topic-per concept thesaurus pattern are the patterns applicable to the segregator.

## Publisher

The application patterns of *self-service* (IBM, 2004) suit the requirements of the publisher. The other relevant patterns are the observer pattern (Gamma et al., 1994) and the publish subscribe pattern (Buschmann et al., 1996). With a wide variety of portal products available in the market, rarely are these patterns implemented ground-up.

## Explorer

The *search pagination* and *item pagination patterns* (Yahoo, n.d.) are the patterns applicable for the explorer in providing the response based on the queries provided by the users. A search engine would need to be developed (Chellappa & Kambhampaty, 1994) that would provide the results of search activities of the user.

## Collaborator

The application patterns for collaboration can address most of the requirements of the collaborator (IBM, 2004). Additionally, whole activity patterns, data patterns, and support patterns listed in DiGiano et al. (2002) can address additional requirements. As in the case of the publisher, most of the functionality is typically implemented using the wide variety of products available.

## Orchestrator

*Orchestration engine* (DiGiano et al., 2002), *orchestration language, orchestration builder,* and *compensating action* are the key patterns for the orchestrator. With BPEL-standard-based products being available in the market, this component is rarely developed ground-up.

## Storage & Network

Patterns for *access integration* and *application integration* (IBM, 2004) are some of the key patterns to address the key requirements of this component at the application level. The integration middleware and storage systems available from several vendors are also needed to meet the requirements at the hardware level.

## MATURITY OF THE KM SYSTEM

The maturity of the KM system can be established based on the extent to which the ASPECTS are implemented. Five levels of maturity can be defined accordingly:

* **Level 1—Initial:** In this initial level, the aggregator and segregator components are implemented to some extent with rudimentary search and retrieval mechanism.
* **Level 2—Publisher:** In the publisher level, the aggregator and segregator components are further implemented, and the publisher component (typically an enterprise portal) is implemented.
* **Level 3—Explorer:** By the time an organization has reached this level, a culture of using KM systems for accessing the explicit knowledge would have set in. Users would demand facilities to search and retrieve information of their interest. The explorer component is implemented by the organization.
* **Level 4—Collaboration:** With the users leveraging the KM system fully for explicit knowledge, the organization focuses on innovative ways of making the tacit knowledge shareable. The organization would be in a position to target a real-time enterprise from a business perspective. The collaboration component is implemented to address the KM needs.

- **Level 5—Orchestration:** A real-time enterprise would be a reality when the organization reached this level. Not only will the business processes be agile, but also the cultural and systemic infrastructure of the organization would be conducive to implement the orchestration component that would bring dynamism to the KM activities.

## CONCLUSION

This chapter discussed the architecting of KM systems. The key components constituting the ASPECTS of KM system were discussed. The relevance of Service-Oriented Architecture to KM was brought out, and the architecture of a generic KM system based on SOA was presented. The patterns for implementing the ASPECTS were discussed, and finally a maturity model for KM systems based on implementation of the ASPECTS was also provided.

## REFERENCES

Abrams, C., & Smith, D. (2003). *Service-oriented business applications show their potential* (Pub. ID: SPA-20-7295). Gartner.

Buschmann, F., Meunier, R., Rohnert, H., Sommerlad, P., & Stal, M. (1996). *Pattern-oriented software architecture—A system of patterns*. New York: John Wiley & Sons.

Calwell, F. (2004), *KM adoption model highlights critical success factors* (Pub. ID: G00123399). Gartner.

Chellappa, M., & Kambhampaty, S. (1994). Text retrieval—a trendy cocktail to address the Dataworld. *Proceedings of IEEE COMPSAC '94.*

DiGiano, C., Yarnall, L., Patton, C., Roschelle, J., Tatar, D., & Manley, M. (2002). Collaboration design patterns: Conceptual tools for planning for the wireless classroom. *Proceedings of WMTE'02.*

Evdemon, J. (2005). *The four tenets of service orientation.* Retrieved from *http://www.bpminstitute.org/articles/article/article/the-four-tenets-of-service-orientation.html*

Foster, T., & Zhao, L. (1999). Cascade. *Journal of Object-Oriented Programming, 11*(9).

Gamma, E., Helm, R., Johnson, R., & Vlissides, J. (1994). *Design patterns: Elements of reusable object-oriented software.* Boston: Addison-Wesley.

Harris, K. (2006). *Knowledge management enables the high performance workplace* (Pub. ID: G00136928). Gartner.

IBM. (2004). *Patterns for e-business.* Retrieved from *http://www28.ibm.com/developerworks/patterns*

Kambhampaty, S., & Chandra, S. (2005). Service-Oriented Architecture for enterprise applications. *Journal of WSEAS Transactions on Business and Economics, 2*(3), 1109-9526.

Rasmus, D. (2003). *Don't bother looking for a knowledge management market* (Pub. ID: RPA-092003-00053). Forrester.

Techquila. (n.d.). *Topic map design patterns for information architecture.* Retrieved from *http://www.techquila.com/tmsinia.html*

Ulrich, F. (2001). Knowledge management systems: Essential requirements and generic design patterns. *Proceedings of the International Symposium on Information Systems and Engineering (ISE'2001)* (pp. 114-121), Las Vegas, NV.

Yahoo. (n.d.). *Design pattern library.* Retrieved from *http://developer.yahoo.com/ypatterns/atoz.php*

# Chapter IX
# Global Knowledge Management Technology Strategies and Competitive Functionality

**William Schulte**
*Shenandoah University, USA*

**Kevin J. O'Sullivan**
*New York Institute of Technology, USA*

## ABSTRACT

*Information and knowledge management technologies and globalization have changed how firms in service industries formulate, implement, and sustain competitive advantage. This research project contributes to our understanding of the relationships between global knowledge management technology strategies and competitive functionality from global IT. Based on field research, this study found that global knowledge management technology strategies have a positive impact on competitive advantage from information technology applications functionality from global IT. This study provides recommendations to international engineering, procurement, and construction industry executives regarding the impact of knowledge management strategies and global information technology on competitive advantage of firms in their industry.*

## RESEARCH ISSUE

Global knowledge management technologies have changed how firms in service industries formulate, implement, and sustain competitive advantage (Schulte, 2004). Moreover, information technology and telecommunications have been driving forces behind the globalization of many industries (Roche & Blaine, 2000). In addition, global information technology has ushered in the knowledge economy and enabled knowledge management to enhance competitive advantage (Stankosky, 2005; Schulte, 1999; Giraldo & Schulte, 2005). Knowledge creating factors managed by governments have also enhanced the innovation of many firms and patent production in industries around the world (Revilak, 2006).

Moreover, the strategic importance of information technology is an established proposition in the information systems and strategic management literature (Roche & Blaine, 2000). In addition, scholars have argued that multinational corporations (MNCs) have improved performance by ensuring that their information technology and knowledge management strategies are congruent with their business and corporate strategies (Giraldo & Schulte, 2004; Stankosky, 2004). In general, knowledge management is a widely accepted factor in creating efficiency, effectiveness, and sustainable competitive advantage (Stankosky, 2004; Schulte & Sample, 2005; Davenport & Prusak, 1997; Drucker, Garvin, Leonard, Straus, & Brown, 1998; Edvinsson & Malone, 1997; Dixon, 2000; Nonaka & Takeuchi, 1995; O'Dell & Grayson, 1998; Schwartz, 2005; Sveiby, 1997; Stewart, 1997; Choo & Bontis, 2002; Liebowitz & Wilcox, 1997; Revilak, 2006).

## RESEARCH QUESTION

This research project will attempt to contribute to our understanding of the relationships between global information technologies, knowledge management, and competitive advantage. Competitive advantage is the most important common denominator in the global information technology, knowledge management, and international corporate strategy literature. This study is an exploration of the factors that contribute to the competitive performance of firms competing in international engineering, procurement, and construction industry. The purpose of this study is to explore the following research question:

To what extent do global information and knowledge management technologies affect the competitive advantage of global organizations in the international engineering, procurement, and construction industry?

This study provides recommendations, based on the results of the research, to international en-gineering, procurement, and construction industry executives about how knowledge management technology strategies can impact functionality competitiveness from information technology applications including knowledge management systems.

## THE INTERNATIONAL ENGINEERING, PROCUREMENT, AND CONSTRUCTION (IEPC) INDUSTRY

Construction is one of the most influential industries in the world (Schulte, 1997, 2004). This position is based on the following nine arguments. First, it is the world's largest industry, representing a significant percentage of the world's total Gross Domestic Product. Because construction is labor intensive, it creates a significant share of global employment, especially in developing countries.

Second, changes in the construction services industry have an exponential impact on the world economy. Construction's impact extends far into the value chain, both upstream and downstream in many industries. Construction projects increase sales in related industries such as heavy equipment, transportation, cement, steel, and financial and other services. Furthermore, the spin-off effect of the industry influences all major industries in the economy, particularly those requiring industrial plant, commercial facilities, or infrastructure construction.

Third, despite recent increases in privatization, regional economic integration, and market liberalization in emerging markets, construction continues to have some degree of government protection worldwide. Many governments on all levels provide local content rules or erect barriers to entry from foreign competitors to ensure the viability of domestic firms.

Fourth, the long-term consequences of the IEPC industry affect many stakeholders in society.

Projects promote higher standards of living and economic development. This fosters an increase in the number and variety of goods and services available to consumers. The spillover creates not only economic, but also social benefits.

Fifth, the IEPC industry is inextricably linked to government. Government is both a major client and a major supplier to contractors. While they are sometimes used as an instrument of a government's domestic and foreign policies, contractors also exert a significant influence on government policy.

Sixth, while its impact on the world economy and government policies is considerable, as discussed above, the IEPC industry is extremely sensitive to macroeconomic adjustments, political changes, and advancements or setbacks in related and even unrelated industries.

Seventh, the industry is also highly concentrated. A relatively small group of very large firms control a significant amount of billings awarded to foreign contractors in the worldwide market.

Eighth, another unique trait is that, unlike most exports, the exported product is constructed almost entirely in the host country.

Finally, construction projects in the IEPC industry typically extend over a long time period. Therefore, success in the industry is affected by a contractor's ability to manage overlapping projects at different stages at different job sites over time, and by building sustainable competitive advantage (Schulte, 1997).

## LITERATURE REVIEW

The new globally competitive information economy increases complexity for information executives to more than they have had to manage in the past. For example, traditional national and regional boundaries are being redrawn by information and Web technologies. Also, regulations, standards, trade policies, tax policies, and other economic and political forces are responding to the needs of the knowledge economy. Social and other external pressures are evolving to keep pace with the global changes. Infrastructure investment priorities are also adapting. Telecommunications infrastructures in many nations are privatizing and moving toward more advanced technologies, leapfrogging ahead of many more economically advanced countries. As global competition increases, the integration of strategic management and information technology will become a more significant factor in the competitive advantage, innovation, and financial performance of firms around the world (Schulte, 1999; Revilak, 2006).

Also, scholars have recently begun to integrate research from different disciplines including international strategic management, global information technology, and knowledge management to explore answers to questions about the management of global information and knowledge management technology. In recent years, studies have been conducted providing support for the strategic impact of global information and knowledge management technology, and competitive advantage in global organizations (Giraldo & Schulte, 2005; Schulte, 2004).

## Knowledge Management and Competitive Advantage

Leaders in global organizations need to develop adaptive knowledge management skills to achieve competitive advantage. They usually formulate strategic plans based on models that do not address complexity and dynamic knowledge workplaces. They also focus on precise metrics instead of patterns generated by the flow of global knowledge. Traditional approaches to gain sustainable competitive advantage are limited. Recent research answered the following research question: Are there any correlations between knowledge management technologies, knowledge flows, communities of practice, and actions conducted to adapt an organization to its external and internal environments? Strong correlations were found using an organizational learning and action framework (Giraldo & Schulte, 2005).

Moreover, scholars have identified the need for an organizational transformation that emphasizes collective knowledge and team development. It is clear in their literature that survival depends on converting the organization into a knowledge-based organization (Drucker, 2001). Knowledge is becoming a critical resource for global success and is a source of competitive advantage (Nonaka & Takeuchi, 1995; Grant & Spender, 1997: Grant, 1997; Spender, 1997). Consequently, efforts in developing collaboration and knowledge management are essential to the survival of the firm that attempts to compete in the global knowledge economy (Doz, Santos, & Williamson, 2001).

Both external and internal knowledge are sources of competitive advantage (Stankosky, 2005). Frameworks have been posited that attempt to understand the flow of knowledge and the knowledge creation process within an organization as a source of competitive advantage (Nonaka & Takeuchi, 1995). Others suggest that a relationship between organizational knowledge and competitive advantage be moderated by the firm's ability to integrate and apply knowledge. Many scholars have explored the impact of accumulating knowledge, creating value, and establishing competitive advantage (Choo & Bontis, 2002; Liebowitz & Wilcox, 1997).

## Global Knowledge Integration and Local Responsiveness Framework

Simon and Grover (1993) explored the strategic use of information technology in international business and developed a framework for information technology applications. The authors explored the use of information technology by applying the global integration and local responsiveness (I/R) framework as proposed by Prahalad and Doz (1987). Their study also explored the dimensions of competitive advantage that theoretically emerges from an overall fit between information

technology strategy and business strategy. Simon and Grover (1993) conclude:

*...the link between IT and international business strategy can define the boundaries of the firm and facilitate its success or failure. The ability to coordinate and control the dispersed activities of these global firms is essential to the attainment of competitive advantage in the global marketplace. The [I/R] framework demonstrates how the fit between a firm's strategic decisions and IT applications can be used to attain competitive advantage in the international environment.* (p. 40)

The transnational solution provides new structures and new leadership requirements to compete globally (Bartlett, Ghoshal, & Birkinshaw, 2003; Johnson, Lenn, & O' Neill). Interestingly, some scholars who discuss global information and knowledge management technology management also applied the global integration/local responsiveness model to help explain the impact of information technology decisions on a firm's competitive advantage (Schulte, 2004; Deans & Ricks, 1993; Palvia, Palvia, & Zigli, 1992). Figure 1 provides a modification of the global integration and local responsiveness framework introducing the knowledge dimension (Schulte, 2004).

*Figure 1. Global knowledge integration/local knowledge responsiveness: International corporate strategy categories (Adapted from Bartlett et al., 2003; Prahalad & Doz, 1987; Schulte, 2004)*

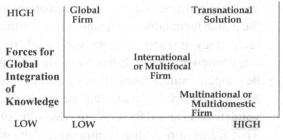

## Global Information and Knowledge Management Technology

The management of global information and technology is a rapidly growing area of interest to researchers in information systems, international management, and strategic management (Roche & Blaine, 2000; Schulte, 1999; Banker, Kauffman, & Mahmood, 1993). Consequently, they argue that the strategic information technology capabilities of management have a positive and significant impact on firm competitiveness (Palvia et al., 1992).

In summary, important conclusions can be derived from the literature on the management of global information and knowledge management technology:

1. Firms competing in the global marketplace that align their information and knowledge management technology capabilities with their overall corporate and business strategies will benefit from increased sustainable competitive advantage.

2. Information and knowledge management technology capabilities are not the primary contributors to this competitive advantage. Technology is an enabler of management capabilities (Schulte & Sample, 2005; Deans & Ricks, 1993; Ives & Jarvenpaa, 1991).

Given the strategic importance of information technology, how can it be measured? The next section of this document addresses the issue of strategic information technology measurement. In the search for reliable tools to measure information technology impacts on competitive advantage, one framework has endured. Not only has it been developed from a foundation in strategic management theory, but it also has been empirically validated and tested for reliability (Schulte, 1999). That framework is the Competitive Advantage Provided by an Information Technology Application (CAPITA) developed by Sethi and King

(1994). The next section of this chapter discusses this useful framework.

## Competitive Advantage Provided by Information Technology Applications

Sethi and King (1994) developed a replicable model and framework to understand the relationships between information technology applications and competitive advantage. They identified attributes that characterize the competitive advantage of the firm. The advantage of this approach is that it provides information about how and why information technology affects competitive advantage.

The CAPITA framework was empirically tested to assess the measurement properties to ensure the framework's usefulness as a research tool by evaluating unidimensionality, convergent validity, discriminant validity, predictive validity, and reliability. According to Sethi and King (1994), "the CAPITA dimensions are positively correlated with each other and...all coefficients are significant. This implies that the CAPITA dimensions accrue multiple benefits to the organization" (p. 1616).

This study borrows from the CAPITA construct to identify and measure the global strategic information technology capabilities and knowledge management strategies of the firm. The CAPITA dimensions used in this study include resource management functionality and resource acquisition functionality. "Resource acquisition functionality measures the impact of the firm's ability to order, acquire and accept a resource. Resource management functionality consists of the impact of IT on the utilization, upgrade, transfer, disposition, accounting and post-acquisition leverage of the firm's resources" (Sethi & King, 1994, p. 1613).

These strategic information technology capabilities are grounded in both the industrial organization economics and the resource-based views of the firm. Functionality competitive advantage theoretical constructs and relevance to firm performance are summarized in Table 1.

*Table 1. CAPITA dimensions supporting theoretical concepts, authors, and relevance to firm performance (Adapted from Sethi & King, 1994, p. 1605; Schulte, 1999)*

| CAPITA Dimension | Theoretical Constructs | Relevance to Firm Performance |
|---|---|---|
| Functionality | Differentiation | Uniqueness |
| | Customer service | Build and maintain customer loyalty |
| | Add value for customers | Increase innovator's market share |
| | New products and services | Change the nature of the industry |
| | Unique product features | Increase market power |

## RESEARCH HYPOTHESIS

Global knowledge management technologies (GKMTs) have become important determinants for international expansion and competitiveness in the IEPC industry. This section of the chapter will discuss the framework hypotheses, revised conclusions, implications, and recommendations for extension and replication of this research.

Based on the literature review, it is logical to ask: What impact does global knowledge management technology strategy have on CAPITA functionality from global information technology? This exploration brings us closer to an approximation of the real relationships between global information and knowledge management technology and competitive advantage in the IEPC industry. The following is the hypothesis generated from the literature review and field interviews:

*H1: As global knowledge management technology strategies increase, CAPITA functionality from global IT increases.*

To test the hypothesis in this study, the independent and dependent variables were calculated and transformed by creating indexes of the means of the items used to measure each construct. The key constructs of interest were CAPITA functionality from global information technologies (GITs) and global knowledge management technology strategies. CAPITA functionality from global IT index was calculated from the responses to the surveys by the CIOs of the firms. The global knowledge management strategy index was calculated from responses from the firm's CEOs.

## DATA COLLECTION AND TARGET SAMPLE

Questionnaires were mailed to the CEO and CIO of the top 225 firms in the international engineering, procurement, and construction industry as defined by the *Engineering News Record*, a top-tier professional journal for the GCS industry. This choice was considered the most appropriate single source. Sethi and King (1998) acknowledged that "the use of multiple respondents, including senior business executives and IT users, would have enriched the data further and eliminated some biases and inaccuracies" (p. 1608).

The population for this study was the Top 225 global contractors as described by the *Engineering News Record*. The response rate was about 20% (46 out of 225) respondent firms, and the population's global market share growth and other measures were compared to ensure representative nature of the sample. This is a typical operation procedure in strategic management research and was used in previous studies (Schulte, 1999).

Given that this study does not attempt to explain firm behavior beyond the population of the top 225 firms, this sample can be used for purposes of statistical inference. This study only generalizes to the industry segment represented by the top 225 firms described by *ENR*. Statistical significance, therefore, is relevant in this case and was used to make statements from the specific sample to the whole industry segment. Moreover, this study does not attempt to claim casualty.

In addition, this study enriched the data collection process and reduced potential limitations by gaining support of *ENR*'s publisher and editor, and other international engineering, procurement, and construction industry opinion leaders. In his study, Schulte (1999) found the items to measure CAPITA functionality from global IT and global knowledge management technology to have a high degree of reliability and construct validity.

Survey measures for CAPITA functionality from global IT are listed in Table 2. The items used to measure global knowledge management technology strategies are summarized in Table 3.

## RELIABILITY OF MEASURES

A key concern in this type of research is ensuring reliable measures—that is, variables that constantly measure the same phenomenon. Strategies to enhance reliability of measures included the following: consistently recording

*Table 2. Survey items used to calculate CAPITA functionality from global IT*

| | **Survey Measure Items**<br>Respondents were asked to respond on a scale from 1 to 7 on statements based on the following effect of global IT on the item. |
| --- | --- |
| CAPITA Functionality from Global IT Variables | • Impact on primary users to monitor the use of the resource<br>• Impact on primary users to upgrade the resource if necessary<br>• Impact on primary users to transfer or dispose of the resource<br>• Impact on primary users to evaluate the overall effectiveness or usefulness of the resource<br>• Impact on primary users to order or put in a request for the resource<br>• Impact on primary users to acquire the resource<br>• Impact on primary users to verify that the resource meets specifications |

*Table 3. Survey items used to calculate global knowledge management technology strategies*

| |
| --- |
| • The main role of foreign operations should be to implement parent company strategies.<br>• New knowledge should be developed at the parent company and then transferred to foreign units.<br>• A firm should provide coordination and control necessary for efficient operations throughout the firm.<br>• A firm's systems should be simultaneously globally efficient, provide local responsiveness, and quickly diffuse organizational innovation.<br>• Solutions should use international standards and a planned common architecture that meets the needs of various-sized foreign operations in diverse environments.<br>• Solutions and applications should be shared across the worldwide organization.<br>• A firm should use universal dictionaries for understanding solutions and applications.<br>• Innovation should be a cooperative activity sharing knowledge between home office and foreign operations.<br>• A firm should build information and communication cost advantages through centralized knowledge management.<br>• A firm's strategy should be focused on worldwide efficiencies from a global information and communications system.<br>• Organization learning should emerge from contacts between home office and foreign operations personnel.<br>• A firm should have strong linkages between the home office and foreign operations based on cooperation and mutual assistance.<br>• A firm should rapidly disseminate innovations while continuing to provide flexibility required to be responsive to local needs of foreign operations.<br>• Foreign operations receive and adapt products and services offered by the parent company to the best advantage in the countries in which they operate.<br>• A firm should centralize its systems to achieve global economies of scale. |

*Table 4. Internal reliability of the constructs in the study using Cronbach's alpha*

| Construct | Cronbach's Alpha |
|---|---|
| **CAPITA Functionality from Global IT** | .9323 |
| **GKMT Score** | .9110 |

data, using continuous rather than discrete data for performance measures, and using multiple items to measure concepts so that the relationships can be empirically analyzed using multiple statistical techniques including cluster analysis and discriminant analysis. As summarized in Table 4, Cronbach's alpha was calculated for the constructs derived from the items in the survey instruments that yielded high reliability.

## CONCLUSION

This study explored the relationships of CAPITA functionality from global IT and GKMT strategy. To that end, correlations and regressions were conducted between GKMT and CAPITA functionality from global IT to test the hypothesis. CAPITA functionality from global IT served as the dependent variable in each case. The independent predictor variable was the global knowledge management technology index. As can be seen in Table 5, CAPITA functionality from global IT is significantly correlated to global knowledge management technology at the $p < .01$ level. Multicollinearity was not an issue.

Based on the data collected, it appears that increases in knowledge management technology strategies will increase the functionality competitive advantage provided by global information technology applications. In this sample of IEPC firms, as GKMT scores increased, CAPITA functionality from global IT also increased as illustrated in Figure 2.

*Table 5. Correlations of CAPITA by GIKMT scores*

| | GKMT SCORE |
|---|---|
| **CAPITA Functionality from Global IT** | .586** |

*** Correlation is significant at the 0.01 level (2-tailed).*

*Figure 2. Plot of CAPITA functionality and GKMT score*

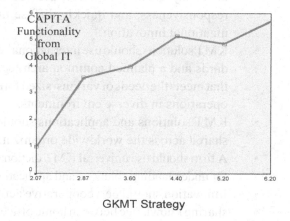

GKMT Strategy

## MANAGERIAL IMPLICATIONS

These findings support a strategy that global information and knowledge management technology should have more recognition and resources in IEPC firms. In addition, GKMT managers in IEPC firms could use these results to negotiate for an influential role in the strategic formulation discussions of the firm. Specific global knowledge management technology strategies are strongly correlated with CAPITA functionality from global IT. This study provides a heuristic guide for IEPC executives to make decisions and formulate global knowledge management technology strategies to achieve competitive advantage from IT applications. The following list provides a summary of strategic guidelines to achieve competitive functionality using global knowledge management technologies.

- The main role of foreign operations should be to implement parent company strategies.
- New knowledge should be developed at the parent company and then transferred to foreign units.
- A firm's KMT should provide coordination and control necessary for efficient operations throughout the firm.
- A firm's KMT systems should be simultaneously globally efficient, provide local responsiveness, and quickly diffuse organizational innovation.
- KMT solutions should use international standards and a planned common architecture that meets the needs of various-sized foreign operations in diverse environments.
- KMT solutions and applications should be shared across the worldwide organization.
- A firm should use universal KMT dictionaries for understanding solutions and applications.
- Innovation should be a cooperative activity sharing knowledge between home office and foreign operations.
- A firm should build information and communication cost advantages through centralized knowledge management.
- A firm's KMT strategy should be focused on worldwide efficiencies from a global information and communications system.
- Organization learning should emerge from contacts between home office and foreign operations KMT personnel.
- A firm should have strong KMT linkages between the home office and foreign operations based on cooperation and mutual assistance.
- A firm should rapidly disseminate KMT innovations while continuing to provide flexibility to respond to local KMT needs of foreign operations.
- Foreign operations should receive and adapt KMT products and services offered by the parent company to the best advantage in the countries in which they operate.
- A firm should centralize its KMT systems to achieve global economies of scale.

Implications for IEPC executives from these strategies include several changes to the management of their firms including the construction value chain. For example, some IEPC firms work 24 hours a day on design projects and proposals as teams share knowledge and engineering drawings on a global intranet. At the end of the workday, the design team in the United States hands off their work and tacit knowledge to the team in Europe, who then passes along their work to the team in Asia. Eight hours later the team in the United States resumes work on the plans with the added knowledge and insight by the entire global design team.

## SUGGESTIONS FOR FUTURE RESEARCH

This was an exploratory study in a single segment of the world's largest service industry. Obviously, much more research, replications, and interpretation must be done. In general, this study calls for more global and interdisciplinary research combining insight from practitioners and theorists from strategic knowledge management, international strategic management, and global information technology. This type of multidisciplinary research is needed to better understand the complex dynamics of a globalizing knowledge economy.

Several areas of research could include the following:

1. The RBV school plays an important role in understanding Global Information and Knowledge Management Technology.
2. The knowledge-based view may provide additional insight into the strategic management of global information and knowledge management technology.

3. Other dimensions of competitive advantage from knowledge and information technologies should be analyzed including efficiencies, innovation, and sustainable competitive advantage.

Clearly, more research must be done to develop a comprehensive understanding of global information and knowledge management technologies and their impact on competitive advantage. Knowledge can be seen as part of the resource-based view of the firm, where global IT knowledge and knowledge creation, application, and storage are strategic capabilities of the firm.

## REFERENCES

Banker, R.D., Kauffman, R.J., & Mahmood, M.A. (Eds.). (1993). *Strategic information technology management: Perspectives on organizational growth and competitive advantage.* Hershey, PA: Idea Group.

Bartlett, C.A., & Ghoshal, S. (1991). Global strategic management: Impact on the new frontiers of strategy research. *Strategic Management Journal, 12,* 5-16.

Bartlett, C.A., Ghoshal, S., & Birkinshaw, J. (2003). *Transnational management: Text and cases* (4th ed.). New York: McGraw-Hill/Irwin.

Choo, C., & Bontis, N. (2002). *The strategic management of intellectual capital and organizational knowledge.* New York: Oxford University Press.

Davenport, T., & Prusak, L. (1998). *Working knowledge.* Boston: Harvard Business School Press.

Deans, P.C., & Karwan, K.R. (Eds.). (1994). *Global information systems and technology: Focus on the organization and its functional areas.* Hershey, PA: Idea Group.

Deans, P.C., & Ricks, D.A. (1993). An agenda for research linking information systems and international business: Theory, methodology and application. *Journal of Global Information Management,* (1), 6-19.

Dixon, N.M. (2000). *Common knowledge: How companies thrive by sharing what they know.* Boston: Harvard Business School Press.

Doz, Y.L., Santos, J., & Williamson, P. (2001). *From global to metanational: How companies win in the knowledge economy.* Boston: Harvard Business School Press.

Drucker, P. (2001). *Management challenges for the 21st century* (1st ed.). New York: Collins.

Drucker P.F., Garvin, D., Leonard, D., Straus, S., & Brown, J.S. (1998). *Harvard business review on knowledge management.* Boston: Harvard Business School Press.

Edvinsson, L., & Malone, M. (1997). *Intellectual capital: Realizing your company's true value by finding its hidden brainpower.* New York: HarperCollins.

Giraldo, J.P., & Schulte, W.D. (2005). An exploration of the effects of knowledge management on global leadership. *Proceedings of the Academy of International Business Southeastern United States Annual Meeting* (pp. 206-217).

Grant, R.M. (1997). The knowledge-based view of the firm: Implications for management practice. *Long Range Planning, 30*(3), 450-454.

Grant, R., & Spender, J.C. (Eds.). (1997). Knowledge and the firm: An overview. *Journal of International Business, 17,* 5-9.

Ives, B., & Jarvenpaa, S.L. (1991). Application of global information technology: Key issues for management. *MIS Quarterly,* 33-49.

Johnson, J.H. Jr., Lenn, D.J., & O'Neill, H.M. (1997). Patterns of competition among American firms in a global industry: Evidence from the U.S. construction equipment industry. *Journal of International Management, 3*(3), 207-239.

Liebowitz, J., & Wilcox, L.C. (1997). *Knowledge elements and its integrative elements.* New York: CRC Press.

Nonaka, I., & Takeushi, H. (1995). *The knowledge-creating company.* New York: Oxford University Press.

Palvia, S., Palvia, P., & Zigli, R. (Eds.). (1992). *The global issues of information technology management.* Hershey, PA: Idea Group.

Prahalad, C.K., & Doz, Y.L. (1987). *The multinational mission: Balancing local demands and global vision.* Boston: The Free Press.

O'Dell, C., & Grayson Jr., C.J. (1998). *If only we knew what we know: The transfer of internal knowledge and best practice.* New York: The Free Press.

Revilak, A. (2006). *Knowledge management and innovation: An analysis of knowledge factors controlled by governments and their impact on patent creation.* Unpublished Doctoral Dissertation, George Washington University, USA.

Ribiere, V., Park, H., & Schulte, W.D. (2004). Critical attributes of organizational culture that promote knowledge management technology success. *Journal of Knowledge Management, 8*(3), 106-117.

Roche, E., & Blaine, M. (Eds.). (1993). *Information technology in multinational enterprises.* Northampton (USA): Edward Elgar.

Schulte, W.D. (2000). The strategic management of global information technology: Theoretical foundations. In E. Roche & M. Blaine (Eds.), *Information technology in multinational enterprises.* Northampton (USA): Edward Elgar.

Schulte, W.D. (2004). Information and knowledge management technologies and competitive advantage in global organizations. *Proceedings of the*

*Academy of International Business Southeastern United States Annual Meeting* (pp. 25-36).

Schulte, W.D. (1997). Is globalocalization the most effective strategic response for international contractors? *Proceedings of the Academy of International Business UK Chapter Annual Meeting* (pp. 455-473).

Schulte, W.D., & Sample, T.L. (2006). Efficiencies from knowledge management technologies in a military enterprise. *Journal of Knowledge Management, 10*(6).

Schwartz, D. (Ed.). (2005). *Encyclopedia of knowledge management.* Hershey, PA: Idea Group.

Sethi, V., & King, W.R. (1994). Development of measures to assess the extent to which an information technology application provides competitive advantage. *Management Science, 40*(2), 1601-1621.

Simon, S.J., & Grover, V. (1993). Strategic use of information technology in international business: A framework for information technology application. *Journal of Global Information Technology, 1*(2), 33-44.

Spender, J.C. (1996). Organizational knowledge, learning and memory: Three concepts in search of a theory. *Journal of Organizational Change Management, 9*(1), 63-78.

Stankosky, M. (Ed.). (2005). *Creating the discipline of knowledge management: The latest in university research.* Oxford: Elsevier Butterworth-Heinemann.

Stewart, T. (1997). *Intellectual capital: The new wealth of organizations.* New York: Doubleday.

Sveiby, K.E. (1997). *The new organizational wealth: Managing & measuring knowledge-based assets.* San Francisco: Berrett-Koehler.

# Chapter X
# Comparing Cultural and Political Perspectives of Data, Information, and Knowledge Sharing in Organisations

**D. Hart**
*Australian National University, Australia*

**L. Warne**
*Defense Science and Technology Organization, Australia*

## ABSTRACT

*This paper raises issues concerning data, information, and knowledge sharing in organisations and, in particular, compares an organisational cultural analysis of why such sharing is often difficult to achieve with an organisational political one. The issues raised are often insufficiently attended to by practitioners who are attempting to build technological information and knowledge management systems. The driver for the paper is that despite impressive advances in technology and its now almost ubiquitous presence in organisations, as well as academic study over several decades, many of the benefits originally expected concerning improved data, information, and knowledge sharing have not materialised as expected. Basic reasons for this lie in the lack of attention to the cultural foundations of organisations and because matters relating to organisational power and political matters are often misunderstood, overlooked, or ignored. These different perspectives are discussed and contrasted in order to tease out the important differences between them and assess the prospects for a synthesis. It is concluded that while there are important commonalities between the two perspectives there are also fundamental differences, notably regarding what are causes and what are effects and, therefore, how to go about effecting change regarding data, information, and knowledge sharing.*

## INTRODUCTION

Flatter organisational hierarchies, decentralised decision-making, and so on, enabled through appropriate use of information technologies for data, information, and knowledge sharing, have been proposed as the way for firms to gain a competitive advantage in today's dynamic and interdependent world, and it may even be that many people in such firms acknowledge this to be true. The question, then, is why do so many efforts and systems that are targeted at enabling such sharing and providing the capabilities it would permit fail as often as they do? If communication and sharing of data, information, and knowledge are the keys to strategic organisational capabilities, then why is it rarely achieved, at least to the extent many think is worthwhile or even essential, when there is little doubt that the technological capability exists to do it (but see Hislop [2002] for a sceptical view regarding knowledge sharing via information technology)?

Knowledge management (KM), like information systems (IS), is derived from, and dependent on, a number of reference disciplines. The richness of both areas could be said to be due, at least partially, to the multiple perspectives of the numerous branches of learning that are applied to the study of the effective use of data, information, and knowledge in organisations. In IS and KM, many heated discussions haven taken place as researchers and practitioners argue their perspectives on everything from basic definitions to the intricacies of IS and KM systems. This is not necessarily a bad situation because often new understandings and innovative solutions are derived from wide-ranging but constructive argument and discussion. This paper is intended to fit this mold — to be a wide-ranging but constructive argument, discussion, and comparison of different views — and is the first of what the authors hope will be a continuing, as well as a useful, series of dialectic discussions on aspects of IS and KM that engage and elicit input from a wider audience as well as encompassing debate about additional perspectives over and above those presented here. More specifically, what we aim to achieve in this paper is to first outline and compare an organisational culture perspective on data, information, and knowledge sharing with an organisational political one (as represented by the views of the two authors). By doing so, we wish to tease out the important differences between them, identify any irreconcilable aspects, and assess the potential for a synthesis. Note, however, that while we have labelled our two perspectives "organisational culture" and "organisational politics" for brevity as well as convenience, it should be recognised that they are two particular instances that may be fairly categorised thus and are not intended as archetypes representative of all such views.

## THEORETICAL BACKGROUND

For more than three decades researchers and practitioners have been concerned about the high failure rate of information systems and, more recently, knowledge management projects (e.g., Ewusi-Mensah & Przasnyski, 1991; Hart & Warne, 1997; Lyytinen & Hirschheim, 1987; Sauer, 1993). As the industry has evolved, the search for factors influencing success and failure has intensified, but, although there may have been incremental improvements, this intensive activity does not seem to have resulted in dramatic changes to the success rate for information systems and knowledge management projects. While definitions and rates of failure continue to be debated, information and the systems that provide it have become an increasingly integral part of modern business life and knowledge generation, and no organisation of any size can exist without them (Applegate, Austin, & McFarlan, 2003; Beynon-Davies, 2002). A variety of factors have been identified by researchers as relevant to, or as contributing causes of, the problems that have been experienced, and we briefly survey these before presenting and comparing our different perspectives later. First, however, we explain why we do not discriminate, in this paper, between data, information, and knowledge — even though they are widely acknowledged to be different although related concepts (e.g., Awad & Ghaziri, 2004).

## Data, Information, and Knowledge

Of data, information, and knowledge, the nature and definition of knowledge remains more controversial than that of the other two. For example, Venzin, von Krogh, and Roos (1998) argue that knowledge has been conceived from three epistemologically distinct perspectives: the cognitivist (as exemplified by Simon, 1993), connectionist (as exemplified by Zander & Kogut, 1995), and autopoetic (as exemplified by Nonaka & Takeuchi, 1995). In addition, it has also been extensively argued that the tacit/explicit distinction represents an important difference of kind when it comes to types of knowledge (Polanyi, 1966). These distinctions, however, tend to impact largely what counts as knowledge, or at least what type of knowledge it is and how or through what mechanisms that knowledge might be shared, rather than *whether* and *why* knowledge — however it is conceived — will or won't be shared. Indeed, it has been argued that it is not possible to share knowledge at all, since knowledge inherently resides in the inaccessible mind of the knower; it is, in fact, only possible to share data (Boisot, 2002) and, arguably, information rather than knowledge itself. We believe, therefore, that the kinds of distinctions outlined previously are of less importance when it comes to the issues in which we are interested, namely assessing and comparing ideas about *whether* and *why*, rather than *what* and *how*, knowledge may or may not be shared. Indeed, we think that at the kind of broad perspective we are taking we can, for the purposes of our discussion, put aside not only differences in conceptions of knowledge but also

the clearer and more widely accepted differences between data and information as well. Thus, while we acknowledge the differences between the concepts of data, information, and knowledge, we treat them together in what follows because we believe that many and perhaps all of the issues we address in this paper affect them in similar if not identical ways.

## Organisations and Data, Information, and Knowledge Sharing

The widespread application of information and communications technologies (ICT) has generally increased the complexity of human workplaces and has placed new demands on the thinking and communication of individuals. In such contexts, traditional rational systematic processes have limitations, and greater demands are made on meta-cognition and intuitive thinking (Crawford, 2003; Woodhouse, 2000). Solving complex problems increasingly involves teams of people with effective communication and cooperation not only within the team itself but also with outsiders such as external stakeholders and those who will be affected by any emerging solution that may be developed. Typically data and information gathering, knowledge generation, and sharing of all these resources are involved. With the wider use of technologies to achieve routine or programmed tasks, the dynamic of human productivity in organisations has shifted into a "meta-realm" of shared activity. Daneshgar, Ray, and Rabhi (2003) note that, in such contexts, it is not only what a person knows that is important but also what they believe should be shared, when, how, and with whom.

Despite the claimed benefits of sharing data, information, and knowledge in organisations, and the undoubted and ever-increasing capabilities of ICT to enable it, sharing evidently remains remarkably difficult. For example, more than a decade ago, Davenport, Eccles, and Prusak (1992) said that "the rhetoric and technology of information management have far out-paced the ability of people to understand and agree on what information they need and then to share it [so] the information-based organization is largely a fantasy," and, arguably, the situation has not changed much since. Kendall and Kendall (2002), discussing the management of e-commerce projects, said "organizational politics can come into play, because often units feel protective of the data they generate and do not understand the need to share them across the organization." Evidently, motivations for sharing data, information, and knowledge—and perhaps even more importantly, motivations for *not* sharing (e.g., Hart, 2002)—need to be better understood. But this understanding needs to be built on an appropriate underlying organisational theory or metaphor (e.g., Morgan, 1997), such as provided by the organisational culture or organisational politics-based views of organisational functioning. Moreover, the chosen theoretical base can be expected to influence the nature of the understanding developed, and it is this aspect on which our paper is focussed.

Despite the impressive advances in both hardware and software information technology over several decades, and its now almost ubiquitous presence in organisations, the experience and research of both the authors and others shows that many of the benefits expected from improved data, information, and knowledge sharing have not materialised. Moreover, the literature puts forward a range of factors relevant to the issue, but it remains unclear which are primary and which are secondary or consequential factors in explaining why data, information, and knowledge sharing in organisations is difficult while at the same time desirable, as it evidently is. As mentioned earlier, the authors have somewhat different perspectives on these matters, one believing that inadequate user requirements analysis and the lack of attention to the cultural foundations of organisations are major factors, and the other thinking that issues relating to ownership, trust, and organisational power and politics are more important. An outline of the different positions follows.

## AN ORGANISATIONAL CULTURE PERSPECTIVE

It is commonly argued that building information and knowledge management systems that people and organisations need and will use effectively is all about understanding how people work in the context of that organisation's culture (e.g., Ahmed, Kok, & Loh, 2002, p. 49). However, it is first necessary to briefly review what we mean by "organisational culture."

Schein (1997) defines organisational culture, or, as he more generally terms it, the "culture of a group" as:

*A pattern of shared basic assumptions that the group learned as it solved its problems of external adaptation and internal integration that has worked well enough to be considered valid and, therefore, to be taught to new members as the correct way to perceive, think and feel in relation to those problems.*

Other definitions differ in detail but most include reference, in one form or another, to:

- Shared values, beliefs and foundational assumptions;
- Common norms of behaviour, customs, practices, rituals, and symbols;
- Shared traditions, myths, meanings and cognitions of the group or organisational world that are inculcated into newcomers through a socialisation process;

and, in what follows, this is the sense in which we use the term "culture" as it applies to organisations.

Individuals belonging to the same organisation (other than, perhaps, a dysfunctional one) can be expected to have, to some degree, a common identity with other organisational members, to share an understanding of their organisational world, and to subscribe, at least in general terms, to their organisation's overall goals. If not, then they would not, or should not, be in that organisation. A common identity gives everyone a similar way of describing and making sense of their world, of determining what is significant and important, and of how to use resources in the environment (Jordan, 1993). Having this common view of the workplace and one's role in it enables effective communication, the development of trust and shared understanding as well as acting to expedite sharing of data, information, and knowledge, and improve learning and work processes. In turn, sharing data, information, and knowledge acts in a positive feedback loop to enhance the common identity and shared understanding on which it is originally founded. Common identity is influenced by issues around goal alignment, cultural and social identity, language, morale, and workplace policies; in short, the organisation's culture.

Common identity does not, however, imply that people in organisations have, or should have, robotic, identical points of view. Of course, individual human beings are unique. But we are social creatures, by and large, and we like to band together under uniting banners, and in an effective organisation where employees feel valued and morale is high, these banners will be shared organisational objectives and a unifying degree of shared understanding. On the other hand, low morale brings about higher levels of alienation toward senior management (Ali, Warne, Agostino, & Pascoe, 2001; Warne, Ali, Pascoe, & Agostino, 2001), and this has obvious implications for the successful progression of organisations to an ideal standard from this common-identity point of view.

Daft and Lewin (1993) have said that organisations increasingly need to make better use of their information systems to achieve flatter hierarchies, decentralised decision-making, a greater capacity for the tolerance of ambiguity, permeable internal and external boundaries, empowerment of employees, the capacity for renewal, self-organising units, and self-integrating coordination. Data, information, and knowledge are strategi-

cally important resources because these types of organisational capabilities are a direct result of sharing, integrating, and applying them. The effective maintenance, communication, transfer, and sharing of information and knowledge is the ubiquitous supportive framework that is needed for the creation and maintenance of strategic organisational outcomes and, if it is not already in place, requires a culture that encourages, supports, and values the efforts of the members of the organisation in achieving them.

Working collaboratively is essential to organisational success and for successful problem solving. Very few people work alone or achieve results by themselves, so the people who interact together and yet have different tasks and responsibilities need to understand what each of them are trying to do, why they are doing it, how they are doing it, and what results to expect. This implies the need to specify and build information systems that give effect to this collaboration, enabling the sharing of data, information, and knowledge so those who need it can find it, access it, and use it when it is required. It is because many organisations now operate in a climate of uncertainty, dynamism, and interdependence that they need to make better use of their information and knowledge-based systems and, among other things, it is this that implies better user requirements analysis for those systems. Improvements in this area, which the existence of an appropriate organisational culture enhances, would provide the ability to build adaptive systems people will use to share the data, information, and knowledge they have or need. Such systems would support the way they want to work and collaborate rather than expecting them to adapt to using whatever systems are built for them, as tends to be the case currently. Organisations, their work, and the problems they face are ever more dynamic, and we continue to build largely static systems for them. However, adding information systems solutions are not always the way to fix problems. First, it is necessary to have a culture of collaboration and sharing and a reward and incentive system that rewards teams rather than individuals, so it is clear the organisation values teamwork and collaboration.

Systems thinking is also tightly coupled with effective mobilisation of data, information, and knowledge resources, and contributes to the development of common identity. Systems thinking, according to Senge (1992), requires a shift of mind—from seeing ourselves as separate to seeing ourselves as connected to, and part of, an organisation or organisational sub-unit. The presence or absence of this type of thinking is closely linked to the nature of the organisational culture and, if present, supported, and encouraged by that culture, is accompanied by generally higher levels of interaction between staff and by higher levels of data, information, and knowledge sharing. Because every individual in an organisation needs information and other resources to solve problems, and since few, if any, ever solve a problem in complete isolation, an individual's network is one of his or her most important resources. Both personal and social networks are an important means of acquiring, propagating, and sharing data, information, and knowledge. Moreover, the individuals in the network can make their own knowledge, expertise, and experience more readily available. In this way, the knowledge and other resources available to any one person, in their work and when problem solving, are multiple, and there is no way it can be thought of as a solitary activity. Again, however, it is the existence of a supportive organisational culture that underpins, and in turn is itself enhanced by, the creation and flourishing of such networks and the benefits they bring.

Apart from satisfying social needs, informal networks also play a pivotal role in knowledge propagation. New knowledge often begins with the individual making personal knowledge available to others as the central activity of knowledge-creating organisations. Through conversations people discover what they know and what others know, and in the process of sharing, new knowledge is created. Technology such as e-mails, faxes, and telephones are invaluable aids in the process of data, information, and knowledge sharing, but they are only supporting tools. Sharing depends on the quality of conversations, formal or informal, that people have, and whether and between whom these conversations occur are dependent on the organisational culture that is in place. Webber (1993) aptly describes it as, "conversations—not rank, title, or the trappings of power—determine who is literally and figuratively 'in the loop' and who is not." Individual and shared perceptions of the organisation, and how it operates, provide an essential backdrop to problem solving within an organisational context. These perceptions may consist of deeply ingrained assumptions, generalisations, or even pictures or images that influence how people within an organisation understand their organisational world and how they should act within it (Senge, 1992), and this is the organisational culture again.

The importance of these perceptions cannot be stressed enough, because they directly influence the construction of individuals' knowledge and understandings that they draw upon in their day-to-day-activities—their shared perceptions. One important example lies in appreciating the ways in which an organisation's formal rules and processes can be bent to achieve a desired outcome. This class of knowledge can empower people to solve problems by expanding the range of solutions that may be available and by giving them confidence to improvise or innovate. Conversely, a lack of knowledge or incorrect perceptions will constrain the types of solutions that can be found.

The role technology plays in all this is as an enabler and aid in developing and supporting the right culture for information and knowledge sharing. An organisational culture that recognises the value of knowledge and its exchange is a crucial element in whether information and knowledge work is successfully carried out or not. Such a culture provides the opportunity for personal contact so that tacit knowledge, which cannot effectively be captured in procedures or represented in documents and databases, can be transferred. For example, Webber (1993) claims that, "conversations are the way knowledge workers discover what they know, share it with their colleagues, and in the process create new knowledge for the organization." In a culture that values knowledge, managers recognise not just that knowledge generation is important for business success but also that it can be nurtured with time and space (Davenport & Prusak, 1998). On the other hand, low morale and its consequent effects on data, information, and knowledge sharing has frequently been coupled with comments about not understanding the motivation or agenda of more senior staff. Lack of understanding not only affects morale but also has an impact on trust, organisational cohesiveness, goal alignment, and common identity, and, consequently, on opportunities and motivation for learning and innovation, and on general productivity.

Finally, while it has to be admitted that in most if not all organisations there are almost certainly going to be people who are motivated primarily by individual needs, power, and politics, and who may even be corrupt or dishonest in their pursuit of their particular aims, this is not generally true. Most people, by contrast, enjoy the experience of working in teams toward shared goals and, provided with the right environment (organisational culture) and means (e.g., technological information or knowledge management systems) that are based on their *real* needs, through effective requirements analysis, for example, will willingly engage in sharing their data, information, and knowledge resources to solve organisational problems and give effect to their work.

## AN ORGANISATIONAL POLITICS PERSPECTIVE

The classical organisational theorists and, to a lesser extent, those belonging to the cultural school, subscribe to the view that organisations are normally characterised by a "philosophy of sharing trust and care for others" (Kakabadse & Parker, 1984). Those for which this is not true tend to be regarded as dysfunctional. However, the power and politics school of organisational thinkers reject this assumption, insisting instead that "power is part of all organizational behaviour" and the effective use of it, which is a political act, "secures both organizational and personal goals in most (if not all) organizational action" (Fairholm, 1993).

The power and political view pictures an organisation as a collection of groups and individuals who are diverse in their aims, beliefs, interests, values, preferences, and perceptions of their organisational world and, to this extent, is compatible with the cultural view. However, it also argues that differences of opinion are common (if not the norm), coalitions form and dissolve, and disagreements, conflict, and political activity are a natural and inevitable part of organisational life. Nevertheless, as Ferris, Fedor, Chachere, and Pondy (1989) say:

*Organizational scientists have had different notions of what constitutes political behaviour. Some have defined organizational politics in terms of the behaviour of interest groups to use power to influence decision making [while] others have focused on the self-serving and organizationally non-sanctioned nature of individual behaviour in organization [and] still others have characterized organizational politics as a social influence process with potentially functional or dysfunctional organizational consequences...or simply the management of influence.*

We see organisational politics in the same light as Checkland and Holwell (1998) and also Pfeffer (1981), the latter of whom says:

*Organizational politics involves those activities taken within organizations to acquire, develop, and use power and other resources to obtain one's preferred outcomes in a situation in which there is uncertainty or dissens[ion] about choices.*

As Sauer (1993) says, "power accrues to those who control resources which are important to others" and, as we have seen, politics entails the use of power to achieve desired ends in the face of dissension. Furthermore, the sources of a particular party's power will be significantly dependent on the pre-existing social and organisational structure, which will largely determine who has what degree of control over which resources. All organisational sections are generally custodians of some form of data, information, and knowledge resources. And the power people have through their control of resources is not just a matter of formally assigned or de-facto ownership but of consciously and actually having arbitrary control over their availability and use. Indeed, there is not only the matter of what data, information, and knowledge individuals and groups in the organisation *actually* own or have control over (and, they think, rightly so) but also what they think or "know" they *should* own or have control over but which in fact they do not. As can be imagined, this may constitute a potent source of conflict and organisational politicking if different parties have significantly differing perceptions in this area. In fact, as roles in an organisation become more defined by the information people and groups hold and control, they will increasingly view that information as a source of power and importance for them, being more protective of its ownership and being less inclined to share it or devolve responsibility for it as a result (Davenport et al., 1992; Hart, 1999).

Arguably, the occurrence of power-based behaviour and organisational politicking when trying to succeed, or even just cope, in a dynamic, interlinked, and mutually dependent environment is less likely when those who need to cooperate communicate effectively. But the effectiveness of communication is highly dependent on the

level of trust between the involved parties, too (Drucker, 1999). A lot of research has demonstrated that the extent to which one individual (and, by extension, a group of individuals as well) trusts another has a significant effect on their willingness to exchange data, information, and knowledge with the other (e.g., Erickson, 1979; Fine & Holyfield, 1996). It has been argued that this is especially true where there is uncertainty or ignorance as to the motives and actions of the other party, particularly with respect to possible actions and outcomes that may result from or be enabled by the act of sharing (Hart, 2004). If these could be predicted with absolute certainty, then trust would not be required but, when they cannot, as in most "real world" circumstances, a degree of trust is necessary to make human action and interaction possible. Concerns over how others might use shared data, information, or knowledge often restricts one's readiness to part with it (Erickson, 1979), and simply belonging to the same organisation may not be enough to provide a basis for the kind of sharing that may, on overtly rational cost-benefit grounds, be both desirable and expected. Moreover, adding information systems to the mix complicates things further since, once a piece of data, information, or knowledge has been committed to such a system, direct control by its original owner over when, why, and with whom it may then be shared will most likely be lost.

Common identity and shared understanding are often spoken of as enabling and in turn being supported by data, information, and knowledge sharing. However, it may be argued that, even if achievable, common identity and shared understanding are always provisional, incomplete, and context-dependent, since they are built upon communicative acts that are always subject to interpretation and, therefore, at least to some extent ambiguous (Marshall & Brady, 2001). Likewise, shared data, information, and knowledge are subject to interpretation, and the meanings derived from them are similarly dependent on context and other actor-dependent factors. Therefore, no attempt at communication, whether person to person or through a technological information or knowledge management system, is ever completely unambiguous.

Indeed, it may be argued that it is never possible to truly achieve shared understanding because each of us, at least in certain important respects, constructs our own reality and individual understanding based on our own prior experience. On this argument, shared understanding can only be achieved, at best, in a limited, provisional, and incomplete sense since each individual interprets the same events or evidence in their own and invariably unique way. Consider, for example, the different views people have of the motivations and meaning of the words and actions of their political leaders, even when these views are derived from exactly the same evidential base. Moreover, even if it could be achieved completely, shared understanding in no way would necessarily entail agreement about the implications of the mutually understood situation. The interests and motivations to action of the different parties who achieved this shared understanding could still diverge dramatically, potentially generating significant power struggles and political activity that could impede further data, information, and knowledge sharing even despite the achieved mutual understanding.

According to the power and political view, organisations are best understood as sites where people and groups interact in pursuit of a range of interests (Dunford, 1992). Some of these interests may be compatible or complementary, in which case limited collaboration may occur; other interests will differ and conflict. This political perspective highlights the complexity and multiplicity of objectives within organisations where outcomes are likely to revolve around the ability to get one's preferences accepted; to have the greatest influence on decisions made and directions taken; where actions can be analysed in terms of power interests; and the mobilisation

of support and negotiation, all of which are not always aligned with the organisation's overall stated objectives. The impact of all this on data, information, and knowledge sharing is, of course, that whether or not it occurs is heavily influenced by, and indivisible from, the political interests and assessments of the various parties involved.

All this is not to indict human beings or their motives either. In fact, it is quite possible for there to be extremely good and ethical reasons for not sharing data, information, or knowledge. Organisations in the defence and security industries are good examples of where this could commonly be so. But even aside from these obvious cases, it may be argued (especially from an individual or group perspective) that it is in some situations better for overall organisational outcomes *not* to share some particular data, information, or knowledge one owns or has in one's possession. This might occur, for instance, if the act of sharing is likely to lead, in the possessor's opinion and for whatever reason, to organisational indecision, less effective or possibly inappropriate action by others, misunderstandings, conflict, or other deleterious effects. Of course, a decision not to share for these types of reasons would not be one to take lightly, but it is possible and perhaps even common that such decisions need to be taken anyway.

Instead, therefore, of trying to "overcome" resistance to sharing, it is important to recognise its sources and to accept that this sort of behaviour is not only endemic to but also more than likely inevitable in many if not all organisations, for the kinds of reasons outlined previously. This means that it is vital to recognise the need of individuals and groups within the organisation to manage their own data, information, and knowledge resources—including deciding with whom, when, how, and why to share them — in accordance with their understanding of their own, others, and their organisation's overall needs. Rather than fighting to defeat their control of these resources, they should be supported in their management of them, which includes *enabling* and making it easy for them to share with other people and groups in the organisation as their understanding, discretion, and willingness dictates, rather than attempting to *force* them to do so. The emergence of the Internet is perhaps both the classic and ultimate example, albeit a non-organisational one, of this kind of process at work. Experience indicates that anything more ambitious or directive is just not going to succeed as well as intended or desired.

## A SUMMARY

Table 1 summarises and contrasts the main standpoints, by general topic area, put forward in the two perspectives outlined earlier.

*Table 1. Main standpoints for organisational culture and politics-based perspective*

| Topic Area | The Organisational Culture-Based Perspective | The Organisational Politics-Based Perspective |
|---|---|---|
| Sharing and the coordination and integration of organisational work | Data, information, and knowledge sharing are necessary for the effective coordination and integration of organisational work | Coordination and integration of organisational work are best effected by *directed* and *selective* data, information and knowledge sharing |
| Shared understanding and common identity | Data, information, and knowledge sharing are both enabled by and improve shared understanding and common identity amongst organisational members | Context is all-important so, other than in a limited and local sense, shared understanding and common identity are unachievable ideals |
| Sharing and organisational alignment | Data, information, and knowledge sharing lead to goal alignment and common purpose amongst organisational members | Data, information, and knowledge sharing occur between organisational members who perceive their goals and purposes are already aligned |
| Sharing and organisational culture and politics | Data, information, and knowledge sharing depend on the creation of an organisational culture that fosters and recognises the value of such sharing, thereby avoiding or reducing political problems | Changing culture is a long, tedious, and difficult process and, in any case, sharing (if it occurs) is more the outcome of normal organisational political motivations and assessment than it is of cultural characteristics |
| Sharing and the communication of meaning | Data, information, and knowledge sharing will enable the free flow of meaningful communication throughout the organisation | Meaning is the result of a process of contextually mediated interpretation; data and information do not, in themselves, carry any inherent meaning |
| Unwillingness to share | Data, information, and knowledge sharing are inhibited by indefensible motives (such as self-interest, power, and politics) inimical to proper organisational functioning | Unwillingness to share data, information or knowledge may be driven by genuine and valid concerns for better organisational functioning as well as by less defensible motivations |
| Approaches to sharing | Wider and more effective data, information, and knowledge sharing can be achieved by better understanding organisational work and system requirements definition, as well as the fostering of a sharing internal culture | Supporting individuals and groups in the management of their own data, information, and knowledge resources, but at the same time enabling and making it easy for them to share with whom and when they see fit, is the way to approach the sharing issue |

## COMPARING THE PERSPECTIVES

Having now outlined and characterised the two perspectives of interest, it should be possible to assess the major differences between them and to see what the prospects might be for some kind of synthesis.

### Causality

Inspection and reflection on the contents of the summary table reveals that one important difference between the two views of data, information, and knowledge sharing relates to causality. That is, which phenomena are causes and which are effects? In broad terms, and admittedly oversimplifying somewhat, the cultural perspective tends to regard data, information, and knowledge sharing as a cause of other desirable organisational effects, rather than the reverse. For example, it is typically argued that sharing is necessary for and, by implication, leads to more effective coordination and integration of organisational activities; improves shared understanding and common identity as well as goal alignment and common purpose among organisational members; reduces political problems; and enhances the flow of meaningful communication. If, therefore, one could establish and embed data, information, and knowledge sharing, then these effects could be expected to follow. By contrast, in at least one important respect, the political perspective sees things the other way around causally, and in other cases denies that the effect claimed by adherents to the cultural view is, in fact, achievable at all through attempts to share data, information, and knowledge. In particular, according to the political perspective, data, information, and knowledge sharing are more a *result* of goal and purpose alignment between organisational actors than they are a *cause* of it. Moreover, according to the cultural perspective, the assumption tends to be that it is necessary to create an organisational culture that would be conducive to and foster data,

information, and knowledge sharing in order to encourage and support the emergence of such sharing. That is, in simplified terms, the direction of the causal link is viewed as being essentially from the creation of the appropriate culture (the cause) to the occurrence of sharing (the effect). Of course, it is not that simple because of feedback effects, but nevertheless the emphasis does tend to be on the creation of an appropriate culture first, as a means of enabling data, information, and knowledge sharing to occur. According to the political perspective, however, while it is usually acknowledged that culture has its effects, it is also viewed as much more resistant to intentional manipulation than is typically assumed by cultural theorists. Instead, data, information, and knowledge sharing are viewed as the outcome of a primarily political (i.e., power-based) process reflecting existing organisational stakeholders and their respective interests and relationships.

### Levers of Change

Consequent upon the causal differences of the two perspectives are important differences regarding how change can be effected, or if indeed it can be effected by intentional action at all. In particular, because the cultural perspective tends to regard data, information, and knowledge sharing as a cause, or at least necessary precursor, of other desired effects, adherents of this view tend to focus primarily on means by which such sharing can be achieved. This accounts for arguments that propose, for example, that if the user requirements definition process in systems development could be improved to the point that the resulting systems actually served the real needs of the users, then data, information, and knowledge sharing would follow naturally. By contrast, those of the political persuasion would tend to argue, however, that it matters not how "good" any technological system might be in enabling data, information, and knowledge sharing—in the technical, design, and usability sense—as such sharing will not occur unless it is compatible with the existing political landscape in the organisation. Accordingly, it is then urged, it is inappropriate and possibly even counter-productive to engage in systems development (no matter how good the user requirements definition process might be) if inadequate attention is paid to this political landscape and, if necessary, effort put into changing it before any systems to support data, information, and knowledge sharing are constructed. Or, if it proves infeasible to significantly alter the political landscape of the relevant parts of the organisation, then such systems should be explicitly designed to be compatible with that landscape. All else is pointless.

## Impediments and Remedies

No matter whether one is of the cultural or political persuasion, it is evident and admitted that getting different parties to share organisational data, information, and knowledge is often difficult to achieve. No disagreement there, but there is some disagreement when it comes to motivations. The culturally oriented view characteristically admits few if any defensible reasons or motives against most data, information, and knowledge sharing, which are essentially regarded as wholly beneficial to the organisation. Any motive or reason standing in the way must therefore be an indication of some organisational dysfunction (e.g., an unwillingness to share may be a symptom of a conflict or a bid for more organisational power or influence). By contrast, the opposite view allows that refusal to share may not necessarily be nefarious, arising as it may through, for example, concerns about possible misinterpretations of significance or meaning by the receiving parties and potentially leading to mistakes or other organisationally deleterious actions. This difference means that cultural adherents draw the conclusion that refusal to share implies that the *people* who are refusing need to be encouraged or educated as to the benefits of sharing (or the organisational culture to which they belong needs

changing) so their refusal can be *overcome*. On the other hand, political adherents accept that sharing will generally only occur between those who are already disposed to do so anyway, and attempts to encourage, educate, or coerce wider or different patterns of sharing are likely not only to be unsuccessful but even counter-productive. It is instead better to make sharing *easier* without attempting to be more directive about what should be shared or with whom, and especially given that the motivations for not sharing may in fact be validly driven by concerns for the overall organisational functioning anyway.

## PROSPECTS FOR A SYNTHESIS

Both the cultural and political views of organisations, among other metaphors, are well known and established (e.g., Morgan, 1997) and have been acknowledged as closely related and complementary (Ferris et al., 1989). Indeed, Ferris et al. (1989), who use the term "myth" to mean "a manifestation of the larger concept of organizational culture," say: "An integration of myths and politics seems to be a quite natural one [because] the content of many myths is often political in nature and myths are used to define the meaning of current political activities." However, while this may be so, according to our analysis there are still some important divergences between these perspectives when it comes to interpreting, understanding, and explaining organisational data, information, and knowledge sharing behaviour.

One potential approach to integrating the two perspectives may be via the concept of sub-cultures. Perhaps it is the case that politically contending parties in an organisation, and, more particularly, those that are reluctant or refuse to share data, information, or knowledge with each other, can generally be identified with different sub-cultures within it. After all, by definition, different sub-cultures hold significantly different value sets, beliefs, assumptions, norms of behaviour, and so on, and these could surely function as a source of power struggles, conflict, and political activity concerning not only data, information, and knowledge sharing but also other areas of organisational activity. Such an identification would, however, imply that political activity regarding data, information, and knowledge sharing would occur much more often between individuals or groups belonging to different sub-cultures than within them and, as far as we are aware, this is a proposition that has yet to be empirically tested. But even if it should turn out to be so, this would most likely still leave some significant differences between what we have termed the cultural and political perspectives regarding organisational data, information, and knowledge sharing, not least in their ascriptions of causality and therefore ideas on how to effect change.

## CONCLUSION

Why is it that so many IS and KM initiatives do not reach their full potential or, at worst, result in failure? Technological tools of ever-increasing sophistication are available for use in achieving the dissemination and sharing of data, information, and knowledge across the organisation. However, despite the existence and capability of these tools, data integration, information sharing, and knowledge management initiatives in many organisations all too often do not deliver the benefits sought from them.

As the two perspectives outlined and contrasted previously are intended to illustrate, the authors argue that the foundational assumptions from which matters of organisational data, information, and knowledge sharing are viewed are an important issue that can materially affect the approaches taken to address these issues. Such foundational assumptions can significantly influence, for example, the ambition and scope of IS-based efforts to support organisational data, information, and knowledge sharing and, if such

efforts fail (for whatever overt reasons), they often fail both spectacularly and expensively for the organisation concerned. It is critical, therefore, to better understand not only what *should* be attempted but also what is *feasible* to attempt and *how* best to attempt it. Understanding the foundations from which one is approaching the problem is, therefore, far from simply an academic exercise as very practical implications attach to its outcome.

The authors and their colleagues are pursuing ongoing research work, involving what are now called network-centric-organisations, intended to illuminate and clarify the kinds of fundamental issues raised in the debate presented in this paper. The results and conclusions of this work will be reported in due course.

## ACKNOWLEDGMENTS

While the views expressed, and any mistakes, are those of the authors, our thanks go to the three anonymous reviewers for their constructive and perceptive analyses and criticisms, which have contributed significantly to improving the overall quality of this paper.

## REFERENCES

Ahmed, P. K., Kok, L. K., & Loh, A. Y. E. (2002). *Learning through knowledge management*. Butterworth Heinemann.

Ali, I., Warne, L., Agostino, K., & Pascoe, C. (2001, June 19-22). Working and learning together: Social learning in the Australian defence organisation. In *Proceedings of Informing Science Conference IS2001 — Bridging Diverse Disciplines* [CD-ROM], Krakow, Poland.

Applegate, L. M., Austin, R. D., & McFarlan, F. W. (2003). *Corporate information strategy and management: Text and cases*. McGraw-Hill Irwin.

Awad, E. M., & Ghaziri, H. M. (2004). *Knowledge management*. Prentice-Hall.

Beynon-Davies, P. (2002). *Information systems: An introduction to informatics in organizations*. Palgrave Publishing.

Boisot, M. (2002). The creation and sharing of knowledge. In C. W. Choo & N. Bontis (Eds.), *The strategic management of intellectual capital and organizational knowledge*. Oxford University Press.

Checkland, P., & Howell, S. (1998). *Information, systems and information systems*. John Wiley & Sons.

Crawford, K. (2003). *Factors affecting learning and communication in organizations: A paper commissioned by the Defence, Science and Technology Organisation (DSTO)*. Creative Interactive Systems Pty Ltd.

Daft, R. L., & Lewin, A. Y. (1993). Where are the theories for the "new" organizational forms? An editorial essay. *Organization Science, 4*, i-vi.

Daneshgar, F., Ray, P. & Rabhi, F. (2003, May 18-21). Knowledge sharing infrastructure for virtual enterprises. In M. Khosrow-Pour (Ed.), *Information Technology & Organizations: Trends, Issues, Challenges & Solutions, 2003 Information Resources Management Association International Conference* (pp. 307-309), Philadelphia, Pennsylvania. Hershey, PA: Idea Group Publishing.

Davenport, T., Eccles, R., & Prusak, L. (1992). Information politics. *Sloan Management Review 34*(1), 53-65

Davenport, T., & Prusak, L. (1998). *Working knowledge: How organizations manage what they know*. Boston: Harvard Business School Press.

Drucker, P. F. (1999, October). Beyond the information revolution. *The Atlantic Monthly*.

Dunford, R.W. (1992). *Organisational behaviour: An organisational analysis perspective*. Sydney: Addison-Wesley.

Erickson, P. E. (1979). The role of secrecy in complex organizations: From norms of Rationality to norms of distrust. *Cornell Journal of Social Relation, 14*(2), 121-138.

Ewusi-Mensah, K., & Przasnyski, Z. H. (1991). On information systems project abandonment: an exploratory study of organizational practices. *MIS Quarterly, 15*(1), 67-86.

Fairholm, G. W. (1993). *Organizational power politics*. Westpot, CT: Praeger.

Ferris, G. R., Fedor, D. B., Chachere, J. G., & Pondy, L. R. (1989). Myths and politics in organizational contexts. *Group and Organization Studies, 14*(1), 83-103.

Fine, G. A., & Holyfield, L. (1996). Secrecy, trust, and dangerous leisure: generating group cohesion in voluntary organizations. *Social Psychology Quarterly, 59*(1), 22-38.

Hart, D. (2002). Ownership as an issue in data and information sharing: a philosophically based view [Special issue]. *Australian Journal of Information Systems*, 23-29.

Hart, D., & Warne, L. (1997). *Information systems defining characteristics: A stakeholder centric view of success and failure* (Technical Paper CS0197). University College UNSW, ADFA.

Hislop, D. (2002). Mission impossible? Communicating and sharing knowledge via information technology. *Journal of Information Technology, 17*, 165-177.

Jordan, B. (1993). Ethnographic workplace studies and computer supported cooperative work. In *Proceedings of Interdisciplinary Workshop on Informatics and Psychology*, Scharding, Austria.

Kakabadse, A., & Parker, C. (Eds.). (1984). *Power, politics, and organizations*. New York: John Wiley & Sons.

Kendall, K. E., & Kendall, J. E. (2002). *Systems analysis and design*. Upper Saddle River, NJ: Prentice-Hall.

Lyytinen, K., & Hirschheim, R. A. (1987). Information system failures: A survey and classification of the empirical literature. *Oxford Surveys in Information Technology*, (4), 257-309.

Marshall, N., & Brady, T. (2001). Knowledge management and the politics of knowledge: Illustrations from complex products and systems. *European Journal of Information Systems, 10*, 99-112.

Morgan, G. (1997). *Images of organization* (new ed.). Sage Publications.

Nonaka, I., & Takeuchi, H. (1995). *The knowledge-creating company: How Japanese companies create the dynamics of innovation*. New York: Oxford University Press.

Pfeffer, J. (1981) Understanding the role of power in decision making. In J. M. Shafritz & J. S. Ott (Eds.), *Classics of organization theory*. Brooks/Cole.

Polanyi, M. (1966). *The tacit dimension*. Doubleday.

Sauer, C. (1993). *Why information systems fail: A case study approach*. Henley-On-Thames, Oxfordshire: Alfred Waller.

Schein, E. H. (1997). *Organizational culture and leadership* (2nd ed.). Jossey-Bass.

Senge, P. M. (1992). *The fifth discipline: The art and practice of the learning organization*. Sydney, NSW: Random House.

Simon, H. A. (1993). Strategy and organizational evolution. *Strategic Management Journal, 14*, 131-142.

Venzin, M., von Krogh, G., & Roos, J. (1998). Future research into knowledge management. In G. Von Krogh, J. Roos, & D. Kleine (Eds), *Knowing in Firms: Understanding Managing and Measuring Knowledge*. Sage Publications.

Warne, L., Ali, I., Pascoe, C., & Agostino, K. (2001, December). A holistic approach to knowledge management and social learning: Lessons learnt from military headquarters [Special issue on knowledge management]. *Australian Journal of Information Systems*, 127-142.

Webber, A. M. (1993, January). What's so new about the new economy? *Harvard Business Review*, 24-42.

Woodhouse, L. B. R. (2000). Personality and the use of intuition: Individual differences in strategy and performance on an implicit learning task. *European Journal of Personality, 4*(2), 157-169.

Zander, U., & Kogut, B. (1995). Knowledge and the speed of the transfer and imitation of organizational capabilities: An empirical test. *Organization Science, 6*(1), 76-92.

*This work was previously published in International Journal of Knowledge Management, 2(2), edited by M. E. Jennex, pp. 1-15, copyright 2006 by IGI Publishing, formerly Idea Group Publishing (an imprint of IGI Global).*

# Chapter XI
# Technology Trends in Knowledge Management Tools

**G. Balmisse**
*KnowledgeConsult, France*

**D. Meingan**
*Knowledge Consult, France*

**K. Passerini**
*New Jersey Institute of Technology, USA*

## ABSTRACT

*A large number of tools are available in the software industry to support different aspects of knowledge management (KM). Some comprehensive applications and vendors try to offer global solutions to KM needs; other tools are highly specialized. In this chapter, state-of-the-art KM tools grouped by specific classification areas and functionalities are described. Trends and integration efforts are detailed with a focus on identifying current and future software and market evolution.*

## BACKGROUND AND DEFINITIONS: A FOCUS ON PEOPLE AND CONTEXT

This chapter focuses on presenting the variety of tools currently available to support KM initiatives and discusses trends in the vendors' arena. However, there are many definitions of knowledge (financial, human resources, information systems, organizational behavior, and strategic management-based definitions) (Alavi & Leidner, 1999) that have resulted in equally many definitions of KM (Davenport & Prusak, 1998; Jennex, 2005). There are many definitions of knowledge (financial, human resources, information systems, organizational behavior, and strategic management-based definitions) (Alavi and Leidner, 1999) that have resulted in equally many definitions of knowledge management (KM) (Davenport and Prusak, 1998; Jennex, 2005). This

*Table 1. Knowledge and context relationships*

| Relationships | | Definitions | Examples |
|---|---|---|---|
| K= I x U where | K= Knowledge<br>I = Information<br>U = Use | **Knowledge**<br>*(Interiorized information put to action)*<br>⇑ | I am in Paris today (*user context*)<br>⇓<br>I am going to wear a coat. |
| I = D x C where | I = Information<br>D = Data<br>C = Context | **Information**<br>*(Data in context)*<br>⇑ | The temperature is $10^0$ Celsius today in Paris |
| | | **Data**<br>*(Raw facts)* | $10^0$ Celsius |

chapter focuses on presenting the variety of tools currently available to support KM initiatives and discusses trends in the vendors' arena. To place the discussion and classification of the tools within the specific framework and organizational view embraced by the authors, an operationa To place the discussion and classification of the tools within the specific framework and organizational view embraced by the authors, an operational definition of knowledge as *information accumulated and assimilated to implement a specific action* is used. Information is *data within a specific context* and data is the *raw facts, without context* (Binney, 2001; Cohen, 1998; Davenport & Harris, 2001). Table 1 summarizes the relationships among the definitions and provides a practical example to illustrate the link between data, information, and knowledge.

The example in Table 1 embeds a clear distinction: information is not transformed into knowledge unless it is accumulated, learned, and internalized by individuals. In addition, it needs to be translated into specific actions. The transformation of information into knowledge is mediated by the "individual actor," who adds value to information by creating knowledge (Davenport & De Long, 1998; Kwan & Cheung, 2006). Thus, knowledge is strictly linked and connected to the individual (or group) who creates it, which may cast doubts on the ability of information systems

tools to effectively support KM and perhaps explain some of the failures of the early tools (Biloslavo, 2005; Chua & Lam, 2005).

It follows that the "visible" part of knowledge—what the literature calls explicit as opposed to the tacit dimension of knowledge (Polanyi, 1966)—is only information regardless of the amount of other individual or project knowledge embedded into it. Therefore, the tools to collect, catalogue, organize, and share knowledge can only transfer information (the explicit knowledge) embedded in various forms and types of documents and media. When the transferred information is put back in the context of the individual recipient, its re-transformation occurs when the object of the transfer is put into action.

Figure 1 diagrams this distinction, giving to information systems a specific transfer or transportation role, rather than a substantial knowledge creation capability. Based on the definitions presented in Table 1, the roles of information management and KM are clearly distinct, even if interconnected. The tools for information management are focused on data and information transfer; the tools for KM are focused on assimilation, comprehension, and learning of the information by individuals who will, then, transform data and information into knowledge.

The key difference between information and KM is the role played by the individual actors

*Figure 1. Information systems and knowledge transfer*

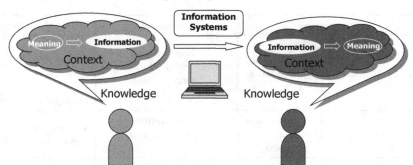

(Adamides & Karacapilidis, 2006; Davenport & Jarvenpaa, 1996; Frank & Gardoni, 2005). KM places people at the center, while information management focuses on the information infrastructure (Janev & Vranes, 2005; Ruiz-Mercader & Merono-Cerdan, 2006); KM focuses on people and their role in the organization. The first failed attempts at KM focused too heavily on tools (and the IT function often led the implementation of KM in organizations) (Davenport & Prusak, 1998). Finally, we have better understood the role played by people and brought back KM into human resources and strategic/leadership management realms (Biloslavo, 2005; Lyons, 2005).

## Knowledge Management Tools Characteristics

Within the aforementioned premises, a KM tool will focus on facilitating individual continuous learning, use, and contextualization of organizational knowledge embedded in people and documents (Alavi & Leidner, 2001). This leads to at least four key functional requirements for KM tools: (1) facilitate information contextualization; (2) intelligently transfer information; (3) facilitate social interactions and networking; and (4) present a customized human-computer interface that meets user needs.

1.  **Facilitate information contextualization.** Nonaka and Konno (1998) discuss the concept of "ba" or shared understanding and shared context. Individuals assimilate information much faster when presented in a familiar context. To facilitate *information contextualization*, metadata on its characteristics and integration within a specific environment must be attached to it before storing. This facilitates easier retrieval and management for the knowledge seeker. Past approaches to full text-based searches on documents yielded limited success, specifically when multiple media formats are stored. In addition, they yielded limited results as they decoupled the document from the context and taxonomy it belonged to. Better results are more often associated with access to the conceptual representation, structure, and links associated with the retrieved documents (Jarvenpaa & Staples, 2000; Turnbow & Kasianovitz, 2005). Sophisticated clustering and indexing search engines, like Vivisimo (www.vivisimo. com), are representative examples in this category.

2.  **Intelligently transfer information.** The transfer of information needs to be aligned with its intended use (Bhatt & Gupta, 2005).

Especially in liability issues that may emerge when the information is decoupled from the context where it is accumulated and transferred (Zhao & Bi, 2006), it is important to implement what we call "*intelligent transfer*" (Junghagen & Linderoth, 2003) Information transfer must occur by taking into account the user, the content, and the time of transfer. A tool that can optimize these three aspects can truly provide information according to the needs of the users, respecting one of the key functional foundations of KM (Argote & Ingram, 2000; Kwan & Cheung, 2006). More development is needed in this area, although upcoming location-aware applications are emerging.

3. **Facilitate social interactions and networking.** Direct communication and verbal knowledge transfer through *social interactions* among individuals is the most natural aspect of knowledge sharing (Huysman & Wulf, 2006). A KM tool must support this social aspect and facilitate exchanges. However, traditional group support tools designed to accomplish a specific objective or task (such as a project) may be ill suited to recreate the spontaneous milieu for the information and knowledge exchanges, which are important to knowledge creation.

Digital socialization tools need to encourage spontaneous as well as casual meetings with multiple views and interactions. Research on ubiquitous social computing (Snowdon & Churchill, 2004) is trying to address these specific needs by creating ad hoc, location–aware, social interaction systems within university campuses. A KM tool that can informally and formally support social interactions needs to accommodate both individual and community synchronous and asynchronous discussions; enable peer reviewing and responses; discussions rankings; and support the management of social network representations and interactions (Van Der Aalst, Reijers et al., 2005).

4. **Present a customized human-computer interface.** The tools must also support *interface customization* and ease of use. The human-computer interface ease of use and usability will drive intention to use and reuse the tools (Jarvenpaa & Staples, 2000; Turnbow & Kasianovitz, 2005). The establishment of swift trust (Hiltz & Goldman, 2005), the error-free interface; the coherent structure and organization will also impact reuse. In addition, the application interface should also be supportive of ergonomics principles and be sociable. Finally, for the

*Figure 2. KM tools framework*

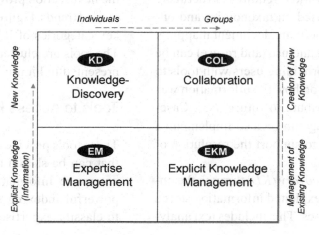

tools to support learning and utilization, they must also be geared to providing visual representations and maps linking taxonomies and documents.

Parallel to the aforementioned roles, which are meant to support individual use, a KM application needs to be designed to sustain KM implementations within the organization. This includes managing existing knowledge and supporting the creation of new knowledge. This process is embedded and thrives on information that is transferred from individuals to groups with a continuous transformation of information into knowledge through contextualization and knowledge discovery.

Figure 2 presents roles and actors linked to KM tools in enterprises and highlights their functions. As described earlier, information is converted into knowledge by individuals and groups, who are the core of the information-to-knowledge transformation process (Rollett, 2003). These tools support KM and new knowledge creation by focusing on:

- *Management of explicit knowledge (EKM)*, with specific focus on the compilation, organization, replenishment, and use of the knowledge base. Compilation and capture of knowledge includes facilitating the creation and publication of information in shared areas. Organization requires structuring information based on taxonomies and ontologies that facilitate document mapping. Replenishment and use (and re-use) can be supported by providing users with tools to add comments on how the information was used and contribute to future uses. Case-based reasoning can be also implemented in repositories to support the resolution of future problems.

- *Knowledge discovery (KD)* through the uncovering of unexploited information stored in large databases. This includes text analy-

sis and mining; knowledge extraction and automatic classification and visualization of patterns; and use of semantic mapping to link documents.

- *Expertise mapping (EM)* tools that link and facilitate knowledge exchanges within the enterprise. These tools go well beyond facilitating finding the right resources (as in employees' directories) because they dynamically ease contacts, follow ups, and communication.

- *Collaboration tools (COL)* for the production of knowledge, coordination, and communication. The production activities provide a static view of the results of team interactions and lessons learned after the exchange. The collaboration activities are more dynamic and support the definition of actors and roles, activities, and tasks throughout the duration of a project. Lastly, communication spaces facilitate direct exchanges among users and, therefore, are important new knowledge creation areas.

## An Overview of KM Tools

A number of tools are currently available to support the functionalities and processes described. Some tools are highly specialized while others try to offer comprehensive solutions to the enterprise. This section briefly lists and describes the tools; the next section provides a brief synthesis of key market trends. Figure 3 presents a summary of the key categories of KM tools and functionalities. The tools are clustered based on the framework presented in Figure 2.

## Tools to Access Knowledge [EKM$_1$]

These tools provide access to explicit knowledge that can be shared and transferred through the enterprise information systems. They rely on powerful indexing systems, including systems to classify expertise based on both content and

*Figure 3. KM tools clusters*

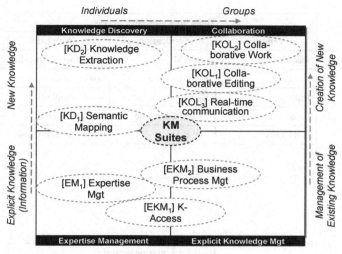

collaboration dynamics and networks within the enterprise (e.g., Entopia K-Bus). Please see Table 1.

## Tools for Semantic Mapping [KD₁]

Semantic mapping is emerging as a fundamental instrument to make sense out of the vast amount of data and information available in increasingly large repositories (Davies & Duke, 2005). Semantic mapping tools are meant to quickly support presentation of information, analysis, and decision making. The extent of interaction with the knowledge map varies by tools, with some tools being mostly static visualizations and others allowing continuous and dynamic interactivity by changing the data views. For example, KartooKM provides many different views from centric mapping; to clustering; topographical maps; interactive trees; closeness and social networks maps; circular maps; and animated charts. Ontology tools are also part of this category as they enable users to organize information and knowledge by groups and schemata that represent the organizational knowledge base (e.g., Ontopia Knowledge Suite, OKS 3.0) (Parpola, 2005). Please see Table 2.

## Tools for Knowledge Extraction [KD₂]

Tools for knowledge extraction support structured queries and replies. They help mining text by interpreting relationships among different elements and documents. Therefore, they help the knowledge seeker in identifying the exact document and the other documents related to his/her queries (e.g., vivisimo.com clustering), resulting in structured and more articulated answers. Some sophisticated data and text analysis tools also support the identification of relationships among concepts, using sound and rigorous statistical association rules (e.g., SPSS). Please see Table 3.

## Tools for Expertise Localization [EM₁]

These tools enable quickly locating the knowledge holders in the enterprise and facilitating collaboration and knowledge exchanges (Huysman & Wulf, 2006). Therefore, they are focused on going beyond simple directories by enabling users to easily capture and organize the results of their project interactions (Coakes & Bradburn, 2005) by quickly locating project expertise and

*Table 1.*

| Tools for knowledge access | | |
|---|---|---|
| **Vendors** | **Applications** | **Web Link** |
| Fast | Fast ESP | www.fastsearch.com |
| Convera | RetrievalWare 8 | www.convera.com |
| Entopia | K-Bus | www.entopia.com |
| Exaled | Exaled Corporate | www.exalead.fr |
| Autonomy Verity | Idol K2 | www.autonomy.com |

*Table 2.*

| Tools for semantic mapping | | |
|---|---|---|
| **Vendors** | **Applications** | **Web Link** |
| Anacubis | Anacubis Connect | www.anacubis.com |
| Inxight | VizServer | www.inxight.com |
| Kartoo | KartooKM | www.kartoo.net |
| MapStan –Amoweba | mapStan | www.amoweba.com |
| **Ontologies** | | |
| Cerebra | Cerebra suite | www.cerebra.com |
| Mondeca | ITM | www.mondeca.com |
| Ontopia | Knowledge suite (OKS 3.0) | www.ontopia.com |
| SchemaLogic | Enterprise suite | www.schemalogic.com |

*Table 3.*

| Tools for knowledge extraction | | |
|---|---|---|
| **Vendors** | **Applications** | **Web Link** |
| ClearForest | ClearForest Text Analysis Suite | www.clearforest.com |
| Intelliseek | Enterprise Mining Suite | www.intellisik.com |
| Insight | InsightSmartDiscovery | www.inxight.com |
| Lingway | Lingway KM | www.lingway.com |
| Temis | Inxight Discovery Extractor | www.temis-group.com |
| **Relationship discovery** | | |
| Grimmersoft | WordMapper | www.grimmersoft.com |
| SPSS | LexiQuest Mine | www.spss.com |

enabling re-use and innovation (e.g., Kankoon Skol). Please see Table 4.

## Tools for Collaborative Editing and Publishing [COL$_1$]

Tools like Vignette and DocuShare enable collaborative editing of documents and the management of the entire document publication cycle. They include systems for document management within the enterprise, as well as more flexible systems such as Wikis and Blog creation tools (like the Movable Type software that enables users to share public spaces within company servers for discussion, comments, and knowledge exchanges) (Frumkin, 2005). Please see Table 5.

## Tools for Collaborative Work [COL$_2$]

These tools enable teams to globally share dedicated spaces for managing the project lifecycle; editing and publishing materials; conducting live discussions and interactions; and maintaining a repository of materials associated with every step of the process (Frank & Gardoni, 2005). For example, using MS SharePoint servers, teams can quickly create password-managed and secure project areas and follow the lifecycle of document creation and exchanges. Other tools (e.g., Tomoye Simplify) are focused on bringing together and facilitating the work of communities of practice (Coulson-Thomas, 2005). Please see Table 6.

## Tools for Real Time Communication [COL$_3$]

These tools overlap with some of the functionalities of the previous category. However, they are specifically focused on live communication exchanges, whiteboarding, and file sharing (e.g., Meeting Center, Yahoo Messenger). Please see Table 7.

## Tools for Business Process Management [EKM$_2$]

These tools can be split into applications for process modeling and tools for workflow management. Process modeling tools focus on designing and optimizing processes (Gronau & Muller, 2005). They formalize and define the elements of the process, assign actors to roles, and identify data sources and flows within the processes (Hlupic, 2003). For example, the Aris Process Platform provides modules for the strategic, tactical, operational, and measurement tasks related to process management. Workflow specific tools, such as Staffware Process suite, are focused on the management of the rules and execution of enterprise processes. They also automate specific operational and analytical steps around the process deployment. Please see Table 8.

## Global Knowledge Management Solutions

Applications in this category are divided in software suites dedicated to KM, such as Knowledge Manager and SK2, and enterprise portal solutions that provide modular applications. For example, portal packages provide collaboration modules; content management; access to repositories and information; process management; text mining; and business intelligence (e.g., Lotus Suites; Plumtree Enterprise Web Suite). Please see Table 9.

## Key Trends and Perspectives in KM Tools

Information systems have continued to evolve and change their role to better respond to the needs of organizations. Until recently, organizations have used information technology to support information management (Ruiz-Mercader & Merono-Cerdan, 2006; Schultze & Leidner, 2002). Therefore, organizational systems have been information

*Table 4.*

| Tools for expertise localization | | |
|---|---|---|
| **Vendors** | **Applications** | **Web Link** |
| Agilence | Expertise Finder | www.agilence.com |
| Kankoon | Kankoon Skol | www.kankoon.com |
| Tacit | ActiveNet | www.tacit.com |

*Table 5.*

| Tools for collaborative editing | | |
|---|---|---|
| **Vendors** | **Applications** | **Web Link** |
| Interwoven | TeamSite6 | www.interwoven.com |
| Open Source | Drupal | www.drupal.org |
| Six Apart | Movable Type | www.movabletype.org |
| Vignette | Vignette V7 Content Services | www.vignette.com/fr/ |
| Xerox | DocuShare4 | http://docushare.xerox.com/ |

*Table 6.*

| Tools for collaborative work | | |
|---|---|---|
| **Vendors** | **Applications** | **Web Link** |
| EMC – Documentum | eRoom | www.documentum.com/eroom |
| IBM / Lotus | QuickPlace | www.lotus.com |
| Affinitiz | Affinitiz | www.affinitiz.com |
| Microsoft | SharePoint Services | www.microsoft.com |
| One2Team | One2Team Pro | www.one2team.com |
| Tomoye | Simplify 4.0 | www.tomoye.com |

*Table 7.*

| Tools for real time collaboration | | |
|---|---|---|
| **Vendors** | **Applications** | **Web Link** |
| Marratech | Marratech e-Meeting Portal | www.marratech.com |
| Microsoft | Live Communication 2003 | www.microsoft.com |
| Microsoft | Windows Messenger | www.microsoft.com |
| WebEx | Meeting Center | www.webex.com |
| Yahoo | Yahoo Messenger | www.yahoo.com |

*Table 8.*

| Tools for business process management | | |
|---|---|---|
| **Vendors** | **Applications** | **Web Link** |
| Boc | Adonis | www.boc-eu.com |
| IDS Sheer | Aris Process Platform | www.ids-scheer.com |
| Mega | Mega Process | www.mega.com |
| **Workflows** | | |
| FileNet | Business Process Manager | www.filenet.com |
| TIBCO | Staffware Process Suite | www.tibco.com |
| W4 | W4 | www.w4.fr |

*Table 9.*

| Global Solutions and Suites | | |
|---|---|---|
| **Vendors** | **Applications** | **Web Link** |
| Ardans | Knowledge Maker | www.ardans.fr |
| Thalès-Arisem | KM Server | www.arisem.com |
| Knowesis | Athanor | www.knowesis.fr |
| Knowings | Knowledge Manager | www.knowings.com |
| Sharing Knowledge | SK2 | www.sharing.com |
| **Portals** | | |
| Autonomy | Portal in a Box | www.autonomy.com |
| HummingBird | Humming Enterprise | www.hummingbird.com |
| IBM | Suite Lotus | www.ibm.fr |
| OpenText | LiveLink | www.opentext.com |
| Oracle | Enterprise Manager, Collaboration Suite, Data Hub | www.oracle.com |
| Plumtree | Enterprise Web Suite | www.plumtree.com |
| Vignette | Vignette V7 | www.vignette.com |

bound and information centric. Today, we have a better understanding that for information to be effectively used by individuals, information systems need to be more people centric and support specific individual needs.

To better leverage the knowledge of individuals in organizations, firms need to understand that employees' daily activities are tightly interconnected to other people and processes in the organization. Therefore, firms need a support system for "the group," rather than an information system designed for individual and autonomous work. In few words, the paradigm needs to shift from an individualistic view of information systems to a collective and collaborative view. For this reason, ubiquitous social computing models (Snowdon & Churchill, 2004) are emerging in several organizations. Many KM tools have been traditionally used in an isolated interaction between the individual and the tool. The new KM logic implies that these tool be seamlessly integrated to manage group discussions, be used by groups, and foster a mix of face-to-face and distant collaboration. The boundaries of collaboration within the enterprise need to evolve. Three key trends are related to this transition.

First, starting from 2002, we have observed a convergence of KM tools (Edwards & Shaw, 2005) through mergers and acquisitions. Market share of pure communication players have become scarce and communication management has been complemented with content management solutions. Or, communication solutions have been integrated with other platforms to support existing tasks (for example, eBay acquisition of Skype to integrate VoIP in the auction transactions). These consolidations have attempted to provide an operational answer to firms faced with capturing the value of current communication interactions by quickly and clearly organizing, storing, and sorting the results of the exchanges through electronic document management solutions. Several vendors of document management solutions have added communication capabilities. Documentum (today part of EMC) bought e-Room; Interwoven acquired i-Manage; and Vignette acquired Intraspect. Following the same trends, actors in the collaboration arena have expanded into the document management realm. IBM/Lotus with Abtrix and Open Text with Ixos.

Second, the concepts of networked enterprises and collaboration have been augmented with the need for exchanges while multitasking. Users will not need to quit the applications they are currently using to augment their work with a synchronous communication component. These components will be easily integrated within the user workspace; will be highly interoperable; and information will be easily transferred across tools and applications. For example, Microsoft offers an integrated SharePoint solution that communicates with office productivity tools (supported by .NET server solutions). IBM/Lotus is also moving quickly in this area with the Lotus Sametime integration of instant messaging, conferencing, and project spaces with Websphere Portal Server.

These platforms are tightly integrated with the proprietary systems they interface with. However even if IBM and Microsoft hold a market advantage in this area, recent trends in the open source market are promoting standardization and alternative interoperable solutions that can be integrated across platforms.

Third, most of the emerging communication needs are focused on supporting individuals in managing communications and collaboration schedules, needs, and requirements. Tools need to integrate with personal information management systems (PIMs) and multiple hardware platforms (PDAs and Smartphone) in order to provide ubiquitous connectivity to an increasingly mobile workforce.

## SUMMARY AND CONCLUSION

In this chapter, we provided a summary overview of the types, functionalities, and clustering of KM solutions. Technical, organizational, and individual factors contribute to knowledge creation. From the technical standpoint, the KM tools need to demonstrate that they are beneficial to the organization, at least based on usage statistics. From the organizational standpoint, the tools must be supplemented with workplace changes that promote knowledge sharing and dissemination through the new platforms, for example, rewarding peer ranking and documents use as practiced by Infosys (Chatterjee & Watson, 2005; Kochikar & Suresh, 2004; Mehta & Mehta, 2005). Lastly, individuals must feel secure that participation and utilization of the tools is not targeted at personnel reduction; rather at personnel enhancement and long-term leadership and growth.

It is the mix of the aforementioned factors, coupled with a clear understanding of the market, the tools, and the drivers for a savvy selection of applications aligned with business needs, which may ultimately support successful KM initiatives.

## ACKNOWLEDGMENT

An earlier version of this chapter was presented at the 2006 University of Tunis-Carthage (UTC) Knowledge Management Forum. Sincere thanks to the UTC conference organizers and Dr. Murray Jennex for the opportunity expand this work for consideration in the *International Journal of Knowledge Management.*

## REFERENCES[1]

Adamides, E. D., & Karacapilidis, N. (2006). Information technology support for the knowledge and social processes of innovation management. *Technovation, 26*(1), 50-59.

Alavi, M., & Leidner, D. E. (1999). Knowledge management systems: Issues, challenges and benefits. *Communications of AIS, 1,* 1-37.

Alavi, M., & Leidner, D. E. (2001). Review: Knowledge management and knowledge management systems: Conceptual foundations and research issues. *MIS Quarterly, 25*(1), 107-136.

Argote, L., & Ingram, P. (2000). Knowledge transfer: A basis for competitive advantage in firms. *Organizational Behavior and Human Decision Processes, 82*(1), 150-169.

Bhatt, G. D., & Gupta, J. N. D. (2005). Interactive patterns of knowledge management in organizations: Insight from a fashion company. *International Journal of Information Technology and Management, 4*(3), 231-243.

Biloslavo, R. (2005). Use of the knowledge management framework as a tool for innovation capability audit. *International Journal of Innovation and Learning, 2*(4), 402-424.

Binney, D. (2001). The knowledge management spectrum—Understanding the KM landscape. *Journal of Knowledge Management, 5*(1), 33-42.

Chatterjee, D., & Watson, R. (2005*).* Infosys technologies limited. Unleashing CIMBA. *Journal of Cases on Information Technology, 7*(4), 127-142

Chua, A., & Lam, W. (2005). Why KM projects fail: A multi-case analysis. *Journal of Knowledge Management, 9*(3), 6-17.

Coakes, E., & Bradburn, A. (2005). *Knowledge management in a project climate.* Hershey, PA: Idea Group Publishing.

Cohen, D. (1998). Toward a knowledge context: Report on the first annual U.C. Berkeley forum on knowledge and the firm. *California Management Review, 40*(3), 22-39.

Coulson-Thomas, C. (2005). Using job support tools to increase workgroup performance. *International Journal of Productivity and Performance Management, 54*(3), 206-211.

Davenport, T. H., & De Long, D. W. (1998). Successful knowledge management projects. *Sloan Management Review, 39*(2), 43-57.

Davenport, T. H., & Harris, J. G. (2001). Data to knowledge to results: Building an analytic capability. *California Management Review, 43*(2), 117-138.

Davenport, T. H., & Jarvenpaa, S. L. (1996). Improving knowledge work processes. *Sloan Management Review, 37*(4), 53-65.

Davenport, T. H., & Prusak, L. (1998). *Working knowledge: How organizations manage what they know.* Boston: Harvard Business School.

Davies, J., & Duke, A. (2005). Next generation knowledge access. *Journal of Knowledge Management, 9*(5), 64-84.

Edwards, J. S., & Shaw, D. (2005). Knowledge management systems: Finding a way with technology. *Journal of Knowledge Management, 9*(1), 113-125.

Frank, C., & Gardoni, M. (2005). Information content management with shared ontologies—At corporate research centre of EADS. *International Journal of Information Management, 25*(1), 55-70.

Frumkin, J. (2005). The Wiki and the digital library. *OCLC Systems and Services, 21*(1), 18-22.

Gronau, N., & Muller, C. (2005). KMDL capturing, analyzing and improving knowledge-intensive business processes. *Journal of Universal Computer Science, 11*(4), 452-472.

Hiltz, S. R., & Goldman, R. (2005). *Learning together online. Research on asynchronous learning.* Mahwah, NJ: Lawrence Erlbaum Associates.

Hlupic, V. (2003). *Knowledge and business process management.* Hershey, PA: Idea Group Publishing.

Huysman, M., & Wulf, V. (2006). IT to support knowledge sharing in communities, towards a social capital analysis. *Journal of Information Technology, 21*(1), 40-51.

Janev, V., & Vranes, S. (2005). The role of knowledge management solutions in enterprise business processes. *Journal of Universal Computer Science, 11*(4), 526-545.

Jarvenpaa, S. L., & Staples, D. S. (2000). The use of collaborative electronic media for information sharing: An exploratory study of determinants. *Journal of Strategic Information Systems, 9*(2-3), 129-154.

Jennex, M. E. (2005). What is Knowledge Management? *International Journal of Knowledge Management, 1*(4), i-iv.

Junghagen, S., & Linderoth, H. C. J. (2003). *Intelligent management in the knowledge economy.* Cheltenham, UK; Northampton, MA: Edward Elgar.

Kochikar, V. P., & Suresh, J. K. (2004). *Towards a knowledge-sharing organization. Some challenges faced on the Infosys journey.* Hershey, PA: Idea Group Publishing.

Kwan, M. M., & Cheung, P.-K. (2006). The knowledge transfer process: From field studies to technology development. *Journal of Database Management, 17*(1), 16-32.

Lyons, P. (2005). A robust approach to employee skill and knowledge development. *Industrial and Commercial Training, 37*(1), 3-9.

Mehta, N., & Mehta, A. (2005). *Infosys technologies, limited.* Hershey, PA: Idea Group.

Nonaka, I., & Konno, N. (1998). The concept of "ba": Building a foundation for knowledge creation. *California Management Review, 40*(3), 40-54.

Parpola, P. (2005). Inference in the SOOKAT object-oriented knowledge acquisition tool. *Knowledge and Information Systems, 8*(3), 310-329.

Polanyi, M. (1966). *The tacit dimension.* London: Routledge and Kegan Paul.

Rollett, H. (2003). *Knowledge management: Processes and technologies.* Boston: Kluwer Academic.

Ruiz-Mercader, J., & Merono-Cerdan, A. L. (2006). Information technology and learning: Their relationship and impact on organizational performance in small businesses. *International Journal of Information Management, 26*(1), 16-29.

Schultze, U., & Leidner, D. E. (2002). Studying knowledge management in information systems research: Discourses and theoretical assumptions. *MIS Quarterly, 26*(3), 213-242.

Snowdon, D. N., & Churchill, E. F. (2004). *Inhabited information spaces: Living with your data.* London; New York: Springer.

Turnbow, D., & Kasianovitz, K. (2005). Usability testing for Web redesign: A UCLA case study. *OCLC Systems and Services, 21*(3), 226-234.

Van der Aalst, W. M. P., Reijers, H. A., Song. (2005). Discovering social networks from event logs. *Computer Supported Cooperative Work (CSCW) An International Journal, 14*(6), 549-593.

Zhao, J. L., & Bi, H. H. (2006). Process-driven collaboration support for intra-agency crime analysis. *Decision Support Systems, 41*(3), 616-633.

## ENDNOTE

[1]   Please note all hyperlinks are valid as of January 2007

# Section III
# Learning

# Chapter XII
# Improving Global Knowledge Management Through Inclusion of Host Country Workforce Input

**Yongsun Paik**
*Loyola Marymount University, USA*

**Charles M. Vance**
*Loyola Marymount University, USA*

**Jeffrey Gale**
*Loyola Marymount University, USA*

**Cathleen A. McGrath**
*Loyola Marymount University, USA*

## ABSTRACT

*Within a framework of international strategy for multinational corporations, this chapter examines the important opportunities afforded by taking a more inclusive approach to the foreign subsidiary host country workforce (HCW). It argues that past international management writing and practice, with its expatriate bias, has neglected consideration of this important resource. Not only can the HCW help expatriate managers be more successful and have a better experience in the host country, but it can contribute to and benefit from the corporate knowledge base, leading to more effective global knowledge management. The authors discuss means by which a multinational corporation can effectively include the HCW in its knowledge management activities.*

## INTRODUCTION

The globalization of the workforce is one of the most significant trends affecting workers in the 21st century (Ivancevich, 1998). Yet there remains a major focus in both the scholarly and practitioner press primarily on the home country workforce—expatriates or parent country nationals from company headquarters—at the expense of other members of the multinational workforce within the global marketplace (Toh & DeNisi, 2003, 2005). With its continued predominant focus on the expatriate, current research in knowledge management and organizational learning on a global scale still reflects an ethnocentric bias (e.g., Paik & Choi, 2005; Bird, 2001; Wong, 2001; Antal, 2001; Bender & Fish, 2000; Downes & Thomas, 2000; Black & Gregersen, 1999). For example, Paik and Choi (2005) found that Accenture, one of the leading global management consulting firms, fell short of fully harnessing and transferring knowledge due to the lack of appreciation for local and regional knowledge. Such one-sided flow of knowledge from the multinational corporation (MNC) headquarters to overseas subsidiaries impedes the potential maximum utilization of knowledge across borders (Kraul, 2003; Bernstein, 2000; Bauman, 1998).

The objective of this chapter is to examine the practical limitations and vulnerabilities resulting from the overemphasis on expatriates and parent country nationals in efforts to achieve effective global knowledge management. Specific ways in which members of the host country workforce (HCW—including third country nationals serving in host country operations) can contribute to effective global knowledge management will be examined, along with strategic implications for MNC competitive advantage when a more inclusive approach to knowledge management and organizational learning is used.

## BACKGROUND

The strategic management literature in recent years has emphasized the "resource-based view" in which firms are characterized as collections of resources and capabilities (Barney, 1991; Peteraf, 1993). This approach recognizes the firm's knowledge base as a major resource with significant potential for providing competitive advantage (Dierick & Cool, 1989). Following the resource-based view, many scholars recognize a company's individual and organizational knowledge as a critical resource that constitutes a sustained competitive advantage (Nonake, 1994; Nonaka & Takeuchi, 1995; Von Krogh et al., 2000). Offering a more dynamic perspective of the resource-based theory, Spender (1996) attempts to provide new insights into knowledge as the basis of a new theory of the firm. As firms are institutions for integrating knowledge (Grant, 1996), internationalization means a process of transferring a firm's knowledge across borders. Internalization theory (Hymer, 1960; Buckley & Casson, 1976; Teece, 1981) further stresses the greater ability of MNCs to utilize their knowledge base. Dunning's (1981) eclectic paradigm further suggests that knowledge as part of firm-specific advantage is a critical rationale for investment and international production. Kogut and Zander (1993) argue that MNCs are efficient specialists in transfer and recombination of knowledge across borders.

Specifically, Gupta and Govindarajan (1991, 2000) have studied knowledge flows in MNCs from an institutional level. Characterizing knowledge flows as similar to capital and product flows and examining flows of "know-how" rather than operational knowledge both to and from subsidiaries, they examine differences based upon subsidiary characteristics such as value of knowledge stock, motivations, richness of transmission channels, and ability to absorb knowledge. As Gupta and Govindarajan point out (2000, p. 474), the idea that multinational enterprises exist because of their ability to exploit knowledge "…does not in any way imply that such knowledge transfers actually take place effectively and efficiently on a routine basis."

Doz, Santos, and Williamson (2002), characterizing much of the knowledge flow in MNCs as projection from the home country, argue that the successful firm in the future needs to go beyond the transnational approach to what they term a "metanational" strategy. Such a strategy would involve organizational activities aimed at sensing and processing complex knowledge involving new sources of technologies, competencies, and market understanding; mobilizing to translate that broadly dispersed knowledge into innovative products/services, business models, and opportunities; and operationalizing these to realize profit potential. They argue that this approach involves far more complex knowledge transfer across the organizational networks than the earlier approaches to strategy.

In order to manage knowledge successfully, organizations must appreciate the value of their intellectual capital at all locations within their organizational boundaries, manage knowledge generation and knowledge flows within their organization, and develop an inclusive organizational culture that values knowledge sharing and organizational learning. In other words, the key to successful knowledge management initiatives is creating contexts in which individuals throughout an organization—not just those from company headquarters—can share information (Stewart, 1997).

However, MNCs often find it difficult to transfer knowledge effectively throughout the organization (Moore & Birkinshaw, 1998; Roos, Krogh, & Yip, 1994). Further complicating the knowledge transfer in MNCs is the nature of the complexity of the domains of knowledge necessary for transfer. The knowledge transfer involves knowledge of higher complexity, including what Doz et al. (2002) term experiential, endemic, and existential knowledge. Similarly, Chait (1998) argues that there are four relevant interlinked domains of organizational knowledge: knowledge content, the firm's business processes, the firm's infrastructure, and culture. All of these domains are relevant for the understanding of effective knowledge transfer.

The past decade has seen tremendous development in the theoretical and practical development of knowledge management. The knowledge management literature consistently adopts Nonaka and Takeuchi's (1995) definition of human knowledge as having two different dimensions: explicit and tacit. Explicit knowledge exists in the "objective world," and can be formally codified and systematically transmitted to others (Lam, 2000). This type of knowledge is commonly expressed in written words or numbers including concrete data, scientific formulas, product specifications, company procedure manuals, and network databases (Nonaka & Takeuchi, 1995; Nonaka & Konno, 1998). On the contrary, knowledge that is highly personal and often difficult to capture and share widely with others is the hallmark of tacit knowledge. Tacit knowledge consists of the "know-how," or learned skills that result from personal experience—that is, learning-by-doing. In other words, tacit knowledge has to do with an employee's "practical expertise" rather than information that can be derived from books or manuals. While MNCs have rather effectively leveraged advances in technology to collect, store, and communicate explicit knowledge through the use of global databases, the effective widespread management of tacit knowledge remains largely elusive (Pfeffer & Sutton, 1999; Cross & Baird, 2000). In order to manage knowledge more successfully, organizations must appreciate the value of their intellectual capital at all locations within their organizational boundaries, manage knowledge generation and knowledge flows within their organization, and develop an inclusive organizational culture that values knowledge sharing and organizational learning.

Therefore, from this perspective, knowledge management incorporates any organizational activity that supports the generation, accounting for, or sharing of knowledge. Ruggles (1998) reports all of these activities as part of corporate knowledge management programs. Each knowledge management activity can be supported by both a technical and behavioral approach. From a technical perspective, significant advances in knowledge management are the result of increased computational power and technological solutions that allow individuals to codify, store, and access more information than ever before. In other words, the codification strategy uses databases and other tangible mediums to formalize and communicate explicit knowledge throughout the company. Systems to encourage knowledge sharing have focused heavily upon explicit knowledge because the two mechanisms for encouraging knowledge flow have been to (1) create a knowledge market (Davenport & Prussak, 1998) that (2) makes it necessary to codify knowledge before it is transferred.

However, from a behavioral perspective, a great deal of knowledge flows through informal connections within organizations, requiring less codification and less tracking of exactly what is shared (Hansen, Nohria, & Tierney, 1999). For those companies primarily undertaking a personalization strategy, there are less tangible factors that influence the way knowledge is collected, transmitted, and utilized. Personalization requires person-to-person interaction, focusing on the sharing of tacit knowledge. This strategy relies heavily on face-to-face communication, with knowledge being viewed as largely personal.

The role of *all* individuals who link different parts of the organization together, including between company headquarters and foreign operations, and within and among the foreign operations themselves, becomes crucial to knowledge sharing within organizations. As the pressures for effective knowledge management gain in intensity as the competitive landscape pushes firms toward transnational strategies and perhaps even a more complex metanational approach, a far richer transfer of knowledge is necessary—featuring both content and domain to provide context for full and clear transfer—than is afforded by the traditional "parent country to subsidiary" efforts dominant in the past.

## MAIN THRUST OF THE CHAPTER: ISSUES, CONTROVERSIES, PROBLEMS

As the ability to transfer knowledge may be the most effective determinant of success, MNCs seeking international expansion should develop systems that enable them to transfer knowledge around the organization as well as to create new knowledge and skills (Welch & Welch, 1994). Given the significance of knowledge transfer to maximize the potential performance of MNCs, what are the most effective means of transferring knowledge throughout the organization? International assignments have been regarded as effective knowledge transfer mechanisms (Bonache & Brewster, 2001; Downes & Thomas, 1999; Conn & Yip, 1997; Taylor, Beechler, & Napier, 1996; Sparrow & Hiltrop, 1994). It is people who have the knowledge that is applied and transferred in the activities developed by the company (Itami, 1987). As such, expatriate managers have been used as a vehicle to transfer knowledge effectively (Black & Gregerson, 1999).

Expatriates can be sent for multiple purposes such as filling a position, management development, and organizational development (Edstrom & Galbraith, 1977). The classic view of the expatriate role presented by early research in international management has been one of a liaison between corporate headquarters and the foreign operation, with important responsibilities of headquarters strategy implementation, performance goal achievement, and increasing MNC control in the foreign operation (Paik & Sohn, 2004; Franko, 1973; Kobrin, 1988; Black, Gregersen, & Mendenhall, 1992; Black & Mendenhall, 1990, 1992). More recently the purpose of the expatriate assignment has expanded to include the expatriate's development of global competencies for building global leadership within the MNC (Mendenhall, Kuhlmann, & Stahl, 2001; Black, Morrision, & Gregersen, 1999; Sparrow & Hiltrop, 1994) and the generation and transfer of new knowledge about foreign markets for enhanced decision making at company headquarters (Downes & Thomas, 1999, 2002; Bender & Fish, 2000; Wong, 2001; Bird, 2001; Kamoche, 1997). This latter purpose is increasingly becoming a major focus of expatriate management research and practice as we continually move toward a global information economy where the effective acquisition and management of knowledge leads to competitive advantage (Doz et al., 2001; Drucker, 2001; Thurow, 2000).

As a testimony to this trend, in her extensive empirical study including MNCs from all parts of the triad, Harzig (2001) found that at both subsidiary and headquarters levels, knowledge transfer is seen as the most important reason for expatriation, while direct expatriate control is seen as least important. In order to transform the individual overseas experiences and acquired knowledge of expatriates into organizational learning at the collective level, it is critical for MNCs to build infrastructures to institutionalize new knowledge so that it flows back and forth between corporate headquarters and the various subsidiaries (Downes & Thomas, 1999). Through international assignments, expatriate managers not only can apply extant knowledge from the headquarters to the overseas subsidiary, but also can acquire new knowledge from the overseas subsidiary that can ultimately be transferred to the parent company.

A competency-based view of the relationship between human resource management and expatriate staffing identified the three different competences that can produce a sustained competitive advantage: input, managerial, and transformation-based competencies (Lado & Wilson, 1994). Of these three competencies, Harvey and Novicevic (2001) suggest that transformation-based competence represents the ability of expatriates required to effectively manage knowledge transfer. Transformation-based competencies are those that enable the foreign subsidiary to transform inputs into outputs and to transfer technology or marketing innovations that facilitate new product and customer relationship development (Lado, Boyd, & Wright, 1992). Transformation-based competencies can play a significant role in global organizations and their subsidiaries. By utilizing competent expatriates with multiple skills, global organizations are developing a resource competency of tacit knowledge that is difficult for global competitors to duplicate. Furthermore, the tacit knowledge gained through expatriates in foreign subsidiaries can be brought back and embedded into the domestic firm-specific routines, which in turn can facilitate organizational learning, resulting in increased global competitiveness (Harvey, 2001; Taylor et al., 1996; Roth & O'Donnell, 1996).

Consistent with arguments in the strategic management literature that emphasize the balance between global integration and local responsiveness (Bartlett & Ghoshal, 1989, 1992; Yip, 1992; Paik & Sohn, 2004), the expatriate management literature generally characterizes the global transfer of knowledge and expertise as a two-way process, where expatriate assignments should be designed to transfer corporate knowledge effectively from headquarters to the overseas subsidiary and to transfer knowledge about specific national markets back to the parent company location as well (Downes & Thomas, 2000). The former process will facilitate global integration or centralization, while the latter process will accommodate localization or decentralization.

Nevertheless, this general body of theoretical and empirical research on expatriate management renders the very limited impression that knowledge only flows from the expatriate manager to the local manager at the foreign subsidiary, not the other way (e.g., Tsang, 2001). Such a unilateral transfer of knowledge could result in some serious consequences to the MNCs' knowledge management. First, MNCs that develop an excessive dependence upon expatriates for foreign market knowledge generation and transfer back to headquarters may eventually face a serious dearth of expatriate participants in this global knowledge management if, according to observed patterns, the number of home country expatriate personnel that are utilized are gradually diminished upon increased MNC internationalization (Downes & Thomas, 2002). Although it is true that companies are often cutting the number of expatriates to save costs, the continued decline in expatriates will present the challenge of developing managers who are equipped with appropriate knowledge and skills to compete in the global market. Second, expatriate assignment failure (represented by premature termination of the foreign assignment or failure to achieve expected performance goals—e.g., see Black & Gregersen, 1999) threatens the reliability and continuity of knowledge management processes.

Third, there can be a significant amount of valuable knowledge lost and damage incurred to knowledge management processes and structures through unsuccessful repatriation (including both underutilization of repatriate tacit knowledge and experience, and repatriate turnover), which continues to be a significant challenge in expatriate career management (Antal, 2001; Bird, 2001; Solomon, 1995). As described by Downes and Thomas (1999), upon losing an experienced expatriate due to ineffective repatriation, a company can lose large amounts of first-hand knowledge about a particular foreign economic context, including information about markets, customers, regulations, and local cultural influence on management practices. In addition, it can forfeit personal knowledge of networks, social connec-

tions, and understanding of company image in the foreign market. Finally, through poor repatriation efforts, companies can subvert formal knowledge and information channels supporting expatriation and its role in knowledge generation for the firm through the formation of informal and damaging channels of information—often with greater credibility than the formal channels—that inform expatriate candidates that the acceptance of a foreign assignment can prove to be very detrimental to their long-term careers.

## SOLUTIONS AND RECOMMENDATIONS

The HCW can play a critical role in addressing the problems identified in the previous section. These potential strategic contributions leading to competitive advantage include:

1. Developing more comprehensive experience databases for guiding professional decision making and practice,
2. Providing more valid pre-departure expatriate training and on-site coaching,
3. Developing a larger and more inclusive globally competent workforce,
4. Gaining an increased awareness about foreign market needs and conditions, and
5. Developing a more flexible corporate mindset that is more open to diverse perspectives and challenges of our global economy.

### Developing More Comprehensive Experience Databases for Guiding Professional Decision Making and Practice

Multinational organizations can potentially enhance decision-making effectiveness and productivity by leveraging knowledge gained by both expatriates and members of the HCW in their subsidiaries around the world. But this more inclusive and comprehensive effort in global knowledge management can prove to be very challenging even for leading MNCs of professional knowledge services.

According to Paik and Choi (2005), Accenture is considered among one of the most successful companies in the consulting industry in which knowledge has always been the primary asset. Accenture's entire knowledge management model is based on one global database system called the Knowledge Exchange (KX). The KX houses approximately 7,000 individual databases, and its primary purpose is to store explicit knowledge—that is, client deliverables, presentations, methodologies, best practices, and other document forms—that can be accessed by its employees through its global network using Lotus Notes. Thus, the KX is the single, most important knowledge generating and transferring tool at Accenture, which causes its entire system to be highly standardized and thereby cost efficient. The KX is absolutely imperative to a consultant's daily work. It is not uncommon for a system user to access knowledge on more than 10 different databases on the KX every day.

The KX was initially established to link its entire global network, pulling expertise and knowledge from around the world into one collective system and uniting the entire organization. However, Accenture's global KX does not provide adequate support or resources for dealing with local and cross-cultural challenges. For example, within Accenture's East Asian offices, global databases are not strictly viewed as the one and only vehicle for knowledge preservation. Without anyone helping them with such time-consuming work, the language barrier and additional time required for translation make it extremely difficult for East Asians to write English abstracts that must accompany their KX contributions. Different language systems and cultures make knowledge transfer especially difficult since, if the context changes, the nature of knowledge also changes (Venzin, 1998).

Accenture also faces cultural complexities that affect the motivation for knowledge sharing in other parts of the world. The rigidity of the KX and the standardization of its practices and work processes have not only effectively prohibited its East Asian employees from making KX contributions, but also have discouraged them from sharing knowledge and conducting business based on personal relationships, which has traditionally been most comfortable and productive for them. East Asian culture is typically a high-context society, with informal socializing and person-to-person communication a large part of accepted business culture (Bhagat, Kedia, Harveston, & Triandis, 2002; Milliman, Taylor, & Czaplewski, 2002; Hall, 1977). Consequently, managers in East Asia seem to be less willing to share their knowledge with those with whom they are not in direct personal contact. The resulting lack of East Asian employee experience-based input into and utilization of the KX is increasingly turning Accenture from "one global firm" largely into "one American firm" that constrains a potential strategic and competitive advantage in effective human knowledge and expertise sharing on a global scale.

Accenture is certainly not alone in unintentionally developing an ethnocentric approach to guiding future decision making on a global scale. Organizations would do well to carefully seek to make their databases more inclusive of local HCW insights and experiences, which would help develop databases that have more sophistication and applicability to diverse foreign market conditions. However, large cross-cultural differences can present significant obstacles to the effective transfer of organizational knowledge across national borders (Bhagat et al., 2002). An important and tangible step forward would be for MNCs to acknowledge the important role of the HCW in knowledge generation and more effectively train their expatriates in facilitating, with appropriate cross-cultural sensitivity, the ongoing involvement and utilization of HCW input.

## Providing More Valid Pre-Departure Expatriate Training and Effective On-Site Expatriate Coaching

In the face of concern for high incidence and cost of expatriate assignment failure and premature return, considerable work has been done to examine the appropriate kinds of knowledge, skills, and abilities to be included in the training of expatriates for foreign assignment (Black & Gregersen, 1999; Adler, 1986). This work typically has recommended the training of general cross-cultural awareness skills (e.g., Copeland & Griggs, 1985) and more customized training content for the host country assignment, including language, customs, and other general country cultural information (Selmer, 1995). Other work has focused on training methods and processes, such as simulations, for effectively delivering the above knowledge, skills, and abilities to optimize expatriate performance (Black & Mendenhall, 1992, 1990).

While this work has made an important contribution to the development of theory and practice for expatriate pre-departure preparation and training, it typically has neglected the HCW as an important source of knowledge input in the design of expatriate training. Apart from the inherent ethnocentricity of this neglect, the value of past approaches to the design of expatriate training may be seriously limited due to their emphasis on generic principles of cross-cultural awareness or on general characteristics of a particular ethnic culture. For example, Paik, Vance, and Stage (1996) found that management style preferences of workforce members across national boundaries can differ dramatically despite the presence of a common Chinese ethnic cultural background, and therefore should not be generalized. The more generic past approaches to the design of expatriate training may not adequately address the specific and unique workplace demands attendant to the expatriate assignment, especially those unique, expatriate assignment-specific workplace

demands involved with HCW management and interpersonal interaction.

This concern for training customization has recently led to the consideration of on-site expatriate learning as a preferred tool to pre-departure training (Mendenhall & Stahl, 2000; Bird, Osland, Mendenhall, & Schneider, 1999). Yet perhaps, in search of expatriate training customization and validity, the answer lies less in when the training is conducted and more in the quality of the knowledge and information input in the training design. From a learning organization perspective, the voice of the relevant HCW unit should be considered in the design of valid, customized, expatriate assignment-specific training. It is possible that by incorporating HCW input into the design of expatriate training, both pre-departure and on-site, HCW perceptions about how management style and particular behaviors affect their work could help optimize expatriate training validity and, ultimately, HCW and foreign assignment productivity.

As suggested by recent research, specific subsidiary data based on surveys of HCW operative employee expectations regarding management style preferences would be useful to include in the expatriate training design for a given foreign operation (Vance & Paik, 2002). Although general information about HCW management style preferences can be useful in preparing an expatriate for an assignment and providing a general framework for understanding a culture, it is possible that norms and preferences regarding appropriate managerial practice and behavior can differ considerably within a given regional or national culture. Specific information should be obtained from the particular HCW corresponding to an expatriate assignment to help refine broad or general cultural portraits to better fit the specific HCW situation.

As part of a comprehensive needs assessment for customized expatriate training, interviews with supervisory and middle-management-level HCW employees could help identify important areas of knowledge and procedure which, based upon their overall past experience, lead to successful knowledge transfer and expatriate performance. The experience of HCW employees in the foreign operation potentially provides a considerable knowledge base that should not be ignored if valid expatriate training is desired. Interviews with HCW managers and supervisors also potentially can expose specific critical incident information, particularly from the HCW's more experienced perspective, which could be used as customized, company-specific lessons learned for expatriate managers regarding behaviors to emulate and those to avoid. These critical incidents can be very useful in developing compelling and valid cases and role-playing scenarios to promote higher levels of learning among expatriates.

HCW managers and supervisors also can serve as ongoing coaches and even mentors to expatriates to help them make decisions that are appropriate for the host country's socioeconomic context, and to maintain positive relations and open communications with all HCW employees (Feldman & Bolino, 1999). This form of HCW training design input, which unlike the previous two categories involves more training *process* than training *content,* can promote effective on-going learning for expatriates while in the field, which is increasingly being considered as the time when the most productive expatriate training occurs (Bird et al., 1999). Past research has found that expatriates with HCW mentors gained an important source of socialization knowledge and support (Black, 1990).

## Developing a Larger, More Inclusive, Globally Competent Workforce

When knowledge management includes the widespread and effective acquisition of critical global business knowledge, skills, and abilities by a broad spectrum of the organization's human resources—wherever they are found in the world—the organization is able to develop

a larger supply of globally competent managers and business leaders. Organizations that focus on expatriates in the development of global competence unwittingly limit their internal global talent pool for future assignment selection. A commitment to the development of all members of the organization, including the foreign HCW, can also help facilitate effective communication and knowledge sharing between expatriates and the HCW in foreign operations. Furthermore, the development of senior HCW managers regarding home country and parent company culture can potentially help those HCW executives better understand and work with key decision makers at MNC headquarters (Vance & Paik, 2001).

Long-term management development experiences of HCW managers at home country headquarters (inpatriation—see Harvey, 1993) can potentially provide a helpful exposure for these HCW managers to an MNC headquarters' corporate culture and the particular style, priorities, and processes of parent company strategic management (Harvey, Price, Speier, & Novicevic, 1999; Harvey & Buckley, 1997). Once they overcome the 'liability of foreignness', inpatriates represent a new source of knowledge transfer that can bridge the cultural gap between headquarters and overseas subsidiaries in effectively implementing MNCs' global strategies (Harvey, Novicevic, Buckley, & Fung, 2005; Harvey & Fung, 1999; Peppas & Chang, 1998). When the HCW manager returns to a senior-level assignment within a foreign operation, working closely with or even replacing expatriate management, he or she should now be able to work more effectively within the context of the strategic direction, goals, and culture of the parent company. But this optimal link by HCW executives to the corporate mindset will likely never be achieved without significant direct work experience and long-term interaction with MNC headquarters. Ultimately, the parent firm will theoretically have more strategic control over this foreign operation than over other operations headed by HCW managers who have not had this in-depth parent company culture/strategy learning experience (Harvey et al., 1999; Kobrin, 1988). The development of the HCW at this senior level through organized efforts of training, multinational team assignments, foreign travel, and extended foreign assignments (including inpatriation) is particularly important in helping to achieve a truly global orientation for the firm where the MNC strategic mindset is also held by senior-level members of the HCW (Black & Gregersen, 1999).

## Gaining an Increased Awareness About Foreign Market Needs and Conditions

HCW managers and executives with frequent information exchange with an MNC headquarter's decision makers (whether by distant communication or during an inpatriate assignment) are positioned to provide helpful input to parent company decision makers who set business policy and performance expectations for those who are given an expatriate assignment. Unlike previously discussed HCW input to expatriate training and subsequent on-site learning about *how* to effectively carry out the expatriate assignment, this form of input benefit relates more to enhancing the validity of just *what* the assignment will be in the first place. In interviewing Mexican HCW managers, Vance and Ensher (2002) noted that often the greatest source of American expatriate poor performance was *not* the lack of appropriate pre-departure training, but rather was due to the inappropriate policies, practices, procedures, and expectations that the expatriate brought as assignment directives from parent company headquarters. What was expected of them for the expatriate assignment was not well grounded in the reality of the host country, leading to unnecessary and avoidable expatriate frustrations and difficulties.

Beyond the level of the expatriate assignment, there are numerous examples of poor and costly decision making on the part of inexperienced,

ethnocentric, and arrogant senior management teams at MNC headquarters who have planned and launched significant international business initiatives without an appropriate understanding of and sensitivity to foreign market needs and socio-political conditions (e.g., Ricks, 1999). Experienced HCW managers, where their inputs are genuinely considered, can potentially provide critical social, political, and economic insights for MNC strategic plans that are directed toward their host country operations.

## Developing a Flexible Corporate Mindset That is More Open to Diverse Challenges of Our Global Economy

Upper-level HCW managers and executives represent a vital source of training design input for shaping the global orientation and multicultural thinking of the company as a whole (Harvey et al., 1999). Their experienced input can lead to the design of very relevant, customized diversity and cross-cultural awareness training for the entire multinational organization which can help draw the corporate mindset away from limiting and dysfunctional ethnocentric patterns of thought and practice. In fact, their presence and meaningful interaction with other home country managers at the parent company headquarters can lead more informally to a greater awareness of differing yet valuable perspectives and experience sets that can enhance the overall global orientation at company headquarters necessary for competing in the global marketplace. Through formal and informal channels, inpatriate managers can potentially infuse knowledge of the host country throughout the global organization and provide a means to enrich the senior management team—now a multicultural management team—by adding a multicultural perspective and cognitive diversity to the process of global strategy development (Harvey et al., 1999; Bartlett & Ghoshal, 1992; Quelch, 1992). And these multicultural strategic management teams can create competitive advantage by increasing creativity and innovation, resulting in more effective managerial decision making and organizational outcomes (Bantel & Jackson, 1989).

## FUTURE TRENDS

The objective of this chapter has not been to disparage or discourage the involvement of expatriates in the overall global knowledge management effort. Rather, this chapter highlights the potential drawbacks of continued imbalance in international management theory and practice, and in particular indicates how the neglect of the potential role of the HCW can render efforts in global knowledge management incomplete at best.

Future research in global knowledge management theory development and practice could make valuable strides by expanding its focus beyond expatriates and parent company nationals to include the voice of the host country workforce. This more inclusive focus will shed new light and generate useful prescriptions related to several potentially strategic contributions of the HCW in global knowledge management as we discussed above. Given that the overall numbers of traditional expatriates continue to decline and the alternative forms of international work arrangements such as virtual or short-term assignments are on the rise, the host country managers are expected to assume many important responsibilities that the home country managers used to handle. It is in this context that the role of the HCW is becoming increasingly important in harnessing and disseminating the critical knowledge generated from business involving overseas subsidiaries, especially as the communication gap between host country managers and HCW employees is much smaller than that between the expatriates and local employees. Yet, it is up to the top management at MNC headquarters to determine how much the company will appreciate the knowledge produced from its overseas subsidiaries, and evaluate its appropriateness and applicability to its global business operations.

## CONCLUSION

Recent research related to global knowledge management has done well to consider the important ways in which expatriates can contribute to the effective generation and utilization of knowledge by MNCs as they compete in our global marketplace. However, this picture of global knowledge management is incomplete without the inclusion of the role of the HCW, both as sources of potentially important knowledge and participants in the MNC knowledge generation and utilization process. Significant contributions of strategic consequence that the HCW can make to the overall effort of knowledge generation and utilization in global knowledge management have been discussed. These include developing more comprehensive experience databases for guiding professional decision making and practice, providing more valid pre-departure expatriate training and on-site coaching, developing a larger and more inclusive globally competent workforce, gaining an increased awareness about foreign market needs and conditions, and developing a flexible corporate mindset that is more open to diverse perspectives and challenges of our global economy.

Our traditionally myopic and ethnocentric view of the parent company workforce, including those on expatriate assignments, as the principal individual-level focal point of studies in international management has typically neglected an important part of the picture—the host country workforce employed in foreign operations. Future research with a more inclusive perspective should expand its heretofore narrow focus and consider more carefully in theory and in practice potential contributions that the HCW can make to the international enterprise, particularly in the vital knowledge generation and utilization activities of global knowledge management.

## REFERENCES

Adler, N.J. (1986). *International dimensions of organizational behavior.* Boston: PWS-Kent.

Antal, A.B. (2001). Expatriates' contributions to organizational learning. *Journal of General Management, 26,* 62-84.

Bantel, K.A., & Jackson, S.E. (1989). Top management and innovations in banking: Does the composition of the top team make a difference? *Strategic Management Journal, 10,* 107-124.

Barney, J. (1991). Firm resources and sustained competitive advantage. *Journal of Management, 17,* 99-120.

Bartlett, C., & Ghoshal, S. (1992). What is a global manager? *Harvard Business Review, 70*(September-October), 124-132.

Bartlett, C., & Ghoshal, S. (1989). *Managing across borders: The transnational solution.* Boston: Harvard Business School Press.

Bauman, Z. (1998). *Globalization: The human consequences.* New York: Columbia University Press.

Bender, S., & Fish, A. (2000). The transfer of knowledge and the retention of expertise: The continuing need for global assignments. *Journal of Knowledge Management, 4,* 125-137.

Bernstein, A. (2000). Backlash: Behind the anxiety over globalization. *Business Week, 3678*(April 24), 38-44.

Bhagat, R.S., Kedia, B.L., Harveston, P.D., & Triandis, H.C. (2002). Cultural variations in the cross-border transfer of organizational knowledge: An integrative framework. *Academy of Management Review, 27,* 204-221.

Bird, A. (2001). International assignments and careers as repositories of knowledge. In M.E. Mendenhall, T.M. Kuhlmann, & G.K. Stahl (Eds.), *Developing global business leaders: Policies, processes, and innovations* (pp. 19-36). Westport, CT: Quorum Books.

Bird, A., Osland, J.S., Mendenhall, M., & Schneider, S.C. (1999). Adapting and adjusting to other cultures. *Journal of Management Inquiry, 8,* 152-165.

Black, J.S. (1990). Locus of control, social support, stress, and adjustment to international transfers. *Asia Pacific Journal of Management, 7,* 1-29.

Black, J.S., & Gregersen, H.B. (1999). The right way to manage expats. *Harvard Business Review, 77*(March-April), 52-63.

Black, J.S., Gregersen, H.B., & Mendenhall, M. (1992). *Global assignments: Successfully expatriating and repatriating international managers.* San Francisco: Jossey-Bass.

Black, J.S., & Mendenhall, M. (1992). A practical but theory-based framework for selecting cross-cultural training methods. *Human Resource Management, 28,* 511-539.

Black, J.S., & Mendenhall, M. (1990). Cross-cultural training effectiveness: A review and a theoretical framework for future research. *Academy of Management Review, 15,* 113-136.

Black, J.S., Morrison, A.J., & Gregersen, H.B. (1999). *Global explorers: The next generation of leaders.* New York: Routledge.

Bonache, J., & Brewster, C. (2001). Knowledge transfer and the management of expatriation. *Thunderbird International Business Review, 43*(1), 145-168.

Buckley, P.J., & Casson, M. (1976). *The future of the multinational enterprise.* London: Macmillan.

Chait, L. (1998). Creating a successful knowledge management system. *Prism,* (2ⁿᵈ Quarter), 83.

Conn, H.P., & Yip, G. (1997). Global transfer of critical capabilities. *Business Horizons, 40*(January-February), 22-31.

Copeland, L., & Griggs, L. (1985). *Going international.* New York: Random House.

Davenport, T., & Prusak, L. (1998). *Working knowledge: How organizations manage what they know.* Boston: Harvard Business School Press.

Dierickx, I., & Cool, K. (1989). Asset stock accumulation and sustainability of competitive advantage. *Management Science, 35,* 1504-1514.

Downes, M., & Thomas, A.S. (2002). Knowledge transfer through expatriation: The U-curve approach to overseas staffing. *Journal of Managerial Issues, 12,* 131-149.

Downes, M., & Thomas, A.S. (2000). The cyclical effect of expatriate satisfaction on organizational performance: The role of firm international orientation. *The Learning Organization, 7*(3), 122-134.

Downes, M., & Thomas, A.S. (1999). Managing overseas assignments to build organizational knowledge. *Human Resource Planning Journal, 22,* 33-48.

Doz, Y.L., Santos, J., & Williamson, P. (2001). *From global to metanational: How companies win in the knowledge economy.* Boston: Harvard Business School Press.

Drucker, P.F. (2001). *Management challenges for the 21st century.* New York: Harper Business.

Dunning, J.H. (1981). *International production and the multinational enterprise.* London: Allen and Unwin.

Edstrom, A., & Galbraith, J.R. (1977). Transfer of managers as a coordination and control strategy in multinational organizations. *Administrative Science Quarterly, 22,* 248-263.

Feldman, D.C., & Bolino, M.C. (1999). The impact of on-site mentoring on expatriate socialization: A structural equation modeling approach. *International Journal of Human Resource Management, 10,* 54-71.

Franko, L.G. (1973). Who manages multinational enterprises? *Columbia Journal of World Business, 8*(Summer), 30-42.

Grant, R. (1996). Toward a knowledge-based theory of the firm. *Strategic Management Journal, 17*(Winter Special Issue), 109-126.

Gupta, A.K., & Govindarajan, V. (1991). Knowledge flows and the structure of control within multinational corporations. *Academy of Management Review, 16,* 768-792.

Gupta, A.K., & Govindarajan, V. (2000). Knowledge flows within multinational corporations. *Strategic Management Journal, 21,* 473-496.

Hall, E.T. (1977). *Beyond culture.* New York: Doubleday/Anchor.

Hansen, M.T., Nohria, N., & Tierney, T. (1999). What's your strategy for managing knowledge? *Harvard Business Review, 77*(March-April), 106-116.

Harvey, M.G. (1993). Inpatriation training: The next challenge for international human resource management. *International Journal of Intercultural Relations, 21,* 393-428.

Harvey, M., & Buckley, M. (1997). Managing inpatriates: Building a global core competency. *Journal of World Business, 32*(1), 67-78.

Harvey, M., & Fung, H. (2000). Inpatriate managers: The need for realistic relocation reviews. *International Journal of Management, 17*(2), 151-159.

Harvey, M., & Novicevic, M.M. (2001). Selecting expatriates for increasingly complex global assignments. *Career Development International, 6*(2), 69-86.

Harvey, M., Novicevic, M., Buckley, M., & Fung, H. (2005). Reducing inpatriate managers liability of foreignness by addressing stigmatization and stereotype threats. *Journal of World Business, 40*(3), 267-280.

Harvey, M.G., Price, M.F., Speier, C., & Novicevic, M.M. (1999). The role of inpatriates in a globalization strategy and challenges associated with the inpatriation process. *Human Resource Planning, 22,* 38-50.

Harzig, A. (2001). An analysis of the functions of international transfer of managers in MNCs. *Employee Relations, 23*(6), 581-598.

Hymer, S. (1960). *The international operations of national firms: A study of direct investment.* Boston: MIT Press.

Itami, H. (1987). *Mobilizing invisible assets.* Cambridge, MA: Harvard University Press.

Ivancevich, J.M. (1998). *Human resource management.* Boston: Irwin/McGraw-Hill.

Kamoche, K. (1997). Knowledge creation and learning in international HRM. *International Journal of Human Resource Management, 8,* 213-225.

Kobrin, S.J. (1988). Expatriate reduction and strategic control in American multinational corporations. *Human Resource Management, 27,* 63-75.

Kogut, B., & Zander, U. (1993). Knowledge of the firm and the evolutionary theory of the multinational corporation. *Journal of International Business Studies, 24,* 625-646.

Kraul, C. (2003). WTO meeting finds protests inside and out. *Los Angeles Times,* (September 11), A3.

Lado, A., Boyd, N., & Wright, P. (1992). A competency-based model of sustainable competitive advantage: Toward a central integration. *Journal of Management, 18*(1), 77-91.

Lado, A., & Wilson, M. (1994). Human resource systems and sustained competitive advantage: A competency-based perspective. *Academy of Management Review, 19,* 699-727.

Mendenhall, M.E., Kuhlmann, T.M., & Stahl, G.K. (Eds.). (2001). *Developing global business leaders: Policies, processes, and innovations.* Westport, CT: Quorum Books.

Mendenhall, M., & Stahl, G. (2000). Expatriate training and development: Where do we go from here? *Human Resources Management, 39*(2&3), 251-265.

Milliman, J., Taylor, S., & Czaplewski, A.J. (2002). Cross-cultural performance feedback in multinational enterprises: Opportunity for organizational learning. *Human Resource Planning, 25*(3), 29-43.

Moore, K., & Birkinshaw, J.M. (1998). Managing knowledge in global service firms: Centers of excellence. *Academy of Management Executive, 12*(4), 81-92.

Paik, Y.S., & Choi, D. (2005). The shortcomings of a standardized global knowledge management system: The case study of Accenture. *Academy of Management Executive, 19*(2), 81-84.

Paik, Y., Segaud, B., & Malinowski, C. (2002). How to improve repatriation management: Are motivations and expectations congruent between the company and expatriates? *International Journal of Manpower, 23*(7), 635-648.

Paik, Y., & Sohn, D. (2003). Expatriate managers and MNCs' ability to control international subsidiaries: The case of Japanese MNCs. *Journal of World Business, 39*(1), 61-71.

Paik, Y., Vance, C.M., & Stage, H.D. (1996). The extent of divergence in human resource practice across three Chinese national cultures: Hong Kong, Taiwan, and Singapore. *Human Resource Management Journal, 6*(2), 20-31.

Peppas, S., & Chang, L. (1998). The integration of inpatriates into rural communities. *Management Decision, 36*(6), 370-377.

Peteraf, M.A. (1993). The resource-based view within the conversation of strategic management. *Strategic Management Journal, 14,* 179-192.

Polanyi, M. (1966). *The tacit dimension.* Garden City, NY: Doubleday and Company.

Quelch, J. (1992). The new country manager. *The McKinsey Quarterly, 4,* 155-165.

Ricks, D.A. (1999). *Blunders in international business* (3rd ed.). Oxford, UK: Blackwell.

Roos, H., Krogh, G., & Yip, G. (1994). An epistemology of globalizing firms. *International Business Review, 4,* 395-409.

Roth, K., & O'Donnell, S. (1996). Foreign subsidiary compensation strategy: An agency theory perspective. *Academy of Management Journal, 39*(3), 678-703.

Ruggles, R. (1998). The state of the notion: Knowledge management in practice. *California Management Review, 40,* 80-89.

Selmer, J. (Ed.). (1995). *Expatriate management: New ideas for international business.* Westport, CT: Quorum Books.

Solomon, C.M. (1997). Return on investment. *Workforce, 2*(4, Global Workforce Supplement), 12-18.

Sparrow, P.R., & Hiltrop, J.M. (1994). *European human resource management in transition.* Englewood Cliffs, NJ: Prentice Hall.

Spender, J.C. (1996). Making knowledge the basis of dynamic theory of the firm. *Strategic Management Journal, 17*(Winter Special Issue), 45-62.

Stewart, T.A. (1997). *Intellectual capital.* New York: Doubleday.

Stroh, L., Gregersen, H., & Black, S. (1998). Closing the gap: Expectations versus reality among repatriates. *Journal of World Business, 33*(2), 111-124.

Taylor, S., Beechler, S., & Napier, N. (1996). Toward an integrative model of strategic international human resource management. *Academy of Management Review, 21*(4), 959-985.

Teece, D.J. (1981). The market for know-how and the efficient international transfer of technology. *Annals of the American Academy of Political and Social Science, 458,* 81-96.

Thurow, L.C. (2000). *Building wealth: The new rules for individuals, companies, and nations in a knowledge-based economy.* New York: Harper Information.

Tsang, E.W.K. (2001). Managerial learning in foreign-invested enterprises in China. *Management International Review, 41,* 29-51.

Vance, C.M., & Ensher, E.A. (2002). The voice of the host country workforce: A key source for improving the effectiveness of expatriate training and performance. *International Journal of Intercultural Relations, 26,* 447-461.

Vance, C.M., & Paik, Y. (2002). One size fits all in expatriate departure training? Comparing the host country voices of Mexican, Indonesian, and U.S. workers. *Journal of Management Development, 21*(7), 557-571.

Vance, C.M., & Paik, Y. (2001, August). Toward a taxonomy of host country national learning process involvement in multinational learning organizations. *Proceedings of the Annual Meeting of the Academy of Management,* Washington, DC.

Welch, D., & Welch, L. (1994). Linking operation mode diversity and IHRM. *International Journal of Human Resource Management, 5,* 911-926.

Wenger, E. (1998). *Communities of practice, learning, meaning and identity.* Cambridge, UK: Cambridge University Press.

Wong, M.M.L. (2001). Internationalizing Japanese expatriate managers: Organizational learning through international assignment. *Management Learning, 32,* 237-251.

Yip, G. (1992). *Total global strategy: Managing for worldwide competitive advantage.* Englewood Cliffs, NJ: Prentice Hall.

# Chapter XIII
# Developing a Standardization Best Practice by Cooperation Between Multinationals

**Henk J. de Vries**
*Erasmus University, The Netherlands*

## ABSTRACT

*This chapter presents a case of knowledge sharing between multinational companies. The companies cooperated to develop a common best practice for the development of company standards through sharing their practices. The chapter describes how this best practice was developed and tested. Experiences in this successful project may help other multinationals also profit from knowledge sharing. Critical success factors are the willingness to be open, the culture of cooperation, and the involvement of academia.*

## INTRODUCTION

Knowledge sharing between multinationals in order to learn from each other is not practiced very often. Corporations may want to protect their proprietary corporate knowledge and restrict sharing anything with others. This chapter, however, shows a case from The Netherlands where six multinational companies managed to develop a common best practice for the development of company standards through sharing their practices.

## BACKGROUND FOR STARTING THE KNOWLEDGE SHARING PROJECT

Large parts of The Netherlands are below sea level. Windmills and nowadays electric pumps are used to keep the polders dry, and all dikes and watercourses have to be in good shape. It was and is a common effort to achieve this. Due to these circumstances, the Dutch developed a tradition of cooperating for common goals, the so-called 'polder model'. This tradition of cooperation applies to the business world as well. This chapter describes a case of cooperation between Dutch multinationals in the area of technical standards.

In 1916, The Netherlands was the first country in the world to establish an independent national standardization organization to develop technical standards for common use—a joint initiative of the national organization of industrialists and the national organization of engineers. Nowadays, 7,000 experts cooperate in committees of this private institute, NEN, to develop national standards and to provide the Dutch input in standards development at the European and international levels. Inherent to this is that NEN functions as a platform for business people to meet in a rather informal setting and to discuss issues of common interest. For standards officers of big chemical and petrochemical industries, such an issue appeared to be the development of standards for their installations.

For companies in process industries, standards for the installations are primarily engineering solutions that define how to design, construct, and maintain manufacturing facilities (Simpkins, 2001). In general, the companies prefer external standards, for example from the ISO (International Organization for Standardization) and API (American Petroleum Institute) (Qin, 2004; Thomas, 2004). However, these do not meet all their needs and, therefore, the companies complement these with their own standards, so-called company standards. A company standard may have the form of: (1) a reference to one or more external standards officially adopted by the company; (2) a company modification of an external standard; (3) a subset of an external standard (for instance, a description of the company's choice of competing possibilities offered in an external standard, or a subset of the topics covered in the external standard); (4) a standard reproduced from (parts of) other external documents, for instance, suppliers' documents; or (5) a self-written standard.

Company standards can improve business performance in terms of efficiency and quality. In the process industry, benefits such as reduction of design and construction costs, procurement costs, training costs, and minimization of design errors and rework have been reported (Simpkins, 2001). The issue raised by the standards officers was how to shape the production of these company standards (standardization activities) in order to maximize the benefits of company standardization.

The Dutch tradition of cooperation includes ties between industry and academia. The standards officers of the process industries expressed their wish to improve company standardization to the chair of standardization at Erasmus University's Rotterdam School of Management. The latter was enthusiastic for a common research project because the question was interesting from a scientific point of view as little research had been done on company standardization. Exceptions include Adolphi (1997), Hesser and Inklaar (1997, Section. 5), Rada and Craparo (2001), Schacht (1991), and Susanto (1988). Professional publications on company standardization include AFNOR (1967), Barnes et al. (1988), Bouma and Winter (1982), British Standards Society (1995), Cargill (1997, pp. 139-146), Nakamura (1993), Ollner (1974), Österreichisches Normungsinstitut (1988), Teal (1990), Toth (1990), Verman (1973, Chapter 7), Verity Consulting (1995), and Wenström, Ollner, and Wenström (2000). The university took the lead in starting the best practice project. The best practice in company standardization should be developed by making an inventory of company practices and relevant literature.

Process industries in The Netherlands include several medium-sized companies and a few large multinational companies. All companies that decided to participate in the project belong to the latter category and include both petrochemical (oil and gas) and chemical industries. Later, a sixth company joined: a U.S.-based chemical industry with a large plant in The Netherlands. All of these companies are in the top five of the world in their market segment, annual turnover in 2005 were between US$1.6 billion and US$307 billion.

Each company promised to provide access to its company and to provide the researchers with all necessary information. The research was carried out by two junior researchers, supervised by a senior researcher (the author of this chapter). A supervising committee was formed consisting of the corporate standardization managers of the companies concerned, a technical officer from NEN—the national standardization institute of The Netherlands, and the president of NKN—the national standards users organization in The Netherlands.

We will now describe the project, in which six subsequent steps can be distinguished. Per step, we will first describe the approach chosen and then the results. A scientific underpinning of the methodology used can be found in De Vries and Slob (2007).

## PROJECT APPROACH AND RESULTS

### Step 1: Getting Acquainted with Business Issue, Companies, People, and Scientific Literature

The project was started by studying the available scientific and professional literature. This study confirmed the expectation that answers to the research question were not available yet and therefore the practical situation in the companies should be the main source of information. Then the junior researchers paid a visit to each of the companies and had a meeting with the standardization officer to get acquainted with him personally and with company standardization in his company. How did he define company standardization? What did his company do in this area, how, and why? This first meeting was more of a chat than an interview, unstructured in order not to be biased by preconceived ideas. It can be seen as a quick scan of company standardization within that company and as a starting point for further systematic research.

### Step 2: Designing a Process Model for Company Standardization

A "best practice" is a practice that is in actual use at some place and which is deemed better than all other practices that are used or known elsewhere. If a practice is acknowledged as "best," it should be fit for being transferred to those other places as well. "Best practice" in company standardization means the best possible contribution of company standardization to business performance (see Figure 1).

Assessing which of the practices in use is the best one requires that appropriate criteria are used to evaluate current practices. Moreover, it is not

*Figure 1. Conceptual model*

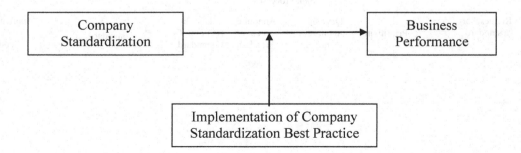

self-evident beforehand that a best practice model is feasible: companies might differ so much that the optimal situation is unique per company and there is no common best practice. Apart from the possible differences per company, the benefits may differ per standard, for example, a safety standard should lead to safe installations, a standard specifying a preference range for pipes should lead to cost savings. These differences hinder a common perception of "best" in "best practice." Therefore, the researchers looked for a more general indicator. In line with the international standards for quality management, "best" might be defined as "maximum user satisfaction" (ISLO, 2000). Then we can distinguish between *direct* users, being people that read the standard, and *indirect* users who use the products, services, systems, and so forth in which the standard has been implemented. Again, however, because of the diversity of standards and user categories, it is difficult to measure user satisfaction and, subsequently, relate it to best practices for standardization. Therefore, this approach seems unfeasible as well.

In their attempt to develop a technical innovation audit, Chiesa, Coughlan, and Voss (1996) faced a similar problem: how to explain successes (and failures) of innovations in terms of business performance. Their basic assumption was that success in innovation is related to good practice in the relevant management processes. Therefore

*Figure 2. Overall best practice in company standardization resulting from best practices of the constituting processes*

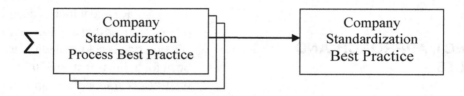

*Figure 3. Process model for company standardization*

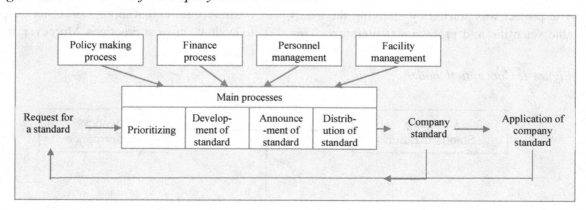

they developed a process model of innovation in which they distinguished four core processes and three supporting processes. The well-functioning of these processes should result in successful innovation. Subsequently, they looked for a best practice per process. This best practice is a set of characteristics of the process that gives the best results.

Innovation and company standardization have a lot in common. Innovation is concerned with the development of a new product or process, or the improvement of an existing product or process. Company standardization concerns the development of a standard which, subsequently, is implemented and affects products or processes. Therefore, Chiesa et al.'s (1996) approach has been taken as a benchmark. Then, the basic assumption is that successful company standards result from well-functioning or, better, 'best' company standardization processes (see Figure 2).

The next question is to determine these processes. Chiesa et al. (1996) could build their process model on existing literature (Roberts, 1988). In the standardization case, the available literature was not workable. However, the researchers had the opportunity to have access to business practice within the six companies. Based on the first impression of company standardization in the companies and the senior researcher's own experience, a process model on company standardization was designed (see Figure 3).

## Core Processes

1.  **Setting Priorities:** Which company standard will be developed and which will not? Who decide(s), based on which criteria (if any)?

2.  **Developing the Standard:** This process consists of the composition of draft versions of the standard, commentary rounds, the writing of the final version, and its approval.

3.  **Introducing the Standard:** The approved standard must be introduced to its users. In this introduction process the benefits of the standard and the reasons for certain choices in the standard can be explained. The more and the better the standard is known to its potential direct users, the higher the chance that they will actually use it and do so in the way intended by the standard's developers. The "promotion" of the standard can also continue after the introduction period.

4.  **Distributing the Standard:** The purpose of this process is to assure that each standard reaches the direct user in a fast and easy way. This can be done by, for instance, subscription, ordering on demand, or in the form of "publishing on demand" using an intranet.

## Facilitating Processes

1.  A *standardization policy* is needed to steer the core processes—a global policy on company level, more detailed on department level.

2.  A *budget* is needed to *finance* the core-processes—standardization activities ask for investments. Costs precede benefits. The break-even point may be after, for instance, three years.

3.  *Human resource management* is a necessary supporting process. Competent *personnel* must realize the established policy.

4.  The core processes are also *facilitated* by IT (e.g., electronic publishing of standards on the intranet) and other tools.

On the right hand side of the model in Figure 3, the required end situation is represented by the concept "Application of the standard." Company standardization can only be a success when the standard is used in practice, and in the right way. A standard that is of a high quality but is not used in practice has no value. Potential direct users must be willing to use the standard and be capable of understanding and using it. On the left-hand side of the model, the beginning of the process is represented by the concept "call for a standard," which represents the requirement for any standard that it is seen as responding to a perceived problem "on the floor."

Finally, at the bottom of the model, a feedback loop is represented. Evaluation of the standard's use may form the basis for withdrawing, maintaining, or changing the standard. The developed standard should be an answer to the question for which it was produced: Are the (potential) users of the standard satisfied? Therefore, user *feedback* to those who have decided to make the standard as well as to the people who have developed it is essential. The figure shows only one overall feedback loop, but in actual (best) practice a feedback loop is required in each of the four steps of the standardization process.

## Step 3: Testing the Process Model and Determining Practices per Process

The process model had to be tested, in the sense that the proposition that the (core and enabling) processes were really in place in business practice was confirmed. This test was a question of pattern matching: Can each of the predefined processes be found, in one form or another, in each of the companies?

Data per company were gathered in the form of interviews, company documents, and personal observation. The process approach appeared to be applicable in each of the companies investigated. No missing processes were reported and each process applied to each company. The model was also presented to the steering group and this group confirmed its correctness. Therefore, the model for company standardization could serve as a basis for the subsequent research steps.

## Step 4: Describing Standardization Process Characteristics per Company

The next step is to describe company standardization process characteristics per company. This description is more an in-between result than that it has value as such, except for the company concerned. In practice, the gathering of data for this step was combined with the gathering of data needed in step 2. There was no pre-defined protocol for interviews other than the process model and the question, asked for each of the processes, of how the company had shaped these processes. It appeared that the way the companies had shaped their processes differed quite a lot.

## Step 5: Determining Best Practice per Process

Chiesa et al. (1996) defined characteristics per process that are associated with success or failure of the process and the overall innovation process, based on available literature. In our approach, similar characteristics were defined in the form of statements. These statements describe a (supposed) best-practice characteristic: "best" in the sense of the expected contribution of the process to the overall success of company standardization. The statements have been developed starting from the observed practice in the six companies, in a team analysis. Company standardization literature, scientific or professional, played a minor role because, in general, it did not provide in-depth best-practice data.

Examples of such statements:

- There is a clear strategic policy on company standardization.
- At the corporate level, there is a clear framework for operating company standardization.

- A 'why document' should be attached to each company standard to provide the underpinning of the most important choices/decisions that were made during standards development.

First we will discuss the first two best-practice statements, both related to the policy process. To make company standardization work, there must be an organizational framework and a policy. There must be enough engagement to the policy by the people who must carry out the standardization activities and their management, and the higher levels of management. In our best practice, top management is represented in company standardization or at least supports it. The most effective way to make this work is by means of a steering group in which the standardization department, (technical) management from business units, and a member of top-level management (e.g., a technical director) are represented. Having a company standardization steering group is an important part of the best practice; we found such a group in some of the investigated companies. Not in the main scientific study on the organization of company standardization (Adolphi, 1997) nor in other scientific literature was the idea of a steering group mentioned. We found it in Dutch professional studies only (e.g., De Gelder, 1989). The British Standards Society (1995, p. 40) mentions a "standards committee," but does not talk about a real steering responsibility. The American National Standards Institute's best practice research (Verity Consulting, 1995) apparently did not find steering groups in the multinational companies they investigated. We considered a steering group to be best practice for reasons of commitment for and support of the standardization activities.

We will now describe how we arrived at the last best practice statement, related to the company standards development process. One of the interviewees mentioned the example of a standard for durability of piping materials related to corrosion. In the case of a pipeline in a dessert, there may be less danger of corrosion, so just applying the standard may lead to an unnecessarily costly design. The why document will explain the assumptions underlying the specifications in the standard so that it may become clear to what extent the design may be changed in the case of deviating circumstances. Then the company should balance the advantages of a cheaper design against the cost of having more diversity in its equipment. This best practice characteristic of having a why document was also found in Brown and Duguid (1991, p. 45).

The result of this step was an 'extended model' consisting of the process model and best practice characteristics per process. We will not list these 102 best practice statements in this chapter, but refer to a paper by De Vries (2006) in which these have been presented.

## Step 6: Testing the Best Practice Model

The last step was to test the best practice model. This was done by presenting the findings to the companies and asking them for feedback.

In order to be able to compare each company with the other companies and the best practice, scorecards were used, again taking the benchmark of Chiesa et al. (1996). Per company, a score was given related to the different statements per process of the model in Figure 3. The score per statement could vary from 1 (not applicable at all) to 5 (very much applicable). The score of 5 is considered to be 'best practice'. For every company the scorecards were filled in both by the companies themselves and by the researchers ('objective party'), and a mean score was determined. The scores were put together with the scores of the other companies. These figures were presented in tables, the most interesting ones also in graphs. This has been done per best practice statement. For every process, the order

*Figure 4. Scorecard graph example: The influence of business units on the strategic policy concerning company standardization*

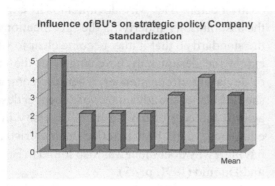

of companies was made differently, in a way that the companies could not recognize which score belonged to which other company.

Figure 4 shows the scorecard for one of the best practice statements related to the policy process: "The business units have sufficient influence on the strategic policy on company standardization (to make sure that their needs in this area are met)." The picture shows seven different bars. The first six represent the scores of the six different companies, the seventh the mean score. In this case, most companies do not score high on this statement. The respondents recognized the importance of involvement of the business units in the formulation of the strategic policy, but just one of the companies had this in place at a sufficient level of quality.

By comparing their own score with the best practice and with the other companies, the cooperating parties could distinguish gaps between their practice and best practice, think about reasons for this gap, and decide on focus and improvement points for their future policy on company standardization. Moreover, besides an overall research-report for all companies, an additional report per company was made with a description of their actual company standardization and the focus points for them to work towards best practice.

Per company, a focus group was formed consisting of the standardization manager and people involved in one or more of the processes. The research findings were presented to each of these groups, thus one session per company. In this session there was also the possibility to discuss the best practice situation in relation to the possibilities of the company. Besides the report, these individual sessions were helpful for the companies to analyze the status of the current situation on company standardization and to identify focus points for its future optimization. So this approach enabled each company to benchmark its company standardization processes against a best practice and to discuss priorities for improvement. The presentations and subsequent discussions within the companies were at the same time an essential element in the scientific approach: each focus group provided feedback on the correctness of the process model and the best practices per process. By taking these as the starting point for the discussion of the situation in the company concerned, comments showed whether or not there was any discussion on the correctness of elements of the best practice model. Discrepancies, if any, between best practices as formulated by the researchers' model and as perceived by the focus groups should be noted.

Every company has its own specific needs, culture, and ways of 'doing', so the best practices may have to be adapted to the specific situation of the company. In fact to their surprise, the researchers found hardly any differences in perceived best practices. The focus groups in the six companies confirmed that the best practice developed was the right one and that it also applied to their organization, so there appeared to be a rather common understanding about which practices were considered to be 'best'. In some cases there were some differences in nuance. For instance, the above-mentioned why document was recognized to be best practice, but the decision whether or not to add it should balance its advantages against the additional time it takes to write it. However, in general, all best practice characteristics were seen by each of the six focus groups as real best practice, so the best practice model passed the test with flying colors.

The six companies differed in scores per best practice characteristic. No one was overall the best or the worst—each one had 'good' as well as 'bad' performances in different areas.

Finally, the best practice found was presented to the steering committee and again its correctness was confirmed.

## CONCLUSION AND DISCUSSION

Based on the existing practices in six companies, completed with some findings from literature, a best practice for company standardization has been developed. This has been done by developing a process model; best practices per process are assumed to result in overall best practice. The best practices per process have been formulated in the form of statements, 102 in total. Both the model and the best practice statements have been tested.

The project can be seen as a successful form of knowledge sharing between multinationals. Critical success factors for this project were: (1) the willingness of the companies to be open, (2) the culture of cooperation, and (3) the involvement of academia.

### The Willingness of the Companies to Be Open

Confidentiality is a core issue in business. Therefore, it is not self-evident that companies are willing to share knowledge—this might be at the cost of their competitive position. In this case, the companies that shared their knowledge did not compete on product level, and they had the common problem to increase or maintain quality and safety of their installations while reducing cost of ownership of these installations. Therefore, it was

not 'dangerous' to be open. Part of the research design, however, was to keep the practices per individual company confidential; only the best practices should be made available. So each of the companies does not know how the five other companies have shaped their company standardization processes. For the academic researchers it was a condition that they could publish the results. In fact, this was more dangerous because the findings might be used by competitors. The Dutch may be naïve at this point, for example, Pakistan could develop an atom bomb using knowledge gathered in a Dutch company, and Philips' IPRs are used in mobile phones without any license fees going to this company. On the other hand, the competitors can see 'only' the best practice model and the 102 best practice statements, while the participating companies also received a special report with a listing of areas for improvement in this particular company. Moreover, the involvement of company people in the project provided a better basis for implementation of changes than 'just' a publication which, moreover, might remain unnoticed. A last reason for not being too afraid of results being published is that the six participating companies can implement changes sooner, not only because of their involvement in the project but also because of the delay related to the scientific review process.

### The Culture of Cooperation

Thanks to the culture of cooperation, the companies could share the wish to start a project and get the project started. In this case, the informal contacts between business experts, the national standardization organization, the national standards users organization, and academia facilitated the start. Because the project was interesting for all participants, all of them were willing to invest time. The only money paid concerned a small allowance for the junior researchers, paid by the six companies.

## The Involvement of Academia

The companies themselves would have lacked the knowledge for a sophisticated benchmarking project. Involving a consultancy firm would have been an option, but such firms would have the disadvantage of lack of knowledge, the project would have been much more expensive, and there might be a danger that the consultancy firm would use the knowledge for advising a competitor.

In this case, knowledge sharing concerned the development and implementation of standards within companies. There is no reason why such knowledge sharing would not apply to other areas, but then the project approach might be different.

The case companies were located in The Netherlands. This country has the advantage of a small size (it is no problem to have a meeting and to return home the same day) and of a culture of cooperation. These advantages apply to some other countries as well, for instance, Switzerland. However, this does not imply that such forms of cooperation are not feasible in other countries or even cross-boarder. Probably success is more a question of willingness to take initiatives and to involve others. Knowledge sharing across company borders can pay off. By choosing to benchmark with non-competitors, the threat of revealing confidential knowledge to competitors can be avoided. Participation in informal professional networks facilitates cooperation. Establishing contacts with academic researchers specialized in the topic of their own profession appeared to be another condition. Then a win-win situation can be possible enabling starting a project at low cost and (therefore) even without formal hierarchical approval. We expect therefore that such a knowledge sharing project could be initiated not only by top managers, but also by middle managers or even in some cases lower managers or specialists in a certain area of expertise, for example, business unit managers, IT managers, quality managers, HR managers, IPR officers and, last but not least, standardization managers.

## FINAL REMARKS

A limitation of the study is that it focuses on a rather broad description of the best practice situation without going into details and without describing how to migrate from the present situation to the new situation. The first was not feasible because of time constraints; the latter was impossible because the present situation differed per company. But in the separate reports per company, suggestions for main steps to improve the present situation have been given.

Additionally, there is also a second way in which the project described in this chapter relates to the theme of this book. Company standardization can be seen as a way to manage (in our case technical) company knowledge. Standardization is a structured way to transfer tacit into explicit knowledge (Nonaka, 1994). Knowledge is recorded (in the standard) and, subsequently, transferred to the other workers/users. In that sense, the research project has resulted in a best practice for a form of knowledge management.

## ACKNOWLEDGMENT

The field research was carried out by Michiel Oly and Florens Slob.

## REFERENCES

Adolphi, H. (1997). *Strategische konzepte zur organisation der betrieblichen standardisierung* (DIN Normungskunde, Band 38). Berlin/Vienna/Zurich: Beuth Verlag.

AFNOR. (1967). *La normalisation dans l'entreprise.* Paris: Association Française de Normalisation.

Barnes et al. (1988). *Development and organization of a company standardization department*

(ISO Development Manual 5). Geneva: International Organization for Standardization.

Bouma, J.J., & Winter, W. (1982). *Standardization fundamentals.* Delft, The Netherlands: Nederlands Normalisatie-Instituut.

British Standards Society. (1995). *PD 3542:1995: Standards and quality management—an integrated approach.* London: BSI.

Brown, J., & Duguid, P. (1991). Organizational learning and communities of practice: Toward a unified view of working, learning and innovation. *Organization Science, 2*(1), 40-57.

Cargill, C. (1997). *Open systems standardization—a business approach.* Upper Saddle River, NJ: Prentice Hall.

Chiesa, V., Coughlan, P., & Voss, C.A. (1996). Development of a technical innovation audit. *Journal of Production Innovation Management, 13*(2), 105-136.

De Gelder, A. (1989). *Opstellen van normen.* Delft, The Netherlands: Nederlands Normalisatie-Instituut.

De Vries, H.J. (2006). Best practice in company standardization. *International Journal for IT Standards and Standardization Research, 4*(1), 62-85.

De Vries, H.J., & Slob, F.J. (2007). Building a model of best practice of company standardization. In J. Dul & T. Hak (Eds.), *Case study methodology in business research.* Oxford, UK: Butterworth Heinemann.

Hesser, W., & Inklaar, A. (Eds.). (1997). *An introduction to standards and standardization* (DIN Normungskunde, Band 36). Berlin/Vienna/Zurich: Beuth Verlag.

ISO. (2000). *ISO 9000:2000: Quality management systems—fundamentals and vocabulary.* Geneva: International Organization for Standardization.

Nakamura, S. (1993). *The new standardization—keystone of continuous improvement in manufacturing.* Portland, OR: Productivity Press.

Nonaka, I. (1994). A dynamic theory of organizational knowledge creation. *Organization Sciences, 5*(1), 14-37.

Ollner, J. (1974). *The company and standardization* (2nd ed.). Stockholm: Swedish Standards Institution.

Österreichisches Normungsinstitut. (1988). *Werknormung in Österreich—ein leitfaden für Normenpraktiker.* Vienna: Österreichisches Normungsinstitut.

Qin, C. (2004). China builds its new petroleum industry around international standards. *ISO Focus, 1*(4), 23-24.

Rada, R., & Craparo, J.S. (2001). Standardizing management of software engineering projects. *Knowledge Technology and Policy, 14*(2), 67-77.

Roberts, E.B. (1988) Managing invention and innovation. *Research and Technology Management, 31*(1), 11-27.

Schacht, M. (1991). *Methodische neugestaltung von Normen als Grundlage für eine Integration in den rechnerunterstützten Konstruktionsprozeß* (DIN Normungskunde, Band 28). Berlin/Cologne: Beuth Verlag.

Simpkins, C.R. (2001). Reengineering standards for the process industries: Process industry practices. In S.M Spivak & F.C. Brenner (Eds.), *Standardization essentials—principles and practice.* New York/Basel: Marcel Dekker.

Susanto, A. (1988). *Methodik zur entwicklung von Normen* (DIN Normungskunde, Band 23). Berlin/Cologne: Beuth Verlag.

Teal, J.L. (1990). Setting the standard for engineering excellence—the people, the process, the competitive edge. *ASTM Standardization News, 17*(6), 32-35.

Thomas, G.A.N. (2004). Standards as a strategic business asset. *ISO Focus, 1*(4), 11-15.

Toth, R.B. (Ed.). (1990). *Standards management—a handbook for profits.* New York: American National Standards Institute.

Verity Consulting. (1995). *Strategic standardization—lessons from the world's foremost compa-* nies. New York: ANSI (not publicly available).

Verman, L.C. (1973). *Standardization—a new discipline.* Hamden, CT: Archon Books, The Shoe String Press.

Wenström, H., Ollner, J., & Wenström, J. (2000). *Focus on industry standards—an integrated approach* (SIS Hb 124:2000, 1st ed.). Stockholm: SIS Förlag.

# Chapter XIV
# The Building of Intellectual Capital Statements in Multinationals:
## Challenges for the Future

**Miltiadis D. Lytras**
*University of Patras, Greece*

**Patricia Ordóñez de Pablos**
*University of Oviedo, Spain*

## ABSTRACT

*Multinational companies (MNCs) are facing important challenges within the current economic context. Rapid technological changes, the globalization of the economy, the existence of increasingly demanding consumers are, among other factors, the origin of the difficulties involved in achieving and sustaining a competitive advantage in the long term. One of the keys for overcoming these difficulties is to manage knowledge-based resources appropriately. However, in order to be able to manage these resources, the multinationals need to know, with complete transparency, just what these resources are, and this is achieved by quantifying them. The quantification of knowledge-based resources and the preparation of intellectual capital statements represent two strategic challenges for the MNCs.*

## INTRODUCTION

The resource-based view of the firm and the literature on knowledge management and organizational learning state that knowledge-based resources are a source of sustained competitive advantage due to their distinctive characteristics: causal ambiguity, social complexity, organizational path dependence, time compression diseconomies, and idiosyncratic value (Barney, 2001; Dierickx & Cool, 1989; Mahoney, 1995; Ordóñez de Pablos, & Peteraf, 2004, 2005; Peteraf, 1993; Reed & DeFillippi, 1990; Wernerfelt, 1984; 1995). These special features of knowledge-based resources require that the organization develops new strategies to manage them.

Knowledge management and intellectual capital literature respectively provide both a conceptual framework and specific tools for the management of intraorganizational and interorganizational knowledge flows in multinational companies (MNCs). Multinational companies consider that the transfer of knowledge flows at the international level represents a source of opportunities and risks.

This chapter has two basic aims. First, it analyzes the complex dynamics of knowledge flow transfers in multinational firms. Second, it addresses the measuring and reporting of knowledge-based resources in MNCs.

## INTELLECTUAL CAPITAL

### Concept and Constructs

Managing knowledge-based resources is not a new problem, and there have been other theories that have tried to tackle it. As Roos et al. (1998) state, intellectual capital is the latest development in this line of research. In particular, the theoretical roots of intellectual capital come from two different streams of research: strategy and measurement. While the first stream studies knowledge management—knowledge creation, acquisition, diffusion, capitalization, conversion, transfer, and storage—the second stream of research focuses on the measuring of intellectual capital. This stream has advanced towards the building of *intellectual capital statements* and the development of international standards on intellectual capital measuring and reporting. Now we are going to focus on the second stream of research: measuring and reporting intellectual capital (Lytras & Pouloudi, 2006).

A broad definition of intellectual capital states it is the difference between the company's market value and its book value. Knowledge-based resources that contribute to the sustained competitive advantage of the firm form intellectual capital. However these resources are not registered in the financial accounts. In contrast with tangible resources, the payoff and value of investments in a firm's current stock of knowledge (intellectual capital) will not appear in the financial accounting until later on. For all these reasons, knowledge-based resources must now being identified, dissected, and analyzed.

An accepted idea in the field is that intellectual capital is formed by three components or subconstructs: human capital (HC), structural capital (SC), and relational capital (RC) (Skandia, 1996).

Human capital reflects the set of knowledge, capabilities, skills, and experience of the employees of the company. It represents the accumulated value of investments in employee training, competence, and the future. It also includes an even more intangible element: employee motivation (Becker, 1964; Skandia, 1996).

Structural capital represents organizational knowledge that has moved from individuals or from the relationships between individuals to be embedded in organizational structures, such as organizational routines, policies, culture, or procedures. Generally, structural capital is divided into technological capital and organizational capital. Technological capital represents industrial and technical knowledge, such as results from R&D and process engineering. Organizational capital includes all aspects that are related to the organization of the company and its decision-making process, for example organizational culture, organizational structure design, coordination mechanisms, organizational routines, planning and control systems, among others (Bontis, Chong, & Richardson, 2000; Skandia, 1996).

Finally, relational capital reflects the value of organizational relationships. In general, it has been accepted that these relationships were mainly focused on customers, suppliers, shareholders, and the administrations, among others, without including the employees, and therefore adopting an external perspective (Ordóñez de Pablos, 2005). However, it is clear that the relationship of a company with its employees creates value, and for this strategic reason it is necessary to bear them in mind. To advance in the study of relational capital, it is convenient to differentiate between internal relational capital and external relational capital. Internal relational capital includes the value of the strategic relationships created between the company and its employees. External relational capital represents the external perspective of relational capital and includes social relations of the company with key agents: customers, suppliers, shareholders and stakeholders, current and potential, regional and national administrations, and the environment, among others.

## Intellectual Capital Measuring Tools

Among these tools for managing a company's stock of knowledge is the Skandia Navigator (Skandia, 1996), the Intellectual Assets Monitor (Sveiby, 1997), and Balanced Scorecard (Kaplan & Norton, 1992, 1993, 1996).

## The Skandia Navigator

In 1991, Leif Edvinsson started to work on the building of intellectual capital tools at Skandia. With the help of Professor Edvinsson, Skandia become world's first company to publish the intellectual capital statement. He also developed two major intellectual capital managing and measuring tools: Skandia Value Scheme and Skandia Navigator (Bounfour & Edvinsson, 2005; Edvinsson, 1997; Edvinsson & Malone, 1997).

The well-known Skandia Value Scheme and the Skandia Navigator are two models for highlighting and describing the evolution of intellectual capital within Skandia. These models visualize value components that make up intellectual capital, as well as the method of managing them and reporting on their development.

Skandia Navigator is designed to provide a balanced picture of the financial and intellectual capital. Its greatest advantage is "the balanced total picture it provides of the operations" (Skandia, 1994, p. 15). The focus on financial results, capital, and monetary flows is complemented by a description of intellectual capital and its development. Indicators that specify both the level and change are highlighted. At Skandia, the intellectual capital ratios are grouped into major focus areas: the customer focus, the process focus, the human focus, and the renewal and development focus.

## Intangible Assets Monitor

The Intangible Assets Monitor represents a theory of stocks and flows which aim to guide managers in the utilization of intangible assets, the identification and renewal of these flows and stocks, and the avoiding of loss. This tool is focused on three types of intangible assets: external structure assets, internal structure assets, and employee competence assets (Sveiby, 1997).

The Swedish firm Celemi uses this intangible assets measuring tool. In its Invisible Balance, Celemi classifies its assets in three main categories: "our clients" (external structure assets), "our organization" (internal structure assets), and "our people" (employee competence assets). Celemi has also developed different tools that assess and better understand its intangible assets. Tango is one example of this. This simulation tool identifies key intangible assets, and measures and manages them in coordination with a firm's tangible assets. Intangible assets are studied at three different levels: (1) growth and renewal, (2) efficiency, and (3) stability of a firm's parameters.

## Balanced Scorecard

It is one of the first tools that aim to create an integral vision of measurement systems for management, including not only financial elements but those non-financial elements (market, internal processes, and learning) that influence organizational performance.

The Balanced Scorecard (BSC) complements the information provided by traditional tools with three additional views: clients, internal and business processes, and learning and growth. They allow controlling the building of capacities and the acquisition of intangible assets needed for future growth. The BSC model proposes that an organization must meet the requirements of three groups of people if it wants to achieve success: investors, customers, and employees (Kaplan & Norton, 1992, 1993, 1996).

## THE DYNAMICS OF KNOWLEDGE FLOWS IN MULTINATIONAL COMPANIES

### Introduction

Multinational corporations have different reasons for global expansion, largely aiming to increase competitive advantage by realizing economies of scale or economies of scope (Harzing & van Ruysseveldt, 2004).

There are stages in the internationalization process and choices in the strategies and related structures adopted by multinational corporations. The range of MNC subsidiary strategies are (Bartlett & Ghoshal, 1989; Perlmutter, 1969):

- **Ethnocentric, Global Strategy:** The control is centralized. Subsidiaries resemble the parent company.
- **Polycentric, Multi-Domestic Strategy:** Control is decentralized. Subsidiaries conform to local practices.
- **Geocentric, Transnational Strategy:** Subsidiaries and headquarters alike adhere to worldwide standards.

## Internal Knowledge Flows in MNCs

Knowledge management in any organization is a complex task. The complexity of this activity increases substantially in the case of a multinational. With respect to the management of knowledge flows within MNCs, we are able to differentiate four dimensions of analysis:

1. Internal knowledge flows within the parent company of the MNC.
2. Internal knowledge flows within the subsidiaries of the MNC.
3. External knowledge flows between parent company-subsidiaries and vice versa.
4. External knowledge flows between subsidiaries.

Managing internal knowledge flows is always easier—obviously within the complexity inherent to the knowledge transfer process—than managing the flows of knowledge between two organizational units (be they parent company-subsidiary or subsidiary-subsidiary).

Basically speaking, the factors that determine the complexity of the knowledge transfer process are:

1. *The tacit character of the knowledge to be transferred:* The greater the tacit component, the more difficult it is for the multinational to carry out this transfer successfully (Nonaka & Takeuchi, 1995; Szulanski, 2003).
2. *Causal ambiguity:* Not knowing the relationships involved in the body of knowledge in question, the relationships between units of knowledge, make transferring it difficult (Dierickx & Cool, 1989; Lippman & Rumelt, 1982).
3. *A "knowledge hoarding" culture:* If the MNC, by way of its organizational policies and style of leadership, has fostered the development of an organizational culture that rewards the hoarding of knowledge as a source of power, the difficulties involved

in the knowledge transfer process will be greater.

4. *Cultural distance:* Here a differentiation must be made between organizational cultural distance and the cultural distance of the country where the MNC is located. The greater the cultural differences between the country of the parent company and the country where the subsidiary is based, for example, the more obstacles there will be to hinder the transfer of knowledge (Hofstede, 1991).

5. *The capacity of absorption:* This is also going to be a determining factor when it comes to receiving or transferring flows of knowledge. If both the parent company and subsidiary company have a good capacity for learning and experience in receiving and sending knowledge flows, this will undoubtedly make transferring knowledge between units easier (Reed & DeFillippi, 1990).

Organizational knowledge transfer is a complex process that faces many obstacles. The tacit nature of knowledge and the diversity of national and organizational cultures are good examples.

There is a correlation between the degree of knowledge transferability and the type of organizational knowledge (Ordóñez de Pablos, 2004a, 2006). Nonaka and Takeuchi (1995) differentiate two knowledge dimensions: epistemological level and ontological level. The first level proposes the existence of explicit and tacit knowledge. Explicit knowledge is knowledge articulated and codified in handbooks, computer programs, databases, and training tools, among other elements. Therefore this type of knowledge is transmissible. However some knowledge-based resources, such as skills—competences, know-how, and experience, for example—cannot be completely codified knowledge, while other resources can be fully codified through standard procedures, computer algorithms, predicting models and theories, formulae, or programs, for example. Tacit knowledge is personal, context specific, and difficult to regularize. It includes cognitive elements—that is, "mental patterns" (diagrams, paradigms, prospects, beliefs, points of view, etc.)—that help individuals to perceive and define their environment. The second level of analysis highlights the existence of knowledge at individual, group, organizational, and interorganizational levels respectively.

Combining these dimensions, we can say that organizations are considered to be depositary of several types of knowledge (explicit and tacit) existing on different levels (individual, group, organizational, and interorganizational). Literature and empirical evidence emphasizes the "stickiness" of tacit knowledge: the transfer of knowledge has more difficulties if the knowledge exhibits a high degree of tacitness.

## MEASURING AND REPORTING KNOWLEDGE-BASED RESOURCES IN MULTINATIONALS

### Brief Historical Review of Intellectual Capital Reporting

MNCs must quantify their available stocks of knowledge. These stocks include the organizational resources based on the knowledge of the parent company and the subsidiaries. At any given moment within each one of these units, there exists a knowledge stock level that, with the passing of time, will subsequently move on to another level as a result of the knowledge flows that exist not only within each organizational unit, but also between them.

Midway through the '90s, a number of innovative companies began, on their own initiative, to publish intellectual capital statements. These are a new type of corporate report that seeks to reflect the company's knowledge map or inventory.

Current accounting standards allow a very small number of intangible resources to be posted if and when these comply with certain conditions, for example, goodwill and patents. However, what happens to the knowledge of the employees? Is it an organizational resource? Does it appear posted in the company's financial statements?

The intangible resources that do not appear reflected in the company's accounting process are not merely limited to the knowledge of the employees. Other knowledge-based resources exist, such as the value of the relationships developed with customers, suppliers, shareholders, competitors, and other agents. Neither must we forget the knowledge that goes into certain organizational policies, structures, culture, and routines.

These intangible resources do not figure into the financial statements. But does that mean that companies should forget to manage them? Is it that they, unlike tangible assets, are unimportant?

Without doubt, knowledge-based resources are a key factor in achieving and sustaining long-term competitive advantage. In order to be able to manage them appropriately, firstly it is necessary to have a clear vision of the stocks of knowledge that exist within the organization, in this case, within the MNC. To achieve this objective, it is vital to measure and quantify these resources.

## The Intellectual Capital Statement

The result of the measurement of knowledge-based resources is a key element for building the intellectual capital report of the company. What is an *intellectual capital statement or report?* According to the Danish Agency for Trade and Industry (2003), the intellectual capital report is:

*...an externally published document, which communicates the company's knowledge management goals, efforts and results. [It] forms an integral part of working with knowledge management within a company. Its statements on the company's efforts to obtain, develop, share and anchor the knowledge resources required to ensure future results. The intellectual capital can contribute*

*to creating value for the company by improving the basis for growth, flexibility and innovation. Its merits lie in expressing the company's strategy for what it must excel at in order to deliver satisfactory products or service.* (p. 13)

An Austrian nanotechnology firm called Nanonet (2003) states that the aim of the intellectual capital report is "to provide a transparent, verifiable overview of the effects of the research funds invested in nanotechnology...it provides a modern communication and control instrument for knowledge-intensive issues" (pp. 2-3). Having a knowledge map of the organizational knowledge is a key issue for MNCs.

Where MNCs are concerned, quantifying knowledge-based resources (intellectual capital) is more complex, in so much as it entails measuring the existing knowledge stock levels not only within the parent company, but also those in the possession of the subsidiaries.

What indicators can be used to quantify the knowledge that exists in an MNC? Two analysis dimensions need to be considered when studying these indicators:

1. The level of knowledge (at the individual, group, and organizational level); and
2. The location of the knowledge (within the parent company or within the subsidiary).

The intellectual capital statement will include a table with two entries. The vertical plane shows the different knowledge stock levels (individual, group, and organizational). In the horizontal plane we shall show the knowledge stocks that exist within the parent company and within the subsidiary, both for the current financial year and for the previous one, thereby providing a comparison of magnitudes.

The type of indicators for MNCs depends on the type of sector in which the company operates. Following recent empirical research on intellectual capital reports published by world leading pioneer firms (Ordóñez de Pablos, 2004b; Ordóñez de Pablos & Edvinsson, 2006), we can propose the indicators listed in Table 1.

Choosing intellectual capital indicators is a complex task. As neither official indicators nor an official intellectual capital guideline exist, companies use those indicators that they deem most opportune to quantify their intellectual capital.

Given the fact that no official directive exists, the MNC is free to decide which specific indicator to use. To do so, it will take into account, among other factors, the sector in which it operates, its activity, the size of the company, and the number of subsidiaries.

If we follow the recommendations for the drawing up of the Intellectual Capital Statement laid down by the 3R Model—developed by Patricia Ordóñez de Pablos at the University of Oviedo, Spain—the MNC should also present the intellectual capital flows account and the intellectual capital memo report (Ordóñez de Pablos, 2004b, 2005a, 2005b).

The intellectual capital flows account will reflect both the increases and the reductions of intellectual capital that occurred during the financial year, with the difference between these being the result. This information will be compiled for each indicator, indicator category, and intellectual capital component as well as at an aggregated level (intellectual capital). Likewise, the objectives for each of the indicators, indicator categories, and intellectual capital components will be specified (Ordóñez de Pablos, 2004b).

The intellectual capital memo shall have to complement and explain the information contained in the intellectual capital statement and in the intellectual capital flows account. In line with traditional accounting plans, the report will include information regarding the company's activity or activities, the standards used to evaluate intellectual capital, as well as events occurring after the closure of the accounts that do not affect these, but knowledge of which will be useful to the users of the intellectual capital accounts.

What advantage does quantifying and reporting on its knowledge-based resources bring to an MNC?

1. Evaluation of the type of existing stocks (strategic knowledge, basic knowledge, residual knowledge, idiosyncratic knowledge).
2. Improved management of these resources, given the fact that they have been quantified and we know where they are located throughout the different organizational units.
3. Knowing the results of the different organizational policies. For example, the influence human resources policies have on the creation of human capital.

## Intellectual Capital and Accounting Policies

Intellectual capital does not appear in the traditional financial report. The explanation is the following. An asset—under *International Accounting Standard Committee* (IASC) literature—is a resource controlled by an enterprise as a result of past events and from which future economic benefits are expected to flow to the enterprise. According to International Accounting Standard (IAS) 38, the list of items that will not make it onto the balance sheet include expenditure on the following items: (a) research, starting-up a business, training, and advertising; and (b) generating internally customer lists, brand names, mastheads, customer loyalty, customer relationships, human capital, structural capital, and publishing titles. These items will not meet the definition of an intangible asset and the recognition criteria. Expenditures on these items will therefore be expended when incurred.

As there are no generally accepted accounting policies for the presentation of the intellectual capital accounts, this is a field currently under development where everything is left to be done in following years.

*Table 1. Intellectual capital report (Sources: Ordóñez de Pablos, 2004b; Ordóñez de Pablos & Edvinsson, 2006)*

| UNIT | PARENT COMPANY | | SUBSIDIARY$_i$ | |
| --- | --- | --- | --- | --- |
| | Year$_t$ | Year$_{t-1}$ | Year$_t$ | Year$_{t-1}$ |
| | | | | |
| HUMAN CAPITAL | | | | |
| **Indicators** <br> • Number of employees <br> • Number of graduate employees <br> • Number of employees holding a doctorate <br> • Total investment in training <br> • Hours of training per employee per year <br> • Number of employees who permanently work abroad <br> • Number of new employees <br> • Number of waivers/relinquishments <br> • Number of competence development plans <br> • Number of career development plans <br> • Average length of service <br> • Number of permanent contracts <br> • Number of employees who have received awards/prizes <br> • Employee job satisfaction index/ratio | | | | |
| RELATIONAL CAPITAL | | | | |
| **Indicators** <br> • Domestic/international market share <br> • Number of strategic customers <br> • Amount invoiced to the five most important customers <br> • Length of the existing customer relationships <br> • % of customers who would recommend the company <br> • New strategic customers gained during the financial year <br> • Investments in relational marketing <br> • Number of relationships with business schools and/or universities <br> • Number of suggestions made by customers <br> • Number of offices equipped with customer satisfaction quantifying systems <br> • Number of management conferences attended <br> • Number of employees speaking/presenting at scientific conferences <br> • Sponsorship agreements <br> • Professional networks <br> • Employees on advisory boards (corporate, political, scientific) <br> • Number of countries in which the company operates <br> • Average number of employees per office <br> • Number of commercial alliances | | | | |
| STRUCTURAL CAPITAL | | | | |

*Continued next page*

*Table 1. Continued*

| Indicators | | | | |
|---|---|---|---|---|
| •      Investment in office equipment | | | | |
| •      Investment in IT equipment | | | | |
| •      IT expenditure per employee | | | | |
| •      Number of visits paid to the organization's Web site on a daily basis | | | | |
| •      Number of visits paid to the organization's Web site on a monthly basis | | | | |
| •      Number of employees with a teleworking option | | | | |
| •      Number of best working practices "posted" on the organization's intranet | | | | |
| •      Number of employees with intranet access out of total number of employees | | | | |
| •      Number of documents shared/distributed via the intranet | | | | |
| •      Number of employees with Internet access out of total number of employees | | | | |
| •      Number of shared-knowledge databases | | | | |
| •      Number of participants in best working practice processes | | | | |
| •      Number of knowledge management projects | | | | |
| •      Number of products/services | | | | |
| •      Number of new products/services | | | | |
| •      Sales volume linked to new products/services introduced over last year | | | | |
| •      Total innovation | | | | |
| •      Accreditations and certifications (environmental and quality) | | | | |
| •      Number of ISO-9000 certifications | | | | |
| •      Number of quality committees | | | | |
| •      Number of improvement groups | | | | |
| •      Number of employees who participate in round tables | | | | |
| •      Environmental investment | | | | |
| •      Number of occupational audits of the company's installations | | | | |
| •      Investment in cultural support projects and solidarity projects | | | | |

Additionally, as there are no standards and/or general accounting policies for the intellectual capital accounts, the reliability of intellectual capital accounts depends on quality data and accumulation methods.

## CHALLENGES FOR REPORTING KNOWLEDGE-BASED RESOURCES IN MNCs

An important challenge is that of the development of official directives—either by the corresponding accounting bodies or by other institutions—that will enable the intellectual capital reporting models drawn up by the companies to be standardized, thereby making it easier to compare and audit them.

The MNCs that still do not quantify their knowledge-based resources must become aware of the importance of these strategic actions and observe the experience and results of those pioneering companies that have been preparing intellectual capital statements for years.

In short, the drawing up of an intellectual capital statement will enable the MNCs to possess a map of their knowledge-based resources that will in turn serve as a route map for making the strategic decisions that will enable them to survive successfully in competitive, complex, and dynamic environments.

## CONCLUSION AND IMPLICATIONS FOR MANAGEMENT

Managers know that managing and measuring knowledge-based resources are key strategic processes for achieving a long-term competitive advantage. These tasks are even more complex in an international context with multiple intra- and interorganizational knowledge flows. The first step towards the management of knowledge-based resources must be the measurement of these resources as well as the building of the intellectual capital statement.

Measuring knowledge stocks in multinational companies is not easy. On the one hand, there are knowledge stocks—as well as flows—within the headquarters of the MNC. On the other, there are knowledge flows and stocks within each subsidiary of the MNC. Additionally there are knowledge flows among the headquarters and the subsidiaries, and among the companies' own subsidiaries.

However, the path to building intellectual capital statements is not easy. Is there an official model for intellectual capital statements? The answer is "No…at least not yet." Then how can MNCs build this report? Should they learn from pioneer firms? Definitely yes!

## REFERENCES

Barney, J.B. (2001). Is the resource-based view a useful perspective for strategic management research? Yes. *Academy of Management Review, 26*(1), 41-56.

Bartlett, C.A., & Ghoshal, S. (1989). *Managing across borders: The transnational solution.* Boston: Harvard Business School Press.

Becker, G.S. (1964). *Human capital.* New York: Columbia University Press.

Bontis, N., Chong, W., & Richardson, S. (2000). Intellectual capital and business performance in Malaysian industries. *Journal of Intellectual Capital, 1*(1), 85-100.

Danish Agency for Development of Trade and Industry (DATI). (2003). *Intellectual capital statements—the new guideline.* Author.

Dierickx, I., & Cool, K. (1989a). Assets stock accumulation and sustainability of competitive advantage. *Management Science, 35*(12), 1504-1511.

Dierickx, I., & Cool, K. (1989b). Assets stock accumulation and sustainability of competitive advantage: Reply. *Management Science, 35*(12), 1512-1513.

Edvinsson, L. (1997). Developing intellectual capital at Skandia. *Long Range Planning, 30*(3).

Edvinsson, L., & Malone, M.S. (1997). *Intellectual capital. Realizing your company's true value by finding its hidden brainpower* (1st ed.). HarperCollins.

Ferner, A. (1997). Country of origin effects and HRM in multinational companies. *Human Resource Management Journal, 7*(1), 19-37.

Gooderham, P.N., & Nordhaug, O. (2003). *International management: Cross-boundary challenges.* Oxford: Blackwell.

Harzing, A., & van Ruysseveldt, J. (Eds.). (2004). *International human resource management* (2nd ed.). London: Sage.

Hofstede, G. (1991). *Cultures and organizations: Intercultural cooperation and its importance to survival.* Glasgow: HarperCollins.

Kaplan, R.S., & Norton, D.P. (1996). Using the balanced scorecard as a strategic management system. *Harvard Business Review,* (January-February), 76.

Kaplan, R.S., & Norton, D.P. (1993). Putting the balanced scorecard to work. *Harvard Business Review,* (September-October), 134-147.

Kaplan, R.S., & Norton, D.P. (1992). The balanced scorecard—measures that drive performance. *Harvard Business Review, 70*(January-February), 72-79.

Lippman, S., & Rumelt, R.P. (1982). Uncertain imitability: An analysis of interfirm differences in efficiency under competition. *Bell Journal of Economics, 13,* 418-438.

Lytras, M., & Pouloudi, N. (2006). Towards the development of a novel taxonomy of knowledge management systems from a learning perspective. *Journal of Knowledge Management, 10*(6), 64-80.

Mahoney, J.T. (1995). The management of resources and the resource management. *Journal of Business Research, 33,* 91-101.

Nanonet. (2003). *Nanonet–Styria intellectual capital report.* Retrieved from *www.nanonet.at*

Nonaka, I., & Takeuchi, H. (1995). *The knowledge-creating company.* Oxford: Oxford University Press.

Ordóñez de Pablos, P. (2001). Relevant experiences on measuring and reporting intellectual capital in European pioneering firms. In N. Bontis & C. Chong (Eds.), *Organizational intelligence: The cutting edge of intellectual capital and knowledge management.* Butterworth-Heinemann.

Ordóñez de Pablos, P. (2004a). Knowledge flow transfers in multinational corporations: Knowledge properties and implications for management. *Journal of Knowledge Management, 8*(4), 105-116.

Ordóñez de Pablos, P. (2004b). A guideline for building the intellectual capital statement: The 3R model. *International Journal of Learning and Intellectual Capital, 1*(1), 3-18.

Ordóñez de Pablos, P. (2005a). Intellectual capital accounts: What pioneering firms from Asia and Europe are doing now. *International Journal of Knowledge and Learning, 1*(3), 249-268.

Ordóñez de Pablos, P. (2005b). Intellectual capital reports in India: Lessons from a case study. *Journal of Intellectual Capital, 6*(1), 141-149.

Ordóñez de Pablos, P. (2006). Transnational corporations and strategic challenges: An analysis of knowledge flows and competitive advantage. *The Learning Organization.*

Ordóñez de Pablos, P., & Edvinsson, L. (2006). *The intellectual capital statements: Evolution and how to get started.* Working Paper.

Ordóñez de Pablos, P., & Peteraf, M. (2004). Managing and measuring knowledge-based resources. *International Journal of Learning and Intellectual Capital, 1*(4), 377-379.

Ordóñez de Pablos, P., & Peteraf, M. (2005). Organizational learning, innovation and knowledge: The creation of a sustained competitive advantage. *International Journal of Learning and Intellectual Capital, 2*(2), 111-113.

Perlmutter, H.V. (1969). The tortuous evolution of the multinational corporation. *Columbia Journal of World Business, 4*(1), 9-18.

Perlmutter, H.V., & Heenan, D.A. (1974). How multinational should your top managers be? *Harvard Business Review, 52*(6), 121-132.

Peteraf, M.A. (1993). The cornerstone of competitive advantage: A resource based-view. *Strategic Management Journal, 14,* 179-191.

Reed, R., & DeFillippi, R. (1990). Causal ambiguity, barriers to imitation and sustainable competitive advantage. *Academy of Management Review, 15*(1), 88-102.

Skandia. (1994). *Visualizing intellectual capital at Skandia.* Supplement to Skandia's 1994 Annual Report.

Skandia. (1996). *Customer value.* Supplement to Skandia's 1996 Annual Report.

Szulanski, G. (2003). *Sticky knowledge: Barriers to knowing in the firm.* London: Sage.

Wernerfelt, B. (1995). The resource-based view of the firm: Ten years after. *Strategic Management Journal, 5*(2), 171-174.

Wernerfelt, B. (1984). A resource based view of the firm. *Strategic Management Journal, 5,* 171-180.

Zahra, S.A., & George, G. (2002). Absorptive capacity: A review, reconceptualization and extension. *Academy of Management Review, 27*(2), 185-203.

# Chapter XV
# Knowledge Management in Research Joint Ventures

**Elena Revilla**
*Instituto de Empresa, Spain*

## ABSTRACT

*As innovation and technology management grow in complexity, the need for interorganizational coop-eration increases. Part of this cooperation requires the understanding of how knowledge management and learning processes may function to support a successful research and development collaboration in multinational enterprises. To further this understanding we introduce a typology to help categorize various collaborative efforts within a research joint venture environment. The typology is based on two dimensions: the locus of the research joint venture knowledge and the knowledge management approach. This matrix leads us to deduce that different research joint venture (RJV) strategies can emerge as a result of these two dimensions. Finally, an evaluation of this relationship is completed using information and practices from data acquired from a broad-based study of European-based RJVs. Implications for research and management of these types of projects are also introduced throughout the chapter.*

## INTRODUCTION

New knowledge (especially technological knowl-edge) is viewed as the foundation for innovation, change, and sustainable competitive advantage. Today, there is no doubt that knowledge is one of the most strategic weapons that can lead to achieving competitive success (Grant, 1996). The primary role of research and development (R&D) within organizations is to create new knowledge or recombine existing knowledge in order to innovate and match with the changing market conditions. Roussel, Saad, and Erickson

(1995) suggest that the only real product of R&D is knowledge. Thus, the R&D process is knowledge intensive: it not only uses existing knowledge but also creates new knowledge, which provides competitive advantage to the firm.

Historically, firms organized R&D internally and relied on outside contract research only for relatively simple functions or products (Mowery, 1983; Nelson, 1990). From this point of view, firms adhered to the following philosophy: *Successful innovation requires control.* Chesbrough (2003) expresses this idea stating that companies must generate their own ideas that they then develop, manufacture, market, distribute, and service themselves. Today, in many industries, global competition, product and process complexity, along with technological advances has made obsolete this idea of an internally oriented approach to R&D, forcing firms to rethink methods for new knowledge acquisition.

During the last few years, useful knowledge beyond the organizational boundary has become widespread, thus companies should not restrict their knowledge attainment only to what was developed in their internal research. For R&D to succeed, knowledge should be collected from all critical sources. This situation has made companies explore innovative ways that embrace and integrate external knowledge in conjunction with internal R&D. Thus, in recent decades there has been unprecedented growth in research joint ventures (RJVs) in order to expand firms' knowledge. Beyond competitive reasons, other explanations to this growth include greater government support and industrial policy, and relaxed regulatory policies. RJVs are seen as mechanisms enabling firms to learn and enter new technological areas, and to deal more effectively with technological and market uncertainty.

In multinational enterprises (MNEs), the success of this strategy depends on the proper transfer of knowledge developed by the RJV. Knowledge transfer concerns have impelled MNEs to provide local subsidiaries with knowledge flows from the RJV, strengthening local competences. MNEs by their nature are network firms. That means that they must be able to leverage their networks to effectively manage dispersed knowledge assets (Mudambi, 2002).

In order to interact effectively with the external environment and integrate the knowledge developed by the RJV, MNEs need to manage knowledge and its related processes. Because knowledge is a critical output of learning, successfully managing the learning process inherently involves the effective management of knowledge. Managing knowledge requires the introduction

of criteria to decide which knowledge factor is most critical for the organization, and to govern these factors and conditions to guide the activities of knowledge acquisition (DiBella & Nevis, 1996). Thus, knowledge management and the knowledge-based view of the firm have become a central theme in innovation and R&D. Some scholars believe that competition is becoming more knowledge based and that the sources of competitive advantage are shifting to intellectual capabilities, away from physical assets (Subramanian & Venkatraman, 1999).

Given that knowledge management is recognized as a critical and central practice in R&D, managers and researchers have lacked management models that could be used as guides in this environment. With an absence of good conceptual models, understanding the effectiveness of knowledge management practices in RJVs is still a difficult task.

In light of this situation, MNEs increasingly demand frameworks to manage the knowledge developed by the RJV. In this chapter, a contingency theory is used to define typology of RJVs and examine the proposition that the characteristics of a RJV's knowledge base, integrated in the concept of the locus of the RJV, has an important influence on its knowledge management choice. Traditionally, contingency theory has focused on such contingency variables as environmental uncertainty, firm size, and firm technology. This chapter's approach, built on recent advances in knowledge management, establishes that the locus of the RJV, which refers to the stage of technical development at which the RJV operates, can be considered a useful contingency variable in its own right.

In order to reach this goal, different conceptualizations of knowledge management are evaluated. Essentially, the published research has these conceptualizations summarized according to two different perspectives (Daft & Huber, 1987; Mirvis, 1996; Garavan, 1997; Gnyawalli & Stewart, 1999; Hansen, Nohria, & Tierney 1999; Prieto, 2003):

the *structural perspective* and the *behavioral perspective*. Other studies have examined the key knowledge characteristics and pointed out their influence on the management of the firm's activities related to acquisition of knowledge (Grantt, 1996). Organizational learning has identified different types of knowledge for the locus of an RJV. The analysis of the above concepts suggests that knowledge management should be consistent with the particular locus of the RJV.

Thus, the core purpose and contribution of this chapter is: (1) to develop a taxonomy of RJVs based on two knowledge management dimensions, the locus of the RJV research and the knowledge management approach; and (2) to determine if differences in knowledge management are dependent on the locus of the RJV. In order to do this, initially, an overview of RJV knowledge creating and transfer processes in MNEs is presented. This background is viewed as fundamentally important to the dimensional discussions. Afterward, RJVs are classified based on two knowledge management dimensions. Each of these dimensions and their theoretical constructs are described and later integrated in this typology. Finally, an evaluation of this relationship is completed using information and practices from data acquired from a broad-based study of European-based RJVs.

## RESEARCH JOINT VENTURES, LEARNING, AND KNOWLEDGE MANAGEMENT IN MNES

The prime motivations for creating an RJV is to access knowledge, which is not yet widely distributed or exploited (Zack, 1999), providing learning opportunities and the potential for value creation. Thus, an RJV is defined as a collaborative agreement in which two or more partner organizations (firms and/or public research organizations) decide to coordinate their R&D activities through a cooperative project and to share the knowledge generated from this joint effort. In ideal situations, partners bring their own knowledge, learned throughout their histories in the form of technology, people, or processes, to the newly created project in the hope that this combination of knowledge will produce benefits for all those concerned. This definition of RJV is similar to that recently used by the Council on Competitiveness (1996) where "partnerships are defined as cooperative arrangements engaging companies, universities, and government agencies and laboratories in various combinations to pool resources in pursuit of a shared R&D objective."

By bringing together firms with different knowledge bases, an RJV creates unique learning opportunities for the partners (Inkpen, 1998). Learning for partners requires connecting people so they can think together, creating environments in which complex knowledge can be interpreted and leveraged (McDermott, 1999). This learning will happen only when R&D managers, scientists, and engineers feel comfortable sharing knowledge with their counterparts in other organizations. In the presence of organizational and national boundaries across which knowledge flows, this can be particularly challenging (Berdrow & Lane, 2003). Differences in language, norms, and mental models often inhibit personal interactions—int eractions that are critical to creating a learning environment for RJVs. Unless the RJV makes deliberate efforts, knowledge generated by a partner remains with the partner. For RJVs to innovate rapidly, it is imperative to make deliberate efforts to manage R&D knowledge. In this respect, an understanding of the acquisition of knowledge for RJVs could benefit RJV managers.

The literature on knowledge management distinguishes two core processes in the acquisition of knowledge for RJVs: (1) the creation of new knowledge through interaction among organizations and (2) the transfer of the existing knowledge from one organization to another (Larsson, Bengtsson, Henriksson, & Sparks 1998).

## The Knowledge Creating Process

The essence of RJVs is the creation of knowledge throughout a creative problem-solving process aimed to enhance the potential of creating innovations as part of an adaptive process to be able to respond to environmental demands. In ideal situations, members of an RJV have a specialized knowledge that frames their attention when they approach a problem. By recognizing and defining problems, and applying knowledge to solve problems, they create new knowledge, both tacit and explicit (Nonaka, Toyama, & Nagata, 2000). Then, by problem solving, an RJV refines the understanding of its environment, increases its absorptive capability, and improves its ability to react appropriately to future stimulus.

The creation of knowledge by an RJV is not just an agglomeration of devices to gain access to an individual firms' knowledge. It should be more than a collection of individual experiences. Senge (1990) considers that for learning to take place at a group level, an alignment of the different individual learning processes is necessary in order to avoid wasted energy. From an organizational learning perspective, it requires a high degree of mutual involvement in problem recognition and problem-solving processes. In the first step, partners must scan, notice, and construct meaning about environmental changes. The recognition of the existence of a problem occurs when some stimuli indicate the need for new actions. These stimuli then lead to the second step, when partners jointly experience new work processes, tasks, technological characteristics, and so forth to solve a problem.

RJV obligates partners to spend considerable time together, discuss and reflect upon their experiences, observe how their colleagues solve tasks and interact with technologies, explain, and give sense to their own actions. RJV members must establish relationships via language and thought in order to coordinate their learning processes.

Dialogue (Isaacs, 1993) has been identified as a key aspect of this integrating process. Each partner exhibits a perception or personal image of the world, and these perceptions will affect the other firms when they are shared during interaction. Individual knowledge needs to be disclosed, shared, and legitimized until it becomes part of group knowledge. RJV knowledge is the result of the construction and interaction of numerous individual firm perspectives during problem recognition and problem-solving processes.

The creation of knowledge by RJVs is especially stimulating in the presence of MNEs. The diversity of national and organizational cultures let RJVs have available a broad set of knowledge, experience, and background, and increase its ability to scan the environmental, recognize the existence of a problem, and solve the problem. Although the presence of such diversity could be positively related to RJV performance, the diversity can also lead to problems in the R&D process by adding situations that increase potential disagreement and conflict. The presence of MNEs stimulates the need to fit new information into RJV members' existing knowledge and presents an opportunity to change their existing theories.

## The Knowledge Transfer Process

The knowledge creating process that happens in the RJV does not guarantee that individual partners benefit from such knowledge on a larger scale. At this point, the problem an organization faces is transferring RJV knowledge to individual organizations. For this transfer to take place, it is essential that RJV knowledge is introduced and materialized in the operational systems of the organization, improving its activities.

Although a RJV is a means through which firms learn, the created knowledge needs to be communicated and integrated into its organizational routines in order to influence organizational effectiveness. An individual organization learns by changing its actual routines (Argyris & Schön, 1978). The intangible nature of knowledge assets prevents knowledge from being completely diffused and subsequently used in the organization, unless "mental models" are simultaneously transferred. Changes in organizational routines and decision rules will not likely take place if mental models are not shared by members (Kim, 1993). Thus, the extent to which these mental models are shared determine their understanding of the problem, fostering its diffusion and facilitating its materialization.

Even in the age of global information and communication systems, the effective knowledge transfer across geographically and cultural boundaries is not a trivial matter. Large MNE firms need to establish efficient internal mechanisms for providing their local subsidiaries with the RJV knowledge (Gerybadze & Reger, 1999). Regardless of these internal mechanisms, the receiver (the local subsidiary) must identify the RJV knowledge as potentially important, and then absorb and exploit it in order to be in position to react as quickly as possible to dynamic changes in relative location advantages.

Cohen and Levinthal (1990) and Lane, Salk, and Lyles (2001) express this idea in terms of "absorptive capacity," which expresses the firm's ability to assimilate new knowledge and make use of the benefits of joint research. Absorptive capacity contributes to innovation because it tends to develop cumulatively and builds on prior related knowledge. Given the intense cumulative nature of scientific knowledge, the local subsidiary's knowledge prior to an RJV influences the effective acquisition and utilization of new knowledge. As Powell, Koput, and Smit-Doerr (1996) argued, knowledge facilitates the use of other knowledge. What can be learned is affected by what is already known. Organizations that possess relevant prior knowledge are likely to have a better understanding of the new knowledge, and can generate new ideas and develop new products. Organizations with a high level of absorptive capacity are likely

to harness new knowledge from an RJV to help their innovative activities. Without such capacity, MNEs cannot learn or transfer knowledge from the RJV.

## RESEARCH JOINT VENTURES: TAXONOMIC FOUNDATIONS

In this section, some background on the two dimensions that will be used in the typology is introduced. The first dimension will be the locus of the RJV knowledge, and the second will focus on the method that knowledge and learning is integrated into an RJV and its membership. This second dimension is defined as the knowledge management approach.

### The Locus of the RJV

As previously stated, RJVs cannot be conceptualized as mere exchange relationships involving the transfer of products or services. An RJV differs from others kinds of collaboration in that the primary motivation for joining an RJV is to gain new knowledge which can be processed and transformed into a competitive asset. Underlying the RJV is the attempt to increase the knowledge base of the organization through a cooperative R&D project.

Among the most widespread elements that influence the RJV's knowledge management are the characteristics of the knowledge to be developed by the R&D process (Winter, 1987). This chapter does not concentrate in separate knowledge characteristics, but as an integrated concept within the general characteristic of locus of the RJV.

Thus, to investigate RJV knowledge management, initially it is defined as the "locus of the RJV" which refers to the stage of technical development at which the RJV operates. The main stages of technical development are: (1) *basic research,* which searches for new concepts or scientific principles, although they may not present any direct application; and (2) *applied research,* which utilizes acquired knowledge from basic research, showing its potential practical contributions to solve known problems. This characterization of basic and applied research is arguably more conceptual than practical, given the considerable gray area between these two extremes of the R&D continuum.

In terms of knowledge, these two stages involve different levels of "radicalness" of its learning process.[1] While applied research focuses on knowledge development from an existing body of knowledge, basic research seeks to construct and acquire new knowledge, adding to the body of knowledge. Viewed broadly, technological change occurs in two extreme forms. In the first situation, the developing knowledge comes from the existing knowledge. In the second situation new knowledge is created with loose connections to existing knowledge.

Basic research introduces new knowledge and competences within the RJV. New knowledge allows the variations needed to provide a sufficient amount of choices to solve problems (March, 1991), improves the possibilities of engendering new ideas or create new knowledge combinations, and allows obsolete knowledge substitution. Applied research includes the application of past experience and competences within the RJV. Using the same knowledge elements reduces the likelihood of errors and false starts, and facilitates the development of routines (Levinthal & March, 1993). It creates a familiarity that allows decomposition of sequenced activities in an efficient order where unnecessary steps can be eliminated (Eisenhardt & Tabrizi, 1995) and can lead to a deeper understanding of concepts, booting the RJV's ability to identify valuable knowledge within them, develop connections between them, and combine them in many different and significant ways (Katila & Ahuja, 2002).

The locus of the RJV can be seen as an important categorization of knowledge assets. Organizational learning has suggested different dimensions

of knowledge to understand the locus of the RJV. Yet, there has been little consistency in classifying knowledge.[2] The focus is on categorizing the intrinsic nature of knowledge associated with RJVs related to the ease of knowledge creation and transfer. The following three dimensions are chosen: tacit-explicit, generic-specific, and autonomous-systemic. These dimensions should not be viewed as dichotomous (i.e., one must fall into one group or another within a given dimension), but rather as a spectrum with two extreme knowledge types at either end.

## The Tacit-Explicit Dimension

Polanyi (1967) distinguishes between tacit and explicit knowledge. This categorization can be thought of as the difference between experiential and articulated knowledge (Simonin, 1999). Explicit knowledge consists of knowledge that can be expressed in symbols and can be communicated through these symbols to other people. Tacit knowledge is difficult to express and communicate to other people because it cannot be codified and articulated. Therefore, tacit knowledge is difficult to pass to others outside the community-of-practice because they will not understand the terminology and basic principles associated with it. In fact, explicit knowledge is revealed by its communication while tacit knowledge is revealed through its application (Spencer & Grant, 1996). Tacit knowledge, accumulated through experience, is often referred to as "learning by doing." According to this categorization, it is expected that the more scientific, and basic, the RJV R&D project, the more explicit the knowledge.

## The Generic-Specific Dimension

This concept is related to what other authors have referred as universal vs. localized knowledge (Bonaccorsi & Piccaluga, 1994). Following these authors, generic knowledge is defined as the scope of its application to various target problem domains, even different from the source domain. Under this respect, generic knowledge is highly universal as opposed to specific knowledge that can only be used within its source domain.

Specific knowledge is more easily appropriated than generic knowledge, even when generic knowledge can be more readily codified. Despite this fact an RJV may have no other option than to look for scientific knowledge when local solutions to specific problems are ineffective or too costly to develop. Generic knowledge, especially intense in basic research projects and at the beginning of the development of the knowledge field, may eventually result in dramatic productivity increases and cost reduction in activity design (e.g., algorithms for parallel computing, new design tools, simulation techniques, and so on), but may be less useful than specific knowledge for the organization. Global time-based competition and a reduced product lifecycle do not allow RJVs to fully market and exploit basic research output, making such research a risky undertaking. The more generic the knowledge is, the more it is capable of producing broad and indiscriminate benefits and providing impetus for future advances in knowledge. Generic knowledge can be categorized as more characteristic of basic research, while specific knowledge is at the applied research locus.

## The Systemic-Autonomous Dimension

This dimension is related to Henderson and Clark's (1990) classification of component and architectural knowledge. It expresses the dependency of the knowledge development process from other innovations or organizational processes. The fewer the functions or knowledge areas that are involved in the R&D project, the more autonomous it is and the further away it usually is from the expected market. Thus, basic research can be implemented as an autonomous process. On the other hand, applied research requires strong feedback between technological users, suppliers, and producers, thus increasing the project organizational dependency between the diverse functional knowledge areas involved in the R&D project.

Autonomous knowledge can exist independently, whereas systemic knowledge cannot or should not be decomposed into independent parts. Because systemic knowledge is typically held organization-wide, it is collective in nature. Moreover, since it is difficult for any one person to understand the whole system, it is typically tacit.

The dimensions of knowledge that have been described facilitate understanding of the knowledge associated to the locus of the RJV. So, it is easy to argue that basic research tends to be more explicit, generic, autonomous, and generally a creator of new knowledge, while applied research that focuses on existing knowledge tends to be more tacit, specified, systemic, and more a transfer mechanism of knowledge.

## Knowledge Management Perspectives

In the previous section, characteristics of RJV based upon the locus of the RJV research were presented. Now this chapter focuses on the second major typological dimension, knowledge management characteristics. The idea of knowledge management has come to the fore in the business literature due to the increased awareness of the importance of knowledge for the organization's prosperity and survival. In particular, the "knowledge-based view of the firm" proposes knowledge as a key firm resource and a source of competitive advantage (Grant, 1996; Kogut & Zander, 1992). Knowledge management refers to identifying, developing, and leveraging knowledge in organizations to help them to compete (Alavi & Leidner, 2001). Broadly speaking, it encompasses any initiative concerned with the creation, acquisition, capture, sharing, and use of knowledge, skills, and expertise, whether these are explicitly labeled as knowledge management or not (Pan & Scarbrough, 1999).

The development of knowledge management in theory and practice involves a wide range of contributions, each bringing their respective experiences, beliefs, and practices. Contemporary knowledge management approaches often reflect the strong divide between those interested in the "technology side" and those emphasizing the "human side" of knowledge management (Alvesson & Karreman, 2001; Gloet & Berrell, 2003). As a result, a wide variety of knowledge management enablers have been addressed in the literature (Leonard, 1995; Lee & Choi, 2003). Among these enablers, culture, structure, people, and information technologies are incorporated into Lee and Choi's (2003) and Chuang's (2004) research model. Gold, Malhotra, and Segars (2001) suggest that a knowledge management infrastructure consists of technology, structure, and culture. Similarly, Van den Brink (2003) classifies knowledge management enablers as social, organizational, and technological factors.

Although there are many organizational knowledge management dimensions, published research has often summarized them according to two different perspectives (Daft & Huber, 1987; Mirvis, 1996; Garavan, 1997; Gnyawalli & Stewart, 1999; Hansen et al., 1999; Prieto, 2003): the *structural perspective* and the *behavioral perspective*. These perspectives are founded on very different theoretical assumptions. The structural vision of knowledge management emerges from the positivist epistemology about learning development in organizations, which is an eminently "mechanic" point of view. The behavioral approach is a result of the constructionist epistemology, which highlights the human, social, and interactive interventions of knowledge management.

The *structural perspective* suggests knowledge is objective, static, universal, and representative of a given external reality that includes objects and events. Accordingly, knowledge management is aimed to represent and reproduce that reality as closely as possible. It is accepted that objective information exists and must be rationally acquired, diffused, and processed between organizational members by implementing and using tangible systems and elements. These systems must comprise the scanning, coordination, and control mechanisms necessary to fit environmental contingencies and reduce the uncertainty of a variety of potential actions (Daft & Lengel, 1986; Daft & Huber, 1987; March & Simon, 1993).

From this point of view, knowledge management is synonymous with the design and employment of technical and structural procedures focused on work processes and information processing. Previous research defines the exchange of information and organization of collaborations as a means for facilitating the integration of R&D. Bonacorsi and Piccaluga (1996) consider information exchange critical in any research activity and identify three dimensions of information exchange that determine the efficiency of the learning process: intensity and frequency of communication between partners, the communication media used for information exchange, and the spatial dimension of information exchange.

The *behavioral perspective* proposes that knowledge often remains in the human mind, related to feelings and experiences. Knowledge is subjective, dynamic, context specific, and embedded in action. As a result, individuals can construct their own reality and modify those constructions on the basis of experience and even context characteristics.

Within this point of view, the primary goal of knowledge management is to analyze and enhance how individuals comprehend events until creating a common understanding as a basis for action. The literature in this area (Weick, 1979; Brown & Duguid, 1991, 1998; Schein, 1993; Hedlund, 1994; Nonaka, 1994) has stated that the potential of organizational members to discern the environment, interpret it, and comprehend it is a social result because knowledge is social and has synergetic attributes. Thus, human behaviors should be aligned towards learning through the adjustment of conditions to develop the human potential. Specifically, it refers to conditions such as transparency, communication, trust, creativity, responsibility, commitment, and initiative.

Both perspectives provide different descriptions about the process of knowledge acquisition. As a consequence, knowledge management initiatives are also different. However, each of these perspectives has limitations that have induced their evolution towards integrative perspectives intended to create a general framework about knowledge management in organizations (Brown & Eisenhardt, 1997; Van der Krogt, 1998; Popper & Lipshitz, 1998, 2000; Choi & Lee, 2001). The integrative idea is to advocate that the structural tools required for work performance as well as for the conditions of the human potential are required to adapt individuals' behavior. Thus, knowledge management in organizations is encouraged by: (1) information mechanisms and coordination systems focused on the processing and analysis of information; and (2) the personal, social, or cultural values that are focused on the development of the human potential as well as on the creation of a shared meaning within organization. The aim is that organizational members will be able to expand their competencies in agreement with the systems established to optimally work in organizations.

## A TWO-DIMENSIONAL TAXONOMY OF RJVS

This section presents a two-dimensional taxonomy by which RJVs may manage their R&D activities and for sharing the knowledge generated by the RJV. Although much of the learning literature addresses the knowledge or content of RJV, the management of knowledge is also important. A focus solely on content of the RJV ignores the complex cognitive and behavioral changes that must occur before a learning "outcome" can be identified (Inkpen & Dinur, 1998).

Figure 1. A two-dimensional taxonomy of RJVs

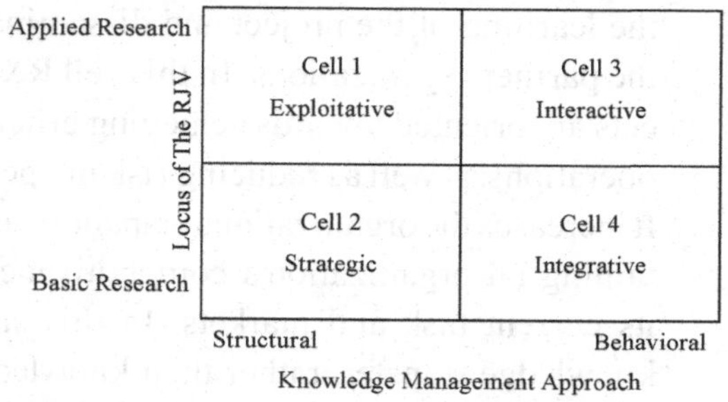

Thus, it is possible to define two critical dimensions that permit us to present a more suitable taxonomy of RJVs. These dimensions are summarized in Figure 1. The first dimension, the locus of the RJV, integrates different characteristics of knowledge and is focused on the stage of applied research at which the RJV operates. This vertical axis clearly delineates R&D projects that use existing knowledge, which is more tacit, specific, and systemic, to solve problems and projects that generate new rules and knowledge—more explicit, generic, and autonomous—to deal with a new problem. The second dimension, along the horizontal axis, is the knowledge management approach that supports the inter-organizational process of knowledge acquisition. The horizontal axis measures the extent to which the RJV focuses more on structural practices vs. behavioral practices to create and transfer knowledge.

Four cells are identified in this taxonomy which are defined as *exploitative, strategic, interactive,* and *integrative*. Each of these cells is further embellished with exemplary cases of actual RJVs. For the sake of anonymity, the companies in these cases are not named.

### Exploitative RJVs

It is posited that RJVs placed in cell 1 on the two-dimensional grid develop R&D projects that are focused on existing knowledge and manage the learning process in a structured way. Knowledge management basically lies in tangible structures and procedures that efficiently capture and retain the learning of the project and disseminate it to the partner organizations. In this cell R&D projects are oriented towards achieving efficiency in operations as well as reducing risk in operations. It increases the organizational capability of maintaining an organization's competitiveness with its current task and markets. In this situation, knowledge transfer, rather than knowledge creation, is essential to the consolidation of activities and competencies.

## Strategic RJVs

In terms of knowledge management, cell 2 shows a similar situation. These types of RJVs support the building of new knowledge, but with a focus not so much on creating knowledge but on capturing and transferring knowledge from the RJV to the partners. The new knowledge is structured and applied according to existing processes. Because the new knowledge in this classification does not pre-exist within the firm, the key challenge is to effectively absorb the new knowledge. These RJVs aim at developing future competitive advantages and thereby enhancing the internal capability to face future changes. In the short term, the benefits are rarely appreciable.

## Interactive RJVs

Cell 3 defines RJVs that increase the scope and depth of existing knowledge by socializing members around certain problems, tasks, and work processes. Knowledge gaps between the members indicate the need to seek new insights, and invest time and energy. Since developing knowledge requires existing experience and knowledge, RJVs build up competencies and skill that, locally applied, generate a better understanding of the key processes or variants of existing products.

## Integrative RJVs

Finally, cell 4 includes RJVs that seek the largest competitive advance. They develop R&D projects that seek to construct and acquire new knowledge and manage the learning process with a behavioral approach, based on innovation, creativity, and trust. Here knowledge creation is something different when compared with the cell 3. In this situation there is no available knowledge where you can judge the relevance for further expansion. In some ways, these RJVs become "corporate revolutionaries" that, with an entrepreneurial behavior, create knowledge that can become imperative to long-term performance. Although creating new knowledge is always risky because it breaks the existing coherence between the new knowledge and the prior knowledge, it produces the highest level of learning, which sometimes changes the definition of a whole market segment.

## Exemplary Taxonomy Cases

### Cell 1: Exploitative RJVs (Applied Research–Structured Knowledge Management)

A good example of this RJV type is an R&D project between a world-class shipyard, a consulting firm, an information technology company, and a mechanical engineering department of a university. The purpose of the project was to define, develop, and introduce practical procedures, methods, and tools to enable different operators within the shipping community to design, maintain, and operate ships and ship systems with high safety, balanced availability, and low owner cost characteristics. The procedures, methods, and tools focused on areas of: information management, logistics support, safety management and quality assurance, maintenance and maintenance management, system design, cost-benefit, and lifecycle costing.

The project could be summarized as follows: endure the ship's life. Anything that could extend the ship's life with information technology was considered. The goal was very broad. This is the reason why the first phase of the project was to analyze the market in order to select the priorities and needs of the shipyards' customers and to clarify and further define the project.

This project was completed in three overlapping and iterative phases. Initially, the state of the art and the expected potential for improvements in the shipping community were discussed, including lower probabilities for safety-related failures and accidents, lower probabilities for failures in ships systems which are related to the timely operation of ships, and lower cost for scheduled and unscheduled maintenance of ships and ships systems. The findings and experiences from this analysis were summarized and transformed into specifications for development of suitable procedures, methods, and tools. These specifications were turned into recommendations for the practical introduction and application of suitable methods, procedures, and tools for improving safety and availability, and to reduce owners' costs. Adaptation of available products was used to improve some of the identified deficiencies. Most of them were composed of available software that was adapted to the specific need.

This R&D project could be considered central for the shipyard's core activities, since this firm is concerned about quality and continuous improvement. Its participation on this RJV was to control future improvements to endure the ship's life. Likewise, the information technology company wanted to develop a product of general utilization in this sector that later could be implemented by other organizations.

This RJV was conceived as a useful tool to aid knowledge transfer. Thus, the RJV defined structural mechanisms (relevant information, documents containing operative solutions, value propositions, technical specifications, programming documents) to be sure that the captured knowledge can be disseminated to other R&D projects or applications. The shipyard company provided expertise in the state of the art of design and production of ships. This knowledge was considered very useful for the identification of needs, possibilities of improvements, and new development in the shipping community. The information technology firm and the university participants combined research and practitioner experts, especially in information technology, to solve operative problems for improving safety, availability, and cost reduction. This RJV project resulted from local adaptation of tools, methods, and processes invented and developed elsewhere. By sharing knowledge in this way, the probability of "re-inventing the wheel" is significantly reduced. Likewise, the available documentation avoids having to spend time tracking down and lets the RJV work efficiently.

## Cell 2: Strategic RJVs (Basic Research–Structured Knowledge Management)

An example of RJV that would fall within this cell is an R&D consortium created to develop a new concept, "The Multimedia Broker." This concept provides an infrastructure for publishers to more easily work with their publication authors and to provide their customers with the tools to query the networked products offered by the publishers.

In this context, this RJV aims at integrating multimedia information retrieval techniques, visual query systems, a federated systems architecture, and transaction systems to provide a service. The system will be constructed with a Web-based infrastructure as the foundation.

This RJV was designed to be an integrated system of a number of independent subsystems, each of whose development was assigned to one of the partners responsible for technical solutions.

Physically, each development partner was going to work independently, with the commitment to satisfy the agreed-upon deadlines for the design and implementation. Electronic mail and the introduction of a system for cooperative work allowed technicians working in three different countries to maintain close cooperation and exchange results. Once the subsystems had been specified, the task of the RJV was to define its interactions and interfaces.

The RJV also defined a work methodology. The work methodology chosen focused on rapid prototyping. Rapid prototyping requires any results to be rapidly translated into an integrated prototype including all independent parts and to proof the whole system functionality. Likewise, at the beginning of the project, a quality plan was decided upon by the RJV management on the software to be developed. The quality plan for software included the definition of nomenclatures, the comments to be included in the program, and the testing procedures to be used. Its aim was to facilitate the integration of the independent efforts of the RJV.

Another important RJV issue was the allocation of the property rights of the results between the different members of the RJV. It was decided that the technical members would have the exclusive property of the parts developed by each one of them. In addition, the participation in the consortium provided the limited right to all partners to use any of the results obtained by the project.

These kinds of RJVs help their partner members attain innovation goals while at the same time sharing the risk of obtaining short-term profitability from new technologies, especially in the initial stages of their development. In this case, the multimedia broker led to detection of areas for technological innovation with the highest possibilities of applications to the business environment. The members of this RJV only become involved in research projects if the results offered innovative solutions to their clients. Thus,

although the RJV must be given the responsibility for creating new knowledge, they were more focused on the definition of the interactions between the partners for capture and transfer of knowledge than in the knowledge creating process, which was the responsibility of individual members. This means that once knowledge is created, the likelihood of capture is very high.

## Cell 3: Interactive RJVs (Applied Research–Behavioral Knowledge Management)

A good illustration of this type of RJV is an alliance created between one of the largest industrial truck manufacturers in the world and a large MNE that develops urban maintenance innovations such as garbage collection, public road cleaning, elimination and treatment of garbage, conservation and cleaning of green zones, building, integral cleaning, and sewage network maintenance. Its aim was to develop two electric hybrid prototypes of refuse trucks that can operate with minimum noise and emission pollution when collecting garbage within congested areas of large European cities.

Since the early 1990s, the partner in the RJV charged with urban maintenance was concerned with town councils' interest in environmental topics. These interests were especially important for pollution and noise-emission-related issues facing collection trucks in difficult-to-access areas such as historical places. To be competitive in such a sensitive market, this company firmly believed that the most advanced technologies had to be incorporated into its services. They were unsatisfied with the performance of the fossil-fuel-based gas engine trucks in reducing gas emissions and noise in difficult access areas. Thus, they concluded that it was necessary to improve upon and experiment with other types of vehicles, especially hybrid trucks that combined the electrical and diesel motors. Once the RJV undertook the challenge, the objective was clear:

the task was to obtain a hybrid vehicle with the same service level as a diesel vehicle, and with no noise and gas emission.

With the RJV goal determined, this company contacted the truck manufacturer to organize a work meeting focusing on the prospects of jointly defining and creating a vehicle that fulfilled the stated objectives. The previous work experience was a determinant for the selection of this partner as the technological collaborator for this new R&D project.

The technology that was to be developed gave the truck manufacturer the opportunity of enabling its managerial staff to build on future breakthroughs in the market, while sharing fixed costs of the R&D of a particular type of vehicle with its clients. In addition to this issue, it provided the possibility of utilizing generic knowledge developed at a scientific level to better satisfy the customer's needs and to improve the relationship with them. Even though the development of this knowledge is vital to the truck manufacturer's core activities, the complexity and the high cost of its development, along with low prospects of large demand, prevented the company from developing the project on its own.

Once both the companies expressed their interest in the R&D project, a collaboration contract was signed. With respect to the property rights on the results of the project, the truck firm would hold the rights on the developments and provide access to the results to the urban maintenance firm for a stipulated time period once the contract ended.

Based on the existing technology, the RJV began with the analysis and assessment of any hybrid vehicle. The results were obtained through joint work that was completed between the two companies. The urban maintenance firm provided the experience from their 4,000 garbage collection trucks and its knowledge about the demands of final users, in this case the town halls. In light of these expressed requirements, the truck company was set to design the truck.

The construction of the prototype was complex and subject to continuous modifications. One of the participants stated that eventually more functions than initially required were added to the vehicle. The urban maintenance firm participated actively in this stage as the client company that was going to use the developed product. It provided knowledge about loading, the work cycles, energy consumption, and other technical specifications.

When the first prototype was finished, it completed a thorough test to detect further possible improvements. In order to complete the test, the urban maintenance firm took over this stage by driving garbage collection trucks through difficult access areas in towns. Simultaneously this prototype was presented at trucking fairs with the purpose of collecting surveys about the interest that had arisen.

With the support of the accumulated knowledge of this prototype, improvements were determined and were assessed by the multidisciplinary team integrated by members of the two companies. Some proposals were implemented during the test. Other proposals required that the vehicle be taken back to the manufacturing site. The feedback cycle between technicians and the customer ended at this test stage. The success of the first vehicle prototype eased decision making for further modifications.

When the second prototype was finished, the urban maintenance firm began to include the option of using this vehicle for urban services maintenance in its competitive bidding clauses. This way it increased the market awareness of environmental issues and made it clear that the hybrid vehicle was a reality. Likewise, the close results of this collection hybrid vehicle to what was demanded by the customer has allowed the truck company to exhibit its capabilities in meeting specific and sometimes complex customer needs.

The main difference of this kind of RJV with respect to the two previous groupings of RJVs is the emphasis on joint work and greater (even contractual) interaction between the partners. Meetings and personnel transfers were included in the means of interacting and for exchanging knowledge. These stronger interactions between customer and supplier also created a basis for broader, more extensive interaction. In fact, the consolidation of this relationship led the maintenance company to opt for this truck firm as the manufacturer of a second-generation collection hybrid truck.

## Cell 4: Integrative RJVs (Basic Research—Behavioral Knowledge Management)

In order to illustrate these kinds of RJVs, a research agreement between several MNEs operating in the international telecommunication market is presented. Two kinds of companies in this RJV are identified: telecommunication operators and telecommunication equipment providers. One of the telecommunication operators had perceived a large demand for automated teller machine (ATM) services and wanted to control future developments in this field. The idea was to develop an ATM switch with lower cost and larger capacity that would be able to support a wide range of services. The project needed to identify participants that had a good reputation in terms of their previous knowledge base in ATM switches and were very interested in completing new work related to ATMs. Therefore, firms with the same ATM interest and a good knowledge base on this issue joined efforts within this RJV.

Since this RJV was focused on radical and breakthrough innovation more than incremental improvements, the partners saw themselves rather as complementary parts than as rival firms. That means that although they operated in the same international markets, in the absence of any apparent rivalry in the short run, the threat was sensed as a long-term concern with no immediate competitive issues that would arise.

In order to define the specifications of the future, a third generation of chips for ATM switches, it needed to gather information about user requirements, review telecommunications standards, and identify the specifications of the ATM switch chip. Because this was a radical innovation beyond mere variants of existing products or technologies, the project was subject to continuous modifications. One of the participants stated that eventually more functions than initially expected were added to the ATM switch chip. The need for continuous consideration of new data, insights, and concepts required a very close inter-company collaboration between the technical staff. The mediums of communication used were electronic mail, fax, telephone, and onsite and offsite meetings.

Creating new knowledge is always a risky activity, even when there is cost sharing for development between the partners. During the project, regulation of the telecommunications sector changed and the operators were not allowed to offer ATM services. When this happened the RJV partners lost interest in chip development for ATM switches and this project. As a result, the customers of these of services looked to other technologies to satisfy their needs, for example, network Internet providers (IP). The less expensive IP network was chosen for providing, if not all, at least part of the services that initially were reserved for ATMs. The problem with the IP network is the low quality of the service offered by them. Even though the ATM offered better quality, it was also more expensive.

However, as time went on, the quality problems of the IP network were more evident and the interest in the chips ATM switch increased. When this situation became clear, the partners decided to reinvigorate and continue with the R&D project. Because these kinds of RJVs do not pay much attention to knowledge transfer issues and the exploitation of knowledge, during the time in which the project was on hiatus due to uncertainties and doubts about the future of ATM technology, a deterioration of the knowledge generated by the RJV resulted with a need to rebuild some knowledge and information.

## EMPIRICAL EVIDENCE IN EUROPE

Just knowing that knowledge management may vary in their levels of structural and behavioral enablers is not particularly compelling. What makes this of interest is that differences in the locus of the RJV may significantly and differentially affect knowledge management. Specially, it is assumed that making sense and understanding differences in the locus of RJV may have implications on the structural and behavioral approach to knowledge management.

Although, in general, knowledge flows in RJV are subject to transmission losses,[3] this problem can be solved using appropriate knowledge management. For example, transmission losses are greater for tacit knowledge than for codified knowledge (Roberts, 2000). The core argument here is that the more explicit the knowledge is, the more easily it is expressed and communicated—either to another individual in the same firm or to another firm. Explicitness means that the creation and transfer of explicit knowledge is relatively easy to accomplish via written documents, frequently supported by computer information systems. In these cases the knowledge exchange is achieved, quickly articulating a common language, so the level of interpersonal interaction between R&D units can be lower.

On the other hand, the acquisition of tacit knowledge requires factors such as intuition, spontaneity, and values or beliefs associated with human development. The higher the level of tacitness of the knowledge involved in the RJV, the higher the frequency and intensity of information exchange through personal channels. In these cases, the knowledge will not flow easily between locations and the establishment of effi-

cient mechanisms for the transfer of knowledge is more necessary.

As a result, the knowledge management approach will be influenced by the nature of the knowledge that is being created and transferred. Szulanski (1996) points out that tacit, context-specific, and ambiguous knowledge is likely the most difficult to transfer within the firm. Along this same line, Revilla, Acosta, and Sarkis (2006) indicate that basic research, whose output tends to be more explicit, generic, and autonomous knowledge, will be managed more according to a techno-structural approach than a behavioral approach. In the case of applied research, the opposite is presumed.

Although the above is equally true whether the knowledge flows are or are not within the MNE, in the presence of geographic borders, there has always been a temptation to introduce regularities and standards for the coordination of knowledge flows. That means that, even in the case of tacit knowledge, many MNEs pursue at least a mixed of structural/behavioral approach. This solution might impede an effective transfer of the knowledge developed by the RJV, since the local variations need for the innovation might not be taken into account. Furthermore, managing the two knowledge management perspectives requires skills most R&D managers do not possess yet.

In order to examine the interaction between the locus of the RJV—the contingency variable—and the knowledge management approach, an empirical study[4] of 98 RJVs located in France, Greece, Ireland, Italy, Spain, Sweden, and the United Kingdom, and involved in cooperative research projects[5] formed between 1990 and 1999, is used. In this study, the locus of RJV, focused on the stage of technological development at which an RJV operates, was characterized as either basic research or applied research. The knowledge management approach was defined as a continuous dimension that integrates behavioral and structural knowledge management practices. It

*Table 2. Impact of knowledge management on the typology of RJVs*

|  | Exploitative | Strategic | Interactive | Integrative | Independence test |
|---|---|---|---|---|---|
|  | Cell 1 | Cell 2 | Cell 3 | Cell 4 |  |
| Mean | 2.85 | 1.54 | 9.50 | 8.14 | Chi-squared |
| Deviation | 1.73 | 2.15 | 1.29 | 2.32 | 4.525 |
| Minimum | -2.00 | -3.00 | 8.00 | 6.00 | Signif. |
| Maximum | 5.00 | 5.00 | 11.00 | 15.00 | 0.003 |
| Size | 39 | 13 | 42 | 4 |  |

assesses the RJV behavioral approach in relation to the RJV structural approach.

When the RJVs are segmented according to the proposed two-dimensional classification of the RJV presented in Figure 1, it is observed that the number of RJVs involved in basic research and focusing on a structural approach of knowledge management is higher than the number of RJVs that develop basic research, which are concentrated on a behavioral knowledge management. Table 2 shows that 76.5% of the RJVs that are involved in basic research are in cell 2 and that only 23.5% are in cell 4. From these observations, one can argue that most basic research relies on a structural approach for knowledge management. The reason for this result could be due to the fact that basic research is more explicit, autonomous, and generic than other types of R&D projects. This result supports Jones and Handry's (1994) contention that structural or technical aspects are more related to explicit knowledge.

However, an analysis of the applied research does not show significant results. Only 51.8% of the RJVs that developed applied research are placed in cell 3 vs. 48.2% placed in cell 1 (see Table 2). These findings do support the argument that applied research is a joint outcome of structural and behavioral knowledge management practices.

The analysis of the means within Table 2 shows that RJVs with applied research characteristics do not present extreme orientations in the knowledge management approach. In these situations, it seems

that RJVs prefer to integrate both approaches. In fact, numerous authors (Brown & Eisenhardt, 1997; Van der Krogt, 1998; Popper & Lipshitz, 1998, 2000; Choi & Lee, 2001) have recognized that knowledge management in organizations is encouraged: (1) by the information mechanism and the coordination systems focused on the processing and analysis of information; and (2) by the personal, social, or cultural tools focused on the development of the human potential as well as on the creation of a shared meaning within organizations. The aim is that organizational members be able to expand their competencies in agreement with the guides established to work optimally in organizations.

## SUMMARY AND CONCLUSION

In this chapter, a topical area is introduced that is of growing interest to organizations, practitioners, and researchers in the knowledge management field. Today many innovations that are being introduced have arisen from RJVs; it is expected that with increased complexity of technology, products and services, and the acceptance of further collaborative organizational efforts, these RJVs will only increase in popularity. Making sense and understanding knowledge management within these types of collaborations has been quite limited. This chapter provides a means to help set a foundation to understand these collaborative efforts in MNEs.

Using literature in the area of research joint ventures, R&D, knowledge management, and organizational learning, a taxonomy of RJVs is introduced. The purpose of any taxonomy is to try to make sense of and further develop evolving ideas and their relationships. Using practical and actual case studies, we exemplify how relationships within these taxonomies may work. An understanding of how RJVs operate in managing their knowledge and learning processes within the locus of the RJVs is beneficial to R&D managers who need to know how to manage or structure the project for greater potential success.

In empirical terms, this chapter shows where RJVs within the given taxonomy are most effective. Thus, we found that RJVs involved in development of new knowledge tend to use a structural knowledge management approach. For applied research the extremes of the knowledge management approach were not evident, which signifies the importance of combining both knowledge management approaches—that is, appropriate structures, systems, and procedures are needed along with personal and cultural values (Popper & Lipshitz, 1998, 2000). Although the knowledge will not be explicit or easy to generalize, such as in the case of applied research, these hybrid knowledge management structures are used frequently by MNEs. The importance of coordination makes both techno-structural and behavioral management tools critical to extend innovation capacity in MNEs.

## REFERENCES

Alavi, M., & Leidner, D.E. (2001). Review: Knowledge management and knowledge management systems: Conceptual foundations and research issues. *MIS Quarterly, 25*(1), 107-136.

Alvesson, M., & Karreman, D. (2001). Odd couple: Making sense of the curious concept of knowledge management. *Journal of Management Studies, 38*(7), 995-1018.

Argyris, C., & Schön, D. (1978). *Organizational learning: A theory of action perspective.* Boston: Addison-Wesley.

Badaracco, J.L. (1991). *The knowledge link.* Boston: Harvard Business School Press.

Bechtold, B.L. (2000). Evolving to organizational learning. *Hospital Material Management Quarterly, 21*(3), 11-25.

Berdrow, I., & Lane, H. (2003). International joint ventures: Creating value through successful knowledge management. *Journal of World Business, 38,* 15-30.

Bonaccorsi, A., & Piccaluga, A. (1994). A theoretical framework for evaluation of university-industry relationships. *R&D Management, 24*(3), 229-247.

Brown, J.S., & Duguid, P. (1998). Organizing knowledge. *California Management Review, 40*(3), 90-111.

Brown, J.S., & Duguid P. (1991). Organizational learning and communities of practice: Towards a unified view of working, learning, and organization. *Organizational Science, 2*(1), 40-57.

Brown, S.L., & Eisenhardt, K.M. (1997). The art of continuous change: Linking complexity theory and time-paced evolution in relentlessly shifting organizations. *Administrative Science Quarterly, 42,* 1-34.

Chesbrough, H., & Teece, D.J. (1996). When is virtual virtuous? Organizing for innovation. *Harvard Business Review, 74,* 65-71.

Chesbrough, W.H. (2003). The era of open innovation. *Sloan Management Review,* (Spring), 35-41.

Choi, B., & Lee, H. (2003). An empirical investigation of KM styles and their effect on corporate performance. *Information & Management, 40*(5), 403-417.

Chuang, S. (2004). A resource-based perspective on knowledge management capability and competitive advantage: An empirical investigation. *Expert Systems with Applications, 27,* 459-465.

Cohen, W.M., & Levinthal, D.A. (1990). Absorptive capacity: A new perspective on learning and innovation. *Administrative Science Quarterly, 35,* 128-152.

Council on Competitiveness. (1996). *Endless frontier, limited resources: U.S. R&D policy for competitiveness.* Washington, DC: Council on Competitiveness.

Daft, R.L,. & Huber, G.P. (1987). How organizations learn: A communication framework. *Research in the Sociology of Organizations, 5,* 1-36.

Daft, R.L., & Lengel, R.H. (1986). Organizational information requirements, media richness and structural design. *Management Science, 32*(5), 554-571.

DiBella, A.J., & Nevis, E. (1998). *How organizations learn.* San Francisco: Jossey-Bass.

Eisenhardt, K.M., & Martin, J.K. (2000). Dynamic capabilities: What are they? *Strategic Management Journal, 21,* 1105-1121.

Garavan, T. (1997). The learning organization: A review and evaluation. *The Learning Organization, 4*(1), 18-29.

Gerybadze, A., & Reger, G. (1999). Globalization of R&D: Recent changes in management innovation in transnational corporations. *Research Police, 28,* 251-274.

Gloet, M., & Berrel, M. (2003). The dual paradigm nature of knowledge management: Implications for achieving quality outcomes in human resource management. *Journal of Knowledge Management, 7*(1), 78-89.

Gnyawali, D.R. (1997). *Creation and utilization of organizational knowledge: An empirical study of the effects of organizational learning on strategic*

*decision making.* Unpublished Doctoral Thesis, University of Pittsburgh, USA.

Gold, A.H., Malhotra, A., & Segars, A.H. (2001). Knowledge management: An organizational capabilities perspective. *Journal of Management Information Systems, 18*(1), 185-214.

Grant, R.M. (1996). Prospering in dynamically-competitive environments: Organizational capability as knowledge integration. *Organization Science, 7*(4), 375-387.

Hagedoorn, J., Link, A.N., & Vonortas, N.S. (2000). Research partnerships. *Research Policy, 29,* 567-586.

Hansen, M.T., Nohria, N., & Tierney, T. (1999). What's your strategy for managing knowledge. *Harvard Business Review,* (March-April), 107-116.

Hedlund, G. (1994). A model of knowledge management and the N-form corporation. *Strategic Management Journal, 15,* 73-90.

Henderson, R.M., & Clark, K.B. (1990). Architectural innovation: The reconfiguration of existing product technologies and the failure of established firms. *Administrative Science Quarterly, 35,* 9-30.

Inkpen, G.P. (1998). Learning, knowledge acquisition, and strategic alliances. *European Management Journal, 16*(2), 223-229.

Inkpen, G.P., & Dinur, A. (1998). Knowledge management processes and international joint ventures. *Organization Science, 9*(4), 454-468.

Isaacs, W.N. (1993). Dialogue, collective thinking, and organizational learning. *Organizational Dynamics,* (Autumn), 24-39.

Katila, R., & Ahuja, G. (2002). Something old, something new: A longitudinal study of search behaviour and new product introduction. *Academy of Management Journal, 45*(6), 1183-1194.

Kim, D.H. (1993). *A framework and methodology for linking individual and organizational learning: Applications in TQM and product development.* Doctoral Thesis, MIT Sloan School of Management, USA.

Kogut, B., & Zander, U. (1992). Knowledge of the firm, combinative capabilities, and the replication of technology. *Organization Science, 383-397.*

Lane, P.J., Salk, J., & Lyles, M.A., (2001). Absorptive capacity, learning, and performance in international joint ventures. *Strategic Management Journal, 22,* 1139-1161.

Larsson, R., Bengtsson, L., Henriksson, K., & Sparks, J. (1998). The interorganizational learning dilemma: Collective knowledge development in strategic alliances. *Organization Science, 9*(3), 285-305.

Lee, H., & Choi, B. (2003). Knowledge management enablers, processes, and organizational performance: An integrative view and empirical examination. *Journal of Management Information Systems, 20*(1), 179-228.

Leonard Barton, D. (1995). *Wellsprings of knowledge. Building and sustaining the sources of innovation.* Boston: Harvard Business School Press.

Levinthal, D.A., & March, J.G. (1993). The myopia of learning. *Strategic Management Journal, 14,* 95-112.

March, J.G. (1991). Exploration and exploitation in organizational learning. *Organization Science, 2*(1), 71-87.

March, J.G., & Simon, H.A. (1958). *Organizations.* New York: John Wiley & Sons.

McDermott, R. (1999). Why information technology inspires but cannot deliver knowledge management. *California Management Review, 40*(4), 103-117.

Mirvis, P.H. (1996). Historical foundations of organizational learning. *Journal of Organizational Change Management, 9*(1), 13-31.

Mowery, D.C. (1983). The relationship between intrafirm and contractual forms of industrial research in American manufacturing, 1900-1940. *Explorations in Economic History, 20,* 351-374.

Mudambi, R. (2002). Knowledge management in multinational firms. *Journal of International Management, 8,* 1-9.

Nelson, R.R. (1990). U.S. technological leadership: Where did it come from and where did it go? *Research Policy, 79,* 119-132.

Nonaka, I. (1994). A dynamic theory of organizational knowledge creation. *Organization Science, 5*(1), 14-37.

Nonaka, I., & Takeuchi, H. (1995). *The knowledge-creating company.* Oxford: Oxford University Press.

Nonaka, I., Toyama, R. & Nagata, A. (2000). A firm as a knowledge-creating entity: A new perspective on the theory of the firm. *Industrial and Corporate Change, 9*(1), 1-20.

Pan, S.L., & Scarbrough, H. (1999). Knowledge management in practice: An exploratory case study. *Technology Analysis & Strategic Management, 11*(3), 359-374.

Polanyi, M. (1967). *The tacit dimension.* Garden City, NY: Doubleday Press.

Popper, M., & Lipshitz, R. (1998). Organizational learning: A structural and cultural approach to organizational learning. *Journal of Applied Behavioural Science, 34*(2), 161-179.

Popper, M., & Lipshitz, R. (2000). Organizational learning: Mechanism, culture, and feasibility. *Management Learning, 31*(2), 181-196.

Powell, W.W., Koput K.W., & Smit-Doerr L. (1996). Interorganizational collaboration and the locus of innovation: Networks of learning in biotechnology. *Administrative Science Quarterly, 41*(1), 116-134.

Prieto, I. (2003). *Una valoración de la gestión del conocimiento para el desarrollo de la capacidad de aprendizaje de las organizaciones. Propuesta de un modelo integrador.* Doctoral Dissertation, Universidad de Valladolid, Spain.

Revilla, E., Acosta, J., & Sarkis, J. (2006). An empirical assessment of a learning and knowledge management typology for research joint ventures. *International Journal of Technology Management, 35*(1/2/3/4), 329-348.

Roussel, P.A., Saad, K.N., & Erickson, T.J. (1995). *Third generation of R&D: Managing the link to corporate strategy.* Cambridge, MA: Harvard Business School Press.

Schein, E.H. (1993). On dialogue, culture and organizational learning. *Organizational Dynamics, 22*(2), 40-51.

Senge, P.M. (1990). *The fifth discipline.* New York: Doubleday.

Shrivastava, P. (1983). A typology of organizational learning systems. *Journal of Management Studies, 20*(1), 7-24.

Simonin, B.L. (1999). Ambiguity and the process of knowledge transfer in strategic alliances. *Strategic Management Journal, 20,* 595-623.

Spencer, J.C., & Grant, R.M. (1996). Knowledge and the firm: Overview. *Strategic Management Journal, 17,* 5-9.

Subramaniam, M., & Venkatraman, N. (1999). The influence of leveraging tacit overseas knowledge for global new product development capability: An empirical examination. In M.A. Hitt, R.G. Clifford, R.D. Nixon, & K.P. Coyne (Eds.), *Dynamic strategic resources.* Chichester: John Wiley & Sons.

Szulanki, G. (1996). Exploring internal stickiness: Impediments to the transfer of best practice within the firm. *Strategic Management Journal, 17,* 27-43.

Tushman, M., & Anderson, P. (1986). Technological discontinuities and organizational environments. *Administrative Science Quarterly, 31,* 439-465.

Van den Brink, P. (2003). *Social, organizational and technological conditions that enable knowledge sharing.* Doctoral Thesis, Technische Universiteit Delft, The Netherlands.

Van der Krogt, F.J. (1998). Learning network theory: The tension between learning systems and work systems in organizations. *Human Resource Development Quarterly, 9*(2), 156-176.

Weick, K.E. (1991). The nontraditional quality of organizational learning. *Organization Science, 2*(1), 116-123.

Winter, S. (1987). Knowledge and competence as strategic assets. In D. Teece (Eds.), *The competitive challenge* (pp. 157-184). Cambridge, MA: Ballinger.

Zack, M.H. (1999). Developing a knowledge strategy. *California Management Review, 41*(3), 125-145.

## ENDNOTES

[1] This concept is related to innovation radicalness, which has been discussed by others (e.g., Tushman & Anderson, 1986).

[2] Learning classifications can be found in Winter (1987), Badaracco (1991), Chesbrough and Teece (1996), and Collins (1993).

[3] It means that the flow of knowledge received by the target will be smaller than the flow transmitted by the source.

[4] For further information, see Revilla et al. (2006).

[5] All the projects are grouped within the following European programs: EU Framework Program, EUREKA Program, or National Programs.

# Chapter XVI
# CRM Practices and Resources for the Development of Customer–Focused Multinational Organizations

**Luciano C. Batista**
*University of Exeter, UK*

## ABSTRACT

*This chapter aims to provide a complete characterization of the different perspectives of customer relationship management (CRM) and its potentialities to support knowledge management practices in a multinational context. It describes the strategic and technological dimensions of CRM and how its adoption supports the development of a learning and customer-focused organization, with special emphasis on multinational corporations. CRM strategic approach entails the adoption of customer-focused initiatives and the development of learning relationships with customers. On the other hand, its technological dimension integrates a variety of different information and communication technologies, which makes a powerful system for improving the process of knowledge acquisition. This way, different subsidiaries of a multinational corporation can develop their learning capability so that they can better identify local market demands. As a result, the corporation is able to more accurately create a global knowledge stock about its different markets in different regions of the world.*

## INTRODUCTION

The current world is witnessing profound developments in the areas of information technology and business strategy. In the technological area, recent developments have led telecommunication technologies to reach a high level of integration with computing technologies and vice versa. This trend has had a strong impact upon society, promoting, among other things, an enlargement of the conceptual focus of information technologies to embrace the notion of relationship technologies. Regarding business strategy aspects, companies are creating a sound and lasting competitive advantage by adopting "relationship" as the word of order. As a matter of fact, the confluence of changing customer demands, emerging marketing and business theories, and available information and communication technologies (ICTs) have been imposing a shift on the way organizations relate to customers. The gap between strategic marketing approaches and ICT deployment has been diminished over time, culminating in integrated business approaches that involve both strategic and technological dimensions at the same time. This chapter focuses on the integration of knowledge management (KM) and customer relationship management (CRM) approaches.

At the same time as the rise of new ICTs, there has been the development of CRM and KM approaches for enhancing both relationship strategies and organizational learning capabilities. For instance, the evolution and integration of different ICT over time enabled the adoption of different and more evolved marketing approaches, giving birth to the present CRM systems. These systems support the development of current relationship strategies, which, in turn, were delineated by the evolution of marketing relationship strategies over time. On the other hand, market knowledge—which is directly related to information about customers and other environmental elements—and internal knowledge have become a strategically important resource for an organization, serving as a basic source of competitive advantage (Cui, Griffith, & Cavusgil, 2005).

In practice, CRM systems provide the functionality that allows an organization to make its customers the focal point of all departments within the firm. This way, the organization will be able to respond to its customers on a continual basis. More specifically, customer information databases and integrated interactivity enable an organization to develop a learning relationship

with its customers, creating organizational capability to differentiate customers and markets, and to develop personalized interactions so that tailored products or services can be offered. In the context of multinational organizations, the adoption of CRM practices and solutions can improve the process of knowledge acquisition in different local markets, allowing multinational corporations to define and develop both local and global strategies according to regional demands. For example, in a multinational environment, CRM allows different subsidiaries to develop long-term learning relationships with their local customers, which makes the creation of specific business intelligence concerning local market demands possible.

In other words, CRM can be considered as a key element for supporting knowledge management in multinational organizations. Its strategic approach entails the adoption of customer-focused initiatives and the development of learning relationships with customers. On the other hand, its technological dimension integrates a variety of different information and communication technologies, which makes a powerful system for improving the process of knowledge acquisition. This way, different subsidiaries of a multinational corporation can develop their learning capability so that they can better identify local market demands. As a result, the corporation is able to more accurately create a global knowledge stock about its different markets in different regions of the world.

The strategic and technological dimensions of CRM are extremely intertwined and, as a matter of fact, the emergence of CRM strategies, concepts, and practices would not be possible without the appearance of new and evolved ICT resources. This chapter aims to provide a complete characterization of the different perspectives of CRM, describing its origins, concepts, paradigms, technologies, and its potentialities to support knowledge management practices. Considering that the adoption of CRM practices and solutions can generate substantial knowledge about an organization's customers, this chapter aims to describe the strategic and technological dimensions of CRM and how its adoption supports the development of a learning and customer-focused organization, with some special emphasis on multinational corporations (MNCs).

By reading this chapter, the reader can get a better and deeper understanding of the following aspects:

- What CRM is
- The strategic and technological dimensions of CRM
- The main challenges of CRM implementation
- CRM measurement aspects
- Practical considerations regarding CRM adoption
- The main CRM supporting roles to KM in a multinational context

## ORIGINS AND CONCEPTS OF CRM

The acronym CRM per se does not explicitly convey what it is about. Sometimes it represents an information system, other times it represents a strategic business approach. Different authors interchangeably use CRM to address one thing or another, which may cause some confusion as to whether they are talking about an information system or a business strategy. The problem is that CRM strategies have emerged together with the information and communication technologies that allowed their practical implementation and feasibility. In terms of technological developments, underlying technologies are becoming less operationally complex and less expensive, and so their facilities and resources are being increasingly used by people, enterprises, and governments. The Internet, for example, is a key information technology that can also be viewed

as a relationship technology. It is perhaps as a consequence of the ubiquity of such technologies that organizations have been focusing on relationship strategies. Turning to the business strategy aspects, companies are creating a sound and lasting competitive advantage by developing long-term learning relationships with their customers. At the same time as the rise of new information and communication technologies, there has been the development of the CRM concepts for implementing relationship strategies that enable sound organizational learning capabilities.

## The Origins of CRM

CRM has its roots in relationship marketing strategies and its antecedents. As a matter of fact, developing good relationships with customers is a very old practice; as Sterne (2000) well illustrates, since the mid-eighteenth century pharmaceutical retailers in Japan have been practicing relationship management with their clients. Individual families are regularly visited by sales representatives, who review the contents of their company-issued medicine cabinets. The items that have been used are replaced, and the items that have not are either removed or replaced according to their expiry dates. Of course, on a small-scale context, such practice is completely feasible; however, on a large-scale context it becomes unviable.

With the development of mass media communications such as the printed press, radio, and TV, companies became able to communicate to millions of people at once. Gummesson (1999) points out that, during the industrial era, mass manufacturing gave birth to mass marketing and mass distribution. There were no technologies to address individuals. As a result, the marketing focus has changed from customer to product and brand recognition. The approach of personalized services was disregarded until new technologies appeared to foster new approaches. Table 1 provides a complete view of the different evolutionary phases of marketing strategies over time.

*Table 1. Evolutionary phases of marketing strategies (Source: Adapted from Ling and Yen, 2001)*

| PHASE | TIME PERIOD | FEATURES | DRAWBACKS |
|---|---|---|---|
| Direct Sales | Since long ago | Small stores; personalized services; intimacy and knowledge about customers; developed loyalty and trust | Cost inefficiency; small scale of business |
| Mass Marketing | After industrial era | Centralized large-scale production; wide-geographic distribution; one-way communication; cost efficiency; measure of success: market share | Does not have the sense of connection; low loyalty |
| Target Marketing | Since mid-1980s | Use IT to target customers by mail or telephone; direct communication with the target; potential reception of direct responses; measure of success: response rate | Interaction at a superficial level, not far enough; lack of more detailed customer data |
| Relationship Marketing | Since 1990s | Develops intimacy by using IT and maintaining mass production and distribution; recognizes that both knowledge and personal interaction yield trust and loyalty | Difficult to implement; involves various business functions; mainly for consumers instead of industry |

Of course, direct sales force and telemarketing efforts have not vanished, nor have mass marketing strategies been totally discarded. Naturally, if a company is successful in acquiring new customers, then at some moment it will reach a large-scale context; consequently it will need mass approaches. In many companies, different marketing strategies are being combined to approach customers. However, it has been reported that there is a lack of cohesion between these strategies, which sometimes leads to confusion as customers receive multiple and uncoordinated messages through separate channels (Ling & Yen, 2001).

Instead of perceiving CRM as a revolutionary business strategy that came to substitute all the ones that preceded it, it would be more coherent to perceive CRM as a business strategy that proposes personal interactions even in a mass context, taking advantage of the strengths of previous approaches. This kind of large-scale personalization is perfectly feasible through the application of current information and communication technologies. Indeed, the availability of highly evolved telecommunication and information technologies was crucial for enabling CRM practices.

## Concepts of CRM

Generically speaking, CRM is a term interchangeably used to refer to ICT or business strategies that improve an organization's capability to develop lasting and learning relationships with its customers. These two perspectives of CRM (technological and strategic) are extremely intertwined; however, CRM is more than a different way of applying existing technological and marketing tools and managing them. From a strategic point of view, CRM can be understood as an organization's broad business strategy, which focuses on building customer-personalized interactions whatever the channel of contact between the organization and its customers (Business Guide, 2000). Given its amplitude, it is fundamental to be aware that the implementation of CRM strategy is not just the responsibility of the marketing department or other customer service sectors. For Ling and Yen (2001), CRM is a broad strategic business process that involves the organization as a whole, spanning across different business functions rather than just within a particular product or business unit. They also affirm that CRM comprises a set of enabling systems that supports a business strategy to build lasting and profitable relationships with customers. A better understanding of customer needs and preferences is the way to enhance customer value, and this aspect is one of the major objectives of CRM.

It can be argued that CRM concepts have also evolved alongside the evolution of information and communication technologies. Making an analogy with Peppers and Rogers' (1993) characterization of today's media, we can identify three important characteristics of today's information technologies: (1) they can address individuals, (2) they are two-way channels, and (3) they are economically accessible. These technological aspects support the implementation of a chief strategy that is at the core of CRM philosophy: the one-to-one approach, which is mainly based on the development of personalized interactions between an organization and its customers. This approach is considered by Kandell (2000), who affirms that CRM involves the use of technology to identify, interact, and track every transaction with individual customers, developing a learning relationship with them. A clearer and more straightforward definition of CRM is provided by Buttle (2004), according to whom:

*CRM is the core business strategy that integrates internal processes and functions, and external networks, to create and deliver value to targeted customers at a profit. It is grounded on high-quality customer data and enabled by IT.* (p. 34)

Taking into account the definitions and concepts we have seen thus far, it is possible to notice that its holistic business approach and information technologies are elements usually present when the CRM subject is addressed. Therefore, it is imperative to further characterize these two dimensions of CRM in a more specific way for further discussion. In the next two sections, we are going to expand on the strategic and technological aspects of CRM.

## STRATEGIC ASPECTS OF CRM

Marketing concerns have progressively shifted from developing, selling, and delivering products to developing and maintaining a mutually satisfying long-term relationship with customers, as enduring relationships with customers provide a unique and sustained competitive advantage that is hard for a competitor to duplicate (Buttle, 1996). This latter argument might explain the fact that recent surveys indicate that CRM is becoming a major element of corporate strategy for many organizations throughout the world, and its implementation is considered a key aspect for the future performance of organizations (Abbott, Stone, & Buttle, 2001; Hansotia, 2002). Looking at some statistics of CRM growth rates, according to a report from The Conference Board,[1] more firms are adopting CRM programs. Fifty-two percent of 96 global firms recently surveyed by The Conference Board have implemented a CRM system or solution. Among these, the top three strategic rationales for implementing CRM were to: (i) increase customer retention/loyalty (94%); (ii) respond effectively to competitive pressures (77%); and (iii) differentiate competitively based on customer service superiority (73%). Across all surveyed firms, half of the total marketing investments were toward driving revenue, while one-third went towards building relationships. The average strategic time horizon employed for the CRM project was almost three years, with an average estimated implementation time of four years. In terms of market value, the numbers show that CRM is a phenomenon not to be ignored. In 2000, Kandell (2000) commented that the CRM market would be worth more than $16 billion by 2003. Two years later, a Gartner Group report showed that organizations worldwide paid $23 billion for CRM services and software, and that amount was expected to rise to $76 billion in 2005 (Pang & Norris, 2002). It can be argued that the differences between the reported numbers were due to different analysis criteria. Despite the differences, the numbers showed that CRM is a billionaire market. The high amounts involved can be explained by the fact that the range of CRM solutions is very broad, and it requires integration and improvements in information and communication technologies to enable the adoption of customer-oriented strategies.

A central practice in CRM strategy is to exploit customer insight and information to create profitable customer relationships (Abbott et al., 2001). Indeed, each customer interaction produces extensive data; the purpose of CRM is to make inferences over this data in order to allow an organization to identify patterns of customers' consuming behavior as well as to identify customers' profiles, needs, wants, and preferences. To achieve continuous improvement, an organization should track the results of customers' interactions and use such knowledge to refine further actions (Ling & Yen, 2001). This practice is reputed to promote the following organizational benefits:

a.  **Retention of existing customers** through the process of anticipating offers according to customers' expectations over time and delivering personalized goods and services according to the customers' profile (Sterne, 2000).

b.  **Acquisition of new customers** by prospecting and analyzing peoples' first contacts so that potential customers' interests can be matched (Buttle, 2004).

c.  **Building of customer loyalty** through the process of listening, understanding, and responding according to customers' needs, wants, and behavior (Business Guide, 2000).

d.  **Raising of customer profitability** through the process of providing high targeted solutions according to the customers' value (Ling & Yen, 2001; Khirallah, 2000).

Other benefits such as the improvement of customer lifetime value, raising of customer satisfaction, execution of faster services, costs reduction, improvement of sales force, better response rates, and so forth are also claimed to be promoted by the adoption of CRM initiatives (Kandell, 2000; Khirallah, 2000; Sterne, 2000; Buttle, 2004). Besides, Silverman (2001) comments that successfully implemented CRM strategies can promote a high return on investment. He argues that statistics from different sources show that organizations that have successfully adopted CRM enjoy higher prices and profit margin, faster growth rates, lower customer turnover, and an increased market share.

The benefits addressed thus far constitute strong reasons for CRM adoption. In order to achieve the organizational benefits we previously commented on, an organization should develop the ability to efficiently and effectively leverage customer information so as to design and implement customer-oriented strategies. The development of customer-focused strategies represents the heart of CRM tenets. As Hansotia says, CRM strategies are:

*...strategies that celebrate differences in customers' values, potentials, needs and preferences. It is about leveraging customer knowledge to get closer to customers by anticipating their needs and communicating intelligently with relevant offers and messages, while all the time nudging them to increase the breadth, depth and length of their relationship with the firm.* (Hansotia, 2002, p. 122)

Moreover, CRM entails the management of customer interactions so that an organization can leverage customer knowledge to design and provide unique services and memorable experiences that customers will value and will be willing to pay for. To have a long-term effect, each experience must exceed expectations adding to the customers' stock of goodwill toward the company. The interactions should be reasonably frequent, error free, and quickly meet customers' needs and wants (Hansotia, 2002).

It is important to point out that, in order to meet customer particularities at a maximum level, customers' differences and common patterns should be observed. These insights are obtained by developing segmentation schemes. As Hansotia (2002) describes, segmentation techniques can be used to characterize and help understand different customer groups. Segmentation methods aim to group customers according to their preferences for products, services, channels of interaction, and the magnitude and frequency of their interactions with an organization. Once different behavioral segments are identified, each segment can be further profiled with additional information, such as survey-based attitudinal and satisfaction data. In the end, the organization will be able to learn, for instance, what the most profitable customers look like, which customers have a high propensity to buy certain products or services, or who the high-risk customers are. Hansotia (2002) also warns that prior to selecting the basic variables and dimensions that will be used to construct the segments on which customers' differences are to be observed, significant discussions should take place.

Indeed, the adoption of CRM strategies requires the commitment of an organization's administrative first echelon, demanding wide organizational discussions that involve not only the chief executive officer (CEO), but also all his or her direct reports. This is because CRM adoption usually presses for fundamental cultural shifts within organizations as well as new forms of organizational structure that might challenge current norms and practices (Abbott et al., 2001). Therefore, it is paramount that an organization revisits its mission statement to certify that it clearly addresses the company's focus on the

customer, ensuring that CRM strategies tie in with the overall organizational mission and related strategies (Hansotia, 2002). This latter aspect is further detailed next.

## Further Strategic Considerations

Strategic management considerations are vital for successful implementations of CRM solutions. Knowing how to introduce strategic changes is the major challenge facing executives acting in a business environment characterized by rapidly advancing technology and fierce competitiveness.

Strategic management deals with the overall direction of an organization, involving decisions regarding very important issues such as financial investments, technological improvements, and the well-being of the people who might be affected by the firm's activities. According to Finlay (2000), the number of people contributing to strategic management has increased considerably over the past decade. This is because organizations are realizing that the implementation of successful change is easier when made by the people responsible for the implementation and by those affected by the change. In practice, lower-level managers interact much more with the organization's main stakeholders, picking up trends in the environment and marketplace, and passing the information to the senior managers who can authorize action. This way, strategic management can be seen as a process where each of an organization's sub-units initiates much of its own strategy, contributing to form the organizational strategy (Thompson, 1997). Despite the advantages, if the process is not conducted in a coordinated manner, the sub-units' initiatives will not be consolidated at a higher organizational level and the solutions will remain fragmented within the sub-unit silos. Another important aspect is that the sub-units' initiatives should meet and strengthen the corporate strategic goals.

Therefore, it is extremely important for an organization to establish and communicate its vision, mission, and strategic goals to all its stakeholders. Basically, the organizational vision can be understood as a view of a future intended by an organization. Based upon this vision, the organization formally states its mission, which is a formal statement of the broad directions that the organization wishes to follow. The mission should contain a broad indication of the organization's offers and customers. Finally, the strategic goals are a formal establishment of an organization's purpose, setting out the scope of the organization's operations. Finlay (2000) warns that suitable goals should be relevant to the mission. This latter aspect is also addressed by Rowe, Mason, Dickel, Mann, and Mockler (1994) when they comment that organizational goals are chosen to align the organization more closely with its values and mission. They also point out that establishing goals and finding strategies that lead there [to the goals] are fairly straightforward tasks. However, there are difficulties when organizations attempt to take the stakeholders' interests into account. This latter concern is shared by Finlay (2000) when he positions the organization's relationships with stakeholders among the major strategic management concerns, namely:

- Matching the organization and its environment
- Initiating and handling both evolutionary and transformational change
- Managing the organization's relationship with stakeholders
- Balancing short- and long-term considerations

Increasingly, diverse groups are making claims as stakeholders in organizations. A stakeholder analysis should begin with the identification of as many relevant stakeholders as possible (Rowe et al., 1994). In the sequence, strategic managers should identify assumptions about the stakeholders in order to figure out the contribution that relationships with them can make to the well-be-ing of the organization, and then to establish and maintain good relationships with them (Thompson, 1997; Rowe et al., 1994).

Buttle (2004) comments that a customer-centric firm is a learning firm that continuously adapts to customer requirements and competitive conditions. To develop customer-oriented strategies, organizations should put the customer first, collecting, disseminating, and using customer information to create better value propositions for customers. Appropriately dealing with massive customer information on a large-scale context is not a simple task; this is when information and communication technologies come onto the scene.

## TECHNOLOGICAL ASPECTS OF CRM

Technology is a crucial factor in the move to CRM. It would not be possible to implement CRM strategies without the use of the current information and communication technologies. In order to implement relationship strategies and exploit their relationship technologies, companies are deploying and integrating CRM systems with their legacy systems, as well as integrating CRM systems with their network channels and the Internet. When well managed, these integrations are reputed to constitute a successful combination of technologies that provide the necessary resources to make the execution of the strategies that will situate a company in a much desired position possible: closer to its customers (Ling & Yen, 2001). Getting closer to customers means developing the ability to know customers' needs and wants in a more accurate, efficient, and effective way, which allows the development of positive, lasting, and learning relationships with customers, hence improving an organization's corporate reputation. The results are extremely significant and positive in terms of long-term strategies and business leveraging.

From a simple perspective, CRM is fundamentally a customer data intensive effort (Hansotia, 2002). We can say that CRM is grounded on generating knowledge from customer data, and the process of knowledge generation is enabled by the deployment of a highly integrated technological infrastructure and the integration of organizational processes. Integration is vital for CRM; without the integration of technological resources and organizational processes, the CRM mechanism will not provide accurate customer information and, as a result, the identification of customer needs and wants will become a helpless guessing game (Business Guide, 2000). The high investments required by CRM adoption can be explained by the fact that the range of CRM solutions is very broad, and it may involve integration and improvements in information and communication technologies. According to Pang and Norris (2002), such integrations and improvements may include:

- Integration of computer telephony that can support call centers' activities, such as voice recognition for directing calls and matching calls against names in a database.
- Customer self-service Web sites that allow the customers themselves to conduct online transactions such as searching for relevant information, downloading forms and software, and requesting services or goods. Reducing a call center's inbound calls by automating the self-service features within the CRM system can result in lower labor and training costs.
- Improvement of business intelligence using segmentation and analytical tools that identify customers' patterns and needs. Detailed customer profiles allow a customized delivery of services and products; these profiles can be generated by CRM analytical tools that allow an organization to quickly identify target populations, this way reducing significantly a marketing cycle time (Berry, 2001).

- Implementation of mass customization processes through which goods and services are individualized to satisfy specific customer needs.

Moreover, CRM systems provide the necessary level of integration to allow seamless coordination between all customer-facing functions. Hence, productivity enhancement can be achieved by customer-facing personnel being able to do customer-related work more quickly and less painfully, since they no longer have to re-type customer information several times and do not have to look up a customer's overall dossier in multiple computer systems (Goldenberg, 2002).

Regarding processes integration, understanding the mechanisms of relationships with stakeholders allows a better definition of organizational processes, which can be seen as the frequency and direction of work and information flows linking the differentiated roles within and between departments of an organization (Hammer, 1996). Indeed, business processes are generally linked together to form a set that delivers a product or service to satisfy a specific stakeholder target—most usually the customers. Competitive success depends on transforming an organization's key processes into strategic capabilities that consistently provide superior value to the customers (Rheault & Sheridan, 2002). Furthermore, Warboys, Kawalek, Robertson, and Greenwood (1999) warn that organizational processes cannot be considered in isolation from the information systems (systems as applications and tools, or systems as infrastructure) that are potentially available.

Regarding the latter issue, one important set of applications that automates and tracks customer processes, as well as integrating these processes with back-office systems, is known as "workflow applications." This characteristic makes workflow products ideally situated to address the demand for CRM solutions. Chambers, Medina, and West (1999) have conducted a comparative assessment of workflow products focusing on how well workflow vendors have adapted their technologies to provide CRM solutions. They found that many of the workflow vendors have indeed responded with product offerings that can handle many of the key application requirements of CRM scenarios. Analyzing four key customer-related scenarios—new order processing, customer complaint handling, new product development, and call center—they identified two main techniques with which workflow vendors began to provide workflow-enabled CRM solutions. These are: (1) providing tightly coupled workflow and CRM capabilities, or (2) offering workflow solutions that can be easily embedded in any CRM platform. According to them, with so many workflow vendors contributing to CRM initiatives, it is clear that workflow as a standalone technology is disappearing and moving toward products that embed productivity, efficiency, and competitive advantage—such as CRM systems.

In fact, as we are going to see next, workflow application is only one of the many technologies that can be involved in the scope of CRM systems.

## Main CRM Components and Functionalities

We previously commented that CRM can be understood as an organization's broad business strategy, which focuses on building personalized interactions with customers whatever the channel of contact between the organization and its customers. Each customer interaction produces extensive data, and the purpose of CRM strategy is to make inferences over this database in order to promote organizational benefits such as retaining existing customers, building customer loyalty, raising customer profitability, and so forth. However, there is no way of implementing any CRM strategy without information technology support. This way, different software developers have been developing a broad number of CRM

systems, applications, or tools that combine existing ICT in different ways.

Generally speaking, the broad categories of CRM solutions involve a set of integrated applications that embody different aspects and functionalities. The core of CRM technologies can be classified into three general areas according to their general roles or purposes (Dean, 2001; Miles, 2002):

1. **Operational:** Technologies that manage customer service activities in storefronts, call-centers, and field service databases. These databases store historical data necessary for the construction of a single view of the customer.

2. **Collaborative:** Technologies that support field self-service applications on the Web, enabling different types of customers to work across a single service channel. This area embraces many communications media, including fax, e-mail, voice calls, text chats, and so forth.

3. **Analytical:** Technologies that provide sifting facilities through data created during customers' interactions to find or generate useful business information. These technologies encompass a collection of tools where data is combined with logical rules in order to generate insight. This area also maintains specific rules for acting on insights.

As we can see, a CRM system is not a single program or technology; it is a set of software, hardware, and network technologies that are integrated together to provide a more complete organizational capability to generate customer knowledge. In a more specific way, McKendrick (2000) describes CRM system or application as an umbrella term involving the four categories of applications below:

- **Sales Force Automation:** This is a set of tools for sales professionals. The set has functionalities such as calendaring, forecasting, contact management, and configuration models.

- **Marketing Automation:** This is a set of tools for automating marketing departments' processes and operations, including Web and traditional marketing campaigns.
- **Customer Service and Support:** This is a set of tools for leveraging and managing information in customer contact centers, such as call-centers or internal helpdesk.
- **Channel and Partner Management:** Also referred to as a partner relationship management (PRM) system, this is a set of tools that supports and tracks activities with distributors, sales channels, resellers, and retailers.

It seems that McKendrick has included PRM systems in the core of CRM applications, considering that partners' demands somehow represent end users' demands and tracking these demands allows a more comprehensive view of customers' needs and wants in general. This aspect is strengthened by Buttle (2004), who comments that partners have access to end consumers; thus, they can provide information on changing customer profiles, customer expectations, or sources of customer satisfaction and dissatisfaction.

Another important category of application called "employee relationship management" (ERM) is also being involved in the reach of CRM solutions (Callaghan, 2002). The reasoning behind this idea is that by using a CRM approach, HR professionals are beginning to better understand employees in a whole new way. More specifically, ERM deploys solutions similar to CRM solutions such as analytical and segmentation tools, smart Internet tools, and interactive technology to care about employees, allowing HR professionals to more accurately identify employees' motivations, needs, and preferences as well as better aligning employment practices to real needs, which minimizes staff turnover and, at the same time,

maximizes staff retention by the definition of more appropriate recruitment profiles. The final results promoted by ERM adoption are better-equipped managers, employee loyalty, empowered employees, improved employee satisfaction, preferred employer status, and reduced costs (Dorgan, 2003).

In terms of system support information technology, there are some computer technologies that should be allocated in order to fully implement a CRM system with all its functionality. It is important to point out that these technologies were not developed exclusively for implementing CRM systems; they were developed in different periods and for several purposes. Their link with CRM exists because their resources and functionalities made the implementation of CRM systems a feasible process. Therefore, they are fundamental to support CRM initiatives. Some of the main technologies that can be considered as core components of CRM systems are:

- **Data Warehouse:** This is a special kind of database that can manage a large amount of data with very high performance; it is generally used to store historical data, and its advanced functionalities allow more flexibility when retrieving information. Most often, the integrations with legacy and external data sources are made through data warehousing technologies. In CRM systems, a data warehouse is generally used as the central customer database that provides a single view of customers. For example, the database can provide key information on customers' orders, requests, problems, and so forth. This sort of information assists service representatives to resolve problems in a more efficient and effective way. Data warehousing technologies are also used as recommendation engines that store predetermined customer treatment recommendations, which are updated after each customer interaction (Todman, 2001; Hansotia, 2002).

- **Data Mining:** This technology combines concepts of statistics and artificial intelligence to help users analyze and extract predictive information from large databases such as, for example, data warehouses. In CRM systems, data mining software uses historical information stored in customer databases to build a model of customer behavior that could be used to predict which customers are more likely to respond to new services and product offers. Such information can then feed other touch point systems such as call centers, e-mail systems, direct mail, and so forth, so that the right customers receive the right offers (Berry & Linoff, 2004). Data mining tools can predict future trends and identify behaviors; this way, businesses are able to make proactive, knowledge-driven decisions.

- **Online Analytical Processing (OLAP):** This technology transforms information stored in databases into a summarized format that allows managers to quickly drill-down on tables and graphics to analyze where a certain problem may have arisen. One of its strongest resources is that the analysis tools can also support decisions in real time; for example, a call-center agent may be promptly informed about customer scoring or predictive measures while the customer is on the telephone. Such a characteristic is called "real-time CRM" by some vendors. Another powerful OLAP functionality involves the setting of trigger points by the users so that they can be automatically informed when, for instance, a customer calls more than a certain number of times in a month (Buttle, 2004).

- **Segmentation Tools:** These technologies provide the functionalities that allow an organization to identify and group its customers according to key characteristics such as demographic, socioeconomic, housing, behavioral characteristics, and so forth. This

way, organizations have a better understanding of their customers' market behavior, tailoring their products and services according to the different customer segments or types present in a database. Customer segments can also be targeted through their preferred media or channels of contact (Doyle, 2002). For Todman (2001), the capability to accurately segment customers is one of the important properties of a data warehouse designed to support a CRM strategy. However, there are other segmentation tools in the market.

Besides the technologies mentioned above, other complementary technologies such as campaign management tools (technologies that support the designing of marketing campaigns and strategies), interfaces to the operational environment, and interfaces to the communications channels can also be allocated by CRM systems.

In practice, customers can interact with organizations through several different channels or means of contact, namely: face to face, by telephone or fax, by post, through the Internet, and so forth. Customer interaction management solutions enable front-office integration, providing an appropriate environment with resources and facilities that allow customer-facing staff to deal with all customer interactions, regardless of the channel of contact. In another layer, workflow functionalities provide integration of front-office with back-office. Workflow solutions play a major role in enabling CRM initiatives to provide a higher quality of service to customers, allowing organizations to design automated processes to enhance the productivity and responsiveness of their workforce (Ling & Yen, 2001). A central data warehouse provides a single customer view, enhancing front-office integration with back-office and integration with legacy systems, and improving organizational performance at the back- and front-office. Data mining and segmentation resources provide the intelligence that allows organizations to better understand their customers' attributes and get better results. Among these technologies, the Internet is one of the most powerful. The adoption of Internet functionalities and capabilities by CRM systems constitutes a specific set of CRM applications termed "e-CRM."

## e-CRM

Electronic CRM or e-CRM can be seen as a set of applications that takes advantage of the potentialities of the Internet environment to implement relationship practices. Indeed, the "Web" is a powerful channel available for organizations to develop and enhance interactions with customers; this is why the Internet has become crucial in supporting CRM efforts. McKendrick (2000) argues that a robust CRM site must have strong customer service functionalities; in addition, the site should also provide interactive chat, browser and application sharing, personalization, e-mail options, and content management. The implementation of such facilities significantly varies from one organization to another; generally speaking, Sterne (2000) describes different evolutionary stages of Internet sites according to the use of e-technologies by organizations:

- **Phase 1:** This is a basic level. Organizations use the Internet only to exhibit catalogs or brochures on their Web sites.
- **Phase 2:** At this phase, organizations include on their Web sites additional information for promoting and selling their products or services.
- **Phase 3:** At this stage, organizations begin to offer additional functionalities and services to assist customers in making decisions or finding solutions on their Web sites.
- **Phase 4:** At this level, the organizations' Web sites have facilities to promote effective customer relationship management through highly interactive mechanisms for both sup-

plying customers with enough information and services, and getting strategic information from customers' interactions.

Based upon the phases above and taking into account the Internet resources, accessibility, and affordability, we can infer that the Web is a popular way for an organization to gradually build customer relationships (from phase 1 to 4). In order to respond to marketing demands and maintain competitiveness, organizations are increasingly considering the strategic value of the Internet as a means of enhancing relationship strategies. E-CRM solutions are situated at the most advanced level of e-technologies applications. Therefore, e-CRM initiatives require a more advanced level of computer and telecommunication organizational infrastructure.

## Wireless CRM

It is important to consider that the evolution of wireless technologies, such as Wireless Access Protocol (WAP) and devices such as mobile phones and personal digital assistants (PDA), may potentially change the face of CRM applications. The rationale for this argument is that salespeople and mobile service personnel will be able to access customer data through Web-enabled handheld devices wherever they may be, cutting companies' expenses and increasing their efficiency. Furthermore, the customers themselves will be able to access service applications using wireless devices. As Songini (2001) illustrates, the General Motors Corporation has a wireless customer relationship management program available to let drivers know what to do when the "check engine" light goes on. McKendrick (2000) also addresses the wireless tendency of CRM systems, commenting that mobile devices will significantly alter the CRM market; the widespread use of wireless and remote technologies will require CRM applications to have multiple entry points and be available on a 24-hours-a-day, 7-days-a-week basis.

Summarizing, the confluence of the technologies we have mentioned thus far, systematically coordinated and integrated by CRM systems, has enabled organizations to sift through large amounts of data to extract invaluable information and knowledge about their customer base. Without these technologies, the adoption of CRM concepts and practices would not be possible. Moreover, the integration of these technologies with other operational systems at the front- and back-ends of organizations provides the necessary seamless collaboration of resources, which is one of the main objectives of CRM. Unfortunately, the integration of different technologies is just the source of the main difficulties that organizations face when adopting CRM initiatives.

## CHALLENGES OF CRM IMPLEMENTATION

CRM is one of many technologies touted as the panacea that led to excessive expectations and a high rate of implementation failure. Previous surveys show that as many as 60% of CRM implementations fail the first time (Silverman, 2001). A close examination of the problem reveals that CRM is an extremely broad area, which involves several categories of solutions and hundreds of products and services that focus on a wide range of business problems and technological opportunities. For instance, CRM embraces a wide range of processes such as product configuration, field service, customer service, and customer analysis (Reddy, 2001). The greatest challenge of implementing CRM initiatives is the deployment and integration of a number of diversified technological resources in different ways so that an organization can ensure that all front-office activities and customer interactions appear seamless to the customers. As Kandell (2000) exemplifies, CRM adoption requires:

- **Integration across all type of interactions:** marketing, sales, service, and support;
- **Integration across all media for interaction:** in-person, telephone, fax, e-mail, web site, and so forth; and
- **Integration across all channels of interactions:** sales force, telemarketing, retail, e-commerce, and so forth.

Moreover, the integration of CRM systems with back-office and legacy systems is also a crucial point for successful implementations. Gartner Group's specialists said that many CRM projects fail because they do not fully leverage and integrate all potential customer channels, and they are not fully integrated with legacy systems and back-office solutions (McKendrick, 2000).

Reddy (2001) mentions that lack of executive sponsorship, too much organizational change, and mismatched technology infrastructure are usually cited as the potential suspects of CRM implementation failure. However, he argues that these symptoms are not the root cause of the failure. Instead, the main cause of failure is the lack of an actionable CRM strategy. This latter argument is strengthened by Silverman (2001) when he comments that CRM can be highly effective if it is implemented in a strategic, focused, and holistic manner. He argues that:

*Typical missteps involve implementing a CRM suite with the hope that it will address all of a company's objectives, a strategy that often ends in disappointment; or implementing a specific solution that is ultimately applied to the wrong problem. Some companies immediately jump into the implementation of a CRM solution without truly understanding the business issue they are trying to address ...The CRM battlefield is littered with failed project corpses resulting from the 'ready, fire, aim' approach. As such, it is important to fully understand and prioritize the business problems or objectives you are trying to address rather than leaping to buy a CRM solution based on a strong vendor demonstration or industry hype.* (Silverman, 2001, p. 90)

Another problematic aspect is the fragmented universe of CRM applications; this characteristic may mislead organizations to wrongly implement CRM solutions. Payne and Frow (2004) address this problem, commenting that many organizations are adopting CRM solutions on a fragmented basis through a range of activities such as help desks, call centers, direct mail, and loyalty cards; and these activities are often not properly integrated. Considering the integration of different channels of interaction as one of the key cross-functional processes in CRM strategy development, they conclude that the adoption of a strategic perspective is fundamental for successful CRM initiatives.

## Cultural Considerations

Organizational values are abstract ideas that underlie beliefs that managers have about the business and about people. Although they are very abstract, vague, and difficult to define, values are revealed by the actions people take, what they think, and how they allocate their time, energy, and skills (Rowe et al., 1994). The shared mindset regarding the basic or implicit assumptions that members of an organization unconsciously carry around with them is the organizational paradigm. In other words, the organizational paradigm can be understood as a set of concepts and perceptions shared by a group that determines how the group views the world (Finlay, 2000). Since the introduction of new technologies almost always requires changes in an organization's strategy and processes, organizational cultural aspects such as values and paradigms may impact positively or negatively on the introduction of innovations. According to Rowe et al. (1994), implementation failures are often attributed to the inability of an organization to

consider its cultural aspects in order to understand how they are influencing the implementation of new strategies or processes within the organization. A positive posture supports the organization's mission and helps achieve its strategies. Contrarily, a negative posture may run counter to the expressed mission and strategies.

Generally, organizational values or paradigms cannot be easily changed. There is evidence that, in some circumstances, people's resistance may slow down radically or even completely impede the adoption of new business models and technologies (Margetts & Dunleavy, 2002). Since CRM implementation entails strategic, procedural, and technological redesign, we may therefore expect organizations adopting CRM initiatives to face resistance problems due to cultural aspects. More specifically, the adoption of customer-oriented strategies requires: (1) revision of organizational mission, posture, and strategic objectives toward customers; (2) process redesign in order to enhance organizational performance; and (3) introduction of new technologies to improve customer experience and staff efficiency. Therefore, it is fundamental to be aware that cultural barriers are potential problems likely to emerge when an organization is adopting CRM concepts and practices.

Through and beyond this, it is important to consider that cultural aspects largely determine the experience of employees in a company, which in turn is reflected in their behavior when interacting with customers (Buttle, 2004). A consequence of this fact is that customer-facing behavior can have a major impact on customers' sense of satisfaction and future buying intentions. One important aspect that strongly impacts on employees' experiences is the accessibility and sharing of customer information across an organization. Buttle (2004) points out that customer-facing employees are in a position where they have significant influence on customer behaviors, perceptions, and expectations; hence, they need to have access to a considerable volume of customer information so that they will be able to tailor their selling efforts and service performance to a specific customer or segment requirements. A potential problem that can emerge from this context is addressed by Bond and Houston (2003), who warn that cross-functional communication can be inhibited by strong functional identities and different customer unit domains. Indeed, previous research has shown that managers from distinct functional areas are likely to perceive strategic decisions from perspectives that originate in different functional subcultures, different self-identities and self-interests, and different beliefs about desired ends and their means of achievement. These differences generate conflict and poor communication among functions and sub-units, hindering the enactment of strategic decisions (Frankwick & Ward, 1994).

## CRM MEASUREMENT ASPECTS

Measuring CRM aspects is still a challenge for most organizations. There is not a common pattern for gauging CRM initiatives. One of the reasons for this difficulty is that the concept of CRM is rather broad and one who wants to measure it should specify very clearly whether what is going to be measured is CRM as a business strategy or CRM as an application system, or even both. Another reason is that the variables considered to be measured vary from one company to another according to the company's activity or business, and these variables can vary even more largely from private to public organizations.

Regarding CRM as a business strategy in the private sector context, most of the attention concerning CRM measurement is focused on return on investment aspects. Two of the most used metrics for measuring the success of CRM efforts are revenue growth and margin growth (Ness, Schroeck, Letendre, & Douglas, 2001). However, some companies still prefer to consider classical parameters such as decreased costs and increased sales to measure CRM benefits (Khirallah, 2000).

Given the amplitude of CRM consequences and effects, we think that the variables or parameters above are insufficient to give us an appropriate measure of CRM benefits.

Other authors consider the impacts that the implementation of CRM strategies can cause on a company's performance, focusing on the main organizational benefits that are supposed to be reached via CRM initiatives. For instance, Sterne (2000) points out the following aspects linked to CRM's payoff:

- Faster service,
- Lower costs,
- Larger profits (profitability),
- Improved retention (loyalty), and
- Higher customer satisfaction.

Khirallah (2000) agrees with Sterne when she affirms that loyalty, profitability, and satisfaction are customers' demonstrations of CRM efficacy. She adds to the list of variables above, suggesting that the following aspects should be considered in the analysis of CRM results, which should also be analyzed in terms of customer segments:

- Customer profitability,
- Customer satisfaction,
- Relationship duration,
- System availability,
- Response time,
- Response rates,
- Cross-sell ratio,
- Market share, and
- Wallet share.

Khirallah (2000) also draws our attention to the analysis of customer satisfaction over time. She claims that the measurement of customer satisfaction would produce a better CRM gauge if the process implied the measurement of customers' satisfaction with the interactions. She justifies her assumption explaining that customer satisfaction is not a static parameter. Actually, the satisfaction of customers oscillates over time according to whether their needs are being attended to or not; moreover, even though previous needs are fully attended to (which raises the satisfaction level), the satisfaction of customers might go down as soon as additional unattended needs appear over time. Based on this aspect, we conclude that although customer satisfaction represents a good indicator of CRM effectiveness, other variables or indicators should also be taken into account in the analysis of CRM impact.

It is important to point out that the variables or indicators above mainly focus on the analysis of CRM results or, we could say, post-CRM adoption analysis. Besides those aspects, it is also important to consider the analysis of pre-CRM factors, which are organizational factors linked to organizational readiness to CRM adoption. Since CRM adoption implies the establishment of customer-focused strategies, enhancement of organizational integration, and improvement of customer interactions, it is crucial to look at the extent to which organization strategies are oriented to customers and how supportive the organizational infrastructure is to the development of such strategies.

## PRACTICAL CONSIDERATIONS AND REFLEXIONS

In our global economy, people's knowledge has become a valuable asset for private companies and governments. Due to the availability of current information and communication technologies such as the Internet, and mobile and wireless resources, customers have more information than they usually had a few years ago and they usually know the companies from which they regularly buy well. The development of lasting and learning relationships between an organization and its customers fosters the creation of mutual trust so that they start sharing responsibilities and interests. For example, through self-service facilities,

customers can verify the availability of products, order their purchases, and trace their orders. On-line access to technical databases, chat resources, and bulletin boards put customers in contact with technical staff and with other customers so that they can mutually help each other.

The development of mass customization capabilities is as important as the ability to conduct personalized interactions. While customization capability refers to an organization's capacity to project and adjust its products and services according to customers' needs, personalized interactions refer to an organization's capacity to deal with customers' singularities and particular needs. Both aspects require the correct identification of every single customer's needs and preferences. Increasing "customer share" might be a better strategy than to increase "market share." The more you know about your customers' business, the better you can serve them. To convince your customers to give you more of their business, let them know much about your business. Do not limit customer relationships within the scope of salespeople only; give your customers access to experts from several areas of the company. Your experts are better able both to identify what your customers' needs and preferences are, and provide more complete and accurate information about your business.

To work with quality, it is necessary to continually observe the view and perception your customers have about the products and services you deliver (Seybold, 2002). According to Seybold (2002) different research has shown that while internal staff members or employees of an organization think their products and services have improved, the external customers think exactly the opposite.

The purpose of CRM solutions and systems is to allow organizations to work with their customers in a learning manner, which yields effective results for both sides. For example, it is becoming quite common for software developers to let their customers test unfinished versions of their products rather than conducting laboratory tests. The result is the creation of a product that more precisely meets users' preferences. Of course, taking advantage of customers' competencies requires some caution: it is necessary to mobilize customer segments according to specific criteria, engage the customers in an active dialogue, and manage their differences. By active dialogue we mean the development of "knowledge-rich" dialogues. Companies should promptly process and share what they learned from the customers to maintain existing dialogues and keep customers' interests alive (Prahalad & Ramaswamy, 2002).

CRM adoption requires deep cultural change, which should mobilize and embrace an organization as a whole. We should be aware that the employees are the people who really interact and establish relationships with customers. Hence, only a sound corporate culture promotes commitment. Many organizations have already realized that it is the internal customers—the employees—who are capable of "delighting" the external customers. Highly motivated employees project their motivation to the external public. This phenomenon helps to build the corporate image itself, which is highly influenced by what is projected by the employees (Davies, Chun, da Silva, & Roper, 2003). Organizations should see their employees as allies to attract, please, and maintain customers. The relationship of an organization with its customers can be seen as a service made by its internal customers to the external ones.

Whatever the strategy, it is important to bear in mind that managing customers' experiences is not the same as managing different products. Rather, managing customers' experiences is managing their interactions and interfaces or channels of contact. As customers' needs change over time, products and services ought to evolve as well and be adjusted over time according to new customers' needs, wants, and preferences.

## Global CRM

Multinational organizations are getting more and more serious about globalizing their CRM programs and taking their CRM strategies to a multinational level. Important considerations should be taken into account by MNCs endeavoring to develop CRM initiatives on a multinational scale. A basic premise is that different countries have different cultures, traditions, symbols, expectations, processes, languages, laws, and so forth. They do business differently, therefore it should be expected that customer behavior or business practices are different across international boundaries. In this sense, the CRM applications and tools used in each country must fit the reality of that country. The reason for this is that cultural customs, language, customer expectations, and privacy laws, for example, all vary from country to country. For this reason, although it is extremely important that an MNC creates global standards for its CRM applications, the company should provide its subsidiaries' business leaders and customer-facing managers with decision-making power to adjust their local CRM applications (Dyche, 2001).

In the multinational arena, a strong global CRM deployment trend is the centralization of customer information. MNCs are creating global customer data infrastructure by implementing a corporate data warehouse that acts as a common repository of customer and business knowledge which is made available to subsidiaries worldwide (Dyche, 2001). This practice is illustrated by Case 1.

In short, multinational organizations are deploying global CRM solutions to better manage their sales and delivery channels worldwide. A usual implementation practice is to centralize customer data in a globally shared data warehouse, which is accessed through a global CRM engine that can interact with local CRM applications that

*Case 1. Kelly Services connected sales network across 30 countries and five continents [Sources: Adapted from Kelly Services (n.d.) and Salesforce (Kelly) (n.d.)]*

Kelly Services, Inc. is a Fortune 500 company headquartered in the U.S., offering staffing solutions including temporary staffing services, staff leasing, outsourcing, and vendor onsite and full-time placement. With clients ranging from small local businesses to blue chip multinationals in various markets from pharmaceuticals to telecommunications, Kelly Services operates in 30 countries and territories providing employment to more than 700,000 employees annually. To manage its highly diverse universe of customers, the company needed a central repository to share sales information between branch managers, sales reps, and recruiters spread throughout 30 different countries. Additional challenges included the need to better capture historical sales information due to staff turnover, and easy remote access to the central repository. Through the adoption of CRM practices and systems, Kelly standardized its tracking and management processes, and provided more than 100 users with anywhere online access to a fully documented sales history on every account anytime. CRM adoption enabled the company to network its global, large account sales force across 30 countries and five continents in a seamless and coordinated manner. Kelly Services now shares real-time data and key account information with minimal internal infrastructure. The solution, which includes multi-language and multi-currency functionalities, increased efficiency and better tracking of sales processes, and allowed easier identification of emerging opportunities and the ability to take action to help close deals. Also, it became smoother to preserve information during staff transitions.

may vary from country to country. This provides global understanding, identification, and tracking of appropriate customer contact channels in any given region, allowing MNCs to better manage their customer interactions around the world.

## CRM AND KNOWLEDGE MANAGEMENT IN MULTINATIONAL ORGANIZATIONS

Considering the CRM strategies, practices, resources, and systems commented on in the previous sections, it is possible to identify a number of potential roles CRM can play to enhance organizational learning capabilities that are also of KM concern.

In general, the development of KM practices entails three interrelated processes, which are mainly concerned with knowledge acquisition, knowledge conversion, and knowledge application (Gold, Malhotra, & Segars, 2001). The knowledge acquisition process is concerned with the development of organizational capabilities to obtain and accumulate knowledge; the knowledge conversion process is more concerned with making existing knowledge useful, which entails the development of organizational capabilities to

organize, integrate, coordinate, and disseminate knowledge. Finally, knowledge application is mainly concerned with the use of knowledge; this entails the development of organizational capabilities to retrieve, share, and apply knowledge (Cui et al., 2005).

The development of these organizational capabilities is especially challenging for multinational corporations (MNCs), which continually seek to establish competitive positions in the global marketplace by developing strategic capabilities through subsidiaries (Kogut & Zander, 1993). To achieve such competitive positions, it is necessary for MNCs' subsidiaries to develop their strategies according to local market demands. As Cui et al. (2005) argue, instead of implementing standardized strategies, MNCs' subsidiaries should have strategic flexibility so that they can develop proactive strategies in accordance with their specific environmental conditions.

In order to efficiently identify and respond to different market conditions and demands, MNCs should develop the learning capability of their subsidiaries. In a global environment, we can see an MNC as a nested learning system in which the learning process occurs at several different but interconnected units at the same time. Monteiro, Arvidsson, and Birkinshaw (2004) point out that the knowledge generated by subsidiaries with strong learning capabilities becomes increasingly valuable to the rest of the organization. Therefore, the knowledge generated in the local environment becomes an essential part of an MNC's knowledge stock.

According to Schneider and De Meyer (1991), external sources are of the utmost importance for the generation of competences in a subsidiary. They argue that external sources can enhance the effectiveness and scope of learning processes. Furthermore, Andersson, Forsgren, and Holm (2002) have found a direct link between external sources and intra-organizational influence on MNC strategy. They argue that the degree of external relations determines the degree of influence. For example, an intensive and long-lasting interaction between a subsidiary and its customers regarding the development of a specific product or service might influence the process of product or service development in the whole MNC (Andersson et al., 2002). This aspect is strengthened by Gammelgaard (2000) when he comments that changes in the customers' taste and attitudes demand the development of entrepreneurial activity, as relationships with customers often lead to requests for modifications of existing products and services, and sometimes, the development of new ones (Gammelgaard, 2000).

Taking into account the aspects mentioned above, we can conclude that the adoption of customer-focused strategies and practices may significantly increase a multinational organization's capacity to generate knowledge. In this sense, CRM can be seen as an enabler for the development of learning capabilities, as the adoption of its concepts, practices, and learning techniques allow the development of business approaches that support knowledge creation and sharing mechanisms.

## CRM Supporting Roles to KM

Knowledge management is a corporate process that involves the development of organizational learning capabilities. It is important to point out that the process of organizational learning is not limited to a mere information system, a data warehouse, or specific analytical tools. Although the adoption of technical solutions makes it feasible for an organization systematically to collect, analyze, process, and disseminate information, strategic and cultural aspects should be carefully observed prior to any technical investment. The adoption of customer-focused strategies is of crucial importance to the processes of knowledge acquisition, conversion, and application. In this context, CRM practices, systems, and tools provide powerful resources to enable effective organizational learning capabilities that can significantly increase a multinational organization's ability to recognize not only customer demands in specific regions of the globe, but also to identify global patterns and common marketing trends that can guide global strategies. In the sequence, we identify and describe the main aspects and areas where CRM can play crucial roles in supporting knowledge management in multinational organizations. Each description is illustrated with a real-life case that shows how different MNCs are deploying their CRM solutions globally.

## Customer Segmentation

Segmentation strategy means that an organization seeks to group its customers according to common patterns and characteristics determined in conformity with previously identified criteria. Segmentation methods are often used to characterize and help with the understanding of different customer groups. More specifically, segmentation aims to group customers according to their preferences for products, services, channels of interaction, and the magnitude and frequency of their interactions with an organization (Hansotia, 2002). This way, organizations can have a better understanding of their customers' wants and needs, tailoring their products and services according to different customer segments or types. In a multinational perspective, CRM segmentation allows the generation of valuable customer knowledge to support the establishment of corporate strategies and services according to the reality of local markets. An example of segmentation practice is illustrated in Case 2 below.

## Customer Personalization

CRM is also seen as an organization's broad business strategy that focuses upon building personalized interactions with customers, whatever the channel of contact between the organization and its customers (Dean, 2001). It proposes personal interactions even in a mass context. Such a large-scale personalization is perfectly feasible through the deployment of CRM systems, applications, and tools (Ling & Yen, 2001). Organizational capability to develop personalized interactions with customers is therefore a remarkable charac-

teristic of organizational focus upon customers. A summary of customers' preferences and profiles in each MNC subsidiary may potentially enhance global strategies. Case 3 shows how the Chase Manhattan Bank is implementing personalization capabilities.

## Channels of Customer Interaction

Customers can interact with organizations through several different channels or means of contact such as telephone, in person, fax, post, e-mail, and so forth (Kandell, 2000). Logically, an organization that offers a diversified number of different contact channels strategically increases the possibility of customer interaction. The integration of such channels in the front-office provides an appropriate environment with resources and facilities that allow customer-facing staff to deal efficiently with all customer interactions regardless of the channel of contact (Sterne, 2000). For Payne and Frow (2004), the integration of different channels of interaction is one of the key cross-functional processes in CRM strategy development. The analysis of the volume of customer interactions per channel is an important source of knowledge that can support MNCs to undertake timely and highly accurate forecasting. This aspect is illustrated in Case 4.

*Case 2. Hard Rock Cafe turned to CRM to help bring customers back into the fold (Source: Jessup and Valacich, 2005)*

Founded in London in 1971, the now U.S.-based Hard Rock Cafe International, Inc. was among the first chains of themed restaurants to come into existence. With 138 venues in 42 countries, and over 30 million customers a year, Hard Rock has become a truly global phenomenon. With the rise of many thematic eateries around the world, Hard Rock turned to CRM to help solidify its footing. In 2000, the company estimated that of its 30 million customers who come to its 138 venues each year, only about 10,000 names were in the company's customer database. The company began a detailed two-year customer survey to build out its data resources and gauge its potential for using CRM. The survey was the backbone of the company's CRM strategy, and it helped to build a database to host about 100,000 names as preferred customers. The database provides real-time customer information for several applications including e-commerce operations. The CRM solution allowed analysis based on different customer segments, and the company was able to figure out how customers responded to e-mail or coupons. It was possible to identify what kind of people were buying and why. By targeting customer preferences, the company increased memorabilia sales by 75% and improved customer service response by 85%. Hard Rock Cafe intends to extend its CRM deployment to the point where it can identify and reward customers at point-of-sale locations (restaurants), rather than exclusively through its member-based programs.

## Workflow

Workflow is an important set of applications that enable the automation and tracking of different customer processes by the integration of front-office with back-office. This characteristic makes workflow products ideally situated to address the demand for CRM solutions (Chambers et al., 1999). Embracing workflow functionalities, CRM systems play a major role in the provision of a higher quality of service to customers, allowing organizations to design automated processes to enhance the productivity and responsiveness of their workforce (Ling & Yen, 2001). Therefore,

*Case 3. Chase Manhattan Bank gets closer to its customers (Sources: Adapted from Ptacek, 2000 and "JPMorgan Chase" ,n.d.)*

> JPMorgan Chase & Co. is a world-leading global financial services firm with assets of $1.3 trillion and operations in more than 50 countries. Under the JPMorgan and Chase brands, the firm serves millions of consumers in the United States and many of the world's most prominent corporate, institutional, and government clients. The U.S. consumer and commercial banking businesses serve customers under the Chase brand. The bank has adopted a CRM system to let its 4,500 relationship managers worldwide share and gain access to constantly changing information about the profitability of their corporate customers. The system makes the managers' jobs easier by keeping them up to date on all aspects of their multinational, multifaceted corporate clients. Chase was one of the first corporate banks to implement CRM techniques that the industry had applied to the retail side. The CRM system has different degrees of customization, allowing managers to use different benchmarks to gauge customers' profitability. Customers and bankers can enter and view relevant information through the Internet. Customers also can get a daily report card on their banking activities and are encouraged to give the bank feedback. The bank is also letting institutional customers send messages to their relationship managers as they observe market events. Video technology will be deployed so that customers and bankers can interact face to face wherever they are around the world. Through an increasing variety of channels, including wireless devices, customers can do online self-service and online tracking.

*Case 4. InFact deployed CRM system to undertake timely and highly accurate forecasting. (Source: Adapted from Oracle, 2006)*

> InFact Group is a global technology consulting organization with a world-class portfolio of customers in three continents. The company provides end-to-end project services, and delivers outsourcing solutions based upon its dedicated development platform in India. After its founding in 2000, the company grew very rapidly, increasing its breadth of customers, extending its global reach, and recruiting more than 60 employees. As a consequence, the company needed to replace the existing legacy systems it relied on to manage a growing number of increasingly complex customer relationships. The company turned to a CRM system to face this challenge. InFact deployed CRM systems in Europe, the U.S., and India to create a single, comprehensive view of its customers and partners across multiple channels and touch-points. By introducing a standard sales, marketing, and service methodology worldwide, the company is able to optimize sales performance by efficiently tracking and qualifying every sales opportunity. InFact can also identify top-performing accounts and conduct rigorous analysis of customer interaction by region, industry, and revenue. CRM has reduced the time it takes to close a sales opportunity by 15%. The system allows the company to undertake timely and highly accurate forecasting. InFact trades in multiple currencies around the world, and it used to take one person up to four days each quarter to pull together all the different currency rates and fluctuation allowances into one consolidated spreadsheet forecast. The new CRM system automatically undertakes all currency conversion, historical exchange rates, and rollups. This saves InFact $33,000 each quarter in reduced overhead. Managers can also analyze customers and prospects by industry, region, and even city. The company has recently targeted 300 companies in Asia Pacific with a direct mail campaign and was able to track the calls coming in from this campaign. It was immediately apparent how many inquiries InFact received and the total cost per lead. By providing one view of the customer, greater visibility into the sales pipeline, and analytic insight into key performance metrics, CRM has helped to transform InFact into a more agile, proactive consultancy, with the tools needed to provide the highest levels of customer service.

the organizational capability to track and/or follow-up automated customer processes also represents integration towards customers. For MNCs, the adoption of workflow functionalities may significantly facilitate and optimize the execution of global business processes. Case 5 shows how an MNC is adopting a CRM system to integrate disparate customer touch points and focus its business processes across the company around customer needs.

## Marketing Knowledge

Obtaining customer information is crucial for allowing MNCs' prompt acquiescence to market demands, which allows the development of better products and services according to local specificities. Also, the analysis of local market demands and trends allows the identification of common points of demand in different regions around the globe; this knowledge helps MNCs to define global strategies for their products and services, as well as target communication with customers and delineate more responsive marketing campaigns. Case 6 shows how Ford is taking its main marketing team to better deliver coordinated cross-border marketing campaigns.

## Customer Information Sharing

This aspect is mainly concerned with customer information gathering and usage. Getting basic information about customers' needs, wants, and preferences allows the development of better strategies for providing immediate responses to different situations and scenarios, which improves MNCs' ability to make complementary plans to respond to different market expectations. The sharing of customer information throughout the

MNC allows better transparency, reporting, and communication across global teams. This aspect is illustrated in Case 7.

## Consistent Global Corporate Image

Employees are the people who really interact and establish relationships with customers. When interacting with customers, MNCs' employees are implicitly building their own corporate image. A positive image can be built when customer-facing employees are empowered to respond to customer needs and when they feel trusted to run the business. Enabling employees to consistently interact with customers in a standardized, but not inflexible manner is how International Business Machines (IBM) Corporation created a consistent corporate image worldwide (Case 8).

In all the illustrative cases presented above, CRM is implicitly supporting knowledge acquisition, knowledge conversion, and knowledge application processes within the multinational organizations addressed. For example, CRM supports knowledge acquisition processes by providing resources to manage the customer interaction channels through which MNCs can obtain and store worldwide customer information in corporate databases. By providing global managers with sharing capabilities to access these corporate databases, as well as integrating the workflow of cross-border processes, CRM is supporting MNCs to integrate, coordinate, and disseminate knowledge. Finally, the segmentation and personalization capabilities provided by CRM solutions, plus marketing campaign management resources and functionalities to adopt standardized relationship processes, strongly support MNCs in the process of retrieving and applying knowledge.

*Case 5. Air Products adopted CRM to support its operations in more than 30 countries (Source: Adapted from "Air Products", n.d.)*

Founded in 1940, Air Products and Chemicals, Inc. has built leading positions in key growth markets such as semiconductor materials, refinery hydrogen, home healthcare services, natural gas liquefaction, and advanced coatings and adhesives. With annual revenues of $8.1 billion, operations in more than 30 countries, and more than 20,000 employees around the globe, the company lacked a common approach for its many divisions to manage the information critical to maintaining its relationships and growing revenue with customers. To allow its employees to focus more attention on customer needs, Air Products is putting into place a CRM system. Companywide access to accurate information about customers, production, and distribution will form the backbone of the company's customer care concept. The CRM system will ultimately integrate disparate touch points, raise the quality of customer interactions, and focus business processes across the enterprise around customer needs. The new system will serve as a repository of information and allow the company to build accurate customer profiles based on the products it sells and the services it offers. A customer portal is expected to strengthen the relationships with customers by making business more convenient and friendly. The portal will be integrated with the corporate CRM system and other business systems so that the new tools and processes will provide customers with a greater level of service than ever before. The ultimate objective is to provide managers with access to customer information all the way through the product cycle, from order commitment to production scheduling to delivery to invoicing, making sure the company gets it right for customers the first time.

*Case 6. Ford's CRM strategy has increased sales and productivity (Sources: Adapted from Ford, n.d.; and IBM, 2006)*

With a recorded net income of $2.5 billion in 2005, Ford Motor Company is a global automotive industry leader based in Dearborn, Michigan. The company manufactures and distributes automobiles in 200 markets across six continents. With about 300,000 employees and 108 plants worldwide, the company's core and affiliated automotive brands include Aston Martin, Ford, Jaguar, Land Rover, Lincoln, Mazda, Mercury, and Volvo. Ford wanted to project a consistent company and product message throughout Europe while ensuring national marketing campaigns were tailored to regional needs. The company also needed to track customer responses and implement a lead qualifying process to focus sales efforts. To achieve these goals, Ford implemented a pan-European CRM solution into its three largest markets—the German, Spanish, and UK operations. Ford then needed to implement a centralized version of its CRM solution into additional markets across Europe, including offices in France, Italy, and Austria. The standardized CRM solution was integrated with key business processes and designed to transform simple marketing campaigns into responsive, targeted communications. The solution included campaign management processes and supporting tools that meet marketing needs at both the local market and pan-European level. This approach works in tandem with the consumer lifecycle management application that tracks marketing campaign responses. The system allows the company to track different communications ranging from a brochure request via the Web site to test drive inquiries to a call center. Identifying and coding the different customer communications set the basis for the solution's lead qualification process that allows customer representatives to prioritize and offer the most appropriate follow-up based on the potential customer's level of interest. The centralized approach enables Ford's main marketing team to better deliver coordinated cross-border marketing campaigns. The CRM initiative has improved customer service with faster, tailored responses to queries. The solution has generated more than 500,000 qualified leads to date.

*Case 7. Nokia customizes CRM solution to meet the needs of sales teams on three continents (Sources: Adapted from www.nokia.com and Salesforce [Nokia], n.d.)*

During the 1980s, Nokia strengthened its position in the telecommunications and consumer electronics markets through a series of European company acquisitions. Since the beginning of the 1990s, Nokia has concentrated on enhancing its core business, telecommunications. Currently, Nokia is the world's largest manufacturer of mobile devices; a leader in equipment, services, and solutions for network operators; and a driving force in bringing mobility to businesses. In 2005, Nokia's net sales totaled EUR 34.2 billion. The company has 15 manufacturing facilities in nine countries, and research and development centers in 11 countries. At the end of 2005, Nokia employed approximately 58,900 people. As Nokia's sales teams used three different reporting systems ranging from spreadsheets to homegrown solutions, it became very difficult to provide real-time visibility into the sales cycle and preserve consistency across different regions and functions. Through the adoption of a CRM solution, Nokia provided its traveling sales force with a customizable system with real-time visibility into business anytime and anywhere. The company is able to customize its CRM system on the fly to respond to changes in business models and requirements. CRM has also provided deeper understanding of customer buying habits and allowed better transparency, reporting, and communication across global teams. This has streamlined sales organization for improved collaboration and productivity, which resulted in a shorter sales cycle and more consistency across different regions and functions.

*Case 8. IBM standardizes its relationship processes (Sources: Adapted from www.ibm.com and ICFAI, 2004)*

With a revenue of $91.1 billion in 2005 and more than 329,000 employees in 75 countries, IBM is the world's largest information technology company. Worldwide, 45,000 business partners and 33,000 suppliers are connected to IBM through the Web. In January 2000, IBM undertook the largest CRM project known at that time. Termed "CRM 2000," the project aimed at ensuring that any point of interface between the company and its customers, through any of its channels of interaction, in any country, was dealt with uniformly, providing the same service level, applying the same tools and information. Ultimately, IBM wanted to show a unified interface to its customers across the world. Four years after the project, the company was well on its way towards achieving its objective, reporting significant improvements in customer satisfaction levels. At that time, IBM's vice president of worldwide CRM deployment said, *"By getting to know our customers better and enabling more effective collaboration around the customer and among multiple IBM organizations involving sales, marketing, and support, we can significantly enhance the value we bring to our customers, while generating additional revenues and cost efficiencies for our company. The concept of 'one IBM' is a cornerstone for the way we serve customers."*

## CONCLUSION

In this chapter we commented on concepts and characteristics of CRM, covering aspects from its origins to supporting roles to KM. The presented theory has shown that the confluence of changing customer demands, emerging marketing theories, and available information technologies have been imposing a shift on the way organizations relate to customers. In contrast to the old economy firm, which was more absorbed in achieving operational excellence through production and service delivery processes, the new economy firm reportedly has the customer at the center of its universe.

On one hand, the evolution of marketing business strategies over time delineated the current characteristics of CRM strategies; on the other hand, the evolution of information and communication technologies enabled the adoption of different and more evolved marketing approaches over time, giving birth to the current CRM systems. These two dimensions of CRM are extremely intertwined and, as a matter of fact, the emergence of CRM strategies, concepts, and practices would not be possible without the appearance of new and evolved ICT resources.

CRM systems provide the functionality that allows an organization to make its customers the focal point of all departments within the firm. This way, the organization will be able to respond to its customers on a continual basis. More specifically, customer information databases and integrated interactivity enable an organization to develop a learning relationship with its customers, creating organizational capability to differentiate its customers through lifetime value segmentation, to develop personalized interactions with customers, and to offer tailored products or services to customers.

A fundamental issue about CRM is that CRM is more than a mere product. If one sees CRM as a system that can be bought and installed in an off-the-shelf manner, then it becomes difficult to harvest the benefits promoted by such an expensive solution. CRM should be seen as a broad business strategy that implies the redevelopment of organizational structures so that there are new service units and new product offerings arranged around a refreshed understanding of customer needs. The real concept of CRM goes beyond the product, implying deep strategic and cultural concerns.

It is possible to identify CRM strategies, practices, and solutions that strengthen and support knowledge management approaches, especially in a more complex and diversified environment such as the one where multinational organizations are inserted. Regarding knowledge about customers, the adoption of customer-focused strategies supported by CRM systems can significantly strengthen the learning capabilities of MNCs' subsidiaries. These capabilities reflect on MNC headquarters in the form of increased corporate capacity to identify local and global trends concerning customers' preferences, cultural aspects, needs, and consumer behavior. This knowledge subsidizes the elaboration of more effective global strategies by multinational organizations.

Of course, CRM does not address the whole myriad of organizational aspects and issues that are of KM concern. Its focus is on developing organizational learning capabilities that can significantly enhance an organizational ability to acquire, process, and apply knowledge about customers. The objective of this chapter was to broadly present CRM characteristics, strategies, concepts, practices, solutions, resources, and concerns that can be explored by multinational organizations with the purpose of supporting the adoption of knowledge management strategies and practices.

# REFERENCES

Abbott, J., Stone, M., & Buttle, F. (2001). Integrating customer data into customer relationship management strategy: An empirical study. *Journal of Database Marketing, 8*(4), 289.

Andersson, U., Forsgren, M., & Holm, U. (2002). The strategic impact of external networks: Subsidiary performance and competence development in the multinational corporation. *Strategic Management Journal,* (23), 979-996.

Air Products. (n.d.). Retrieved October 18, 2006, from *http://www.airproducts.com/AboutUs/index. asp*

Berry, J. (2001). On the hunt for the right CRM metrics. *InternetWeek,* (April 9), 49.

Bond, E., & Houston, M. (2003). Barriers to matching new technologies and market opportunities in established firms. *Journal of Product Innovation Management, 20*(2), 120.

Business Guide. (2000). *Customer relationship management.* London: Caspian.

Buttle, F. (2004). *Customer relationship management—concepts and tools.* Oxford: Elsevier Butterworth-Heinemann.

Buttle, F. (1996). *Relationship marketing: Theory and practice.* London: Paul Chapman.

Callaghan, D. (2002). PeopleSoft widens CRM reach. *eWeek, 19*(50), 18.

Chambers, B., Medina, R., & West, K. (1999). Customer relationship management, the new battlefield for workflow. *Document World, 4*(4), 18.

Cui, A., Griffith, D., & Cavusgil, S. (2005). The influence of competitive intensity and market dynamism on knowledge management capabilities of multinational corporation subsidiaries. *Journal of International Marketing, 13*(3), 32-53.

Davies, G., Chun, R., da Silva, R., & Roper, S. (2003). *Corporate reputation and competitiveness.* London: Routledge.

Dean, J. (2001). Better business through customers. *Government Executive, 33*(1), 58.

Dorgan, M. (2003). Employee as customer: Lessons from marketing and IT. *Strategic HR Review, 2*(2), 10.

Doyle, S. (2002). Software review: Communication optimization—the new mantra of database marketing. Fad or fact? *Journal of Database Marketing, 9*(2), 185-191.

Dyche, J. (2001). *The CRM handbook: A business guide to customer relationship management.* Boston: Addison Wesley Professional (Information Technology Series).

Finlay, P. (2000). *Strategic management—an introduction to business and corporate strategy.* London: Financial Times Prentice Hall.

Ford. (n.d.). *Overview.* Retrieved October 20, 2006, from *http://www.ford.com/en/company/about/overview.htm*

Frankwick, G., & Ward, J. (1994). Evolving patterns of organizational beliefs in the formation of strategy. *Journal of Marketing, 58*(2), 96.

Gammelgaard, J. (2000). How foreign subsidiaries develop into integrated competence centers. In J. Larimo & S. Kock (Eds.), *Recent studies in interorganizational and international business research: Proceedings of the University of Vaasa* (report 58, pp. 164-181).

Gold, A., Malhotra, A., & Segars, A. (2001). Knowledge management: An organizational capabilities perspective. *Journal of Management Information Systems, 18*(1), 185-214.

Goldenberg, B. (2002, May). *Barton Goldenberg's advice: The truth about customer relationship management.* Retrieved September 10, 2002, from *http://www.crmcommunity.com*

Gummesson, E. (1999). *Total relationship management.* Oxford: Butterworth-Heinemann.

Hansotia, B. (2002). Gearing up for CRM: Antecedents to successful implementation. *Journal of Database Marketing, 10*(2), 121.

Hammer, M. (1996). *Beyond reengineering.* London: HarperCollins.

IBM. (2006, January). *Ford Motor Company's integrated CRM and marketing functions generate increased sales leads.* Retrieved October 20, 2006, from *http://www-306.ibm.com/software/success/cssdb.nsf/CS/GJON-6KWLL4?OpenDocument&Site=igsww*

ICFAI. (2004). *IBM's e-CRM initiatives* (case code ITSY044). Retrieved October 21, 2006, from *http://www.icmr.icfai.org/casestudies/catalogue/IT%20and%20Systems/ITSY044.htm*

Jessup, L., & Valacich, J. (2005). *Information systems today—why IS matters* (2nd/international ed.). Englewood Cliffs, NJ: Prentice Hall.

JPMorgan Chase. (n.d.). *About JPMorgan Chase.* Retrieved October 17, 2006, from *http://www.jpmorganchase.com/cm/cs?pagename=Chase/Href&urlname=jpmc/about*

Kandell, J. (2000). CRM, ERM, one-to-one—decoding relationship management theory and technology. *Trusts & Estates, 139*(4), 49.

Kelly Services. (n.d.). *A people company, staffing the world.* Retrieved October 16, 2006, from *http://www.kellyservices.com/web/global/services/en/pages/about_us.html*

Khirallah, K. (2000). Customer relationship management: How to measure success? *Bank Account & Finance,* (Summer), 21.

Kogut, B., & Zander, U. (1993). Knowledge of the firm and the evolutionary theory of the multinational corporation. *Journal of International Business Studies, 24*(4), 625-646.

Ling, R., & Yen, D. (2001). Customer relationship management: An analysis framework and implementation strategies. *Journal of Computer Information Systems, 41*(3), 82.

Margetts, H., & Dunleavy, P. (2002, April). *Cultural barriers to e-government.* Report HC704-III, National Audit Office, The Stationary Office, London.

McKendrick, J. (2000). The bottom line on CRM: Know thy customer. *ENT, 5*(20), 40.

Miles, J. (2002). CRM for citizens. *Government Computer News, 21*(29).

Monteiro, L., Arvidsson, N., & Birkinshaw, J. (2004). Knowledge flows within multinational corporations: Why are some subsidiaries isolated? *Proceedings of the Academy of Management Conference 2004* (p. B1).

Ness, J., Schroeck, M., Letendre, R., & Douglas, W. (2001). The role of ABM in measuring customer value. *Strategic Finance,* (March), 32.

Oracle. (2006, June). *InFact group reduces sales cycle times by 15%.* Retrieved October 17, 2006, from *http://www.oracle.com/customers/snapshots/infact-siebel-casestudy.pdf*

Pang, L., & Norris, R. (2002). Applying customer relationship management (CRM) to government. *Journal of Government Financial Management, 51*(1), 40.

Payne, A., & Frow, P. (2004). The role of multichannel integration in customer relationship management. *Industrial Marketing Management, 33*(6), 527.

Peppers, D., & Rogers, M. (1993). *The one to one future.* New York: Currency Doubleday.

Prahalad, C., & Ramaswamy, V. (2002). Co-opting customer competence. *Harvard Business Review on Customer Relationship Management,* 1.

Ptacek, M. (2000). Chase revs up corporate CRM system. *American Banker, 165*(156), 1.

Reddy, R. (2001). Through a lens smartly. *Intelligent Enterprise, 4*(5), 66.

Rheault, D., & Sheridan, S. (2002). Reconstruct your business around customers. *Journal of Business Strategy, 23*(2), 38.

Rowe, A., Mason, R., Dickel, K., Mann, R., & Mockler, R. (1994). *Strategic management—a methodological approach* (4th ed.). New York: Addison-Wesley.

Salesforce (Kelly). (n.d.). *Kelly Services connects sales network across 27 countries and five continents with Salesforce.* Retrieved October 17, 2006, from *http://www.salesforce.com/customers/snapshot.jsp?customer=kelly*

Salesforce (Nokia). (n.d.). *Nokia easily customizes Salesforce to meet the needs of sales teams on three continents.* Retrieved October 17, 2006, from *http://www.salesforce.com/customers/snapshot.jsp?customer=nok*

Schneider, S., & De Meyer, A. (1991). Interpreting and responding to strategic issues: The impact of national culture. *Strategic Management Journal, 12*(4), 307-320.

Seybold, P. (2002). Get inside the lives of your customers. *Harvard Business Review on Customer Relationship Management,* 27.

Silverman, R. (2001). CRM dichotomies. *Intelligent Enterprise, 4*(8), 90.

Songini, M. (2001). Wireless technology changes the face of CRM. *Computerworld, 35*(7), 20.

Sterne, J. (2000). *Customer service on the Internet* (2nd ed.). New York: John Wiley & Sons.

Thompson, J. (1997). *Strategic management—awareness and change* (3rd ed.). London: International Business Press.

Todman, C. (2001). *Designing a data warehouse—supporting customer relationship management.* Englewood Cliffs, NJ: Prentice Hall.

Warboys, B., Kawalek, P., Robertson, I., & Greenwood, M. (1999). *Business information systems—a process approach.* Berkshire: McGraw-Hill.

## ENDNOTE

[1] A respected, not-for-profit, non-partisan organization that brings leaders—who represent a variety of major industries—together to find solutions to common problems and objectively examine major issues having an impact on business and society (*www. conference-board.org*); in *Journal of Business Strategy (2001), 22*(6).

Chapter XVII

# Organizational Learning Process:
## Its Antecedents and Consequences in Enterprise System Implementation

**W. Ke**
*Clarkson University, USA*

**K. Kee Wei**
*City University of Hong Kong, Hong Kong*

## ABSTRACT

*This chapter uses organizational learning as a lens to study how firms implement enterprise system. The core research questions are: what are the critical organizational factors affecting organizational learning in ES implementation? How do these elements shape the learning process and thereby influence ES implementation outcomes? To address these questions, we conducted comparative case study with two organizations that have recently adopted ES and achieved significantly different results. Based on the empirical findings, we propose a framework that describes how organizational factors affect the four constructs of organizational learning in ES implementation context – knowledge acquisition, information distribution, information interpretation and organizational memory.*

## INTRODUCTION

Over the past few years, enterprise systems (ES) have generated much interest among researchers and practitioners as a potential means to enhance organizational agility (Sambamurthy et al. 2003; Davenport 1998). While interest and investment in ES have been rising steadily, actual experiences with ES have exhibited more ambiguity. Some studies report improvements in efficiency and effectiveness from ES adoption, yet others find that the expected gains are far beyond reach (Al-Mashari 2000). It is imperative to conduct research that can make sense of the apparently inconsistent ES adoption results.

Most of extant research on ES focuses on discrete critical success factors leading to on time and within budget implementation (e.g., Bingi et al. 1999; Holland et al., 1999; Parr & Shanks 2000; Sumner 1999). Yet, to leverage the business value of ES, it is not sufficient to simply adopt and install the system. Rather, employees and the organization as a whole must learn how to apply the technology effectively while they are implementing the system (Fichman & Kemerer, 1997; Cooper & Zmud, 1990; Purvis et al., 2001; Argyris 1977; Attewell 1992). The learning process plays a critical role in shaping IT adoption results (Tippins & Sohi, 2003). Hence studying how different forces affect the organizational learning process allows us to understand what leads to different ES implementation outcomes.

In this chapter, we use organizational learning as a lens to study how firms implement ES. Extant ES literature alludes to organizational learning sporadically and most of them do so in a cursory fashion, except the work of Robey et al. (2001) and Scott and Vessey (1999). Different from these studies, this chapter studies all the four constructs of the underlying learning process involved in ES implementation—knowledge acquisition, information distribution, information interpretation and organizational memory (Huber, 1991). The core research questions are: What are the critical organizational factors affecting organizational learning in ES implementation? How do these elements shape the learning process and thereby influence ES implementation outcomes? To address these questions, we collect data by conducting case studies with two firms that have implemented ES within budget and on time, but with significant different outcomes.

This chapter makes three principal contributions. First, drawing on the rich data of two organizations' experiences, the chapter generates an understanding of the organizational learning associated with ES implementation. Second, dealing with the complex links traced in context, this chapter adds substantive content

to our understanding of the central role played by organizational factors in the organizational learning enacted in ES implementation. Such an understanding has been absent from the research and practice discourses on ES. Third, the chapter integrates our research findings with the more formal insights available from the IS implementation and organizational learning literature. It facilitates researchers and practitioners to explain, anticipate, and evaluate organizational learning process associated with the ES adoption. This chapter is organized as follow: first, we briefly describe theoretical background of this study. Second, we discuss our research methodology. Third, we present the empirical findings that emerged from our case study. Last is our discussion and conclusion.

## THEORETICAL BACKGROUND

Firms' ability to apply IT effectively in their business activity explains the different outcomes of their IT adoption (Feeny & Wilcocks, 1998; Armstrong & Sambamurthy, 2001; Boynton et al., 1994; Cooper & Zmud, 1990; Sethi & King, 1994). When technologies are first introduced, they impose a substantial burden on the adopter in terms of the knowledge needed to understand and use them effectively (Attewell, 1992; Argyris, 1977; Fichman & Kemerer, 1997; Purvis et al., 2001). Organizations must undergo an intensive learning process to bridge the gap between what they have known and what the new technology requires them to know. Thus, the effectiveness of the organizational learning process plays a critical role in shaping IT adoption results. Indeed, this argument has been widely tested to be valid by the IS implementation literature (e.g., Boynton et al., 1994; Purvis et al., 2001; Fichman & Kemerer, 1997; Ciborra & Lanzara, 1994; Pentland, 1995; Lyytinen & Robey, 1998; Wastell, 1999).

Organizational learning is defined as a process enabling the acquisition of, access to and revision of organizational memory, thereby providing direction to organizational action (Robey et al., 2002). As cognitive entities, organizations are capable of observing their own actions, experimenting to discover the effects of alternative actions, and modifying their actions to improve performance (Filol & Lyles, 1985). The breadth and depth of organizational learning are positively related to its four constructs—knowledge acquisition, information distribution, information interpretation and organizational memory (Huber 1991). Knowledge acquisition is the process by which knowledge is obtained (Tippins & Sohi, 2003; Robey et al., 2002; Huber, 1991). Information distribution is the process by which knowledge obtained is shared through formal and informal channels (Maltz & Kohli, 1996; Slater & Narver, 1995). Information interpretation is the process by which functional units reach a consensus with regard to the meaning of information (Slater & Narver, 1995; Tippins & Sohi, 2003; Daft & Weick, 1984) and organizational memory refers to organizations' storing knowledge for future use (Walsh & Ungson, 1991; Huber, 1991).

Extant ES literature alludes to organizational learning sporadically and most of them do so in a cursory fashion, except the work of Robey et al. (2002) and Scott and Vessey (1999). In addition, the literature suggests a list of critical success factors for ES implementation, such as leadership (Lee & Sarkar, 1999), top management support and change management (Al-Mashari, 2000). But there is no study explicitly linking these factors with organizational learning enacted in ES implementation. Different from the extant studies, our research studies how organizational factors affect the learning process, which determines ES implementation outcomes.

## RESEARCH METHODOLOGY

To address our research questions, we employ a case study methodology. As an empirical inquiry investigating a contemporary phenomenon within its real-life context, case study is particularly appropriate when examining "how" and "why" research questions (Yin, 1990). Given the nature of our research question and desire to obtain rich explanations of organizational learning process in ES implementation, a case study methodology is the most appropriate.

We selected two organizations for their similarities as well as their differences (Glaser & Strauss, 1967), paying attention to theoretical relevance and purpose. With respect to relevance, our selection process ensured that the substantive area addressed—the on-time and within budge implementation of ES—was kept of similar. As the purpose of the research is to generate insight into how organizational factors affect organizational learning enacted and thereby ES implementation outcomes, differences were sought in organizational conditions, such as the motivation of adopting ES, user training methods and adoption outcomes. We first conducted study with CPM—a PC and computer peripheral manufacturing company with 800 employees located in south China. The second company we studied was MEM which was a division of a publicly listed multinational electronic manufacturing company. This division had 750 employees and was located in the North of China.

In both research sites, we collected data by using multiple methods: unstructured and semi-structured interviews, archival sources, and observation. This triangulation across various techniques of data collection provides multiple perspectives on an issue, supplies more information on emerging concepts, and yields stronger substantiation of constructs and allows for cross-checking (Yin, 1990; Eisenhardt, 1989; Pettigrew, 1990).

In this study, we had both investigators make visits to the case study sites together so that we could avoid biases due to one single researcher's perception. In particular, we followed Eisenhardt and Bourgeois' (1988) strategy and had one re-

*Table 1. Amount of interviewees*

| CPM | | MEM | |
|---|---|---|---|
| **Interviewee's Title** | **Count** | **Interviewee's Title** | **Count** |
| Senior VP in Marketing | 1 | Senior VP | 1 |
| Senior VP in Manufacturing | 1 | General Manager | 1 |
| CIO | 1 | Vice General Manager | 1 |
| Departmental Manager | 4 | Departmental Manager | 5 |
| Line Worker | 5 | Line Worker | 4 |

searcher handling the interview questions, while the other recording notes and observations. This tactic allows the interviewer to have perspective of personal interaction with the informant, while the other investigator retains a different and more distant view. The interviews we conducted are shown in Table 1. Each interview last between one and one and a half hours. They were all tape-recorded and transcribed within 24 hours after the interview.

## Data Analysis

We analyzed data within each site, as well as across the two sites. Given the qualitative nature of data collected, we avoided biases by using the iterative approach of data collection, coding, and analysis. Within CPM—the first site—we relied more on open-ended and generative interview questions. After these interviews, both authors independently read the transcripts of interviews and categorized data into concepts of salient organizational factors, major organizational learning activities and implementation outcomes. The lists of concepts were compared and contrasted. Any difference was further examined and verified with the informants. This process yielded a broad set of concepts, which guided our second field study conducted in MEM.

Following the constant comparative analysis method suggested by Glaser and Strauss (1967), we systematically compared MEM's experiences with those of CPM. Data collected from MEM were first sorted into concepts generated by CPM's data. However, the list of concepts did not accommodate some findings emerging from MEM. For example, the mistrust among mid-level managers led us to study the organizational culture's effect, which did not seem to be salient to us in CPM's case. In this kind of situations, we went back to CPM to collect data related with these new concepts. The iteration between data and concepts ended when we had enough concepts to explain experiences of both sites.

## RESEARCH FINDINGS

### Organizational Factors and Organizational Learning in CPM

#### ES Vision

The vision of adopting ES was formulated when CPM was in a crisis. Its management decision-making and inter-departmental coordination became ineffective due to its fast business expansion—more than 25% annual growth rate for four years in a row. As described by the CIO:

*Our management encountered severe difficulties due to the lack of information support. The business data located in fragmented systems were inconsis-*

tent and difficult to reconcile... The coordination between departments was chaotic. For example, our accounting system didn't record the sales long after the goods were delivered and we didn't detect these mistakes until we did physical count.

In addition to the internal difficulties, CPM faced a more and more competitive market and profit margins of its major products were diminishing. To cope with these problems, the top management decided to expand its business scope and adopt the advanced packaged software enterprise system. As explained by the CIO:

*The packaged software in the market was a solution to integrate our system and streamline our business processes... It (ES adoption) is part of our business strategic plan... In addition adopting an integrated system, we expected to change our practices and organizational structure in the light of ES functionalities.*

With a "transform" vision of ES adoption, CPM treated it as an investment and was committed to it with slack resources. These resources allowed CPM to acquire ES knowledge by hiring consultants (the Consulting Group in our later description), whose service cost USD400,000. The consultant group transferred its system knowledge to CPM by helping the firm choose the right software/hardware, configure the system and train end users. In addition, the consultants transferred the knowledge of process-oriented methodology to CPM and taught CPM managers how to use tools to draw business process diagrams. The external knowledge provided by the Consulting Group was critical to jump start CPM's ES project, as commented by the IT manager:

*ES is much more complicated than our old systems. Without the external knowledge from the consultants, I don't think we would be able to get it implemented successfully.*

Also, as described by the senior VP of manufacturing:

*Though I had heard of the concept of process-oriented thinking, but I didn't know how to describe our business practices by using the tools until I attended the classes... These business process diagrams were really helpful and greatly facilitated our sharing of business process ideas.*

Equipped with process-oriented knowledge and graphically describing business process techniques, CPM managers were able to discuss business practices by representing business processes with a uniform set of notations. It enhanced the effectiveness of communications and facilitated information interpretation—another construct of organizational learning (this sub-process is described in later sections).

## Advocacy of ES Vision

The necessity of adopting ES was first perceived by the CEO who had led the firm since it was first set up in 1988. In a top management meeting, CEO presented his idea about ES adoption and asked for attendants' comments. After studying the feasibility of adopting ES for two weeks, the top management formulated its ES vision and started to communicate the vision with mid-level managers. The managers were called upon to embrace this vision and influence their subordinates by articulating the vision as much as possible. In addition, flyers, posters and brochures about ES were widely distributed. Within two weeks, the message of adopting ES was disseminated across the organization. As described by a line worker about employees' reaction to ES adoption decision:

*Some people thought it would be a good opportunity for the firm and individuals to learn, while others were worried about losing their jobs after ES adoption. It took a while for us to be convinced that we would benefit from ES adoption.*

Employees' concerns were addressed by the CEO in an assembly meeting, in addition to the departmental meetings. By clearly explaining the rationale for ES adoption, CEO assured employees that their jobs would be secure as long as the firm grew healthily, which required employees to endeavor as a unit toward a common goal—enhancing the firm's competitiveness and make ES adoption a success. As explained by a line worker:

*Since implementing ES was a must-do project for our company's survival, it didn't make sense for us to resist it ... If we accepted the project positively and tried to gain some ES knowledge, mostly likely we would keep our jobs and upgrade ourselves. Especially, a lot of firms were adopting ES. With the ES knowledge gained from the project, we would be more competitive in the job market.*

His comments were conferred by another line-worker:

*It was a good opportunity for us to learn this advanced technology ... Being positive and supportive was a smarter choice than being worried and resistant.*

The advocacy of ES vision allowed CPM to win the majority's support. It also motivated the employee to contribute, receive and capture ES knowledge. This was revealed by the employees' passion and persistence in learning ES after work twice a week for two nearly months. In recalling the learning experience, one line worker described to us that:

*Though we had to perform our job duty as before, staying overtime to learn ES was not unbearable. Since we were excited about this learning opportunity and looking forward to seeing the system implemented successfully. That kind of feelings made us to take a positive approach and better able to put up with the fatigue.*

The employees' endeavor in learning ES allowed CPM to distribute knowledge to the right people. The system knowledge was first transferred to the IT group, which would be responsible for the maintenance and support of the system. Also, knowledge on each module adopted was transferred to all relevant employees by formal training courses. Though the users were mainly trained to master the knowledge on the modules related to their work, a lot of employees proactively studied other modules and how different modules were inter-related. In addition, power users were formally assigned in each business unit. These power users learnt about "why" and "how", in addition to "what". Such knowledge empowered them to be able to re-configure the system and make necessary adjustment of parameters to meet the requirement of special events.

## Administrative Structure Support

CPM set an administrative structure for the project, which included a steering committee, working committee, project function groups, IT group and Consulting Group. The steering committee was consisted of the members of top management team, while working committee consisted of senior managers who were respected and trusted in the organization. The project function groups were made up by the managers and key employees of every department. The six members of Consulting Group were from a highly-reputable consulting firm specializing in ES adoption. These committees/groups were delegated with appropriate responsibility and authority to make decisions related to ES implementation. For example, the responsibilities of the working committee included formulating project plans and ensuring the progress of the project, guiding, organizing and promoting the interaction among function groups, analyzing and proposing solutions to problems of business process optimization, organizing managerial and technical training courses, and being in charge of job specifications and standardizing work procedures.

The administrative structure served as a formal communication channel in CPM's learning ES, which was especially important for the acquisition of business knowledge and information interpretation. It called for regular/irregular meetings that allowed people to have formal and informal information exchange. For example, the function groups met four times a week to generate the diagrams of business process status quo and redesigning the firm's business processes. According to the inventory manager:

*Being a member of the function group made me better understand what role I should play in this project... The meetings and social gatherings provided us chances to communicate with each other. In addition to getting jobs done, they also enhanced cohesion and trust among us, which made coordination and cooperation issues much easier... It helped a lot with our reaching consensus on the business processes spanning departmental boundaries.*

## Control Scheme

To ensure that employees would learn and master knowledge required to apply ES effectively, the firm made employees' performance in the ES implementation an important part of individuals' and business units' annual evaluation. For example, it accounted for 60% of the CIO's annual evaluation. As commented by the manufacturing manager:

*This evaluation scheme made it clear to everyone that he must be responsible for what he did and how he performed throughout the ES implementation process... I think this evaluation scheme was really helpful in encouraging people to put in their effort... As we would also be evaluated as a business unit, we were encouraged to help each other in learning how to use the system.*

In addition, CPM formulated strict controlling rules, i.e., only when the employees passed skill tests on ES, would they be allowed to take up jobs using the system. Employees who failed these tests would have to undergo the training again or be assigned to do some other jobs. In addition to providing incentives to learning ES, these control schemes ensured minimum operation and manufacturing disruptions after the system went live.

## Top Management Involvement

The committee members attended all business process- redesign meetings and training workshops on process-oriented methodology. Also, the steering committee evaluated and approved the refined business process and ES implementation plan. As commented by a mid-level manager:

They worked together with us, even though we had to work overtime continuously for months. Their personal involvement in the project made us well aware of the importance of the project and inspired us to work hard on it... Also, with their presence in the meetings, we could make decisions on business process changes on the spot, which facilitated the project's progress.

In addition to enhancing employees' morale and facilitating the project progress, top management brought constructive ideas and sound judgments on the refined business processes. Due to their possession of knowledge that was not available to mid-level managers, top management was able to challenge the business model proposed by the groups and evaluate different proposals, which ensured that the most suitable model was adopted.

## Organizational Structure and Culture

CPM was organized divisionally with business units representing its major business areas. It had a culture that emphasized cooperation among employees and across functional units. Especially, the management emphasized employees' job satisfaction and career development. The firm organized many formal and informal social gatherings every year, in addition to providing free lunches for employees in its canteen. As commented by the senior VP of marketing:

*These social gatherings allowed employees from different, maybe not directly related, departments to know each other ... It helped us build cohesive and trusting culture.*

The firm's culture enabled people to share different opinions openly, which was critical for the organizational learning in ES implementation. In the sub-process of information interpretation, all groups and committees came together to discuss about the possibilities of redesigning the organization's business processes. The discussions mainly focused on further improvement of business processes within department and the management of activities spanning departmental boundaries and ad hoc business events. Trusting and cohesive culture facilitated the reaching of consensus on how to get jobs done, as described by the marketing manager:

*We benefited a lot from the innovative ideas provided by people from other departments ... We freely expressed our opinion and discussed in greater details when there was any disagreement. While trying to fight for our department, we also tried to put ourselves in others' shoes. There was nothing that couldn't be worked out. Especially, we could always pass controversial issues to the Boss. He had the last say.*

With the shared understanding about what the best business practices were after ES implementation, CPM was able to update its organizational memory according to changes in its organizational structure, business processes and management white paper. The information distribution and interpretation sub-processes decided the types of

organization memory for this project. First, all the activities happened during the ES implementation were recorded in the computer system as part of the project. These documents facilitated the review, coordination and communication during and after the ES implementation. Second, the organization memory had humans as carriers. All end users and power users passed ES tests and became carriers of knowledge on how to interact with the system. They served as instructors to new comers of their departments, using the operation documentation of each module compiled by IT group. In addition, function group and committee members are the carriers of knowledge on business processes.

## Organizational Factors and Organizational Learning in MEM

### ES Vision

Aiming to cut purchasing cost and reduce lead time, headquarter of MEM decided to integrate the databases in different sites located in different countries. Following this strategy, MEM was required to adopt ES which had been implemented in headquarter and some other sites. ES implemented in MEM had its configuration and business processes exactly the same as those in other sites.

With the aim to cut cost by ES adoption, MEM was tight with resources contributed to ES project. The knowledge about new business processes and system was acquired by learning from the Expert Team sent by headquarter. The experts spoke different language from MEM employees. Due to the language barrier, it was difficult for MEM employee to capture the knowledge transferred by the experts, just as described by the personnel manager:

*Language barrier was a big problem. I couldn't understand them clearly. Even worse, it was hard for them to understand my questions. Sometimes it became so frustrating that I just kept silent. And that might have passed a wrong message, and made them thought that I didn't have any problems in understanding what they said.*

Though the employees complained about the difficulties in learning and suggested hiring native speaking consultants, the top management decided not to do so due to two main reasons: (1) high consulting fee; (2) consultants' lack of knowledge about business processes to be adopted. The senior VP believed that as long as employees in MEM put in enough effort, the language barrier problem could be get around. Hiring consultants was regarded as a waste of money and violated the principle of ES adoption—cost saving.

## Advocacy of ES Vision

In one meeting, the general manager informed the top and mid-level managers of headquarter's decision on implementing ES at MEM and explained the rationale for this adoption. Different from CPM, the vision was not passed to employees at lower levels. Neither did all the mid-level managers align with this vision. As told by the sales manager:

*With all the data shared among different sites, it meant that the discount we offered to our clients would be monitored by other sales people. That would lead us (sales representatives) to compete against each other by offering higher discount rates. It would harm both the interests of our division and the company as a whole. In my opinion, the adoption of ES was a big strategic mistake.*

Some employees were against ES adoption because of their fear of losing jobs after ES adoption. As described by the purchasing manager:

*The system was bad for each division. With central sourcing, we would lose autonomy in selecting our own supplies… Since the Boss emphasized*

*cost saving, most likely we would be replaced by the system.*

Overall, employees regarded the project owned by headquarter and stayed distant from it. With the lack of support from employees, especially some key mid-level managers, the morale of learning ES was low. MEM employees received knowledge transferred by the Expert Team passively and did not endeavor to capture the knowledge, which was reflected in their making excuses for skipping or postponing ES lessons.

## Administrative Structure Support

MEM did not set up a specific administrative structure to support the ES implementation project, but had the experts from headquarter to lead the project, with assistance of IS department. The Expert Team was in change of project plan and training organization. Throughout the project, the information flew mainly from the experts to MEM and there was an insufficiency of communication among MEM employees. This arrangement affected the effectiveness of information distribution and interpretation, due to the lack of inputs from MEM employees.

Treating MEM employees as knowledge receivers, the Expert Team adopted a hierarchical approach to transfer ES knowledge, i.e., the Expert Team trained the mid-level managers and the managers trained their subordinates. In these trainings, the experts verbally explained the standardized business practices set by headquarter and showed the managers how to enter and retrieve data from the system. Each manager was shown how to use the module related to his/her work only. The managers passed what they had learned to their subordinates in a similar way. Regarding the trainings, a manager made such comments;

*The experts just told me what to do, rather than why I should do it that way. So after they left, I was totally lost when I encountered problems. As I was the only one who learned this module with the experts, I couldn't seek help from others within our firm...I was not confident to give advice to my subordinates when they had problems with the system.*

Also, a line worker told us:

*The system was too complex to me and learning experiences were really frustrating... It seemed to me that none of the people in our division really knew the system. Basically we just learned by trial and error... So our skepticism about the system's capability in supporting our operation turned out to be right.*

This training method led to little ES knowledge overlapping within the firm and the lack of administrative structure deprived the chance for employees to share what they had learned. Thus, the firm did not have managers who knew well about new business processes across department boundaries. The low degree of information distribution made MEM encounter great problems in information interpretation, which was described as "there was little shared understanding of business processes coming along with the system."

## Control Schemes

The top management assumed that all the employees would put in their best efforts in learning ES and participate in ES project proactively, so the firm did not set up any reward scheme for the employees' performance in the project. Neither did they formulate any control scheme to ensure that employees were able to interact with the system appropriately before the system went live. This lack of control scheme, coupled with employees' attitude towards the project, did not provide employees enough incentives to seek for and capture ES knowledge.

## Top Management Involvement

Trusting the Expert Team's capability, the top management did not participate in the project as much as in CPM. On the contrary, they almost left the project completely in the hands of the Expert Team, though they checked whether the project was progressing as expected from time to time. The general manager told us:

*The Expert Team from headquarter was very experienced in ES implementation after undertaking many projects in other sites. Leaving the project to them was the best choice for us.*

With the lack of top management involvement, MEM lost the chance to study the feasibility of copying all business processes from headquarter, as commented by one manager:

*Some of the new business processes did not suit our division. I think it would be very helpful if our boss discussed with the Expert Team and got them (business processes) modified... Well, the processes implemented were so alien to us.*

## Organizational Structure and Culture

MEM was organized as a matrix with control coming directly from the general manager. It had a particularly competitive culture. The employees' career path was "up or out." The turnover rate was higher than other companies in the same industry. So the employees needed to focus on excel themselves individually. The working relationship was described as "more competitive than cooperative" by one manager.

This culture made employees concerned about what they talked about and unwilling to share their ideas freely. When the general manager called for meetings after realizing the lack of knowledge overlapping and mutual understanding of business practices, the participants chose to be silent most of the time, as described by the general manager:

*I really didn't know what went wrong. They simply didn't want to share their ideas openly. If I was in the meeting, I would lead the discussion and they would talk. But without my presence, the meetings* were so silent. But I was too busy to attend all their meetings.*

In addition, a manager explained to us:

*Some managers didn't get along well and were afraid of being backstabbed. So they wouldn't talk*

*Table 2. Differences of organizational factors in CPM and MEM*

| Organizational Factor | CPM | MEM |
|---|---|---|
| ES Adoption Vision | Transform | Informate up |
| Advocacy of ES Vision | Strong advocacy across the firm | Limited dissemination |
| Top Management Involvement | Actively participated in key decision making | Left the decisions to the Expert Team from HQ |
| Administrative Structure Support | Steering and Working Committees and Functional Groups | No formal structure at MEM side |
| Control Scheme | Strict rules on the assignment jobs related with ES | No control scheme |
| Organizational Structure and Culture | Cohesive and trusting | Competitive and mistrusting |
| Employee's Attitude | Enthusiastic | Resistant and suspicious |

*Table 3. Differences between organizational learning in CPM and MEM ES implementation*

| Org. Learning Sub-Process | CPM | MEM |
|---|---|---|
| Knowledge Acquisition | -System knowledge and process-oriented methodology were acquired from the consultants- Business process status quo was acquired from organizational memory | -System knowledge and new standardized business process information were acquired from experts at headquarter |
| Information Distribution | -System configuration information was distributed to the IT group and power users in every business unit<br>-System operation knowledge was distributed to all end users<br>-Information about business processes was shared among business units | -System operation knowledge and information about business processes were distributed to the relevant mid-level managers by the experts<br>-Mid-level managers passed what they had learned to the end users |
| Information Interpretation | - Function groups and working committee worked together to streamline the business process, focusing on the activities spanning departmental boundaries and non-routine practices | -Little information interpretation during ES implementation |
| Organizational Memory | -All information related to the project was documented in computer-based repositories<br>-Standard system operation manuals were compiled<br>-Humans were certified and became organizational memory carriers | -Humans were the main organizational memory carriers<br>-System configuration files were archived |

*freely. Even with General Manager's presence, they chose to avoid critical problems existing in their departments... Also, some of us just didn't feel like sharing what we had learned with each other, since our exclusive possession of knowledge made us valuable to the firm.*

Due to the limited information distribution and little information interpretation, there was insufficient organizational memory to guide ES application. Humans were the main organizational learning carriers in MEM, especially the mid-level managers. In addition, the business process changes were not followed by corresponding organizational structure changes. MEM ended up having a function-oriented organizational structure and process-oriented business practices. This situation, coupled with insufficient understanding of business practices across the organization, caused confusion about job specification of posts spanning functional units.

To summarize our research findings described in the above sections, we present the major differences between organizational factors (Table 2) and the organizational learning processes enacted in CPM and MEM ES implementation (Table 3).

These differences between the organizational learning processes enacted in ES implementation by CPM and MEM caused significant different implementation outcomes, though both firms managed to get the system implemented within budget and on time. We categorized these outcomes into the following: further business process refinement, users' capability to apply the system effectively and appropriately, more effective and efficient departmental coordination, better decision making, solid organizational memory and enhanced business performance. To avoid the complexity of presentation, we list our findings one by one, following the order of the above-mentioned aspects of implementation outcomes.

## ES Implementation Outcomes in CPM

1.  By implementing ES, CPM managers learned to evaluate different business practices by analyzing the efficiency and effectiveness of business processes. The group and committee members learned process-oriented methodology, thus they were able to change business processes without the help from the consultant after the system went live. According to the senior VP in Marketing, "we now have a team to keep studying our business processes and continuously refine them. I think this is the most important gain from ES project."

2.  The end users and power users mastered system knowledge. End users were effective in interacting with the system. The firm did not run into any chaos due to end users' operation mistakes. In addition, power users were able to reconfigure the system to cater for the requirements of ad hoc events and new business processes.

3.  By solving many problems together throughout the ES implementation project, managers knew each other better and established a more trusting relationship. This relationship, coupled with their knowledge about business practices across the whole organization, made inter-departmental coordination more effective and efficient.

4.  With real time operational data stored in the central database, the management was able to make more informed decisions and respond to market changes more swiftly.

5.  With many different types of organizational memory carriers and overlapping knowledge among employees, the firm was able to maintain its organizational memory integrity when some key players left for ES consulting jobs.

6.  With the support of ES, the amount of bad debts was reduced by four million US dollars

in year 2002. In addition, the firm succeeded in getting around the dealership and set up their own distribution channel across the country. As described by the Senior VP of Marketing: *Without the ES, it wouldn't be possible for us to manage the inventory across the country on our own. By getting rid of the dealership, our profit margin was increased significantly.*

## ES Implementation Outcomes in MEM

1.  There was insufficient understanding of business processes among managers. Since the business processes implemented in the system were straightforward to the Expert Team, they were not aware of the necessity of sharing the rationales for these business practices with MEM managers. This caused managers' incapability in handling ah hoc events and system errors. Thus, MEM had to turned to the Expert Team at headquarter whenever problems came up. But being lo-cated in different time zones—a difference of 13 hours, MEM couldn't get response from the experts promptly. The efficiency promised by the ES system was greatly comprised.

2.  End users could not interact with the system appropriately. The central database was often corrupted by individuals' mistaken operation. Due to the lack of knowledge about the inter-relationship between different modules, they did not take actions to inform related parties of these errors immediately. This allowed the mistakes to cascade across the whole system and caused operation and manufacturing disruptions. Eight months after the within budget and on time implementation of the ES, MEM kept experiencing difficulties and encountered problems with this system. MEM had to limit the assess privilege of most users or simply switch to manual operation for some processes.

3.  With the lack of common understanding of how jobs were done across departmental

*Table 4. Differences of implementation outcomes in CPM and MEM*

| Implementation Outcomes | CPM | MEM |
|---|---|---|
| Relationship between business units | Trusting and valuing each other | Mistrusting and competitive |
| Inter-department coordination | Became more effective and efficient | Coordination was difficult due to lack of business practice knowledge |
| Managerial decision making | Got timely and accurate information support | Couldn't use the information due to the inaccuracy of data |
| Loss due to employee turnover | Did not lose organizational memory | Big loss of organizational memory due to resignation of some key mid-level managers |
| End user's interaction with the system | Effective and appropriate | Their mistakes caused manufacturing and operation disruption |
| Capability to deal with ad hoc events | Could handle special events without help from consultant | Must turn to experts at HQ |
| Significant impact on business performance | Decreased bad debts by about 4 million USD in 2002 and set up distribution channels without new hiring | Inventory cost increased by about 2 million USD in 2003 |

boundaries, inter-departmental coordination was chaotic and relationship between some managers became mistrusting.

4. Since the central database was corrupted often, managers could not make decisions based on these data. Also, since MEM abandoned the old system after ES went life, it ended up that managerial decision making could not get the right data support for months.

5. MEM also suffered a loss of organizational memory because of the leaving of some key end users and managers. Due to the limited information distribution and little information interpretation throughout the ES project, the manager became the single carrier of knowledge transferred by the Expert Team. This knowledge structure made MEM vulnerable to personnel turnovers.

6. The operation cost was increased rather than decreased, due to the end user' inappropriate interactions with the system. For example, its inventory cost was increased by two million US dollars in 2003.

The major differences between these two firm's ES implementation outcomes can be summarized by Table 4.

Developed from these two organizations' experiences, the process of organizational learning in ES implementation can be described with a model (Figure 1). This model shows the major organizational factors that emerged as salient from our data analysis. Also, it encompasses how these organizational factors affect the four constructs of organizational learning. This process is proposed as an initial formulation of the key concepts and interactions that portray organizational learning in ES implementation. No claim is made that the concepts and interactions presented here are exhaustive. Further organizational learning studies on ES implementation should modify or extend the ideas presented here.

In this model, the four organizational learning constructs are influenced by organizational factors as follow:

A. Influenced by environmental and organizational contexts, the top management formu-

*Figure 1. Organizational factors affecting organizational learning in ES implementation*

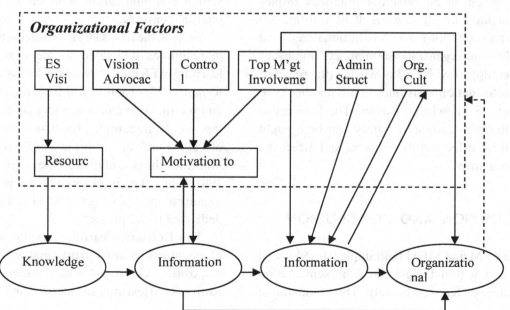

lates ES vision. Guiding by this vision, the organization decides the amount of resources committed to the project, which leads to different ways of knowledge acquisition. The knowledge acquired directly affects the amount of knowledge that is distributed in the organization.

B. The organization takes action to distribute knowledge to its relevant employees. This sub-process is influenced by advocacy of ES vision, top management's involvement and control scheme mediated by employees' motivation to receive and capture knowledge. The end users' learning experiences either reinforce or change their perception about ES adoption, which in turn influences their learning motivation. On the other hand, the breadth and depth of information distribution influences information interpretation.

C. Top management's involvement, the administrative structure and organizational culture, trust in particular, decide the effectiveness and outcomes of information interpretation. The interaction process in information interpretation may affect organizational culture.

D. With top management involvement, the consensus on business practices implemented in ES (the result of information interpretation) was institutionalized and become organizational memory. Employees equipped with ES knowledge (the result of information distribution) are another type of ES knowledge carrier. The knowledge in organizational memory can be brought forth affect future learning and affect the organization.

## DISCUSSION AND CONCLUSION

While CPM and MEM both implemented ES on time and within budget, their implementation outcomes differ significantly. The comparative analysis method, which allows contrasting CPM with MEM on a common set of concepts, suggest that these differences can be attributed to variations in the organizational learning process which was affected by organizational factors including the firm's ES vision, organizational culture, the ad hoc administrative structure for ES adoption, employees' motivation to learn ES, leaders' advocacy of ES vision, the top management's involvement and control scheme. To enhance the internal validity and generalizatility of theory building from this case study, we tie our findings to existing literature (Eisenhardt, 1989).

First, the attitude of the organization's "power elites" is important for ES implementation outcomes. Institutional leadership goes to the essence of the process of institutionalization, concurring with Armstrong and Sambamurthy's findings (1999). It is particularly needed for ES implementation, which represents a transition to alternative ways of getting jobs done across the whole organization. The central responsibility of the top management is to ensure individuals and the organization as whole learn how to apply ES effectively. This responsibility can be carried out through four key functions: advocacy of ES vision, personal involvement in the learning, setting up formal communication channels and ordering internal conflicts.

Second, the firm's IT vision affects the amount of resources dedicated to the organizational learning in ES implementation. Firms with transformative IT vision would treat ES adoption as an investment and devote adequate resources to the project. In contrast, the firm with the vision of "automate" or "informate up" would try to minimize the cost of ES adoption (Scott-Morton, 1991). Thus, the vision about ES adoption affects organizational learning, mediated by the resources dedicated to the project.

Third, effective learning depends on a culture of openness, mutual trust, and a self-critical disposition. Consistent with the literature of organizational learning and learning in information system development, the accessibility to expertise and trusting working environment help the business units and individuals overcome learning anxiety and learn faster. (Schein, 1998; Wastell, 1999). Anxiety and uncertainty about sharing "private" knowledge lead to the avoidance of authentic engagement in identifying and solving substantive problems.

Fourth, knowledge structure characterized by extensive knowledge overlaps and information exchange among managers is important for successful ES implementation outcomes. The information exchange enriches organizational knowledge structure and consequently enhances the firm's absorptive capacity (Boynton et al. ,1994; Purvis et al., 2001; Cohen & Levinthal, 1990). In turn, such knowledge and enhanced absorptive capacity enable rich dialogues among managers through which truly innovative ES applications arise (Lind & Zmud, 1991; Watson, 1991). Also, know-how and know why about the innovation should be distributed to system users. Transferring why and how knowledge to the end users can instill confidence and a sense of control, which helps users to deal with ad hoc events.

In order to ensure that the study's results can be placed in an appropriate context as well as to enable future research, it is important to examine the limitations of this study. First, we neglect the socialization of learning process from the individual to the organizational level, which might offer insights into how learning process can be correctly managed. Second, both organizations we conducted the study with are in a culture of high collectivism. Some strategic conducts applicable in this culture might not be appropriate for another culture. Future research on the issues we do not address in this chapter can extend our understanding of organizational learning in ES implementation.

## REFERENCES

Al Mashari, M., & Zairi, M. (2000). The effective application of SAP R/3: A proposed model of best practice. In *Logistics Information Management*, Bradford (pp. 156-166).

Argyris, C., & Schon, D. (1978). *Organizational learning: A theory of action research.* Reading, MA: Addison-Wesley.

Armstrong, C.P., & Sambamurthy, V. (1999). Information technology assimilation in firms: The influence of senior leadership and IT infrastructures. *Information Systems Research, 10*(4), 304-327.

Attewell, P. (1992). Technology diffusion and organizational learning: The case of business computing. *Organization Science, 3*(1), 1-19.

Bingi, P., Sharma, M.K., & Godla, J. (1999). Critical issues affecting an ERP implementation. In *Information systems management* (pp. 7-14). Boston.

Boynton, A.C., Zmud, R.W., & Jacobs, G.C. (1994). The influence of IT management practice on IT use in large organizations. *MIS Quarterly, 18*(3), 299.

Carroll, J.S., Rudolph, J.W., & Hatakenaka, S. (2002). Learning from experience in high-hazard organizations. *Research in Organizational Behavior, 24*, 87-137.

Ciborra, C.U., & Lanzara, G.F. (1994). Formative contexts and information technology: Understanding the dynamics of innovation in organizations. *Accounting, Management and Information Technology, 4*(2), 61-86.

Cooper, R.B., & Zmud, R.W. (1990). Information technology implementation research: A technological diffusion approach. *Management Science, 36*(2), 123.

Crossan, M.M., Lane, H.W., & White, R.E. (1999). An organizational learning framework: From intuition to institution. *Academy of Management Review, 24*(3), 522-537.

Daft, R.L., & Lengel, R.H. (1986). Organizational information requirements, media richness and structural design. *Management Science, 32,* 554-571.

Davenport, T.H. (1998). Putting the enterprise into the enterprise system. *Harvard Business Review,* 121-131.

Eisenhardt, K.M. (1989). Building theories from case study research. *Academy of Management Review, 14*(4), 532-550.

Eisenhardt, K.M., & Bourgeois, L.J.I. (1988). Politics of strategic decision making in high-velocity envi. *Academy of Management Journal, 31*(4), 737-734.

Feeny, D.F., & Willcocks, L.P. (1998). Core IS capabilities for exploiting information technology. *Sloan Management Review,* 9-21.

Fichman, R.G., & Kemerer, C.F. (1997). The assimilation of software process innovations: An organizational learning perspective. *Management Science, 43*(10), 1345-1363.

Fiol, C.M., & Lyles, M.A. (1985). Organizational learning. *Academy of Management Review, 10,* 803.

Harris, S.G., & Sutton, R.I. (1986). Functions of parting ceremonies in dying organizations. *Academy of Management Journal, 29*(1), 5-30.

Holland, C.P., & Light, B. (1999). A critical success factors model for ERP implementation. *IEEE Software,* 30-36.

Huber, G.P. (1991). Organizational learning: The contributing processes and the literatures. *Organization Science, 2*(1), 88-115.

Lind, M.R., & Zmud, R.W. (1991). The influence of a convergence in understanding between technology providers and users on information technology innovativenss. *Organization Science, 2*(2), 195-217.

Lyytinen, K., & Robey, D. (1999). Learning failure in information systems development. *Information Systems Journal,* (9), 85-101.

Markus, M.L., Axline, S., Petrie, D., & Tanis, C. (2000). Learning from adopters' experiences with ERP: Problems encountered and success achieved. *Journal of Information Technology, 15*(4), 245-265.

Orlikowski, W.J. (1993). CASE tools as organizational change: Investigating increment. *MIS Quarterly,* 309-332.

Parr, A., & Shanks, G. (2000). A model of ERP project implementation. *Journal of Information Technology, 15*(4), 289-303.

Pettigrew, A. (1988). *Longitudinal field research on change: Theory and practice.* National Science Foundation Conference on Longitudinal Research Methods in Organizaitons, Austin, TX.

Purvis, R.L., Sambamurthy, V., & Zmud, R.W. (2001). The assimilation of knowledge platforms in organizations: An empirical investigation. *Organization Science, 12*(2), 117-135.

Robey, D., Ross, J.W., & Boudreau, M.C. (2002). Learning to implement enterprise systems: An exploratory study of the dialectics of change. *Journal of Management Information Systems, 19*(1), 17-46.

Sambamurthy, V., Bharadwah, A., & Grover, V. (2003). Shaping agility through digital options: Reconceptualizing the role of information technology in contemporary firms. *MIS Quarterly, 27*(2), 237-263.

Scott, J.E., & Vessey, I. (2000). Implementing enterprise resource planning systems: The role of learning from failure. *Information Systems Frontiers, 2*(2), 213-232.

Scott-Morton, M.S. (Ed.). (1991). IT-induced business reconfiguration. In *The corporation of the 1990s: Information technology and organizational transformation* (pp. 3-23). Oxford University Press.

Sethi, V., & King, W.R. (1994). Development of measures to assess the extent to which an inf. *Management Science*, 1601-1627.

Schein, E.H. (1993). How can organizations learn faster? The challenge of entering the green room. *Sloan Management Review*, 85-92.

Sumner, M. (2000). Risk factors in enterprise-wide/ERP projects. *Journal of Information Technology, 15*(4), 317-327.

Walsh, J. P., & Ungson, G. R. (1991). Organizational memory. *Academy of Management Review, 16*(1), 57-91.

Wastell, D. (1999). Learning dysfunctiona in information systems development: Overcoming the social defenses with transitional objectives. *MIS Quarterly, 23*(4), 581-600.

Yin, R.K. (1994). *Case study research: Design and methods.* Thousand Oaks, CA: Sage Publications.

Watson, R.T. (1990). Influences on the IS manager's perceptions of key issues: Information scanning and the relationship with the CEO. *MIS Quarterly*, 217.

Zmud, R.W. (1984). An examination of 'push-pull' theory applied to process innovation in knowledge work. *Management Science*, 727.

*This work was previously published in Journal of Global Information Management, 14(1), edited by F. Tan, pp.1-22, copyright 2006 by IGI Publishing, formerly Idea Group Publishing (an imprint of IGI Global).*

# Section IV
# Leadership

# Chapter XVIII
# Managing Knowledge Diversity in Distributed Organizational Structures

**Claude Paraponaris**
*Université de la Méditerranée, France*

## ABSTRACT

*Knowledge in organizations can be compared with human memory. There is no unique place for creating and conserving knowledge. Knowledge in multinationals realizes its potential with various tools of management. The diversity of tools leads to the issue of coordinating levels of management. How can one manage different tools of KM without disrupting the knowledge creating process? To address this issue we analyze several knowledge management strategies of high-technology industries (computer, telecommunications, and pharmacy). In these cases diversity encourages implementation of knowledge management tools. The precision of these tools indicates the firm's competence in managing and diffusing knowledge. An important conclusion that can be drawn is that several factors (redundancy, diversity, discussion, and duration) can reinforce these competences and, in fact, network mechanisms in organizations.*

*As a result, the management community has come to realize that what an organization and its employees know is at the heart of how the organization functions.* (Davenport & Prusak, 1998)

## INTRODUCTION: EPISTEMOLOGICAL CONCEPT OF KNOWLEDGE MANAGEMENT

### The Field of Knowledge Management

Knowledge in organizations can be compared with human memory. There is no single place for creating and conserving knowledge. Consequently it is essential to take account of the full diversity of existing modes of knowledge.

Several studies have emphasized the need to develop knowledge management in order to make use of an organization's cognitive heritage (Nonaka, 1990). Thus knowledge management is inevitably contingent, since it must be tailored to each firm's structures and processes (Tsoukas, 1996). These studies also underscore the diversity of ways in which knowledge can be managed, capitalized, diffused, and combined (Nonaka & Takeuchi, 1995).

The question is to ascertain how the various resources required to accumulate and diffuse knowledge can be linked together. Like Tsoukas (1996), we know that "the knowledge firms need to draw upon is also inherently indeterminate." It is not that knowledge is 'out there' in bits and pieces and just needs to be collected and assembled in one encyclopedic database.

Approaches to the nature of knowledge and the modes of knowledge management are proliferating. Several recent syntheses (Management Science, 2003; Easterby-Smith & Lyles, 2003) have described the epistemological and methodological differences between the various approaches.

Like Davenport, DeLong, and Beers (1998), we know that "knowledge is information combined with experience, context, interpretation and deliberation." This is a reminder not to ignore the contextualized nature of knowledge. "Knowledge is constructed and functions through a process of productive cooperation among individuals as well as through interactions between those individuals and the cognitive devices within which they operate" (Poitou, 1997). Cognitive devices are defined as "organised and consolidated sets of intellectual objects,[1] linked to each other and arranged spatially for the purpose of producing goods or knowledge" (Poitou, 1997).

Knowledge management is usually described as a process (Swan, 1999) that can take several paths:

*Table 1. Comparison of Simoni's (2005) three approaches to knowledge management*

|  | **Examples** | **Advantages** | **Limitations** |
|---|---|---|---|
| **Objectification Approaches** | Expert systems Knowledge systems Project memories | Specific approach to the capitalization of knowledge | Cost/utility ratio Local in nature |
| **Socialization Approaches** | Communities of practice | Knowledge management practices arise out of practices and interactions | Conceptual Operational |
| **Organizational Approaches** | Multimodal approach Action on contexts | Integrative and diversified | Poorly differentiated nature of the processes involved Developed for knowledge creation |

- Creation;
- Sharing (including transfer and, in some cases, diffusion); and
- Retention (location and capture of knowledge in codified form).

There are in fact three main approaches to knowledge management. Simoni (2005) provides a very precise classification and analysis of these approaches, which we adopt as a starting point for this chapter.

## TAKE ACCOUNT OF THE EXPLICIT DIMENSION AND THE TACIT DIMENSION

Approaches of the *objectification* type emphasize the codification of knowledge. Knowledge is regarded as an object that can be precisely described, captured, and moved from one place to another. Thus various methods are put forward for capturing and formalizing knowledge at the end of large-scale projects or for retaining strategic expertise within a firm. There are many methods for formalizing the principles of project design.

These methods have a certain degree of relevance to the conservation of knowledge, but since they take no account of socio-organizational context, they do not encourage the diffusion of knowledge.

Approaches of the *socialization* type are based on analysis of the functioning of communities of practice (Brown & Duguid, 1991, 1998, 2000). In this approach, learning is part of a social process, defined as "social interactions among individuals engaged in a shared practice." Communities of practice are the locus for the creation and diffusion of knowledge. This knowledge is, so to speak, attached to its context. The diffusion of knowledge requires social media, such as *translators* capable of formulating one community's interests from the perspective of another community, *intermediaries* operating in several communities to facilitate

the flow of knowledge, and *boundary objects* that provide opportunities to compare the practices of several communities.

In their turn, these approaches offer some highly relevant insights (the social contextualization of knowledge and the possibility of transfer) with limitations as to the recommendations for capitalization.

## ANALYZE KNOWLEDGE DIVERSITY IN DISTRIBUTED ORGANIZATIONAL STRUCTURES

Some studies adopt a dichotomous approach to knowledge management choices, depending on the activities in question. In one case, the aim is to prioritize the organization's control of the formalization and diffusion of knowledge (Stein & Zwass, 1995), while in the other it is to encourage its members' creative practices (Conklin, 1992; Nonaka & Konno, 1998). In this way, two major knowledge capitalization strategies are formulated (Hansen, Nohria, & Tierney, 1999):

- **Codification:** When a firm faces recurrent problems, systematic codification with storage in databases is used so that knowledge can be easily accessed and used by employees.
- **Socialization:** When a firm faces one-off problems and expectations, then it is preferable for knowledge to remain tacit and be shared by means of direct contacts between employees. This is the personalization model, in which firms prioritize a culture of mobility and dialogue between individuals based on interpersonal networks.

This dichotomy is not sufficient to understand and formalize the various knowledge management processes. A third approach is absolutely necessary, one that does not simply pit the objectification and socialization approaches against each other, but seeks rather to consider a combination of the two approaches within organizations. The socialization approaches are useful for understanding creative processes, while the objectification approaches shed light on the need to accumulate knowledge and the demands this places on organizations.

Through what processes might their advantages be brought together and what processes will help to make them partially complementary? So-called 'organizational' approaches to knowledge management offer a way forward. Approaches of this kind highlight the diversity of the modes of knowledge generation (Davenport & Prusak, 1998, pp. 52-67): internal and external acquisition, rental, dedicated resources, merger, adaptation, and networks. They focus on the factors that might influence knowledge management (Szulanski, 1996). These factors are inherent in the very structure of knowledge and individuals' capacities for learning, hence the interest in examining means of facilitating knowledge creation. Some studies give prominence to the idea that knowledge creation cannot be managed. Excessive use of knowledge objectification procedures and computer systems is criticized. The studies by Von Krogh, Ichijo, and Nonaka (2000), for example, are concerned with relations within organizations and seek to identify the attitudes likely to facilitate knowledge creation at the various stages of its development within organizations.

Any attempt to develop an organizational approach to knowledge management must give priority to organizational dynamics, and in particular the dynamic of the actors involved, of the relations between them, and of the management processes.

## ORGANIZATIONAL APPROACH AND MANAGEMENT TOOLS

Taking as our starting point the observation that knowledge is contextualized, it can be assumed that each of the means deployed to manage knowledge is specific. If this is so, the organization is made up of a set of means deployed for the purposes of knowledge management, the effects of which are not necessarily complementary. It seems to us particularly interesting to examine how these specific means are integrated into a coherent and homogeneous approach.

To this end, we draw on two observations: the diversity of the roles attributed to management tools and the ambidexterity of management processes.

## Management Tools

Management tools can be defined as follows: "any sets of reasoning or knowledge formally linking a certain number of variables stemming from an organisation and designed to carry out the different traditional management tasks" (Moisdon, 1997). Management tools can be considered in a wider sense as "all formal means of organisation. In this respect not only management data reports, expert systems and linear programmes can be considered as management tools but also structures, management by objectives contracts and evaluation interviews" (David, 2001).

A management tool can assume several roles (see Table 2). The best-known one is the creation of conformity (conformation) in order to achieve a previously defined optimum. However, it may be used to examine the functioning of an organization (in order to reveal the factors that determine organizational functioning and then to go beyond or change them). It can sometimes support change by acting as a medium for the gradual construction of shared representations. Finally, it may open the way to the exploration of new paths by challenging and transforming the technical knowledge that currently prevails within a firm.

This approach to management tools contributes a great deal to an understanding of how organizations based on the diffusion of experience function, since it provides a means of going beyond the assumed antinomy between knowledge creation and capitalization tools.

*Table 2. The four roles of management tools (Sources: David, 2001; Moisdon, 1997)*

| Role of Tool | Definition |
|---|---|
| Conformation | Standardize behavior in order to comply with an 'optimum' state claimed by the tool. |
| Investigating the way the organization works | Confronting the tool and the organization leads to a clarification of the latter's 'laws': the tool reveals the determining factors in the organization and helps actors to imagine new development patterns. |
| Supporting change | The starting point is not the wish to introduce a new tool but to design tools that accompany and aid change that has been decided previously. The tool acts a medium for the gradual construction of shared representations. |
| Exploring new paths | The tool not only serves to transform organizational rules, but also to challenges and transforms 'technical' knowledge. |

## Ambidextrous Organization

Ambidextrous organization (Duncan, 1976; Tushman & Moore, 1988; Tushman & O'Reilly, 1996) is a notion developed with regard to the management of innovation. Based on a characterization of the various management processes, this approach adopts an evolutionary perspective in order to highlight the need to combine two types of process: one an essentially bureaucratic process that tends to standardize organizational structures, the other essentially uncertain with regard to both purpose and timeframe.

Drawing on these two observations, we analyze the structures, processes, and tools used in knowledge management. Our analysis reveals devices at various levels, responsibility for which falls to separate actors within the firm: R&D organization, academic collaborations, internal networks, multiple personnel evaluations, and databases. We describe these devices in the third part of this chapter, while their ability to establish coherence is analyzed in the fourth part.

This chapter discusses the question of distributed organizational structures with integrated knowledge systems in the field of R&D management. We argue that:

- Knowledge management processes in multinational organizations make use of a wide range of management tools.

- This diversity of tools creates the problem of how to coordinate different levels of management. How can there be a diversity of KM tools without disrupting the knowledge creating process?

In order to address this issue, we analyze several knowledge management strategies in the following industries: IT, telecommunications, and pharmaceuticals.

- First, we use the concept of network to discuss the dispersion of knowledge. We highlight the key characteristics of networks by exploring two of the main spaces in which knowledge is created, namely technological alliances and R&D projects.

- The following section argues that diversity encourages the implementation of knowledge management tools. The precision of these tools is an indication of a firm's competence in managing and diffusing knowledge. Several of the main tools of knowledge management are outlined.

- The final section draws conclusions about a conceptual framework for dealing with the various ways in which knowledge can be managed. The adoption of decentralized management structures gives rise to "linkage errors." These errors are a product of the gap between "what is required" and "what is available." One important conclusion that can be drawn for this work is that several factors can reduce this gap and, in fact, reinforce network devices in organizations. We identify these key factors.

## THE CONCEPT OF NETWORK TO DISCUSS THE DISPERSION OF KNOWLEDGE

### Global R&D in MNCs

How has the globalization of multinationals' R&D activities developed? And what are the consequences for knowledge management?

The main trend, which first became evident in the 1980s, is an increase in the scale of activities (Gerybadze & Reger, 1999; Lam, 2003; Pearce, 1999). This trend was first set in motion by American companies and is particularly pronounced in the pharmaceutical and electronics industries.

What is the main reason for this increase in activity? The global dispersion of R&D has been driven by firms' needs to acquire new knowledge and capabilities and to gain access to unique human resources (Cantwell, 1995; Florida, 1997; Kuemmerle, 1997, 1999). The aim is to tap into resources (ideas, links to the market, expertise) in order to develop, from a single unit, innovations for the global market.

The modes of coordinating international R&D activities are often organized around network structures. Networks emerge as the most sophisticated organizational forms which make it possible to explain the extension of multina-tionals' knowledge and experience base. The advantages of network structures have been the subject of a more general analysis by Miles and Snow (1986).

Networks are presented as the means of organizing the various R&D remits and making them complement each other. Networks are used to forge links between research activities and development activities that are more or less strongly coordinated functionally, spatially, and epistemically.

These studies show that extension of the knowledge base is the main driver for the increased globalization of R&D activities. But this extension also leads to a diversification of the spaces in which knowledge is created. This diversification makes the management of knowledge flows even more complex for multinationals.

Thus the globalization of R&D activities can be investigated in terms of the gradual structuring of networks. This is an encouragement to examine the difficulties that could not be dealt with by the earlier organizational forms but have been addressed by the network structures that have been put in place (see Box 1).

This development reflected the search for better ways to foster innovation. It was achieved by diversifying knowledge sources and bringing R&D centers closer together.

As a result, the distinctions between centralization and decentralization, or even between a local or global approach, are no longer relevant because of the transnational configuration. This is based on the need to differentiate both roles as well as modes of coordination. From this point of view, Ghoshal and Bartlett (1993) define the modern multinational as an "inter-organisational network" or as a "network embedded in an external network."

This chapter develops the questions of knowledge management within decentralized structures by taking support from the experience of several multinationals (see Box 2).

*Box 1. Technology-driven, market-driven, and R&D networks*

A historical analysis of R&D organizations is provided by Roussel, Saad, and Erickson (1991), as well as by Reger and Von Wichert-Nick (1997). These authors outline the evolution of R&D organizations from the 1980s onwards. They identify three main modes of organization. The first is technology-driven and is organized around a centralized research unit that supplies the development units. Innovation is based on the expansion of scientific knowledge and using it to meet development needs. The second is more market-driven, the aim being to manage knowledge flows the opposite way round. The third and final mode combines the best elements of each of the previous modes by putting in place coordination networks. According to the authors, there have been two major periods in the development of knowledge networks.

In the first period, during the 1980s, firms devolved their previously centralized R&D activities to decentralized business units. R&D had previously been centralized in order to obtain economies of scale as part of industrial strategies based on the technologies they had already assimilated. Thus a central laboratory was responsible for developing these technologies by playing a major role in the coordination of technological cooperation. However, the main failing of this arrangement was that insufficient account was taken of commercial constraints, and it was this that provided the justification for the decentralization of R&D resources to operational units. The task of these decentralized units was to be more closely involved in the development of product policy, with more attention being paid to marketing and the technological possibilities. This brought the actors involved in the design of new products closer together, with spectacular results in terms of development times. However, this specification of resources also contributed to the increased diversity of knowledge creation spaces.

In the second period, during the 1990s, some abuses of the new arrangement began to creep in: the business units' decision-making autonomy sometimes turned into technological independence vis-à-vis the multinational group. In fact, various problems emerged. Since each R&D unit was supposed to respond to the needs of its commercial controller, it could scarcely justify its autonomous exploratory and collaborative activities. On the other hand, there was little opportunity for the R&D units to coordinate with each other. Finally, it was becoming difficult to accumulate knowledge. In order to gain greater control over the diversity of the results produced by innovation projects, central managements sought to centralize R&D activities again, but this time in a different way. Since it was not possible to return to the previous situation, it was decided to put in place network organizational structures. This led to the emergence of corporate labs, which reflected the need to split short- and medium-term activities from long-term ones and, above all, to put in place knowledge capitalization systems. The task of these laboratories was to centralize knowledge and disseminate it to any units that expressed a need for it. They did not operate like the central laboratories of the past. Their physical and human resources were distributed among several subsidiaries and were required to operate as part of a network. This second period constituted the third generation of R&D.

*Box 2. Multinational strategies for knowledge management*

A research network[2] was allowed to study for several years (1999-2004) a sample of multinationals (see Appendix). The sample of large firms was selected from among those operating in the IT, telecommunications, and pharmaceuticals markets. The focus of these firms' activities is on technological innovation of the market. Almost all of them share a strategic focus on a tightly defined area of activity (achieved through transfer of assets, acquisitions, and mergers) and a commitment to a large number of technological alliances. Their strategies are implemented through their involvement in R&D, the organization of which has been through several significant changes over the last decade. Their R&D laboratories are now integrated into networks and enjoy a high degree of autonomy when it comes to exploiting sources of knowledge (pre-project studies, alliances, diffusion of knowledge within the subsidiary).

Operating within network structures means that knowledge can be created in a large number of different spaces. Furthermore, that knowledge can be diffused through a variety of different structures. This raises the question of the balance between autonomy (creation) and control (diffusion). What types of coordination might facilitate knowledge transfer?

In fact, network structuring is an attempt to tackle an old problem. Studies of organizational memory (Stein & Zwass, 1995) show that knowledge is always divided between management processes, individuals, artifacts, and partner organizations. This knowledge is never centralized in a single location but distributed among various parts of an organization (Walsh & Ungson, 1991).

## SPACES IN WHICH KNOWLEDGE IS CREATED

The increasing diversity of knowledge creation spaces within multinational networks raises various types of questions, each of which relates to complementary research agendas. Each one reflects the increasing diversification of knowledge and the management issues that arise as a consequence.

## Technological Alliances

According to Nonaka (1994), one of the main reasons why firms engage in cooperative ventures is to accelerate learning and appropriation by gaining access to partners' competences and creating new competences. Doz and Hamel (2000) summarize the main aspects of alliance management and suggest that firms are seeking three main types of advantage:

• Co-option of partners in order to establish networks;
• Co-specialization in order to combine hitherto unique and differentiated resources, competences, and knowledge; and
• Learning and appropriation of new expertise.

Several studies have examined the difficulties of managing alliances and the ensuing need to develop a particular competence in collaboration and alliance management (Kogut, 1989). There is some measure of complementarity between the external acquisition of technologies, through alliances for example, and internal R&D activities based on innovation projects (Hamel, 1991; Powell, 1996). Complementarity between groups collaborating with each other inside a firm and their counterparts outside the firm (i.e., alliance partners) is identified as a factor in determining success (Hagedoorn & Schakenraad, 1994). More generally, the learning processes that may take place at these two levels are complementary and even tend to be mutually reinforcing (Cohen & Leninthal, 1990; Duysters & Hagedoorn, 2000).

According to Gulati (1995, 1999), firms enter into alliances with a view to positioning themselves at the center of networks that will enable them to

build up 'social capital', which in turn will help them gain access to technological resources. However, while the forming of alliances may be a successful cooperative principle, knowledge still has to be transferred from the alliance partners to the relevant units within the firm (Lambert, 1993).

To this end, Goodman and Sproull (1990) define the conditions for joining a network. They analyze the organizational modes that facilitate effective participation in network-based activities. They concluded that participation in a network requires a mode of organization that itself relies on network structures. Goodman and Sproull show that organizing a firm as a network involves putting in place several entities that are decentralized to the point of competing with each other.

## R&D Projects

Project-based organization constitutes an attempt to break down the operational sequentiality and compartmentalization resulting from functional structures, with the aim of accelerating the development of new products or services by encouraging rapid decision making (Larson & Gobeli, 1988; Clark, Hayes, & Wheelwright, 1992). The means of coordination are temporary (Declerck, Debourse, & Navarre, 1983), the aim being to establish the conditions under which creativity can flourish: "The purpose of a project is to bring together different but complementary forms of professional expertise by constructing links between different specialties" (Garel et al., 2003).

R&D projects are, by definition, spaces in which new knowledge is constructed, with the learning processes that take place within them being defined as the development of a new knowledge base (Purser, Pasmore, & Tenkasi, 1992). According to Maidique and Zirger (1985), projects are spaces characterized by learning by doing. Kogut and Zander (1992) specify the two types of knowledge that are acquired in the course of a project:

- information constructed in the various technical spheres and the expertise developed by the actors as a means of solving problems; and
- information on the possession and sharing of the information by the actors, as well as expertise relating to project management.

These different types of information are incorporated into the actors' cognitive structures without any specific means being used to evaluate them. The development of knowledge actually raises several questions pertaining to project management in particular and to the development of organizations in general.

The cognitive and professional diversity found within a project team is likely to give rise to interactions that carry major risks of failure. These risks include a lack of synergy between the participants, failure to adhere to deadlines and budgets, and results that are not consistent with the project objectives (Jehn et al., 1999). The difficulties of managing this diversity simply increase when a project developed with geographically dispersed teams is conceived with the aim of diffusing knowledge within a multinational R&D network (Schweiger, 1998).

In fact, succeeding projects generate a profusion of knowledge that is not necessarily used subsequently (Prusak, 1997). What is at stake in a project is more the creation of knowledge than the memorization of that knowledge within a firm's structures. Meyers and Wilemon (1989) have drawn attention to the need to protect the learning that takes place in the course of R&D projects. According to these authors, team composition and the management of individual members before and after a project contribute to the diffusion of the lessons learned between projects. It is the network formed by the totality of employees inside and outside the project team that is identified as the medium for the development of a firm's knowledge.

## KNOWLEDGE NETWORKS: BETWEEN DIVERSITY AND COORDINATION

In fact in both cases (alliances and projects), networks play a role in bringing activities, resources, and actors into relationship with each other (Håkansson, 1989). These two cases are among the most illustrative of the challenges facing knowledge management.

After all, the strategic approach adopted by multinationals could be characterized as an attempt to combine two trends: the diversification of the knowledge being mobilized in order to innovate, on the one hand, and the coordination of the various units involved, on the other. This attempt to combine two contrary trends impacts on all multinationals' activities:

- The objective is to create proximity between units that threaten to become increasingly remote from each other, not only in spatial terms but also strategically (see the difficulties with second-generation R&D) and, above all, in terms of the gap between their needs to advance knowledge.
- The attempt to coordinate disparate activities is also part of the effort to go beyond the 'centralization-decentralization' dilemma that multinationals face when deciding on the organizational structures to adopt. This applies, for example, to technological alliances. Alliances, which are experiments in decentralization, are beneficial to firms only if they manage to absorb knowledge in order to transfer it to activities that need to draw on such knowledge.
- Exactly the same applies to projects, since a capacity for the inter-temporal transfer of knowledge seems necessary in order to initiate new research that will pave the way for innovation.

Thus while diversity is deliberately sought after, it raises some fairly significant organizational issues if the resources being developed within multinationals are to be brought together. "The dispersedness of knowledge is an important driver of organizational problems" (Becker, 2001). From this perspective, networks seem to be a new organizational form that make it possible to manage this diversity of knowledge.

But how exactly does the management of this knowledge proceed? How is the knowledge created within a particular space in a multinational identified and evaluated as relevant to other spaces? What resources are committed to such evaluation and who is responsible for it? Finally, how is the knowledge transferred from the space in which it was created to other spaces?

## ORGANIZATIONAL DEVICES AND KNOWLEDGE MANAGEMENT

### The Notion of Device

Organizational devices consist of sets of linked management tools distributed within an organization in order to facilitate the creation, capitalization, and diffusion of knowledge (Paraponaris, 2001).

The management tools of which such devices consist are not all used directly or solely for the purposes of knowledge management. Their very presence within the organizations means they are likely to be used to that end, although they were not necessarily designed and put in place for that reason. The coexistence of several management tools and their possible use for a cognitive purpose constitutes a significant management challenge. Linking the tools to form a device and then linking the various knowledge management devices within an organization is a practical problem that raises many significant design issues.

## THE VARIOUS DEVICES IDENTIFIED AND ANALYZED

### R&D Structures

The evolution of R&D structures was being driven by the scale of the investment decided on by general management and the need to develop innovations quickly. As a result, mobilization of the available knowledge had become a strategic lever. R&D activities are organized in two main blocks:

*Table 3. The devices and their tools (creation or capitalization)*

| Devices | Management Tools | Purposes |
|---|---|---|
| R&D structures | Allocations of assignments<br>Gatekeepers<br>R&D information system | Organization of R&D<br>Centralizing and distributing information<br>Facilitating internal and external collaborations |
| Codification of experience | Project management<br>Technical databases | Homogenization through technical information<br>Technical documentation for R&D work<br>Product development documentation |
| Technical community | Forums<br>Internal benchmarking | Technical upgrading<br>Management of technological assets |
| Evaluation of competences | Project manager's evaluation<br>Annual appraisal<br>Promotion up technical workers' scale<br>Quarterly interviews | Competence management |

- In the first, corporate laboratories are charged with the long-term exploration of technologies.
- In the second, a multiplicity of development units located in the business units are responsible for development of the technologies and product design.

This division of labor had to be put in place by multinationals when it became evident that the decentralization of R&D management to business unit level had led to a dispersion of knowledge. The corporate labs' role as catalysts in the creation of knowledge has been emphasized (Von Krogh, 1997).

Third-generation R&D is a mode of organization based on network structures that have an internal and an external dimension. The internal element of the network serves to structure the exchanges between the two sets of R&D activities, while the external element is concerned with the structuring of each level of R&D activity with different partners through alliances and collaborative ventures.

This knowledge management device is the one put in place most deliberately by the managements of multinationals. In doing so, they made the formal structures of R&D departments the main means for the organization and capitalization of knowledge. Nevertheless, these formal structures do not account for all the knowledge capitalization operations that take place, as may be suggested by the difficulties of maintaining links between the two main sets of R&D activities.

The multinationals structured their networks in different ways. In the telecommunications multinational that had been attempting to incorporate the provision of telecommunications services more closely into the design of its corporate communications systems, the two areas of R&D activity were experiencing difficulties in coordinating their activities. The knowledge generated in the two areas was not of the same kind, and the actors were finding it difficult to

discuss common problems. The business units' customer orientation and the academic collaborations of the central laboratory could not be combined seamlessly to advance the company's technological development.

In the other IT multinational, which had outsourced much of its exploratory R&D activities to major research laboratories, the objective was to organize the absorption of knowledge at the level of the units responsible for developing new IT units. Knowledge transfer was proving to be difficult. The main reason lay in each partner's organizational configurations. The firm had a traditional bureaucratic mode of functioning, whereas its scientific partners were engaged in a number of projects, the results of which were disseminated freely within the scientific community.

It is undoubtedly in the pharmaceutical industry that the use of network structures in the organization of R&D encounters the greatest difficulties. One of the principal reasons for this is the trend towards concentration that has gathered pace in the industry over the last decade. This trend has given rise to competition between the laboratories in the various companies that have merged and to difficulties in assimilating the different corporate cultures.

The main knowledge management tools deployed in support of the role of networked R&D units depend to a large extent on the competences of a few professionals.

After all, the dual internal/external network put in place for the purposes of knowledge management operate on the basis of third-generation structures and devices for collaboration with the academic world (student placements, joint supervision of theses, joint laboratories, and technological platforms designed to facilitate knowledge absorption). The means developed within these devices are managed by senior researchers or engineers. In many cases, a single person fulfils this role within an establishment. This individual is responsible for determining the direction of relations with partners and initiating the transfer of knowledge to the laboratories and business units. This role is in fact that of gatekeeper as defined by Allen (1977). We will show subsequently the way in which this role is linked to other functions.

## Internal Codification of Knowledge: Databases and Project Management

This second device is made up of a set of tools very close to approaches of the 'objectification of knowledge' type. This is the most explicit mode of knowledge management, as well sometimes the only mode. Two main tools are deployed.

### Project Management

Project management's main guidelines are managed centrally by project management teams in each of the R&D units. The project management teams lay down standardized operational guidelines for each of the teams engaged in exploratory or R&D projects.

Thus a multinational pharmaceutical firm that is the result of several mergers and has evolved from its original core business in chemicals into a biotechnology company has set up a design center that lays down in detail the procedures for launching and supervising a project. In each of the subsidiaries, a project manager is responsible for applying the procedures and circulating them among the project leaders. The progress made and the final outcomes of projects are distributed to the various project management teams by means of the electronic documents that accompany every project. These documents are processed centrally by the design center, which compares the efficiency of each project in terms of deadlines, cost, and technical quality, and identifies the new scientific and technical knowledge produced.

### Technical Databases

Technical databases constitute the most widely used 'dedicated' knowledge management tool. They synthesize accumulated experience in the areas of product design, patents, design procedures and software, technical tests, and quality procedures more generally. The technical database centralizes and makes 'up-to-date' information available. Various databases may coexist, depending on the technological fields being explored. R&D employees both feed information into these databases and consult them. (There is no space here to discuss the questions raised by these operations).

These two types of tools perform the additional function of bringing order to the diversity of experience within a multinational. This 'tidying up' is justified by management as a means of coordinating the diversity of practices in the various subsidiaries. These practices are a product of societal and cultural approaches to employment and economic activity that are never homogeneous. The standardization of management methods and tools is a way of bringing the different practices in the subsidiaries closer together. Although diversity is actively sought out by multinational companies, the conditions under which such diversity is implemented are also being adjusted in order to encourage the internal diffusion of experiences. Against this background, the management of knowledge is one of the issues at stake in attempts to strike a balance between organizational unity and diversity.

### Technical Communities

This third device differs from the previous one while being complementary to it. A firm's technical communities have a power that frequently collides with corporate strategy. There is a long tradition of studies of these conflicting practices, many of which draw on the work of Gouldner (1957). Technical communities occupy an important position in high-tech multinationals. Their development can be understood by applying the principles of 'communities of practice'.

In this case, professionals accumulate the knowledge they produce for themselves and diffuse it within expert circles for whom scientific progress is of greater significance than the organization's projects. Company management can make use of these communities by maintaining communications or encouraging them to flourish.

In the multinationals, most notably in telecommunications, the number and size of projects make the circulation of knowledge within the various departments problematic. A forum has been set up in each business unit whose task it is to present proposals for technological developments and experience reports. Each proposal is collectively examined and selected or rejected by management. Those proposals that are adopted receive support by being promoted among members of the business unit. Thus knowledge can be diffused through presentation of proposals for exploratory projects. The presentations are not intended to be directly productive (i.e., to lead to the launch of a new project), but rather to strengthen the cohesion of the technical community.

In another multinational active in the electronics and telecommunications businesses, the technical community is well established and comprises some 300 people. It is divided into areas of competence in order to exploit the scientific and technical knowledge generated in the course of exploratory programs and R&D projects. Community members are consulted by management when programs and projects are being selected, and they also sit on promotion committees for engineers.

Community members themselves define the modes of knowledge capitalization by dis-

seminating information through the channels that exist in the various units (unit and technological group directors and project leaders). The functioning of the community is managed through meetings, technological forums, and electronic exchanges.

## Evaluation of Competences

This device is the most complex one because of the diversity of actors and management processes involved. It relies for the most part on tools for evaluating the competences and results of R&D employees. These tools were developed primarily for use in HRM systems, and include appraisals, remuneration, and promotion. Use of such tools requires input from several managers: HRM managers, project managers, technological program directors, and members of the technical community.

## The Annual Appraisal

The annual interview involves an evaluation of each employee's results or his or her competences, or even both. In preparation for the interview, a 360-degree feedback procedure is carried out, with several actors being canvassed for their opinions of the employee in question, and the employee is also requested to carry out a self-appraisal.

The interview is conducted by a human resources manager who is not familiar with the employee's work and competences. This is why the procedure outlined above is used, since it draws essentially on the opinions of those in charge of the technological group to which the employee is permanently attached and of the manager of the project team to which he or she is more specifically affiliated. The project manger's assessment is decisive, to the extent that it relates directly to the individual's actual work and his or her behavior within the team. In the self-appraisal, the employee is asked to evaluate the results of his or work at time 't' relative to the commitments taken on at 't – 1'. Thus the appraisal interview is structured around these two categories of information. The resulting appraisal leads to the award of an overall mark or grade that serves as a basis for differentiated recompense in the form of a bonus.

## Promotion up the Scale for Technical Scale

R&D employees have opportunities for career progression in terms of technical expertise. In the multinationals we studied, the scales for technical staff have between six and eight grades, each of which corresponds to a particular level of professional experience and pay. Those who reach the top of the scale acquire the status of 'technical leader', which makes them eligible for promotion to project leader or technological group director. In some cases, this expertise is sufficient qualification for the role of technical advisor to the technical communities.

The promotion process is managed by committees of experts (technical leaders and representatives of the HR department). These committees receive applications from the various R&D sites within a particular area (Americas, Europe, Asia). The committees undertake an initial selection process. Applicants are evaluated by means of a reference system, with both committee members and applicants' immediate colleagues having an opportunity to provide their own input.

## The Quarterly Interviews

This interview is conducted by the employee's n + 1: the laboratory director in the case of occupational group leaders and project leaders, occupational group leaders for other staff. This type of interview is explicitly a reassurance tool that is used to evaluate an employee's level of involvement, to record his or her expectations, and to discuss the unit's objectives. In fact, it provides an opportunity to compare individual aspirations with more collective considerations.

These latter are formalized on the basis of 'criteria of excellence': leadership ability, ability to understand the company's strategic development, customer orientation, ability to analyze information, responsibility for human resources (expertise and cognitive abilities), expertise in management processes, and ability to interpret a company's results.

## Evaluation by Project Leaders

As Boutellier, Gassman, and Von Zedtwitz (1999) note:

*Most decisions nowadays are made in teams ... Thus the project leader is at the heart of organizational learning, and the production of new knowledge. In global projects, this role becomes even more important, since the project leader is often the only team member who knows all the other participants through frequent travelling.*

At this level, evaluations are in fact carried out with reference to projects and are reused in the processes outlined above. They are conducted regularly by means of project reviews and standard procedures for defining and evaluating technical and commercial performance.

The various evaluations bring into play to some extent R&D employees' cognitive activities: the technological areas they have covered, the knowledge development processes they have been involved in, the problems they have solved in context, and the relations they maintain with their colleagues, which are also sources of knowledge.

These evaluations are linked to each other more through functional managers than by databases. In this way, they can make a significant contribution to knowledge capitalization.

It remains to be shown how these various devices are linked. In doing so, we will also be able to identify the factors that determine the success of a diversified approach to knowledge management in multinationals.

## CONNECTING THE DEVICES: THE FACTORS CONTRIBUTING TO THE SUCCESS OF DIVERSIFIED KNOWLEDGE MANAGEMENT

The devices analyzed above are controlled by various levels of management, the coordination of which is a subject for discussion, for example: evaluation at project level/evaluation by HR departments, identification of technological capabilities by general management/identification within technical communities.

These devices point to the existence of tangled networks. What are these networks? Several of them can be identified within these devices. The first is the firm's large international network which, from its base in the parent company, attempts to coordinate the activities of its subsidiaries (third-generation R&D structures, technical databases). Then there are the networks formed by the scientific and technological alliances managed by the subsidiaries' laboratories (gatekeepers, technical communities) and the internal networks used to disseminate experience (evaluation within and around projects, technical communities, forums).

In each of these networks, the problem of striking a balance between two necessary but contradictory trends rears its head: creativity vs. control in the first case, diversity vs. complementarity of partners in the second, and exploration and capitalization in the third. From this point of view, there is certainly a similarity between the major strategic questions facing multinationals and the organizational issues encountered in knowledge management. In fact, there are several dilemmas in need of resolution here, sufficient to justify close examination of the principles governing the interlinking of the knowledge management devices.

An initial dilemma concerns the search for diversity. While multinationals need cognitive diversity, the concomitant diversity of tools deployed in knowledge creation and capitalization dies give rise to coordination problems. The desired diversity is present right at the outset!

A second dilemma arises out of the functioning of the networks. The distribution of R&D activities by means of networks makes it easier to discern the emergence of radical technologies and is sufficient justification for implementing exploratory projects on a decentralized basis. However, attempts to diffuse experiences within third-generation R&D networks come up against a number of difficulties. For example, it has proved difficult to transfer technology from an alliance, and problems with knowledge capitalization have been encountered at the end of R&D projects.

Benveniste (1994) noted that management within decentralized structures encounters problems in solving "linkage errors." These errors are created by the gap between "what is required" and "what is available."

The answers to the following series of questions are intended to shed further light on the difficulties encountered in establishing links between devices.

### What is Being Connected?

From a normative point of view, establishing links between the management tools that constitute a device and then between the devices is essential if a multinational's networks are to function effectively. From a positive point of view, however, the value of a contextualized concept of knowledge and an organizational approach to knowledge management should not be ignored. According to the definition offered by Davenport et al. (1998), each tool has to deal with information produced by actions and individuals in specific contexts; this information is subject to different interpretations as well as to further investigation. There are various points at which contextualized knowledge is translated into more refined forms and then from these forms into yet others.

In fact the tools and devices cannot connect themselves. On the other hand, the information that can be extracted by means of these tools and devices can be linked together by individuals operating in several devices at the same time.

## Who is Doing the Connecting?

In their various papers, Von Krogh, Nonaka, and Ichijo (1997, 2000) warn against a belief in the effectiveness and efficiency of the 'chief knowledge officer'. In fact, the authors outline several complementary roles likely to foster links between individuals involved in knowledge creation. They identify 'knowledge and technology transfer'[3] of several categories of actors, including corporate labs, middle managers, and strategists.

Corporate labs perform the role allocated to them, namely to generate knowledge and make it accessible to the various actors. Strategists usually have considerable experience in their particular area of expertise: they are in charge of R&D departments and are members of the technical communities. These actors are working on company projects in order to achieve technological progress. In their view, their company's competitiveness is synonymous with the success they can make their teams achieve in the development of technologies.

Middle managers play a key role in connecting the various devices. As project leaders, technological group managers, or members of a technical community, these managers are in contact with the contexts in which knowledge is created. They work with their collaborators to resolve design questions, with their actions aimed at matching needs with sources of knowledge.

## Where are These Connections Made?

In essence, the devices are brought into contact with each other by managers during meetings: appraisal committees, forums, technical community meetings, and so forth. Potentially, however, the entire organization is the general space within which tools and devices can be connected. This observation raises the question of organizational design. Following the approach developed by Nonaka and Takeuchi (1998), we adopt the 'middle-top-bottom' model. These authors have demonstrated the limitations of the two best-known approaches with reference to Japanese companies. These are, firstly, the hierarchical model, which is said to foster the objectification of knowledge and the centralization of information systems, and the 'bottom-top' model, with its horizontal structures that function in a way similar to the communities of practice. The 'middle-top-bottom' model is more than a compromise between the two standard models, since its aim is to link local actions to the strategic objectives set by general management. The objective in fact is to set up a monitoring system within the organization in order to exploit all possible opportunities to diffuse experiences.

## How are These Connections Made?

Analysis of the various case studies reveals the difficulties involved in knowledge transfer. The exchanges that can be effected between the various devices improve the diffusion of knowledge. The actors most heavily involved in these exchanges are middle managers, who have the advantage of operating in several knowledge creation and capitalization spaces. They are the actors most called on when it comes to establishing links between other actors and the tools they are manipulating. Consequently, the establishment of links between the various devices is dependent on the quality of the relations that are established between middle managers themselves, and between those same managers and the other actors involved in design projects or in managing the firm's various core businesses. Thus it is middle managers' competences that emerge as the preferred levers in establishing connections between the devices.

These managers' memories and their perceptions of the technological issues at stake guide their actions when they meet at an engineers' promotion committee or in a forum at which the various proposals of the day are to be examined. It is essentially through the middle managers' abilities that that links are established between sources of knowledge and latent needs that the connections between devices are made.

## THE FACTORS DETERMINING THE SUCCESSFUL FUNCTIONING OF NETWORKS

Multinationals' network-based organizational structures have been put in place in order to establish a balance between creativity and control of knowledge. The purpose of our study was to assess the extent to which this balance can be maintained by reconciling the various modes of knowledge management. This led us to include the diversity of knowledge and then the diversity of means (tools and devices) in our analysis. Thus the efficient functioning of network-based structures depends on the effectiveness of the knowledge management devices.

Examination of the ways in which links are established between these devices reveals four factors determining efficiency: redundancy of the information-detecting devices, the diversity of the actors within the devices, opportunities for discussion, and long-term thinking.

Redundancy of the information-detecting devices is often presented as a factor in the reliability of control and monitoring systems. The various management tools deployed in each of the devices can be used to produce information about the same item of knowledge. Thus the results of a technological exploration may be recorded in a database, gathered together during a project review, and presented at a technological forum.

The diversity of actors in knowledge capitalization processes is another decisive factor. The actors in question are project managers, scientific and technical information specialists, technologi-

cal groups managers, forum convenors, or even HR managers. This diversity is a diversity of approaches to the modes of knowledge production and diffusion. It enriches the knowledge capitalization processes.

The third factor supplements the previous ones, since it increases the opportunities for redundancy and diversity. The opportunities in question take the form of meetings and discussions involving middle managers that are actually organized in order to facilitate exchanges between the various approaches and options for knowledge capitalization. The forums are one of the spaces for debating the technological developments to be prioritized. The various appraisal and promotion interviews also provide opportunities for middle managers to discuss the experiences of R&D employees. These spaces can be compared with the 'information channels' that facilitate access to strategic knowledge identified by Nahapiet and Ghoshal (1998).

The fourth factor in determining success is a long-term approach to the first three factors. Redundancy, diversity, and spaces for debate and discussion will not have positive effects unless a long-term approach is adopted. An approach of this kind makes it possible to stabilize relations and establish fixed points for knowledge capitalization.

## GENERAL LESSONS

These factors determining success can be subjected to further analysis. Indeed, two more lessons need to be drawn in terms of management.

Our analysis of multinational networks reveals that they are established in two stages. In the first stage the diversity of knowledge required as input for R&D projects is created. This diversity is accompanied by a segmentation of knowledge management into four separate devices, each one put in place to process part of the knowledge produced (explicit or tacit) and to handle one aspect of its management (creation or capitalization). In the second stage, the various devices are coordinated by various means, which may give rise to a very considerable degree of complexity within the organization. The numerous links between the various subsystems can be managed by applying four simple principles. We have defined these principles as the factors determining the success of knowledge management.

Our two-stage analysis has similarities with that of Lawrence and Lorsch (1967). For these authors, the objective in the first stage is to differentiate the organization's subsystems on the basis of their scientific, technico-economic, and market environments. It is this analysis that is the inspiration for current strategies of breaking down organizations into small units. In order to reduce the dispersion of knowledge, these units are given the opportunity to organize their own problem solving (Rycroft & Kash, 1999). However, there is a considerable risk that these decentralized units will become strategically remote from each other (see the difficulties inherent in second-generation R&D). This then leads to the second phase, in which the differentiated systems are integrated with each other. This integration involves coordinating the organization as a whole. The more diversified the subsystems are, the greater the need for integration will be. The integration process has to be designed to match the degree of differentiation. The means of integration described by Lawrence and Lorsch (1967) are very similar to the modes of coordinating the devices that we have identified. These means include direct contact between managers, liaison committees, and departments; interdepartmental rules (budgets); and matrix structures.

The second lesson concerns the management tools and means of integration brought into play as part of the knowledge capitalization process. Detailed analysis of the means of integration reveals that they are essentially different and

that each of them can be used to pursue several different objectives simultaneously.

The various devices contribute in their own ways to knowledge creation and capitalization. However, some of them (third-generation structures, databases, project management tools) rely on knowledge objectification, while the others (forums, communities, evaluation committees) are characterized by a high degree of autonomy. This is what Dougherty (1996) found with regard to innovation processes. Organizing innovation involves seeking a balance between deterministic, top-down approaches and the emergent modes of organization. Such a balance requires that responsibility for innovation successes and failures be shared at all levels of the organization.

This balance is all the more necessary since the knowledge management tools that are deployed can be used to fulfill several different objectives. In this regard, one can speak of organizational ambidexterity (Duncan, 1976; Tushman & Moore, 1988; Tushman & O'Reilly, 1996). In addition to their principal purposes, databases and project management tools, for example, can be used to bring order to the management practices of the various subsidiaries of a multinational company. Project evaluation procedures provide opportunities for appraising, in part at least, the employees working on those projects. And a tool like the individual appraisal interview can be used simultaneously to evaluate competences and accumulate knowledge within an R&D department.

Finally, this second lesson sheds light on the complexity of integration devices. The main conclusion to be drawn here is not that a specific mode of coordination should be adopted; rather, the organization should be structured around the notion that each knowledge management tool can fulfill several different objectives. In this way, managers can be provided with a wide variety of information, which will be of help to them in linking their actions to the processes emerging within the organization's structures.

## CONCLUSION

The aim of this chapter has been to investigate the way in which multinationals could avoid the risk of developing 'linkage errors' within their decentralized structures, errors which arise out of the gap between the knowledge that is required and the knowledge that is available.

Having shown how to search for diversity proceeds within multinationals, we analyzed the means that can be used to facilitate the diffusion of knowledge within these large organizations. This analysis produced a number of results. Let us highlight, firstly, the need to clarify the definition of knowledge and of the modes of knowledge management that we have adopted. The factors that determine the success of knowledge management in large, decentralized organizations must be set alongside the complexity of the devices identified in the various studies. The quality of knowledge diffusion depends on the quality of the links between these devices. One of the main challenges is to mark out the routes by which access to knowledge can be gained. The factors that determine success emphasize the complexity of these links, since each of the devices is associated with several management tools which, in turn, produce non-homogeneous information.

Consequently, our results also offer some lessons for the management of multinational networks. Several management principles can be identified.

The first is undoubtedly to take control of the diversity of processes involved in knowledge creation and capitalization within organizations. Any attempts to establish such control must strike a balance between control and creativity, and thus between intentions that are not always compatible. The second concerns the privileging of informational redundancy over centralized systems for accumulating experience. The third and final principle concerns the measures to be taken in order to foster meetings and exchanges between the main managers in charge of processes linked directly or indirectly to the activities of R&D employees.

Identification of these management principles should encourage us to explore further aspects of the quality of relations between actors within organizations.

## REFERENCES

Allen, T.J. (1977). *Managing the flow of technology.* Cambridge, MA: The MIT Press.

Bartlett, C., & Ghoshal, S. (1987). Managing across borders: New organizational responses. *Sloan Management Review*, (Autumn), 43-53.

Bartlett, C., & Ghoshal, S. (1987). Managing across borders: New strategic management. *Sloan Management Review*, (Winter), 7-17.

Becker, M.C. (2001). Managing dispersed knowledge: Organizational problems, managerial strategies and their effectiveness. *Journal of Management Studies, 38*(7), 1037-1051.

Benveniste, G. (1994). *Twenty-first century organization: Analyzing current trends, imagining the future.* San Francisco: Jossey-Bass.

Boutellier, R., Gassman, O., & Von Zedtwitz, M. (1999). *Managing global innovation.* New York: Springer.

Brown, J.S., & Duguid, P. (2000). Balancing act: How to capture knowledge without killing it. *Harvard Business Review*, (May-June), 3-7.

Brown, J.S., & Duguid, P. (1998). Organizing knowledge. *California Management Review, 40*(3), 90-111.

Brown, J.S., & Duguid, P. (1991). Organizational learning and communities-of-practice: Toward a unified view of working, learning and innovation. *Organization Science, 2*(1), 40-57.

Cantwell, J.A. (1995). The globalisation of technology: What remains of the product cycle model? *Cambridge Journal of Economics, 19,* 155-174.

Clark, K.B., Hayes, R.H., & Wheelwright, S.C. (1988). *Dynamic manufacturing, creating the learning organization.* New York: The Free Press.

Conklin, E.J. (1992). Capturing organizational memory. In D. Coleman (Ed.), *Proceedings of GroupWare'92* (pp. 133-137). San Mateo, CA: Morgan Kaufmann.

Davenport, T.H., & Prusak, L. (1998). *Working knowledge. How organizations manage what they know.* Boston: Harvard Business School Press.

Davenport, T.H., DeLong, D.W., & Beers, M.C. (1998). Successful knowledge management projects. *Sloan Management Review, 40,* 43-57.

David, A. (2001). Models implementation: A state of the art. *European Journal of Operational Research, 134,* 459-480.

Declerck, R., Debourse, J.P., & Navarre, C. (1983). *Méthode de direction générale: Le management stratégique.* Paris: Hommes et Techniques.

Doz, Y., & Hamel, G. (2000). *L'avantage des alliances.* Dunod.

Dougherty, D. (1996). Organizing for innovation. In S.R. Clegg & W.R. Nord (Eds.), *Handbook of organization studies.* Sage.

Duncan, R.B. (1976). The ambidextrous organization: Designing dual structures for innovation. In R.H. Kilmann, R.L. Pundy, & D.P. Slevin (Eds.), *The management of organization: Strategy and implementation.* New York: North Holland.

Easterby-Smith, M., & Lyles, M.A. (Eds.). (2003). *Blackwell handbook of organizational learning and knowledge management.* Blackwell.

Florida, R. (1997). The globalization of R&D: Results of a survey of foreign-affiliated R&D laboratories in the USA. *Research Policy, 26,* 85-103.

Gerybadze, A., & Reger, G. (1999). Globalization of R&D: Recent changes in the management of innovation in transnational corporations. *Research Policy, 28,* 251-274.

Gouldner, A.W. (1957). Cosmopolitans and locals: Towards an analysis of latent social roles. *Administrative Science Quarterly,* (December), 281-306.

Gulati, R. (1995). Social structure and alliance formation pattern: A longitudinal analysis. *Administrative Science Quarterly, 40,* 619-642.

Gulati, R. (1999). Network location and learning: The influence of network resources and firm capabilities on alliance formation. *Strategic Management Journal, 20*(5), 397-420.

Håkansson, H. (1989). *Corporate technological behavior: Cooperation and networks.* London: Routledge.

Hansen, M.T., Nohria, N., & Tierney, T. (1999). What's your strategy for managing knowledge? *Harvard Business Review,* (March-April), 106-116.

Janet, P. (1936). *L'intelligence avant le langage.* Paris: Flammarion.

Kogut, B. (2000). The network as knowledge: Generative rules and the emergence of structure. *Strategic Management Journal, 21,* 405-425.

Kogut, B., & Zander, U. (1992). Knowledge of the firm: Combinative capabilities and the replication of technology. *Organization Science, 3*(3), 383-397.

Kuemmerle, W. (1999). The drivers of foreign direct investment into research and development: An empirical investigation. *Journal of International Business Studies, 30*(1), 1-25.

Lam, A. (2003). Organizational learning in multinationals: R&D networks of Japanese and U.S. MNEs in the UK. *Journal of Management Studies, 40*(3), 673-703.

Lambert, G. (1993). Variables clés pour le transfert de technologie et le management de l'innovation. *Revue Française de Gestion,* (94), 49-72.

Lawrence, P.R., & Lorsch, J.W. (1967). *Organization and environment. Differentiation and integration.* Boston: Harvard University Press.

Maidique, M.O., & Zirger, B.J. (1985). The new product learning cycle. *Research Policy,* (14), 299-313.

Management Science. (2003). Managing knowledge in organizations: Creating, retaining and transferring knowledge. *Management Science,* (April Special Edition).

Meyers, P.W., & Wilemon, D. (1989). Learning in new technology development team. *Journal of Product Innovation Management,* (6), 79-88.

Miles, R., & Snow, C. (1992). Causes of failure in network organizations. *California Management Review, 34*(4), 53-72.

Miles, R., & Snow, C. (1986). Organizations: New concepts for new forms. *California Management Review, 28*(3), 62-73.

Moisdon, J.C. (Ed.). (1997). *Du mode d'existence des outils de gestion.* Paris: Séli-Arslan.

Nahapiet, J., & Ghoshal, S. (1998). Social capital, intellectual capital, and the organizational advantage. *Academy of Management Review, 23*(2), 242-266.

Nonaka, I. (1990). Redundant, overlapping organization: A Japanese approach to managing the innovation process. *California Management Review,* (Spring), 27-38.

Nonaka, I., & Konno, N. (1998). The concept of "Ba": Building foundation for knowledge creation. *California Management Review, 40*(3), 40-54.

Nonaka, I., & Takeuchi, H. (1995). *The knowledge creating company: How Japanese companies create the dynamics of innovation.* New York: Oxford University Press.

Paraponaris, C. (2003). Third generation R&D and strategies for knowledge management. *Journal of Knowledge Management, 7*(5), 96-106.

Paraponaris, C. (2001). The organization of R&D and the management of cooperation: Controlling a diversity of knowledge sources. In E. Verdier (Ed.), *Higher education system and innovation* (pp. 55-89). European Commission Report Number 1-1054.

Pearce, R.D. (1999). Decentralized R&D and strategic competitiveness: Globalized approaches to generation and use of technology in multinational enterprises. *Research Policy, 28,* 157-178.

Pelz, D.C., & Andrews, F.M. (1966). *Scientists in organizations.* New York: John Wiley & Sons.

Pettigrew, A.M. (1990). Longitudinal field research on change: Theory and practice. *Organization Science, 1*(3), 267-292.

Pettigrew, A.M. (1987). Context and action in the transformation of the firm. *Journal of Management Studies, 24*(6), 649-670.

Poitou, J.P. (1997). Building a collective knowledge management system: Knowledge-editing versus knowledge-eliciting techniques. In G.C. Bowker, L. Gasser, S.L. Star, & W. Turner (Eds.), (pp. 235-256).

Porter, M. (Ed.). (1986). *Competition in global industries.* Boston: Harvard Business School Press.

Purser, R.E., Pasmore, W.A., & Tenkasi, R.V. (1992). The influence of deliberations on learning in new product development teams. *Journal of Engineering and Technology Management,* (9), 1-28.

Roussel, P.A.., Saad, K.N., & Erickson, T.J. (1991). *Third generation R&D. Managing the link to corporate strategy*. Boston: Harvard Business School Press.

Rycroft, R.W., & Kash, D.E. (1999). *The complexity challenge—technological innovation for the 21st century*. London: Pinter.

Simoni, G. (2005). *Capitaliser les connaissances générées dans les projets de R&D: Pour un leadership intégratif et situationnel*. Unpublished Doctoral Dissertation, Université de la Méditerranée, France.

Stein, E.W., & Zwass V. (1995). Actualizing organizational memory with information systems. *Journal of Information Management, 6*(2), 85-117.

Szulanski, G. (1996). Exploring internal stickiness: Impediments to the transfer of best practice within the firm. *Strategic Management Journal, 17*(Winter Special Issue), 27-43.

Tsoukas, H. (1996). The firm as a distributed knowledge system. *Strategic Management Journal, 17*(Winter Special Issue), 11-25.

Tushman, M.L., & Moore, P. (1988). *Readings in the management of innovation*. Ballinger.

Tushman, M.L., & O'Reilly III, C.A. (1996). Ambidextrous organizations: Managing evolutionary and revolutionary change. *California Management Review, 38*(4), 8-30.

Von Krogh, G. (1998). Care in knowledge creation. *California Management Review, 40*(3), 133-154.

Von Krogh, G., Ichijo, K., & Nonaka, I. (2000). *Enabling knowledge creation. How to unlock the mystery of tacit knowledge and release the power of innovation*. Oxford: Oxford University Press.

Von Krogh, G., Nonaka, I., & Ichijo, K. (1997). Develop knowledge activists! *European Management Journal, 15*(5), 475-483.

Von Krogh, G., Roos, J., & Slocum, K. (1994). An essay on corporate epistemology. *Strategic Management Journal, 15*, 53-71.

Von Zedtwitz, M., & Gassmann, O. (2002). Market versus technology drive in R&D internationalization: Four different patterns of managing research and development. *Research Policy, 31*, 569-588.

Walsh, J.P., & Ungson, G.R. (1991). Organizational memory. *Academy of Management Journal, 16*(1), 57-90.

Zanfei, A. (2000). Transnational firms and the changing organization of innovation activities. *Cambridge Journal of Economics, 24*, 515-542.

# ENDNOTES

[1] An intellectual object is defined as an object or device that has the capacity to develop the practical and technical intellectual approaches inherent in artifacts (Janet, 1936). The idea is that manipulation of an object not only gives rise to knowledge of the object itself, but also develops or improves cognitive capacities in such a way that the subject may extend the cognitive processes developed while discovering the object (and developed thanks to it) to new objects. For example, when a firm acquires capital goods. it learns nothing as a socio-economic entity; rather, it acquires intellectual objects that are capable of developing the intellectual capacities of members of its workforce.

[2] CBS–University of Kent (United Kingdom. Pr Alice Lam). CRIS International (Germany and California. Christoph Büchtemann). Dinamia–University of Lisbon (Portugal. Luisa Olivera). Institute for Advanced Studies (Austria. Kurt Mayer). Lest–University of Aix–Marseille (France. Eric Verdier). Lirhe–University of Toulouse (France. Pr Jean-Michel Plassard).

[3] The purpose of these units is to diffuse locally created knowledge rapidly and systematically. They operate mainly in a coordinating role and generally work to the timescale of projects or contracts—that is, they take a short-term approach.

## APPENDIX: THE MULTINATIONALS STUDIED

| Firms | Sectors | Employees | R&D Budget as % of Turn-over |
|---|---|---|---|
| Agilent Technology | IT | 47,000 | 10.0% |
| Alcatel Space | Telecoms | 100,000 | 9.0% |
| Bull | IT | 21,000 | 5.9% |
| Canon | IT | 75,000 | 7.5% |
| Ericsson | Telecoms | 100,000 | 15.0% |
| Fabre | Pharmaceuticals | 7,000 | 20.0% |
| Hewlett Packard | IT | 124,600 | 7.7% |
| HMR (2) | Pharmaceuticals | 38,109 | 17.0% |
| ICI | Pharmaceuticals | 58,000 | 2.5% |
| ICL | IT | 22,250 | 2.9% |
| Kapsch | Telecoms | 1993 | 13.0% |
| Merck | Pharmaceuticals | 57,000 | 12.0% |
| Motorola | Telecoms | 130,000 | 9.0% |
| Nortel | Telecoms | 76,700 | 14.0% |
| Pfizer | Pharmaceuticals | 46,000 | 17.0% |
| Racal Electronics | Telecoms | 10,000 | 6.0% |
| RPRorer (2) | Pharmaceuticals | 26,000 | 17.5% |
| Siemens | Telecoms | 440,000 | 8.0% |

# Chapter IXX
# Knowledge Management Success:
## Roles of Management and Leadership

**Vittal S. Anantatmula**
*Western Carolina University, USA*

## ABSTRACT

*Globalization and free market philosophy characterize the current economic environment of increased competition, and it has posed far greater challenges than ever for organizations to meet customer needs and demands. The global competition is compelling organizations to develop products and services faster, cheaper, and better in order to sustain competitive advantage in the marketplace. Twenty-first century economy is setting new trends and unique styles of business operations because of continuous advancement of information technology and communication technologies. These technologies have offered more avenues to conduct business effectively and efficiently. Many organizations participating in the global economy have two distinct features associated with their operations, outsourcing and virtual teams, which have become feasible because of these technological advances. These two features have an impact on how organizations manage knowledge, and they deserve further discussion.*

## OUTSOURCING AND VIRTUAL TEAMS

Outsourcing is a common business practice because it helps acquire quality services and expertise at a lower cost. General Motors, Toyota, Siemens, Hewlett-Packard, General Electric, and IBM—among many other major organizations—are using outsourcing as a strategy to cut down costs.

Also, global economy is compelling organizations to establish operating divisions and factories close to marketplaces and other strategic locations where the labor costs are cheaper. Consequently, virtual teams are integral to many organizations in the current economy. A case in point is Infosys Technologies Limited—one of the leading software consultants in the world. The company has a conference room in Bangalore, India that can hold a virtual meeting of the key players from its entire global supply chain on a super-size screen to integrate project functions and work as an effective project team (Friedman, 2005).

These virtual teams span various time zones, different languages and cultures, and possess a wide range of competencies and skills. Needless to say, outsourcing and consequent virtual teams are challenging the traditional structures of organizations.

Two questions come to our mind: How do they impact the way organizations run their business operations? And how do they impact the manager's role? It is critical for organizations to find answers to these questions. More importantly, both these distinct features—outsourcing and virtual teams—have one thing in common: the explicit and tacit knowledge of the organization is no longer confined within the organization. The daunting task that faces organizations is how to manage knowledge resources to gain and sustain competitive advantage. In this chapter, we will attempt to address all these important questions.

## KNOWLEDGE MANAGEMENT

Intense competition, indecisive consumers, and globalization are some of the driving forces that have led to increased interest in studying how knowledge is used, applied, and leveraged. This has led to placing greater emphasis on understanding and developing better frameworks for assessing knowledge management effectiveness, thereby determining its impact on bottom-line business results (Lim & Ahmed, 2000).

A recent study (Nidiffer & Dolan, 2005) observed that in the current economy, top management priorities are building virtual teams with a minimum of face time, clearly defining work, measuring cybernetic worker productivity, and managing employee communications across time zones. These priorities are relevant to projects and processes of several management functions including knowledge management (KM) and have a

significant impact on a manager's role. It is obvious that technology plays a critical role in supporting management's efforts to meet these priorities.

Before we discuss knowledge and knowledge management further, it is important to have a common understanding of these terms.

## Data, Information, Knowledge and Knowledge Management

The word "data" generally refers to numerical facts collected together for reference. According to Ellis (2003), the distinction is that data are the facts that are organized into information; when used by someone to solve a problem, information in turn becomes personal knowledge (see Figure 1). When we convert it to explicit knowledge, it becomes an intellectual asset that can be shared within an organization.

Information is a subset of knowledge, which denotes understanding of the information. Knowledge is derived from thinking, and it is a combination of information, experience, and insight. This insight, in turn, is developed with the use of tacit knowledge. Deriving knowledge from information requires human judgment, and is based on context and experience. As a resource, knowledge increases its value with use. Ironically, knowledge will remain dormant and not very useful until it is reflected in action (Rad & Anantatmula, 2005).

*Figure 1. Relation between data, information, and knowledge*

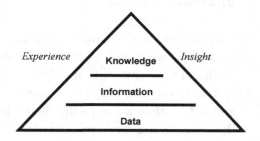

The primary focus of knowledge management is to utilize information technology and tools, business processes, best practices, and culture to develop and share knowledge within an organization, and to connect those who possess knowledge to those who do not. In this definition of KM, the keywords are developing and sharing knowledge. Thus, important functions of KM are creating and transferring knowledge.

Developing and sharing knowledge should lead to performance improvements at an individual level then at an organizational level. With this premise, organizations are using KM systems to improve their business performance. KM has several advantages: importantly, it presents an opportunity to develop processes that would help to prevent from continually reinventing the wheel. KM and consequent intellectual capital offer unique competitive advantage to an organization because it is not easy to replicate.

## IT and KM

Information technology (IT) refers to a combination of computer-related hardware and software systems intended to develop and manage data and information. Organizations invest in technology systems to improve business performance and sustain competitive advantage. Several research studies link IT and/or KM systems to improved organizational performance (Ahn & Chang, 2002; Jennex & Olfman, 2002; King, 2002; Marchand, Kettinger, & Rollins, 2000). Marchand et al. (2000) found that information operation, which measures an organization's capabilities to effectively manage and use information, influences business performance.

It is common experience that IT facilitates efficient storage and quick retrieval of large amounts of data and information. From a KM perspective, however, IT is considered useful for efficient conversion between data and information, but it is a rather poor alternative for converting information into knowledge (Ra, 1997). Prieto and Rivella (2004), citing research studies, suggested that conversion from information to knowledge is best accomplished by human actions; however, they reminded us that humans are slow as compared to IT systems for converting data into information.

In a research study to explore the relation between IT, KM, and business performance, Martin, Hatzakis, Lycett, and Macredia (2004) showed that KM can be seen as a holistic way to manage the complex relation between business and IT. Martin et al. contend that effective KM, which promotes one vision and improved communication, will have a direct impact on the ability of firms to bridge the gap between IT and end users, thereby impacting organizational performance.

A recent research study (Anantatmula & Kanungo, 2005)—after identifying measures of effectiveness for technology (IT and KM) and project performance, and studying the relationship among these measures—suggested that organizations should develop technology systems to meet specific business and project needs, and they should not be designed in isolation with the assumption that people will use it for productive purposes. Anantatmula and Kanungo (2005) concluded that developing technology systems to meet specific business and project needs will help link technology with business results.

From these research findings, one can see IT in conjunction with KM as a remedy to address the issue of converting information into useful knowledge.

## KM AND ORGANIZATIONAL PERFORMANCE

In the previous section, we discussed the relation between IT and KM with reference to organizational performance and business results. However, it is people who make use of these systems, and thus it is imperative to understand the extent to which these systems help people in their day-to-day activities. Earlier discussions suggested that KM acts as a bridge between IT and end users. So, our focus in this section is to understand the impact of KM on people and the consequent impact on organizational performance.

A research study to assess KM success that included 147 organizations in 21 countries identified improved communication enhanced collaboration, improved employee skills, better decision making, and improved productivity as the most useful outcomes of KM (Anantatmula, 2005). Using interpretive structural modeling (ISM) to develop relations among these outcomes, Anantatmula and Kanungo (2006) showed that enhanced collaboration leverages employee skills in the context of decision making to influence productivity and quality.

In principle, KM criteria must be guided by an organization's goals and bottom-line results. If KM initiatives do not contribute to an organization's business performance, top management would not support such initiatives. However, these research findings revealed that KM efforts result in soft measures, which are not directly tied to end results. These results also imply that KM outcomes are difficult to measure and all of them are people-related factors, which emphasize the importance of management and leadership roles in directing KM efforts successfully.

Discussions so far have set the platform to discuss management and leadership roles in successful implementation of KM. For this purpose, we have discussed the business environment of global economy and the consequent impact of such virtual teams and outsourcing; the relation among IT, KM, and organization performance; and finally, outcomes of KM initiatives and their relation with business performance. With this as background, we will now examine the management and leadership roles in the successful implementation of KM.

## KM: CREATION AND TRANSFER OF KNOWLEDGE

We have identified creation and transfer of knowledge as the two important functions of KM. Knowledge creation and, more specifically, knowledge transfer can happen only when more than one person is involved.

### Knowledge Creation

With respect to knowledge creation, KM deals with two activities:

- Preserving and using existing knowledge, and
- Creating new knowledge.

Existing knowledge includes both tacit and explicit knowledge. Creating new knowledge involves a great deal of interaction of people with the processes and among people within the organization.

Before we discuss knowledge creation, we must understand the term *tacit knowledge*. Individuals—by virtue of having knowledge that cannot necessarily be verbalized as the knowledge that is intuitive and unarticulated—always know more than they can express and explain. This is known as tacit knowledge, which may sometimes become an important factor of competitive advantage. An important goal of KM is to tap into this tacit knowledge, and make it explicit and accessible within the organization to achieve better business results. Possessing knowledge about a situation or an event should enable people to make better decisions or act more rationally (Martin, 2000).

Needless to say, knowledge creation requires people to participate and interact with each other. KM must employ both formal and informal organizational structures to accomplish the creation and dissemination of knowledge. Nonaka's model

(1994) is a process of knowledge creation and dissemination using tacit and explicit knowledge within the organization. The underlying concept of knowledge creation and dissemination is learning.

A well-defined learning process serves as a prerequisite for knowledge accumulation and organizational learning. Individual learning—a pre-condition to organizational learning—is characterized by thinking, personal experience, needs and motives, interests and values, level of difficulty of the task at hand, and manifestation of behavioral changes (see Figure 2). On the other hand, organizational learning is characterized by collective thinking and creation of shared frame of reference. Organizational learning is defined as a process by which the organization's knowledge and value-base is changed, thus leading to improved problem solving, which in turn leads to increased capacity for action (Probst & Buchel, 1997).

While individual learning is associated with tacit knowledge, organizational learning makes use of explicit knowledge. Employees tend to develop optimum processes while performing tasks within the rules of the organization. Subsequently, organizations gain knowledge by documenting these processes, and by using these documents as reference material for sharing it within the organization. Through replicating these processes, organizations acquire additional knowledge, which becomes independent of individuals who developed the original processes.

## Knowledge Transfer

The present global economy—from the knowledge standpoint—distinguishes itself from earlier ones due to the size of knowledge base, innovation, and the technological advances that facilitate knowledge transfer. One of the main challenges of KM is to facilitate knowledge transfer among people within the organization (Alavi & Leidner,

*Figure 2. Individual learning vs. organizational learning (Adopted from Probst & Buchel, 1997)*

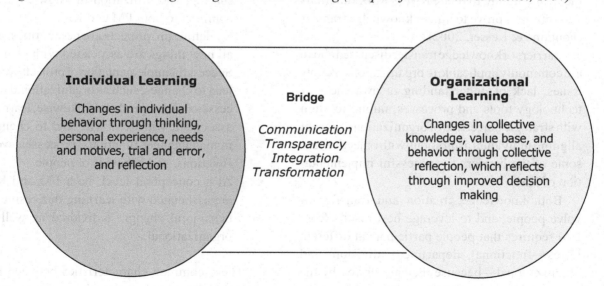

2004). Many people consider knowledge as power and perceive it as a form of job security. Consequently, they would not like to share their personal knowledge with their colleagues. The inherent issue is lack of trust. It is obvious that people issues are considered important in knowledge transfer, and research supports this contention (Disterer, 2001).

Research on software development teams has shown that other obstacles that lead to absence or ineffective knowledge transfer are lack of awareness about the KM, low information quality, low usage, and time-consuming maintenance of KM systems (Komi-Sirvio et al., 2002). These obstacles can be considered as general and applicable to KM systems in other work environments as well. Thus, it is important to develop KM systems keeping in view these obstacles. Special attention to increase the use of KM tools and maintaining quality will help develop sustainable KM systems and knowledge transfer. Also, KM systems should be aimed to support strategic objectives of the organization. Studies have shown that failure to align KM with the strategic goals, creation of knowledge repositories without explicitly defining the intentions behind them, and failure to relate KM to work functions and activities prove to hinder knowledge transfer (Fontaine & Lesser, 2002).

Barriers of knowledge transfer discussed above are commonly applicable to organizations. People issues, lack of understanding or awareness of technology tools and processes, failure to align with strategic objectives of organizations, and not aligning individual aspirations with objectives are some of the barriers to successful implementation of KM.

Both knowledge creation and transfer involve people, and to leverage best results from KM requires that people participate at different levels—functional, department, division, and organizational—because they are driven by the need to share knowledge at all these levels to enhance knowledge transfer, collaboration, and

innovation. As such, being a member of a team is an inevitable feature of modern work life (Smith, 2001). Therefore, management and leadership of these teams and KM systems influence the success of KM.

## KM SUCCESS FACTOR MODEL

Before we analyze the role of management and leadership of a KM system, we need to understand the characteristics of KM. Like any other initiative, KM is considered a project. According to Rad and Anantatmula (2005), some of the common features of KM and project management (PM) are:

- Improving performance through learning is a common theme to formalized project management (PM) and knowledge management, albeit KM focuses on knowledge in all areas beyond managing projects. Specifically, knowledge development, transfer, and utilization are common functions to both.
- Effective communication is a critical success factor for both PM and KM.
- Acquisition, creation, transfer, retention, sharing, and utilization of knowledge are common to both PM and KM.
- By definition, projects are new entities, and all new things are associated with change. Successful implementation of projects would lead to changes, such as organizational processes and new products. Likewise, learning associated with KM will lead to changes in management functions, processes, work functions, and behavior of people.
- At a conceptual level, both PM and KM are associated with learning that results in behavioral change; individual as well as organizational.

These common characteristics between PM and KM help to analyze the roles of management and leadership of KM by relating to a research study on management and a leadership role for project management performance (Anantatmula, 2006). One distinction with KM systems is that IT plays a major facilitating role for KM systems. Using this study and literature review, eight factors were identified, which have significant influence on successful implementation of KM.

## KM Success Factors

### Create Clarity

Clarity in defining goals and outlining likely outcomes is important during the early stages of KM initiative. Otherwise, we may fail to identify some of the important requirements of the KM system. As a consequence, the KM system will be perceived as a failure, and incorporating these requirements at a later stage may not help.

### Define Roles and Processes

In general, many employees, in addition to their primary responsibilities and functions, participate in KM efforts for knowledge creation and sharing. Therefore, formal definition and approval of roles and processes is very important. Clear assignments of roles and responsibilities without ambiguity or overlapping responsibilities are important for conflict resolution and productivity.

### Communicate Expectations

Defining and establishing expectations from all the stakeholders is imperative for KM success, and if we fail to do so, KM efforts will eventually result in both perceived and actual incidences of not delivering expected results. Objective and formally defined processes in developing knowledge repositories and effective dissemination of these processes and results are some of the means to communicate what is expected of all stakeholders.

### Employ Consistent Processes

Organizations tend to manage KM with no formal processes. Mandating consistent and formal processes would encourage greater participation and contribution. Participation in knowledge development and sharing the new knowledge within the group and throughout the organization are the tenets of KM systems, and consistent process is the means to implement these policies.

### Establish Trust

Trust is critical for knowledge sharing and teamwork. An environment of trust is influenced by the organizational culture, which can promote transparency, openness in communication, and collaboration. Needless to say, clear definition of roles and responsibilities promotes team effectiveness.

### Facilitate Organizational Support

A significant success factor to implement KM systems is to gain support and participation from key personnel representing all the functions in the organization and top management. Obtaining organizational support is one of the challenges. Resources are generally controlled by functional managers, and their collaboration to KM efforts is a prerequisite to successful implementation of KM. Failure to facilitate organizational support would lead to ineffective use of KM systems and ultimate failure.

### Manage Outcomes

KM efforts require resources, and therefore, management would expect results that would indicate better business performance. As is true with projects, most perceptions of failure and success of KM systems are based on unspoken and personal indices. As a result, different people assess the same project differently (Rad, 2002). Therefore, there is a need for a set of performance indices that formalize the process and make explicit what is implicit in these seemingly subjective evaluations. Such an organized performance evaluation system would promote excellence.

## Facilitate IT Support

IT systems support electronic storage in miniscule size, and efficient and fast retrieval of large amounts of data. Thus, IT serves KM systems well in effective communication and developing KM tools such as electronic yellow pages, knowledge repositories, intranet, and virtual communities of practice. Organizations should—when developing IT systems—focus on specific business needs.

## ISM Research Methodology

Using these success factors and based on interpretive structural modeling (ISM) to obtain input from KM professionals, a management and leadership model is developed (see Figure 3). ISM was developed by Warfield (1973) and involves structuring of goals and objectives into a hierarchical framework. In this study, the set of KM factors described above was used to develop an understanding of the shared underlying mental model in which these factors operate.

ISM is selected for two reasons: first, human brains have limitations in dealing with complex problems of a significant number of elements and relations among elements (Waller, 1975); second, input data quality is better because unlike surveys, which collect data on perceptions, ISM uses an interactive discussion method to collect data, thereby compelling the participant in the research study to analyze carefully the relations among these factors. Thus, it brings out tacit knowledge of participants in the study.

ISM allows structuring a complex problem of many elements while considering two elements

only at a time. Thus, it is useful for developing policies and strategies, in addition to solving complex problems. ISM is used to develop a model because we usually function with mental models or relations or systems. It is useful because structure determines behavior (Senge, 1990).

The results in Figure 3 represent the mental models of those who participated in the study. Therefore, they are subject to interpretation and that is why it is called the interpretive structural model. These arrows represent "leads to," and these relations are tenable.

As can be seen in Figure 3, organizational support and IT infrastructure are the independent variables; they are required to be present for a KM system to be successful. An effective KM will result in establishing trust among the participating and contributing employees. It will also establish a system to manage its outcomes.

## KM: ROLE OF MANAGEMENT AND LEADERSHIP

Leadership and management roles are entwined, and the distinction between management and leadership is not always obvious. Classical functions such as planning, organizing, and controlling are considered within the boundaries of management.

*Figure 3. Role of management and leadership*

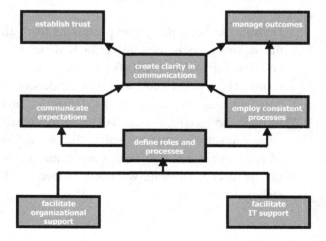

Management is also concerned with decision making—specifically related to processes and functions—to improve operational efficiency and effectiveness. Leadership is concerned with motivation and support to people in order to realize their potential and achieve challenging and difficult goals. Among the leadership styles, situational leaders focus on various tasks and relationship behaviors (Hersey & Blanchard, 1996), and transformational leaders may inspire followers, meet their developmental needs, and encourage new approaches and more effort toward problem solving (Selzer & Bass, 1990).

Resource integration and efficient and effective use of their utilization are important tenets of management and they help manage complexity. Leadership, on the other hand, has its efforts directed towards convincing people about the need to change, aligning them to a new direction and motivating people to work together to achieve KM objectives under difficult and demanding work environments.

As is true with projects, uniqueness, complexity, and unfamiliarity are some of the characteristics of KM when it is initiated in an organization. Thus, these efforts are often associated with significant changes in working culture. As a consequence, leadership is a determinant of success as it provides vision and ability to cope with change (Kotter, 1999). Additionally, the role of management and leadership in creating and transferring knowledge within an organization is more challenging because of the dynamic nature of the organization structure and culture as a result of virtual teams and outsourcing.

## Management

KM is aimed at making use of people in enhancing the knowledge base of the organization. To provide clarity and purpose, roles of individuals participating in the KM initiative and processes associated with KM must be clearly defined first. Without such formal definition and approval of roles, KM would lack support from top management and functional managers. Defining the roles and processes would logically lead to developing formal processes that would facilitate an understanding of the organizational requirements needed to support KM internally and externally.

A KM system cannot be left to voluntary participation. KM must encourage people to interact within and across disciplines and functions; each person brings specific expertise and experience. Defining each member's role would help in creating and sharing of knowledge. Consistent processes aid in managing a diverse group of people from different functions and divisions. By defining the roles and process, and by identifying the organizational support needs, managers can successfully lead teams and effectively accomplish the expected outcomes. It would also help managers define and manage KM goals and outcomes.

In the context of virtual teams and outsourcing, management should make a prudent and informed choice to identify areas of knowledge that can be shared among all the groups. To facilitate effective communication in a virtual team, extensive use of technology tools such as intranets, videoconferencing, electronic yellow pages, and electronic bulletin boards of virtual communities of practice is desirable. For effective use of these tools and knowledge transfer, management should encourage free flow of information, and archive all the relevant and useful information. Usually, outsourcing is a choice for hiring expertise or quality of work at a lower cost. These tasks could be either familiar or unfamiliar to the parent organization, and in either case, outsourcing provides an opportunity to learn and enhance organizational knowledge.

## Leadership

By defining processes and roles, and communicating what is expected of all the members of the KM community, one can establish both predictability and openness. Both predictability and openness, in turn, can be used to develop expectations and manage outcomes. Trust and open communication are essential to nurture human relationships; predictability and openness are important factors in establishing trust (Gray & Larsen, 2005). Establishing trust in virtual teams—where face-to-face interaction is limited or non-existent—is a challenging task. Effective and frequent communication using technology can be a solution. With virtual teams, organizations usually employ electronic media for written communication and group meetings (videoconferencing).

By communicating clearly and effectively, managers can establish an environment of openness and transparency. It can lead to a work environment where team members willingly share information, experiences, and knowledge. These factors also instill trust—among all the participants—in their leader. Trust, in turn, encourages participants to collaborate, network, and innovate. Ring (1996) analyzed trust at the interpersonal level and found it as a precursor to forming ongoing networks. Although it should evolve mutually, trust is more important for leaders as they try motivating participating employees to accomplish a vision and to realize goals. And by establishing trust, leaders can also mitigate conflicts, a deterrent to knowledge creation and transfer.

Because people are motivated by challenges and opportunities to further their career goals, participants are almost always interested in accomplishing personal and professional goals in addition to completing their routine responsibilities. Therefore, it is imperative that KM leadership understand and support the personal aspirations of the people and align them with the objectives of the organization.

As a prerequisite to successful implementation of KM in organizations, leadership of the organization is responsible for practicing strategic planning and systems thinking approaches, making best use of resources, fostering a culture that encourages open dialogue and team learning, and

finally, for encouraging and rewarding risk taking, learning, and knowledge sharing.

## Organizational Support

Research has shown that top management involvement, KM leadership, and the culture of the organization are important driving factors based on which a successful KM system can be built (Anantatmula & Kanungo, 2007). With the involvement of top management, KM initiatives will gain support and active participation of the senior executives of the organization. Top management involvement would also ensure that KM initiatives will have strategic focus. The research has also indicated that competent leadership of a KM initiative combined with the support from the top management would lead to budgetary support for KM initiatives.

Organization culture that encourages open and transparent communication among the employees of the organization would lead to increased collaboration and knowledge sharing at hierarchical levels of the organization, which leads to knowledge sharing. Increased communication with the aid of standard processes, along with technology infrastructure, make it easy and enhance collaboration.

The organization should have a structure that facilitates personal interactions and supports communities of practice to capture tacit and explicit knowledge within the organization, and this structure should be extended to virtual teams and outsourcing personnel in applicable areas through appropriate communication tools. Likewise, technology (both IT and KM) infrastructure should promote the efficient capture of explicit knowledge and support knowledge sharing within and outside the organization by developing processes and systems that are easy to use.

The organization should identify means and provide opportunities for individual learning, and link it to organizational learning and business performance. Such organizations should develop metrics to measure the results of learning and challenge people to perform better by setting tougher targets.

In conclusion, KM initiative—during its implementation stage—has to deal with complexity and changes under multiple constraints. It is characterized by newness, time and budget constraints, uncertainty, uniqueness, complexity, and demanding expectations. Therefore, leadership assumes greater importance during the implementation stage. Once the KM system is in place, it becomes process oriented and well defined, and the emphasis shifts to management functions.

## CONCLUSION

Organization culture that encourages open and transparent communication among the employees would lead to increased collaboration and knowledge sharing at hierarchical levels of the organization. Increased communication with the aid of standard processes, along with technology infrastructure, make it easy and enhance collaboration.

Technology and communication systems are influencing the way we do business today. Organizations participating in the global economy and their markets have no boundaries. In this business environment of increased competition and customer demands, knowledge and knowledge workers are assuming greater importance. Virtual teams and outsourcing are commonly practiced and offer challenges to the management and leadership roles in implementing KM successfully.

## REFERENCES

Ahn, J., & Chang, S. (2002). Valuation of knowledge: A business performance-oriented methodology. *IEEE Computer Society*.

Alavi, M., & Leidner, D.E. (2001). Knowledge management and knowledge management systems—conceptual foundations and research issues. *MIS Quarterly, 25*(1).

Anantatmula, V. (2004). *Criteria for measuring knowledge management efforts in organizations.* Doctoral Dissertation in Publication, References Number 3123064, UMI Dissertation Services.

Anantatmula, V. (2005). Outcomes of knowledge management initiatives. *International Journal of Knowledge Management, 1*(2), 50-67.

Anantatmula, V. (2006, July 16-19) Improving project performance through leadership and technology. *Proceedings of the Project Management Institute Research Conference,* Montreal, Canada.

Anantatmula, V., & Kanungo, S. (2005). Role of information technology and knowledge management in influencing project performance. *Proceedings of IEMC 2005* (pp. 599-603).

Anantatmula, V., & Kanungo, S. (2007, January 3-6). Modeling enablers and barriers for successful KM implementation. *Proceedings of the Hawaii International Conference on System Sciences* (HICSS).

Disterer, G. (2001). Individual and social barriers to knowledge transfer. *Proceedings of HICSS34.*

Ellis, K. (2003). K-span: Building a bridge between learning and knowledge management. *Training, 40*(10), 46.

Fontaine, M.A., & Lesser, E. (2002). *Challenges in managing organizational knowledge.* Technical Report, IBM Institute for Knowledge-Based Organizations, USA.

Friedman, T. (2005). *The world is flat: A brief history of the twenty-first century.* New York: Farrar, Straus and Giroux.

Gray, C.F., & Larson, E.W. (2005). *Project management: The managerial process.* New York: McGraw-Hill.

Hersey, P., & Blanchard, K. (1996). Great ideas revisited: Revisiting the life-cycle theory of leadership. *Training & Development, 50*(1), 43-47.

Jennex, M.E., & Olfman, L. (2002). Organizational memory/knowledge effects on productivity, a longitudinal study. *Proceedings of the 35ᵗʰ IEEE Hawaii International Conference on System Sciences.*

King, W.R. (2002). IT capabilities, business processes, and impact on the bottom line. *Information Systems Management, 19*(2), 85-87.

Kotter, J.P. (1999). *John P. Kotter on what leaders really do.* Boston: Harvard Business School Press.

Lim, K.K., & Ahmed, P.K. (2000). Enabling knowledge management: A measurement perspective. *Proceedings of CMIT 2000.*

Marchand, D.A., Kettinger, W.J., & Rollins, J.D. (2000). Information orientation: People, technology and the bottom line. *Sloan Management Review, 41*(4), 69-80.

Martin, B. (2000). Knowledge management within the context of management: An evolving relationship. *Singapore Management Review, 22*(2), 17-36.

Martin, V.A., Hatzakis, T., Lycett, M., & Macredie, R. (2004). Building the business/IT relationship through knowledge management. *Journal of Information Technology Cases and Applications, 6,* 2.

Nidiffer, K., & Dolan, D. (2005). Evolving distributed project management**.** *IEEE Software,* (September/October), 63-72.

Nonaka, I. (1994). A dynamic theory of organizational knowledge creation. *Organization Science, 5*(1), 14-37.

Prieto, I.M., & Revilla, E. (2004). Information technologies and human behaviors as interacting knowledge management enablers of the organizational learning capacity. *International Journal of Management Concepts and Philosophy, 1*(3), 175-197.

Probst, G., & Buchel, B. (1997). *Organization learning.* London: Prentice Hall.

Ra, J.W. (1997). The informal structure of project organizations. *Proceedings of the Portland International Conference on Management and Technology* (PICMET) (p. 392).

Rad, P.F., & Anantatmula, V. (2005). *Project planning techniques.* Vienna, VA: Management Concepts.

Selzer, J., & Bass, B. (1990). Transformational leadership: Beyond initiation and consideration. *Journal of Management, 16*(4), 693-703.

Senge, P.M. (1990). *The fifth discipline: The art & practice of learning organization.* New York: Doubleday.

Smith, G. (2001). Making the team. *IEE Review, 47*(5), 33-36.

Waller, R.J. (1975). Application of interpretive structural modeling to priority-setting in urban systems management. In M. Baldwin (Ed.), *Portraits of complexity* (Battelle Monograph No. 9). Columbus, OH: Battelle Memorial Institute.

Warfield, J.N. (1973). Intent structures. *IEEE Transactions on Systems, Man, and Cybernetics, 3*(2).

# Chapter XX
# Strategic Knowledge Management in Matrix Multinational Organizations

**Alan M. Thompson**
*Production Services Network Ltd., Scotland*

## ABSTRACT

*This chapter looks at managing knowledge workers within the business environment of a matrix-organized multinational organization, using oil and gas contractor Production Services Network for illustration. It looks at the influence of business needs, and human and organizational culture and strategic factors on KM; the importance of communicating business drivers; and adverse demographics; it also outlines some future trends that managers and KM staff in multinational matrix organizations should be preparing for. It is hoped that discussing examples of KM in practice, within the context of globalization, demographic changes, and rapid developments in technology, markets, and business relationships, will ground some familiar theory in some new and evolving territory, providing interest to both academics and practitioners.*

## INTRODUCTION

This chapter looks at managing knowledge workers within the business environment of a matrix-organized multinational organization. The organization Production Services Network (PSN) is used for illustration purposes. PSN provides operational support within the global oil and gas industry, and faces that industry's challenges of cyclical demand; an aging workforce; the need for highly skilled, highly mobile workers; and rapid technological development. The matrix model within PSN takes the form of staff and contrac-tor workers reporting to both a functional head, who is a discipline specialist, and an assignment manager, who is a business specialist. Managing knowledge workers within this context presents both opportunities and obstacles. This chapter looks at how PSN's knowledge management team negotiates these, with reference to some of the latest literature on the subject. It looks specifically at how each company's distinct business imperatives for managing knowledge influence how they manage their knowledge workers, with particular reference to PSN; human and organizational culture, and strategic factors; the importance of communicating business drivers; and adverse demographics. An outline is offered of some future trends for which managers and KM staff in multinational matrix organizations should be preparing.

## BACKGROUND

Matrix organizations have been around for much longer than knowledge management as we know it today. Within PSN, the reasons for organizing the company on matrix principles stem from the nature of the business. PSN provides oil and gas companies with operational support for their production platforms and processing facilities around the world. For more than 20 years, the company was a wholly owned subsidiary of the global support company KBR, in turn part of the Halliburton Company, headquartered in Houston, Texas. PSN was purchased by its management team in May 2006 and continues to operate on a global basis from its headquarters in Aberdeen, Scotland. PSN has experienced considerable expansion over the last five years, mainly by developing its non-UK business. It has around 7,000 employees working in more than 20 countries across five continents and is organized on the matrix principle to provide the core business services of engineering, maintenance, and operation services to customers. The matrix principle gives the company necessary flexibility.

The oil and gas industry is cyclical (Yergin, 1991). For the support sector of the industry, this means managing the peaks and troughs associated with not only the oil price, but with varying demand for gas, which has become more of an internationally traded commodity in recent times. Cyclicality also affects asset maintenance and modifications, as the discovery of new oil fields has slowed but not ceased, while increased innovation is required to extend the production life of existing older fields.

In light of this cyclicality, there is a business need to move people and sometimes the execution of activities around efficiently, while ensuring all people are all suitably competent, experienced, and informed for each project assignment. A project assignment is the industry term used to describe a group of people with a wide variety of skill sets dedicated or assigned to support a particular oil or gas production asset or group of assets for a particular client. The cornerstone knowledge management practice of using previously learned methods to inform the solutions of the future is particularly relevant to this mobile workforce; how this relevance interacts with workforce perceptions will be discussed later.

The matrix management model offers flexibility because the dual line responsibility arrangement of people reporting to both a function head and a project assignment leader ensures a reliable supply of competent people, conversant with the organization's methods on project assignments. It permits relatively rapid updating and dissemination of improved working practices, because there is a desire by functional heads to ensure their people are kept up to date, while the assignment leader keeps focus sharply on the specific demands of the contract with the customer. The driver for the functional heads is associated with work practices, improvements, and increased competencies, and tends towards a medium-term horizon; for the project assignment manager, the main focus is on the delivery of his or her particular project assignment goals, mostly on a shorter timescale.

Modern matrix organizations tend to be relatively 'flat' organizations, which frequently are observed to have a middle-management layer populated by fewer people, many of whom have become overburdened in more recent times and who have little spare time. If we factor in that this industry also has a relatively high proportion of short-term contract workers, the reader may begin to understand the sometimes conflicting complexity of knowledge management issues which need to be balanced as a consequence.

The contract knowledge workers represent a significant core competency whose skill levels are on a par with the staff workforce and who are rewarded well because they could be laid off at short notice. There is a need from the organization's viewpoint for them to share rather than hoard information, and to exhibit behaviors indistinguishable from those of the long-term personnel. A potential conflict here stems from the widespread belief that hoarding knowledge increases the value of the knowledge worker to the organization, and hence the remuneration attainable. While that suggests a behavioral pattern mitigating against sharing, research by Thompson (2004), who tested the hypotheses that the mode of employment (staff vs. contract) had an impact on knowledge sharing, indicated the widely held belief that contract workers do not contribute as much as staff personnel in a collaborative environment was untrue. Thus, the pros and cons of knowledge management and contract workers are not as straightforward as they first appear.

## THE BUSINESS IMPERATIVE FOR MANAGING KNOWLEDGE, AND HOW THAT INFLUENCES MANAGING KNOWLEDGE WORKERS IN A MATRIX ORGANIZATION MODEL

While it might be said that this form of matrix management drives a certain amount of knowledge sharing within the organization, this is quite different than fulfilling a knowledge management function. The business imperative for PSN to actively manage its knowledge reflects four major operational changes in the oil and gas support industry which have taken place over the last 10 years or so.

Previously, the reward mechanism centered upon the amount of man-hours sold, with each man-hour attracting a profit element. In more recent times however, partially as a result of the maturity of the industry, the mechanism has moved towards directly linking the profit attainable by the support company to the amount of oil and gas produced, or to plant availability, or to a mixture of both. Given that the assets being supported are all aging, this change in the reward mechanism makes it harder for the support organizations to make profit. Thus there is a considerable incentive for service companies to re-use prior work wherever possible, supported by a relatively recent realization among clients that bespoke solutions are wasteful of *their* money rather than that of the service company, and so bespoke solutions have become less frequently sought by client organizations. There is absolutely no incentive for service companies or their oil company clients to re-invent solutions.

Further, as the rate of discovery of new fields slows down, the support industry has responded by developing innovative modification solutions for field life extensions for these older fields. A common feature in this latter scenario is that the time to carry these out must be much more rapid than in previous times. There is a paradox here of course, in that while all operating companies like to think of themselves as innovative, they are frequently risk-averse in terms of being first to use new ways of doing business because the rewards are less certain!

An additional driver for active managing of knowledge is the realization by client and support organizations alike that there is an increasing shortage of experienced personnel due to demographic factors, particularly in Western cultures (Drucker, 2001).

These factors have driven a strong business need to ensure that prior work is carefully noted, both in terms of what to repeat (let's do more of that) and to avoid (let's NOT do that again), succinctly put by Browne (1997), former chairman of BP:

*Our philosophy is simple: every time we do something again, we should do it better than last time.*

There is a need to make all such information on prior work, good practices, and so on readily available to all parts of the organization everywhere to support global expansion.

A further business environmental change in the same period is the emergence of 'partnering' or 'alliancing' contracts, intended to make the client and support organizations work more collaboratively, rather than in a master/servant mode of operation, as was previously more common. This may be due to recognition among the client organizations, of the increasing expertise and sophistication of the support organization; whatever the reason, collaboration is premised on knowledge sharing, which places a requisite on competing support organizations to have a better managed resource to sell.

## HUMAN FACTORS RELATED TO MANAGING KNOWLEDGE WORKERS

In asking personnel to work in a more collaborative way, we have noted, as have many observers of organizational behavior decades apart (e.g., Handy, 1981; Davenport, 2005), that there are many barriers, most conveniently grouped together for the purpose of discussion as being in the organizational culture category. This section looks at the role of the middle manager, an essential facilitator of KM within the matrix organization, while simultaneously embedded in the organizational culture. An example is given of how PSN uses its middle managers to align staff with organizational objectives that prioritize KM. This is contextual-

ized with a summary of the typical attitudes that middle managers and KM staff alike encounter, and that constitute a large part of the culture that still has to be changed.

Development of KM is a culture shift and thus a change of habits, and like any culture shift it takes people away from their *comfort zones,* resulting in many unspoken barriers arising. Middle management is in a position to help make KM succeed when they have time, but equally they can be significant obstacles, too (DeLong, 2004). The matrix organization structural model adds complications to this because of the relative flatness of such organizations. This reduces the time available to the middle management to engage in what many of them see as additional tasks to the 'day job', compounded by reductions in the numbers of middle managers in most Western culture organizations generally, which can be traced back to the downsizing initiatives of the late 1990s.

One area where middle management can help is to encourage personnel to take the time to become familiar with the new techniques and technology as an investment for their future. Another is by including KM-related objectives in personnel performance reviews, such as rewarding collaborative behavior. The KM team can support this by providing 'model' KM-related objectives.

In PSN, the 'line of sight' concept, in itself a cultural change over the last 10 years, has become embedded within the company personnel appraisal scheme. It means that every person in the organization can demonstrate how his or her activities align with the strategic aims of the organization, focusing on the categories of vision, strategy, objectives, and plans. Middle managers commonly receive some mandatory criteria, such as safety and integrity, whereby they have to show how the activities of each of their subordinates contribute to safety and integrity. This is a shared process, where the manager asks each member of his or her team to consider what they do or what more they could do to meet the mandatory criteria. In addition to this, the manager helps his or her reports to set targets which are clearly aligned with strategic aims, where necessary, making explicit the contribution of daily tasks to global corporate movement and direction. While the matrix organization style supports KM by providing some impetus for driving knowledge through the organization, line-of-sight appraisal attempts to emphasize cohesion of purpose, which is another aid to effectively managing knowledge, though not strictly speaking a KM function in itself.

Line-of-sight appraisal is used more directly to support KM because being very good at KM and knowledge transfer is an important part of PSN's strategy. The PSN vision is very much associated with the concept of a network operational mode; therefore, setting objectives and planning are in alignment with that vision. Further, in a matrix organization it is not as difficult to normalize that approach as might be the case in a more hierarchical organization, because of the line and function relationship. On the other hand, managers need to guard against a project assignment variant of what Byrne (2002) described as:

*An organization's 'obsessive' desire to accumulate and value knowledge can lead to individuals establishing knowledge protectorates, inefficient in use of time and investment...not aligned to the organizational goals.*

The following statements, collected by the KM team from individuals during the development of the PSN KM program, illustrate some of the barriers KM teams come across, and which middle managers encounter often more tacitly when individuals are asked to change the way they carry out their work. Readers may recognize people they know from these descriptions!

## "It's *My* Knowledge" (and therefore my power)!

This is a common finding and is frequently linked to 'expert power'. Often the only person who

values such knowledge is the owner of it, and he or she equates it to having some form of power within the organization that others do not. If, however, that knowledge is not known about by others, and subsequently shared and used, then it is sterile, useless to both the organization AND the individual possessing it; the organization, being unaware of it, can make little or no use of it, while the individual believes him or herself to be more valuable than he or she is. As Davenport (2005) points out:

*Knowledge is all the knowledge workers have—it's the tool of their trade, the means of their production. It's therefore natural that they would have difficulty relinquishing or sharing it in such a way that their own jobs might be threatened.*

Yet sharing knowledge is much more powerful for both individual and organization, because in the most straightforward respect, the organization can recognize and reward the individual, as well as seek and carry out work that is more highly rewarded. In a matrix organization, the potential for reward to the individual is increased, because the opportunity to communicate and collaborate is increased; in a globally networked organization, the potential positive impact of a particularly timely and or relevant act of knowledge sharing is multiplied further still.

## "I'm *Supposed* to Know" (and I don't want to reveal that I am no longer up to date).

This perception often exists when senior people have become less familiar with the day-to-day work they have left behind in their career path. However, in more recent times, as more and more people re-train or refresh their skill sets, the norm of only qualifying as a young person and never returning to the classroom or updating skills acquired earlier has changed. As a consequence, recognizing one's own limitations is becoming seen as the more mature approach. This can be complemented with much easier ways to search the organization for someone who "knows what I need to know." Within PSN there is an online database of staff expertise, experience, and areas of interest called SkillFinder, which is similar to Hewlett-Packard's Connex, Motorola's Compass, and BP Connect; the organization also has a profusion of Web-based communities of practice. Evidence has shown that more and more personnel are making use of these tools, rather than relying on just themselves and the people around them. The rapid expansion of tertiary education, increasingly via virtual campuses, promotes this behavioral change in the outside world, while back in the world of work, professional organizations are increasingly placing an obligation on members to demonstrate continuous professional development (CPD) to maintain their membership. In many organizations, such as PSN, CPD is an inherent part of the annual appraisal system.

## "Who *is* That Guy Anyway?"

This is a well-known problem, sometimes called the 'not invented here' syndrome, where people regard only those they know personally as credible and valid sources of help. In a matrix organization, it can be argued that this approach is less prevalent, because part of the role of the functional lead people is to negate any effects of a 'silo' mentality which can otherwise creep in. In any case, when people think about this syndrome, they realize that sooner or later, half the people they know will have retired or moved into different lines of work, and their pool of knowledge workers from whom they can draw experience becomes smaller. Thus it makes sense to develop, renew, and replace contacts and mutual trust across the entire organization. Several KM sources refer to this in terms of the social network within organization, and how knowledge brokering, where it takes place, can greatly assist with the development of reciprocal trust.

## "*I* Haven't the Time—I'm Much Too Busy."

The perception of knowledge sharing as an additional, rather than a fundamental task is widespread. In the case of engineers supporting oil and gas production, it is also a relatively recent misconception. In the engineering profession generally, as with many professional knowledge workers, there is a long history of sharing new techniques, with some European professional engineering learned societies going back over 150 years. Given the normal churn of employees in the oil and gas support industry, it is inevitable that some unstructured knowledge transfer will take place. In a matrix organization this is encouraged, but it is prudent to place such activity under the guardianship of functional heads to maintain or preferably raise standards so as to gain competitive edge. Behrend's (2006) description of knowledge transfer relationships between people lists "central connectors," "brokers," and "peripheral actors." He also points out, referring to the client/contractor company relations, "In today's co-operative-cum-competitive business there is a high chance that organizations experience deviation between the intended and actual knowledge flows." The matrix organization's role flexibility allows the middle manager, taking knowledge transfer relationships into account, to narrow the gap between intended and actual knowledge flows.

## "It's *Not 'Macho'* to Ask."

In any organization, it is likely that an observer will come across people who just will not change, frequently because they have reached a stage in their working life when they genuinely believe they know all there is to know about their work sphere and will not accept that they could do something better. They will be left behind, while the rest of the world moves on, similar to the last typesetter in London's Fleet Street lamented being the last, while everybody else moved over to computer-driven typesetting. In male-dominated industries this attitude might be seen as machismo, in other areas it might be viewed as an outmoded interpretation of professional pride. In either case, what the KM practitioner or middle manager views as a behavior or belief, the worker may see as an important part of his or her identity. The flatter structure of a matrix organization makes it easier to see the spread of new ways of working, but can equally work against the seeding of new initiatives. Similarly the mobile contractor workforce may be useful for transmitting industry trends, but this works equally for positive and less positive trends.

## STRATEGIC FACTORS RELATED TO MANAGING KNOWLEDGE WORKERS

Above we have looked at some of the issues around why workers are reluctant to share knowledge, and the militating effects of a matrix, multinational organization. The main issue faced by managers, is: Who owns the truth?

In a matrix organization individuals may find themselves suffering from organizational conflict between the line and function management command chains each seeking different reports. Dual reporting, where the same raw data is used but interpreted differently, is wasteful and presents the manager with the task of trying to determine which version of the story, from the different reporting lines, is most accurate. This can be further complicated when, for example, one reporting line seeks information for a customer, while the other seeks feed into management information on the entire company. In a perfect world, when everything is going well, these conflicts may be negligible, but from time to time things do not go so well. When that happens, there is a need to justify variances or at least explain them, and that can bring in interpretations of the facts, leading in turn to conflict or simply to managers being

distracted sorting out the facts. By the time the truth is determined, the opportunities for intervention may be reduced. In turn, the effort expended goes against the strategic intention of having a responsive, reliant, and flexible operation—one of the sought-after features of a matrix organization. A further cause of conflict comes from the friendly, but sometimes not at all friendly, rivalry between various project assignment teams.

This issue can be considerably mitigated if every part of the organization is working from the same raw data, and the algorithms associated with the relevant reporting are transparent, understood, and consistent. Clearly there is a greater likelihood of that happening if the business managers understand the processes thoroughly, and even more so if they collaborate towards conflict avoidance, rather than conflict resolution.

With a matrix organization, when KM collaborative techniques are used supportively, there is a superb opportunity for conflicts to be removed. How is this done? The starting point is for those involved, in this case with reporting, to collaborate on what each needs from the raw data. They must fully understand all of the business flows and collaborate on that regularly, because such flows alter over time and in accordance with individual clients. Further, if the organization is sufficiently enlightened to make use of an intermediary, sometimes called a knowledge broker, then the collaboration will be more fruitful and more rapid. However, the overall objective needs to be avoidance of a repetition of the conflict, and so the broker's role needs also to include assisting the wider organization to learn and not replicate a similar conflict on some other project assignment.

The role of the knowledge broker is particularly important in a matrix organization, because there is considerable scope for brokers to make contacts across the entire organization, compared with the up-across-down communications found in hierarchical organizations. Velasquez and Odem (2005) describe the benefits of knowledge brokers in another part of the oil and gas industry. Each community of practice in their organization (Halliburton) has a full-time knowledge broker, who is in an advantageous position to connect knowledge seekers with solutions, or those who have the know-how to help. Incidentally, the role of broker in Halliburton is seen as a career development role for an individual, because the broker gains as an individual by being able to network on a grand scale.

## COMMUNICATING BUSINESS DRIVERS FOR STRATEGIC KM

Build it—but they will not come. Whoever coined the phrase "one need only build a better mousetrap and the world will beat a path to your door" was wrong. There will always be a need to inform people of what you have to offer them, pointing out why it will benefit them. There are many examples of grand IT schemes developed and released only to be found to be underused, which all too often comes as a surprise to the developers. One of the main reasons for this is almost certainly a failure to communicate the business need for the new application, closely followed by specially designed and responsive user training.

In a multinational matrix company, there are particular difficulties with such launches. Apart from the more obvious ones of geography and time zones, the soft issues of less face-to-face contact can foster the perception in the eyes of the user that the new system is something being done *to* them, rather than *for* them. Within PSN, the strategy has been for the trainers to make the extra effort needed to make contact with personnel in other time zones, even if it means carrying out contact in the middle of the night for the trainers. This is one example of the "implied psychological contract" (Handy, 1981) between trainer and pupil—if the trainer will go the 'second mile', it obligates the trainee to pay greater attention to

the content. At the same time it builds up trust in areas where previous contact has been non-existent, sparse, or perhaps always timed to suit the HQ time zone.

## ADVERSE DEMOGRAPHICS

The demographic problem of people retiring (Economist, 2006b) and taking their know-how with them is acute in most Western cultures, and one source indicating the extent of this can be found in Paylow, Hickman, and Zappa (2006), based on the demographic profile of the age spread of the Society of Petroleum Engineers' membership. PSN's demographics are less onerous, because of a recent sustained and aggressive graduate recruitment policy. This however has altered the problem into one where the challenge is to put old heads on young shoulders. Again, the matrix organization, supported by a strong KM input, has a specific role here, because there is a chance to turn a threat into an opportunity. By training the new graduates in KM-centric ways of working, and combined with their tendency to be quicker to adopt new technology, the graduates have become knowledge transfer advocates as they travel about during their early professional development.

## FUTURE TRENDS

This section looks at the future for managing knowledge workers in the matrix-organized multinational organization. Davenport (2005) describes some of the future challenges, and one central point is the difficulty of determining what will be important for the future, as it is unlikely that everything held in the heads of those currently in the organization will be useful for the future. Keeping in mind this need to be able to work with the unknowable, the main issues outlined below are differentiating between information transfer and knowledge transfer, making knowledge transfer happen, managing this without conventional metrics, leading by example, dealing with changing demographics, and rewarding personnel.

It is a matter of observation that more and more information is available, particularly to those who work at an Internet PC. This seemingly unstoppable trend on the one hand offers more people more information, possibly to the point of overload; yet as Prusak (2006) points out, it still takes the same time to carry out some activities as it did 100 years ago. The distinction he makes of course is between information and knowledge, and many KM practitioners would recognize that as an issue. Business managers, particularly those in a matrix organization, need to recognize and respond to the new challenges associated with knowledge transfer, and be sure that they are clear on the difference between information transfer and knowledge transfer.

From the point of both information and knowledge transfer, a matrix organization has a head start in this respect because there are already two lines of linkage from an individual knowledge worker into the wider organization.

The seemingly relentless progress in technology to handle and distribute information is an issue for all future managers, but for KM managers the more pertinent issue is the possibility of some parts of the organization falling behind others in their ability to handle information. Sometimes this

*Figure 1. Bias towards 'push' technologies (Source: "Thinking for a living", by T.H. Davenport, U.S. 2003 survey of 439 respondents with access to all media listed*

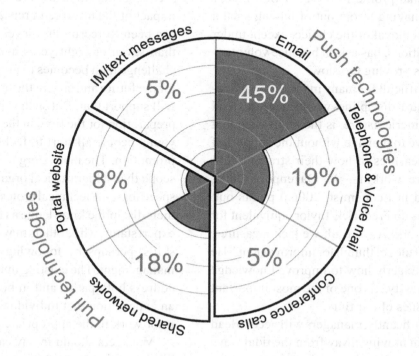

is described as a variation of the digital divide, although it is a matter of enablers and behaviors rather than access and technology. Prusak's (2006) example of learning surgery online is a superb illustration of the difference between transferring information, which can be done with medical texts, and transferring knowledge, which relies on personal interactions and relationships. The information needs of a globally expanding organization may be met in some part by more technologically advanced global databases, but their knowledge needs are dependent on the development and support of soft skills.

Managers will need to find ways to work with the relatively soft issues of knowledge transfer, gently but resolutely steering their organization onwards to meet the business strategic intent. They will need to strike a balance between direct instruction and 'soft paternalism' (Economist, 2006c) to achieve this. An example of this latter point can be seen in a recent shift in PSN away from merely encouraging all personnel to opt to have a personal profile in the PSN SkillFinder database, to having to opt out of having such a profile. The removal of the choice, except under certain conditions, has arisen because voluntary inclusion was proving too slow.

Equally difficult for many managers, particularly in the 'hard' disciplines where measures tend to be of a numeric nature, is the realization that they may have to manage without the support of numerical measures of how their strategic KM initiatives are working. As Davenport (2005, also reported in Economist, 2006a) points out: "Alas, there is no Frederick Taylor equivalent for knowledge work. As a result we lack measures, methods and rules of thumb for improvement." He concludes: "Exactly how to improve knowledge work productivity…is one of the most important economic issues of our time."

More significantly, managers will need to lead by example in moving away from the tidal wave of information overload, sometimes referred to as push technology (e-mail being an illustration of that), towards encouraging personnel to engage in collaboration, where they pull the information they need for their daily work, as a function of choices they have made as informed individuals. A recent survey, again from Davenport (2005), illustrates below the present imbalance of contact methods, suggesting more push than pull.

Managers will need to manage the difficult issues surrounding detrimental demographic shifts. In the context of the oil and gas support industry, singularly featured by its cyclical nature, the president of the Society of Petroleum Engineers (Sprunt, 2006) makes an important observation that "while companies watch their age distribution and complain about them, they hire in response to activity, and activity follows oil price." That is to say, attempting to counteract the effects of an aging industry by hiring lots of youngsters in response to cyclical trends, sets in motion more demographic waves, encountering the same career milestones at roughly the same time, as they work their way through an organization. While many sectors of the industry are ill-prepared for the impact of the upsurge in retrial, PSN's response has been to recruit at a level five times greater than seven or eight years ago. The managerial challenge then becomes to prepare these recruits for the future and ensure the organizational ethos will support that. But such support also includes preparation for the time in the future when these young people all start to feel they are due some promotion. The matrix organization offers more scope than a hierarchical organization in this respect, for some technical professionals will deepen their discipline knowledge as they move towards expert status, while others may instead widen their skills, perhaps by following careers in project management. The existing management needs to address both paths, and in both cases articulate an expectation that individuals will fully utilize prior work in the appropriate context.

Managers should in any case periodically review how they reward their personnel, but in the knowledge-intensive future, they are also likely to have to take into account some means of rewarding people for what they share collaboratively, rather than for what they know (Davenport & Volpel, 2001). Managers in a matrix organization will need to take particular care over how they operate such schemes. One trap they might fall into stems from the very structure of a matrix organization—that of inadvertently developing a two-class culture, where personnel assigned to a particular project assignment may share in project assignment-sponsored performance incentive schemes, possibly associated with KM, while their central support function colleagues are excluded. It is likely that the design of any knowledge sharing or collaborative working incentive scheme will need to take care to avoid such divisions, if it is to be effective across the entire organization.

## CONCLUSION

The example of PSN is indicative of many companies in that it is faced with a changing market, evolving relationships with both customers and employees, and a certainty that technology will continue to change much more rapidly than people change. Organizational structure has a large part to play in how organizations deal with these issues, but even a relatively progressive structure like the matrix model has a lot to gain from strategic knowledge management and considered management of knowledge workers. Initiatives like line-of-sight appraisal, which builds cohesion of purpose; dual reporting, which increases employee input into the organization; and the growth in continuing professional development—all are pro-KM, but they do not amount to managing knowledge workers. Traditional KM tools like skills databases, knowledge brokers, and communities of practice are as essential as ever, but in an unknowable future; perhaps the best plan is to ensure that the KM strategy is fully aligned with the business needs, organizational structure, corporate culture and goals, and manage knowledge workers as if

they are human beings, rather than anonymous workers. That is to say, allow for the fact that what some of your workers regard as knowledge may not be beneficial to your organization; make the most of the reality that your workers are valuable commodities in a globalized employment market and so are likely to follow their best interests and move around; and remember that most of them cannot read the minds of the KM team or anyone else. Matrix organizations increase the visibility of each part of the organization, so the manager of knowledge workers must make sure that the view is productive, for instance, by implementing more pull than push technology, and by brokering relationships. Multinational organizations have potential access to great diversity in knowledge content and style, but realizing that access again depends on the ability to build personal relationships and tools that support such relationships.

Observation of some of Europe's larger companies (e.g., BP, Nokia, and Philips) that operate globally suggests that even organizations of that size, often organized on variations of the matrix model, experience times of reorganization and invariably stress. Arguably, it is even more important during such times that the contribution from the KM program is perceived as both positive and part of the overall business strategy. This will be particularly true during times of global expansion or mergers. KM teams can serve their organizations well, if they can get the balance of threat and opportunity right, while at the same time addressing the human and international aspects of the organization.

## REFERENCES

Behrend, F.D. (2006). Collaborate today, compete tomorrow: techniques for KM in inter-organizational relationships. *KM Review, 8*(6), 24-27.

Browne, J. (1997). Unleashing the power of learning. *Harvard Business Review,* (September/October), 147-168.

Byrne, R. (2001). Employees: Capital or commodity? *The Learning Organisation, 8*(1), 44-50.

Davenport, T.H. (2005). *Thinking for a living* (p. 45). Boston: Harvard Business School Press.

Davenport, T.H., & Volpel, S.C. (2001). The rise of knowledge towards attention management. *Journal of Knowledge Management, 5*(3), 212-221.

DeLong, D.W. (2004). *Lost knowledge: Confronting the threat of an aging workforce* (ch. 11). New York, Oxford University Press.

Drucker, P. (2001). The next society: A survey of the near future. *The Economist,* (November 3), 1-22.

Economist. (2006a). Thinking for a living: Knowledge workers need a new kind of organization *The Economist,* (January 19 special report).

Economist. (2006b). The fertility bust: Very low birth rates in Europe may be here to stay. *The Economist,* (February 11), 46.

Economist. (2006c). The avuncular state: The new paternalism. *The Economist,* (April 8 special report), 75-77.

Handy, C. (1981). *Understanding organizations* (pp. 39-45). Harmondsworth, Middlesex: Penguin.

Paylow, K., Hickman, A., & Zappa, D. (2006, April 11-13). Identifying future leaders through knowledge management. *Proceedings of the 2006 Society of Petroleum Engineers Intelligent Energy Conference and Exhibition* (ref. SPE 99898), Amsterdam.

Prusak, L. (2006). The world is round. *Harvard Business Review,* (April), 18-20.

Sprunt, E.S. (2006). Where will the next generation come from? *Journal of Petroleum Technology,* (June), 12.

Thompson, A.M. (2004). *The impact of the mode of employment of personnel engaged in the oil & gas support industry on knowledge sharing.* Unpublished Masters Research Dissertation, Robert Gordon University Business School, Scotland.

Velasquez, G., & Odem, P. (2005, October 9-12). Harnessing the wisdom of crowds—case study. *Proceedings of the 2005 Society of Petroleum Engineers Annual Technical Conference* (ref. SPE 95292), Dallas, TX.

Yergin, D. (1991). *The prize: The epic quest for oil, money and power* (ch. 36). London: Simon & Schuster.

# Chapter XXI
# A Cross–National Comparison of Knowledge Management Practices in Israel, Singapore, the Netherlands, and the United States

**Ronald D. Camp II**
*University of Regina, Canada*

**Leo-Paul Dana**
*University of Canterbury, New Zealand*

**Len Korot**
*Institute for Global Management, USA*

**George Tovstiga**
*Arthur D. Little Ltd., Switzerland*

## ABSTRACT

*The purpose of this chapter is to explore organizational knowledge-based practices. A distinguishing feature of the successful post-Network Age enterprise is its intrinsic entrepreneurial character that manifests itself in key organizational knowledge practices relating to organizational culture, processes, content, and infrastructure. The chapter reports on the outcome of field research in which entrepreneurial firms in four geographic regions were analyzed with the help of a diagnostic research tool specifically developed for profiling organizational knowledge-based practices. The diagnostic tool was applied in firms located in the U.S.'s Silicon Valley, Singapore, The Netherlands, and Israel. Key practices that were found to be common to leading-edge firms in all regions included: a propensity for experimentation, collective knowledge sharing, and collective decision making. The chapter describes the research in terms of a cross-cultural comparison of the four regions, derives key determinants of competitiveness, and profiles regional characteristics that enhance innovation and entrepreneurship.*

## CONCEPTUAL BACKGROUND

In post-industrial, knowledge-based economies, knowledge management has become a critical success factor. This is especially true for entrepreneurial organizations pursuing innovation strategies. The pressures associated with this rapidly changing, increasingly competitive global niche make knowledge and knowledge management vital to these innovative, entrepreneurial organizations. A small but telling example of the importance of knowledge management in innovation would be the NEC factory in Honjo, Japan, which "has been replacing assembly-line robots with human workers, because human flexibility and intelligence makes them more efficient at dealing with change" (Davenport & Prusak, 1998, p. 15).

Knowledge is more than data or information. It is the integration of information, experience, context, ideas, intuition, skill and lessons learned, interpretation, and reflection that creates added value for a firm (Dana, Korot, & Tovstiga, 2005; Davenport & Prusak, 1998). Placing information in a context, questioning the underlying assumptions and deep logic that led to a piece of knowledge, and suggesting its next steps is an important aspect of knowledge management (Senge, Kleiner, Roberts, Ross, & Smith, 1994) and an important contributor to the innovative use of knowledge in new contexts, markets, or applications (English & Baker, 2006). Innovation, then, is the process by which knowledge is transformed into new or significantly modified products and/or services that establish the firm's competitive edge (Dana et al., 2005).

Nonaka and Takeuchi (1995) define two realms of knowledge: "tacit" and "explicit." Explicit knowledge is easily identifiable, easy to articulate, capture, and share. Explicit knowledge is the stuff of normal science (Kuhn, 1970), well-understood processes and outcomes amenable to step-by-step explanations in books, manuals, and reports. By contrast, tacit knowledge consists predominantly of intuition, feelings, perceptions, and beliefs,

often difficult to express and therefore difficult to capture and transfer. Of the two, tacit knowledge often carries the greater value in dynamic environments in that it is difficult to copy, creates competitive advantage, and is the essence of innovation processes, helping knowledge workers to combine their ability and experiences to rapidly respond to environmental changes with new ideas (Keskin, 2005; Nonaka & Takeuchi, 1995).

Managing knowledge and innovation in the post-Network Age is a multidimensional challenge. It requires understanding and application of four inextricably linked domains (see Figure 1): culture, content, process, and infrastructure (Dana et al., 2005). Each of these domains has a tacit as well as an explicit dimension. In Figure 1, the solid areas indicate an estimation of the explicit knowledge portion of each domain. The open areas estimate the relative proportion of the tacit knowledge for each of the four domains (Birchall & Tovstiga, 1998; Chait, 1998; Tovstiga & Korot, 2000).

*Figure 1. Organizational knowledge domains (Source: Dana, Korot, & Tovstiga, 2005)*

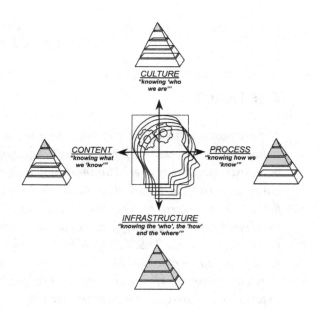

## Knowledge Culture or "Knowing Who We Are"

It is in this domain that the values, beliefs, and behavioral norms are played out. Knowing who we are involves a general transmission of rituals, organizational routines, and stories (Davenport, De Long, & Beers, 1998). It is the most elusive domain, but the prime determinant in the success of knowledge management. It is here where we find the cutting distinction between Industrial Age and Network Age enterprises.[1] With reference to Schein's (1992) three levels, culture ranges from the highly explicit, visible organizational structures and procedures ("artifacts") to those highly tacit, largely out-of-awareness, deeply imprinted core attitudes, beliefs, and assumptions that guide an individual's behavior.

## Knowledge Content or "Knowing What We Know"

This domain comprises the organization's stock of strategically relevant knowledge—both explicit and tacit. It exists in the organization in the form of:

- **Experiential Knowledge:** Highly tacit, derived from previous experience, and often difficult to articulate, it includes tricks of the trade and insights into innovative approaches (Davenport et al., 1998).
- **Formal Knowledge:** The foundation for practice, is refined, documented, and highly explicit in nature. It includes the body of accepted theory, illustrations of successful applications, and comparisons to observations and experiments (Kuhn, 1970).
- **Emerging Knowledge:** Both tacit and explicit, emerging at the interface of highly innovative and cross-disciplinary interactions in the firm such as new product development projects (Dana et al., 2005).

## Knowledge Infrastructure or "Knowing the *Who*, the *How*, and the *Where*"

This domain encompasses all functional elements in the firm that support and facilitate the management of knowledge. Information and communication technology is one element that helps knowledge workers to access knowledge located in any of three domains: the external knowledge domain, the structured internal knowledge domain, and the informal internal knowledge domain, where knowledge resides in the minds of people rather than in a structured, document-based form (Davenport et al., 1998). For many organizations, knowledge management stops with information and communication technology. But, knowledge infrastructure is much more—it includes the carriers of knowledge such as cross-functional, cross-national project teams. Fluid processes (Maira, 1998) and flexible teams taking advantage of knowledge maps that encourage professionals to share information on people, projects, organizations, and tools in their working field (van den Berg & Popescu, 2005) ensure the rapid transfer of knowledge across complex and shifting internal and external organizational boundaries. Microsoft, for example, has developed expert networks that make the knowledge competencies necessary for software development explicit and match development team needs with relevant experts (Davenport et al., 1998).

## Knowledge Process or "Knowing How We Know"

A firm's knowledge process domain incorporates how knowledge is created, converted, transferred, applied, and ultimately discarded. In order to be applied, knowledge needs to be actionable (Senge et al., 1994). Knowledge creation requires combining theory and core knowledge in practice (Deming, 1994). Applying and discarding knowledge involves implementing policies and practices that evaluate the effectiveness of knowledge and its application (Argyris, 1993), and challenging deep assumptions and the reasoning that led up to current knowledge (Senge et al., 1994). Knowledge conversion involves four processes identified by Nonaka and Takeuchi (1995): "socialization" (tacit to tacit), "internalization" (explicit to tacit), "externalization" (tacit to explicit), and "combination" (explicit to explicit).

Knowledge processes also involve roles played by knowledge workers in the firm (Tovstiga, 1999). In high-tech firms these processes need to cope with the fact that firms must often work hard to overcome an inherent predisposition of engineers not to seek help in solving problems (Davenport et al., 1998). This suggests that in high-tech firms, effective knowledge processes will be characterized as actively bringing knowledge workers together to create, convert, transfer, apply, and discard knowledge.

## Related Concepts and Research

In this chapter, we examine organizational practices in four different regions of the world. In the field of comparative management, much writing and research has been devoted to understanding the influence of national culture on organizational behavior and practices. Culture can be defined as a shared system of meanings and ideas regarding how to live (Namenwirth & Weber, 1987) that affect patterned ways of thinking, feeling, and reacting (Kroeber & Kluckholn, 1952), and the characteristic way of perceiving the man-made part of one's environment (Triandis, 1972).

Hofstede's (1980, 1991) landmark cross-national survey of IBM has catalyzed a number of studies in which cultural dimensions drawn from Hofstede and others have been used to examine a broad range of topics. For example, recent studies have used these cultural dimensions to look at national differences in achievement motivation (Sagie & Elizur, 2001), at the relationship

between national culture and capital structure (Chui, Lloyd, & Kwok, 2002), and at the role of culture in initial trust development (Camp, 2003). The prevailing conclusion drawn from cross-national studies like these is that national culture similarities override similarities in management thinking and processes.

In the case of knowledge management, culture might affect the process in several ways. For example, individuals from collectivist cultures might be expected to more readily share information and knowledge with work team members than would their more individualistic counterparts. Dawar, Parker, and Price (1996) found that power distance (PD), the extent to which people accept that power is distributed unequally within a society, and uncertainty avoidance (UA), the extent to which members of society feel the need to cope with anxiety by minimizing uncertainty through strict laws and rules for behavior, are inversely related to both a society's general openness to objective sources of new information and to general information-seeking activities. Hofstede (1980) found that cultures that score low in UA take an empirical approach to knowledge, while countries that score high on UA are more inclined to seek absolute "truth."

By contrast, other authors assert that at different times the salience of organizational culture, professional culture, or national culture may dominate (Karahanna, Evaristo, & Srite, 2005). Weisinger and Trauth (2002) assert that how a firm enacts a particular business practice is dependent upon the context in which the firm operates. Furthermore, for multinational IT companies "a culture of local practices is influenced by multiple contexts, including that of the home and host countries, the corporation, and the IT industry" (Weisinger & Trauth, 2002, p. 310). Korot (1989, 1997), in a study of 17 high-tech start-ups in Ireland, the UK, and France, pursued the hypothesis that there is a high-technology subculture that transcends national culture boundaries. Likewise, Robert Locke and Katja Schöne assert that in the 1990s the Silicon Valley was a high-tech entrepreneurial center that drove thinking around the world about the correct ways to pursue high-technology entrepreneurialism (Batiz-Lazo, 2005). One such piece of received wisdom is that rapid knowledge transfer is a key to organizational success (English & Baker, 2006).

In the case of high-technology sectors, where workers may be characterized as interacting with multiple communities, behavior is likely to vary with the context (Weisinger & Salipante, 2000), and thus professional culture may be dominant as is seen with the emphasis on quality in engineering. Pursuing the concept of a high-technology subculture that is cross-national in nature, Tovstiga, Korot, and Dana (2000) compared eight knowledge-driven organizations in The Netherlands, 31 in Singapore, and 30 in the Silicon Valley, and concluded these firms demonstrated remarkably similar key practices and underlying cultural values. Likewise, Keskin found that the "relationships between tacit oriented [knowledge management] strategy, explicit oriented [knowledge management] strategy and firm performance…in Turkey…were similar with the empirical studies completed in developed and western countries" (2005, p. 174). Weisinger and Trauth (2002) found that the Irish IT industry was moving away from traditional Irish culture toward a culture characteristic of the IT industry, with an egalitarian approach to worker-manager interactions.

## NATIONAL/REGIONAL CULTURAL CONTEXT

*Wired* magazine rated 46 regions around the globe as high-technology centers. Each region was evaluated on each of four factors, with scores on each factor ranging from 1 (low) to 4 (high) (Hillner, 2000). The four factors are as follows:

1. The ability of area universities and research facilities to develop new technologies and to provide skilled knowledge professionals,
2. The presence of established companies and multinationals to provide expertise and economic stability,
3. The population's entrepreneurial drive to start new ventures, and
4. The availability of venture capital to ensure that ideas make it to market.

According to Wired, Singapore was rated 7, Israel 15, and the Silicon Valley 16. Using the same criteria, Dana et al. (2005) assigned The Netherlands a rating of 10. Summaries of the national/regional cultural context for each of the areas compared in this study are given in the next section.

### Silicon Valley

The Silicon Valley, an area 35 miles long and 10 miles wide, south of San Francisco, is the most concentrated source of technological innovation in the world. Despite the economic downturn precipitated by the bursting of the dot.com bubble, the Silicon Valley is in another cycle of innovation (Levy, 2002). Fuelled by an extraordinary fusion of technical talent, imagination, and capital, and unhampered by traditional Industrial Age management constraints, the more than 6,500 technology companies located in the Valley continue to set the pace for globally driven entrepreneurship (Dana et al., 2005). Factors surrounding knowledge management and innovation in the Silicon Valley include the following:

- A relatively egalitarian national culture (hofstede, 1980) that within the valley encourages questioning processes, assumptions, and so forth across organizational levels (Brown & Eisenhardt, 1997);

- An individualistic national culture that emphasizes individual competence and competitiveness (Hofstede, 1980);
- A regional culture that amply rewards innovation and risk-taking, and accepts failure as a natural consequence of experimentation (Brown & Eisenhardt, 1997);
- A global perspective in which product marketing and manufacturing knows no geographical boundaries (dana et al., 2005)—While the united states averages 3.3 Migrants per 1,000 population (gesource, 2006), 40% of the region's population were born outside the united states (joint venture, 2006);
- A multi-ethnic, young workforce driven by the opportunity to be on the frontier of innovation and by the possibility of creating personal wealth (Dana et al., 2005);
- A dense population, providing access to a deep, constantly refreshed pool of talent—in 2003 2.44 Million people lived in the silicon valley (joint venture, 2006);
- A critical mass of universities and research laboratories that provide r&d resources for technology transfer (Stanford, University of California, Xerox and Fuji Parcs, NASA Ames Research Center, Lawrence Livermore Laboratory)—40% of residents in the valley have at least a bachelor's degree (joint venture, 2006);
- A continuous transfer of knowledge, both tacit and explicit, within and between organizations in formal and informal forums, in coffee houses and restaurants, and through the constant movement of people from company to company—technology "geeks" continue to transfer knowledge, and figure out how to translate their ideas into fundable, commercial applications, and this continual exchange is enhanced by an advanced, broad, networked infrastructure (Dana et al., 2005); and

- Access to venture capital—the valley still remains the major global source of venture capital, with us$6 billion invested in 2001 (Dana et al., 2005).

## Israel

Israel, ranked third in the industrialized world (behind the United States and The Netherlands) in terms of university degrees per capita, rivals the Silicon Valley in technology innovation. This extraordinary base of knowledge professionals, coupled with high expenditures on research and development, has enabled Israel to transform itself into a technology-driven economy. High-tech products and services now account for three-quarters of Israeli exports (Dana et al., 2005).

Akin to the Silicon Valley, high-technology enterprise in Israel is represented by the presence of major companies such as IBM, Intel, Microsoft, Motorola, and AT&T, and by the generation of indigenous new technology ventures (Dana et al., 2005). Factors surrounding knowledge management and innovation in Israel include the following:

- A culture that is both more egalitarian (low power distance) and more collectivist than Americans' (Sanyal & Guvenli, 2004), supporting cooperative knowledge development and use;
- A culture high in uncertainty avoidance that leads to a preference for a regulated environment and an urge to work relatively hard (Black, 1999), but may also dampen the adoption of new ideas or behaviors (Dawar et al., 1996);
- An emphasis on higher education and technology innovation—Israel has 145 scientists and technicians per 10,000 workers, compared to 85 in the united states (Sanyal, & Guvenli, 2004), and Israel has 14 qualified engineers per 1,000 workers vs. 8 Per

1,000 for the U.S. And 7.5 Per 1,000 for the Netherlands (Dana et al., 2005);

- A critical mass for technological innovation, with more than 25% of the Israeli workforce employed in the technical professions (Sanyal, & Guvenli, 2004) and a concentration of technology parks and technology incubators (Dana et al., 2005);

- Low immigration—in recent years Israel has had 0 immigrants per 1,000 population (Gesource, 2006); and

- A country ranked third in the world in entrepreneurial activity by the global entrepreneurship monitor, attracting investors and multinationals (Dana et al., 2005).

## Singapore

Only 646 square kilometers in area, Singapore is home to almost 100,000 entrepreneurs, the majority of this being small family enterprises. Early entrepreneurs in Singapore were middlemen in the international trade of spices between Indonesia and Europe. In 1869, the inauguration of the Suez Canal made Singapore an important node along the route from England to Australia; this made Singapore a distribution hub for international trade. The British promoted commerce and this attracted entrepreneurs to Singapore.

Singapore became an independent republic in 1965. Until 1985, it relied on foreign multinationals to industrialize the economy. Then, a recession prompted the state to focus efforts on promoting entrepreneurship. In 1995, the Singapore Productivity and Standards Board was created. It undertook to promote entrepreneurship, and to help enterprises expand (Dana et al., 2005).

In the last 20 years, the Singaporean government has invested heavily in moving into a technology-centered future with the goal of establishing Singapore as Southeast Asia's financial and high-tech hub (Wikipedia, 2006). Every other home has a personal computer, taxis are rigged

with GPS systems, and Singapore ONE is the world's only nationwide high-speed broadband network (Dana et al., 2005). Factors surrounding knowledge management and innovation in Singapore include the following:

- A culture characterized by uncertainty avoidance, where people prefer a regulated environment (McNamara, 2004);

- A culture where both Chinese and Malay influence individuals to accept subtle social stratification and defer to authority (McNamara, 2004), with an emphasis on loyalty and hierarchy (Noordhoff, Pauwels, & Odekerken-Schroder, 2004);

- An Asian tiger where Confucian dynamism and collectivism have been credited with underpinning Singapore's "economic miracle" (McNamara, 2004);

- A diverse, Eastern population where there are 10.3 migrants per 1,000 population (GEsource, 2006)—ethnically, Singapore's population is 76.8% Chinese, 13.9% Malay, 7.9% Indian, and 1.4% other, and in addition, residents of the city-state speak several native languages: Mandarin 35%, English 23%, Malay 14.1%, Hokkien 11.4%, Cantonese 5.7%, Teochew 4.9%, Tamil 3.2%, other Chinese dialects 1.8%, and other 0.9% (CIA, 2006);

- Government policies support innovation and technology development—Singapore's education policy has focused on developing skilled workers (Wikipedia, 2006), and at the tertiary level, Singapore has three universities, five polytechnics, and the Institute of Technical Education, all supporting the development of technology-based enterprises (Ministry of Education, 2006);

- Hardware, software, and IT industries generate more than US$7 billion in revenue (Dana et al., 2005), accounting for 48% of Singapore's total industrial output (Wikipedia, 2006); and

- In 1985, the Small Enterprise Bureau of Singapore was introduced to create schemes for entrepreneurs and to provide a one-stop service for small enterprises—at the time US$100 million was set aside for the promotion of Singaporean entrepreneurs, and currently, venture capital can come from the extended family, from Chinese clan associations, and from venture capital firms (Acs & Dana, 2001).

## The Netherlands

This small nation, approximately twice the size of the state of New Jersey with a population of 16 million, ranks second only to the United States in terms of university degrees per capita, providing a rich source of technical professionals and knowledge workers. The graduates of Dutch technical universities typically move into large enterprises or government agencies (Dana et al., 2005).

The Netherlands' prosperous and open economy, heavily dependent upon foreign trade, is noted for stable industrial relations, moderate unemployment and inflation, and an important role as a European transportation hub (CIA, 2006). The services sector, primarily trade, financial services, and government contributes 50% of the GDP; 25% of the GDP is represented by industrial activity—food processing, chemical, petroleum refining, electrical machinery, and microelectronics (Dana et al., 2005). High-technology activity is found primarily in large companies such as Philips with few indigenous high-technology entrepreneurial firms (Dana et al., 2005). The Netherlands is one of the leading European nations for attracting foreign direct investment (CIA, 2006). Factors surrounding knowledge management and innovation in The Netherlands include the following:

- A network-type culture characterized by high individualism, low power distance, and low uncertainty avoidance (Bigoness & Blakely, 1996) that is expected to lead to a generally high level of objective information seeking—this type of culture is also expected to emphasize equality, cooperation, mutual independence, and harmonization of interests between heterogeneous groups (Noordhoff et al., 2004) leading to the development and exchange of new knowledge;
- A long history of tolerance toward diversity, with 2.8 migrants per 1,000 population (GEsource, 2006);
- A country strong in universities and research facilities (Dana et al., 2005) with a history of excellence in tertiary science education preparing students for research and high-skill professions—scientific publications per capita are the sixth highest in the Organization for Economic Cooperation and Development (OECD, 2006);
- Some of the earliest technologies parks were founded in The Netherlands—these still function as hot beds for innovation and are traditionally linked with technical universities and research labs (Dana et al., 2005);
- High-technology activity is found primarily in large companies such as Philips with few indigenous high-technology entrepreneurial firms (Dana et al., 2005); and
- A business climate characterized as moderately strong in terms of the presence of established companies and multinationals, but weak in entrepreneurial drive and the availability of venture capital (Dana et al., 2005).

If regional infrastructure and culture are key drivers for knowledge management practices and high-technology innovation, then, based on the preceding regional differences, we hypothesize:

- **H1:** There will be significant differences between the four regions in knowledge management practices of high-tech firms.
- **H2:** The Knowledge Practices Survey results for the highest performing organizations will be found in the Silicon Valley and in Israel, with lower performing organizations found in The Netherlands and Singapore.

## METHODOLOGY

### Research Sample

The survey data for this study was collected from managers and technical professionals in knowledge-intensive organizations: 32 Silicon Valley enterprises, 26 Israeli enterprises, 30 Singaporean enterprises, and 8 Dutch enterprises. Surveys were distributed to each of the organizations by the researchers or by internal research assistants. The average return rate was 45%. The firms that were surveyed in each of the four regions were drawn from a broad spectrum of medium-high and high-tech industry sectors, including computer hardware and software, biotech, bio-medicine, and telecommunications. The study sample included both region-specific start-ups as well as established multinationals.

### Survey Instrument

Respondents completed the Knowledge Practices Survey (KPS) instrument developed by Tovstiga and Korot (1999). The instrument consists of 21 items which tap into the four major domains of knowledge management described previously: knowledge culture, knowledge content, knowledge infrastructure, and knowledge process. In the survey respondents are asked to give their perceptions of the current practices within their organizations and how important they consider a specific practice to be on the basis of a five-point Likert-type scale. A response of "1" indicates that

a respondent believes that a low level of activity is appropriate for a given practice, such as knowledge transfer, or that the respondent's perception is that his or her organization engages in a low level of activity for that practice. A response of "5" represents a high level of desired activity or perceived practice.

Knowledge content encompasses items 1-5 in Figures 2-7. These items include: where knowledge resides (item 1), sources of knowledge (item 2), knowledge dissemination (item 3), and knowledge flow (item 4). Knowledge culture encompasses items 6-11 in Figures 2-7. These items include learning focus (item 6), experimentation (item 7), participation (item 8), organizational structure (item 10), and openness and trust (item 11). Knowledge infrastructure encompasses items 12-17 in Figures 2-7. These items include: access to key knowledge or knowledge storage (item 13), sharing of knowledge (item 14), and degree of interpersonal networking (item 15). Knowledge process encompasses items 18-21 in Figures 2-7. These items include: strategy process (item 18), learning process (item 19), and gap management (item 20). In each of these figures, knowledge content is in the upper right quadrant, knowledge culture is in the lower right quadrant, knowledge infrastructure is in the lower left quadrant, and knowledge process is in the upper left quadrant.

The diagnostic tool used in this study, the Knowledge Practices Survey, was created to measure knowledge management practices in these four domains. In this survey, respondents indicate their perceptions of both the level at which each of the elements in each of these four domains should be performed and the current practices within their firms in regards to the elements of the four domains.

### Assessment of the KPS Instrument

Robertson (2001) and McCall (2001) assessed the internal consistency reliability of the instrument using Cronbach's alpha. A sample of 142 respondents representing three Silicon Valley firms and one firm in The People's Republic of China yielded coefficients ranging from 0.76 to 0.91, exceeding the generally accepted standard for reliability estimates of 0.70 (Nunally, 1978). This implies that the KPS subscales are sufficiently homogeneous and that the subscale items do measure the same construct satisfactorily.

The survey instrument was translated into and back translated from the native language for the four geographic locations. However, the majority of the companies chose the English language version of the survey. This may reflect the reality that for high-technology, knowledge-intensive companies around the globe, English and "technotalk" are rapidly becoming universal. Given that language guides cognition, and a lack of significant difference within countries between those who completed English and translated versions of the scales, the data also suggest a reasonably high level of construct equivalence across the samples.

## RESEARCH FINDINGS

Research findings in Figures 2 to 6 are taken from Dana et al. (2005).

*Figure 2. Knowledge management practice and significance in Silicon Valley (Source: Dana, Korot, & Tovstiga, 2005)*

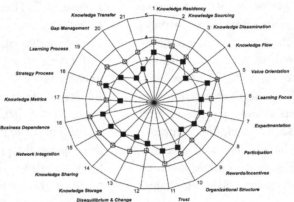

**Note:** KPS results – comparison of perceived "current" (■) practices vs. "importance" (□)

*Figure 3. Knowledge management practice and importance in Israel (Source: Dana, Korot, & Tovstiga, 2005)*

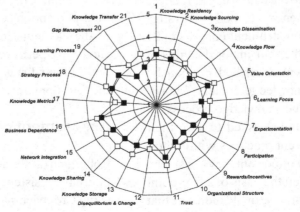

**Note:** KPS results – comparison of perceived "current" (■) practices vs. "importance" (□)

*Figure 4. Knowledge management practice and importance in Singapore (Source: Dana, Korot, & Tovstiga, 2005)*

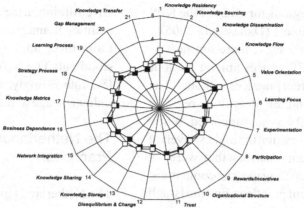

**Note:** KPS results – comparison of perceived "current" (■) practices vs. "importance" (□)

*Figure 5. Knowledge management practice and importance in The Netherlands (Source: Dana, Korot, & Tovstiga, 2005)*

**Note:** KPS results – comparison of perceived "current" (■) practices vs. "importance" (□)

*Figure 6. Overall comparison of knowledge management practice (Source: Dana, Korot, & Tovstiga, 2005)*

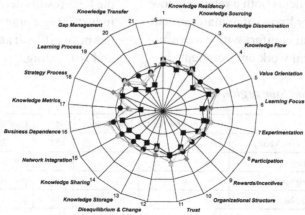

**Note:** KPS results – comparison of perceived "current" practices – Silicon Valley (◆), Israel (▲), Singapore (●), Netherlands (■)

## Analysis of the Findings

Averages of the four regions for all 21 of the KPS items are shown in Table 1 (Dana et al., 2005).

Contrary to Hypothesis 1, there are no statistically significant differences among the four regions in terms of current practices, although The Netherlands lags behind the other three regions. Likewise, Hypothesis 2 was not supported. While Silicon Valley firms did exhibit the highest levels of knowledge management practices, they were not significantly higher than Singaporean companies' knowledge management practices, and the Israeli companies' practices were the same as companies from Singapore. However, further data analysis showed significant gaps between current practices and importance assigned to these practices in the Silicon Valley and The Netherlands. While the gap between practice and importance in Israel was close to significant, no significant practice/importance gap was found in Singapore.

Our interpretation of these results is that knowledge workers in both Silicon Valley and Israel are highly motivated with a strong sense of their own capabilities, but with their organizations falling short of employee expectations. The major gaps both groups identify are centered on lack of *openness* and *access to knowledge,* limited *sharing of knowledge across both internal and external boundaries* and the lack of *opportunity for training and development.* The minimal gap between current practices and importance in Singapore probably reflects both a relatively low level of expectation for knowledge management practices and a cultural comfort with a more authoritarian, hierarchical work environment.

## Additional Analyses

Given the initial lack of support for our hypotheses, additional analyses of the data were conducted. From these analyses, results from two regions stood out: The Netherlands and the Silicon Valley. Interestingly, these findings correspond to industrial age and network age distinctions.

## The Netherlands and Industrial Age Practices

The Netherlands group shows the lowest level of current practices in virtually every area of managing knowledge and innovation. Compared to the other three regions, there is a very significant gap between current practices and the perceived importance of those practices. In follow-up discussions with respondents (Dana et al., 2005), what emerged was a perception among employees that there is a major discrepancy between what top management preaches and what is actually practiced. In the employees' view, management espouses creating a much more open, collaborative, team-oriented corporate culture (consistent with network age concepts), but is unable to relinquish its traditional grasp on knowledge and decision-making power (consistent with industrial age practices). This discrepancy has been magnified as the Dutch government is withdrawing subsidies and demanding that organizations such as IT consulting groups stand on their own. As the KPS results demonstrate, this transition from industrial age practices to network age practices has been difficult and, for the employees, painful and frustrating.

*Table 1. Averages of the four regions*

|  | Current Practices | Importance | Gap | Gap Significance |
|---|---|---|---|---|
| Silicon Valley | 3.01 | 3.56 | 0.55 | p < .05 |
| Israel | 2.96 | 3.30 | 0.34 | p < .10 |
| Singapore | 2.96 | 3.14 | 0.18 | p > .10 |
| The Netherlands | 2.65 | 3.83 | 1.18 | p < .05 |

## Leading-Edge Companies and Network Age Practices

To get an even clearer picture of the knowledge management practices that drive innovation, we drew from our total research sample those companies that we characterize as "leading-edge." The firms in this sub-sample are all from Silicon Valley. To be included in this sub sample, the KPS average current practices score must be above 3.5 and the technology driving the firms must be regarded by the investment community as state of the art. For these leading-edge firms, the average scores in the four domains are:

1. Knowledge content = 3.7.
2. Knowledge culture = 3.6.
3. Knowledge infrastructure = 3.7.
4. Knowledge process = 3.2.

When comparing current practices to perceived importance, two intriguing reversals from the expected emerge—experimentation and de-pendence on external networking ("Knowledge Metrics" in Figure 7) were both felt to be less important than currently practiced. Follow-up interviews with members of these firms revealed a need to slow experimentation and give the organization an opportunity to digest and solidify new products and processes (Dana et al., 2005). In terms of external networking, there was a feeling of information overload accompanied by an expressed need for more internal focus. This finding is consistent with Allen, Tushman, and Lee's finding that "when product development engineers decrease their average level of external communication but at the same time allow a few of their members to maintain or increase their external communication, their performance is enhanced" (1979, p. 702). For most technologists, technological problems are defined in organization-specific terms. It therefore takes a significant amount of time to understand the way outsiders' perspectives differ from those of their own organizational colleagues and to translate between their own system and outside systems (Allen et

*Figure 7. Knowledge management practice and importance in leading-edge firms (Dana et al., 2005)*

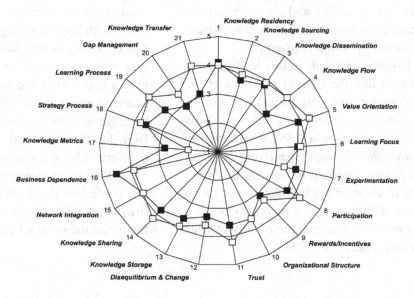

**Note:** KPS results – comparison of perceived "current" (■) practices vs. "importance" (□)

al., 1979). From this analysis they concluded that to maximize performance, firms engaged in developing sophisticated technology need informal processes to deal with this issue of translation time, such as utilizing gatekeepers with an unusually high ability to quickly translate external information and knowledge. In the current context, the felt need for more internal focus may indicate the realization that to capitalize on the knowledge gained from external networking requires taking more time to translate that knowledge into their own system.

The four areas where current practice falls significantly short of perceived importance are *flow of knowledge throughout the organization, openness and trust, learning process,* and *tacit knowledge transfer.* In interviews, members of these firms related these gaps to their intense sense of urgency—to a concern about staying ahead of fierce competition. Under this stress, management sometimes fails to communicate key information, generating barriers to information flow and some lack of trust. This constant pressure to create and get new products to market leaves little time for members of the organization to get together informally, thereby reducing the opportunity to generate trust within a high-tech team (Edmondson, 1999), and also prevents the organization from investing time and resources in professional development programs.

What is strikingly clear in this leading-edge KPS profile is that the current practices of the firms demonstrate an extraordinary commitment to *constant experimentation, open and collective sharing of knowledge, dissemination of that knowledge through formal and informal networks, flexible strategy, loose organizational structures, dedication to customer needs,* and *a team-centered, participative management culture.* This profile is the epitome of network age organizations (Dana et al., 2005).

## CONCLUSION

What this study partially demonstrates is that professional culture, regional culture, and infrastructure affect knowledge management in innovative, high-technology, knowledge-driven organizations. For some regions there appears to be a symbiosis between regional culture and infrastructure and competitive knowledge management practices. The Silicon Valley and Singapore appear to most clearly demonstrate that symbiosis. Both the *Wired* ranking and the results from the KPS leading-edge analysis coincide, illustrating the powerful interdependency between knowledge management and innovation practices within organizations and a region's infrastructure. In spite of this there appears to be a tension between practice as shaped by regional culture and its importance as an element of professional culture. It is also worth noting that as all of the "leading-edge" companies reside in the Silicon Valley, the benchmark for the professional IT/high-tech culture followed by companies worldwide also resides in the Silicon Valley. For these leading-edge companies, professional and regional culture may be more aligned than are the professional and regional cultures for firms located in other regions.

Although conforming to the practices of its Silicon Valley competitors, Singapore also demonstrates a symbiosis between regional cultural values and norms and knowledge management practices and priorities. While actual knowledge management practice is not significantly different from the other three regions, there appears to be a comfort with the status quo and little appetite for risk-taking and experimentation. This may suggest that professional culture drives behavior until a firm is competitive within an industry, but beyond that point the national culture reasserts itself.

We had expected the implementation of knowledge processes in Israel to be somewhere between the Silicon Valley and Singapore. However, the Israeli results show that, though this country is culturally different from the Silicon Valley (more collectivist and egalitarian with a higher discomfort with uncertainty), it is very akin in terms of infrastructure and the drive for high-technology innovation. This may suggest that the Israeli's competitive nature drives them to be as competitive as their best rivals, and thus professional culture completely dominates regional culture in the Israeli high-tech sector.

On the other hand this may be a function of cultural dimensions not considered at the outset of this project, such as universalism, a desire to consistently apply what is found to be the best universal way to behave (Trompenaars & Hampden-Turner, 1998). Cosmopolitan members of Israeli society, such as knowledge workers (Florida & Gates, 2002), have worked hard to preserve universalist world views in this region (Hirschl, 2004). At the same time, a dominant element of the Israeli identity includes modernization (Frenkel, 2005). It may be that the levels of knowledge management adopted in Israeli high-tech firms are a function of applying these cultural values across high-tech sectors to search for and implement universal best practices found within the sector, even if some of these practices seem inconsistent with other Israeli cultural values.

The Netherlands has an unexpectedly high gap between knowledge management importance and practice. This gap exists in spite of an espoused commitment by organizations and government to encourage the development of more open, innovative, self-reliant technology/knowledge-driven organizations. However, this follows a long period in which European investment in IT development has lagged the United States and in which labor rigidities have hindered adapting to new market realities (Economist, 2000). In this case both the gap and the general frustration may be primarily a function of infrastructure issues.

Our results appear to show the importance of professional culture and both regional culture and infrastructure in knowledge management practice. We believe that the area we have chosen for this study—the bond between regional culture and infrastructure, and the creation of highly innovative organizations within the region—is valuable in that it can illuminate the key regional and organizational factors essential to entrepreneurial development.

Knowledge management is critical for high-tech innovation. Employees in the most successful high-tech firms feel that time pressures lead to knowledge management practices that hurt performance. This suggests that companies in these industries need to employ knowledge management practices that address culture and infrastructure issues that affect the time required to assimilate relevant external knowledge. Some of these practice issues are highlighted here:

- **Knowledge Content:** While tacit knowledge may offer greater competitive advantage, time-based pressures that reduce informal interpersonal interactions may be reducing the ability of high-tech workers to effectively transfer this information within the organization. Experiential and emerging knowledge are the types most likely affected by time pressures. Therefore managers of knowledge workers need to allow them time to effectively exchange these types of information.

- **Knowledge Culture:** For knowledge management practices, effects of national culture appear to have less effect on high-tech firms than do professional culture. If anything, national culture moderates professional culture in high-tech firms. This finding supports past research that has concluded the importance of utilizing key elements of a professional culture for high-tech innovation.

- **Knowledge Infrastructure and Processes:** High-tech organizations need to take more time for knowledge management. They may also need to rethink the processes used to access and incorporate external knowledge. High-tech organizations need to further develop structures to quickly assess time-sensitive external knowledge and integrate it into internal knowledge. Given the belief of workers in the most effective organizations that less organizational time should be spent dealing with external knowledge, perhaps high-tech firms should look at identifying appropriate employees as gatekeepers. Future research needs to investigate optimal processes for accessing and integrating external information.

## LIMITATIONS AND FUTURE RESEARCH

Before concluding, it is worth discussing some of the limitations and implications for future research. First, this chapter shares a limitation common to the research into knowledge management. Knowledge management refers to a broad range of practices used by organizations to identify, create, represent, and disseminate knowledge, and encourage awareness and learning. Furthermore, the field of knowledge management is a continually evolving discipline that includes disparate streams of theory development and research about issues such as intellectual capital, organizational learning, enabling organizational practices, and enabling technologies. This chapter has only addressed a small subset of issues within this domain.

Second, we must acknowledge limitations that are more specific to this project. This study looked at a limited set of regional cultures. A larger set should be studied in the future. Likewise, the current study only looked at high-tech firms operating in volatile economic/technological environments. Future studies should look at knowledge man-

agement practices and priorities across multiple industries, facing a variety of environmental factors such as capacity, complexity, and volatility, and in a greater variety of countries.

Methodologically, this project relied on self-reports of respondents regarding their own sense of the relative importance of each of the items in the KPS and of actual practice within their own organizations. Future research should expand on this project through the addition of alternative methods, such as in situ observations of extant project teams, analysis of project records, and so forth. In addition, findings from such observations should be linked to project outcomes.

A final limitation addressed here pertains to the time-bound nature of this study. Given that knowledge management is a process that occurs through time, it would be appropriate to undertake a longitudinal study that captures more of the time-related issues uncovered in this study.

## REFERENCES

Acs, Z., & Dana, L.P. (2001). Contrasting two models of wealth redistribution. *Small Business Economics, 16*(2), 63-74.

Allen, T.J., Tushman, M.L., & Lee, D.M.S. (1979). Technology transfer as a function of position in the spectrum from research through development to technical services. *Academy of Management Journal, 22*(4), 694-708.

Argyris, C. (1993). *Knowledge for action.* San Francisco: Jossey-Bass.

Batiz-Lazo, B. (2005). Review of the book *The entrepreneurial shift: Americanization in European high-technology management education. Management Decision, 43*(3), 464-465.

Bigoness, W.J., & Blakely, G.L. (1996). A cross-national study of managerial values. *Journal of International Business Studies, 27*(4), 739-748.

Birchall, D.W., & Tovstiga, G. (1998, November). Methodology for assessing the strategic impact of a firm's knowledge portfolio. *Proceedings of the 8th International Forum on Technology Management,* Grenoble, France.

Black, B. (1999). National culture and high commitment management. *Employee Relations, 21*(4), 389.

Brown, S.L., & Eisenhardt, K.M. (1997). The art of continuous change: Linking complexity theory and time-paced evolution in relentlessly shifting organizations. *Administrative Science Quarterly, 42*(1), 1-34.

Camp, R.D. II. (2003). *Effects of national culture on trust development: A study of Canadian and Japanese business students.* Doctoral Dissertation, University of British Columbia, Canada (ProQuest Dissertations and Theses AAT NQ79204).

Chait, L. (1998). Creating a successful knowledge management system. *Prism,* (2nd Quarter), 83.

Chui, A.C.W., Lloyd, A.E., & Kwok, C.C.Y. (2002). The determination of capital structure: Is national culture a missing piece of the puzzle? *Journal of International Business Studies, 33*(1), 99-128.

CIA. (2006). *The world factbook.* Washington, DC: Central Intelligence Agency. Retrieved March 24, 2006, from *http://www.cia.gov/cia/publications/factbook/countrylisting.html*

Dana, L.-P., Korot, L., & Tovstiga, G. (2005). A cross-national comparison of knowledge management practices. *International Journal of Manpower, 26*(1), 10-22.

Davenport, T.H., De Long, D.W., & Beers, M.C. (1998). Successful knowledge management projects. *Sloan Management Review, 39*(2), 43-57.

Davenport, T.H., & Prusak, L. (1998). *Working knowledge: How organizations manage what they know.* Boston: Harvard Business School Press.

Dawar, N., Parker, P.M., & Price, L.J. (1996). A cross-cultural study of interpersonal information exchange. *Journal of International Business Studies, 27*(3), 497-516.

Deming, W.E. (1994). The need for change. *Journal for Quality and Participation, 17*(7), 30-31.

Economist. (2000). Economic indicators for The Netherlands. *The Economist, 144*(1).

Edmondson, A. (1999). Psychological safety and learning behavior in work teams. *Administrative Science Quarterly, 44*(2), 350-383.

English, M.J., & Baker, W.H. Jr. (2006). Rapid knowledge transfer: The key to success. *Quality Progress, 39*(2), 41-48.

Florida, R., & Gates, G. (2002). Technology and tolerance. *The Brookings Review, 20*(1), 32-35.

Frenkel, M. (2005). The politics of translation: How state-level political relations affect the cross-national travel of management ideas. *Organization, 12*(2), 275-301.

GEsource. (2006). Country comparison tool. *GEsource World Guide.* Retrieved March 24, 2006, from *http://www.gesource.ac.uk/worldguide/*

Goleman, D. (1995). *Emotional intelligence: Why it can matter more than IQ.* New York: Bantam Books.

Hillner, J. (2000). Venture capitals. *Wired,* (July).

Hirschl, R. (2004). Constitutional courts vs. religious fundamentalism: Three Middle Eastern tales. *Texas Law Review, 82*(7), 1819.

Hofstede, G. (1980), *Culture's consequences: International differences in work-related values.* Beverly Hills, CA: Sage.

Hofstede, G. (1991). *Cultures and organizations.* London: McGraw-Hill.

Joint Venture. (2006). *Silicon Valley index*. San Jose, CA: Joint Venture. Retrieved March 23, 2006, from *http://www.jointventure.org/publications/index/2005index/2005index/changingdemo.html*

Karahanna, E., Evaristo, J.R., & Srite, M. (2005). Levels of culture and individual behavior: An integrative perspective. *Journal of Global Information Management, 13*(2), 1-20.

Keskin, H. (2005). The relationships between explicit and tacit oriented KM strategy, and firm performance. *Journal of American Academy of Business,* (1), 169-175.

Korot, L. (1997). *A cross-cultural comparison of the organizational cultures of hi-tech start-up ventures.* Paper presented to the Executive MBA Group, Pepperdine University, USA.

Korot, L. (1989, January). Technoculture: Leading edge to European integration or an organizational anomaly? *Proceedings of the 17th Annual Conference of the Association for Business Simulation and Experiential Learning,* Honolulu, HI.

Kroeber, A.L., & Kluckholn, C. (1952). *Culture: A critical review of concepts and definitions.* New York: Vintage Books.

Kuhn, T.S. (1970). *The structure of scientific revolutions* (2nd ed., enlarged). Chicago: University of Chicago Press.

Levy, S. (2002). Welcome back to Silicon Valley: How the dot-com crash saved technology. *Newsweek,* (March), 25.

McCall, C.H. (2001, November). An empirical examination of the Likert scale: Some assumptions, development, and cautions. *Proceedings of the 80th Annual CERA Conference,* South Lake Tahoe, CA.

Maira, A.N. (1998). Connecting across boundaries: The fluid-network organization. *Prism,* (1st Quarter), 23.

McNamara, J.R. (2004). The crucial role of research in multicultural and cross-cultural communication. *Journal of Communication Management, 8*(3), 322-334.

Ministry of Education. (2006). *Ministry of Education Singapore.* Retrieved March 24, 2006, from *http://www.moe.gov.sg/*

Namenwirth, J.Z., & Weber, R.P. (1987). *Dynamics of culture.* Boston: Allen & Irwin.

Nonaka, I., & Takeuchi, H. (1995). *The knowledge creating company.* New York: Oxford University Press.

Noordhoff, C., Pauwels, P., & Odekerken-Schroder, G. (2004). The effect of customer card programs: A comparative study of Singapore and The Netherlands. *International Journal of Service Industry Management, 15*(3/4), 351-360.

Nunally, J.C. (1978). *Psychometric theory.* New York: McGraw-Hill.

OECD. (2005). Economic survey of The Netherlands 2005: Making better use of knowledge creation in innovation activities. *Economic Survey of the Netherlands 2005.* Paris: Organization for Economic Cooperation and Development. Retrieved March 27, 2006, from *http://www.oecd.org/document/14/0,2340,en_2649_201185_35822542_1_1_1_1,00.html*

Robertson, E.D. (2001). Personal communications.

Sagie, A., & Elizur, D. (2001). Entrepreneurship and culture as correlates of achievement motive: A multifaceted approach. *International Journal of Entrepreneurship and Innovation Management, 1*(1), 34-52.

Sanyal, R.N., & Guvenli, T. (2004). Perception of managerial characteristics and organizational performance: Comparative evidence from Israel, Slovenia, and the USA. *Cross Cultural Management, 11*(2), 35-57.

Schein, E.H. (1992). *Organizational culture and leadership* (2nd ed.). San Francisco: Jossey-Bass.

Senge, P., Kleiner, A., Roberts, C., Ross, R., & Smith, B. (1994). *The fifth discipline fieldbook: Strategies and tools for building a learning organization.* New York: Currency Doubleday.

Tovstiga, G. (1999). Profiling the knowledge worker in the knowledge-intensive organization: Emerging roles. *International Journal of Technology Management, 18*(5/6/7/8), 731-744.

Tovstiga, G., & Korot, L. (2000). Knowledge-driven organizational change: A framework. *International Journal of Entrepreneurship and Innovation Management, 1*(1), 22-23.

Tovstiga, G., & Korot, L. (1999). Profiling the twenty-first century knowledge enterprise. In R. Wright & H. Etamad (Eds.), *Research in global strategic management.* Greenwich, CT: JAI Press.

Tovstiga, G., Korot, L., & Dana, L.P. (2000, September). International entrepreneurship: A cross-cultural comparison of knowledge management practices. *Proceedings of the 2nd Annual McGill Conference on International Entrepreneurship: Researching New Frontiers,* Montreal, Canada.

Triandis, H.C. (1972). *The analysis of subjective culture.* New York: John Wiley & Sons.

Trompenaars, F., & Hampden-Turner, C. (1998). *Riding the waves of culture: Understanding diversity in global business.* Toronto: McGraw-Hill.

van den Berg, C., & Popescu, I. (2005). An experience in knowledge mapping. *Journal of Knowledge Management, 9*(2), 123-128.

Weisinger, J.Y., & Salipante, P.F. (2000). Cultural knowing as practicing: Extending our conceptions of culture. *Journal of Management Inquiry, 9*(4), 376-390.

Weisinger, J.Y., & Trauth, E.M. (2002). Situating culture in the global information sector. *Information Technology & People, 15*(4), 306-320.

Wikipedia. (2006). *Singapore.* Retrieved March 24, 2006, from *http://en.wikipedia.org/wiki/Singapore*

## ENDNOTE

[1]  Industrial Age organizations are characterized by hierarchically organized, systemic management controls. Creativity and imagination are the exclusive domain of a few people at the top of an enterprise. Good workers perform highly precise, structured, and repetitious tasks in a disciplined manner, but with little or no personal initiative. Conversely, Network Age organizations tend to be highly decentralized, relying on continuous innovation and employee involvement at all levels. In order to meet dynamic customer expectations, employees in these organizations must be able to adapt rapidly without waiting for external direction (Goleman, 1995)

# Chapter XXII
# Developing a Global CRM Strategy

**M. Shumanov**
*Monash University, Australia*

**M. Ewing**
*Monash University, Australia*

## ABSTRACT

*While the managerial rationale for adopting customer relationship management (CRM) has been fairly well articulated in the literature, research on strategy development is scant. Moreover, reports of "CRM failures" in the popular business press have done little to inspire confidence. To date, what little research has been conducted in the area of CRM strategy development has been confined to a single country (often the U.S.). Global CRM strategy development issues have yet to be specifically addressed, particularly which elements of CRM strategy should be centralised/decentralised. The present study examines the complexities of global CRM strategy using the case of a leading financial services company. Interviews are conducted in 20 countries. Global Head Office and external IT consultant perspectives are also considered. Our findings confirm that a hybrid approach has wide practical appeal and that subsidiary orientation towards centralisation/decentralisation is moderated by firm/market size and sophistication.*

## INTRODUCTION

Recent advances in information technology (IT) have enhanced the possibilities for collecting customer data and generating information to support marketing decision making. CRM has been heralded by some as being the key to delivering superior business performance by focusing organisational efforts towards becoming more customer-centric and responsive (Davenport, Har-

ris, & Kohli, 2001; Puschman & Rainer, 2001). However, others have cautioned that increasing information may actually *increase* the complexity of the decision-making process thereby adversely affecting decision-making performance (Van Bruggen, Smidts, & Wierenga, 2001).

Much of the extant academic literature on CRM has focused on identifying antecedents and consequences (e.g., Bull, 2003; Day & Van den Bulte 2002; Kotorov, 2003; Ryals & Knox,

2001). CRM has been variously conceptualised as (1) a process (e.g., Day & Van den Bulte, 2002; Galbreath & Rogers, 1999; Srivastava, Shervani, & Fahey, 1998); (2) a strategy (e.g., Croteau & Li, 2003; Verhoef & Donkers, 2001); (3) a philosophy (e.g., Fairhurst, 2001; Reichheld, 1996); (4) a capability (e.g., Peppers, Rogers, & Dorf, 1999) and (5) a technology (e.g., Shoemaker, 2001). Although there is clearly more to CRM than technology (Day & Van den Bulte, 2002; Reinartz, Krafft, & Hoyer, 2004), it is important to recognise that technology does play a central role in supporting the seamless integration of multiple customer touch points. IT also enables organisations to collect, store, develop, and disseminate knowledge throughout the organisation (Bose 2002; Crosby & Johnson, 2001). Customer knowledge is critical for successful customer relationship management (Crosby & Johnson, 2000; Davenport et al., 2001; Hirschowitz, 2001).

## CRM Defined

The importance of technology in enabling CRM is exemplified by the attempts at defining the concept. CRM has been defined as the alignment of business strategies and processes to create customer loyalty and ultimately corporate profitability enabled by technology (Rigby, Reichheld, & Schefter, 2002). In a similar vain, Ryals (2002) defines it as the lifetime management of customer relationships using IT. E-CRM is defined as the application of customer relationship management processes utlising IT and relies on technology such as relational databases, data warehouses, data mining, computer telephony integration, Internet, and multi-channel communication platforms in order to get closer to customers (Chen & Chen, 2004; Fjermestad & Romano, 2003). In many respects e-CRM is a tautology in that without "e," or technology, there would be no CRM. We therefore standardise on the term CRM throughout the paper.

As a business philosophy, CRM is inextricably linked to the marketing concept (Kotler, 1967) and market orientation, which stresses that firms must organise around, and be responsive to, the needs of customers (Kohli & Jaworski, 1990; Narver & Slater, 1990). From a capability perspective, CRM needs to be able to gather intelligence about current and prospective customers (Campbell, 2003; Crosby & Johnson, 2000; Davenport et al., 2001; Zablah, Bellenger, & Johnston, 2004) and apply that intelligence to shape its subsequent customer interactions. Furthermore, CRM processes need to acknowledge that relationships develop over time, have distinct phases, and are dynamic (Dwyer, Schurr, & Oh, 1987). Adopting this view highlights that CRM processes are best thought of as longitudinal phenomena. The interesting feature for firms is that they should interact and manage relationships with customers differently at each stage (Srivastava et al., 1998). Essentially, CRM involves the systematic and proactive management of relationships from initiation to termination across all channels (Reinartz et al., 2004). Another aspect of the relationship continuum is that not all relationships provide equivalent value to the firm. CRM requires firms to allocate resources to customer segments based on the value of the customer segment to the firm (Zablah et al., 2004; Zeithaml, Rust, & Lemon, 2001).

## CRM Strategy

A high degree of CRM process implementation is characterised as where firms are able to adjust their customer interactions based on the life-cycle stages of their customers and their capacity to influence or shape the stages (i.e., extending relationships, Reinartz et al., 2004). Standardising CRM processes enables consistent execution to customers across all delivery channels. Successful CRM also requires organisational alignment (employee reward systems, organisational structure, training procedures) and investments in CRM technology. Interestingly, the level of technological sophistication of CRM technology makes no contribution to economic performance and supports the view that CRM is more than just software (Reinartz et al., 2004).

CRM can be conceptualised at three levels: (1) company wide, (2) functional, and (3) customer facing (Buttle, 2004). This study adopts the company-wide definition of CRM which views CRM as a core customer-centric business strategy focused on acquiring and retaining profitable customers (Buttle, 2004). This requires a customer-centric business culture, formal reward and recognition systems that promote employee behaviours that enhance customer satisfaction and the sharing of customer information and its conversion into useful knowledge.

Unfortunately, CRM's potential has, in many instances, failed to be realised. Successful implementation requires the adoption of a customer-centric business strategy and a redesign of functional activities, workflows, and processes (Galami, 2000; Nelson & Berg, 2000). Some organisations have begun focusing their business strategy around their customers and capturing, sharing, and applying customer knowledge to deliver superior service and customisation (Mitchell, 1998).

However, despite the rhetoric, empirical research on CRM strategy development is scarce. In particular, work on the vexing standardisation/localisation issue is lacking. In this increasingly globalised economy, it is surprising that researchers have overlooked cross-national differences and global CRM strategy issues. To address these gaps, the present study will seek to explore in depth the issues surrounding standardisation versus localisation of CRM strategy development. A case study of a leading financial services company is used to explore these issues. The paper reviews the localisation/centralisation literature, describes the study to be undertaken, and based on the findings draws a number of conclusions regarding global CRM strategy development and highlights areas worthy of future research.

## GLOBAL CRM STRATEGY

In an increasingly competitive and complex market environment, multi-national enterprises (MNE's) are under constant pressure to re-assess the degree of autonomy they grant to their local subsidiaries. While headquarters are likely to have more expertise on strategic matters, local subsidiaries are likely to have more information on operational issues and be more responsive to dynamics impacting their specific market. Within a specific MNE context, centralisation refers to where decision making is vested largely with the global parent company (Cray, 1984). By contrast, decentralised organisations are defined as those where each subsidiary has a high degree of autonomy in making decisions on processes and products relevant to the needs of the local market (Edwards, Ahmad, & Moss, 2002).

There is some empirical evidence to suggest that although subsidiaries of global parent organisations may be given some autonomy in making operating decisions, strategic decision making is invariably controlled by the parent organisation (Bowman, Farley, & Schmittlein, 2000), which can be manifested through IT (Roche, 1996). Moreover, IT provides an efficient and effective decision support system to transfer information from the local subsidiary into the parent company's reporting models, increasing the capacity of headquarter management to engage in local company decision making (Clemmons & Simon, 2001; McDonald, 1996). Using a case study approach, Ciborra and Failla (2000) found that IBM failed in its vision for global CRM because of their fixation for standardisation and centralisation and the use of IT to enforce behaviours. Furthermore, they concluded that this variation in CRM adoption at the country level and unique regulatory requirements made the concept of "global CRM" tenuous at best, although they acknowledge that CRM is a "powerful weapon for centralisation" (Ciborra & Failla, 2000, p. 122).

This desire for greater parent company control is a function of perceived risk. That is, the greater the perceived level of risk, the greater the desire for active decision making (Garnier, 1982). The types of decisions likely to require parent company decision making include capital expenditure; acquisitions and divestments; and funding. A criticism of centralised decision making is that it is expensive and that local subsidiaries are unable to react quickly to changes in local market dynamics (Harris, 1992). There is some empirical evidence to suggest that organisations with decentralised decision making performed better than those organisations characterised as having centralised decision making with respect to marketing (Ozsomer & Prussia, 2000). Moreover, highly centralised organisations make less contribution to their host country in terms of investment, knowledge transfer, and management expertise than their decentralised counterparts (Fina & Rugman, 1996).

We have adopted a typology developed by Barlett and Ghoshal (1989) to classify the predisposition of organisations for a globalised/localised orientation. They describe organisations as: global, international, multi-national, and transnational. A global organisation is characterised as driven by the need for global efficiency, while having structures that are more centralised in their strategic and operational decisions. An international organisation is characterised as transferring and adapting the parent company's knowledge or expertise to foreign subsidiaries. The parent retains influence and control, but to a lesser extent than a classic global structure. A multi-national organisation manages its subsidiaries as though they were components of a portfolio of multi-national entities with headquarters exercising low control and low coordination. Finally, a transnational organisation seeks a balance between global integration and local responsiveness. This type of organisation has structures considered to be both centralised and decentralised simultaneously. Transnational firms have higher degrees of coordination with

low control dispersed throughout the organisation. Using this typology, our focal firm can be characterised as a global organisation. That is, they employ structures that are more centralised in their strategic and operational decisions, and their products are homogenous throughout the world. Given a centralised structure, most of the decisions are made at headquarter level and imposed on subsidiaries.

## Agency Theory

We use agency theory (Ross, 1973) as the theoretical foundation for describing the relationship between headquarters and country subsidiaries. Agency theory refers to the basic agency structure of a principal and agent who are engaged in cooperative behaviour, but having differing goals and attitudes to risk (Ross, 1973). In our research, the principal is headquarters and the agent is the subsidiary organisation. Goal differences, risk tolerance differences, and information asymmetry can create problems in agency relations (Eisenhardt, 1985). The first general problem is differences in the goals of principal and agents. Agents may act in their own self-interest at the expense of the principal. Secondly, principals and agents may have different tolerances towards risk. In the context of CRM strategy development, the principal is likely to have a lower risk tolerance than the agent. The third problem, asymmetric information arises when one party has more information than the other, or when one party prefers to keep some information private.

There are two types of agent behaviour that could be detrimental to the principal. The first, adverse selection might refer to a subsidiary's misrepresentation of its ability to undertake/implement CRM. The second moral hazard refers to the fact that the agent may not act as diligently as anticipated in carrying out the will of the principal. However, agency theory proposes that better information management systems can reduce the agency problem and provide the principal with greater control and is consistent with our earlier discussion on global CRM strategy development. Control may take the form of behaviour-based or outcome-based strategies. Both rely on the principal's ability to evaluate the performance of the agent, either on a behaviour-by-behaviour basis or at the end of the project based on its outcome (Eisenhardt, 1985).

From the principal's perspective, adopting an outcome-based control strategy is likely to be difficult given that the principal would need to wait until the long-term outcomes became known. Consequently, a behaviour-based control strategy may be preferred by the principal in CRM strategy development. The degree of knowledge that the principal (headquarters) has about the agent (wholly owned subsidiary) in terms of market characteristics, customer profile, and processes, enables headquarters to more effectively monitor and control a subsidiary's behaviour (Kirsch, 1996). This is likely to mitigate the risk of subsidiaries acting in their own self-interest at the expense of the entire organisation. Agency theory (Ross, 1973) is therefore useful in addressing our research questions: what aspects of CRM strategy should be centralised/localised? and what are some of the complexities of cross-national CRM strategy development? Another fundamental concept is the level of involvement between the principal and agent in implementation. For instance, if the agent is able to customise the CRM implementation to reflect their country's requirements, then the principal has less ability to control the behaviour of local country CRM managers compared to where the local subsidiary is required to implement a standardised CRM solution. However, the control dichotomy needs to be balanced to avoid implementation failure particularly where headquarters does not have an in-depth understanding of local market conditions. Furthermore, where a standardised implementation is imposed, it is important to consider the level of knowledge and dynamic learning mechanisms that will need to be created in the local subsidiary to address system failures.

We also examined the channel coordination literature (i.e., Frazier, 1999; Frazier & Rody, 1991; Hunt & Nevin. 1974), which describes the relationship between buyer and seller involving a distribution channel. However, given that this research seeks to examine the relationship between headquarters and its subsidiaries, agency theory offers a more robust theoretical foundation with respect to CRM strategy development. The channel coordination literature relates more to relationships characterised as involving a distribution channel, rather than describing the parent-subsidiary relationship.

## METHOD

### Data Collection

Understanding both substantive and methodological context permits the reader to put the research into context and thus derive deeper meaning from the findings (Johns, 2001). Data were derived using the case study method and utilising a multi-sample longitudinal research design (Yin, 1994). Case studies enable the development of deep insights into respondent beliefs and assist in theory development (Beverland, 2001). Bonoma (1985), Hirschman (1986), and Deshpande (1983) have all advocated for greater application of qualitative research methods in marketing. In order to avoid cueing subjects into a desired response, respondents were asked fairly general questions on the topic in order to elicit themes (Strauss & Corbin, 1992). Specifically, two "grand tour" questions (McCracken, 1988) were asked. The first related to issues surrounding local subsidiary decision-making empowerment in relation to CRM strategy. The second, on what CRM processes and systems should be centralisation versus decentralisation. Each participant was also sent a copy of the final transcript for comment. Any comments were noted and the results adjusted accordingly (Johnston, Leach, & Liu, 1999). The research questions were

*Table 1. First round sample characteristics*

| Subsidiary | Person Interviewed | Function |
|---|---|---|
| 1. | **Senior Consultant CRM Project** | Strategic |
| 2. | **Customer Relations Manager** | Strategic |
| 3. | **Marketing Manager** | Operational |
| 4. | **Leader CRM** | Strategic |
| 5. | **Customer Service Manager** | Strategic |
| 6. | **CRM Manager** | Operational |
| 7. | **Marketing Manager** | Operational |
| 8. | **CRM Director** | Strategic |
| 9. | **CRM Manager** | Operational |
| 10. | **CRM Manager** | Strategic |
| 11. | **Senior Consultant - XYZ Consulting** | Strategic |

*Table 2. Second round sample characteristics*

| Subsidiary | Person Interviewed | Function |
|---|---|---|
| 1. | **Marketing Manager** | Operational |
| 2. | **CRM Manager** | Operational |
| 3. | **Customer Relations Manager** | Strategic |
| 4. | **CRM Manager** | Operational |
| 5. | **Marketing Manager** | Operational |
| 6. | **Leader CRM** | Strategic |
| 7. | **CRM & Corporate Sales Manager** | Operational |
| 8. | **Manager CRM & Internet Marketing** | Operational |
| 9. | **Marketing Manager** | Operational |
| 10. | **Marketing Manager** | Operational |
| 11. | **Marketing Manager** | Operational |
| 12. | **CRM Director** | Strategic |
| 13. | **CRM Programs Manager** | Operational |
| 14. | **CRM Manager** | Operational |
| 15. | **Manager Prospecting & New Media** | Operational |

then e-mailed to sample 1 respondents with a statement thanking them for participating in the initial depth interviews and reiterating the purpose of the research. This was broadly described as seeking to gain an understanding of global CRM strategy development complexities with the aim of sharing the eventual findings across the whole group. In order to cross validate the results using a different group of respondents, we e-mailed the same two research questions to a second sample of respondents coupled with a statement describing the research. The objective was to assess the robustness of the initial sample findings with a separate sample of respondents (Deshpande, Farley, & Webster, 1993).

Two rounds of interviews were conducted with managers having a functional responsibility for CRM in their respective national subsidiary. Whether CRM respondents were responsible for CRM strategy or implementation was dependent on the level of the respondent within the organisation. Invariably, more senior respondents were responsible for strategy formulation. We had a mix of both strategic and operational CRM respondents (see Tables 1 and 2). The first sample consisted of CRM representatives from the following subsidiaries: Australia, Belgium, Germany, Italy, Netherlands, Spain, Switzerland, United Kingdom, and United States. To improve construct validity, interviews were also conducted with the internal strategy department at headquarters and with external consultants assisting in CRM strategy formulation. This provided a strategic level view of the vision for CRM from a Group/HQ perspective (Deshpande, 1983; Johnston et al., 1999). Details of first round respondents are presented in Table 1.

The first round of interviews was conducted by one of the authors over the telephone (Holbrook, Green, & Krosnick, 2003) and recorded/transcribed in order to assist in thematic analysis. The transcribed data was then edited and any additional data was integrated to develop a case summary. Details of second-round respondents

are presented in Table 2. Australia, Germany, Netherlands, Spain, and Switzerland were represented in both samples, although in this case an alternative respondent, having responsibility for CRM, was interviewed.

## FINDINGS

In reporting our results, we quote actual statements made by respondents in order to improve the validity of the findings for the reader (Eisenhardt, 1989; Yin, 1994).

## Perceived Complexities of Global CRM Strategy Development

The general consensus of both samples suggested that they are limited in their ability to make strategic decisions. *"[Subsidiaries] get a very strong framework from headquarters."* Most respondents also anticipate that strategic decision-making is unlikely to become more devolved. Some respondents noted a distinction between strategic decision-making in terms of IT and operations: *"I must say that the CRM project on the IT side is very much directed by the project group at head office. On the other hand, nobody asks us if CRM processes are in place and actively managed"* and *"CRM initiatives particularly system related are being governed on a global or regional basis [and the subsidiary] probably does not have an overriding influence on it."* An exception to this is country X, where the different stage of CRM development in that market has meant that *"[head office] kind of gave us the ability to operate outside of their purview."*

Respondents in both samples noted cultural differences and maturity of markets as contributing to the complexity of global CRM strategy development. For instance, *"local cultural differences make it difficult to offer standardised CRM tools."* Another respondent noted *"no one central system can accommodate all of the* differences that exist." And another: "*what works great in one country may not work at all in another country.*" Another perceived complexity was the capacity to meet all the different subsidiary requirements. "*The number of countries and the differences in market size and maturity creates another layer of complexity.*" And "*you have to deal with a lot of market specifics—market-specific business processes and market-specific system adaptations.*" Process concerns were also articulated, "*...existing local IT systems and related business processes cause issues when trying to overlay a global IT system.*" Interestingly, hardly any respondents considered software-related issues as potential barriers to CRM strategy development, which may reflect their view that CRM is more than just software. However, one respondent noted, "*fractured information flows between head office and local subsidiaries results in misinformation regarding CRM developments.*" And another respondent (in the second sample) raised the issue of cross functionality: "*CRM can't be implemented easily because it is cross functional.*" Some respondents also noted that "*country-specific legislation also needs to be considered.*"

## Standardised Across Markets or Tailored to Local Market Requirements?

On the question of whether CRM processes and systems should be centralised, or decentralised, a "hybrid" approach has practical merit. That is, embracing a centralised CRM IT system which can then be configured by subsidiaries to meet local market requirements. The perceived benefits of this approach are that it is cost and resource efficient. Nearly all agreed that there were considerable advantages to centralisation. For example, "*If you just let every country do what they wanted, it would be chaos. Everybody would come up with unique solutions, there would be double investments and duplication of effort,*

*there would no cooperation and I think the organization would suffer.*" And "*centralise as much as possible and localise as little as possible.*" A small market perspective was that "*we feel that some sort of centralisation in one country can very much benefit smaller countries due to budget constraints impeding their ability to develop their own systems.*" The general consensus was that decentralisation would be inefficient in terms of resource utilisation, costs, and duplication of effort. On the other hand, they did recognise that complete centralisation would lead to a situation of inflexibility. "*If you do everything on a central basis, one size fits all, then you are going to end up with inertia of the organization—think global act local.*" There was some dissension on whether centralisation was more cost efficient than localisation. "*From a high level perspective [centralisation] might be cheaper, but down the road, one country will have a couple of hundred requirements, another country will also have another couple of hundred and the question is whether it is going to be worth it. The money that you and everyone is going to spend for changes will be [the] same as having a local solution.*" The answer seems to be somewhere in the middle. "*In my opinion, I think it makes sense to develop them centrally and to adapt to local requirements. Each market is different and has different cultures, has different issues and so to develop things centrally makes sense because of development costs. But each market has to adapt them locally.*" And, "*You may need to develop some tools that are able to have some consistency at its core, but which can then be configured to meet local needs, because its in the local market where you have got to survive.*" And "*a centralised CRM tool is cost efficient and easy to update if you want to further develop the tool. If it is decentralised, then each country may spend a lot of financial resources doing that. The negative thing is that it doesn't take into account the local needs of the market.*"

Another perspective viewed lack of market-specific information as a potential barrier to centralisation. *"My perspective is that markets know more what they need than the central department. I think the processes are not that different from country to country, but the key integration points are different for each market and are not well understood by headquarters. I think that when you try and bring a group approach to a specific problem its not going to work."* Another respondent noted the possibility for resistance, *"...what I can see, there is high resistance [to a centralised tool] from the markets because they want a lot of customisation which is not allowed and that causes a lot of problems."* Similarly, *"I think that CRM processes should be decentralised because of the respective market idiosyncrasies and it is important to set common objectives and standards and pursue them. In my opinion, centralisation is much more expensive [compared to localisation] because of the customisation costs."* One respondent noted that performance measurement also needs to be standardised in order to enable comparability. *"Success measurement KPIs need to be defined so that the performance of one market can be objectively compared against another market."*

One respondent suggested a set of guiding principles or framework could be utilised to assist in providing some direction, but ultimately subsidiaries would be responsible for decision making given their more intimate understanding of the market. *"I think there needs to be a strategic framework which is applicable for all subsidiaries all over the world and you can act within this framework to bring in your own experience, bring in your market-specific issues."* Another respondent noted that an alternative to the centralisation-decentralisation dichotomy is clustering markets based on similar characteristics and then applying a common approach. *"It might be a European solution for say all European countries, 'an Americas solution' for North and South America and so forth."*

## Global Strategy

Local subsidiaries are often not empowered to make strategic decisions with respect to CRM. This may be a function of the perceived risk (Garnier, 1982). This finding is consistent with Bowman et al. (2000) who found that strategic decision making was controlled by the parent company. There also appears to be some dissension on whether the organisation has achieved a global strategy for CRM. *"Is there one [a global strategy]? To my mind we have only managed to derive some more or less binding rules for the subsidiaries, which tell them the 'do's', and 'don'ts' in treating their customers. A concise strategy focused on retention and acquisition to my mind does not yet exist."* In summing up, one respondent noted that, *"CRM is really about the business first and the business processes. The system should be designed to support this, not the other way round."* A number of large market respondents noted that there should be a global platform for knowledge management. *"We need to capture the key learnings from each market and leverage off these for the next country."* And *"lets stay connected and learn from each other."*

## Cross-National Differences

In comparing differences between countries a clear pattern begins to emerge: two countries are demonstrably more advanced in terms of CRM implementation than the other 18, who are largely still in a passive "data collection" phase, not yet using customer data in their marketing strategies to anywhere near its full potential. The two advanced countries, by contrast, are well ahead of the curve—using advanced customer analytics for segmentation purposes to proactively manage customer relationships. The other interesting dynamic within this context is the fact that Head Office has largely allowed the advanced country "to get on with it" and granted them a high degree of autonomy. Among the other 18, there is another fairly obvious partition, between more advanced and less advanced. We say obvious because the split is fairly predictable and is driven by country size, stage of economic/social development, and market size. Basically, mature versus developing economies.

There also appears to be a feeling that the group strategy favours large markets and the needs of smaller subsidiaries in emerging markets are subordinated. *"There needs to be more attention paid to the smaller [market] solution and strengthening central support."* And *"from the point of view of small markets, you might think that decisions are sometimes based on the big market."*

## DISCUSSION

Most respondents recognised the many advantages of standardisation. They could see the merit in having a universal strategic framework to guide the CRM process. They acknowledged that IT systems should be standardised to avoid resource duplication and any possible re-inventing of the wheel. This was particularly evident in smaller and/or less developed markets. However, a number of problems with standardisation were also acknowledged. These included inability to factor into account cultural differences/idiosyncrasies, country-specific legislation, and complexities arising from the inherently cross-functional nature of CRM. Thus, somewhat predictably, calls for a hybrid approach can de deduced from the data. However, based on the strength of arguments and also drawing on the literature, we conclude that local adaptation needs to be well justified and should be viewed more as the exception rather than the norm.

## Theory-Building and Managerial Implications

This paper makes at least two significant contributions to the extant CRM literature. First, given the lack of empirical research in the area, it extends on earlier work on the complexities of global CRM strategy development (Ciborra & Failla, 2000; Massey, Montoya-Weiss, et al. 2001). Findings confirm that there is a lack of clarity regarding what the important antecedents are to global CRM success. The more mature markets in this study seem to have a better developed understanding of the importance of these dimensions and invest resources in enhancing their competencies in these areas. Second, we have shed some light on the perennial standardisation/adaptation question and have provide a preliminary framework of what elements may be amenable to centralisation and which to localisation. For global CRM managers and strategists, the findings suggest that a centralised approach has merit. Indeed, the majority of CRM functionality could well be centrally located, with the more customer-centric elements driven at the subsidiary level. The benefit of this approach is that it improves control and coordination while reducing transaction costs (Clemmons & Simon, 2001).

## Limitations and Future Research

A number of limitations of this research are noted. First, the non-random selection of respondents introduced an element of judgement into the sampling process. Furthermore, for the majority of subsidiaries, a single informant may not accurately represent the entire view of the organisation. However, it was felt that the manager identified as responsible for CRM activities was the most qualified to respond to in-depth interview questions. Another limitation of this study is that it only involves a single organisation in a single industry and therefore the results may not be generalisable to other organisations or industries. The researchers attempted to mitigate the limitations of the sample by utilising two respondent samples (Deshpande et al., 1993). A problem also arises in attempting to find a suitable second informant in small subsidiaries, and some initial respondents may object to having a cross-validation process. Finally, stringent university "Ethics in Research Involving Humans" guidelines prevented us from identifying verbatim quotes with individual respondents because that would compromise respondent anonymity.

A number of directions for future research have emerged from this exploratory study. First, a study examining global CRM strategy development across industries would be useful to test the generalisability of these findings. In addition, further research is required to examine the relative importance of those global CRM factors we have identified and test whether there are some other factors which contribute to global CRM complexity, which have been overlooked in the current study. Also further work is required to quantify the cost-benefit of localisation versus centralisation. It is not clear whether the inflexibility that a centralised CRM tool mandates compensates for the anticipated cost benefits. It may be that the costs of local market customisation erode these cost benefits. An interesting stream for future research would be to attempt to develop a framework that provides organisations with some insights into the required sequencing of CRM activities consistent with stage of implementation in order to build a solid foundation for the development of further CRM capabilities. Finally, from a cross-cultural perspective, the applicability of a stage model to global CRM implementation is worth considering.

## REFERENCES

Barlett, C., & Ghoshal, S. (1989). *Managing across borders. The Transnational Solution.* Boston: Harvard Business School Press.

Beverland, M. (2001). Contextual influences and the adoption and practice of relationship selling in a business to business setting: An exploratory study. *Journal of Personal Selling & Sales Management, 21*(3), 207-215.

Bonoma, T. (1985). Case research in marketing: Opportunities, problems, and a process, *Journal of Marketing Research, 22,* 199-208.

Bose, R. (2002). Customer relationship management: Key components for IT success. *Industrial Management and Data Systems, 102*(½), 89-97.

Bowman, D., Farley, J., & Schmittlein, D. (2000). Cross national empirical generalisation in business services buying behaviour. *Journal of International Business Studies, 31*(4), 667.

Bull, C. (2003). Strategic issues in customer relationship management (CRM) implementation. *Business Process Management Journal, 9*(5), 592-602.

Buttle, F. (2004). *Customer relationship management.* Oxford, UK: Elsevier Butterworth-Heinemann.

Campbell, A. (2003). Creating customer knowledge competence: Managing customer relationship management programs strategically. *Industrial Marketing Management, 32*(5), 375.

Chen, Q., & Chen, H. (2004). Exploring the success factors of eCRM strategies in practice. *Database Marketing & Customer Strategy Management, 11*(4), 333-343.

Ciborra, C., & Failla, A. (2000). Infrastructure as a process: The case of CRM in IBM. In C. Ciborra (Ed.), *From control to drift: The dynamics of corporate information infrastructures* (pp. 105-124). Oxford University Press.

Clemmons, S., & Simon, S. (2001). Control and coordination in global ERP configuration. *Business Process Management Journal, 7*(3), 205-215.

Cray, D. (1984). Control and coordination in multinational corporations. *Journal of International Business Studies,15*(2) 85-98.

Crosby, L. and Johnson, S. (2001). Technology: friend or foe to customer relationships. *Marketing Management, 10* (4), 10-11.

Croteau, A. M., & Li, P. (2003). Critical success factors of CRM technological initiatives. *Canadian Journal of Administrative Sciences, 20*(1), 21-34.

Davenport, T. H., Harris, J. G., & Kohli. (2001). How do they know their customers so well? *Sloan Management Review, 42*(2), 63-73.

Day, G., & Van den Bulte, C. (2002). *Superiority in customer relationship management consequences for competitive advantage and performance.* Marketing Science Institute.

Deshpande, R. (1983). Paradigms lost: On theory and method in research in marketing. *Journal of Marketing, 47*(4), 101-111.

Deshpande, R., Farley, J., & Webster, F. (1993). Corporate culture, customer orientation and innovativeness. *Journal of Marketing, 57*(1), 23-38.

Dwyer, R., Schurr, P., & Oh, S. (1987). Developing buyer-seller relationships. *Journal of Marketing, 51*(2), 11-28.

Edwards, R., Ahmad, A., & Moss, S. (2002). Subsidiary autonomy: The case of multinational subsidiaries in Malaysia. *Journal of Internal Business Studies, 33*(1), 183.

Eisenhardt, K. (1985). Agency theory: An assessment and review. *Academy of Management Review, 14*(1), 57-74.

Eisenhardt, K. (1989). Building theories from case study research. *Academy of Management Review, 14*(4), 532-550.

Fairhurst, G. (2001). Values at work: Employee participation meets market pressure at mondragon. *Communication Theory, 11*(2), 242.

Fina, E., & Rugman, A. (1996). A test of internalization theory and internationalization theory: The Upjohn company. *Management International Review, 36*(3), 199-214.

Fjermestad, J., & Romano, N. (2003). Electronic customer relationship management: Revisiting the general principles of usability and resistance An integrative implementation framework. *Business Process Management Journal, 9*(5), 572-591.

Frazier, G. (1999). Organizing and managing channels of distribution. *Journal of the Academy of Marketing Science, 27*(2), 226-240.

Frazier, G., & Rody, R. (1991, January). The use of influence strategies in interfirm relationships in industrial product channels. *Journal of Marketing, 55*, 52-69.

Galami, J. (2000). *Strategic analysis report: CRM IT requirements and strategies for payer prganisations.* Gartner Group.

Galbreath, J., & Rogers, T. (1999), Customer Relationship Leadership: A Leadership and Motivation Model for the Twenty-First Century Business, *The TQM Magazine, 11* (3), 161-171

Garnier, G. (1982). Context and decision making autonomy in the foreign affiliates of US multinational corporations. *Academy of Management Journal, 25*(4), 893-909.

Harris, G. (1992). International marketing centralisation. *European Business Journal, 4*(3), 50-55.

Hirschman, E. (1986). Humanistic inquiry in marketing research: Philosophy, method and criteria. *Journal of Marketing Research, 23,* 237-249.

Hirschowitz, A. (2001). Closing the CRM loop: The 21st century marketer's challenge: Transforming customer insight into customer value. *Journal of Targeting, Measurement and Analysis for Marketing, 10*(2), 168-179.

Holbrook, A., Green, M., & Krosnick, J. (2003). Telephone versus face-to-face interviewing of national probability samples with long questionnaires. *Public Opinion Quarterly, 67*(1), 79-125.

Hunt, S., & Nevin, J. (1974). Power in a channel of distribution: Sources and consequences. *Journal of Marketing Research, 11*(1), 186-193.

Johns, G. (2001). In praise of context. *Journal of Organizational Behavior, 22*(1), 31-40.

Johnston, W., Leach, M., & Liu, A. (1999). Theory testing using case studies in business to business research. *Industrial Marketing Management, 28,* 201-213.

Kirsch, L. (1996). The management of complex tasks in organizations: Controlling the systems development process. *Organization Science, 7*(1), 1-22.

Kohli, A., & Jaworski, B. (1990). Market orientation: The construct, research propositions, and managerial implications. *Journal of Marketing, 62*(4), 20-35.

Kotler, P. (1967). *Marketing management: Application, planning, implementation and control.* Upper Saddle River, NJ: Prentice Hall.

Kotorov, R. (2003). Customer relationship management: Strategic lessons and future directions. *Business Process Management Journal, 9*(5), 566-571.

Massey, A. P., Montoya-Weiss, M. M., et al. (2001). Re-engineering the customer relationship: Leveraging knowledge assets at IBM. *Decision Support Systems, 32*(2), 155-170.

McCracken, G. (1988). *The long interview, qualitative research methods.* Newbury Park, CA: Sage.

McDonald, W. (1996). Influences on the adoption of global marketing decision support systems: A

management perspective. *International Marketing Review, 13*(1), 33-46.

Mitchell, P. J. (1998). Aligning customer call center for 2001. *Telemarketing and Call Center Solutions, 16*(10), 64-69.

Narver, J., & Slater, S. (1990). The effect of a market orientation on business profitability. *Journal of Marketing, 54*(4), 20-36.

Nelson, S., & Berg, T. (2000). *Customer relationship management: An overview.* Gartner Group.

Ozsomer, A., & Prussia, G. (2000). Competing perspectives in international marketing strategy: Contingency and process models. *Journal of International Marketing, 8*(1), 27-51.

Peppers, D., Rogers, M., & Dorf, B. (1999). Is your company ready for one-to-one marketing? *Harvard Business Review, 77*(1), 151-161.

Puschmann, T., & Rainer, A. (2001). Customer relationship management in the pharmaceutical industry. In *Proceedings of the 34th Hawaii International Conference on System Sciences.*

Reichheld, F. (1996). Learning from customer defections. *Harvard Business Review, 74*(2), 56-68.

Reinartz, W., Krafft, M., & Hoyer, W. (2004). The customer relationship management process: Its measurement and impact on performance. *Journal of Marketing Research, 61*(1), 293-305.

Rigby, D., Reichheld, F., & Schefter, P. (2002, February). Avoid the four perils of CRM. *Harvard Business Review, 80*(2), 101.

Roche, E. (1996). Strategic alliances—An entrepreneurial approach to globalisation. *Journal of Global Information Management, 4*(1), 34.

Ross, S. (1973). The economic theory of agency: The principal's dilemma. *The American Economic Review Proceedings, 63,* 134-139.

Ryals, L. (2002). Measuring risk and returns in the customer portfolio. *Journal of Database Marketing, 9*(3), 219-227.

Ryals, L., & Knox, S. (2001). Cross functional issues in the implementation of relationship marketing through customer relationship management. *European Management Journal, 19*(5), 534.

Shoemaker, M. (2001). A framework for examining IT enabled market relationships. *Journal of Personal Selling & Sales Management, 21*(2), 177-186.

Srivastava, R., Shervani, T., & Fahey, L. (1998). Market based assets and shareholder value: A framework for analysis. *Journal of Marketing, 62*(1), 2-18.

Strauss, A., & Corbin, J. (1992). *Basics of qualitative research: Grounded theory procedures and techniques.* Newbury Park, CA: Sage.

Van Bruggen, G., Smidts, A., & Wierenga, B. (2001). The powerful triangle of marketing data, managerial judgement, and marketing management support systems. *European Journal of Marketing, 25*(7/8), 796-814.

Verhoef, P., & Donkers, B. (2001). Predicting customer potential value: An application in the insurance industry. *Decision Support Systems, 32*(2), 189.

Yin, R. (1994). *Case study research: Design and methods.* Thousand Oaks, CA: Sage.

Zablah, A. R., Bellenger, D. N., & Johnston, W. J. (2004). An evaluation of divergent perspectives on customer relationship management: Towards a common understanding of an emerging phenomenon. *Industrial Marketing Management, 33*(6), 475-489.

Zeithaml, V., Rust, R., & Lemon, K. (2001). The customer pyramid: Creating and serving profitable customers. *California Management Review, 43*(4), 118-146.

*This work was previously published in International Journal of E-Business Research, 3(2), edited by I. Lee, pp. 70-82, copyright 2007 by IGI Publishing, formerly Idea Group Publishing (an imprint of IGI Global).*

# Compilation of References

Abbott, J., Stone, M., & Buttle, F. (2001). Integrating customer data into customer relationship management strategy: An empirical study. *Journal of Database Marketing, 8*(4), 289.

Abrams, C., & Smith, D. (2003). *Service-oriented business applications show their potential* (Pub. ID: SPA-20-7295). Gartner.

Acs, Z., & Dana, L.P. (2001). Contrasting two models of wealth redistribution. *Small Business Economics, 16*(2), 63-74.

Adamides, E. D., & Karacapilidis, N. (2006). Information technology support for the knowledge and social processes of innovation management. *Technovation, 26*(1), 50-59.

Adler, N.J. (1986). *International dimensions of organizational behavior.* Boston: PWS-Kent.

Adolphi, H. (1997). *Strategische konzepte zur organisation der betrieblichen standardisierung* (DIN Normungskunde, Band 38). Berlin/Vienna/Zurich: Beuth Verlag.

AFNOR. (1967). *La normalisation dans l'entreprise.* Paris: Association Française de Normalisation.

Ahmed, P. K., Kok, L. K., & Loh, A. Y. E. (2002). *Learning through knowledge management.* Butterworth Heinemann.

Ahn, J., & Chang, S. (2002). Valuation of knowledge: A business performance-oriented methodology. *IEEE Computer Society.*

Air Products. (n.d.). Retrieved October 18, 2006, from *http://www.airproducts.com/AboutUs/index.asp*

Akrich, M. (2000). The description of technical objects. In W. Bijker & J. Law (Eds.), *Shaping technology/building society: Studies in sociotechnical change* (pp. 205-224). Cambridge: The MIT Press.

Al Mashari, M., & Zairi, M. (2000). The effective application of SAP R/3: A proposed model of best practice. In *Logistics Information Management*, Bradford (pp. 156-166).

Alavi, M., & Leidner, D. (2001). Knowledge management and knowledge management systems: Conceptual foundations and research issues. *MIS Quarterly, 25*(1), 107-136.

Alavi, M., & Leidner, D. E. (1999). Knowledge management systems: Issues, challenges and benefits. *Communications of AIS, 1,* 1-37.

Alavi, M., & Leidner, D. E. (2001). Review: Knowledge management and knowledge management systems: Conceptual foundations and research issues. *MIS Quarterly, 25*(1), 107-136.

Alavi, M., & Leidner, D.E. (2001). Knowledge management and knowledge management systems—conceptual foundations and research issues. *MIS Quarterly, 25*(1).

Alavi, M., & Leidner, D.E. (2001). Review: Knowledge management and knowledge management systems: Conceptual foundations and research issues. *MIS Quarterly, 25*(1), 107-136.

Alavi, M., Kayworth, T., & Leidner, D. (2005). *Organizational and sub-unit values in the process of knowledge management* (Working Paper). Baylor University.

Ali, I., Warne, L., Agostino, K., & Pascoe, C. (2001, June 19-22). Working and learning together: Social learning in the Australian defence organisation. In *Proceedings of Informing Science Conference IS2001 — Bridging Diverse Disciplines* [CD-ROM], Krakow, Poland.

Allee, V. (2004). 360-degree transparency and the sustainable economy. *World Business Academy, 18*(2).

Allen, T.J. (1977). *Managing the flow of technology.* Cambridge, MA: The MIT Press.

Allen, T.J., Tushman, M.L., & Lee, D.M.S. (1979). Technology transfer as a function of position in the spectrum from research through development to technical services. *Academy of Management Journal, 22*(4), 694-708.

Alvesson, M., & Karreman, D. (2001). Odd couple: Making sense of the curious concept of knowledge management. *Journal of Management Studies, 38*(7), 995-1018.

American Productivity and Quality Center (APQC). (1996). *Knowledge management: Consortium benchmarking study final report.* Retrieved on April 3, 2000, from http://www.store.apqc.org/reports/Summary/know-mng.pdf

American Teleservices Association. (2002). *Consumer study.* Retrieved February 17, 2006, from *http://www.ataconnect.org/IndustryResearch/ConsumerStudy2002.html*

Anandarajan, M., Igbaria, M., & Anakwe, U. (2000). Technology acceptance in the banking industry: A perspective from a less developed country. *Information Technology and People, 13*(4), 298-312.

Anantatmula, V. (2004). *Criteria for measuring knowledge management efforts in organizations.* Doctoral Dissertation in Publication, References Number 3123064, UMI Dissertation Services.

Anantatmula, V. (2005). Outcomes of knowledge management initiatives. *International Journal of Knowledge Management, 1*(2), 50-67.

Anantatmula, V. (2006, July 16-19) Improving project performance through leadership and technology. *Proceedings of the Project Management Institute Research Conference,* Montreal, Canada.

Anantatmula, V., & Kanungo, S. (2005). Role of information technology and knowledge management in influencing project performance. *Proceedings of IEMC 2005* (pp. 599-603).

Anantatmula, V., & Kanungo, S. (2007, January 3-6). Modeling enablers and barriers for successful KM implementation. *Proceedings of the Hawaii International Conference on System Sciences* (HICSS).

Andersson, U., Forsgren, M., & Holm, U. (2002). The strategic impact of external networks: Subsidiary performance and competence development in the multinational corporation. *Strategic Management Journal,* (23), 979-996.

Antal, A.B. (2001). Expatriates' contributions to organizational learning. *Journal of General Management, 26,* 62-84.

Applegate, L. M., Austin, R. D., & McFarlan, F. W. (2003). *Corporate information strategy and management: Text and cases.* McGraw-Hill Irwin.

Argote, L., & Ingram, P. (2000). Knowledge transfer: A basis for competitive advantage in firms. *Organizational Behavior and Human Decision Processes, 82*(1), 150-169.

Argyris, C. (1993). *Knowledge for action.* San Francisco: Jossey-Bass.

Argyris, C., & Schon, D. (1978). *Organizational learning: A theory of action research.* Reading, MA: Addison-Wesley.

Armstrong, C.P., & Sambamurthy, V. (1999). Information technology assimilation in firms: The influence of senior leadership and IT infrastructures. *Information Systems Research, 10*(4), 304-327.

Arthur, J. (1994). Effects of human resource systems on manufacturing performance and turnover. *Academy of Management Journal, 37,* 670-687.

Attewell, P. (1992). Technology diffusion and organizational learning: The case of business computing. *Organization Science, 3*(1), 1-19.

Austin, J.L. (1962). *How to do things with words.* Cambridge, MA; Harvard University Press.

Avgerou, C. (1998). How can IT enable economic growth in developing countries? *Information Technology for Development, 8*(1), 15-29.

Avgerou, C. (2001). The significance of context in information systems and organizational change. *Information Systems Journal, 11*(1), 43-63.

Avgerou, C. (2002). *Information systems and global diversity.* Oxford: Oxford University Press.

Awad, E. M., & Ghaziri, H. M. (2004). *Knowledge management.* Prentice-Hall.

Bada, A. (2000). *Global practices and local interests: Implementing technology-based change in a developing country context.* Unpublished doctoral dissertation, London School of Economics and Political Science, London.

Badaracco, J.L. (1991). *The knowledge link.* Boston: Harvard Business School Press.

Bagnara, S., & Marti, P. (2001). Human work in call centers: A challenge for cognitive ergonomics. *Theoretical Issues in Ergonomic Science, 2*(3), 223-237.

Baldwin, T., Magjuka, R., & Loher, B. (1991). The perils of participation: Effects of choice of training on trainee motivation and learning. *Personnel Psychology, 44,* 51-65.

Baltahazard, P. A., & Cooke, R. A. (2003). *Organizational culture and knowledge management success: Assessing the behavior-performance continuum* (Working Paper). Arizona State University West.

Banker, R.D., Kauffman, R.J., & Mahmood, M.A. (Eds.). (1993). *Strategic information technology management:*

*Perspectives on organizational growth and competitive advantage.* Hershey, PA: Idea Group.

Bantel, K.A., & Jackson, S.E. (1989). Top management and innovations in banking: Does the composition of the top team make a difference? *Strategic Management Journal, 10,* 107-124.

Barata, K., Kutzner, F., & Wamukoya, J. (2001). Records, computers, resources: A difficult equation for sub-saharan Africa. *Information Management Journal, 35*(1), 34-42.

Barlett, C., & Ghoshal, S. (1989). *Managing across borders. The Transnational Solution.* Boston: Harvard Business School Press.

Barnes et al. (1988). *Development and organization of a company standardization department* (ISO Development Manual 5). Geneva: International Organization for Standardization.

Barney, J. (1991). Firm resources and sustained competitive advantage. *Journal of Management, 17,* 99-120.

Barney, J.B. (2001). Is the resource-based view a useful perspective for strategic management research? Yes. *Academy of Management Review, 26*(1), 41-56.

Bartlett, C., & Ghoshal, S. (1987). Managing across borders: New strategic management. *Sloan Management Review,* (Winter), 7-17.

Bartlett, C., & Ghoshal, S. (1992). What is a global manager? *Harvard Business Review, 70*(September-October), 124-132.

Bartlett, C.A., & Ghoshal, S. (1991). Global strategic management: Impact on the new frontiers of strategy research. *Strategic Management Journal, 12,* 5-16.

Bartlett, C.A., Ghoshal, S., & Birkinshaw, J. (2003). *Transnational management: Text and cases* (4th ed.). New York: McGraw-Hill/Irwin.

Batiz-Lazo, B. (2005). Review of the book *The entrepreneurial shift: Americanization in European high-technology management education. Management Decision, 43*(3), 464-465.

Bauman, Z. (1998). *Globalization: The human consequences*. New York: Columbia University Press.

Bawden, D. (2001). Information overload. *Library and Information Briefings, 92*.

Beasty, C. (2005). Outsourcing south of the border. *Customer Relationship Marketing*, (April), 13.

Bechtold, B.L. (2000). Evolving to organizational learning. *Hospital Material Management Quarterly, 21*(3), 11-25.

Becker, G.S. (1964). *Human capital*. New York: Columbia University Press.

Becker, M.C. (2001). Managing dispersed knowledge: Organizational problems, managerial strategies and their effectiveness. *Journal of Management Studies, 38*(7), 1037-1051.

Behrend, F.D. (2006). Collaborate today, compete tomorrow: techniques for KM in inter-organizational relationships. *KM Review, 8*(6), 24-27.

Benbya, H., & Belbaly, N.A. (2005). Mechanisms for knowledge management system effectiveness: An exploratory analysis. *Knowledge and Process Management Journal, 12*(3), 203-216.

Bender, S., & Fish, A. (2000). The transfer of knowledge and the retention of expertise: The continuing need for global assignments. *Journal of Knowledge Management, 4*, 125-137.

Bennett, J.L. (2001). Change happens. *HR Magazine*, 149-156.

Benveniste, G. (1994). *Twenty-first century organization: Analyzing current trends, imagining the future*. San Francisco: Jossey-Bass.

Berdrow, I., & Lane, H. (2003). International joint ventures: Creating value through successful knowledge management. *Journal of World Business, 38*, 15-30.

Bernstein, A. (2000). Backlash: Behind the anxiety over globalization. *Business Week, 3678*(April 24), 38-44.

Berry, J. (2001). On the hunt for the right CRM metrics. *InternetWeek*, (April 9), 49.

Beverland, M. (2001). Contextual influences and the adoption and practice of relationship selling in a business to business setting: An exploratory study. *Journal of Personal Selling & Sales Management, 21*(3), 207-215.

Beynon-Davies, P. (2002). *Information systems: An introduction to informatics in organizations*. Palgrave Publishing.

Bhagat, R.S., Kedia, B.L., Harveston, P.D., & Triandis, H.C. (2002). Cultural variations in the cross-border transfer of organizational knowledge: An integrative framework. *Academy of Management Review, 27*, 204-221.

Bhatt, G. D., & Gupta, J. N. D. (2005). Interactive patterns of knowledge management in organizations: Insight from a fashion company. *International Journal of Information Technology and Management, 4*(3), 231-243.

Bigoness, W.J., & Blakely, G.L. (1996). A cross-national study of managerial values. *Journal of International Business Studies, 27*(4), 739-748.

Biloslavo, R. (2005). Use of the knowledge management framework as a tool for innovation capability audit. *International Journal of Innovation and Learning, 2*(4), 402-424.

Bingi, P., Sharma, M.K., & Godla, J. (1999). Critical issues affecting an ERP implementation. In *Information systems management* (pp. 7-14). Boston.

Binney, D. (2001). The knowledge management spectrum—Understanding the KM landscape. *Journal of Knowledge Management, 5*(1), 33-42.

Birchall, D.W., & Tovstiga, G. (1998, November). Methodology for assessing the strategic impact of a firm's knowledge portfolio. *Proceedings of the 8th International Forum on Technology Management*, Grenoble, France.

Bird, A. (2001). International assignments and careers as repositories of knowledge. In M.E. Mendenhall, T.M.

Kuhlmann, & G.K. Stahl (Eds.), *Developing global business leaders: Policies, processes, and innovations* (pp. 19-36). Westport, CT: Quorum Books.

Bird, A., Osland, J.S., Mendenhall, M., & Schneider, S.C. (1999). Adapting and adjusting to other cultures. *Journal of Management Inquiry, 8,* 152-165.

Black, B. (1999). National culture and high commitment management. *Employee Relations, 21*(4), 389.

Black, J.S. (1990). Locus of control, social support, stress, and adjustment to international transfers. *Asia Pacific Journal of Management, 7,* 1-29.

Black, J.S., & Gregersen, H.B. (1999). The right way to manage expats. *Harvard Business Review, 77*(March-April), 52-63.

Black, J.S., & Mendenhall, M. (1990). Cross-cultural training effectiveness: A review and a theoretical framework for future research. *Academy of Management Review, 15,* 113-136.

Black, J.S., & Mendenhall, M. (1992). A practical but theory-based framework for selecting cross-cultural training methods. *Human Resource Management, 28,* 511-539.

Black, J.S., Gregersen, H.B., & Mendenhall, M. (1992). *Global assignments: Successfully expatriating and repatriating international managers.* San Francisco: Jossey-Bass.

Black, J.S., Morrison, A.J., & Gregersen, H.B. (1999). *Global explorers: The next generation of leaders.* New York: Routledge.

Bloor, G., & Dawson, P. (1994). Understanding professional culture in organizational context. *Organization Studies, 15*(2), 275-295.

Boisot, M. (2002). The creation and sharing of knowledge. In C. W. Choo & N. Bontis (Eds.), *The strategic management of intellectual capital and organizational knowledge.* Oxford University Press.

Bonaccorsi, A., & Piccaluga, A. (1994). A theoretical framework for evaluation of university-industry relationships. *R&D Management, 24*( 3), 229-247.

Bonache, J., & Brewster, C. (2001). Knowledge transfer and the management of expatriation. *Thunderbird International Business Review, 43*(1), 145-168.

Bonache, J., & Brewster, C. (2001). Knowledge transfer and the management of expatriation. *Thunderbird International Business Review, 43*(1), 145-168.

Bonache, J., & Fernandez, Z. (1997). Expatriate compensation and its link to the subsidiary strategic role: A theoretical analysis. *International Journal of Human Resource Management, 8*(4), 457-475

Bond, E., & Houston, M. (2003). Barriers to matching new technologies and market opportunities in established firms. *Journal of Product Innovation Management, 20*(2), 120.

Bond, M.H. (Ed.). (1996). *The handbook of Chinese psychology.* New York: Oxford University Press.

Bonoma, T. (1985). Case research in marketing: Opportunities, problems, and a process, *Journal of Marketing Research, 22,* 199-208.

Bontis, N., Chong, W., & Richardson, S. (2000). Intellectual capital and business performance in Malaysian industries. *Journal of Intellectual Capital, 1*(1), 85-100.

Bose, R. (2002). Customer relationship management: Key components for IT success. *Industrial Management and Data Systems, 102*(½), 89-97.

Bouma, J.J., & Winter, W. (1982). *Standardization fundamentals.* Delft, The Netherlands: Nederlands Normalisatie-Instituut.

Boutellier, R., Gassman, O., & Von Zedtwitz, M. (1999). *Managing global innovation.* New York: Springer.

Bowlby, J. (1969). *Attachment and loss* (vol. I). New York: Basic Books.

Bowman, D., Farley, J., & Schmittlein, D. (2000). Cross national empirical generalisation in business services buying behaviour. *Journal of International Business Studies, 31*(4), 667.

Boynton, A.C., Zmud, R.W., & Jacobs, G.C. (1994). The influence of IT management practice on IT use in large organizations. *MIS Quarterly, 18*(3), 299.

Bresman, H., Birkinshaw, J., & Nobel, R. (1999). Knowledge transfer in international acquisitions. *Journal of International Business Studies, 30*(3), 439-462.

Brewster, C. (1993). Developing a "European" model of human resource management. *International Journal of Human Resource Management, 4*(4), 765-785.

Brewster, C., Communal, C., Farndale, E., Hegewisch, A., Johnson, G., & van Ommeren, J. (2001). *The HR healthcheck. Benchmarking HRM practices across the UK and Europe* (report published by Cranfield University School of Management and Financial Times). Englewood Cliffs, NJ: Prentice Hall.

British Standards Society. (1995). *PD 3542:1995: Standards and quality management—an integrated approach.* London: BSI.

Broadbent, M., Weill, P., & St. Clair, D. (1999). The implications of information technology infrastructure for business process redesign. *MIS Quarterly, 23*(2), 159-182.

Brown, J.S., & Duguid, P. (1991). Organizational learning and communities-of-practice: Toward a unified view of working, learning and innovation. *Organization Science, 2*(1), 40-57.

Brown, J.S., & Duguid, P. (1998). Organizing knowledge. *California Management Review, 40*(3), 90-111.

Brown, J.S., & Duguid, P. (2000). Balancing act: How to capture knowledge without killing it. *Harvard Business Review,* (May-June), 3-7.

Brown, J.S., Denning, S., Groh, K., & Prusak, L. (2005). *Storytelling in organizations: Why storytelling is transforming 21st century organizations and management.* Burlington, MA: Elsevier Butterworth-Heinemann.

Brown, S. J., & Duguid, P. (2000). Balancing act: How to capture knowledge without killing it. *Harvard Business Review, 78*(3), 73-80.

Brown, S.L., & Eisenhardt, K.M. (1997). The art of continuous change: Linking complexity theory and time-paced evolution in relentlessly shifting organizations. *Administrative Science Quarterly, 42,* 1-34.

Browne, J. (1997). Unleashing the power of learning. *Harvard Business Review,* (September/October), 147-168.

Buckley, P.J., & Casson, M. (1976). *The future of the multinational enterprise.* London: Macmillan.

Bull, C. (2003). Strategic issues in customer relationship management (CRM) implementation. *Business Process Management Journal, 9*(5), 592-602.

Burnes, B., & James, H. (1995). Culture, cognitive dissonance and the management of change. *International Journal of Operations and Production Management, 15*(8), 14-22.

Buschmann, F., Meunier, R., Rohnert, H., Sommerlad, P., & Stal, M. (1996). *Pattern-oriented software architecture—A system of patterns.* New York: John Wiley & Sons.

Business Guide. (2000). *Customer relationship management.* London: Caspian.

Buttle, F. (1996). *Relationship marketing: Theory and practice.* London: Paul Chapman.

Byrne, R. (2001). Employees: Capital or commodity? *The Learning Organisation, 8*(1), 44-50.

Calaberese, F. (2000). *A suggested framework of key elements defining effective enterprise knowledge management programs.* Unpublished doctoral dissertation, George Washington University, Washington, DC.

Call, D. (2005). Knowledge management—not rocket science. *Journal of Knowledge Management, 9*(2), 19-31.

Callaghan, D. (2002). PeopleSoft widens CRM reach. *eWeek, 19*(50), 18.

Calwell, F. (2004), *KM adoption model highlights critical success factors* (Pub. ID: G00123399). Gartner.

Camp, R.D. II. (2003). *Effects of national culture on trust development: A study of Canadian and Japanese business students.* Doctoral Dissertation, University of British Columbia, Canada (ProQuest Dissertations and Theses AAT NQ79204).

Campbell, A. (2003). Creating customer knowledge competence: Managing customer relationship management programs strategically. *Industrial Marketing Management, 32*(5), 375.

Cantwell, J.A. (1995). The globalisation of technology: What remains of the product cycle model? *Cambridge Journal of Economics, 19,* 155-174.

Cargill, C. (1997). *Open systems standardization—a business approach.* Upper Saddle River, NJ: Prentice Hall.

Carroll, J.S., Rudolph, J.W., & Hatakenaka, S. (2002). Learning from experience in high-hazard organizations. *Research in Organizational Behavior, 24,* 87-137.

Center for Research into Management of Expatriation on the New Forms of International Working. (2002). *Executive report.* Cranfield, UK: Cranfield School of Management.

Chait, L. (1998). Creating a successful knowledge management system. *Prism,* (2nd Quarter), 83.

Chambers, B., Medina, R., & West, K. (1999). Customer relationship management, the new battlefield for workflow. *Document World, 4*(4), 18.

Chatman, J. A., & Barsade, S. G. (1995). Personality, organizational culture, and cooperation: Evidence from a business simulation. *Administrative Science Quarterly, 40*(3), 423-443.

Chatterjee, D., & Watson, R. (2005*).* Infosys technologies limited. Unleashing CIMBA. *Journal of Cases on Information Technology, 7*(4), 127-142

Checkland, P., & Howell, S. (1998). *Information, systems and information systems.* John Wiley & Sons.

Chellappa, M., & Kambhampaty, S. (1994). Text retrieval—a trendy cocktail to address the Dataworld. *Proceedings of IEEE COMPSAC '94.*

Chen, Q., & Chen, H. (2004). Exploring the success factors of eCRM strategies in practice. *Database Marketing & Customer Strategy Management, 11*(4), 333-343.

Chesbrough, H., & Teece, D.J. (1996). When is virtual virtuous? Organizing for innovation. *Harvard Business Review, 74,* 65-71.

Chesbrough, W.H. (2003). The era of open innovation. *Sloan Management Review,* (Spring), 35-41.

Chiesa, V., Coughlan, P., & Voss, C.A. (1996). Development of a technical innovation audit. *Journal of Production Innovation Management, 13*(2), 105-136.

Chin, W., & Gopal, A. (1995). Adoption intention in GSS relative importance of beliefs. *Data Base, 26*(2/3), 42-63.

Chinese Culture Connection. (1987). Chinese values and the search for culture-free dimensions of culture. *Journal of Cross-Cultural Psychology, 18*(2), 143-164.

Chittum, R. (2004). Call centers phone home. *Wall Street Journal,* (June 9), B1.

Choi, B., & Lee, H. (2003). An empirical investigation of KM styles and their effect on corporate performance. *Information & Management, 40*(5), 403-417.

Choo, C., & Bontis, N. (2002). *The strategic management of intellectual capital and organizational knowledge.* New York: Oxford University Press.

Chow, C.W., Deng, F.J., & Ho, J.L. (2000). The openness of knowledge sharing within organizations: A comparative study in the United States and the People's Republic of China. *Journal of Management Accounting Research, 12,* 65-95.

Chua, A., & Lam, W. (2005). Why KM projects fail: A multi-case analysis. *Journal of Knowledge Management, 9*(3), 6-17.

Chuang, S. (2004). A resource-based perspective on knowledge management capability and competitive advantage: An empirical investigation. *Expert Systems with Applications, 27,* 459-465.

Chui, A.C.W., Lloyd, A.E., & Kwok, C.C.Y. (2002). The determination of capital structure: Is national culture a missing piece of the puzzle? *Journal of International Business Studies, 33*(1), 99-128.

CIA. (2006). *The world factbook.* Washington, DC: Central Intelligence Agency. Retrieved March 24, 2006, from *http://www.cia.gov/cia/publications/factbook/countrylisting.html*

Ciborra, C., & Failla, A. (2000). Infrastructure as a process: The case of CRM in IBM. In C. Ciborra (Ed.), *From control to drift: The dynamics of corporate information infrastructures* (pp. 105-124). Oxford University Press.

Ciborra, C.U., & Lanzara, G.F. (1994). Formative contexts and information technology: Understanding the dynamics of innovation in organizations. *Accounting, Management and Information Technology, 4*(2), 61-86.

Clark, K.B., Hayes, R.H., & Wheelwright, S.C. (1988). *Dynamic manufacturing, creating the learning organization.* New York: The Free Press.

Clarke, T. (2006). Why Indian summer is drawing to a close. *PrecisionMarketing,* (May 12), 14-15.

Clegg, C.H. (2004). *Best practices in telephone customer service.* Portland, OR: Portland Research Group.

Clemmons, S., & Simon, S. (2001). Control and coordination in global ERP configuration. *Business Process Management Journal, 7*(3), 205-215.

Coakes, E., & Bradburn, A. (2005). *Knowledge management in a project climate.* Hershey, PA: Idea Group Publishing.

Coakes, E., Willis, D., & Clarke, S. (Eds.). (2002). *Knowledge management in the sociotechnical world: The graffiti continues.* London: Springer-Verlag.

Coase, R.H. (1937). The nature of the firm. *Economica, 4*(16), 386-405.

Cohen, D. (1998). Toward a knowledge context: Report on the first annual U.C. Berkeley forum on knowledge and the firm. *California Management Review, 40*(3), 22-39.

Cohen, W., & Levinthal, D. (1990). Absorptive capacity: A new perspective on learning and innovation. *Administrative Science Quarterly, 35,* 128-152.

Conklin, E.J. (1992). Capturing organizational memory. In D. Coleman (Ed.), *Proceedings of GroupWare '92* (pp. 133-137). San Mateo, CA: Morgan Kaufmann.

Conn, H.P., & Yip, G. (1997). Global transfer of critical capabilities. *Business Horizons, 40*(January-February), 22-31.

Conner, K.R., & Prahalad, C.K. (1996). A resource based theory of the firm: Knowledge versus opportunism. *Organization Science, 7*(5), 477-501.

Consumer Reports. (2006). Computer technical support survey. *Consumer Reports,* (June), 21.

Cooper, R.B., & Zmud, R.W. (1990). Information technology implementation research: A technological diffusion approach. *Management Science, 36*(2), 123.

Copeland, L., & Griggs, L. (1985). *Going international.* New York: Random House.

Coulson-Thomas, C. (2005). Using job support tools to increase workgroup performance. *International Journal of Productivity and Performance Management, 54*(3), 206-211.

Council on Competitiveness. (1996). *Endless frontier, limited resources: U.S. R&D policy for competitiveness.* Washington, DC: Council on Competitiveness.

Cox, T. (2001). *Creating the multicultural organization: A strategy for capturing the power of diversity.* San Francisco, CA: Jossey-Bass.

Crawford, K. (2003). *Factors affecting learning and communication in organizations: A paper commissioned by the Defence, Science and Technology Organisation (DSTO).* Creative Interactive Systems Pty Ltd.

Cray, D. (1984). Control and coordination in multinational corporations. *Journal of International Business Studies, 15*(2) 85-98.

Crosby, L. and Johnson, S. (2001). Technology: friend or foe to customer relationships. *Marketing Management, 10* (4), 10-11.

Crossan, M.M., Lane, H.W., & White, R.E. (1999). An organizational learning framework: From intuition to institution. *Academy of Management Review, 24*(3), 522-537.

Croteau, A. M., & Li, P. (2003). Critical success factors of CRM technological initiatives. *Canadian Journal of Administrative Sciences, 20*(1), 21-34.

Csikszentmihalyi, M. (1997). *Finding flow: The psychology of engagement with everyday life*. New York: Basic Books.

Cui, A., Griffith, D., & Cavusgil, S. (2005). The influence of competitive intensity and market dynamism on knowledge management capabilities of multinational corporation subsidiaries. *Journal of International Marketing, 13*(3), 32-53.

Daft, R. L., & Lewin, A. Y. (1993). Where are the theories for the "new" organizational forms? An editorial essay. *Organization Science, 4*, i-vi.

Daft, R.L,. & Huber, G.P. (1987). How organizations learn: A communication framework. *Research in the Sociology of Organizations, 5*, 1-36.

Daft, R.L., & Lengel, R.H. (1986). Organizational information requirements, media richness and structural design. *Management Science, 32*(5), 554-571.

Dalkir, K. (2005). *Knowledge management in theory and practice*. Oxford: Elsevier Butterworth-Heinemann.

Damodaran, L., & Olphert, W. (2000). Barriers and facilitators to the use of knowledge management systems. *Behaviour & Information Technology, 19*(6), 405-413.

Dana, L.-P., Korot, L., & Tovstiga, G. (2005). A cross-national comparison of knowledge management practices. *International Journal of Manpower, 26*(1), 10-22.

Daneshgar, F., Ray, P. & Rabhi, F. (2003, May 18-21). Knowledge sharing infrastructure for virtual enterprises. In M. Khosrow-Pour (Ed.), *Information Technology & Organizations: Trends, Issues, Challenges & Solutions, 2003 Information Resources Management Association International Conference* (pp. 307-309), Philadelphia, Pennsylvania. Hershey, PA: Idea Group Publishing.

Daniels, D. (2003). Self-service: Creating value with natural language search. *Call Center Magazine, 16*, 8-9.

Danish Agency for Development of Trade and Industry (DATI). (2003). *Intellectual capital statements—the new guideline*. Author.

Darley, W. (2001). The Internet and emerging e-commerce: Challenge and implications for management in sub-saharan Africa. *Journal of Global Information Technology Management, 4*(4), 4-18.

Das, A. (2003). Knowledge and productivity in technical support work. *Management Science, 49*(4), 416-431.

Das, G. (1993, March-April). Local memoir of a global manager. *Harvard Business Review*, 38-47.

Datamonitor. (2003). *Call centers in the United States. Industry profile*. New York: Author (reference code: 00720758).

Davenport, T. H., & De Long, D. W. (1998). Successful knowledge management projects. *Sloan Management Review, 39*(2), 43-57.

Davenport, T. H., & Harris, J. G. (2001). Data to knowledge to results: Building an analytic capability. *California Management Review, 43*(2), 117-138.

Davenport, T. H., & Jarvenpaa, S. L. (1996). Improving knowledge work processes. *Sloan Management Review, 37*(4), 53-65.

Davenport, T. H., & Prusak, L. (1998). *Working knowledge: How organizations manage what they know*. Boston: Harvard Business School.

Davenport, T. H., De Long, D. W., & Beers, M. C. (1998). Successful knowledge management. *Sloan Management Review, 39*(2), 43-57.

Davenport, T. H., Harris, J. G., & Kohli. (2001). How do they know their customers so well? *Sloan Management Review, 42*(2), 63-73.

Davenport, T., & Prusak, L. (1998). *Working knowledge.* Boston: Harvard Business School Press.

Davenport, T., & Prusak, L. (1998). *Working knowledge: how organizations manage what they know.* Cambridge, MA: Harvard Business School Press.

Davenport, T., Eccles, R., & Prusak, L. (1992). Information politics. *Sloan Management Review 34*(1), 53-65

Davenport, T.H. (1998). Putting the enterprise into the enterprise system. *Harvard Business Review,* 121-131.

Davenport, T.H. (2005). *Thinking for a living* (p. 45). Boston: Harvard Business School Press.

Davenport, T.H., & Prusak, L. (1998). *Working knowledge. How organizations manage what they know.* Boston: Harvard Business School Press.

Davenport, T.H., & Volpel, S.C. (2001). The rise of knowledge towards attention management. *Journal of Knowledge Management, 5*(3), 212-221.

Davenport, T.H., De Long, D.W., & Beers, M.C. (1998). Successful knowledge management projects. *Sloan Management Review, 39*(2), 43-57.

Davenport, T.H., DeLong, D.W., & Beers, M.C. (1998). Successful knowledge management projects. *Sloan Management Review, 40,* 43-57.

David, A. (2001). Models implementation: A state of the art. *European Journal of Operational Research, 134,* 459-480.

Davies, G., Chun, R., da Silva, R., & Roper, S. (2003). *Corporate reputation and competitiveness.* London: Routledge.

Davies, J., & Duke, A. (2005). Next generation knowledge access. *Journal of Knowledge Management, 9*(5), 64-84.

Davis, F.D. (1989). Perceived usefulness, perceived ease of use, and user acceptance of information technology. *MIS Quarterly, 13,* 319-340.

Dawar, N., Parker, P.M., & Price, L.J. (1996). A cross-cultural study of interpersonal information exchange. *Journal of International Business Studies, 27*(3), 497-516.

Dawson, K. (2004). Customers: Not as happy as you think. *Call Center Magazine, 17,* 16-22.

Day, G., & Van den Bulte, C. (2002). *Superiority in customer relationship management consequences for competitive advantage and performance.* Marketing Science Institute.

De Gelder, A. (1989). *Opstellen van normen.* Delft, The Netherlands: Nederlands Normalisatie-Instituut.

De Vries, H.J. (2006). Best practice in company standardization. *International Journal for IT Standards and Standardization Research, 4*(1), 62-85.

De Vries, H.J., & Slob, F.J. (2007). Building a model of best practice of company standardization. In J. Dul & T. Hak (Eds.), *Case study methodology in business research.* Oxford, UK: Butterworth Heinemann.

Deal, T.E., & Kennedy, A.A. (1982). *Corporate cultures: The rites and rituals of corporate life.* Boston: Addison-Wesley.

Dean, J. (2001). Better business through customers. *Government Executive, 33*(1), 58.

Deans, P.C., & Karwan, K.R. (Eds.). (1994). *Global information systems and technology: Focus on the organization and its functional areas.* Hershey, PA: Idea Group.

Deans, P.C., & Ricks, D.A. (1993). An agenda for research linking information systems and international business: Theory, methodology and application. *Journal of Global Information Management,* (1), 6-19.

Deci, E., & Ryan R. (1985). *Intrinsic motivation and self-determination in human behavior.* New York : Plenum Press.

Declerck, R., Debourse, J.P., & Navarre, C. (1983). *Méthode de direction générale: Le management stratégique.* Paris: Hommes et Techniques.

Delaney, J., & Huselid, M. (1996). The impact of human resource management practices on perceptions of organizational performance. *Academy of Management Journal, 39*(4), 949-969.

Delery, J. (1998). Issues of fit in strategic human resource management: Implications for research. *Human Resource Management Review, 8,* 289-309.

Delery, J., & Doty, H. (1996). Modes of theorizing in strategic human resource management: Tests of universalistic, contingency, and configurational performance predictions. *Academy of Management Journal, 39*(4), 802-835.

Delios, A., & Bjorkman, I. (2000). Expatriate staffing in foreign subsidiaries of Japanese multinational corporations in the PRC and the United States. *International Journal of Human Resource Management, 11*(2), 278-293.

Delisi, P. (1990). Lessons from the steel axe: Culture, technology, and organizational change. *Sloan Management Review,* 83-93.

DeLong, D. W., & Fahey, L. (2000). Diagnosing cultural barriers to knowledge management. *Academy of Management Executive, 14*(4), 113-127.

DeLong, D.W. (2004). *Lost knowledge: Confronting the threat of an aging workforce* (ch. 11). New York, Oxford University Press.

Deming, W.E. (1994). The need for change. *Journal for Quality and Participation, 17*(7), 30-31.

Deshpande, R. (1983). Paradigms lost: On theory and method in research in marketing. *Journal of Marketing, 47*(4), 101-111.

Deshpande, R., Farley, J., & Webster, F. (1993). Corporate culture, customer orientation and innovativeness. *Journal of Marketing, 57*(1), 23-38.

DiBella, A.J., & Nevis, E. (1998). *How organizations learn.* San Francisco: Jossey-Bass.

Dierickx, I., & Cool, K. (1989). Asset stock accumulation and sustainability of competitive advantage. *Management Science, 35,* 1504-1514.

Dierickx, I., & Cool, K. (1989a). Assets stock accumulation and sustainability of competitive advantage. *Management Science, 35*(12), 1504-1511.

Dierickx, I., & Cool, K. (1989b). Assets stock accumulation and sustainability of competitive advantage: Reply. *Management Science, 35*(12), 1512-1513.

DiGiano, C., Yarnall, L., Patton, C., Roschelle, J., Tatar, D., & Manley, M. (2002). Collaboration design patterns: Conceptual tools for planning for the wireless classroom. *Proceedings of WMTE'02.*

Disterer, G. (2001). Individual and social barriers to knowledge transfer. *Proceedings of HICSS34.*

Dixon, N.M. (2000). *Common knowledge: How companies thrive by sharing what they know.* Boston: Harvard Business School Press.

Dorgan, M. (2003). Employee as customer: Lessons from marketing and IT. *Strategic HR Review, 2*(2), 10.

Dougherty, D. (1996). Organizing for innovation. In S.R. Clegg & W.R. Nord (Eds.), *Handbook of organization studies.* Sage.

Downes, M., & Thomas, A. (2000). Knowledge transfer through expatriation: The U-curve approach to overseas staffing. *Journal of Management Issues, 12*(2), 131-149.

Downes, M., & Thomas, A.S. (1999). Managing overseas assignments to build organizational knowledge. *Human Resource Planning Journal, 22,* 33-48.

Downes, M., & Thomas, A.S. (2000). The cyclical effect of expatriate satisfaction on organizational performance: The role of firm international orientation. *The Learning Organization, 7*(3), 122-134.

Downes, M., & Thomas, A.S. (2002). Knowledge transfer through expatriation: The U-curve approach to overseas staffing. *Journal of Managerial Issues, 12,* 131-149.

Downing, J. (2004). 'It's easier to ask someone I know:' Call center technicians' adoption of knowledge management tools. *Journal of Business Communication, 41*(2), 166-192.

Downing, J. (in press). Using customer contact center technicians to measure the effectiveness of online help systems. *Technical Communication.*

Doyle, S. (2002). Software review: Communication optimization—the new mantra of database marketing. Fad or fact? *Journal of Database Marketing, 9*(2), 185-191.

Doz, Y., & Hamel, G. (2000). *L'avantage des alliances.* Dunod.

Doz, Y.L., Santos, J., & Williamson, P. (2001). *From global to metanational: How companies win in the knowledge economy.* Boston: Harvard Business School Press.

Doz, Y.L., Santos, J., & Williamson, P. (2001). *From global to metanational: How companies win in the knowledge economy.* Boston: Harvard Business School Press.

Drucker P.F., Garvin, D., Leonard, D., Straus, S., & Brown, J.S. (1998). *Harvard business review on knowledge management.* Boston: Harvard Business School Press.

Drucker, P. (2001). *Management challenges for the 21st century* (1st ed.). New York: Collins.

Drucker, P. (2001). The next society: A survey of the near future. *The Economist,* (November 3), 1-22.

Drucker, P. F. (1999, October). Beyond the information revolution. *The Atlantic Monthly.*

Drucker, P.F. (2001). *Management challenges for the 21st century.* New York: Harper Business.

Duncan, R.B. (1976). The ambidextrous organization: Designing dual structures for innovation. In R.H. Kilmann, R.L. Pundy, & D.P. Slevin (Eds.), *The management of organization: Strategy and implementation.* New York: North Holland.

Dunford, R.W. (1992). *Organisational behaviour: An organisational analysis perspective.* Sydney: Addison-Wesley.

Dunning, J.H. (1981). *International production and the multinational enterprise.* London: Allen and Unwin.

Dwyer, R., Schurr, P., & Oh, S. (1987). Developing buyer-seller relationships. *Journal of Marketing, 51*(2), 11-28.

Dyche, J. (2001). *The CRM handbook: A business guide to customer relationship management.* Boston: Addison Wesley Professional (Information Technology Series).

Earl, M. (2001). Knowledge management strategies: Towards taxonomy. *Journal of Management Information Systems, 18*(1), 215-233.

Earley, P.C. (1993). East meets west meets mid-east: Further explorations of collectivistic and individualistic work groups. *Academy of Management Journal, 36*(2), 319-348.

Earley. (1994). Self or group? Cultural effects of training on self-efficacy and performance. *Administrative Science Quarterly, 39*(1), 89-117.

Easterby-Smith, M., & Lyles, M.A. (Eds.). (2003). *Blackwell handbook of organizational learning and knowledge management.* Blackwell.

Ebsco. (2005a). Busy signals. *Economist,* (September 9), 60. Retrieved March 3, 2005, from *http://www.ebsco.com*

Ebsco. (2005b). Offshore contact centers. *MarketWatch: Global Round-Up, 4*(October), 229-230. Retrieved February 15, 2006, from *http://www.ebsco.com*

Economist. (2000). Economic indicators for The Netherlands. *The Economist, 144*(1).

Economist. (2006a). Thinking for a living: Knowledge workers need a new kind of organization *The Economist,* (January 19 special report).

Economist. (2006b). The fertility bust: Very low birth rates in Europe may be here to stay. *The Economist,* (February 11), 46.

Economist. (2006c).The avuncular state: The new paternalism. *The Economist,* (April 8 special report), 75-77.

Edmondson, A. (1999). Psychological safety and learning behavior in work teams. *Administrative Science Quarterly, 44*(2), 350-383.

Edstrom, A., & Galbraith, J.R. (1977). Transfer of managers as a coordination and control strategy in multinational organizations. *Administrative Science Quarterly, 22,* 248-263.

Edvinsson, L. (1997). Developing intellectual capital at Skandia. *Long Range Planning, 30*(3).

Edvinsson, L., & Malone, M.S. (1997). *Intellectual capital. Realizing your company's true value by finding its hidden brainpower* (1ˢᵗ ed.). HarperCollins.

Edwards, J. S., & Shaw, D. (2005). Knowledge management systems: Finding a way with technology. *Journal of Knowledge Management, 9*(1), 113-125.

Edwards, L. (2004). Overseas call centers can cost firms goodwill. *Marketing News,* (April 15), 21.

Edwards, R., Ahmad, A., & Moss, S. (2002). Subsidiary autonomy: The case of multinational subsidiaries in Malaysia. *Journal of Internal Business Studies, 33*(1), 183.

Eisenhardt, K. (1985). Agency theory: An assessment and review. *Academy of Management Review, 14*(1), 57-74.

Eisenhardt, K. (1989). Building theories from case study research. *Academy of Management Review, 14*(4), 532-550.

Eisenhardt, K.M., & Bourgeois, L.J.I. (1988). Politics of strategic decision making in high-velocity envi. *Academy of Management Journal, 31*(4), 737-734.

Eisenhardt, K.M., & Martin, J.K. (2000). Dynamic capabilities: What are they? *Strategic Management Journal, 21,* 1105-1121.

El Sawy, O. (2001). *Redesigning enterprise processes for e-business.* Boston: Irwin/McGraw-Hill.

Ellis, K. (2003). K-span: Building a bridge between learning and knowledge management. *Training, 40*(10), 46.

English, M.J., & Baker, W.H. Jr. (2006). Rapid knowledge transfer: The key to success. *Quality Progress, 39*(2), 41-48.

Enz, C. (1986). *Power and shared values in the corporate culture.* Ann Arbor, MI: University of Michigan Press.

Erickson, P. E. (1979). The role of secrecy in complex organizations: From norms of Rationality to norms of distrust. *Cornell Journal of Social Relation, 14*(2), 121-138.

Evans, P., Pucik, V., & Barsoux, J. (2002). *The global challenge.* New York: McGraw-Hill Irwin.

Evdemon, J. (2005). *The four tenets of service orientation.* Retrieved from *http://www.bpminstitute.org/articles/article/article/the-four-tenets-of-service-orientation.html*

Ewusi-Mensah, K., & Przasnyski, Z. H. (1991). On information systems project abandonment: an exploratory study of organizational practices. *MIS Quarterly, 15*(1), 67-86.

Fairell, D., Kaka, N., & Stürze, S. (2005). Ensuring India's offshoring future. *McKinsey Quarterly,* 74-83.

Fairholm, G. W. (1993). *Organizational power politics.* Westpot, CT: Praeger.

Fairhurst, G. (2001). Values at work: Employee participation meets market pressure at mondragon. *Communication Theory, 11*(2), 242.

Feeny, D.F., & Willcocks, L.P. (1998). Core IS capabilities for exploiting information technology. *Sloan Management Review,* 9-21.

Feinberg, R.A., Kim, I., Hokama, L., de Ruyter, K., & Keen, C. (2000). Operational determinants of caller satisfaction in the call center. *International Journal of Service Industry Management, 11,* 131-141.

Feldman, D.C., & Bolino, M.C. (1999). The impact of on-site mentoring on expatriate socialization: A structural equation modeling approach. *International Journal of Human Resource Management, 10,* 54-71.

Ferner, A. (1997). Country of origin effects and HRM in multinational companies. *Human Resource Management Journal, 7*(1), 19-37.

Ferris, G. R., Fedor, D. B., Chachere, J. G., & Pondy, L. R. (1989). Myths and politics in organizational contexts. *Group and Organization Studies, 14*(1), 83-103.

Fichman, R.G., & Kemerer, C.F. (1997). The assimilation of software process innovations: An organizational learning perspective. *Management Science, 43*(10), 1345-1363.

Fina, E., & Rugman, A. (1996). A test of internalization theory and internationalization theory: The Upjohn company. *Management International Review, 36*(3), 199-214.

Fine, G. A., & Holyfield, L. (1996). Secrecy, trust, and dangerous leisure: generating group cohesion in voluntary organizations. *Social Psychology Quarterly, 59*(1), 22-38.

Finlay, P. (2000). *Strategic management—an introduction to business and corporate strategy.* London: Financial Times Prentice Hall.

Fiol, C.M., & Lyles, M.A. (1985). Organizational learning. *Academy of Management Review, 10,* 803.

Fjermestad, J., & Romano, N. (2003). Electronic customer relationship management: Revisiting the general principles of usability and resistance An integrative implementation framework. *Business Process Management Journal, 9*(5), 572-591.

Flores, F., & Spinosa, C. (1998) *Information technology & people* (vol. 11, no. 4, pp. 351-372). MCB University Press (0959-3845 Reflections).

Florida, R. (1997). The globalization of R&D: Results of a survey of foreign-affiliated R&D laboratories in the USA. *Research Policy, 26,* 85-103.

Florida, R., & Gates, G. (2002). Technology and tolerance. *The Brookings Review, 20*(1), 32-35.

Fontaine, M.A., & Lesser, E. (2002). *Challenges in managing organizational knowledge.* Technical Report, IBM Institute for Knowledge-Based Organizations, USA.

Ford. (n.d.). *Overview.* Retrieved October 20, 2006, from *http://www.ford.com/en/company/about/overview.htm*

Foss, N., & Pedersen, T. (2002). Transferring knowledge in MNCs: The role of sources of subsidiary knowledge and organizational context. *Journal of International Management, 8,* 49-67.

Foster, T., & Zhao, L. (1999). Cascade. *Journal of Object-Oriented Programming, 11*(9).

Frank, C., & Gardoni, M. (2005). Information content management with shared ontologies—At corporate research centre of EADS. *International Journal of Information Management, 25*(1), 55-70.

Franko, L.G. (1973). Who manages multinational enterprises? *Columbia Journal of World Business, 8*(Summer), 30-42.

Frankwick, G., & Ward, J. (1994). Evolving patterns of organizational beliefs in the formation of strategy. *Journal of Marketing, 58*(2), 96.

Frazier, G. (1999). Organizing and managing channels of distribution. *Journal of the Academy of Marketing Science, 27*(2), 226-240.

Frazier, G., & Rody, R. (1991, January). The use of influence strategies in interfirm relationships in industrial product channels. *Journal of Marketing, 55,* 52-69.

Frenkel, M. (2005). The politics of translation: How state-level political relations affect the cross-national travel of management ideas. *Organization, 12*(2), 275-301.

Friedman, T. (2005). *The world is flat: A brief history of the twenty-first century.* New York: Farrar, Straus and Giroux.

Frumkin, J. (2005). The Wiki and the digital library. *OCLC Systems and Services, 21*(1), 18-22.

Gadman, S. (2003) Adaptive innovation: Interdependent approaches to knowledge creation and organisational transformation. *Journal of Management Systems.*

Galami, J. (2000). *Strategic analysis report: CRM IT requirements and strategies for payer prganisations.* Gartner Group.

Galbraith, J. (1977). *Organizational design.* Reading, MA: Addison Wesley.

Galbreath, J., & Rogers, T. (1999), Customer Relationship Leadership: A Leadership and Motivation Model for the Twenty-First Century Business, *The TQM Magazine, 11* (3), 161-171

Gamma, E., Helm, R., Johnson, R., & Vlissides, J. (1994). *Design patterns: Elements of reusable object-oriented software.* Boston: Addison-Wesley.

Gammelgaard, J. (2000). How foreign subsidiaries develop into integrated competence centers. In J. Larimo & S. Kock (Eds.), *Recent studies in interorganizational and international business research: Proceedings of the University of Vaasa* (report 58, pp. 164-181).

Garavan, T. (1997). The learning organization: A review and evaluation. *The Learning Organization, 4*(1), 18-29.

Garnier, G. (1982). Context and decision making autonomy in the foreign affiliates of US multinational corporations. *Academy of Management Journal, 25*(4), 893-909.

Gerybadze, A., & Reger, G. (1999). Globalization of R&D: Recent changes in management innovation in transnational corporations. *Research Police, 28,* 251-274.

GEsource. (2006). Country comparison tool. *GEsource WorldGuide.* Retrieved March 24, 2006, from *http://www. gesource.ac.uk/worldguide/*

Giraldo, J.P., & Schulte, W.D. (2005). An exploration of the effects of knowledge management on global leadership. *Proceedings of the Academy of International Business Southeastern United States Annual Meeting* (pp. 206-217).

Gittell, J. (2003). *The Southwest Airlines way.* New York: McGraw Hill.

Gloet, M., & Berrel, M. (2003). The dual paradigm nature of knowledge management: Implications for achieving quality outcomes in human resource management. *Journal of Knowledge Management, 7*(1), 78-89.

Gnyawali, D.R. (1997). *Creation and utilization of organizational knowledge: An empirical study of the effects of organizational learning on strategic decision making.* Unpublished Doctoral Thesis, University of Pittsburgh, USA.

Gold, A. H., Malhotra, A., & Segars, A. H. (2001). Knowledge management: An organizational capabilities perspective. *Journal of Management Information Systems, 18*(1), 185-214.

Gold, A., Malhotra, A., & Segars, A. (2001). Knowledge management: An organizational capabilities perspective. *Journal of Management Information Systems, 18*(1), 185-214.

Goldenberg, B. (2002, May). *Barton Goldenberg's advice: The truth about customer relationship management.* Retrieved September 10, 2002, from *http://www. crmcommunity.com*

Goldschmidt, W.R. (1960). *Exploring the Ways of Mankind.* New York: Holt, Rinehart, and Winston.

Goleman, D. (1995). *Emotional intelligence: Why it can matter more than IQ.* New York: Bantam Books.

Gooderham, P.N., & Nordhaug, O. (2003). *International management: Cross-boundary challenges.* Oxford: Blackwell.

Gouldner, A.W. (1957). Cosmopolitans and locals: Towards an analysis of latent social roles. *Administrative Science Quarterly,* (December), 281-306.

Grady (Goetz), V., & Hamner, M. (2004). The effect of technological change on organizational effectiveness. *American Society of Engineering Managers Practice Periodical, 1*(2).

Grady (Goetz), V., & Hamner, M. (2004, October). The deterioration from an organizational loss of stability into an organizational LOE. *Proceedings of the 2004 American Society Engineering Management National Conference*, Alexandria, VA.

Grady, V. (2005). *Studying the effect of loss of stability on organizational behavior: A perspective on technological change*. Unpublished Doctoral Dissertation, George Washington University, USA.

Grady-Goetz, V., & Hamner, M. (2003, October). Identifying behavioral symptoms in the workplace that can evolve into an organizational loss of effectiveness. *Proceedings of the 2003 American Society Engineering Management National Conference*, St. Louis, MO.

Grant, R. (1996). Toward a knowledge-based theory of the firm. *Strategic Management Journal, 17*(Winter Special Issue), 109-126.

Grant, R., & Spender, J.C. (Eds.). (1997). Knowledge and the firm: An overview. *Journal of International Business, 17*, 5-9.

Grant, R.M. (1996). Prospering in dynamically-competitive environments: Organizational capability as knowledge integration. *Organization Science, 7*(4), 375-387.

Grant, R.M. (1996). Toward a knowledge based theory of the firm. *Strategic Management Journal, 17*, 109-122.

Grant, R.M. (1997). The knowledge-based view of the firm: Implications for management practice. *Long Range Planning, 30*(3), 450-454.

Gray, C.F., & Larson, E.W. (2005). *Project management: The managerial process*. New York: McGraw-Hill.

Gregersen, H., & Black, J. (1992). Antecedents to commitment to a parent company and a foreign operation. *Academy of Management Journal, 35*(1), 65-90.

Gronau, N., & Muller, C. (2005). KMDL capturing, analyzing and improving knowledge-intensive business processes. *Journal of Universal Computer Science, 11*(4), 452-472.

Grove, A. (1996). *Only the paranoid survive—how to exploit the crisis points that challenge every company and career*. New York: Doubleday.

Guest, D. (1997). Human resource management and performance: A review and research agenda. *International Journal of Human Resource Management, 8*(3), 263-276.

Gulati, R. (1995). Social structure and alliance formation pattern: A longitudinal analysis. *Administrative Science Quarterly, 40*, 619-642.

Gulati, R. (1999). Network location and learning: The influence of network resources and firm capabilities on alliance formation. *Strategic Management Journal, 20*(5), 397-420.

Gummesson, E. (1999). *Total relationship management*. Oxford: Butterworth-Heinemann.

Gupta, A. K., & Govindarajan, V. (2000). Knowledge management's social dimension: Lessons from Nucor Steel. *Sloan Management Review, 42*(1), 71-80.

Gupta, A., & Govindarajan, V. (2000). Knowledge flows within MNCs. *Strategic Management Journal, 21*, 473-496.

Gupta, A., & Singhal, A. (1993). Managing human resources for innovation and creativity. *Research Technology Management, 36*(3), 41-48.

Gupta, A.K., & Govindarajan, V. (1991). Knowledge flows and the structure of control within multinational corporations. *Academy of Management Review, 16*, 768-792.

Gupta, A.K., & Govindarajan, V. (2000). Knowledge flows within multinational corporations. *Strategic Management Journal, 21*, 473-496.

Hagedoorn, J., Link, A.N., & Vonortas, N.S. (2000). Research partnerships. *Research Policy, 29*, 567-586.

Håkansson, H. (1989). *Corporate technological behavior: Cooperation and networks*. London: Routledge.

Hall, E.T. (1977). *Beyond culture*. New York: Doubleday/Anchor.

Hammer, M. (1996). *Beyond reengineering.* London: HarperCollins.

Handy, C. (1981). *Understanding organizations* (pp. 39-45). Harmondsworth, Middlesex: Penguin.

Hansen, M. (1999). The search-transfer problem: The role of weak ties in sharing knowledge across organization subunits. *Administrative Science Quarterly, 44,* 82-111.

Hansen, M. T., Nohria, N., & Tierney, T. (1999). What's your strategy for managing knowledge? *Harvard Business Review, 77*(2), 106-115.

Hansen, M., Nohria, N., & Tierney, T. (1999). *What's your strategy for managing knowledge?* HBR.

Hansotia, B. (2002). Gearing up for CRM: Antecedents to successful implementation. *Journal of Database Marketing, 10*(2), 121.

Hargadon, A. B. (1998). Firms as knowledge brokers: Lessons in pursuing continuous innovation. *California Management Review, 40*(3), 209-227.

Harhoff, D., Henkel, J., & von Hippel, E. (2002, May). *Profiting from voluntary information spillovers: How users benefit by freely revealing their innovations.* Working Paper, MIT Sloan School of Management, USA.

Harris, G. (1992). International marketing centralisation. *European Business Journal, 4*(3), 50-55.

Harris, H. (2002). Strategic management of international workers. *Innovations in International HR, 28*(1), 1-5.

Harris, H., Brewster, C., & Sparrow, P. (2003). *International human resource management.* London: CIPD

Harris, K. (2006). *Knowledge management enables the high performance workplace* (Pub. ID: G00136928). Gartner.

Harris, S.G., & Sutton, R.I. (1986). Functions of parting ceremonies in dying organizations. *Academy of Management Journal, 29*(1), 5-30.

Hart, D. (2002). Ownership as an issue in data and information sharing: a philosophically based view

[Special issue]. *Australian Journal of Information Systems*, 23-29.

Hart, D., & Warne, L. (1997). *Information systems defining characteristics: A stakeholder centric view of success and failure* (Technical Paper CS0197). University College UNSW, ADFA.

Hart, S.L., & Milstein, M.B. (2003). Creating sustainable value. *Academy of Management Executive, 17*(2).

Harvey, J.B. (1988). *The Abilene Paradox: And other meditations on management.* New York: John Wiley & Sons.

Harvey, J.B. (1999). *How come every time I get stabbed in the back my fingerprints are on the knife? And other meditations on management.* San Francisco: Jossey-Bass.

Harvey, M., & Buckley, M. (1997). Managing inpatriates: Building a global core competency. *Journal of World Business, 32*(1), 67-78.

Harvey, M., & Fung, H. (2000). Inpatriate managers: The need for realistic relocation reviews. *International Journal of Management, 17*(2), 151-159.

Harvey, M., & Novicevic, M.M. (2001). Selecting expatriates for increasingly complex global assignments. *Career Development International, 6*(2), 69-86.

Harvey, M., Novicevic, M., Buckley, M., & Fung, H. (2005). Reducing inpatriate managers liability of foreignness by addressing stigmatization and stereotype threats. *Journal of World Business, 40*(3), 267-280.

Harvey, M.G. (1993). Inpatriation training: The next challenge for international human resource management. *International Journal of Intercultural Relations, 21,* 393-428.

Harvey, M.G., Price, M.F., Speier, C., & Novicevic, M.M. (1999). The role of inpatriates in a globalization strategy and challenges associated with the inpatriation process. *Human Resource Planning, 22,* 38-50.

Harzig, A. (2001). An analysis of the functions of international transfer of managers in MNCs. *Employee Relations, 23*(6), 581-598.

Harzing, A., & van Ruysseveldt, J. (Eds.). (2004). *International human resource management* (2nd ed.). London: Sage.

Hasan, H., & Gould, E. (2001). Support for the sense-making activity of managers. *Decision Support Systems, 31*(1), 71-86.

Hay Acquisition Company I. (1993). *Personal values questionnaire.*

Hedlund, G. (1994). A model of knowledge management and the N-Form corporation. *Strategic Management Journal, 15,* 73-90.

Hedlund, G. (1994). A model of knowledge management and the N-form corporation. *Strategic Management Journal, 15,* 73-90.

Hegel, G.W.F. (1979). *The phenomenology of spirit* (A.V. Miller, trans.). Oxford: Oxford University Press.

Heidegger, M. (1962 [1937]). *Being and time* (J. Macquarrie & E. Robinson, trans.). Oxford: Basil Blackwell.

Heidegger, M. (1977). The question concerning technology. In *The question concerning technology and other essays.* New York: Harper and Rowe.

Heijden, H. (2003). Factors influencing the usage of Web sites: The case of a generic portal in The Netherlands. *Information & Management, 40,* 541-549.

Heller, M. (2004). Outsourcing. *Workforce Management, 83,* 95-97. Retrieved May 17, 2006, from *http://www.ebsco.com*

Henderson, R.M., & Clark, K.B. (1990). Architectural innovation: The reconfiguration of existing product technologies and the failure of established firms. *Administrative Science Quarterly, 35,* 9-30.

Hersey, P., & Blanchard, K. (1996). Great ideas revisited: Revisiting the life-cycle theory of leadership. *Training & Development, 50*(1), 43-47.

Hesser, W., & Inklaar, A. (Eds.). (1997). *An introduction to standards and standardization* (DIN Normungskunde, Band 36). Berlin/Vienna/Zurich: Beuth Verlag.

Hillmer, S., Hillmer, B., & McRoberts, G. (2004). The real costs of turnover: Lessons from a call center. *Human Resource Planning, 27*(3), 34-41. Retrieved February 17, 2006, from *http://www.ebsco.com*

Hillner, J. (2000). Venture capitals. *Wired,* (July).

Hiltz, S. R., & Goldman, R. (2005). *Learning together online. Research on asynchronous learning.* Mahwah, NJ: Lawrence Erlbaum Associates.

Hirschl, R. (2004). Constitutional courts vs. religious fundamentalism: Three Middle Eastern tales. *Texas Law Review, 82*(7), 1819.

Hirschman, E. (1986). Humanistic inquiry in marketing research: Philosophy, method and criteria. *Journal of Marketing Research, 23,* 237-249.

Hirschowitz, A. (2001). Closing the CRM loop: The 21st century marketer's challenge: Transforming customer insight into customer value. *Journal of Targeting, Measurement and Analysis for Marketing, 10*(2), 168-179.

Hislop, D. (2002). Linking human resource management and knowledge management via commitment: A review and research agenda. *Employee Relations, 25*(2), 182-202.

Hislop, D. (2002). Mission impossible? Communicating and sharing knowledge via information technology. *Journal of Information Technology, 17,* 165-177.

Hlupic, V. (2003). *Knowledge and business process management.* Hershey, PA: Idea Group Publishing.

Hofstede, G. (1980), *Culture's consequences: International differences in work-related values.* Beverly Hills, CA: Sage.

Hofstede, G. (1980). *Culture's consequences: International differences in work-related values.* Beverly Hills, CA: Sage.

Hofstede, G. (1991). *Cultures and organizations.* London: McGraw-Hill.

Hofstede, G. (1997). *Cultures and organizations — Software of the mind*. New York: McGraw Hill.

Holbrook, A., Green, M., & Krosnick, J. (2003). Telephone versus face-to-face interviewing of national probability samples with long questionnaires. *Public Opinion Quarterly, 67*(1), 79-125.

Holland, C.P., & Light, B. (1999). A critical success factors model for ERP implementation. *IEEE Software,* 30-36.

Hollman, L. (2002). The power of knowledge management software. *Call Center Magazine, 15*(1), 30-38.

Holman, D., Epitropaki, O., & Fernie, S. (2001). Understanding learning strategies in the workplace: A factor analytic investigation. *Journal of Occupational and Organizational Psychology, 74*, 675-681.

Holsapple, C., & Joshi, K. (1999, January 3-6). Description and analysis of existing knowledge management frameworks. In *Proceedings of the Thirty-Second Hawaii International Conference on System Sciences.*

Holsapple, C., & Joshi, K. (2000). An investigation of factors that influence the management of knowledge in organizations. *Journal of Strategic Information System, 9*(2-3), 235-261.

Holsapple, C., & Joshi, K. (2001). Organizational knowledge resources. *Decision Support Systems, 31*(1), 39-54.

Huber, G.P. (1991). Organizational learning: The contributing processes and the literatures. *Organization Science, 2*(1), 88-115.

Huener, L., von Krogh, G., & Roos, J. (1998). Knowledge and the concept of trust. In von Krogh, Rood, & Klein (Eds.), *Knowing in firms, understanding, managing and measuring knowledge.* London: Sage.

Hunt, S., & Nevin, J. (1974). Power in a channel of distribution: Sources and consequences. *Journal of Marketing Research, 11*(1), 186-193.

Huselid, M. (1995). The impact of human resource management practices on turnover, productivity, and corporate financial performance. *Academy of Management Journal, 38*(3), 635-672.

Huselid, M., Jackson, S., & Schuler, R. (1997). Technical and strategic human resource management effectiveness as determinants of firm performance. *Academy of Management Journal, 40*(1), 171-188.

Husted, K., & Michailova, S. (2002). Diagnosing and fighting knowledge sharing hostility. *Organizational Dynamics, 31*(1), 60-73.

Huysman, M., & Wulf, V. (2006). IT to support knowledge sharing in communities, towards a social capital analysis. *Journal of Information Technology, 21*(1), 40-51.

Hwang, Y. (2005). Investigating enterprise systems adoption: Uncertainty avoidance, intrinsic motivation, and the Technology Acceptance Model. *European Journal of Information Systems, 14*, 150-161.

Hymer, S. (1960). *The international operations of national firms: A study of direct investment.* Boston: MIT Press.

IBM. (2004). *Patterns for e-business.* Retrieved from *http://www28.ibm.com/developerworks/ patterns*

IBM. (2006, January). *Ford Motor Company's integrated CRM and marketing functions generate increased sales leads.* Retrieved October 20, 2006, from *http://www-306.ibm.com/software/success/cssdb.nsf/CS/GJON-6KWLL4?OpenDocument&Site=igsww*

ICFAI. (2004). *IBM's e-CRM initiatives* (case code ITSY044). Retrieved October 21, 2006, from *http://www.icmr.icfai.org/casestudies/catalogue/IT%20and%20Systems/ITSY044.htm*

Ichniowski, C., Shaw, K., & Prennushi, G. (1997). The effects of human resource management practices on productivity: A study of steel finishing lines. *The American Economic Review,* (June), 291-313.

Igbaria, M., Livari, J., & Maragahh, H. (1995). Why do individuals use computer technology? A Finnish case study. *Information & Management, 29*(5), 227-238.

INDEHELA-Methods project. (1999). Retrieved on March 2, 2003, from http://www.uku.fi/atkk/indehela/

Inkpen, G.P. (1998). Learning, knowledge acquisition, and strategic alliances. *European Management Journal, 16*(2), 223-229.

Inkpen, G.P., & Dinur, A. (1998). Knowledge management processes and international joint ventures. *Organization Science, 9*(4), 454-468.

International Crops Research Institute for Semi-Arid Tropics (ICRISAT). (2001). *People first!* (Medium Term Plan 2002-2004). Patancheru AP, India.

Isaacs, W.N. (1993). Dialogue, collective thinking, and organizational learning. *Organizational Dynamics,* (Autumn), 24-39.

ISO. (2000). *ISO 9000:2000: Quality management systems—fundamentals and vocabulary.* Geneva: International Organization for Standardization.

Itami, H. (1987). *Mobilizing invisible assets.* Cambridge, MA: Harvard University Press.

Ivancevich, J.M. (1998). *Human resource management.* Boston: Irwin/McGraw-Hill.

Ives, B., & Jarvenpaa, S.L. (1991). Application of global information technology: Key issues for management. *MIS Quarterly,* 33-49.

Janet, P. (1936). *L'intelligence avant le langage.* Paris: Flammarion.

Janev, V., & Vranes, S. (2005). The role of knowledge management solutions in enterprise business processes. *Journal of Universal Computer Science, 11*(4), 526-545.

Jarvenpaa, S. L., & Staples, D. S. (2000). The use of collaborative electronic media for information sharing: An exploratory study of determinants. *Journal of Strategic Information Systems, 9*(2-3), 129-154.

Jarvenpaa, S. L., & Staples, S. D. (2001). Exploring perceptions of organizational ownership of information and expertise. *Journal of Management Information Systems, 18*(1), 151-183.

Jennex, M. E. (2005). What is Knowledge Management? *International Journal of Knowledge Management, 1*(4), i-iv.

Jennex, M.E., & Olfman, L. (2002). Organizational memory/knowledge effects on productivity, a longitudinal study. *Proceedings of the 35th IEEE Hawaii International Conference on System Sciences.*

Jessup, L., & Valacich, J. (2005). *Information systems today—why IS matters* (2nd/international ed.). Englewood Cliffs, NJ: Prentice Hall.

Johns, G. (2001). In praise of context. *Journal of Organizational Behavior, 22*(1), 31-40.

Johnson, G. (1992) Managing strategic change — Strategy, culture and action. *Long Range Planning, 25*(1), 28-36.

Johnson, J.H. Jr., Lenn, D.J., & O'Neill, H.M. (1997). Patterns of competition among American firms in a global industry: Evidence from the U.S. construction equipment industry. *Journal of International Management, 3*(3), 207-239.

Johnston, W., Leach, M., & Liu, A. (1999). Theory testing using case studies in business to business research. *Industrial Marketing Management, 28,* 201-213.

Joint Venture. (2006). *Silicon Valley index.* San Jose, CA: Joint Venture. Retrieved March 23, 2006, from *http://www.jointventure.org/publications/index/2005index/2005index/changingdemo.html*

Jordan, B. (1993). Ethnographic workplace studies and computer supported cooperative work. In *Proceedings of Interdisciplinary Workshop on Informatics and Psychology*, Scharding, Austria.

JPMorganChase. (n.d.). *About JPMorganChase.* Retrieved October 17, 2006, from *http://www.jpmorganchase.com/cm/cs?pagename=Chase/Href&urlname=jpmc/about*

Junghagen, S., & Linderoth, H. C. J. (2003). *Intelligent management in the knowledge economy.* Cheltenham, UK; Northampton, MA: Edward Elgar.

Kakabadse, A., & Parker, C. (Eds.). (1984). *Power, politics, and organizations*. New York: John Wiley & Sons.

Kambhampaty, S., & Chandra, S. (2005). Service-Oriented Architecture for enterprise applications. *Journal of WSEAS Transactions on Business and Economics, 2*(3), 1109-9526.

Kamoche, K. (1997). Knowledge creation and learning in international HRM. *International Journal of Human Resource Management, 8,* 213-225.

Kandell, J. (2000). CRM, ERM, one-to-one—decoding relationship management theory and technology. *Trusts & Estates, 139*(4), 49.

Kanungo, S., Sadavarti, S., & Srinivas, Y. (2001). Relating IT strategy and organizational culture: An empirical study of public sector units in India. *Journal of Strategic Information Systems, 10*(1), 29-57.

Kaplan, R.S., & Norton, D.P. (1992). The balanced scorecard—measures that drive performance. *Harvard Business Review, 70*(January-February), 72-79.

Kaplan, R.S., & Norton, D.P. (1993). Putting the balanced scorecard to work. *Harvard Business Review,* (September-October), 134-147.

Kaplan, R.S., & Norton, D.P. (1996). Using the balanced scorecard as a strategic management system. *Harvard Business Review,* (January-February), 76.

Karahanna, E., Evaristo, J.R., & Srite, M. (2005). Levels of culture and individual behavior: An integrative perspective. *Journal of Global Information Management, 13*(2), 1-20.

Karsten H. (2000). *Weaving tapestry: Collaborative information technology and organizational change*. Doctoral dissertation, Jyvaskyla Studies in Computing, No 3.

Katila, R., & Ahuja, G. (2002). Something old, something new: A longitudinal study of search behaviour and new product introduction. *Academy of Management Journal, 45*(6), 1183-1194.

Keegan, A., & Turner, J. (2002). The management of innovation in project-based firms. *Long Range Planning, 35,* 367-388.

Kelly Services. (n.d.). *A people company, staffing the world.* Retrieved October 16, 2006, from *http://www.kellyservices.com/web/global/services/en/pages/about_us.html*

Kendall, K. E., & Kendall, J. E. (2002). *Systems analysis and design*. Upper Saddle River, NJ: Prentice-Hall.

Keskin, H. (2005). The relationships between explicit and tacit oriented KM strategy, and firm performance. *Journal of American Academy of Business,* (1), 169-175.

Khirallah, K. (2000). Customer relationship management: How to measure success? *Bank Account & Finance,* (Summer), 21.

Kierkegaard, S. (1985). *Fear and trembling* (A. Hannay, trans.). London: Penguin.

Kim, D.H. (1993). *A framework and methodology for linking individual and organizational learning: Applications in TQM and product development*. Doctoral Thesis, MIT Sloan School of Management, USA.

Kim, L. (2001). Absorptive capacity, co-operation, and knowledge creation: Samsung's leapfrogging in semiconductors. In I. Nonaka & T. Nishiguchi (Eds.), *Knowledge emergence—social, technical, and evolutionary dimensions of knowledge creation* (pp. 270-286). Oxford: Oxford University Press.

King, J., Gurbaxani, V., Kraemer, K., McFarlan, F., Raman, K., & Yap, C. (1994). Institutional factors in information technology innovation. *Information Systems Research, 5*(2), 139-169.

King, W.R. (2002). IT capabilities, business processes, and impact on the bottom line. *Information Systems Management, 19*(2), 85-87.

Kirsch, L. (1996). The management of complex tasks in organizations: Controlling the systems development process. *Organization Science, 7*(1), 1-22.

Klein, K.J., & Ralls, R.S. (1995). The organizational dynamics of computerized technology implementation: A review of the literature. In M.W. Lawless & L.R. Gomez-Media (Eds.), *Advances in global high-technology management* (pp. 31-79). New York: JAI Press.

Kobrin, S.J. (1988). Expatriate reduction and strategic control in American multinational corporations. *Human Resource Management, 27,* 63-75.

Kochikar, V. P., & Suresh, J. K. (2004). *Towards a knowledge-sharing organization. Some challenges faced on the Infosys journey.* Hershey, PA: Idea Group Publishing.

Kogut, B. (2000). The network as knowledge: Generative rules and the emergence of structure. *Strategic Management Journal, 21,* 405-425.

Kogut, B., & Zander, U. (1992). Knowledge of the firm, combinative capabilities and the replication of technology. *Organization Science, 3*(3), 383-397.

Kogut, B., & Zander, U. (1992). Knowledge of the firm, combinative capabilities, and the replication of technology. *Organization Science,* 383-397.

Kogut, B., & Zander, U. (1992). Knowledge of the firm: Combinative capabilities and the replication of technology. *Organization Science, 3*(3), 383-397.

Kogut, B., & Zander, U. (1993). Knowledge of the firm and the evolutionary theory of the multinational corporation. *Journal of International Business Studies, 24,* 625-646.

Kogut, B., & Zander, U. (1993). Knowledge of the firm and the evolutionary theory of the multinational corporation. *Journal of International Business Studies, 24*(4), 625-646.

Kogut, B., & Zander, U. (1996). What firms do. Coordination, identity and learning. *Organization Science, 7*(5), 502-518.

Kohli, A., & Jaworski, B. (1990). Market orientation: The construct, research propositions, and managerial implications. *Journal of Marketing, 62*(4), 20-35.

Korot, L. (1989, January). Technoculture: Leading edge to European integration or an organizational anomaly? *Proceedings of the 17th Annual Conference of the Association for Business Simulation and Experiential Learning,* Honolulu, HI.

Korot, L. (1997). *A cross-cultural comparison of the organizational cultures of hi-tech start-up ventures.* Paper presented to the Executive MBA Group, Pepperdine University, USA.

Korpela, M. (1996). Traditional culture or political economy? On the root causes of organizational obstacles of IT in developing countries. *Information Technology for Development, 7,* 29-42.

Korpela, M., Mursu, A., & Soriyan, H. A. (2001). Two times four integrative levels of analysis: A framework. In N. Russo, B. Fitzgerald, & J. DeGross, (Eds.), *Realigning research and practice in information systems development. The social and organizational perspective* (pp. 367-377). Boston: Kluwer Academic Publishers.

Kotler, P. (1967). *Marketing management: Application, planning, implementation and control.* Upper Saddle River, NJ: Prentice Hall.

Kotorov, R. (2003). Customer relationship management: Strategic lessons and future directions. *Business Process Management Journal, 9*(5), 566-571.

Kotter, J.P. (1999). *John P. Kotter on what leaders really do.* Boston: Harvard Business School Press.

KPMG Management Consulting. (1998). *Knowledge management: Research report.*

Kraul, C. (2003). WTO meeting finds protests inside and out. *Los Angeles Times,* (September 11), A3.

Krebsbach, K. (2004). Lessons from the dark side: Avoiding mistakes in overseas outsourcing. *Bank Technology News,* (May), 31, 54.

Kroeber, A.L., & Kluckholn, C. (1952). *Culture: A critical review of concepts and definitions.* New York: Vintage Books.

Kuemmerle, W. (1999). The drivers of foreign direct investment into research and development: An empirical investigation. *Journal of International Business Studies, 30*(1), 1-25.

Kuhn, T.S. (1970). *The structure of scientific revolutions* (2nd ed., enlarged). Chicago: University of Chicago Press.

Kwan, M. M., & Cheung, P.-K. (2006). The knowledge transfer process: From field studies to technology development. *Journal of Database Management, 17*(1), 16-32.

Lado, A., & Wilson, M. (1994). Human resource systems and sustained competitive advantage: A competency-based perspective. *Academy of Management Review, 19*, 699-727.

Lado, A., Boyd, N., & Wright, P. (1992). A competency-based model of sustainable competitive advantage: Toward a central integration. *Journal of Management, 18*(1), 77-91.

Lai, H., & Chu, T. (2000, January 4-7). Knowledge management: A theoretical frameworks and industrial cases. In *Proceedings of the Thirty-Third Annual Hawaii International Conference on System Sciences* [CD/ROM].

Laine-Sveiby, K. (1991). *Foretagil kulturmoten. tre finlandska foretag och ders svenska dotterbolag.* En Etnologisk Studie (diss) Akedemitryck Edsbruk.

Lam, A. (2003). Organizational learning in multinationals: R&D networks of Japanese and U.S. MNEs in the UK. *Journal of Management Studies, 40*(3), 673-703.

Lambert, G. (1993). Variables clés pour le transfert de technologie et le management de l'innovation. *Revue Française de Gestion,* (94), 49-72.

Lane, P., & Lubatkin, M. (1998). Relative absorptive capacity and interorganizational learning. *Strategic Management Journal, 19,* 461-477.

Lane, P., Salk, J., & Lyles, M. (2001). Absorptive capacity, learning, and performance in international joint ventures. *Strategic Management Journal, 22*(12), 1139-1161.

Larsson, R., Bengtsson, L., Henriksson, K., & Sparks, J. (1998). The interorganizational learning dilemma: Collective knowledge development in strategic alliances. *Organization Science, 9*(3), 285-305.

Lateef, A. (1997). *A case study of Indian software industry.* International Institute for Labor Studies, New Industrial Organization Programme, DP/96/1997.

Lau, T., Wong, Y., Chan, K., & Law, M. (2001). Information technology and the work environment — Does IT change the way people interact at work? *Human Systems Management, 20*(3), 267-280.

Laursen, K., & Foss, N. (2003). New HRM practices, complementarities, and the impact on innovation performance. *Cambridge Journal of Economics, 27,* 243-263.

Lawrence, P.R., & Lorsch, J.W. (1967). *Organization and environment. Differentiation and integration.* Boston: Harvard University Press.

Leavitt, H. J. (1965). Applied organizational change in industry: structural, technological, and humanistic approaches. In J. March (Ed.), *Handbook of organizations* (pp. 1144-1170), Chicago: Rand McNally & Co.

Lee, H., & Choi, B. (2003). Knowledge management enablers, processes, and organizational performance: An integrative view and empirical examination. *Journal of Management Information Systems, 20*(1), 179-228.

Lee, R., & Cole, R. (2003). The Linux model of software quality development and improvement." In International Association of Quality (Ed.), *Quality in the 21st century: Perspectives on quality and competitiveness sustained performance.* ASQ Press.

Leonard Barton, D. (1995). *Wellsprings of knowledge. Building and sustaining the sources of innovation.* Boston: Harvard Business School Press.

Leonard-Barton, D. (1995). *Wellsprings of knowledge: Building and sustaining the sources of innovation.* Cambridge, MA: Harvard Business School Press.

Levinthal, D.A., & March, J.G. (1993). The myopia of learning. *Strategic Management Journal, 14,* 95-112.

Levy, S. (2002). Welcome back to Silicon Valley: How the dot-com crash saved technology. *Newsweek,* (March), 25.

Lewin, K. (1951). *Field theory in social science.* New York: Harper and Row.

Lieber, R. (2002). 'Operator, I demand an automated Menu.' *Wall Street Journal,* (July 30), D1.

Liebowitz, J., & Wilcox, L.C. (1997). *Knowledge elements and its integrative elements.* New York: CRC Press.

Lim, K.K., & Ahmed, P.K. (2000). Enabling knowledge management: A measurement perspective. *Proceedings of CMIT 2000.*

Lind, M.R., & Zmud, R.W. (1991). The influence of a convergence in understanding between technology providers and users on information technology innovativenss. *Organization Science, 2*(2), 195-217.

Ling, R., & Yen, D. (2001). Customer relationship management: An analysis framework and implementation strategies. *Journal of Computer Information Systems, 41*(3), 82.

Lippman, S., & Rumelt, R.P. (1982). Uncertain imitability: An analysis of interfirm differences in efficiency under competition. *Bell Journal of Economics, 13,* 418-438.

Lyles, M., & Salk, J. (1996). Knowledge acquisition from foreign parents in international joint ventures: An empirical examination in the Hungarian context. *Journal of International Business Studies,* (Special Issue), 877-903.

Lynch, J.J. (1977). *The broken heart: The medical consequences of loneliness.* New York: Basic Books.

Lyons, P. (2005). A robust approach to employee skill and knowledge development. *Industrial and Commercial Training, 37*(1), 3-9.

Lyytinen, K., & Hirschheim, R. A. (1987). Information system failures: A survey and classification of the empirical literature. *Oxford Surveys in Information Technology,* (4), 257-309.

Lyytinen, K., & Robey, D. (1999). Learning failure in information systems development. *Information Systems Journal,* (9), 85-101.

Lyytinen, K., Mathiassen, L., & Ropponen, J. (1998). Attention shaping and software risk — A categorical analysis of four classical risk management approaches. *Information Systems Research, 9*(3), 233-255.

MacDuffie, J. (1995). Human resource bundles and manufacturing performance: Flexible production systems in the world auto industry. *Industrial & Labor Relations Review, 48*(2), 197-221.

Mahoney, J.T. (1995). The management of resources and the resource management. *Journal of Business Research, 33,* 91-101.

Maidique, M.O., & Zirger, B.J. (1985). The new product learning cycle. *Research Policy,* (14), 299-313.

Maier, R., & Remus, U. (2001, January 3-6). Toward a framework for knowledge management strategies: Process orientation as strategic starting point. In *Proceedings of the 34th Hawaii International Conference on Systems Sciences* [CD/ROM].

Maira, A.N. (1998). Connecting across boundaries: The fluid-network organization. *Prism,* (1st Quarter), 23.

Malhotra, Y. (2002). Is knowledge management really an oxymoron? Unraveling the role of organizational controls in knowledge management. In D. White (Ed.), *Knowledge mapping and management* (pp. 1-13). Hershey, PA: Idea Group.

Malhotra, Y. (2004). Desperately seeking self-determination: Key to the new enterprise logic of customer relationships. *Proceedings of the Americas Conference on Information Systems,* New York.

Management Science. (2003). Managing knowledge in organizations: Creating, retaining and transferring knowledge. *Management Science,* (April Special Edition).

March, J.G. (1991). Exploration and exploitation in organizational learning. *Organization Science, 2*(1), 71-87.

March, J.G., & Simon, H.A. (1958). *Organizations.* New York: John Wiley & Sons.

Marchand, D.A., Kettinger, W.J., & Rollins, J.D. (2000). Information orientation: People, technology and the bottom line. *Sloan Management Review, 41*(4), 69-80.

Margetts, H., & Dunleavy, P. (2002, April). *Cultural barriers to e-government.* Report HC704-III, National Audit Office, The Stationary Office, London.

Markus, L., & Robey, D. (1998). Information technology and organizational change: Causal structure in theory and research. *Management Sciences, 34*(5), 583-598.

Markus, M.L., Axline, S., Petrie, D., & Tanis, C. (2000). Learning from adopters' experiences with ERP: Problems encountered and success achieved. *Journal of Information Technology, 15*(4), 245-265.

Marshall, N., & Brady, T. (2001). Knowledge management and the politics of knowledge: Illustrations from complex products and systems. *European Journal of Information Systems, 10*, 99-112.

Martin, B. (2000). Knowledge management within the context of management: An evolving relationship. *Singapore Management Review, 22*(2), 17-36.

Martin, V.A., Hatzakis, T., Lycett, M., & Macredie, R. (2004). Building the business/IT relationship through knowledge management. *Journal of Information Technology Cases and Applications, 6,* 2.

Martin, X., & Salomon, R. (2003). Knowledge transfer capacity and its implications for the theory of the multinational corporation. *Journal of International Business Studies, 34*(4), 345-356.

Marwick, A.D. (2001). Knowledge management technology. *IBM Systems Journal, 40*(4), 814-830.

Massey, A. P., Montoya-Weiss, M. M., et al. (2001). Re-engineering the customer relationship: Leveraging knowledge assets at IBM. *Decision Support Systems, 32*(2), 155-170.

McCall, C.H. (2001, November). An empirical examination of the Likert scale: Some assumptions, development, and cautions. *Proceedings of the 80th Annual CERA Conference,* South Lake Tahoe, CA.

McCracken, G. (1988). *The long interview, qualitative research methods.* Newbury Park, CA: Sage.

McDaniel, C. (2006). *2006 call center employment outlook.* Available from M.E.R. Inc., 866-991-3555.

McDermott, R. (1999). Why information technology inspires but cannot deliver knowledge management. *California Management Review, 40*(4), 103-117.

McDonald, W. (1996). Influences on the adoption of global marketing decision support systems: A management perspective. *International Marketing Review, 13*(1), 33-46.

McKendrick, J. (2000). The bottom line on CRM: Know thy customer. *ENT, 5*(20), 40.

McKinney, V., & Gerloff, E. (2004). *Interorganizational systems partnership effectiveness.* Retrieved from *http://hbs.baylor.edu*

McNamara, J.R. (2004). The crucial role of research in multicultural and cross-cultural communication. *Journal of Communication Management, 8*(3), 322-334.

Mehta, N., & Mehta, A. (2005). *Infosys technologies, limited.* Hershey, PA: Idea Group.

Mendenhall, M., & Stahl, G. (2000). Expatriate training and development: Where do we go from here? *Human Resources Management, 39*(2&3), 251-265.

Mendenhall, M.E., Kuhlmann, T.M., & Stahl, G.K. (Eds.). (2001). *Developing global business leaders: Policies, processes, and innovations.* Westport, CT: Quorum Books.

Meyers, P.W., & Wilemon, D. (1989). Learning in new technology development team. *Journal of Product Innovation Management,* (6), 79-88.

Miles, J. (2002). CRM for citizens. *Government Computer News, 21*(29).

Miles, R., & Snow, C. (1986). Organizations: New concepts for new forms. *California Management Review, 28*(3), 62-73.

Miles, R., & Snow, C. (1992). Causes of failure in network organizations. *California Management Review, 34*(4), 53-72.

Milliman, J., Taylor, S., & Czaplewski, A.J. (2002). Cross-cultural performance feedback in multinational enterprises: Opportunity for organizational learning. *Human Resource Planning, 25*(3), 29-43.

Minbaeva, D. (2007). Knowledge transfer in MNCs. *Management International Review,* (forthcoming).

Minbaeva, D., & Michailova, S. (2004). Knowledge transfer and expatriation practices in MNCs: The role of disseminative capacity. *Employee Relations, 26*(6), 663-679.

Minbaeva, D., Pedersen, T., Bjorkman, I., Fey, C., & Park, H. (2003). MNC knowledge transfer, subsidiary absorptive capacity and knowledge transfer. *Journal of International Business Studies, 34*(6), 586-599.

Miner, J., & Crane, D. (1995). *Human resource management: The strategic perspective.* HarperCollins College.

Ministry of Education. (2006). *Ministry of Education Singapore.* Retrieved March 24, 2006, from *http://www. moe.gov.sg/*

Mirvis, P.H. (1996). Historical foundations of organizational learning. *Journal of Organizational Change Management, 9*(1), 13-31.

Mitchell, P. J. (1998). Aligning customer call center for 2001. *Telemarketing and Call Center Solutions, 16*(10), 64-69.

Moisdon, J.C. (Ed.). (1997). *Du mode d'existence des outils de gestion.* Paris: Séli-Arslan.

Monteiro, L., Arvidsson, N., & Birkinshaw, J. (2004). Knowledge flows within multinational corporations: Why are some subsidiaries isolated? *Proceedings of the Academy of Management Conference 2004* (p. B1).

Moore, G., & Benbasat, I. (1991). Development of an instrument to measure the perceptions of adopting an information technology innovation. *Information Systems Research, 2*(3), 192-222.

Moore, K., & Birkinshaw, J.M. (1998). Managing knowledge in global service firms: Centers of excellence. *Academy of Management Executive, 12*(4), 81-92.

Morales-Gomez, D., & Melesse, M. (1998). Utilizing information and communication technologies for development: the social dimensions. *Information Technology for Development, 8*(1), 3-14.

Morgan, G. (1997). *Images of organization* (new ed.). Sage Publications.

Mowday, R., & McDade, T. (1979). Linking behavioral and attitudinal commitment: A longitudinal analysis of job choice and job attitude. *Academy of Management Proceedings.* Atlanta: AOM.

Mowery, D., Oxley, J., & Silverman, B. (1996). Strategic alliances and interfirm knowledge transfer. *Strategic Management Journal, 17,* 77-91.

Mowery, D.C. (1983). The relationship between intrafirm and contractual forms of industrial research in American manufacturing, 1900-1940. *Explorations in Economic History, 20,* 351-374.

Mudambi, R. (2002). Knowledge management in multinational firms. *Journal of International Management, 8,* 1-9.

Mumford, E. (1993). *Designing human systems for health care: The ETHICS method.* Chesire: Eight Associates.

Mumford, E., & Weir, M. (1979). *Computer systems in work design — The ETHICS method: Effective technical and human implementation of computer systems.* Exeter: A. Wheaton & Co.

Nahapiet, J., & Ghoshal, S. (1998). Social capital, intellectual capital, and the organizational advantage. *Academy of Management Review, 23*(2), 242-266.

Nakamura, S. (1993). *The new standardization—keystone of continuous improvement in manufacturing.* Portland, OR: Productivity Press.

Namenwirth, J.Z., & Weber, R.P. (1987). *Dynamics of culture.* Boston: Allen & Irwin.

Nanonet. (2003). *Nanonet–Styria intellectual capital report.* Retrieved from *www.nanonet.at*

Narver, J., & Slater, S. (1990). The effect of a market orientation on business profitability. *Journal of Marketing, 54*(4), 20-36.

Nathanson, D., Kazanjian, R., & Galbraith, J. (1982). Effective strategic planning and the role of organization design. In P. Lorange (Ed.), *Implementation of strategic planning* (pp. 91-113). Englewood Cliffs, NJ: Prentice Hall, Inc.

Nelson, R.R. (1990). U.S. technological leadership: Where did it come from and where did it go? *Research Policy, 79,* 119-132.

Nelson, S., & Berg, T. (2000). *Customer relationship management: An overview.* Gartner Group.

Ness, J., Schroeck, M., Letendre, R., & Douglas, W. (2001). The role of ABM in measuring customer value. *Strategic Finance,* (March), 32.

Nidiffer, K., & Dolan, D. (2005). Evolving distributed project management. *IEEE Software,* (September/October), 63-72.

Noer, D.M. (1993). *Healing the wounds: Overcoming the trauma of layoffs and revitalizing downsized organizations.* San Francisco: Jossey-Bass.

Nonaka, H., & Takeuchi, I. (1995). *The knowledge creating company.* Oxford: Oxford University Press.

Nonaka, I. (1990). Redundant, overlapping organization: A Japanese approach to managing the innovation process. *California Management Review,* (Spring), 27-38.

Nonaka, I. (1994). A dynamic theory of organizational knowledge creation. *Organization Sciences, 5*(1), 14-37.

Nonaka, I., & Konno, N. (1998). The concept of "ba": Building a foundation for knowledge creation. *California Management Review, 40*(3), 40-54.

Nonaka, I., & Takeuchi, H. (1995). *The knowledge creating company: How Japanese companies create the dynamics of innovation.* New York: Oxford University Press.

Nonaka, I., Toyama, R. & Nagata, A. (2000). A firm as a knowledge-creating entity: A new perspective on the theory of the firm. *Industrial and Corporate Change, 9*(1), 1-20.

Noordhoff, C., Pauwels, P., & Odekerken-Schroder, G. (2004). The effect of customer card programs: A comparative study of Singapore and The Netherlands. *International Journal of Service Industry Management, 15*(3/4), 351-360.

Nunally, J.C. (1978). *Psychometric theory.* New York: McGraw-Hill.

O'Dell, C., & Grayson Jr., C.J. (1998). *If only we knew what we know: The transfer of internal knowledge and best practice.* New York: The Free Press.

O'Dell, C., & Grayson, C. J. (1998). If only we know what we know: Identification and transfer of best practices. *California Management Review, 40*(3), 154-174.

O'Reilly, C. A., Chatman, J., & Caldwell, D. F. (1996). Culture as social control: Corporations, cults, and commitment. *Research in Organizational Behavior, 18,* 157-200.

O'Sullivan, K.J., & Stankosky, M. (2004). The impact of KM technology on intellectual capital. *Journal of Information and KM, 3*(4), 331-346.

Odedra, M., Lawrie, M., Bennett, M., & Goodman, S. (1993). International perspectives: Sub-saharan Africa: A technological desert. *Communications of the ACM, 36*(2), 25-29.

OECD. (2005). Economic survey of The Netherlands 2005: Making better use of knowledge creation in innovation activities. *Economic Survey of the Netherlands 2005.* Paris: Organization for Economic Cooperation and

Development. Retrieved March 27, 2006, from *http:// www.oecd.org/document/14/0,2340,en_2649_201185_ 35822542_1_1_1_1,00.html*

Okunoye, A., & Karsten, H. (2001, June 10-12). Information technology infrastructure and knowledge management in sub-saharan Africa: Research in progress. In *Proceedings of the Second Annual Global Information Technology Management (GITM) World Conference*, Dallas, TX.

Okunoye, A., & Karsten, H. (2002a). Where the global needs the local: Variation in enablers in the knowledge management process. *Journal of Global Information Technology Management, 5*(3), 12-31.

Okunoye, A., & Karsten, H. (2002b, January 7-10). ITI as enabler of KM: Empirical perspectives from research organisations in sub-saharan Africa. In *Proceedings of the 35th Hawai'i International Conference on Systems Sciences*, Big Island, Hawaii.

Okunoye, A., & Karsten, H. (2003). Global access to knowledge in research: Findings from organizations in sub-saharan Africa. *Information Technology and People, 16*(3), 353-373.

Okunoye, A., Innola, E., & Karsten, H. (2002, September 24-25). Benchmarking knowledge management in developing countries: Case of research organizations in Nigeria, The Gambia, and India. In *Proceedings of the 3rd European Conference on Knowledge Management*, Dublin, Ireland.

Ollner, J. (1974). *The company and standardization* (2nd ed.). Stockholm: Swedish Standards Institution.

Oracle. (2006, June). *InFact group reduces sales cycle times by 15%*. Retrieved October 17, 2006, from *http:// www.oracle.com/customers/snapshots/infact-siebel- casestudy.pdf*

Ordóñez de Pablos, P. (2001). Relevant experiences on measuring and reporting intellectual capital in European pioneering firms. In N. Bontis & C. Chong (Eds.), *Organizational intelligence: The cutting edge of intellectual capital and knowledge management.* Butterworth-Heinemann.

Ordóñez de Pablos, P. (2004a). Knowledge flow transfers in multinational corporations: Knowledge properties and implications for management. *Journal of Knowledge Management, 8*(4), 105-116.

Ordóñez de Pablos, P. (2004b). A guideline for building the intellectual capital statement: The 3R model. *International Journal of Learning and Intellectual Capital, 1*(1), 3-18.

Ordóñez de Pablos, P. (2005a). Intellectual capital accounts: What pioneering firms from Asia and Europe are doing now. *International Journal of Knowledge and Learning, 1*(3), 249-268.

Ordóñez de Pablos, P. (2005b). Intellectual capital reports in India: Lessons from a case study. *Journal of Intellectual Capital, 6*(1), 141-149.

Ordóñez de Pablos, P. (2006). Transnational corporations and strategic challenges: An analysis of knowledge flows and competitive advantage. *The Learning Organization.*

Ordóñez de Pablos, P., & Edvinsson, L. (2006). *The intellectual capital statements: Evolution and how to get started.* Working Paper.

Ordóñez de Pablos, P., & Peteraf, M. (2004). Managing and measuring knowledge-based resources. *International Journal of Learning and Intellectual Capital, 1*(4), 377-379.

Ordóñez de Pablos, P., & Peteraf, M. (2005). Organizational learning, innovation and knowledge: The creation of a sustained competitive advantage. *International Journal of Learning and Intellectual Capital, 2*(2), 111-113.

Orlikowski, W., & Barley, S. (2001). Technology and institutions: What can research on information technology and research on organizations learn from each other. *MIS Quarterly, 25*(2), 145-165.

Orlikowski, W.J. (1993). CASE tools as organizational change: Investigating increment. *MIS Quarterly*, 309-332.

Österreichisches Normungsinstitut. (1988). *Werknormung in Österreich—ein leitfaden für normenpraktiker.* Vienna: Österreichisches Normungsinstitut.

Ozsomer, A., & Prussia, G. (2000). Competing perspectives in international marketing strategy: Contingency and process models. *Journal of International Marketing, 8*(1), 27-51.

Paik, Y., & Sohn, D. (2003). Expatriate managers and MNCs' ability to control international subsidiaries: The case of Japanese MNCs. *Journal of World Business, 39*(1), 61-71.

Paik, Y., Segaud, B., & Malinowski, C. (2002). How to improve repatriation management: Are motivations and expectations congruent between the company and expatriates? *International Journal of Manpower, 23*(7), 635-648.

Paik, Y., Vance, C.M., & Stage, H.D. (1996). The extent of divergence in human resource practice across three Chinese national cultures: Hong Kong, Taiwan, and Singapore. *Human Resource Management Journal, 6*(2), 20-31.

Paik, Y.S., & Choi, D. (2005). The shortcomings of a standardized global knowledge management system: The case study of Accenture. *Academy of Management Executive, 19*(2), 81-84.

Palmer, J. (2004). Qualities and capacities of interaction. *Proceedings of the Mindful Leadership Program,* Isle of Man, UK.

Palvia, S., Palvia, P., & Zigli, R. (Eds.). (1992). *The global issues of information technology management.* Hershey, PA: Idea Group.

Pan, S., & Scarbrough, H. (1998). A socio-technical view of knowledge — Sharing at Buckman Laboratories. *Journal of Knowledge Management, 2*(1), 55-66.

Pan, S.L., & Scarbrough, H. (1999). Knowledge management in practice: An exploratory case study. *Technology Analysis & Strategic Management, 11*(3), 359-374.

Pang, L., & Norris, R. (2002). Applying customer relationship management (CRM) to government. *Journal of Government Financial Management, 51*(1), 40.

Paraponaris, C. (2001). The organization of R&D and the management of cooperation: Controlling a diversity of knowledge sources. In E. Verdier (Ed.), *Higher education system and innovation* (pp. 55-89). European Commission Report Number 1-1054.

Paraponaris, C. (2003). Third generation R&D and strategies for knowledge management. *Journal of Knowledge Management, 7*(5), 96-106.

Park, H., Ribiere, V., & Schulte, W.D. (2004). Critical attributes of organizational culture that promote KM technology implementation success. *Journal of KM, 8*(3), 106-116.

Parpola, P. (2005). Inference in the SOOKAT object-oriented knowledge acquisition tool. *Knowledge and Information Systems, 8*(3), 310-329.

Parr, A., & Shanks, G. (2000). A model of ERP project implementation. *Journal of Information Technology, 15*(4), 289-303.

Paylow, K., Hickman, A., & Zappa, D. (2006, April 11-13). Identifying future leaders through knowledge management. *Proceedings of the 2006 Society of Petroleum Engineers Intelligent Energy Conference and Exhibition* (ref. SPE 99898), Amsterdam.

Payne, A., & Frow, P. (2004). The role of multichannel integration in customer relationship management. *Industrial Marketing Management, 33*(6), 527.

Pearce, R.D. (1999). Decentralized R&D and strategic competitiveness: Globalized approaches to generation and use of technology in multinational enterprises. *Research Policy, 28,* 157-178.

Pelz, D.C., & Andrews, F.M. (1966). *Scientists in organizations.* New York: John Wiley & Sons.

Peppas, S., & Chang, L. (1998). The integration of inpatriates into rural communities. *Management Decision, 36*(6), 370-377.

Peppers, D., & Rogers, M. (1993). *The one to one future.* New York: Currency Doubleday.

Peppers, D., Rogers, M., & Dorf, B. (1999). Is your company ready for one-to-one marketing? *Harvard Business Review, 77*(1), 151-161.

Perlmutter, H.V. (1969). The tortuous evolution of the multinational corporation. *Columbia Journal of World Business, 4*(1), 9-18.

Perlmutter, H.V., & Heenan, D.A. (1974). How multinational should your top managers be? *Harvard Business Review, 52*(6), 121-132.

Peteraf, M.A. (1993). The cornerstone of competitive advantage: A resource based-view. *Strategic Management Journal, 14,* 179-191.

Peteraf, M.A. (1993). The resource-based view within the conversation of strategic management. *Strategic Management Journal, 14,* 179-192.

Pettigrew, A. (1988). *Longitudinal field research on change: Theory and practice.* National Science Foundation Conference on Longitudinal Research Methods in Organizaitons, Austin, TX.

Pettigrew, A. M. (1987). Context and action in the transformation of the firm. *Journal of Management Studies, 24*(6), 649-670.

Pettigrew, A.M. (1990). Longitudinal field research on change: Theory and practice. *Organization Science, 1*(3), 267-292.

Pfeffer, J. (1981) Understanding the role of power in decision making. In J. M. Shafritz & J. S. Ott (Eds.), *Classics of organization theory.* Brooks/Cole.

Pfeffer, J., & Cohen, Y. (1984). Determinants of internal labor markets in organizations. *Administrative Science Quarterly, 29*(4), 550-573.

Pinsonneault, A., & Rivard, S. (1998). Information technology and the nature of managerial work: From the productivity paradox. *MIS Quarterly, 22,* 3.

Poitou, J.P. (1997). Building a collective knowledge management system: Knowledge-editing versus knowledge-eliciting techniques. In G.C. Bowker, L. Gasser, S.L. Star, & W. Turner (Eds.), (pp. 235-256).

Polanyi, M. (1966). *The tacit dimension.* Garden City, NY: Doubleday and Company.

Polanyi, M. (1966). *The tacit dimension.* London: Routledge and Kegan Paul.

Polanyi, M. (1967). *The tacit dimension.* Garden City, NY: Doubleday Press.

Popper, M., & Lipshitz, R. (1998). Organizational learning: A structural and cultural approach to organizational learning. *Journal of Applied Behavioural Science, 34*(2), 161-179.

Popper, M., & Lipshitz, R. (2000). Organizational learning: Mechanism, culture, and feasibility. *Management Learning, 31*(2), 181-196.

Porter, M. (Ed.). (1986). *Competition in global industries.* Boston: Harvard Business School Press.

Powell, W. W., & DiMaggio, P. J. (Eds.). (1991). *The new institutionalism in organizational analysis.* Chicago, University of Chicago Press.

Powell, W.W., Koput K.W., & Smit-Doerr L. (1996). Inter-organizational collaboration and the locus of innovation: Networks of learning in biotechnology. *Administrative Science Quarterly, 41*(1), 116-134.

Prahalad, C., & Ramaswamy, V. (2002). Co-opting customer competence. *Harvard Business Review on Customer Relationship Management,* 1.

Prahalad, C.K., & Doz, Y.L. (1987). *The multinational mission: Balancing local demands and global vision.* Boston: The Free Press.

Prieto, I. (2003). *Una valoración de la gestión del conocimiento para el desarrollo de la capacidad de aprendizaje de las organizaciones. Propuesta de un modelo integrador.* Doctoral Dissertation, Universidad de Valladolid, Spain.

Prieto, I.M., & Revilla, E. (2004). Information technologies and human behaviors as interacting knowledge management enablers of the organizational learning capacity. *International Journal of Management Concepts and Philosophy, 1*(3), 175-197.

Probst, G., & Buchel, B. (1997). *Organization learning.* London: Prentice Hall.

Prusak, L. (2006). The world is round. *Harvard Business Review,* (April), 18-20.

Ptacek, M. (2000). Chase revs up corporate CRM system. *American Banker, 165*(156), 1.

Pucik, V. (1988). Strategic alliances, organizational learning, and competitive advantage: The HRM agenda. *Human Resource Management, 27*(1), 77-93.

Purser, R.E., Pasmore, W.A., & Tenkasi, R.V. (1992). The influence of deliberations on learning in new product development teams. *Journal of Engineering and Technology Management,* (9), 1-28.

Purvis, R.L., Sambamurthy, V., & Zmud, R.W. (2001). The assimilation of knowledge platforms in organizations: An empirical investigation. *Organization Science, 12*(2), 117-135.

Puschmann, T., & Rainer, A. (2001). Customer relationship management in the pharmaceutical industry. In *Proceedings of the 34th Hawaii International Conference on System Sciences.*

Qin, C. (2004). China builds its new petroleum industry around international standards. *ISO Focus, 1*(4), 23-24.

Quelch, J. (1992). The new country manager. *The McKinsey Quarterly, 4,* 155-165.

Quinn, R. E., & Rohrbaugh, I. (1983). A spatial model of effectiveness criteria: Towards a competing values approach to organizational analysis. *Management Science, 29*(3), 363-377.

Ra, J.W. (1997). The informal structure of project organizations. *Proceedings of the Portland International Conference on Management and Technology* (PICMET) (p. 392).

Rad, P.F., & Anantatmula, V. (2005). *Project planning techniques.* Vienna, VA: Management Concepts.

Rada, R., & Craparo, J.S. (2001). Standardizing management of software engineering projects. *Knowledge Technology and Policy, 14*(2), 67-77.

Rasmus, D. (2003). *Don't bother looking for a knowledge management market* (Pub. ID: RPA-092003-00053). Forrester.

Raymond, E.S. (1999). *The cathedral and the bazaar: Musings on Linux and open source by an accidental revolutionary.* Cambridge, MA: O'Reilly.

Reddy, R. (2001). Through a lens smartly. *Intelligent Enterprise, 4*(5), 66.

Reed, R., & DeFillippi, R. (1990). Causal ambiguity, barriers to imitation and sustainable competitive advantage. *Academy of Management Review, 15*(1), 88-102.

Reichheld, F. (1996). Learning from customer defections. *Harvard Business Review, 74*(2), 56-68.

Reinartz, W., Krafft, M., & Hoyer, W. (2004). The customer relationship management process: Its measurement and impact on performance. *Journal of Marketing Research, 61*(1), 293-305.

Revilak, A. (2006). *Knowledge management and innovation: An analysis of knowledge factors controlled by governments and their impact on patent creation.* Unpublished Doctoral Dissertation, George Washington University, USA.

Revilla, E., Acosta, J., & Sarkis, J. (2006). An empirical assessment of a learning and knowledge management typology for research joint ventures. *International Journal of Technology Management, 35*(1/2/3/4), 329-348.

Rheault, D., & Sheridan, S. (2002). Reconstruct your business around customers. *Journal of Business Strategy, 23*(2), 38.

Ribiere, V., & Sitar, A.S. (2003). Critical role of leadership in nurturing a knowledge-supporting culture. *KM Research and Practice,* 39-48.

Ribiere, V., Park, H., & Schulte, W.D. (2004). Critical attributes of organizational culture that promote knowledge management technology success. *Journal of Knowledge Management, 8*(3), 106-117.

Richardson, R. (2004). *The whole and its parts.* Retrieved from *www.Dr.Rob.info*

Ricks, D.A. (1999). *Blunders in international business* (3rd ed.). Oxford, UK: Blackwell.

Ridderstrale, J., & Nordstrom, K. (2004). *The Karaoke capitalism: Management for mankind.* Financial Times.

Rigby, D., Reichheld, F., & Schefter, P. (2002, February). Avoid the four perils of CRM. *Harvard Business Review, 80*(2), 101.

Roberts, E.B. (1988) Managing invention and innovation. *Research and Technology Management, 31*(1), 11-27.

Robertson, E.D. (2001). Personal communications.

Robey, D., Ross, J.W., & Boudreau, M.C. (2002). Learning to implement enterprise systems: An exploratory study of the dialectics of change. *Journal of Management Information Systems, 19*(1), 17-46.

Roche, E. (1996). Strategic alliances—An entrepreneurial approach to globalisation. *Journal of Global Information Management, 4*(1), 34.

Roche, E., & Blaine, M. (Eds.). (1993). *Information technology in multinational enterprises.* Northampton (USA): Edward Elgar.

Rogers, E.M. (1995). *Diffusion of innovations* (4th ed.). New York: The Free Press.

Rollett, H. (2003). *Knowledge management: Processes and technologies.* Boston: Kluwer Academic.

Roos, H., Krogh, G., & Yip, G. (1994). An epistemology of globalizing firms. *International Business Review, 4,* 395-409.

Ross, S. (1973). The economic theory of agency: The principal's dilemma. *The American Economic Review Proceedings, 63,* 134-139.

Roth, K., & O'Donnell, S. (1996). Foreign subsidiary compensation strategy: An agency theory perspective. *Academy of Management Journal, 39*(3), 678-703.

Roussel, P.A., Saad, K.N., & Erickson, T.J. (1995). *Third generation of R&D: Managing the link to corporate strategy.* Cambridge, MA: Harvard Business School Press.

Roussel, P.A.., Saad, K.N., & Erickson, T.J. (1991). *Third generation R&D. Managing the link to corporate strategy.* Boston: Harvard Business School Press.

Rowe, A., Mason, R., Dickel, K., Mann, R., & Mockler, R. (1994). *Strategic management—a methodological approach* (4th ed.). New York: Addison-Wesley.

Rubenstein-Montano, B., Liebowitz, J., Buchwalter, J., McCaw, D., Newman, B., Rebeck, K., & The Knowledge Management Methodology Team. (2001). A systems thinking framework for knowledge management. *Decision Support Systems, 31*(1), 5-16

Ruggles, R. (1998). The state of the notion: Knowledge management in practice. *California Management Review, 40*(3), 80-89.

Ruiz-Mercader, J., & Merono-Cerdan, A. L. (2006). Information technology and learning: Their relationship and impact on organizational performance in small businesses. *International Journal of Information Management, 26*(1), 16-29.

Ryals, L. (2002). Measuring risk and returns in the customer portfolio. *Journal of Database Marketing, 9*(3), 219-227.

Ryals, L., & Knox, S. (2001). Cross functional issues in the implementation of relationship marketing through customer relationship management. *European Management Journal, 19*(5), 534.

Rybczynski, W. (1983). *Taming the tiger: The struggle to control technology.* New York: Viking Press.

Rycroft, R.W., & Kash, D.E. (1999). *The complexity challenge—technological innovation for the 21st century.* London: Pinter.

Sagie, A., & Elizur, D. (2001). Entrepreneurship and culture as correlates of achievement motive: A multifaceted approach. *International Journal of Entrepreneurship and Innovation Management, 1*(1), 34-52.

Salesforce (Kelly). (n.d.). *Kelly Services connects sales network across 27 countries and five continents with Salesforce.* Retrieved October 17, 2006, from *http://www.salesforce.com/customers/snapshot.jsp?customer=kelly*

Salesforce (Nokia). (n.d.). *Nokia easily customizes Salesforce to meet the needs of sales teams on three continents.* Retrieved October 17, 2006, from *http://www.salesforce.com/customers/snapshot.jsp?customer=nok*

Sambamurthy, V., Bharadwah, A., & Grover, V. (2003). Shaping agility through digital options: Reconceptualizing the role of information technology in contemporary firms. *MIS Quarterly, 27*(2), 237-263.

Sanyal, R.N., & Guvenli, T. (2004). Perception of managerial characteristics and organizational performance: Comparative evidence from Israel, Slovenia, and the USA. *Cross Cultural Management, 11*(2), 35-57.

Sauer, C. (1993). *Why information systems fail: A case study approach.* Henley-On-Thames, Oxfordshire: Alfred Waller.

Schacht, M. (1991). *Methodische neugestaltung von normen als grundlage für eine integration in den rechnerunterstützten konstruktionsprozeß* (DIN Normungskunde, Band 28). Berlin/Cologne: Beuth Verlag.

Schäfer, G., Hirschheim, R., Harper, M., Hansjee, R., Domke, M., & Bjorn-Andersen, N. (1988). *Functional analysis of office requirements: A multiperspective approach.* Chichester: Wiley.

Schein, E. (1985). *Organizational culture and leadership.* San Francisco: Jossey-Bass.

Schein, E. (1992). *Organizational culture and leadership.* San Francisco: Jossey-Bass.

Schein, E. (2003). *DEC is dead, long live DEC: Lessons on innovation, technology and the business gene.* San Francisco: Berrett-Koehler.

Schein, E. H. (1985). *Organizational culture and leadership.* San Francisco, CA: Jossey-Bass.

Schein, E. H. (1997). *Organizational culture and leadership* (2nd ed.). Jossey-Bass.

Schein, E.H. (1992). *Organizational culture and leadership* (2nd ed.). San Francisco: Jossey-Bass.

Schein, E.H. (1993). How can organizations learn faster? The challenge of entering the green room. *Sloan Management Review,* 85-92.

Schein, E.H. (1993). On dialogue, culture and organizational learning. *Organizational Dynamics, 22*(2), 40-51.

Schneider, S. C., & Barsoux, J.-L. (1997). *Managing across cultures.* London: Prentice Hall.

Schneider, S., & De Meyer, A. (1991). Interpreting and responding to strategic issues: The impact of national culture. *Strategic Management Journal, 12*(4), 307-320.

Schulte, W.D. (1997). Is globalocalization the most effective strategic response for international contractors? *Proceedings of the Academy of International Business UK Chapter Annual Meeting* (pp. 455-473).

Schulte, W.D. (2000). The strategic management of global information technology: Theoretical foundations. In E. Roche & M. Blaine (Eds.), *Information technology in multinational enterprises.* Northampton (USA): Edward Elgar.

Schulte, W.D. (2004). Information and knowledge management technologies and competitive advantage in global organizations. *Proceedings of the Academy of International Business Southeastern United States Annual Meeting* (pp. 25-36).

Schulte, W.D., & Sample, T.L. (2006). Efficiencies from knowledge management technologies in a military enterprise. *Journal of Knowledge Management, 10*(6).

Schultze, U., & Boland, R. (2000). Knowledge management technology and the reproduction of knowledge work practices. *Journal of Strategic Information Systems, 9*(2-3), 193-213.

Schultze, U., & Leidner, D. E. (2002). Studying knowledge management in information systems research: Discourses and theoretical assumptions. *MIS Quarterly, 26*(3), 213-242.

Schwartz, D. (Ed.). (2005). *Encyclopedia of knowledge management.* Hershey, PA: Idea Group.

Scott, J.E., & Vessey, I. (2000). Implementing enterprise resource planning systems: The role of learning from failure. *Information Systems Frontiers, 2*(2), 213-232.

Scott, W. (1998). *Organizations: Rational, natural and open systems.* Upper Saddle River, NJ: Prentice-Hall.

Scott-Morton, M.S. (Ed.). (1991). IT-induced business reconfiguration. In *The corporation of the 1990s: Information technology and organizational transformation* (pp. 3-23). Oxford University Press.

Searle, J.R. (1975). *Speech acts.* Cambridge: Cambridge University Press.

Selmer, J. (Ed.). (1995). *Expatriate management: New ideas for international business.* Westport, CT: Quorum Books.

Selzer, J., & Bass, B. (1990). Transformational leadership: Beyond initiation and consideration. *Journal of Management, 16*(4), 693-703.

Sena, J., & Shani, A. (1999). Intellectual capital and knowledge creation: Towards an alternative framework. In J. Liebowitz, (Ed.), *Knowledge management handbook.* Boca Raton: CRC Press.

Senge, P. M. (1992). *The fifth discipline: The art and practice of the learning organization.* Sydney, NSW: Random House.

Senge, P., Kleiner, A., Roberts, C., Ross, R., & Smith, B. (1994). *The fifth discipline fieldbook: Strategies and tools for building a learning organization.* New York: Currency Doubleday.

Senge, P., Kleiner, A., Roberts, C., Ross, R.G., & Smith, B. (1999). *The dance of change: The challenges to sustaining momentum in learning organizations* (1st ed.). New York: Doubleday.

Senge, P.M. (1990). *The fifth discipline: The art & practice of learning organization.* New York: Doubleday.

Sethi, V., & King, W.R. (1994). Development of measures to assess the extent to which an information technology application provides competitive advantage. *Management Science, 40*(2), 1601-1621.

Seybold, P. (2002). Get inside the lives of your customers. *Harvard Business Review on Customer Relationship Management, 27.*

Shoemaker, M. (2001). A framework for examining IT enabled market relationships. *Journal of Personal Selling & Sales Management, 21*(2), 177-186.

Shrivastava, P. (1983). A typology of organizational learning systems. *Journal of Management Studies, 20*(1), 7-24.

Silverman, R. (2001). CRM dichotomies. *Intelligent Enterprise, 4*(8), 90.

Simon, H. A. (1993). Strategy and organizational evolution. *Strategic Management Journal, 14*, 131-142.

Simon, S. (2001). The impact of culture and gender on Web sites: An empirical study. *The DATA BASE for Advances in Information Systems, 32*(1), 18-37.

Simon, S.J., & Grover, V. (1993). Strategic use of information technology in international business: A framework for information technology application. *Journal of Global Information Technology, 1*(2), 33-44.

Simoni, G. (2005). *Capitaliser les connaissances générées dans les projets de R&D: Pour un leadership intégratif et situationnel.* Unpublished Doctoral Dissertation, Université de la Méditerranée, France.

Simonin, B. (1999a). Transfer of marketing know-how in international strategic alliances: An empirical investigation of the role and antecedents of knowledge ambiguity. *Journal of International Business Studies, 30*(3), 463-490.

Simonin, B. (1999b). Ambiguity and the process of knowledge transfer in strategic alliances. *Strategic Management Journal, 20*(7), 595-623.

Simonin, B.L. (1999). Ambiguity and the process of knowledge transfer in strategic alliances. *Strategic Management Journal, 20,* 595-623.

Simpkins, C.R. (2001). Reengineering standards for the process industries: Process industry practices. In S.M Spivak & F.C. Brenner (Eds.), *Standardization essentials—principles and practice.* New York/Basel: Marcel Dekker.

Skandia. (1994). *Visualizing intellectual capital at Skandia.* Supplement to Skandia's 1994 Annual Report.

Skandia. (1996). *Customer value.* Supplement to Skandia's 1996 Annual Report.

Smith, G. (2001). Making the team. *IEE Review, 47*(5), 33-36.

Snowdon, D. N., & Churchill, E. F. (2004). *Inhabited information spaces: Living with your data.* London; New York: Springer.

Solomon, C.M. (1997). Return on investment. *Workforce, 2*(4, Global Workforce Supplement), 12-18.

Songini, M. (2001). Wireless technology changes the face of CRM. *Computerworld, 35*(7), 20.

Sparrow, P.R., & Hiltrop, J.M. (1994). *European human resource management in transition.* Englewood Cliffs, NJ: Prentice Hall.

Spencer, J.C., & Grant, R.M. (1996). Knowledge and the firm: Overview. *Strategic Management Journal, 17,* 5-9.

Spender, J.C. (1996). Making knowledge the basis of dynamic theory of the firm. *Strategic Management Journal, 17*(Winter Special Issue), 45-62.

Spender, J.C. (1996). Organizational knowledge, learning and memory: Three concepts in search of a theory. *Journal of Organizational Change Management, 9*(1), 63-78.

Spinosa, C., Flores, F., & Dreyfus, H.L. (2001). *Disclosing new worlds—entrepreneurship, democratic action and the cultivation of solidarity.* Cambridge, MA: MIT Press.

Spitz, R.A. (1983). *Rene A. Spitz: Dialogues from infancy* (R.N. Emde, ed.). New York: International Universities Press.

Spitz, R.A., & Wolf, K. (1946). Anaclitic depression: An inquiry into the genesis of psychiatric conditions in early childhood, II. *The Psychoanalytic Study of the Child, 2,* 313-342.

Sprunt, E.S. (2006). Where will the next generation come from? *Journal of Petroleum Technology,* (June), 12.

Srivastava, R., Shervani, T., & Fahey, L. (1998). Market based assets and shareholder value: A framework for analysis. *Journal of Marketing, 62*(1), 2-18.

Stankosky, M. (Ed.). (2005). *Creating the discipline of knowledge management: The latest in university research.* Oxford: Elsevier Butterworth-Heinemann.

Stein, E.W., & Zwass V. (1995). Actualizing organizational memory with information systems. *Journal of Information Management, 6*(2), 85-117.

Sterne, J. (2000). *Customer service on the Internet* (2nd ed.). New York: John Wiley & Sons.

Stewart, R. (1982). A model for understanding managerial jobs and behavior. *Academy of Management Review, 7*(1), 7-14.

Stewart, T. (1997). *Intellectual capital: The new wealth of organization.* New York: Double Day.

Stewart, T.A. (1997). *Intellectual capital.* New York: Doubleday.

Straub, D. (1994). The effect of culture on IT diffusion: Email and fax in Japan and the US. *Information Systems Research, 5*(1), 23-47.

Straub, D., Keil, M., & Brenner, W. (1997). Testing the technology acceptance model across cultures: A three country study. *Information & Management, 31*(1), 1-11.

Strauss, A., & Corbin, J. (1992). *Basics of qualitative research: Grounded theory procedures and techniques.* Newbury Park, CA: Sage.

Stroh, L., Gregersen, H., & Black, S. (1998). Closing the gap: Expectations versus reality among repatriates. *Journal of World Business, 33*(2), 111-124.

Subramaniam, M., & Venkatraman, N. (1999). The influence of leveraging tacit overseas knowledge for global new product development capability: An empirical examination. In M.A. Hitt, R.G. Clifford, R.D. Nixon, & K.P. Coyne (Eds.), *Dynamic strategic resources.* Chichester: John Wiley & Sons.

Subramaniam, M., & Venkatraman, N. (2001). Determinants of transnational new product development capability: Testing the influence of transferring and deploying tacit overseas knowledge. *Strategic Management Journal, 22,* 359-378.

Sumner, M. (2000). Risk factors in enterprise-wide/ERP projects. *Journal of Information Technology, 15*(4), 317-327.

Susanto, A. (1988). *Methodik zur entwicklung von normen* (DIN Normungskunde, Band 23). Berlin/Cologne: Beuth Verlag.

Sveiby, K. (1996). *What is knowledge management?* Retrieved on March 4, 2000, from http://www.sveiby. com.au/KnowledgeManagement.html

Sveiby, K.E. (1997). *The new organizational wealth: Managing & measuring knowledge-based assets.* San Francisco: Berrett-Koehler.

Szulanki, G. (1996). Exploring internal stickiness: Impediments to the transfer of best practice within the firm. *Strategic Management Journal, 17,* 27-43.

Szulanski, G. (1996). Exploring internal stickiness: Impediments to the transfer of best practice within the firm. *Strategic Management Journal, 17*(Winter Special Issue), 27-43.

Szulanski, G. (2000). Appropriability and the challenge of scope: Banc One routinizes replication. In G. Dosi, R. Nelson, & S. Winter (Eds.), *The nature and dynamics of organizational capabilities.* New York: Oxford University Press

Szulanski, G. (2003). *Sticky knowledge: Barriers to knowing in the firm.* Thousand Oaks, CA: Sage.

Taylor, S., Beechler, S., & Napier, N. (1996). Toward an integrative model of strategic international human resource management. *Academy of Management Review, 21*(4), 959-985.

Teal, J.L. (1990). Setting the standard for engineering excellence—the people, the process, the competitive edge. *ASTM Standardization News, 17*(6), 32-35.

Techquila. (n.d.). *Topic map design patterns for information architecture.* Retrieved from *http://www.techquila. com/tmsinia.html*

Teece, D.J. (1981). The market for know-how and the efficient international transfer of technology. *Annals of the American Academy of Political and Social Science, 458,* 81-96.

Tessler, S., & Barr, A. (1997). *Software R&D strategies of developing countries* (Position Paper). Stanford Computer Industry Project.

The World Bank Group, Data and Map. (2004). Retrieved December 27, 2004, from http://www.worldbank.org/ data/countrydata/ictglance.htm

Thomas, G.A.N. (2004). Standards as a strategic business asset. *ISO Focus, 1*(4), 11-15.

Thomas, R., Roosevelt, R., Thomas, D., Ely, R., & Meyerson D. (2002). *Harvard Business Review on managing diversity.* Boston: Harvard Business Review Publishing.

Thompson, A.M. (2004). *The impact of the mode of employment of personnel engaged in the oil & gas support industry on knowledge sharing.* Unpublished Masters Research Dissertation, Robert Gordon University Business School, Scotland.

Thompson, J. (1997). *Strategic management—awareness and change* (3rd ed.). London: International Business Press.

Thurow, L.C. (2000). *Building wealth: The new rules for individuals, companies, and nations in a knowledge-based economy.* New York: Harper Information.

Tiwana, A. (2002). *The knowledge management toolkit.* Englewood Cliffs, NJ: Prentice Hall.

Todman, C. (2001). *Designing a data warehouse—supporting customer relationship management.* Englewood Cliffs, NJ: Prentice Hall.

Toth, R.B. (Ed.). (1990). *Standards management—a handbook for profits.* New York: American National Standards Institute.

Tovstiga, G. (1999). Profiling the knowledge worker in the knowledge-intensive organization: Emerging roles. *International Journal of Technology Management, 18*(5/6/7/8), 731-744.

Tovstiga, G., & Korot, L. (1999). Profiling the twenty-first century knowledge enterprise. In R. Wright & H. Etamad (Eds.), *Research in global strategic management.* Greenwich, CT: JAI Press.

Tovstiga, G., & Korot, L. (2000). Knowledge-driven organizational change: A framework. *International Journal of Entrepreneurship and Innovation Management, 1*(1), 22-23.

Tovstiga, G., Korot, L., & Dana, L.P. (2000, September). International entrepreneurship: A cross-cultural comparison of knowledge management practices. *Proceedings of the 2nd Annual McGill Conference on International Entrepreneurship: Researching New Frontiers,* Montreal, Canada.

Triandis, H.C. (1972). *The analysis of subjective culture.* New York: John Wiley & Sons.

Trist, E. (1981). The socio-technical perspective. The evolution of sociotechnical systems as conceptual framework and as an action research program. In A. Van de Ven, & W. Jotce (Eds.), *Perspectives on organization design and behavior* (pp. 49-75). New York: John Wiley & Sons.

Trompenaars, F., & Hampden-Turner, C. (1998). *Riding the waves of culture: Understanding diversity in global business.* Toronto: McGraw-Hill.

Tsang, E. (1999). The knowledge transfer and learning aspects of international HRM: An empirical study of Singapore MNCs. *International Business Review, 8,* 591-609.

Tsang, E.W.K. (2001). Managerial learning in foreign-invested enterprises in China. *Management International Review, 41,* 29-51.

Tsoukas, H. (1996). The firm as a distributed knowledge system. *Strategic Management Journal, 17*(Winter Special Issue), 11-25.

Tsoukas, H., & Vladimirou, E. (2001). What is organizational knowledge? *Journal of Management Studies, 38,* 973-993.

Turek, N. (2002). Call centers: Here, there, and everywhere. *InformationWeek,* (October 23), 168-174.

Turkle, S. (1995). *Life on the screen: Identity in the age of the Internet.* New York: Simon and Schuster.

Turnbow, D., & Kasianovitz, K. (2005). Usability testing for Web redesign: A UCLA case study. *OCLC Systems and Services, 21*(3), 226-234.

Tushman, M., & Anderson, P. (1986). Technological discontinuities and organizational environments. *Administrative Science Quarterly, 31,* 439-465.

Tushman, M.L., & Moore, P. (1988). *Readings in the management of innovation.* Ballinger.

Tushman, M.L., & O'Reilly III, C.A. (1996). Ambidextrous organizations: Managing evolutionary and revolutionary change. *California Management Review, 38*(4), 8-30.

U.S. Department of Labor, Bureau of Labor Statistics (2005). *Customer service representatives.* Retrieved February 17, 2006, from *http://www.bls.gov/oco/ocos280.htm*

Ulrich, F. (2001). Knowledge management systems: Essential requirements and generic design patterns. *Proceedings of the International Symposium on Information Systems and Engineering* (ISE'2001) (pp. 114-121), Las Vegas, NV.

Urch-Druskat, V., & Wolff, B.S. (2001). *Building the emotional intelligence of groups.* HBR.

Van Bruggen, G., Smidts, A., & Wierenga, B. (2001). The powerful triangle of marketing data, managerial judgement, and marketing management support systems. *European Journal of Marketing, 25*(7/8), 796-814.

van den Berg, C., & Popescu, I. (2005). An experience in knowledge mapping. *Journal of Knowledge Management, 9*(2), 123-128.

Van den Brink, P. (2003). *Social, organizational and technological conditions that enable knowledge sharing.* Doctoral Thesis, Technische Universiteit Delft, The Netherlands.

Van der Aalst, W. M. P., Reijers, H. A., Song. (2005). Discovering social networks from event logs. *Computer Supported Cooperative Work (CSCW) An International Journal, 14*(6), 549-593.

Van der Krogt, F.J. (1998). Learning network theory: The tension between learning systems and work systems in organizations. *Human Resource Development Quarterly, 9*(2), 156-176.

Vance, C.M., & Ensher, E.A. (2002). The voice of the host country workforce: A key source for improving the effectiveness of expatriate training and performance. *International Journal of Intercultural Relations, 26,* 447-461.

Vance, C.M., & Paik, Y. (2001, August). Toward a taxonomy of host country national learning process involvement in multinational learning organizations. *Proceedings of the Annual Meeting of the Academy of Management,* Washington, DC.

Vance, C.M., & Paik, Y. (2002). One size fits all in expatriate departure training? Comparing the host country voices of Mexican, Indonesian, and U.S. workers. *Journal of Management Development, 21*(7), 557-571.

Velasquez, G., & Odem, P. (2005, October 9-12). Harnessing the wisdom of crowds—case study. *Proceedings of the 2005 Society of Petroleum Engineers Annual Technical Conference* (ref. SPE 95292), Dallas, TX.

Venkatesh, V., & Davis, F.D. (2000). A theoretical extension of the Technology Acceptance Model: Four longitudinal field studies. *Management Science, 46*(2), 186-204.

Venzin, M., von Krogh, G., & Roos, J. (1998). Future research into knowledge management. In G. Von Krogh, J. Roos, & D. Kleine (Eds), *Knowing in Firms: Understanding Managing and Measuring Knowledge.* Sage Publications.

Verhoef, P., & Donkers, B. (2001). Predicting customer potential value: An application in the insurance industry. *Decision Support Systems, 32*(2), 189.

Verity Consulting. (1995). *Strategic standardization—lessons from the world's foremost companies.* New York: ANSI (not publicly available).

Verman, L.C. (1973). *Standardization—a new discipline.* Hamden, CT: Archon Books, The Shoe String Press.

Von Hippel, E. (2002). Innovation by user communities: Learning from open source software. *Sloan Management Review, 42*(4), 82-86.

Von Hipple, E., & Von Krogh, G. (2003). Exploring the open source software phenomenon: Issues for organization science. *Organization Science.*

von Krogh, G. (1998). Care in knowledge creation. *California Management Review, 40*(3), 133-153.

Von Krogh, G. (1998). Care in knowledge creation. *California Management Review, 40*(3), 133-154.

Von Krogh, G. (2002). The communal resource and information system. *Journal of Information Systems, 11*(2).

Von Krogh, G., & Roos, J. (Eds.). (1996). *Managing knowledge: Perspectives on cooperation and competition.* London: Sage.

Von Krogh, G., Ichijo, K., & Nonaka, I. (2000). *Enabling knowledge creation. How to unlock the mystery of tacit knowledge and release the power of innovation.* Oxford: Oxford University Press.

Von Krogh, G., Nonaka, I., & Ichijo, K. (1997). Develop knowledge activists! *European Management Journal, 15*(5), 475-483.

Von Krogh, G., Roos, J., & Slocum, K. (1994). An essay on corporate epistemology. *Strategic Management Journal, 15,* 53-71.

Von Krogh, G., Roos, J., & Slocum, K. (1996). In G. Von Krogh & J. Roos (Eds.), *Managing knowledge: Perspectives and cooperation and competition.* London: Sage.

Von Krogh, G., Spaeth, S., & Lakhani, K.R. (2003). Community joining and specialization in open source software innovation: A case study. *Research Policy, 32,* 1217-1241.

Von Zedtwitz, M., & Gassmann, O. (2002). Market versus technology drive in R&D internationalization: Four different patterns of managing research and development. *Research Policy, 31,* 569-588.

Vroom, V. (1964). *Work and motivation.* New York/London/Sydney: John Wiley & Sons.

Wallach, E. J. (1983, February). Individuals and organizations: The cultural match. *Training and Development Journal,* .

Waller, R.J. (1975). Application of interpretive structural modeling to priority-setting in urban systems management. In M. Baldwin (Ed.), *Portraits of complexity* (Battelle Monograph No. 9). Columbus, OH: Battelle Memorial Institute.

Walsh, J. P., & Ungson, G. R. (1991). Organizational memory. *Academy of Management Review, 16*(1), 57-91.

Walsh, J.P., & Ungson, G.R. (1991). Organizational memory. *Academy of Management Review, 16,* 57-91.

Walsh, J.P., & Ungson, G.R. (1991). Organizational memory. *Academy of Management Journal, 16*(1), 57-90.

Walsham, G. (2001). *Making a world of difference: IT in a global context.* New York: John Wiley and Sons.

Warboys, B., Kawalek, P., Robertson, I., & Greenwood, M. (1999). *Business information systems—a process approach.* Berkshire: McGraw-Hill.

Warfield, J.N. (1973). Intent structures. *IEEE Transactions on Systems, Man, and Cybernetics, 3*(2).

Warne, L., Ali, I., Pascoe, C., & Agostino, K. (2001, December). A holistic approach to knowledge management and social learning: Lessons learnt from military headquarters [Special issue on knowledge management]. *Australian Journal of Information Systems,* 127-142.

Washington, M., & Hacker, M. (2005). Why change fails: Knowledge counts. *Leadership & Organization Development Journal, 26*(5/6).

Wassenar, A., Gregor, S., & Swagerman, D. (2002). ERP implementation management in different organizational and cultural settings. In *Proceedings of the European Accounting Information Systems Conference,* Copenhagen Business School, Copenhagen, Denmark.

Wastell, D. (1999). Learning dysfunctiona in information systems development: Overcoming the social defenses with transitional objectives. *MIS Quarterly, 23*(4), 581-600.

Watson, R.T. (1990). Influences on the IS manager's perceptions of key issues: Information scanning and the relationship with the CEO. *MIS Quarterly,* 217.

Watson, S. (1998). Getting to "aha!" companies use intranets to turn information and experience into knowledge — And gain a competitive edge. *Computer World, 32*(4), 1.

Webber, A. M. (1993, January). What's so new about the new economy? *Harvard Business Review,* 24-42.

Weeks, J., & Galunic, C.A. (2003). *Theory of the cultural evolution of the firm: The interorganizational ecology of memes.* INSEAD.

Weick, K.E. (1991). The nontraditional quality of organizational learning. *Organization Science, 2*(1), 116-123.

Weick, K.E., & Quinn, R.E. (1999). Organizational change and development. *Annual Psychology Review, 50,* 361-386.

Weill, P., & Vitale, M. (2002). What IT infrastructure capabilities are needed to implement e-business models? *MIS Quarterly Executive, 1*(1), 17-34.

Weisinger, J., & Trauth, E. (2002). Situating culture in the global information sector. *Information Technology and People, 15*(4), 306-320.

Weisinger, J.Y., & Salipante, P.F. (2000). Cultural knowing as practicing: Extending our conceptions of culture. *Journal of Management Inquiry, 9*(4), 376-390.

Welch, D., & Welch, L. (1994). Linking operation mode diversity and IHRM. *International Journal of Human Resource Management, 5,* 911-926.

Wenger, E. (1998). *Communities of practice, learning, meaning and identity.* Cambridge, UK: Cambridge University Press.

Wenger, E. C., & Snyder, W. M. (2000). Communities of practice: The organizational frontier. *Harvard Business Review, 78*(1), 139-145.

Wenström, H., Ollner, J., & Wenström, J. (2000). *Focus on industry standards—an integrated approach* (SIS Hb 124:2000, 1st ed.). Stockholm: SIS Förlag.

Wernerfelt, B. (1984). A resource based view of the firm. *Strategic Management Journal, 5,* 171-180.

Wernerfelt, B. (1995). The resource-based view of the firm: Ten years after. *Strategic Management Journal, 5*(2), 171-174.

Wiggins, B. (2000). *Effective document management: Unlocking corporate knowledge.* Gower: Aldershot.

Wikipedia. (2006). *Singapore.* Retrieved March 24, 2006, from *http://en.wikipedia.org/wiki/Singapore*

Williamson, O.E. (1985). *The economic institutions of capitalism.* New York: The Free Press.

Winograd, T., & Flores, F. (1987). *Understanding computers and cognition.* Norwood, NJ: Ablex.

Winter, S. (1987). Knowledge and competence as strategic assets. In D. Teece (Ed.), *The competitive challenge.* Ballinger.

Wong, M.M.L. (2001). Internationalizing Japanese expatriate managers: Organizational learning through international assignment. *Management Learning, 32,* 237-251.

Woodhouse, L. B. R. (2000). Personality and the use of intuition: Individual differences in strategy and performance on an implicit learning task. *European Journal of Personality, 4*(2), 157-169.

Yahoo. (n.d.). *Design pattern library.* Retrieved from *http://developer.yahoo.com/ypatterns/atoz.php*

Yates, J., & Orlikowski, W. (2002). Genre systems: Structuring interaction through communicative norms. *Journal of Business Communication, 39,* 13-35.

Yergin, D. (1991). *The prize: The epic quest for oil, money and power* (ch. 36). London: Simon & Schuster.

Yi, M.Y., Fiedler, K.D., & Park, J.S. (2006). Understanding the role of individual innovativeness in the acceptance of IT-based innovations: Comparative analyses of models and measures. *Decision Sciences, 37*(3), 393-426.

Yin, R. (1994). *Case study research: Design and methods.* Thousand Oaks, CA: Sage.

Yip, G. (1992). *Total global strategy: Managing for worldwide competitive advantage.* Englewood Cliffs, NJ: Prentice Hall.

Zablah, A. R., Bellenger, D. N., & Johnston, W. J. (2004). An evaluation of divergent perspectives on customer relationship management: Towards a common understanding of an emerging phenomenon. *Industrial Marketing Management, 33*(6), 475-489.

Zack, M.H. (1999). Developing a knowledge strategy. *California Management Review, 41*(3), 125-145.

Zahra, S.A., & George, G. (2002). Absorptive capacity: A review, reconceptualization and extension. *Academy of Management Review, 27*(2), 185-203.

Zander, U., & Kogut, B. (1995). Knowledge and the speed of the transfer and imitation of organizational capabilities, *Organization Science, 6*(1), 76-92.

Zander, U., & Kogut, B. (1995). Knowledge and the speed of the transfer and imitation of organizational capabilities: An empirical test. *Organization Science, 6*(1), 76-92.

Zanfei, A. (2000). Transnational firms and the changing organization of innovation activities. *Cambridge Journal of Economics, 24,* 515-542.

Zeithaml, V., Rust, R., & Lemon, K. (2001). The customer pyramid: Creating and serving profitable customers. *California Management Review, 43*(4), 118-146.

Zellmer-Bruhn, M. (2003). Interruptive events and team knowledge acquisition. *Management Science, 49,* 514-528.

Zhao, J. L., & Bi, H. H. (2006). Process-driven collaboration support for intra-agency crime analysis. *Decision Support Systems, 41*(3), 616-633.

Zmud, R. W. (1984). An examination of 'push-pull' theory applied to process innovation in knowledge work. *Management Science,* 727.

# About the Contributors

**Kevin J. O'Sullivan** is assistant professor of management and director of global academic administration at the New York Institute of Technology, USA. He has more than 16 years of IT experience in multinational firms and consulting both in the private and public sector in American, Middle Eastern, European, and Far Eastern cultures. Dr. O'Sullivan has delivered professional seminars to global Fortune 100 organizations on subjects such as global collaboration, knowledge management, information security, and multinational information systems. His research and development interests include knowledge management, intellectual capital security, and information visualization. He serves on the editorial board of the *Journal of Information and Knowledge Management* and is associate editor of *VINE: The Journal of Information and Knowledge Management Systems*.

\*\*\*

**Vittal S. Anantatmula** has worked in the petroleum and power industries for several years as an electrical engineer and project manager. As a consultant, he worked with the World Bank, Arthur Andersen, and other international consulting firms. Dr. Anantatmula is a certified project management professional and certified cost engineer. He is a member of PMI and AACE. His academic qualifications include BE (Electrical Engineering), MBA, MS (Engineering Management), and DSc (Engineering Management). He has several publications in various journals and presented more than 20 papers in prestigious and international conferences.

Dr. Anantatmula is a faculty member of the College of Business, Western Carolina University. Prior to joining Western Carolina, he worked as the program director of the Project Management Program, School of Business, George Washington University, USA.

**Luciano C. Batista** is an associate research fellow in the School of Business and Economics at the University of Exeter, UK. Since 2001, he has been researching several aspects of customer relationship management (CRM), from implementation strategies to information and communication technologies requirements. He has published in several international conferences on information systems, e-government, and corporate reputation, in Europe and in the U.S. Currently, he is researching integrated CRM and business process management approaches, and their underlying theories. He is also researching the role of manage-processes in the building and sustaining of long-term organizational competitive advantage.

**Ronald D. Camp II** is assistant professor of organizational behavior and international business in the Faculty of Business Administration at the University of Regina, Canada. He holds a BA from Whitworth

College, an MM from the Atkinson Graduate School of Management at Willamette University, and a PhD from the Suader School of Business at the University of British Columbia. In addition to his work in knowledge management, he has studied the effects of culture on collaboration and trust within and between organizations. His articles have appeared in publications such as the *Journal of International Entrepreneurship and Organizational Behavior* and *Human Decision Processes.*

**Thippaya Chintakovid** is a doctoral student in the College of Information Science and Technology, Drexel University, USA. Her research interests are HCI, knowledge management, and end user software support. She is doing research on gender and end user software support, and the effects of intrinsic motivation, gender, and user perceptions in end user applications at work.

**Leo-Paul Dana** is senior advisor to the World Association for Small and Medium Enterprises, and tenured at the University of Canterbury. He was formerly deputy director of the International Business MBA Program at Singapore's Nanyang Business School. He also served on the faculties of McGill University and INSEAD. He holds BA and MBA degrees from McGill University, and a PhD from the Ecole des Hautes Etudes Commerciales. He has an extensive research background studying entrepreneurship in different cultures and is the author of a number of books and articles on the subject. He is the founder of the *Journal of International Entrepreneurship.*

**Henk J. de Vries** is associate professor of standardization in the Department of Management of Technology and Innovation at RSM Erasmus University, The Netherlands. His education and research concern standardization from a business point of view. From 1994 until 2003, he worked with NEN, Netherlands Standardization Institute, in several jobs, being responsible for R&D towards the end of his tenure. Since 1994, he has held an appointment at Erasmus University's School of Management, and since 2004, he has worked full time at Erasmus. Professor de Vries is the author of more than 200 publications, including several books on standardization.

**Joe R. Downing** earned his PhD from Rensselaer Polytechnic Institute and is an assistant professor of corporate communication at Southern Methodist University, USA. His research has appeared in the *American Communication Journal, Communication Education, Journal of Business Communication, Public Relations Review,* and *Technical Communication.* For the past three years he has worked with American Airlines to chronicle the airline's employee crisis response to the 9/11 attack. He is currently working with an inbound sales account at a U.S.-based call center to study how technicians' communication skills affect their sales conversion rate.

**Leslie Gadman** is managing director at Duke Corporate Education, a carve-out of the custom executive education practice of Duke University's Fuqua School of Business. Dr. Gadman holds responsibility for the design and delivery of custom executive education to global corporations. He works out of Duke CE's London office. Prior to joining Duke, he served on the faculty of the International Business School on the Isle of Man, specializing in enterprise and innovation behavior studies. In addition to his academic experience, he is a former Cap Gemini consultant and advisor to multinational firms and new ventures in several countries, including the United States, Switzerland, France, Lebanon, Jordan, and the United Kingdom. He is the author of *Power Partnering: A Strategy for Excellence in the 21st Century* and, with Cary Cooper, of the forthcoming *Open Source Leadership.* He has published in the *Leadership*

*& Organizational Development Journal,* the *Journal of Management Science,* the *Asian Journal on Quality,* and *MIT Sloan Management Review,* among others. His research interests include strategic innovation; cooperative strategies; strategic processes, including organizational learning, knowledge, and competence development; and strategic management practices in emerging industries. He holds a PhD in organizational behavior from the University of Lancaster.

**Jeffrey Gale** is professor of management at Loyola Marymount University in Los Angeles where his primary teaching and research is in the areas of strategic management and international strategy. He holds SB and SM degrees from the Sloan School of Management at MIT and a PhD from the Anderson Graduate School of Management at UCLA. In addition, he holds a JD from UCLA and is a member of the California Bar. Dr. Gale has been an active consultant on strategy issues for over two decades and has also served as an outside director in two financial services firms. Prior to joining LMU, he held faculty positions at the University of Washington and the University of Texas at Dallas, as well as visiting appointments at UCLA, Ben-Gurion University in Israel, and Katholieke Universitat in Leuven, Belgium.

**James D. Grady III** received his residency training and an MSc in oral and maxillofacial surgery at the University of North Carolina at Chapel Hill in 1974. He has been a principal presenter at practice management seminars entitled: "Enhancing Productivity" and "Conflict Management" at the American Association of Oral and Maxillofacial Surgeons Annual Meetings in 1995, 1996, 1997, and "Office Management for the OMS Practice" in 1998. His contributions include a chapter in *Oral and Maxillofacial Surgery, Volume I: Anesthesia/Dentoalveolar Surgery/ Practice Management* (WB Saunders. 2000).

**Victoria M. Grady** completed her doctor of science degree in engineering and technology management at George Washington University in May 2005. She holds an MSM in the management of technology from the University of Alabama in Huntsville and a BS in accounting from Birmingham-Southern College. Dr. Grady is currently an assistant professorial lecturer in the Organizational Science Department at George Washington University, USA. Her research focuses on the exploration of the integral relationship between organizational behavior and the impact of continuous change.

**Shankar Kambhampaty** has been involved for 17 years in architecture, design, development, and management for a number of software projects executed globally. During this time, he has also played a key role in development of software products that have been exhibited in AIIM and COMDEX shows. Mr. Kambhampaty has architected solutions for banking and financial services, insurance, retail, health care, and transportation and logistics verticals. He has written papers for international conferences on several topics related to architecting solutions. He holds a master's degree in electrical engineering with specialization in digital systems from the Indian Institute of Technology, and he is a Microsoft Certified Architect and IBM-Certified On-Demand Solution Designer V2.

**Len Korot** is retired from Pepperdine University in California, and is currently affiliated with the Institute for Global Management, USA. He has done much work in knowledge-driven organizational change.

**Miltiadis D. Lytras** earned his PhD, MBA, and BSc from Athens University of Economics and Business (AUEB). He is a faculty member in both the Computers Engineering and Informatics Department (CEID) and the Department of Business Administration at the University of Patras. He's also a faculty member in the Technology Education and Digital Systems Department at the University of Piraeus. Since 1998, he has been a research officer in ELTRUN, the research center in the Department of Management Science and Technology at AUEB. His research focuses on Semantic Web, knowledge management and e-learning, with more than 50 publications in these areas. He has co-edited nine special issues in international journals and has authored/edited six books. He is the founder of the Semantic Web and Information Systems Special Interest Group in the Association for Information Systems (http://www. sigsemis.org) as well as the co-founder of AIS SIG on Reusable Learning Objects and Learning Design (http://www.sigrlo.org). He serves as the Editor-in-Chief for three international journals, while acting as an associate editor or editorial board member in seven other journals.

**Cathleen A. McGrath** currently serves as an associate professor of management in the College of Business Administration at Loyola Marymount University, USA. She teaches courses in organizational behavior, management, and social network analysis. Her research interests focus on the application of experimental and computational methods to understand behavior in organizations. Specifically she works on social network analysis, social network data visualization, and computational organization theory. She received her PhD from the H.J. Heinz III School of Public Policy and Management at Carnegie Mellon University in 1998.

**Dana B. Minbaeva** earned her PhD from the Copenhagen Business School, Denmark, where she currently serves as assistant professor of human resource management. Her work has been published in the *Journal of International Business Studies, Management International Review, Employee Relations,* and *Personnel Review.* Her current research focuses on human resource management, knowledge sharing, and transfer in multinational corporations.

**Patricia Ordóñez de Pablos** is professor of business administration and accountability, Faculty of Economics, University of Oviedo, Spain. She is executive editor of the *International Journal of Learning and Intellectual Capital* and *International Journal of Strategic Change Management.* Her research focuses on intellectual capital measuring and reporting, knowledge management, organizational learning, human resource management, and Chinese management.

**Kevin J. O'Sullivan** is assistant professor of management and director of global academic administration at the New York Institute of Technology, USA. He has more than 16 years of IT experience in multinational firms and consulting both in the private and public sector in American, Middle Eastern, European, and Far Eastern cultures. Dr. O'Sullivan has delivered professional seminars to global Fortune 100 organizations on subjects such as global collaboration, knowledge management, information security, and multinational information systems. His research and development interests include knowledge management, intellectual capital security, and information visualization. He serves on the editorial board of the *Journal of Information and Knowledge Management* and is associate editor of *VINE: The Journal of Information and Knowledge Management Systems.*

**Yongsun Paik** is a professor of international business and management in the College of Business Administration, Loyola Marymount University, USA. He holds a PhD in international business from the University of Washington, USA. His primary research interests focus on international human resource management, global strategic alliances, and Asian Pacific business studies. He has recently published articles in such journals as the *Journal of World Business, Academy of Management Executive, Academy of Management Learning and Education, Management International Review, Journal of International Management, Business Horizons, International Journal of Human Resource Management, Journal of Management Inquiry, Human Resource Management Journal,* among others. He is an editorial board member of the *Journal of World Business* and the *Thunderbird International Business Review.*

**Claude Paraponaris** is assistant professor of human resource management and strategic management at the University of Méditerranée, France. He specializes in technological innovation and knowledge management, and has conducted research in several industries, including computer software and hardware, life-sciences, logistics, and transportation.

He teaches courses on human resource management, management of innovation, project management, and management theory. He has published two books on networks, human resource management, and innovation, as well as numerous articles in journals such as the *Journal of Knowledge Management, International Journal of Human Resource Management,* and *Revue de Gestion des Ressources Humaines* (France). He is an editorial board member of *Management Decision.*

**Elena Revilla** is a professor of operations management at the Instituto de Empresa, Spain. She holds a doctoral degree in business administration from the Universidad de Valladolid. She also holds an MA in science and technology from Universidad Carlos III, Spain. She holds a post-doctoral fellowship at North Carolina University, USA. Her articles have been published in academic and professional journals, including the *Journal of the Operations Research Society, Management Learning, Journal of High Technology Management, International Journal of Technology Management, Management Research, The Learning Organization Journal,* and the *Harvard-Deusto Business Review.* Her research interests are in knowledge management, organizational learning, innovation, and new product development.

**Vincent M. Ribiere** is assistant professor of MIS at the New York Institute of Technology, USA. He received his doctorate in knowledge management from George Washington University and a PhD in management sciences from Paul Cézanne University, France. He teaches, conducts research, and consults in the area of knowledge management and information systems. He has presented various research papers at different international conferences on knowledge management, organizational culture, information systems, and quality, as well as publishing in various refereed journals and books. He is a contributing editor and reviewer to journals focused on knowledge management.

**William Schulte** is an associate professor and Sam Walton Free Enterprise fellow in the Harry F. Byrd Jr. School of Business of Shenandoah University, USA. He was a founding research associate of the Institute for Knowledge and Innovation of George Washington University, where he previously taught, as well as at the Tobin College of Business of St. John's University in New York and the School of Management at George Mason University. Dr. Schulte is on the editorial advisory board of the *Journal of Knowledge Management* and *Management Decision.* His research includes scores of books, chapters, articles, proceedings, cases, and presentations on knowledge management, social entrepreneurship, innovation, and international management for journals and conferences of international scholarly organizations. He received his bachelor's and master's degrees from LSU, and his PhD from the School of Business and Public Management of George Washington University.

**Alan M. Thompson** is global KM manager for Production Services Network (PSN) headquartered in Aberdeen, Scotland. Following a career in shipbuilding and marine consultancy, he has been in the Oil & Gas industry since 1980, initially working for Oil Majors. He joined PSN in 1994 and has held a variety of project management roles for over 30 years. A chartered naval architect and European registered engineer by profession, he holds a BA in applied mathematics and an MBA specializing in project management and organizational development. In 2004 he earned an MSc in knowledge management from the Aberdeen Business School of Robert Gordon University, where he is a guest lecturer.

**Charles M. Vance** holds graduate degrees in instructional technology and organizational behavior from Syracuse University and Brigham Young University, respectively. He teaches graduate and undergraduate courses in areas of management and human resources at Loyola Marymount University. In the 2005-2006 school year, he completed two Fulbright teaching and research appointments in Austria and China. He has a recent book co-authored with Yongsun Paik entitled *Managing a Global Workforce* (M.E. Sharpe, 2006). He has been actively involved as a consultant in training and curriculum development the U.S. and abroad, including South America, Western Europe, and Asia.

**Qiping Zhang** is an assistant professor of Information and Computer Science at Long Island University, USA. She is interested in facilitating productive collaborations of individuals who are geographically and culturally distributed. Her work not only includes just communication technologies, but also cultural issues that arise in intercultural, distributed collaborations. She has presented papers for conferences of ACM, ICKM, ALISE, and the International Congress of Psychology, and she has published papers in journals including *JIKM*. Dr. Zhang holds a PhD and an MS in information science from the University of Michigan, and MS and BA degrees in cognitive psychology from Peking University.

# Index

## A

anaclitic depression 107, 108

## B

buy-in 58

## C

call centers 53–60
CAPITA framework 130, 133
ClientLogic 57, 58
commitment-based value networking 29
cultural
  differences 44
  values 41, 44
culture 41–51, 325
customer
  relationship management (CRM) 227–252
    definition 343–345
    global strategy 342–355, 344–346
      agency theory 345–346
      findings 348–351
    implementation 240–242
      and cultural considerations 241–244
    measurement 242–243
    origins 229–231
    strategies 231–234, 343–350
    technologies 234–240

## D

data
  analysis 88–89
  collection 88
diffusion 29

## E

electronic
  customer relationship management (e-CRM) 239
employee
  behavior 108–112
enterprise systems (ES) 256–270
  administrative structure 261–262, 264–265
  control scheme 262, 265
  implementation 258
    outcomes 267–270
  management involvement 262, 265
  organizational structure and culture 262–263, 265–267
  vision 259–261, 263–264
explicit
  dimension 277

## G

global
  diversity 64–65
  knowledge
    integration 129

management 168–177
    technologies (GKMTs) 131
globalization 168

# H

host country workforce (HCW) 172–177
human resources 3
    management (HRM) 1–27

# I

in-group/out-group relationships 41–51
innovation 29–37
intellectual
    capital 196–198
        accounting policies 201–206
        measuring tools 197–198
            balanced scorecard 197–198
            intangible assets monitor 197
            Skandia navigator 197
        statement 200–201
international
    engineering, procurement, and construction
        (IEPC) industry 127–128

# K

knowledge
    content 325
    culture 325
    disclosure 29
    dispersion 280–281
    diversity ananlysis 277–278
    diversity management 276–293
    diversity managment
        toosl 278–280
    exchange (KX) 173–177
    infrastructure 325
    management (KM) 63–78, 84–103, 105–
        116, 138–151, 276–277, 300–301
        and competitive advantage 128–129
        approaches 84–85
        aspects 123–124
        communities 93–94
        cultural impact 91–92
        global strategies 126–135
        intranet projects 89–90
        knowledge creation 302–303
        knowledge transfer 303–305
        leadership roles 306–309
        Lotus Notes 90–91
        organizational

devices 284–288
    performance 301–302
    perspectives 213–216
    practices 324–338
        finding analysis 334–336
        in Israel 328–329
        in Silicon Valley 327–328
        in Singapore 329–330
        in The Netherlands 330–331
    processes 76
    projects 114–116
    solutions 120
        evolutionary approach 120
        hybrid approach 120
        product-based approach 120
    success 299–309
        factors 304–306
    systems
        architecture 119–125
        components 120–121
        maturity 124–125
    technologies 106–107
    tools 56–59, 152–166
        characteristics 154–156
        decision tree 57–58
        key trends 159–162
        online help tool 57
        overview 156–159
    networks 283–284
        success factors 291
    process 325
    resources 76
    sharing 40–51
        project 183–185
            approach 185–191
            results 185–191
    transfer process 210–211
    worker 55, 60
        management 314–317, 317–318
        retirement problem 318
Kontext Aware FRAmework (KAFRA) 65–78
    framework 69–76

# L

Leavitt's diamond organization model 66
local responsiveness framework 129

# M

matrix multinational organizations 311–322
    background 312–313

multinational corporations (MNCs) 1–5, 9–17, 21–
    22, 170–177, 183–192
  and academic involvement 192
  and customer relationship management (CRM)
      245–249
  and knowledge management (KM) 245–249
  culture of cooperation 191
  intellectual capital statements 195–206
  knowledge
    flow 198–199
      resource measurement 199–203
      resource reporting 203–204
  openess 191
multinational enterprises (MNEs) 208

**N**

nearsourcing 55–56

**O**

organizational
  change (OC)
    group 93, 95
    management 107–108
  culture 85–87, 97–100
    perspective 138, 140–143, 147–148
  innovation 3–5, 23
  knowledge 106
  learning 3–5, 257–258
  loss of effectiveness (LOE) 107–113
  politics
    perspective 143–146, 147–148
outsourcing 54–55, 55, 60–62, 61–62, 299–
    300, 373–396

**P**

personnel 3–5

**R**

research
  joint venture (RJV) 207–223
    taxonomic foundations 211–215
    taxonomy 215–221
research and develoment (R&D)
  projects 282–284
resource-based view 168

**S**

service-oriented architecture (SOA) 121–123
Singapore 329

socio-technical
  systems 65–66
successful diversified knowledge management
    289–291

**T**

tacit
  dimension 277
team rooms 93
technological alliances 282

**U**

utilization 29

**V**

value
  networking
    model 32–35
    strategy 30–32
      closed source adaption 31
      open source innovation 31–32
vitual
  teams 299–300

**W**

wireless
  access protocol (WAP) 239
  customer relationship management 239–240